Weirdumentary

**Ancient Aliens,
Fallacious Prophecies,
and Mysterious Monsters
from 1970s Documentaries**

***Dedicated to my dear sisters,
Lee Ann and Lana Renae***

ISBN: 9781627311571

**Feral House
1240 W Sims Way #124
Port Townsend WA 98368
www.feralhouse.com
info@feralhouse.com**

Designed by Ron Kretsch

Weirdumentary

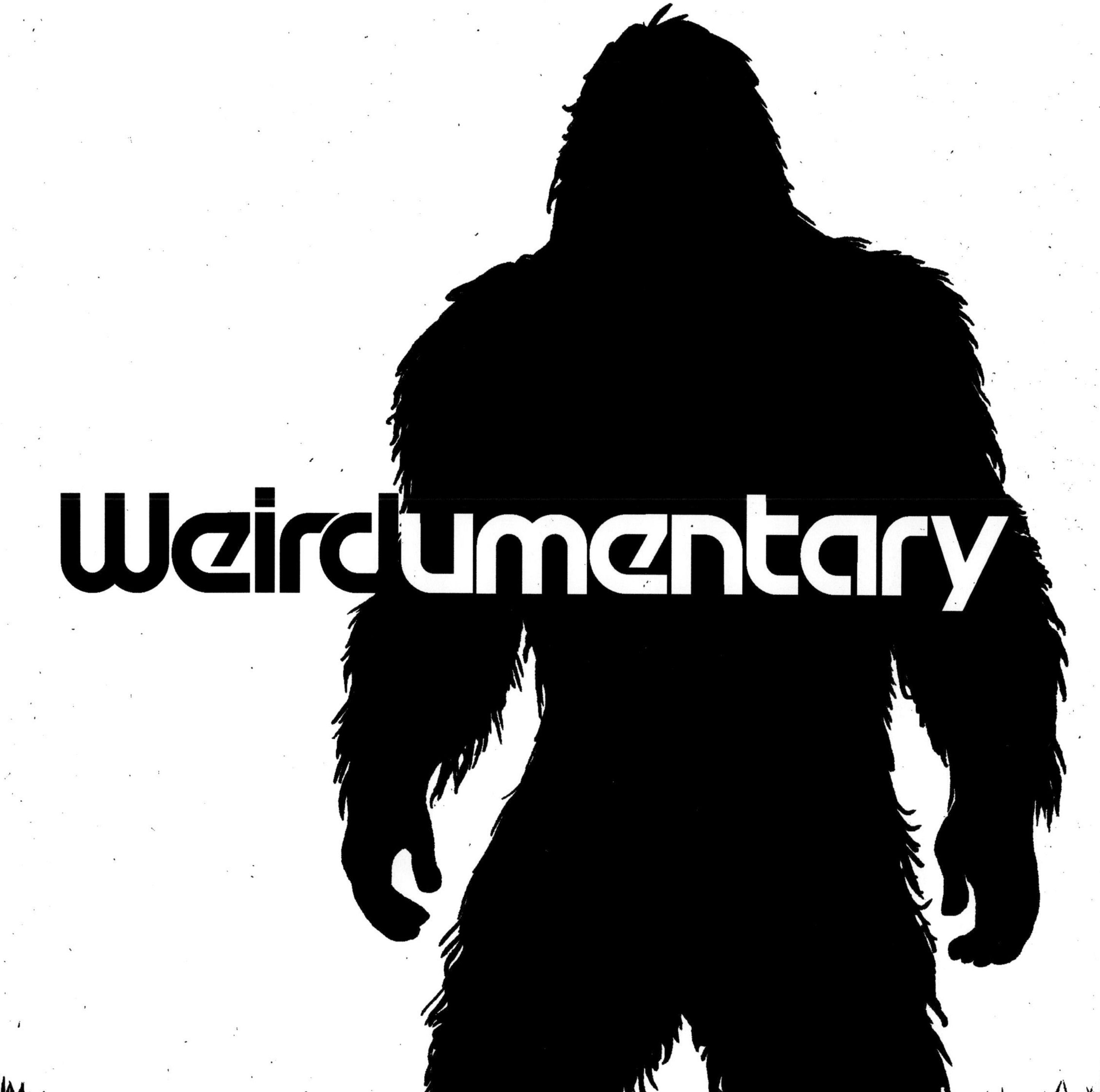

Ancient Aliens, Fallacious Prophecies, and Mysterious Monsters from 1970s Documentaries

By Gary D. Rhodes

Foreword by Stephen R. Bissette

Opposite:
Promotional image for *BEYOND AND BACK*,
Sunn Classic Pictures, 1978

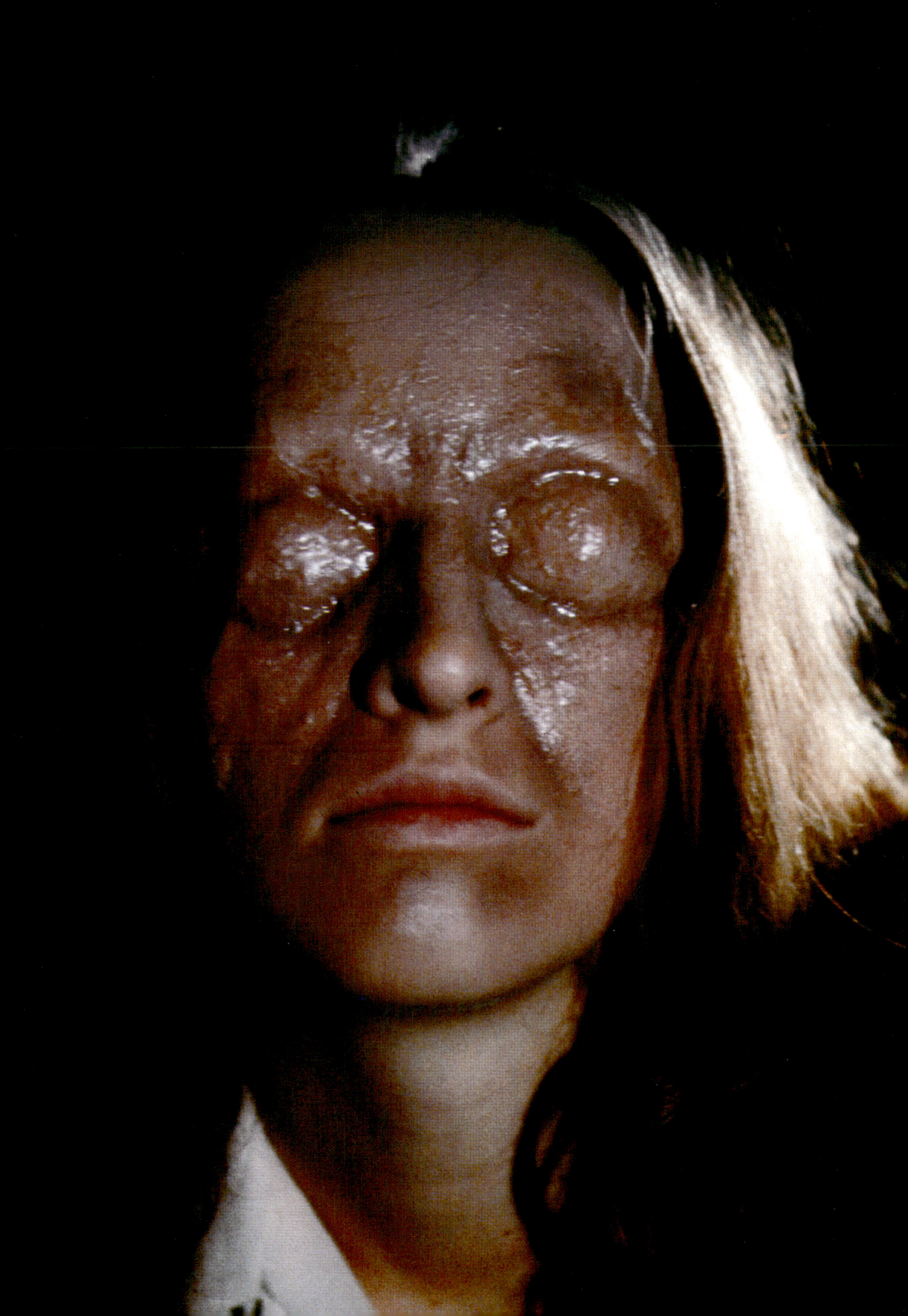

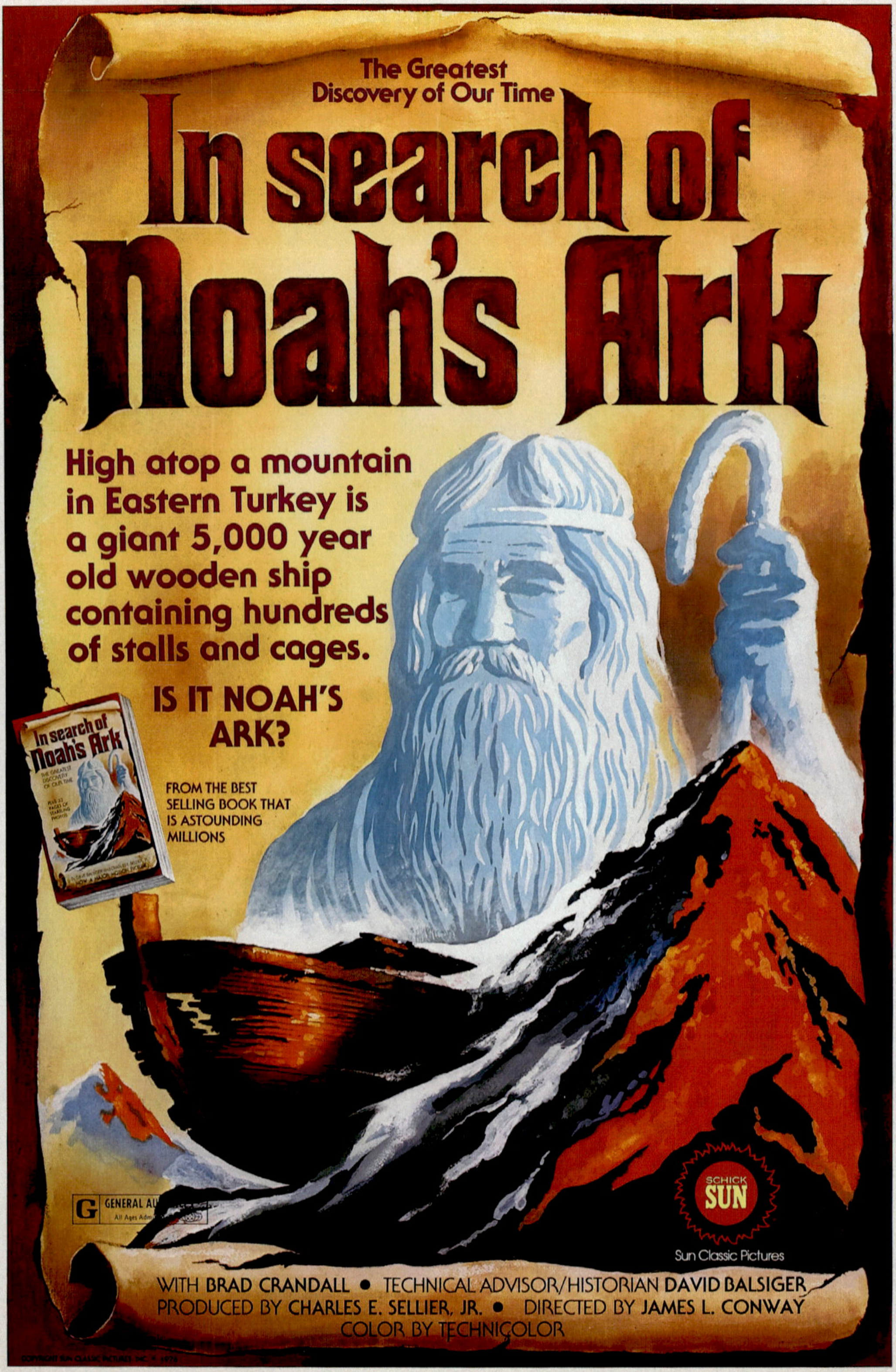
The Greatest
Discovery of Our Time
In search of
Noah's Ark
High atop a mountain
in Eastern Turkey is
a giant 5,000 year
old wooden ship
containing hundreds
of stalls and cages.
IS IT NOAH'S
ARK?
FROM THE BEST
SELLING BOOK THAT
IS ASTOUNDING
MILLIONS
SCHICK
SUN
Sun Classic Pictures
WITH BRAD CRANDALL • TECHNICAL ADVISOR/HISTORIAN DAVID BALSIGER
PRODUCED BY CHARLES E. SELLIER, JR. • DIRECTED BY JAMES L. CONWAY
COLOR BY TECHNICOLOR
COPYRIGHT SUN CLASSIC PICTURES INC. © 1976

Foreword (is fore-armed) a cautionary text

BY STEPHEN R. BISSETTE

I still remember a chilly afternoon when a college friend and I were deciding what movie to catch that night. We were eager for a change of pace. We both wanted to see something unlike anything we'd ever seen, and we both laughed out loud when we opened the newspaper to find *In Search of Noah's Ark* (1977) was definitely the oddest title opening that very night.

Well, what the hell, then, it was decided: Sunn Classic Pictures was going to get our money, and we were going to force ourselves to sit through every nanosecond, however whacked or wretched it turned out to be. Typical of such films, we were, and we were not, disappointed—it was awful, but entertainingly awful—neither were we convinced, nor converted.

Lest you need further evidence, a couple of years later the same amigo and I crossed paths and before we caught up with one another on the many changes in our respective lives, he smiled wickedly and said, "So, tell me you've already seen *In Search of Hysterical Jesus*!" He was referring, of course, to the latest Sunn Classics epic *In Search of Historic Jesus* (1979), and yes, it turned out we'd both separately, joyously inflicted ourselves with it (or it upon ourselves), and yes, we had a good laugh talking about it. I still call it *In Search of Hysterical Jesus,* and I'm not sorry if that offends anyone, because I tell ya, the movie deserves any scorn one might heap upon it.

But we're not here to talk about religious movies—or are we? Why, yes, I think we are!

Yes, these *were* religious movies, as surely as Cecil B. DeMille parted the Red Sea not once but twice—it's just that they weren't associated with accepted organized religions *per se*, except it turned out many (if not most) of the movies were bankrolled by Mormons a.k.a. Church of Jesus Christ of Latter-day Saints devotees. But I'm not referring to that. The Weirdumentaries were artifacts of what had become devotional texts by the 1970s. These were essentially the strange fruit of a variety of alternative belief systems, pseudo-religions, a new brand of faith that cast wider nets for converts than any revivalist preacher ever dared.

Believers (and curious non-believers: hey, it's all money at the box office, as long as it gets asses into theater seats) in Bigfoot, ancient aliens, UFOs, suspect archaeology, political conspiracies, "life after death" experiences, possession, the occult (but

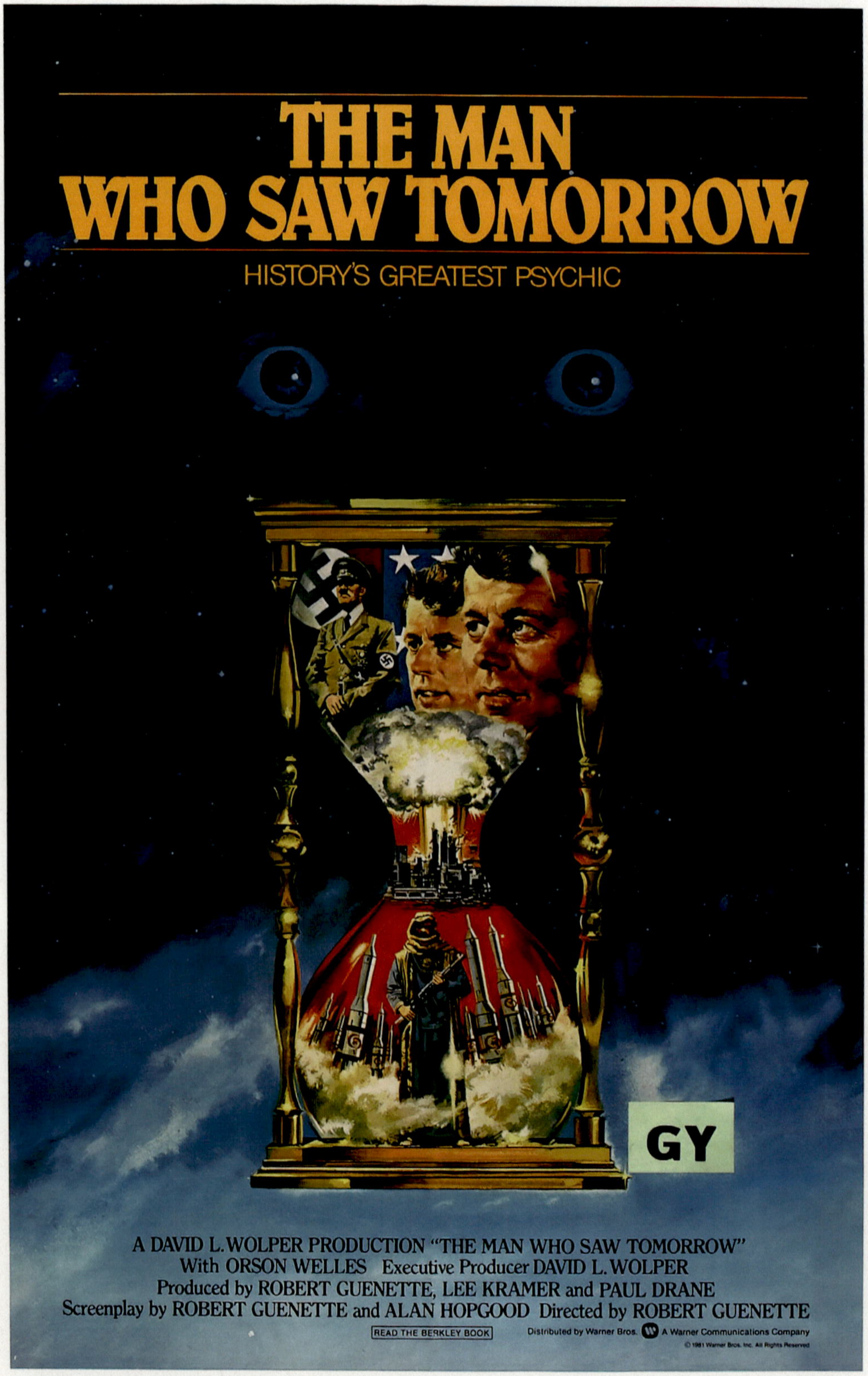
THE MAN
WHO SAW TOMORROW
HISTORY'S GREATEST PSYCHIC
GY
A DAVID L. WOLPER PRODUCTION "THE MAN WHO SAW TOMORROW"
With ORSON WELLES Executive Producer DAVID L. WOLPER
Produced by ROBERT GUENETTE, LEE KRAMER and PAUL DRANE
Screenplay by ROBERT GUENETTE and ALAN HOPGOOD Directed by ROBERT GUENETTE
READ THE BERKLEY BOOK
Distributed by Warner Bros. A Warner Communications Company
© 1981 Warner Bros. Inc. All Rights Reserved

none of the sex magick stuff, mind you), the Bermuda Triangle, faith healing, psychic surgery, paranormal phenomena, and all manner of what my New England folklorist friend Joseph A. Citro prefers to call "stories that might not be fiction" were now *everywhere*. What had been relatively obscure niche cult interests and obsessions indulged by the likes of *Fate* magazine had exploded into mainstream populist Americana and G-rated family entertainments. At some point in the 1960s, the seeming polar opposition of the spaced-out youth counterculture and the Bible Belt conservative Christian agendas were either abducted by aliens and mated, or they collided and fused together in the netherworld we only read about in paperbacks by Frank Edwards or Hans Holzer, men's mags like *Argosy*, and tabloids like Generoso Pope Jr.'s post-gore era *The National Enquirer* (the paper went UFO- and occult-crazy in the late 1960s; *The Weekly World News* wasn't launched until 1979, for those who think I'm off my oats).

In his introduction to this marvelous book, Gary D. Rhodes properly cites the cultural landmarks of *Erinnerungen an die Zukunft/ Chariots of the Gods?* and *2001: A Space Odyssey* as a turning point in the chronology. Gary also establishes his timeline for this comprehensive overview of a bastard genre between Academy Award nominee *Chariots of the Gods* in 1970 and *The Man Who Saw Tomorrow* eleven years later, and that's as rational a set of guidelines as anyone could posit for such an inherently irrational spread of such curious feature films.

But I'm here to tell you, things were going astray long before the devout Church of Jesus Christ of Latter-day Saints (LDS, a.k.a. Mormon) moguls at Sunn Classic Pictures (a.k.a. Sunn International Pictures a.k.a. Schick Sunn Classic Pictures a.k.a., later, Taft International Pictures) were using high-tech computers to calculate how to fleece more rubes than anyone ever had before. And oh, man oh man, did the money pour in. For every *The Life and Times of Grizzly Adams* (1974) family wildlife offering, Sunn Classic's Charles E. Sellier, Jr. also released something like *The Mysterious Monsters* or *The Amazing World of Psychic Phenomena* (both 1976). Warner Bros. finally jumped on the bandwagon with Orson Welles pontificating about Nostradamus and his dire prophecies, and though he happily cashed the paycheck, Welles reportedly dissed *The Man Who Saw Tomorrow* saying "one might as well make predictions based on random passages from the phone book." Let's not forget Orson Welles had, in his way, already mounted his own pre-emptive retort to the entire genre with *F for Fake* (1973).

Before Erich von Däniken's arrival on the best-selling paperback starships, cinematic snake-oil sales geniuses from Kroger Babb to Dwain Esper to Ron and June Ormond were doing their utmost to fleece susceptible potential audiences. These cine-carnies paved the way for the 1970s wave of weirdness even Nostradamus couldn't have foreseen. Before the 1960s and '70s ushered in a fresh four-walling bonanza (Gary will elucidate the particulars of four-walling to you, patient reader), documentaries skirted the indifference of more mainstream movie distribution constraints by renting public venues and presenting lectures and self-made nonfiction film chronicles of various expeditions. Herbert Ponting bought back his documentary *The Undying Story of Captain Scott* (1913)—his chronicle of the tragic Captain Scott Antarctic expedition—from the Gaumont Company to re-release it, with his live presentation of slides and lecture, and score a major hit in 1914 (including a May 1914 Buckingham Palace Royal Command Performance). Which is, as Dr. Rhodes mentions herein, pretty much what von Däniken later did for *Chariots of the Gods?*, including the 3,000-plus lectures.

Back in 1920, Lowell Thomas couldn't kindle distributor interest in releasing his quintet of documentaries on the campaigns of notoriously publicity-shy T.E. Lawrence (a.k.a. Lawrence of Arabia), so he rented New York's Century Theater himself, and two of the features became such hits that he moved them to Madison Square Garden, subsequently touring England, Australia, and America.[1] And so it went, too, for Martin and Osa Johnson, Robert Flaherty, Merian C. Cooper and Ernest B. Schoedsack, on into the sound era. When Walt Disney completed the half-hour True-Life Adventure *Seal Island* (1948), his distributor RKO balked, so Disney went off on his own and rented two theaters (Los Angeles and California); only after *Seal Island* made money (it eventually won an Oscar) did RKO come around to releasing it nationally, and that's how the popular True-Life Adventure series began. When distributors shunned Bruce Brown's surfing documentary *The Endless Summer* (1966), Brown went coast-to-coast renting any public venue he could find (including high schools) offering "Free Smith and Gordon surfboard" contests at some playdates to drum up interest; settling in to New York City's Kips Bay Theater, *The Endless Summer* played for a full year, prompting Don Rugoff of Cinema 5 distribution to negotiate a wider national theatrical run. Leading by example, Brown initiated the four-wall distributor strategies fiction filmmakers like Tom Laughlin (with *Billy Jack*, 1971) and nonfiction (and pseudo-nonfiction) outfits like Sunn Classic Pictures refined in the 1970s.

But those were genuine documentaries, the work of real pioneers. The die was cast for the Weirdumentary whenever shameless hucksters cobbled together something reel that wasn't real, and passed it off as a documentary. When early silent movie producer Colonel Selig was denied permission to accompany Teddy Roosevelt on his 1909 African safari, Selig faked his own Roosevelt expedition in his Chicago studio and had a major hit with *Hunting Big Game in Africa* (1909). When opportunists William S. Campbell and Nat Spitzer formed Congo Pictures to wed new shot-in-California sequences (bogus scenes of "native" African women being seized by gorillas, including 'gorilla man' Charles Gemora) with footage from a lawsuit-tainted African travelogue (Lady Grace Mackenzie and Hal Sintzenich's 1915 expedition feature *Heart of Africa*) to unleash *Ingagi* (1930), the roadshow was an incredible moneymaker (prompting RKO, who owned some of the theaters *Ingagi* scored in, to bankroll their own ape-kidnaps-woman adventure-romance, *King Kong*, which made its fortune without pretending to be anything except an audacious fantasy).

Armand Denis and André Roosevelt's Balinese exotic *Goona Goona* (a.k.a. *The*

---

1 Kevin Brownlow covered these films, and more, in the essential *The War, The West, and the Wilderness* (1979, Alfred A. Knopf, Inc.), which I highly recommend.

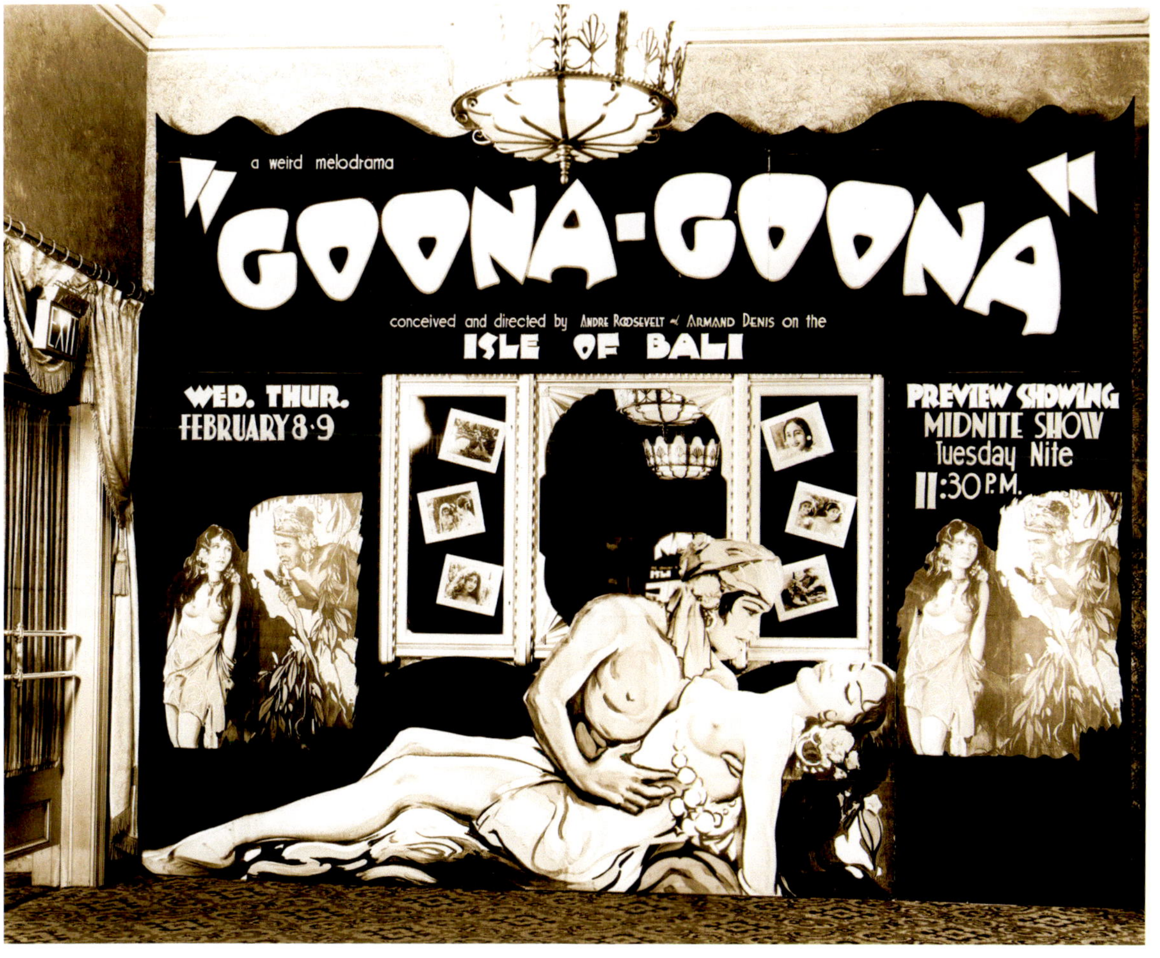

Kriss, 1930) lured Depression-era audiences with its titillating tapestry of authentic 1928 expedition footage (including topless native women) and a spicy prince-and-servant romantic conflict; it was popular enough that its title was adopted as street slang for any and all saucy tropical tribal exploitation exotica. The goona-goona genre lasted into the 1960s, as films like *Gow the Killer* (1934) were repackaged and re-released (as *Cannibal Island*, 1956) and showman Kroger Babb toured the African "adult entertainment" *Kwaheri* (1964; "The Universe Holds Its Breath at the Audacity of Man!"). I'm moved to mention Kroger Babb and William Beaudine's Lawton, Oklahoma-filmed Cinecolor Passion Play recreation *The Lawton Story of "The Prince of Peace"* (a.k.a. *The Lawton Story* a.k.a. *The Prince of Peace*, 1949), an agonizingly impoverished Christian roadshow epic (a grueling two hours in length) that Babb milked for almost a decade. Babb's Okie opus was the real predecessor to *In Search of Noah's Ark* and *In Search of Hysteri*—excuse me, *Historic Jesus*. Sunn Classic Pictures was surely modeled on the "it's no sin to make a profit" exploitation legacy of Babb's Hygienic Productions a.k.a. Modern Film Distributors (Babb scored unrecorded millions for over two decades off his 1945 sex education feature *Mom and Dad*).

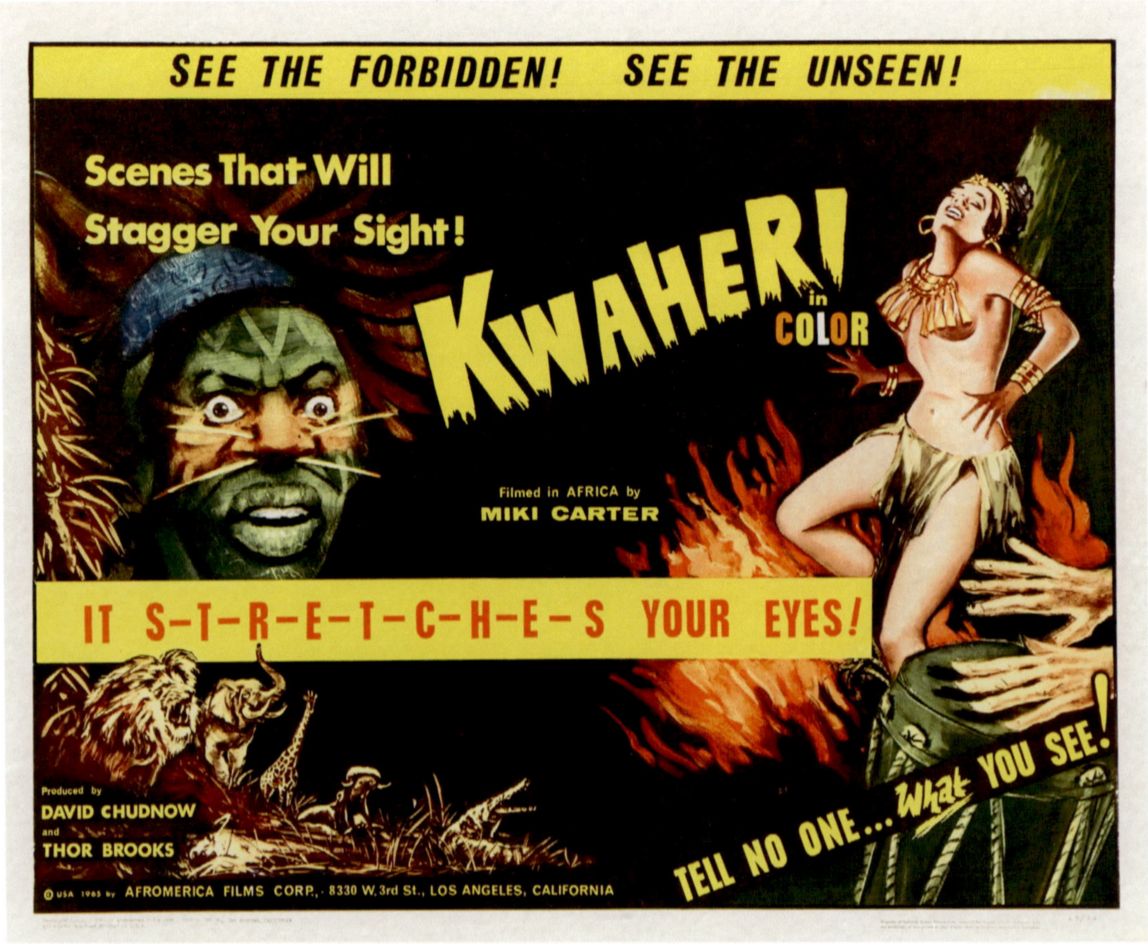

But the 1970s brand of hucksterism was, in another way, completely different. One of the most curious components of the 1970s Weirdumentary success story is how utterly clean, wholesome, family-friendly, and *sexless* it all was.

Who needed either the Oldest Profession *or* Old-Time Religion when we had Nostradamus, UFOs, Bigfoot, the Bermuda Triangle, and spoon-curling Uri Geller?

Somewhere between newsreel shorts like *The Flying Saucer* (1950) and *The Flying Saucer Mystery* (1952), and completely whacked feature film successors like G. Brook Stanford and W. Gordon Allen's *Overlords of the U.F.O.* (1976), something ... happened.

Some of what happened percolated up from the far fringes of the industry. Just as the goona-goona of the 1930s–1960s transmuted into the mondo movies of the 1960s–1970s, the lurid crime exposés and propagandistic anti-Nazi, anti-Japanese, anti-Communist 'hate movies' emerging from WWII (*Hitler's Strange Love Life, Menace of the Rising Sun,* etc.) and the Cold War (*Slaves of Stalin, We Will Bury You!,* etc.) paved the way for twenty-first-century political provocateur "documentaries" by Michael Moore and Dinesh D'Souza (in polar opposition to one another in every way). Similarly, long-forgotten esoteric-in-their-day paranormal fare of the 1950s and 1960s anticipated the explosion of Weirdumentaries in the 1970s.

Reflecting their personal fascination with UFOs and the paranormal, Ron and June Ormond dubbed the West German short film *Fliegende Untertassen* (1953) into *Attack of The Flying Saucers* (1956), co-featured with *The Eternal Question* (1956), framing dramatizations of UK psychic case histories (from an unfinished British production) with narrative inserts by Ormond and an intro with Charlie Chaplin, Jr. lending pseudo-celebrity name recognition to the proceedings. Thus, the Ormonds packaged the first proto-Weirdumentary double bill of its kind. The very same year United Artists rolled out the semi-documentary *Unidentified Flying Objects: The True Story of Flying Saucers* a.k.a. *UFO* (1956). *UFO* was sold as a nonfiction film, fabricating a fictionalized but earnest account of then-ongoing government investigations climaxing with the 1952 Washington, D.C., sightings. The film didn't cheat audiences, ending with a compilation of genuine amateur UFO film footage, blurry but compelling images the filmmakers helpfully rewind and replay in slow motion.

A little over a decade later, the famous October 20, 1967 Roger Patterson-Bob Gimlin 16mm color footage of a Bigfoot photographed at Bluff Creek in Northern California made its first documentary appearance nine months after the encounter was filmed, licensed to BBC producer Ronald Webster's TV documentary *Bigfoot: America's Abominable Snowman.* Hosted by Dr. John Napier (Curator of Mammals, Smithsonian Institute), the special was an interview-format investigation (with naturalist/cryptozoologist Ivan T. Sanderson prominently featured) broadcast on the BBC2 on Saturday, July 27, 1968. As part of the deal, Patterson received a print of the BBC2 documentary, which he and his brother-in-law Albert DeAtley, Jr. promptly added new introductory footage to and released regionally in 1969 under the same title, *Bigfoot: America's Abominable Snowman.* With a reported thirty-eight prints eventually being road-showed throughout the Northwest and Midwest, this non-narrative short feature was a first, but its regional four-wall release was fleeting. Portions of the film were subsequently folded into Lawrence Crowley's *Bigfoot Man or Beast* (1972), a shy-of-a-half-hour short booked with wildlife documentaries *North Country* and the National Film Board of Canada acquisition *Cry of the Wild.* By then, Charles B. Pierce's Texarkana-filmed *The Legend of Boggy Creek* (1972) had become *the* breakthrough Sasquatch sort-of-documentary of the decade.

It's impossible in the span of a single foreword to summarize what led to American and international documentaries derailing into increasingly aberrant and outré territories (but I've tried, oh I've tried). Suffice to acknowledge that it *did* happen, and that words like "bizarre" don't even begin to cover how truly out-to-lunch the so-called "documentaries" playing in rural and urban neighborhood theaters, drive-in screens, and metropolitan movie palaces truly had become.

It doesn't matter how it happened, but it happened. Populist "documentaries" went from being militaristic propaganda or Irwin Allen stock-footage-compilation reels, or the somber province of world travelers like Lowell Thomas and narrators like David Brinkley, to becoming ... *something else.* All the signs were there, in hindsight, but who was really thinking it would, it *could,* go so far off the beaten tracks?

Before he was cranking out SF TV series in the 1960s to become the self-made master-of-disaster for the 1970s, back in 1953 Irwin Allen won the Best Documentary Feature Academy Award by stringing exotic oceanic found footage into *The Sea Around Us.* Fine, that's fine; but by the 1960s, the signs were there: just follow a trio of the decade's Best Documentary Feature winners, and tell me we weren't heading for weird times.

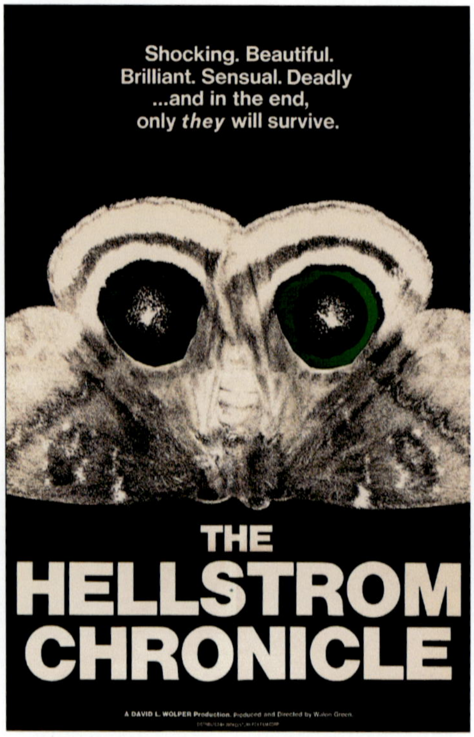

• Joseph E. Levine's sensationalistic ad campaign for the Oscar-winning French ethnographic doc *Le Ciel et la Boue / The Sky Above, The Mud Below* (1961) was emblematic of the *Mondo Cane* era of stamina-and-stomach-testing shockumentaries to follow (and yes, *Mondo Cane* was nominated for an Academy Award, too, for Best Original Song);

• The Best Doc Feature Oscar went to a completely speculative slice of anti-nuclear-weapon agitprop science fiction, Peter Watkins' produced-by-but-never-broadcast-by-the-BBC *The War Game* (1966);

* Yes, it's true, Dr. Harald Reinl's *Chariots of the Gods?* was nominated for Best Documentary Feature in 1970. It lost to *Woodstock*, which was and is fine: either way, one could say that the hippies won.

• The very next year, true documentarians were outraged when the apocalyptic semi-SF "will insects outlive man?" *The Hellstrom Chronicle* from Walon Green and David L. Wolper beat out Marcel Ophüls' Holocaust epic *Le Chagrin et la Pitié / The Sorrow and the Pity* (1969; U.S. release 1972). Take that, Vichy toadies to the Third Reich! Dr. Nils Hellstrom was right. The miraculously microphotographed insects indeed won out, after all.

Then, the year after that, the evangelism exposé *Marjoe* took the Oscar. Can I get a hallelujah, brothers and sisters?

No wonder 1970s documentaries veered so far afield, opening mind-muddling doorways into the fifth dimension, beyond that which is known to man, inhabiting a dimension as vast as space and as timeless as infinity—with our guides, Rod Serling, Peter Graves, and others lending gravitas to whatever crazy speculative archaeological extremes, cryptozoological curiosities, assassination theories, or Biblical bombast could be properly pre-packaged for easy pre-digestion. After all, wasn't Peter Graves the first-ever cinematic alien abductee (see *Killers from Space,* 1954); didn't he make *Mission: Impossible* seem possible every week? Didn't Rod Serling bring *The Twilight Zone* right into our own homes? Who could have been more trustworthy guides?

The blurring between science fiction and the "new" pseudo-science speculative "fact" in this 1970s breed of "documentary" cannot be overstated. It was self-evident we were heading in that direction, via the encouraged confusion between the Alaska-set Cold War espionage drama *The Flying Saucer* (1950) and the nonfiction newsreel *The Flying Saucer* (also 1950), between the Ormonds' short *Attack of the Flying Saucers* and Columbia's wholly SF feature *Earth vs. the Flying Saucers* (both 1956), the latter claiming to be based upon Major Donald Kehoe's 1953 best-selling investigative nonfiction book *Flying Saucers from Outer Space.*

There is an evolutionary genre metamorphosis at play: the almost documentary-like investigative procedural flavor that lends the giant-ant classic *Them!* (1954) its impact (including the incorporation of nature footage of ant colonies as a narrative exposition tool) is inverted for the documentary-as-science-fiction conceit of the entomological epic *The Hellstrom Chronicle*, which mesmerized audiences with intimate nature microphotography by cinematographers like Ken Middleham. The latter in turn prompts director Saul Bass to employ Middleham to convincingly present the speculative evolution of ants into the new dominant terrestrial species in *Phase IV* (1973). Neither *Them!* nor *Phase IV* were packaged or promoted as documentaries, but *The Hellstrom Chronicle* very successfully was, echoing passages of the Academy-Award-winning Disney True-Life Adventure *The Living Desert* (1953, a feature initially inspired by doctoral student N. Paul Kenworthy's footage of a tarantula and a wasp locked in a life-or-death struggle). In turn, *The Hellstrom Chronicle* providing the template (sans any apocalyptic SF frame) for the internationally popular French documentary *Microcosmos: Le peuple de l'herbe / Microcosmos* (1996).

By the 1970s, the firewalls dividing documentary from speculative fantasy were no longer required, encouraged, or sustained: they were, willfully, eroded, collapsed, dissolved. The calculated confusion between science fact and science fiction was *essential* to the films this book lovingly illuminates.

Before Erich von Däniken, before Stanley Kubrick, and roughly in tandem (to the very year) with Kubrick's *2001* co-creator Arthur C. Clarke's revelatory novel *Childhood's End* (1953), a BBC TV miniseries, *The Quatermass Experiment* by writer Nigel Kneale and producer/director Rudolph Cartier, introduced a wholly fictional scientist/explorer, Quatermass. Before the close of the 1950s, Quatermass would discover something buried in London that would propose the very same premise of both *2001* and *Chariots of the Gods:* in Gary's words, "aliens landed on Earth and helped early man." The notion had popped up in various pulp SF stories prior to 1950—the year Clarke's catalytic short story "Guardian Angel" was first published (*New Worlds* #8, Winter 1950), planting the seed for Clarke's breakthrough success with *Childhood's End*—but it was without a doubt Kneale and Cartier who most firmly posited and popularized the notion of alien intervention reshaping mankind's evolutionary development with their third *Quatermass* opus, *Quatermass and the Pit* (originally telecast December 22, 1958–January 26, 1959, and a Merry Christmas and Happy New Year to you, too). Between the prominent examples of Clarke (with *Childhood's End*) and Kneale and Cartier (with *Quatermass and the Pit*), the seeds of both *2001* and *Chariots of the Gods* were firmly planted in pop cultural soil that would soon be sprouting bizarre beanstalks and magic beans aplenty. Even the Hammer Films color feature adaptation of *Quatermass and the Pit* handily predates the arrival of von Däniken's best-seller: produced and completed by Hammer in

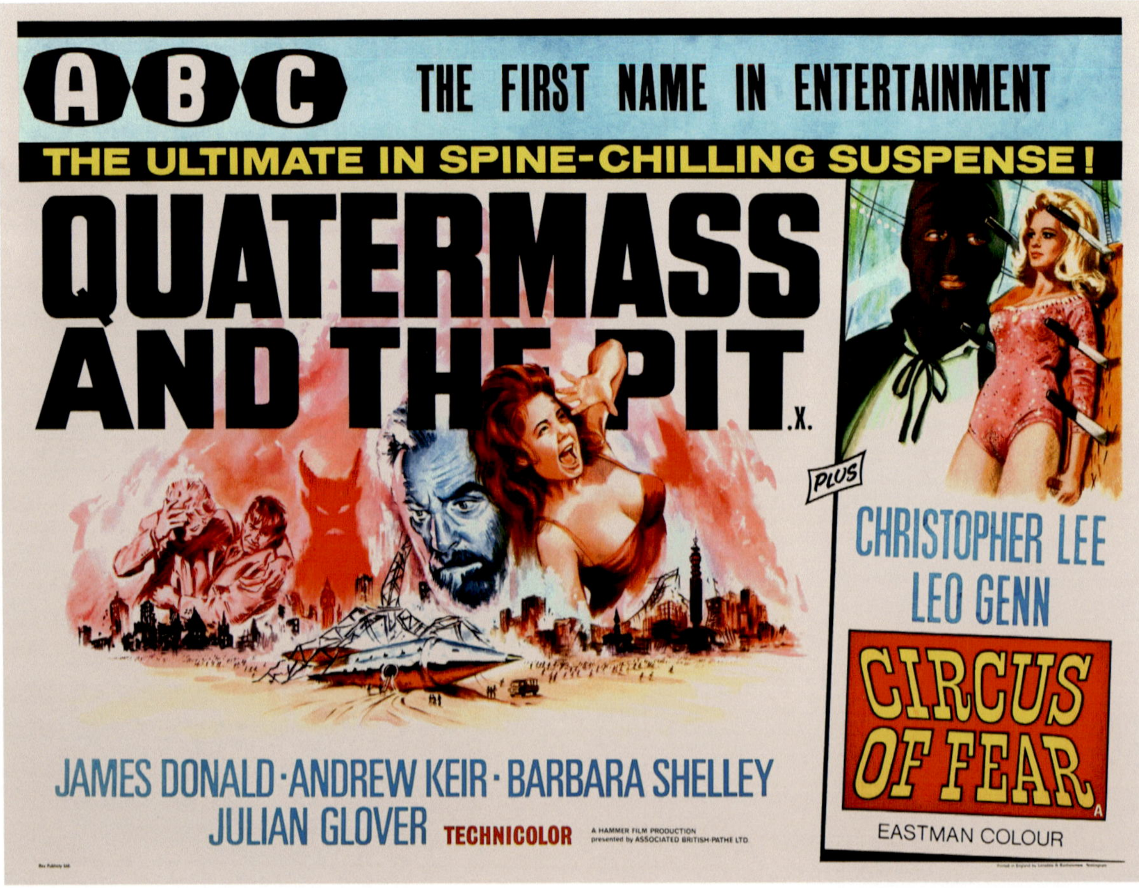

1967, opening in the UK in November 1967, released in the U.S. as *Five Million Years to Earth* by 20th Century Fox in February 1968 (but failing at the box office). Hammer's feature beat Econ-Verlag's first German edition of the von Däniken book (first UK and U.S. editions, 1969) *and* beat *2001* to the screen (*2001* opened early April 1968 in the U.S., mid-May in the UK, then slowly rolled out theatrically after its prestige Cinerama opening venues). *Five Million Years to Earth* later debuted on one of the CBS-TV network movie showcases (*CBS Late Movie,* if memory serves), reaching a wider American audience than found it at the local theater or drive-in—but by then, *2001* and *Chariots of the Gods?* had cast their spell farther, wider, and the pop culture's absorption of Kneale's novel-in-1959 SF concept was complete.

So, von Däniken was essentially repackaging *Quatermass and the Pit,* in his way. And he scored, big-time. And now, the belief that aliens shaped mankind's evolution is spoken of casually as fact (especially by those who claim not to accept either science or evolution). It's now fact, and yet not fact. The concept became an ongoing plot point on Chris Carter's popular SF/aliens & government conspiracy series *The X-Files*, but I'm still gobsmacked when Nigel Kneale's conceit pops up almost word-for-word as he originally scripted it.

I'm still addicted to UFOlogical documentaries (never-ending successors to some of the films Gary includes in this book), but I had to push the pause button, rewind, and make sure I'd heard what I thought I heard in *Mirage Men* (2014) during an interview with journalist Linda Moulton Howe (filmmaker/author of *A Strange Harvest*, 1980, and *Strange Harvests*, 1993). Howe talks about a covert meeting with infamous (in UFO and paranormal circles) U.S. government operative Richard Doty, who showed her "secret documents" in Kirtland Air Force Base in Albuquerque, New Mexico. One of these was entitled *Briefing Paper for The President Of The United States Of America On Unidentified Aerial Vehicles*, and Howe quotes a passage: "...These extraterrestrials manipulated DNA in already-evolving primates to create homo sapiens." Later in the documentary, the filmmakers cite "Project Garnet," a document stating, "All questions and mysteries about the evolution of Homo sapiens on this planet have been answered and this project is closed." Quatermass, we need you!

How, then, can one keep one's wits? How to negotiate this cultural and pop-cultural minefield?

Hey, good luck, Bunky. I for one think Dr. Rhodes has provided us with a long-overdue and essential map with this overview. The only downside I've found, personally, is that now I'm aching to excavate *Mysteries from Beyond the Triangle* (1978), a title I never gave a rat's ass about until today, when Gary pointed out how impossible-to-find-and-see it is.

Gary has wrestled mightily with what to call these bastard cinematic offspring of Charles Fort's writings, men's "sweat mag" articles, and all that came before. The title of the tome you hold in your hands is decisive, but I sympathize with the struggle: Daftumentary, Wackumentary, Crockumentary, Fortumentary, and the titular Weirdumentary are each in their own way judgmental and pejorative monikers, but things could be worse. Weirdomentary, for instance, would assert a judgmental assessment of the target audience, would it not? What a difference that "u" makes.

Having devoured this entire book and supped upon its delicious delirium, I wholeheartedly endorse cartographer-of-the-craziest-docs-ever Gary's ultimate distillation of titles. I remind the reader that yes, it's true, these *all* rolled out across North American screens at a time when audiences turned out *en masse* to see such movies.

If that seems incomprehensible to you, let me remind you that I only paid to see *In Search of Noah's Ark* one time. Such fare now dominates cable networks and streaming services 24/7 (remember when the History Channel and Animal Planet actually relied on fact-based programming?), and that millions upon millions of viewers pay that cable and/or internet access bill month after month after month.

My, how times haven't changed.

Stephen R. Bissette
June 2021, Mountains of Madness, VT

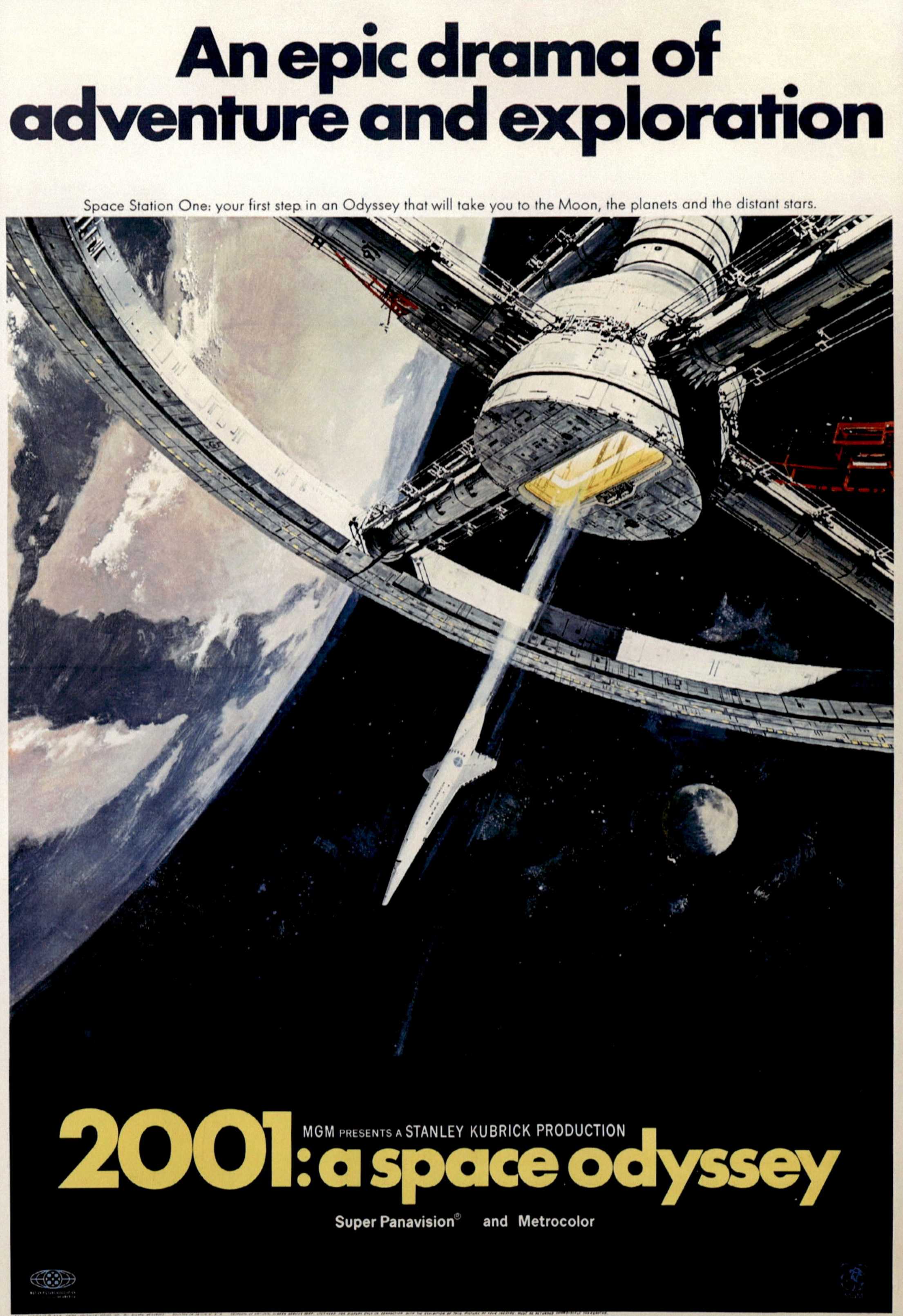
An epic drama of
adventure and exploration
Space Station One: your first step in an Odyssey that will take you to the Moon, the planets and the distant stars.
MGM PRESENTS A STANLEY KUBRICK PRODUCTION
2001: a space odyssey
Super Panavision® and Metrocolor

Introduction

**"A procession of the damned.
By the damned, I mean the excluded.
We shall have a procession of data that Science has excluded.
Battalions of the accursed, captained by pallid data that I have exhumed, will march. You'll read them—or they'll march. Some of them livid and some of them fiery and some of them rotten."**

— Charles Fort, *The Book of the Damned* (1919)

Stanley Kubrick's film *2001: A Space Odyssey* became a hit in the spring of 1968, breaking records in cities like Los Angeles, Washington, D.C., and Boston. The movie struck a chord with audiences spellbound by its special effects and psychedelic imagery. As the in-crowd agreed, *2001* really was the "ultimate trip."

Some four years in the making, the monumental film underwent evolutions during its production. Kubrick shot head-and-shoulders interviews with scientists and astrophysicists to ground various sections of the film with clear narrative explanation. He didn't use them, but *2001* retains a nonfiction vibe thanks to its extreme attention to detail and scientific accuracy. The film's slow pace also feels like documentary, the camera holding deliberately on many of the sites that it sees.

All that said, *2001* was a head-puzzler. What did it mean? And who or what was behind its mysterious black monoliths?

The Catholic Legion of Decency answered those questions with God, a Christian God, and commended *2001* to the faithful. They weren't alone. *Rolling Stone* wrote about a moviegoer at the Los Angeles Cinerama who leapt from his seat screaming "It's God! It's God!" Praise the Lord, and pass the science fiction.

For other viewers, Arthur C. Clarke's book-of-the-film became a way to clear up *2001*'s opacity. The answers it held hardly suggested a deity pulling the puppet strings of humanity. Aliens, however undefined, were at the end of the Star Gate. And aliens had helped the australopithecines at the very "Dawn of Man." *Sight and Sound* observed that *2001* was the "source of considerable pleasure as much to the UFO spotters as to the Bible readers." A big tent, this universe of ours.

When prodded by *Playboy* magazine in 1968, Kubrick provided a response that mediated the God-Alien debate: "these [alien] beings would be gods to billions

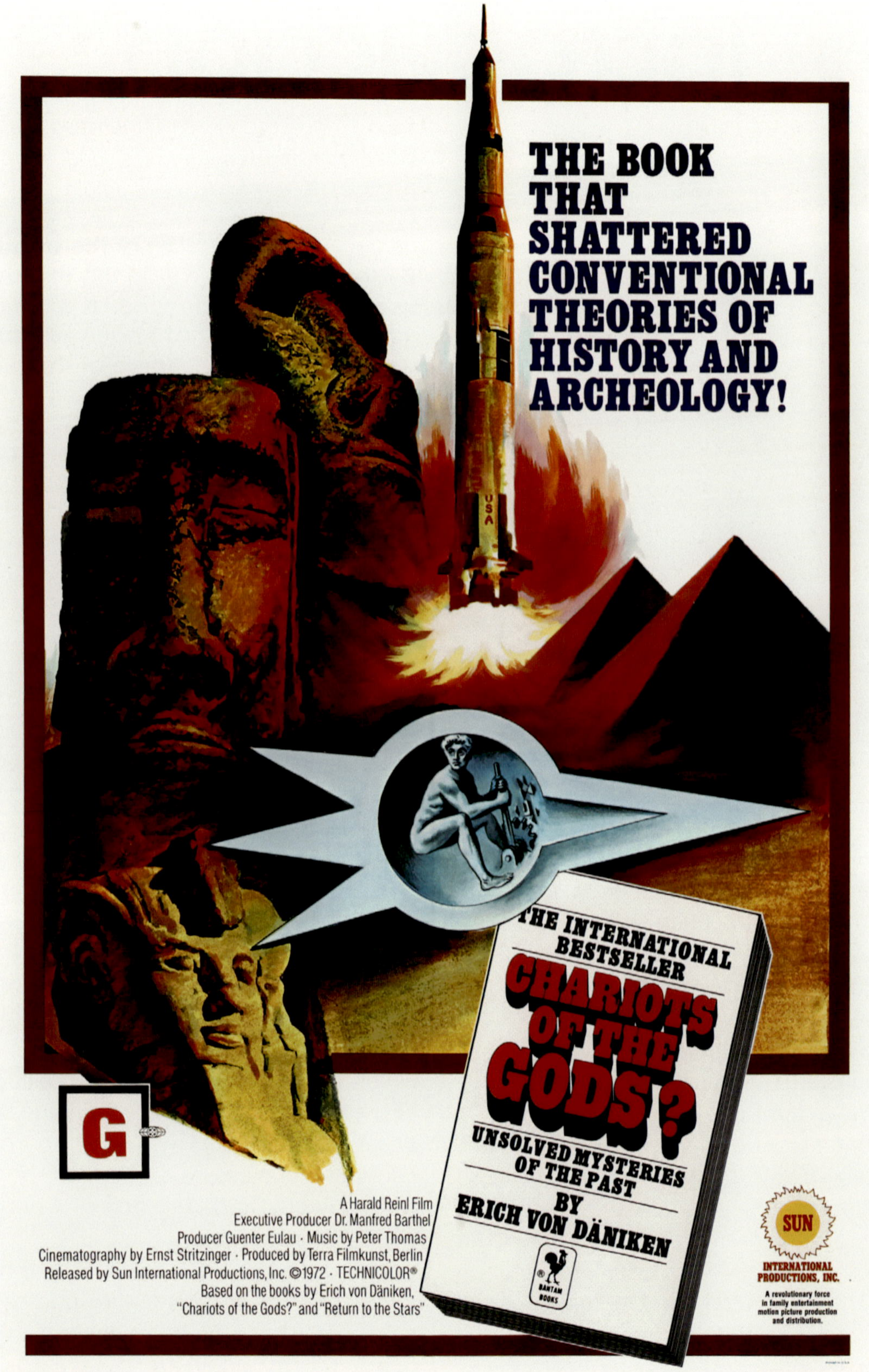

THE BOOK THAT SHATTERED CONVENTIONAL THEORIES OF HISTORY AND ARCHEOLOGY!
USA
THE INTERNATIONAL BESTSELLER
CHARIOTS OF THE GODS?
UNSOLVED MYSTERIES OF THE PAST
BY
ERICH VON DÄNIKEN
BANTAM BOOKS
G
A Harald Reinl Film
Executive Producer Dr. Manfred Barthel
Producer Guenter Eulau · Music by Peter Thomas
Cinematography by Ernst Stritzinger · Produced by Terra Filmkunst, Berlin
Released by Sun International Productions, Inc. ©1972 · TECHNICOLOR®
Based on the books by Erich von Däniken,
"Chariots of the Gods?" and "Return to the Stars"
SUN
INTERNATIONAL PRODUCTIONS, INC.
A revolutionary force
in family entertainment
motion picture production
and distribution.

of less advanced races in the universe, just as man would be a god to an ant that somehow comprehended man's existence. ... [Aliens like those in *2001*] would be incomprehensible to us except as gods; and if the tendrils of their consciousness ever brushed men's minds, it is only the hand of God we could grasp as an explanation."

OF GODS AND ALIENS:

In 1968, while *2001* was thrilling audiences, Erich von Däniken copyrighted his book *Chariots of the Gods? Unsolved Mysteries of the Past* in the United States. European editions appeared as early as 1968, though American readers had to wait until the following year for publication.

Born in 1935 in Zofingen, Switzerland, von Däniken went to school at the Catholic Collége Saint-Michel in Fribourg. While there, he devoted much of his time to studying religious texts. Never completing his formal education, von Däniken went to work at a five-star Swiss hotel. By the mid-1960s, he was its managing director.

His interests in ancient civilizations increased to the point that he developed the theory for which he would become world-renowned. "Ancient Astronauts," as von Däniken calls them, visited Earth in centuries past. They gave important knowledge and assistance to peoples across the globe. But von Däniken realized he needed to visit the places that held the secrets of extraterrestrial influence.

Taking some 400,000 Swiss francs from the hotel, von Däniken journeyed to Peru, Easter Island, Mexico, Lebanon, Egypt, and elsewhere in search of proof for his theory. His pilgrimages yielded much in the way of "evidence," but his findings were temporarily bittersweet. His employers charged him with embezzlement, and von Däniken spent a small amount of time in jail. The hotelier-turned-traveler became a prisoner of his own device.

Chariots of the Gods? hit bookstores while its author was behind bars. It was a best-seller in Germany and then in the United States.

The book fascinated readers with a wide array of examples supporting its thesis, but even under mild scrutiny most of what he wrote falls apart. Some evidence was seemingly invented (a clay pot that was not "ancient"), and some evidence seemingly distorted (the Sirius-based Egyptian calendar). Biblical quotations are cited out of context (Ezekiel's visions), and revelatory mathematical formulas offered proof of nothing (the area of the base of the Pyramid of Cheops divided by twice its height is allegedly the figure Pi). Carl Sagan was one of many to puncture holes in the *Chariots*' big wheels, but they kept a-turning, and the proud von Däniken kept a-burning.

"EvD" soon wrote such follow-up books as *Gods from Outer Space* (1970), *The Gold of the Gods* (1972), *In Search of Ancient Gods: My Pictorial Evidence for the Impossible* (1973), *Miracles of the Gods: A New Look at the Supernatural* (1974), and various others. By 2018, over 67 million copies of his forty books were in print. So sayeth his website. He has also given over 3,000 lectures, or, put another way, perhaps, the same lecture 3,000 times.

As early as 1972, the *Washington Post* declared that Erich von Däniken was "almost a cult figure."

THE NEW AGE IS UPON US:

2001: A Space Odyssey and *Chariots of the Gods?* proposed similar stories; aliens landed on Earth and helped early man. And both spoke in loud voices to the counterculture of the sixties and seventies, which openly questioned traditional religions and morality while seeking new paths to replace the old. Counterculture ideologies were eclectic, fragmented, and even contradictory. Adherents struggled for a utopian ideal, but they were hardly bound by consistent doctrine.

Tied to past interests in occultism, psychic phenomena, secret lore, magic, astrology, and paganism, the counterculture also embraced an amalgam of current events, including UFO sightings. Other factions pondered the individual's ties to the whole of life on Earth and to life after death. Anti-materialism, holistic medicine, ecology, channeling, reincarnation: these are but a few of the topics that sparked interest and controversy at the time and in the ensuing decades. Go ask your local guru, or go ask Alice, provided she measures at least ten feet tall.

These thoughts gripped Americans far beyond the confines of the counterculture. Ivan T. Sanderson's writing on cryptozoology and vortices gripped many readers. The CIA's Stargate Project undertook experiments on psychic spying and remote viewing. Jimmy Carter saw a UFO. And Uri Geller bent spoons on TV, either with his mind or with his hands. As Ken Kesey told us, "The hell with facts! We need stories!"

In 1974, the *Los Angeles Times* described "widespread popular interest in theories that mix the supernatural with 'science,' providing a *deus ex machina* for alleged mysteries of science." Such theories combined the "pseudo-scientific" with the "semi-spiritual." The result? A "movement among a growing number of people who earnestly seek new religious foundations based on a naturalistic, scientific explanation of the universe—with room for the supernatural."

What we can take from this brief history is that in many ways the question *becomes* the answer. The sheer act of questioning the status quo is as much or more important than any particular answer that might emerge from, say, studying Egyptology or Visitors from Outer Space. The unyielding ambiguity of *2001: A Space Odyssey* offers such a challenge; moviegoers walk away only with the ability to ask questions. And it's the very punctuation mark in the title of *Chariots of the Gods?* that underscores the desire to question, to always question. Indeed, von Däniken once proudly announced that his book contains 238 question marks.

And so we enter the realm of the "What If?", a realm where those two words alone are more crucial than any that follow.

Pondering these imponderables in 1975, the *Wall Street Journal* noticed a type of "urban voodoo" had caught fire after the publication of *Chariots of the Gods?* And filmmakers were more than ready to go do that cinematic voodoo that they do so well.

THE WEIRDUMENTARY

In 1970, Harald Reinl directed the German film *Erinnerungen an die Zukunft*, which translates as *Memories of the Future*. It was based on von Däniken's theories. In America, it was retitled *Chariots of the Gods*, with no question mark.

That landmark documentary inaugurated a new formula: pseudoscience conveyed through wonderful cinematography and unforgettable music, as well as rhetorical questions and visual juxtapositions that led us to believe, kinda-sorta, in ancient aliens. It had to be, even if it wasn't. Reinl was a genius.

Enter Alan Landsburg, the producer who brought von Däniken into American living rooms by transforming parts of Reinl's documentary into *In Search of*

Ancient Astronauts (1973) and *In Search of Ancient Mysteries* (1974). Those TV movies stirred another chemical into the mix: a famous narrator already associated with the bizarre, in this case Rod Serling.

Landsburg was one of the generals of the Made-for-TV movie. He had earned his stripes working for Wolper Productions, his name appearing on programs ranging from Jacques Cousteau to *National Geographic*. Of him, Wolper once said, "Alan wasn't a triple-threat man, he was a quadruple. He could write, produce, direct, and he was a good businessman on top of it all."

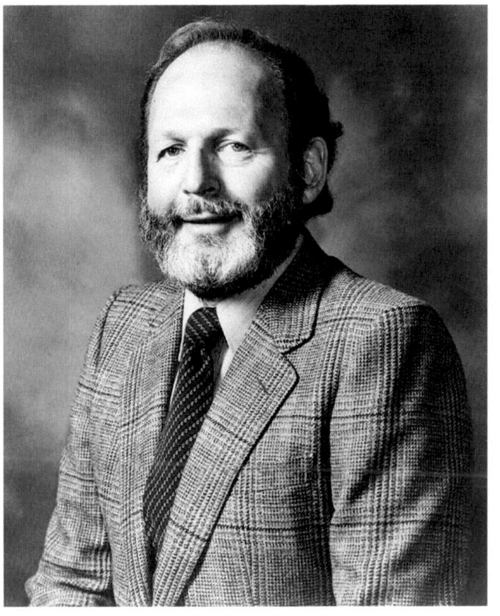

ALAN LANDSBURG

Landsburg became one of the key figures in this new genre, writing books with his wife Sally that he adapted into films. He also initiated a tactic that others would adopt: opening narration that told us we were about to watch the most startling film ever seen.

"We're not trying to present definite answers," Landsburg once said, "just to ask possible questions." His post-von Däniken credits included the TV series *In Search Of...* (1976–82), hosted by Leonard Nimoy.

But the original Reinl-Landsburg formula needed more juice. Enter Charles B. Pierce, who wrote, directed, and shot *The Legend of Boggy Creek* in 1972. Chronicling the Fouke Monster, an Arkansas variation on Bigfoot, Pierce created a semi-documentary that relied heavily on recreations of events, dramatizations with plenty of, well, drama. That was the final key ingredient necessary for the new genre to be complete.

THE SUNN ALSO RISES

Charles E. "Chuck" Sellier, Jr., Vice President of Sun International Productions, which had begun operation in 1970, declared that his company was in pursuit of a "lost audience." He meant the "entire family unit," as G-rated film fare appealing to young and old had become nearly obsolete. As one of the company's cinematographers would tell the press, "I am not judging anything done by anyone else, but I feel providing entertainment families can view together is a very satisfying thing to do."

Originally based in Salt Lake City, Sun distributed Reinl's *Chariots of the Gods* in U.S. theaters in 1973. Two years later, the company released Landsburg's *The Outer Space Connection* (1975). That was all in addition to Sellier ramping up Sun's own productions, producing more pseudo-science documentaries in the 1970s than anyone else.

In 1975 or so, the company changed its name to Sun Classic Pictures. In 1976, it changed its name again, this time to Schick Sunn Classic Pictures, with Schick Labs being its parent company and Sun spelled with two "N"s for reasons unknown. Anyhow, "Sunn Classic" remains the best remembered of these monikers, and the best remembered company involved in the new genre. It even augmented the formula with a particular movie set, one that I call the Office of Knowledge, in which the on-screen host was surrounded by books

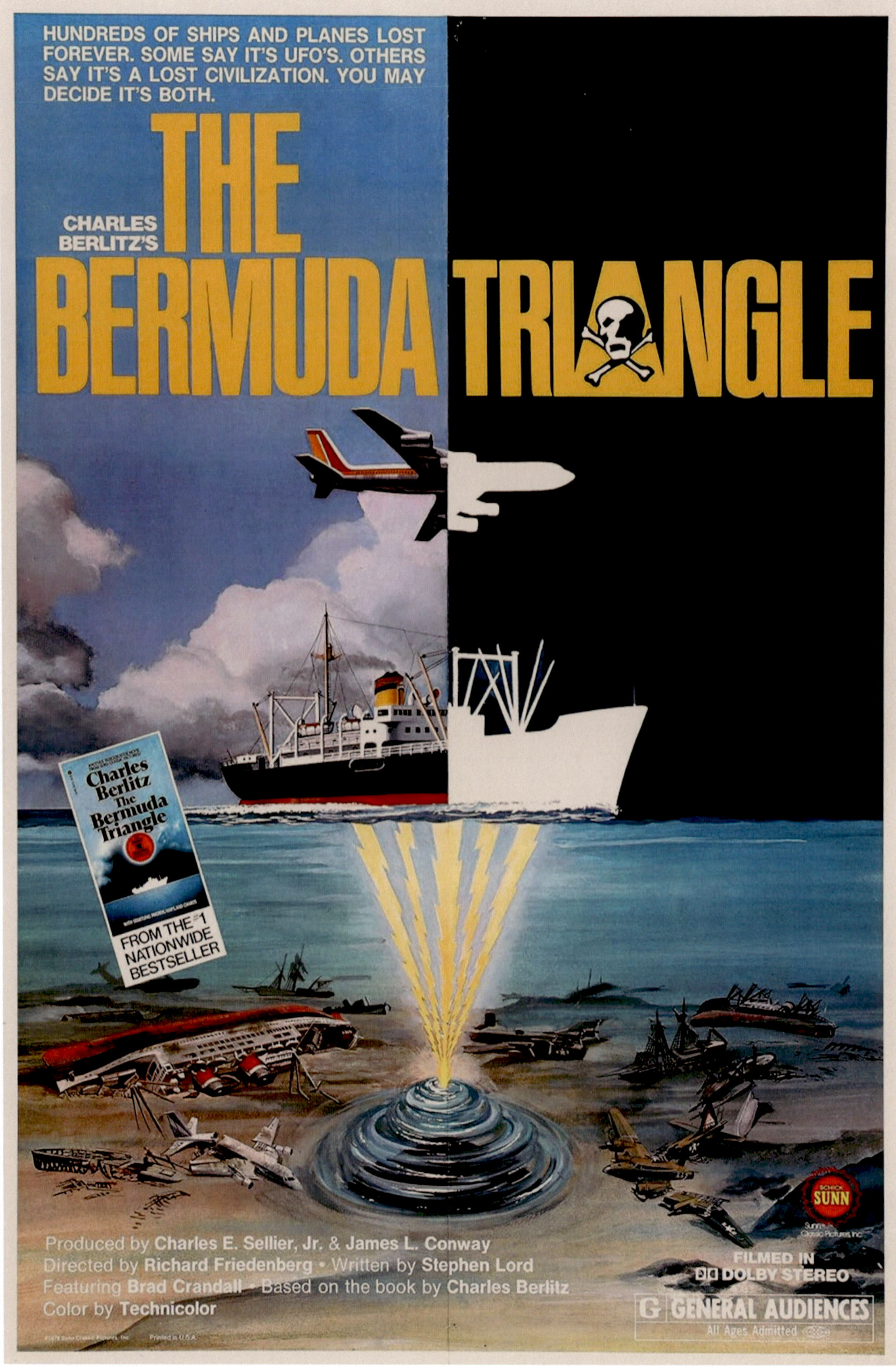
HUNDREDS OF SHIPS AND PLANES LOST FOREVER. SOME SAY IT'S UFO'S. OTHERS SAY IT'S A LOST CIVILIZATION. YOU MAY DECIDE IT'S BOTH.
CHARLES BERLITZ'S
THE BERMUDA TRIANGLE
Charles Berlitz The Bermuda Triangle
FROM THE #1 NATIONWIDE BESTSELLER
Produced by Charles E. Sellier, Jr. & James L. Conway
Directed by Richard Friedenberg • Written by Stephen Lord
Featuring Brad Crandall • Based on the book by Charles Berlitz
Color by Technicolor
SUNN
FILMED IN DOLBY STEREO
G GENERAL AUDIENCES
All Ages Admitted

and artifacts that gave the appearance of veracity and academic rigor.

Test marketing developed by Skinner Behavioral Science Studies helped Sunn to determine its potential audiences and their movie preferences, in part by conducting surveys of shoppers at malls and grocery stores. Sellier and Co. fed the data into a computer. The results enabled the company to decide which films to produce, as well as "the best days of the week to book a given film, which neighborhoods contain the highest concentration of potential ticket buyers, [and] what television spots should be bought to reach the specific target market." A type of "blitzkrieg advertising" followed, as did book tie-ins, a carryover from Alan Landsburg.

Another secret of Sunn's success was the decision to "four-wall" its pictures. Instead of just renting their films, Sunn sometimes rented the theaters that screened them, even sending their own staff to help with the ballyhoo. Sell the sizzle, and rent the cinematic restaurant where it's served. In 1975, a higher-up at the National Association of Theater Owners observed that companies like Sunn "merchandise film like Procter & Gamble would a new bar of soap." Sellier agreed, claiming, "Movies can be made the same as any mass-market product."

Make no mistake, Sunn believed it had mastered the skill of risk reduction. By 1977, Sellier was even talking about long-range weather forecasts factoring into its evaluation about dates and locations for premiering new films.

American Cinematographer magazine reported on all of this, as well as a "$500,000 modernistic communications system that links a fleet of some 90 vehicles with production crews, administrative and postproduction facilities."

The same article importantly added, "there is also a pervasive sense of camaraderie. People with unfulfilled visions are finding open minds and doors. They come to make a movie, and stay to build a career."

The mid- to late seventies also saw the company expand its offices into London and Australia, enlarge its book publishing division (Sunn Classic Books), and launch a merchandising division before *Star Wars* action figures arrived at department stores.

Put another way, the industry trade *Boxoffice* declared the "Sunn is shining." The cool kids agreed.

The critics did not. Of *Charles Berlitz's The Bermuda Triangle* (1979), *Daily Variety* wrote:

> *As with the other Sunn films, recollections from people, both living and dead, who have experienced the phenomenon in question, are reenacted in a silly, unconvincing fashion. So-called experts with degrees and credentials are carted out in front of the camera to add weight to the arguments. Brad Crandall narrates, tying together the bits and pieces.*

To lesser men we leave these petty slights. As I see it, Sunn had perfected an art form, a very profitable art form, crystallizing a new genre for a new age.

ENSORCELLED

In 1978, the *Independent Film Journal* described the Sunn Classic formula as a "highly dubious genre, a fairly recent hybrid form." And so we must ask, what should we call this particular art form?

To be sure, production companies and critics had a difficulty naming the genre, repeatedly using terms like "documentary" and "docu-drama." But these words

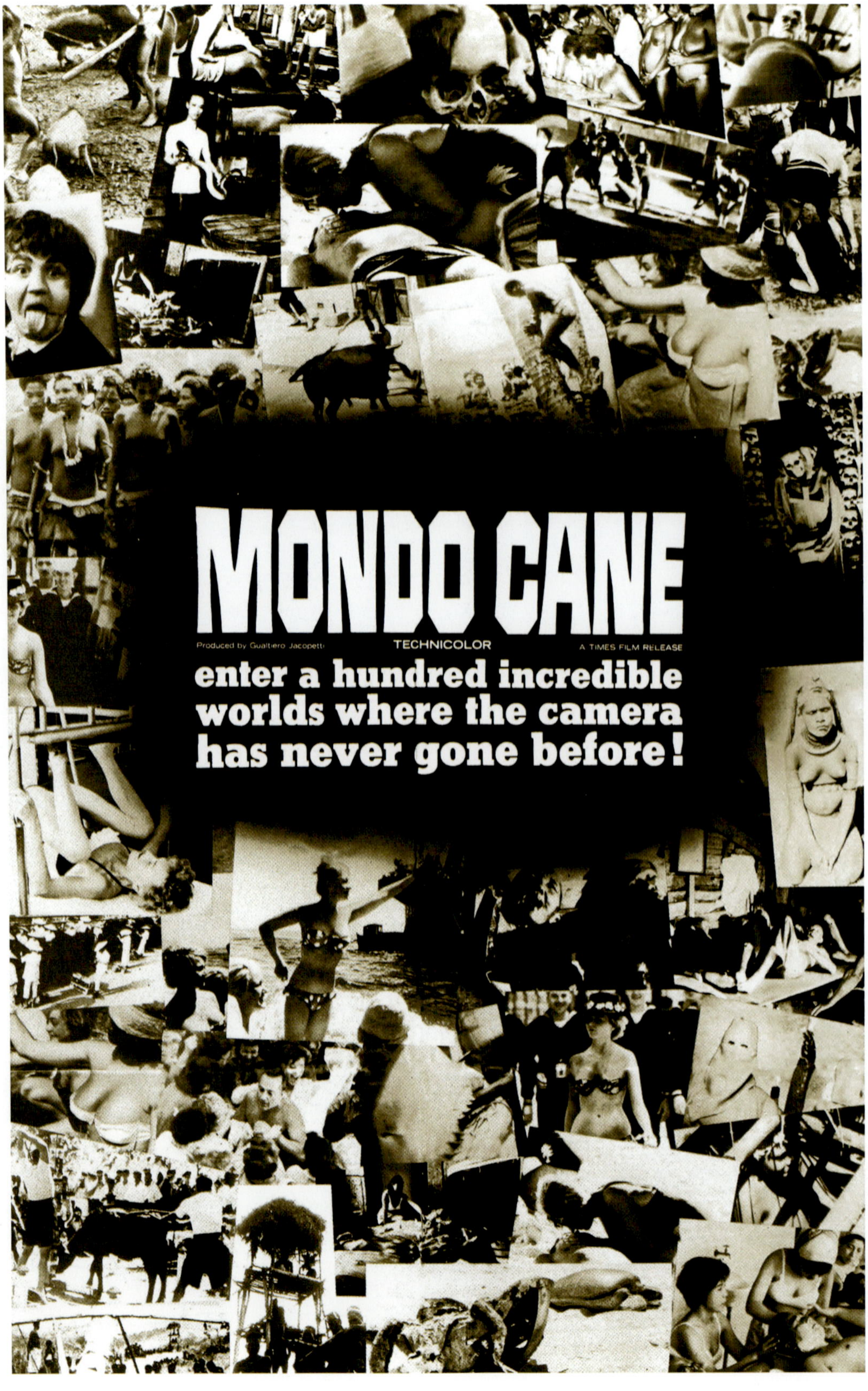
MONDO CANE
Produced by Gualtiero Jacopetti
TECHNICOLOR
A TIMES FILM RELEASE
enter a hundred incredible worlds where the camera has never gone before!

hardly fit the fun pseudo-science at play. As the *Hollywood Reporter* said of *The Legend of Boggy Creek* in 1972, "the film is not and makes no pretense at being a straightforward documentary." (Thank the gods and aliens, I say in response.)

And so repurposing old terms will not suffice. Consider "Mondo," a term used for 1960s-era films beginning with *Mondo Cane* (1962). They featured far more shocking and grisly content than this new genre, and they were certainly not aimed at the whole family. No, a unique form, however dubious, deserves its own name.

Choosing how to best identify this group of films is no easy task, as the book's structure illustrates. Section II focuses on Ancient Aliens, Section III on UFOs, Section IV on the Bermuda Triangle, Section V on the Paranormal, Section VI on Mysterious Monsters, Section VII on Speculative History, and Section VIII on Prophecies. (And Section I, in case you're wondering, concentrates on cinematic precursors to these wondrously weird films.)

Put another way, these films include everything from the Loch Ness Monster to the "conspiracy" to assassinate Lincoln. Rara avis, yes. They cover a vast terrain, geographically, intellectually, spiritually, and historically, but they also adhere to that special formula, one prescription for all the many topics that ail us.

The less kind among us might create words like "Daftumentary," "Wackumentary," or—best of all—"Crockumentary," but that far I cannot go. For one like myself who so often wishes to dwell in Tiahuanaco or on Easter Island, to plant those flags would seem unkind. I love these films, in large measure because they are pseudo-science.

My friend Robert Guffey, author of *Cryptoscatalogy* (2012) and *Chameleo* (2015), suggested the most accurate name: "Fortumentary," after Charles Fort, the famed writer and researcher of "anomalous phenomena." The adjective "Fortean" has become a descriptive term for subjects and events that challenge scientific norms, with the *Fortean Times* sold at quality newsstands since 1976. As Robert has observed, the films under review represent "the Unexplained, the Paranormal, and General High Strangeness."

For the sake of being user-friendly, specifically to those unaware of Fort, I have opted instead for "Weirdumentary." The term "weird" suggests all that is at stake in this film genre: the fantastic, the bizarre, the preternatural, the unnatural, the unearthly, and the uncanny. More archaic uses of "weird" invoked the control of fate or destiny, and those concerns also surface in these pages.

In terms of the films catalogued herein, the Weirdumentary formula is always present, even if in varying degrees. A few films of the era, such as the Orson Welles-narrated *Who's Out There* (1975) and the William Shatner-narrated *Universe* (1976), aren't included because they don't qualify, despite titles that suggest otherwise. A couple of others that probably do fit are so obscure as to not be preserved at archives or circulate among collectors, alas. Perhaps they swirl in the maelstrom of the Super-Sargasso Sea. Perhaps they will someday wash ashore. Perhaps…

Until that time, I offer my own procession of the damned: individual entries of approximately eighty films and television programs that form the corpus of the Weirdumentary, a unique movie genre. To those who created them, I offer my undying thanks, in this universe and all others. And to those who love them, I offer my deepest gratitude. Enjoy, or at least endure.

Gary D. Rhodes, Ph.D.
2024

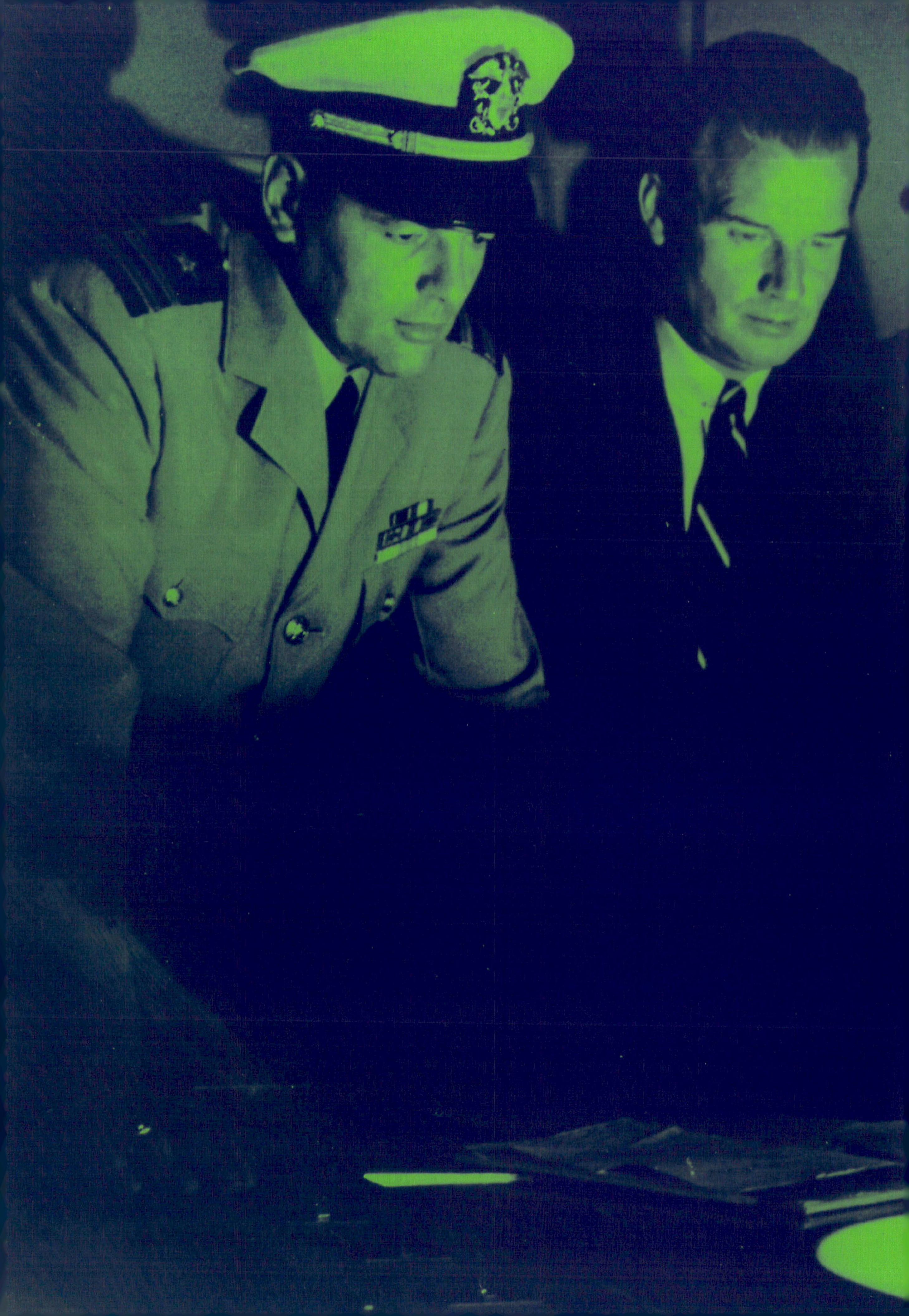

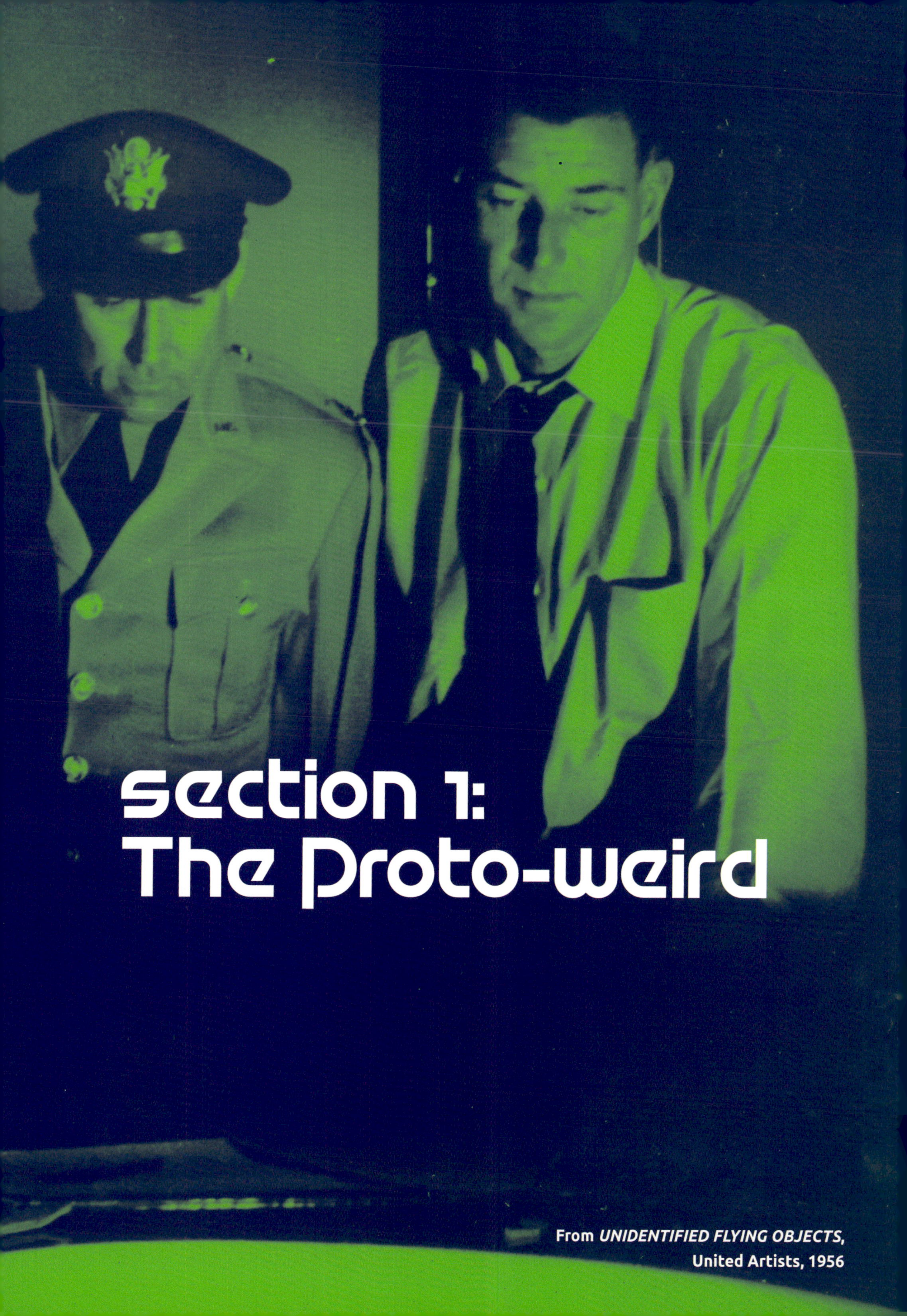

section 1: The Proto-weird

From *UNIDENTIFIED FLYING OBJECTS*, United Artists, 1956

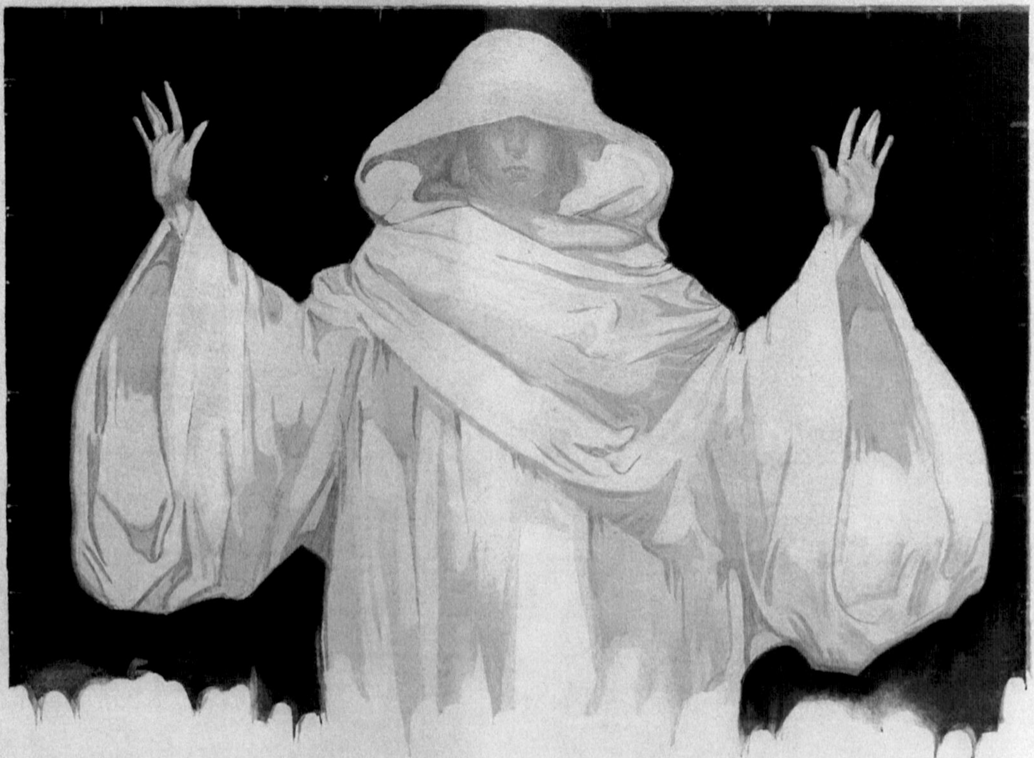

Did you ever see a spirit?

Whether you ever did or not you should see

Is Conan Doyle Right?

Two parts

Sir Arthur Conan Doyle, a very distinguished Englishman, says this life is merely the vestibule for the Hereafter; that we take up life in the next world just where we leave it off here; that he is in constant communication with those who have passed on; and that their message is one of Hope and encouragement to mankind.

Sir Arthur is honest in his beliefs; there are others who are not, who seek to profit from the tears of the bereaved. This great two reel picture shows up the fakers and the crooks who seek to commercialize Spiritualism.

Everybody in your community is either for or against Doyle's beliefs. It's the biggest topic and the biggest little picture of the day. Play it up and PROFIT.

Written by
Cullom Holmes Ferrell

Pathépicture
TRADE MARK

Directed by
John J. Harvey

Is Conan Doyle Right?
(1923)

It was never grammatically correct to spell the word "weird" as "wierd," but writers did it, time and again, during the nineteenth and early twentieth centuries. Perhaps we could, between friends, at least for fun, refer to this the proto-Weirdumentaries in this section as "Wierdumentaries," the spelling evoking the era under review, an era long before the likes of Harald Reinl's *Chariots of the Gods* (1970).

Don't care to join me in such weird wordplay, in such strange shenanigans? Fair enough, I suppose. But I'll remember it, if not in this life, then in the next.

Whatever we call these precursors, the first of them to appear on-screen was *Is Conan Doyle Right?* (1923).

Are there ghosts? Can we talk to them? Do they talk to us? Do they even want to talk to us?

Spiritualism, at least modern spiritualism, began in 1848 thanks to Kate and Margaret Fox, who spoke to the dead. Or not. Their spirit rapping ignited a national craze, but decades later they admitted to faking the whole thing. After that, Margaret recanted her recantation.

By that time, the Fox sisters didn't matter as much, in part because there were so many spiritualists, and not just in America. Talking with the dead was popular in Europe, including England, where it caught the fancy of no less than Sir Arthur Conan Doyle, creator of Sherlock Holmes.

Ghosts and fake ghosts alike populated the cinema in its earliest days, as did silly spiritualists. As early as 1899, the Edison Manufacturing Company distributed *A Visit to the Spiritualist*, which one review called the "funniest of all moving magic films."

Films generally concentrated on spiritualist frauds, including the first documentary on the subject, *Spiritualism Exposed!* (1913). Over the course of three reels, real-life medium Eva Ray and "Professor" Fred Curtis fulfilled the title mission. *Variety* reported, "all the tricks known to the mediums and the spooks from the other world are exposed via the film." This now-lost film also featured—according to *Billboard*—a "heart-interest story." Whether that meant between ghosts, humans, or some interbreeding of the two, I know not.

Another lost film, *Is Conan Doyle Right?*, is of particular interest to those of us in pursuit of the proto-weird. Two reels in length, this Pathé film was directed by John J. Harvey and written by Cullom Holmes Ferrell.

Motion Picture News suggested that the question posed in the film's title was indeed explored:

> *The present picture, while depicting the fraudulent practices of the great army of fake mediums, is in no way a condemnation of the spiritualism movement and does*

not indict all spiritualistic practitioners as cheats. The serious and sincere phase of the movement is presented as well as the deceptive elements which have been prospering at the expense of too credulous patrons.

By contrast, *Moving Picture World* told readers, "While this subject hints slightly at a possible foundation for spiritualism, it leaves small argument in favor of it."

That *Is Conan Doyle Right?* wanted to answer its own question in the negative is fairly evident in this advertising copy:

Sir Arthur is honest in his beliefs; there are others who are not, who seek to profit from the tears of the bereaved. This great two-reel picture shows up the fakers and the crooks who seek to commercialize Spiritualism.

It was as if the film was the inverse of the later Weirdumentary, only a nod to the paranormal and a concentration on not-so-fun world of the skeptics.

Put another way, no one in this movie—or in the audience, apparently—gets to say howdy to Captain Howdy. But the sheer emphasis on the question in its title makes this little number about mediums an important step as we rock on to Weirdumentary Avenue.

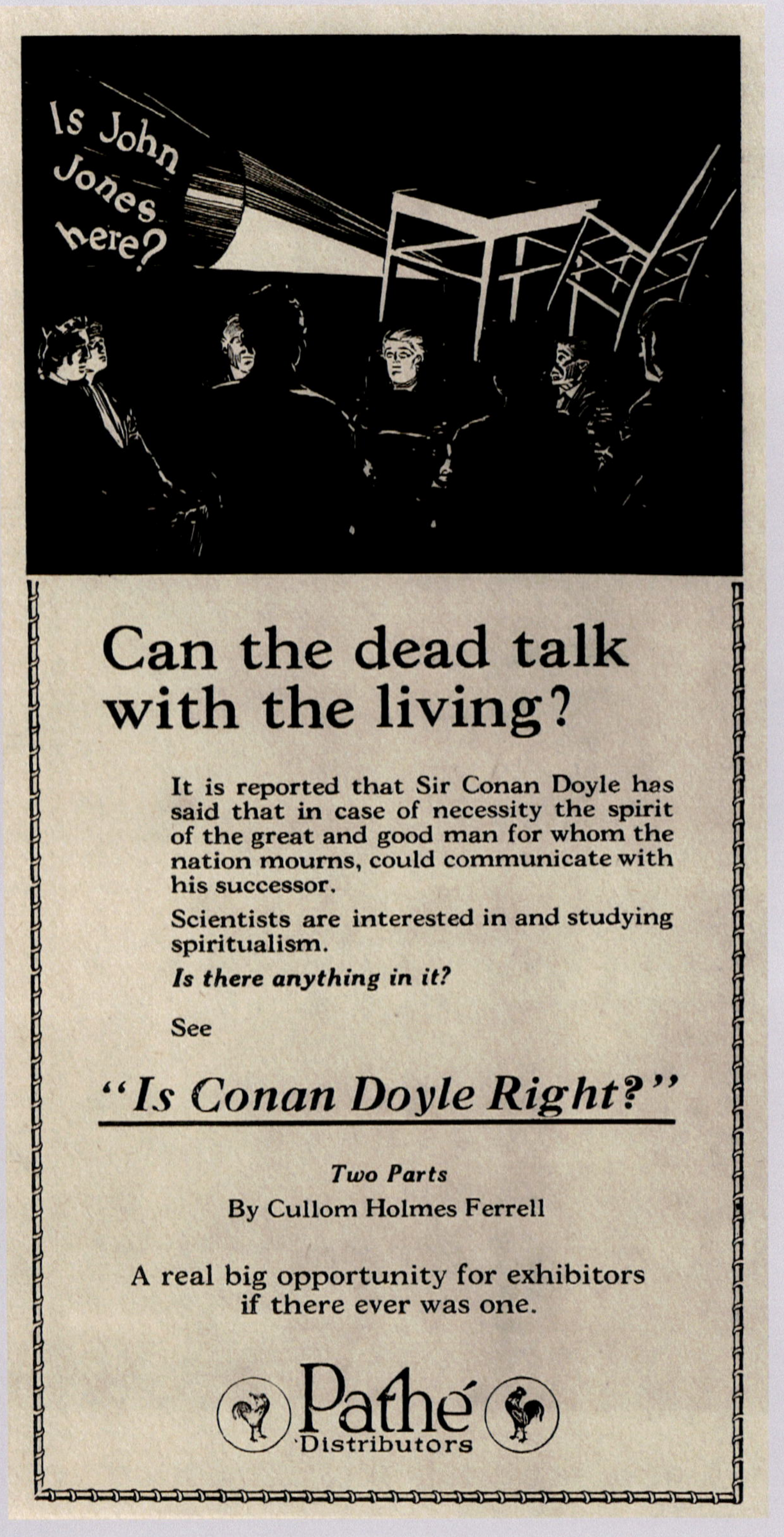

Curiosities

(1930–1932)

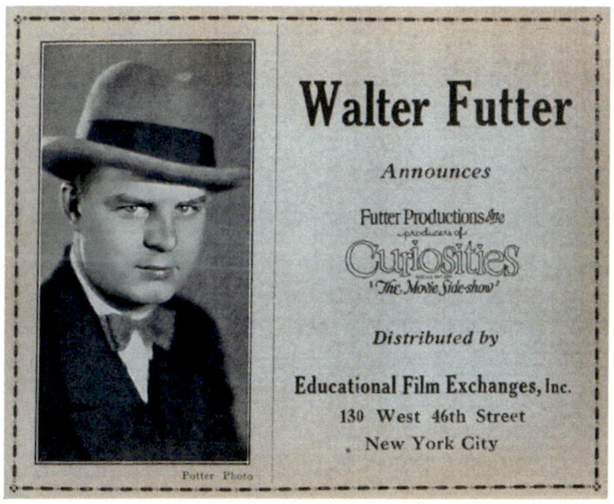

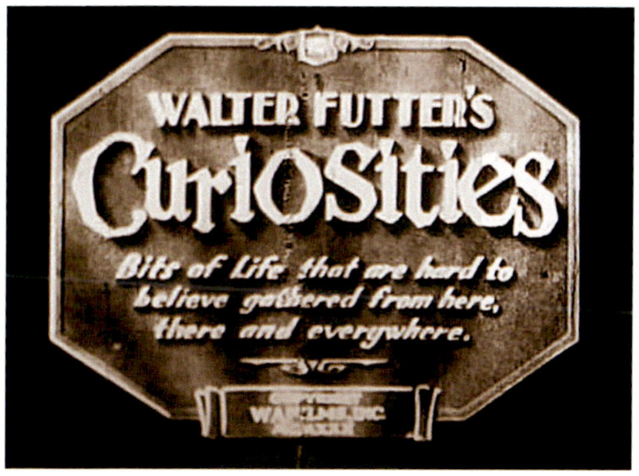

Within these pages must appear the name Robert L. Ripley. He initially appeared on-screen in *Believe It or Not!,* a series of Vitaphone short subjects produced and released from 1930 to 1932. Odd stories, sometimes weird, but not Weirdumentaries. That said, Ripley did bring a bit of the bizarre into the American movie bazaar.

Warner Bros. released a similar series called *Strange as It Seems* (1930–1934). Strange stories, yes. Weirdumentaries, no, not any more than *Believe It or Not!* But *Strange as It Seems* regularly featured low-budget historical re-enactments, an element that became crucial for Weirdumentaries.

It was Walter's Futter's *Curiosities,* a series of short subjects also introduced in—guess what—1930, that is of the greatest import for the likes of us. Futter promoted them as "bits of life that are hard to believe gathered from here, there and everywhere."

In the very first *Curiosities* film, one story is particularly noteworthy: *Voodooism is the Worship of the Serpent.* Filmed in Haiti, some of the footage presents beautiful scenery and everyday life in Port-au-Prince. Other images depict the beating of drums and frenetic dancing at an alleged voodoo ceremony. The short also refers to the midnight sacrifice of a three-year-old child, but it shows us nothing of the kind.

More fascinating still is a *Curiosities* short released in December 1931. According to *Movie Age*:

> *Walter Futter shows how dead men work in the Island of Haiti in his most recent* Curiosities, *which are released by Columbia Pictures. According to the natives, voodoo rites make it possible to animate the bodies of the deceased and keep them working in the fields. Other novelties including the mystery of the crown of thorns, the oddest junkyard in the world, proof that the state of Wyoming was once at the bottom of the ocean, and the secret of how ships are put in bottles.*

Motion Picture Daily added that J.P. Medbury, the narrator, who usually cracked jokes, delivered his "monologue is more in a straight vein, getting away from the kidding stuff in describing the clips."

Here was a more serious tone, as well as the very first on-screen appearance of zombies—whether real, fake, or somewhere in between—coming over six months before Victor Halperin's feature film *White Zombie* (1932) with Bela Lugosi.

Equally interesting is Futter's *Voodooland* (1932, a.k.a. *Voodoo Land*), which was an entry in a different series, *Travelaughs. The Film Daily* called it:

> *A trip through the island of Haiti with J.P. Medbury as the wisecracking off-stage lecturer. First are shown some of the various native occupations and primitive methods, most of the work being done by women while the men specialize in loafing. Then after following a series of countryside trails, the scene of the voodoo ceremonies is reached. This spectacle is nothing very special, just a little hip shaking and drinking, but the comedy comments by Medbury make it quite amusing.*

A surviving print exhibits what *Film Daily* described, though Medbury's jokes would be best understood as dumb, unfunny, and racist. (Unfortunate that I've misplaced my long cane, because this jerk needs to be yanked offstage.)

But there was one advance in *Voodooland*. Rather than being one story among many, *Voodooland* features a singular narrative, as would most of the later Weirdumentaries.

In the 1950s, Futter developed a widescreen lens for movie projectors. In my book, though, his panoramic vision was already on display in the thirties.

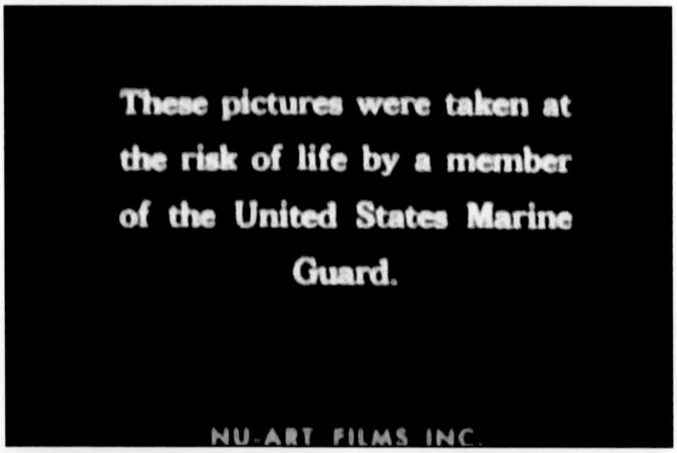

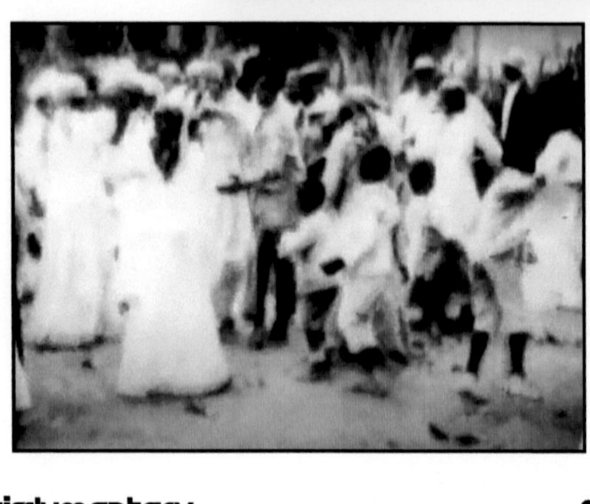

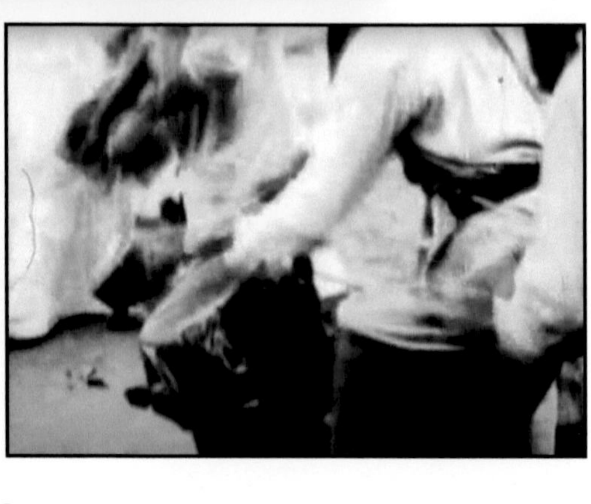

Ingagi

(1930)

"Congo Pictures Ltd. Present ..." a horribly racist documentary, one that provoked enormous interest and controversy upon its original release, and one that was thought lost for decades. Thanks to a rediscovered print and restoration, we can now explore the exotic country of Weirdonia.

Ingagi actually takes place in Africa. Several other racist travelogues were released in the thirties, *Africa Speaks!* (1930) among them. But *Ingagi* is distinctive enough in its awfulness to require its presence herein.

Let's first consider what the opening text tells us: "Portraying the thrilling adventures of Sir Hubert Winstead, F.A.S., during his two years' expedition into the hitherto unknown regions of Darkest AFRICA."

Winstead and his partner planned their trip as a typical smash-and-grab imperialist robbery, collecting "specimens" for transport back to Jolly Old England. They did just that, apparently. But they also heard an "unbelievable and fantastic" story that they had to pursue. What was it? The "suspense" evaporates even before the opening text finishes:

> *In the Ingagi country there exists a tribe who annually give one of their women to the Gorillas (Ingagi). This sacrifice seems to be part of a tradition which, in the superstitious minds of these natives, protects them from the raids of these beasts.*

So, three years before King Kong fell in love with Fay Wray, we have the allegedly true tale of interspecies sex, right here on our show.

Speaking of chronologies, *Ingagi* came about thirty-eight years before the MPAA rating system, and thus before the either offensive or attractive label "X-Rated."

Not to worry, though, because the bulk of this eighty-two-minute movie has nothing to do with bestiality. Instead, it's a brew of footage filmed in Africa and Los Angeles, playing so fast and loose with the truth as to give us whiplash.

The "Ingagi" section of the film doesn't show up until the final fifteen minutes. "Could these tales be true?" our narrator asks. The answer is no, of course, but that's in real life. In reel life, the answer is a big yes.

The (attempted) sacrifice of a bare-breasted woman occurs in the very last five minutes, on the heels of an "all-night ceremony."

The chosen victim sits on a log, awaiting her new pal, which is either to be a gorilla or a guy in a mediocre costume. (It's the latter.)

He carries her off, and she screams like someone "possessed." A member of the crew shoots the "gorilla," and thus the woman is saved from her "inhuman" fate.

Motion Picture News reported that crowds in Los Angeles "fought and pushed their way into the Orpheum to see *Ingagi*." (Curious George brought all of his racist pals, apparently.)

To be sure, *Ingagi* received some backlash in 1930, not only for its sensationalism, but also its fakery. One trade publication called it a "Barnum attraction," advising exhibitors to promote it as a "freak piece of entertainment."

Back to our original question, though. Why do we need to chronicle this horrifying nonsense on our journey? After all, most Weirdumentaries didn't fake their evidence, even if they showed questionable footage like the Patterson-Gimlin Bigfoot film of 1967.

The rationale for inclusion here is because *Ingagi* proved how much money an exploitation documentary on a bizarre topic could generate at the box office in an era—like most of the twentieth and twenty-first centuries—when it's been hard for any nonfiction or "nonfiction" film to even get a theatrical release.

Believe it or not, one serious description of *Ingagi* in 1930 called it a "scientific thriller." What I'd call this racist tripe is best not mentioned in polite or even impolite company.

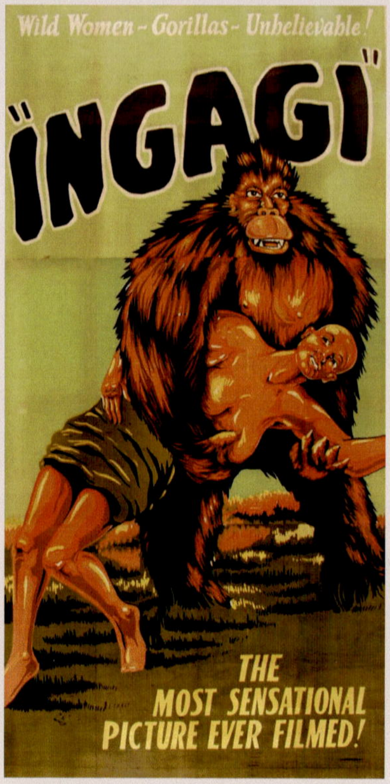

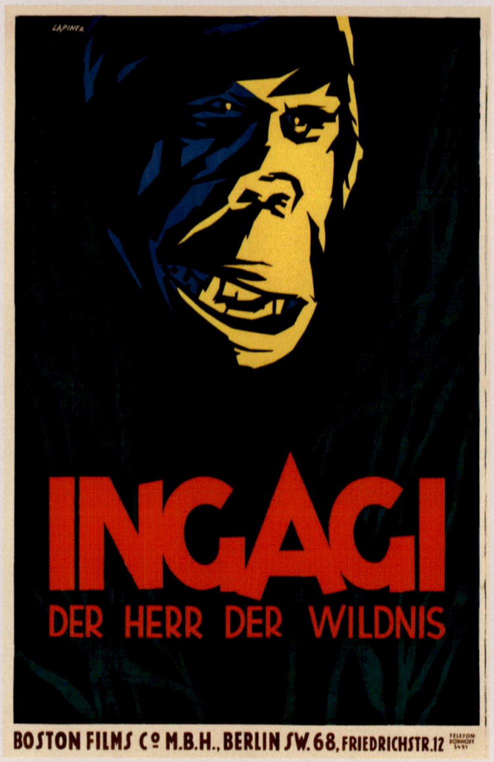

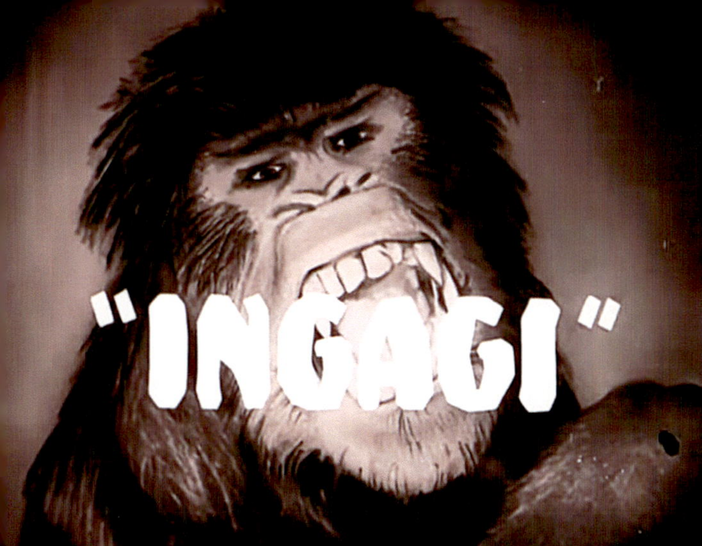

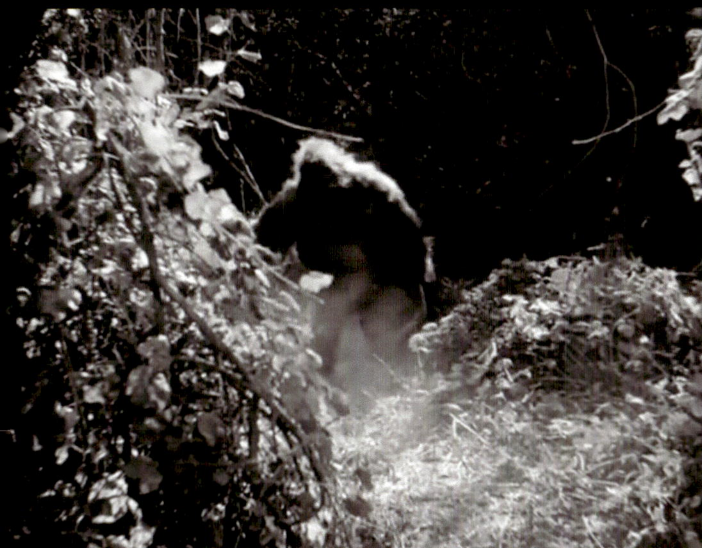

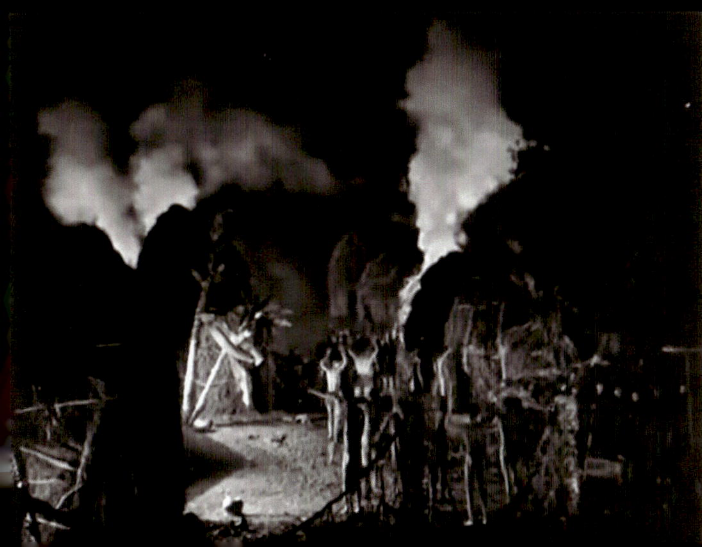

HAYS BARS "INGAGI" FILM.

Movie of Jungle Life Called Nature Faking by Business Bureau.

LOS ANGELES, June 11 (AP).—Fred Beetson, executive vice president of the Association of Motion Picture Producers, said today he had received a telegram from President Will H. Hays announcing that "we will not show the motion picture 'Ingagi,' which depicts African jungle life.

The National Better Business Bureau declared in a statement the picture was "nature faking."

"INGAGI," FAKE AMERICAN FILM, HITS NEW SNAG

Federal Government Files Charge

WASHINGTON, May 15.—"Ingagi," that insidious film of African life—a la Hollywood—is in bad again, this time with the government.

The federal trade commission charges that Congo Pictures, Ltd., producers of the film, "have been and are now using unfair methods of competition in interstate commerce."

The charge is based on the fact that "the company culled the feature from film libraries and assembled it into a complete continuous film and that newspaper advertising pictures, copy and reading matter make many false, deceptive and misleading statements."

The government further charges that "some of the scenes were made in or about the city of Los Angeles."

All respondents in the case have been notified that the hearing on the charges will take place May 15 in the offices of the federal trade commission. No commission attorneys have as yet been asigned, nor has response been heard from the Congo Pictures, Ltd., or any of the individuals named.

These men include N. H. Spitzer, president of Congo; William Alexander, vice president; W. S. Campbell, secretary, and H. D. Smith.

The picture is still being shown, according to the commission.

What Do You Think?

(1937-1939)

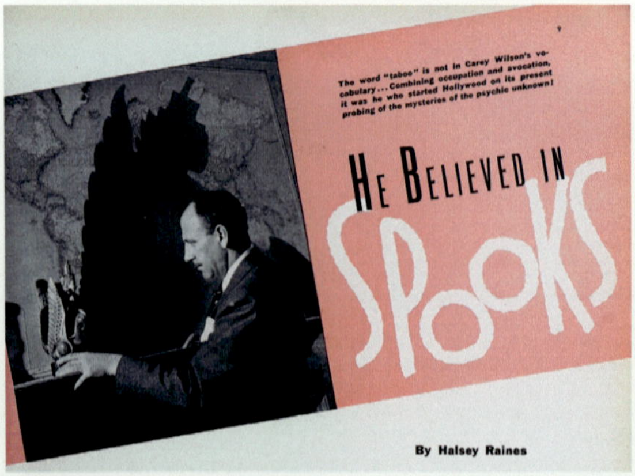

One of the ventricles beating deep in the very heart of the Weirdumentary is the question mark. Whatever topic—no matter how unbelievable or unprovable—can be broached just as long as it's phrased in the form of a question.

Carey D. Wilson, film salesman turned scenario writer, was working at MGM in the late thirties when he decided to produce and narrate a short subject on psychic phenomena. It would be one reel, meaning approximately ten minutes in length.

He later recalled that "virtually all his studio acquaintances dismissed the suggestion as impractical, verging too far from reality and sober fact." But his persistence eventually paid off. Wilson "received reluctant permission to go ahead with one subject."

Directed by Jacques Tourneur, *What Do You Think?* was the result. *The Film Daily* wrote:

> *Looks like a real novelty and one that will meet with strong response from that big section of the public interested in psychic phenomena. Carey Wilson tells the story, which purports to be an actual experience of a young man saved from death by an auto collision by the voice of his mother who is thousands of miles away. Other strange phenomena are present in the youth's experience, such as the vision of a dead woman's body on his bed, which later turns out to be the woman who is killed in the auto crash. The point is that the youth would have been the victim instead of the other if his mother's voice had not delayed him for the fraction of a minute.*

Motion Picture Daily also reviewed the short, coming to the beautiful conclusion that "It is all rather strange."

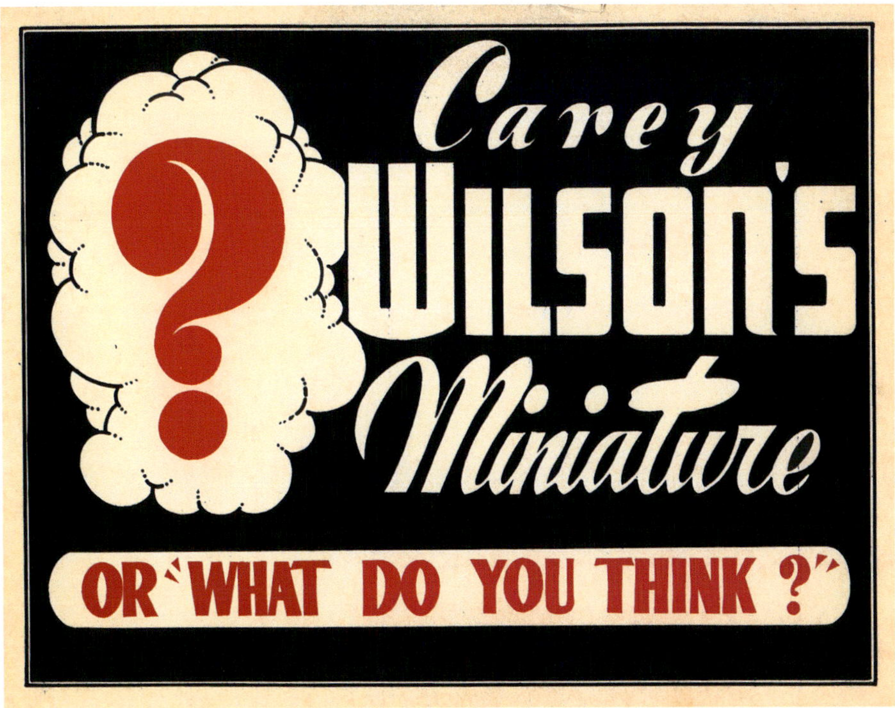

Wilson later admitted that he was the "youth" depicted in the story. He also announced:

> *I am a firm believer of communication with the dead and because I believe that thousands of others are, we are treating the question very seriously. We will make as many of these little pictures as we can find real incidents upon which to base them. If possible, we [will] find some scientific explanation for the occurrence that will raise a question of what really caused it. In this way we leave the idea of psychic phenomena open to debate.*

MGM claimed to have received more than one thousand letters during the first month that *What Do You Think?* played theaters.

The film's success caused Wilson to search for more stories, which ranged from ghost dogs to reincarnation. MGM promoted them as "subjects investigating the mysteries of metaphysics and psychic phenomena." According to *Motion Picture Daily*, *What Do You Think No. 2* (1938) was:

> *Another interesting cinematic venture into the realm of the supernatural. The film should have good reception where the audience found the initial number of interest. The slight plot ... concerns the near commission of murder by a young and jealous husband who saw a woman resembling his wife in a doctor's arms. The narrative is shrewdly ended with a deduction that leaves the conclusion hanging in mid-air.*

The Film Daily added, "The psychic and spiritualist fans will go for it." The same trade would also call the overall series "controversial," apparently using the term as a compliment.

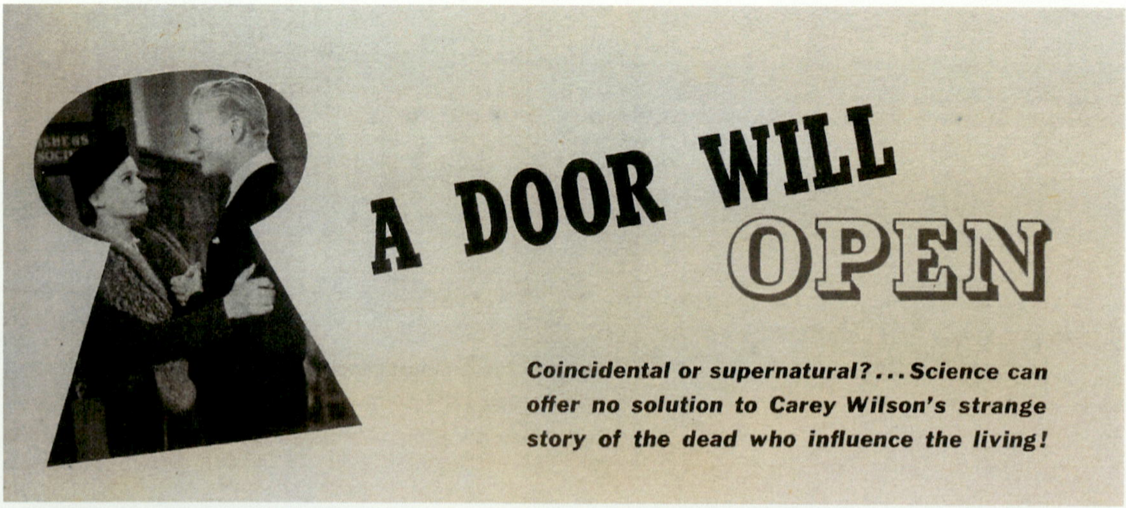

Of *A Door Will Open* (1939), another short in the *What Do You Think?* series, *Boxoffice* told readers:

> *Another Carey Wilson excursion into supernatural phenomena that has great possibilities for successful presentation to the average audience. It concerns the rise of a pianist and the weird contributions to his success by his dead mother-in-law. Serious stuff and a bit on the different side.*

Motion Picture Herald added, "The film poses the question whether the events were coincidental or of the supernatural."

Of the entire series, a journalist said, "Although Mr. Wilson's own paranormal experiences and study of psychic literature have brought him a conviction of personal survival and communication after death, he has zealously kept any individual interpretation of his screen episodes from his narrative text. The problem there, he feels, is to present the greatest amount of mentally stimulating entertainment in the most unbiased fashion."

Unbiased, I don't know. That's a question mark. But it's clear that Carey D. Wilson needs to be better known for the doors that he opened, thus helping us to break on through to the weird side.

Nostradamus

(1938–1944)

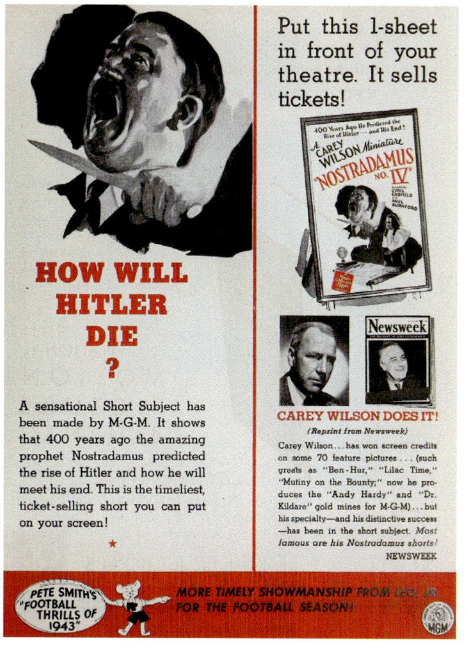

According to studio publicity, MGM had "more stars than there [were] in the heavens." But there were stars in the actual heavens as well, lots of them. And some folks read them like a book and then wrote books about them.

Which brings us to the sixteenth-century French astrologer and seer Nostradamus. And his quatrains, of course, all those many vague and cryptic quatrains.

And it also brings us to Carey D. Wilson, our friend behind the *What Do You Think?* series (1937–39, see entry). As one magazine article wrote:

> *He saw enormous public appeal values in the amazing prophecies made about the war today, by Miguel de Nostradamus, who died five hundred years ago. The Prophecies have been available for half a thousand years, but it took Carey Wilson to remove them from dusty archives, to make them into the most startling short subjects ever filmed.*

When *Nostradamus* was released in 1938, MGM publicity proclaimed, "Here is a short that will be heard round the world!" Wilson produced and narrated it, while John Burton portrayed the title character in its proto-weird dramatizations. Of the eleven-minute film, *Motion Picture Herald* told readers:

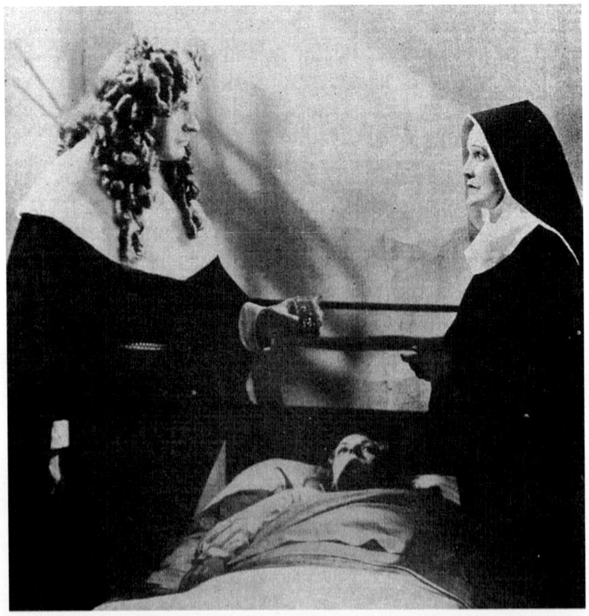

> *The material offered in this newest number from the Historical Mysteries group studies a subject that should hold a greater audience response than the customary high degree of attention given these intriguing short queries. It offers the strange success of a certain psychic individual... Nostradamus, whose name has been coined into the word 'nostrum,' to foretell coming events. A learned medico of the middle ages, Nostradamus wrote a tome called* Prophetic Centuries *in which are contained forecasts of happenings such as the London Fire of 1666, the tragic fate of Louis XVI, Marie Antoinette, and the military career of the little Corsican corporal. The riddling of the future is done in historical and entertaining accuracy.*

Motion Picture Daily was duly impressed as well, calling *Nostradamus* as an "unusually fine subject."

The film's success meant the public wanted more, and that's exactly what MGM gave them. *More About Nostradamus* (1941) returned Wilson as narrator and Burton as actor for another eleven-minute short. *Motion Picture Daily* explained:

> *The prophecies of the French seer of the 16th century are dramatized by Carey Wilson in a dramatic sequel to the original* Nostradamus *of two years ago. The film first depicts dramatically the death of the nobleman who desecrated Nostradamus' tomb, just as predicted. It then follows Nostradamus' book of predictions,* Prophetic Centuries, *and depicts how they are borne out in such historical developments as Britain's defeat of the Spanish armada, the World War, and various episodes in the second World War. Nostradamus also wrote of the U.S. entry into the present war and of a vanquished German nation. The effect is startling.*

A bit more about *More About Nostradamus*: it was nominated for an Academy Award in the Best Short Subject category. (Carry on, Carey, and don't even try to keep us calm!)

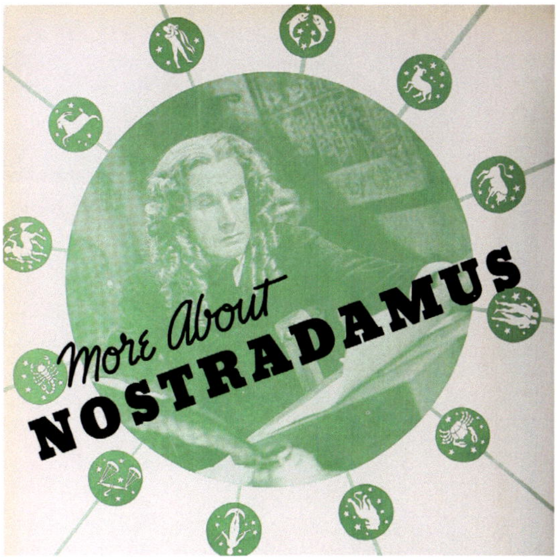

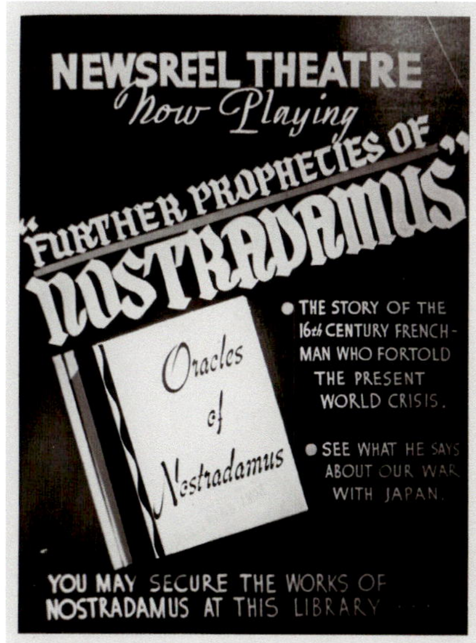

Of the old seer and his predictions, *Boxoffice* told readers, "This is the kind of stuff it seems that audiences relish." Apparently they did, because MGM released *Further Prophecies of Nostradamus* in 1942. Another eleven minutes, another round of Wilson and Burton. According to *Motion Picture Daily*:

> *Here's Nostradamus again and, with intelligent presentation of the subject ... In recent issues Wilson illustrated how the predictions of the 16th-century French seer materialized. In this he depicts a photostat copy of the original Nostradamus book of prophecies, follows through on the method of interpretation, and then points out recent developments in the present war which have borne out the predictions. At the outset, Nostradamus is pictured as an outstanding scientist who, following the death of his wife and children, undertakes to look into the future.*

Nostradamus worked in quatrains; so did Carey Wilson and MGM. The fourth and final subject of this run was *Nostradamus IV* (1944). More than the others, it concentrated on the application of his old prophecies to then-current events. *Showmen's Trade Review* described it as follows:

> *Carey Wilson again takes the audience into a survey of the amazing predictions of a strange 16th-century philosopher and their bearing on current historical happenings. In principal the reel deals with predictions of the downfall of Hitler and the means by which he may die. ... A very good short for any program."*

"How will Hitler Die?" MGM ads for *IV* asked, adding that the prophet had already told everyone the answer four centuries earlier. The short's specific answer had to do with his "traitorous henchmen, Hermann Goering or Heinrich Himmler," which wasn't completely wrong, but certainly not correct.

In 1946, *The Hollywood Reporter* announced that Wilson planned to make a Nostradamus feature out of his four short subjects. Alas, he did not.

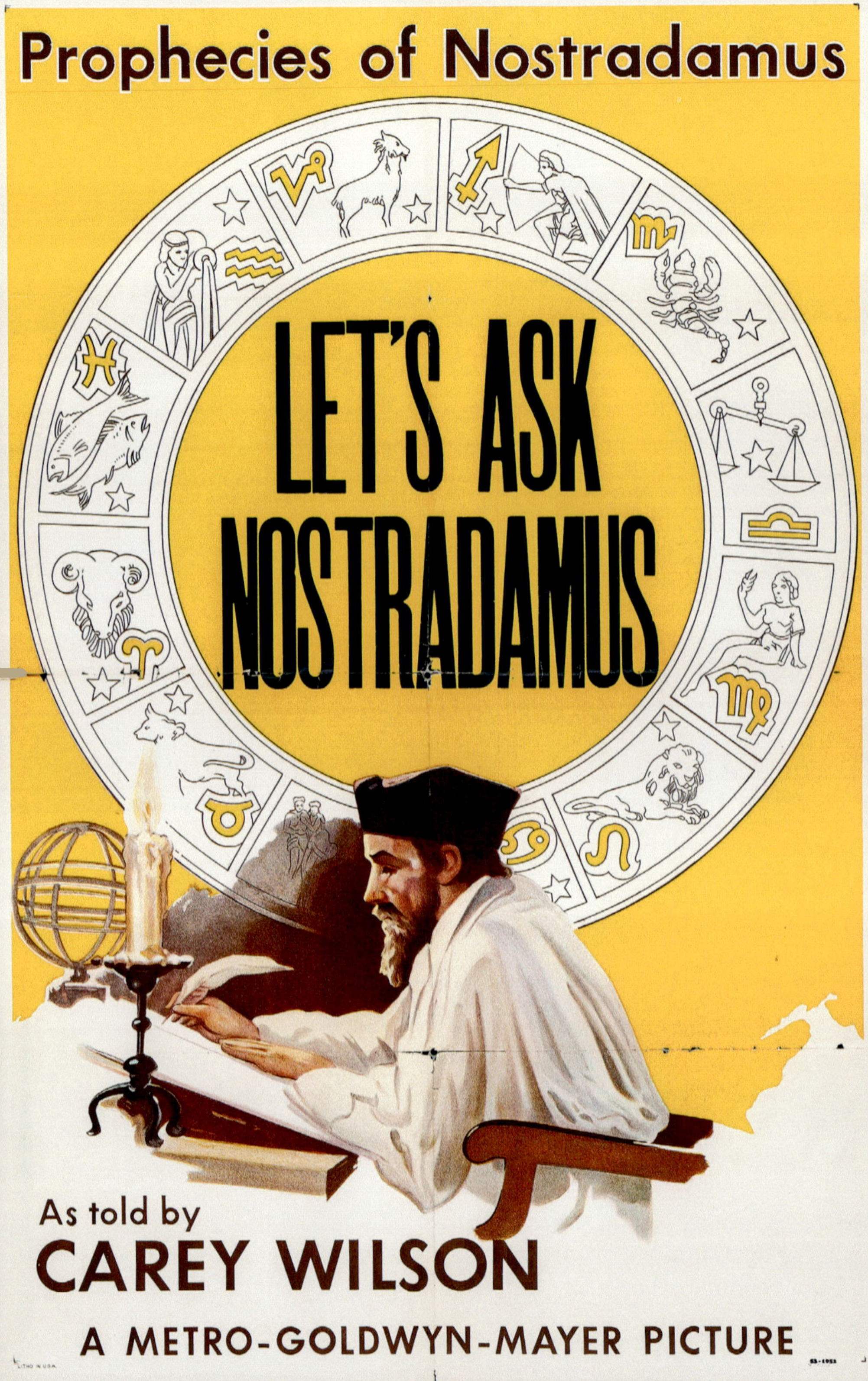
Prophecies of Nostradamus
LET'S ASK NOSTRADAMUS
As told by
CAREY WILSON
A METRO-GOLDWYN-MAYER PICTURE
LITHO IN U.S.A.

Prophecy of Nostradamus

(1953)

Such good news, and news that almost anyone could have predicted, even without speaking in quatrains. In 1952, *Boxoffice* announced, "After an eight-year hiatus, MGM is resuming production of its Nostradamus short subjects by scheduling four to be produced and written by Carey Wilson, who turned out the first group."

The new film series led Wilson to write a short article about Nostradamus, telling readers:

> *It's bad enough that for the past ten years I've been accused of translating and interpreting the prophecies of Nostradamus, the 16th-century Swami, to suit my own purposes—or rather the purposes of the little MGM one-reel featurettes about Nostradamus, the man who dared to put into writing his predictions of the future. Yes, such accusation is bad enough, but recently I was accused of inventing Nostradamus! I didn't.*

Nope. Nada. Not a bit of it. Nostradamus was real. Wilson certainly didn't create him, but he does deserve credit for creating the modern interest in him.

And he was back in action with what became a trio of new MGM short subjects, the overall series title being *Prophecy of Nostradamus.*

Why bring the old boy back? The title of the first ten-minute short explains it as well as it could be: *Nostradamus Says So!* (1953). Of the demanding sage and his new flick, *Boxoffice* explained:

> *For the first time in eight years, Carey Wilson has produced another in the series which attracted some attention in the early 1940s. Turning the leaves of Nostradamus' volumes, the narrator picks out many prophecies which are applicable to today's events. One of his amazing 16th-century predictions includes a vision of the atom bomb. Shots of the modern-day version of his prophecies are then shown.*

Wilson's second film in the new series was *Let's Ask Nostradamus* (1953). Why not, yes, why not indeed? But let's keep it to a single, ten-minute reel. *Boxoffice* wrote:

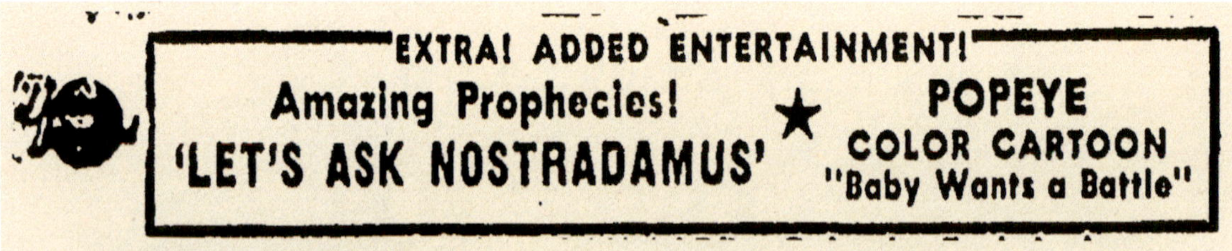

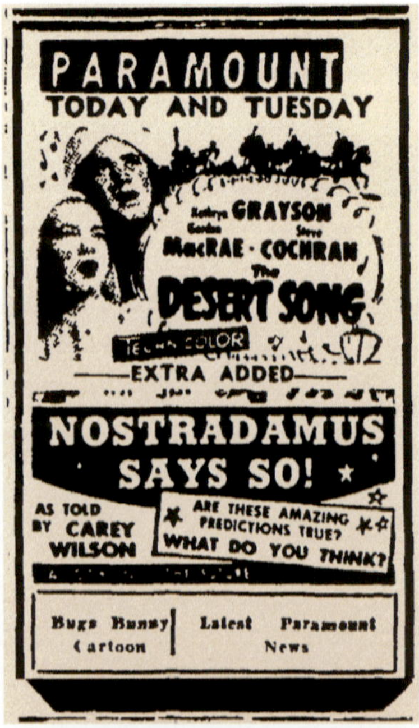

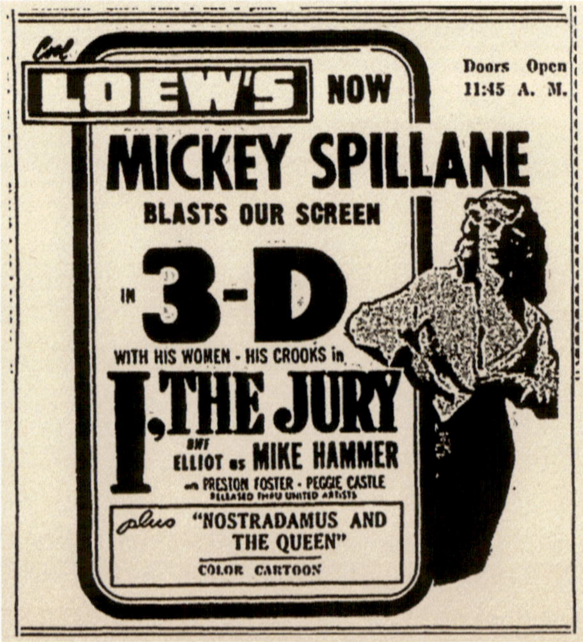

> *Carey Wilson again delves into early French history to point out the prognostications of [an] era fraught with troubles and killings. Several of Nostradamus' quotations are read which prophesy events which took place later, including the ultimate beheading of Louis XVI, his queen and his mistress, Madame Du Barry.*

Speaking of royalty, there was *Nostradamus and the Queen* (1953), the last short in the series. Again, from *Boxoffice*:

> *Like the earlier shorts in this series, this has educational value, but it is only mildly entertaining. Dipping into the well-preserved volumes written by ... Nostradamus, the producer shows how his insights into the future have come true. Many of the things that happened to Catherine de Medici and the royalty of France were predicted by Nostradamus.*

And so went the final ten minutes that Carey D. Wilson spent with the old (mis)fortune-teller.

Wilson retired from MGM in 1954, taking advantage of a pension plan at the studio. I need no crystal ball to understand that he had well earned it.

Unidentified Flying Objects
the true story of flying saucers

(1956)

"We are grateful to the following for appearing personally in this Motion Picture to tell their experiences in their own words…"

So goes the opening text of *Unidentified Flying Objects*, the list that follows being of real people. The architects of the weird are starting to build the bridge of credibility.

"We wish to thank all the people who appear in this picture in the many sections of the country where this film was made."

That second bit of text keeps building the bridge by implying exhaustive research and numerous shooting locations.

"Our special gratitude to Mr. Tom Towers, an active Los Angeles newspaper reporter, who enacts the role of Mr. Albert M. Chop."

The third bit of text dips under the bridge, under the boardwalk even, as we learn that everything we're about to see isn't true.

"The Montana and Utah films of UFOs will be shown during the picture exactly as they were photographed. They will again be shown at the end of the picture in various densities and speeds to enable you to further examine the objects."

This fourth bit of text not only helps us forget that last palaver about dramatizations, but also attracts our attention. This bridge is vertical, up to the stars, baby.

"These films will be made available to established Scientific Research Institutions upon request."

We got nothin' to hide. The fact that we haven't already sent these films to such eggheads means nothin' at all.

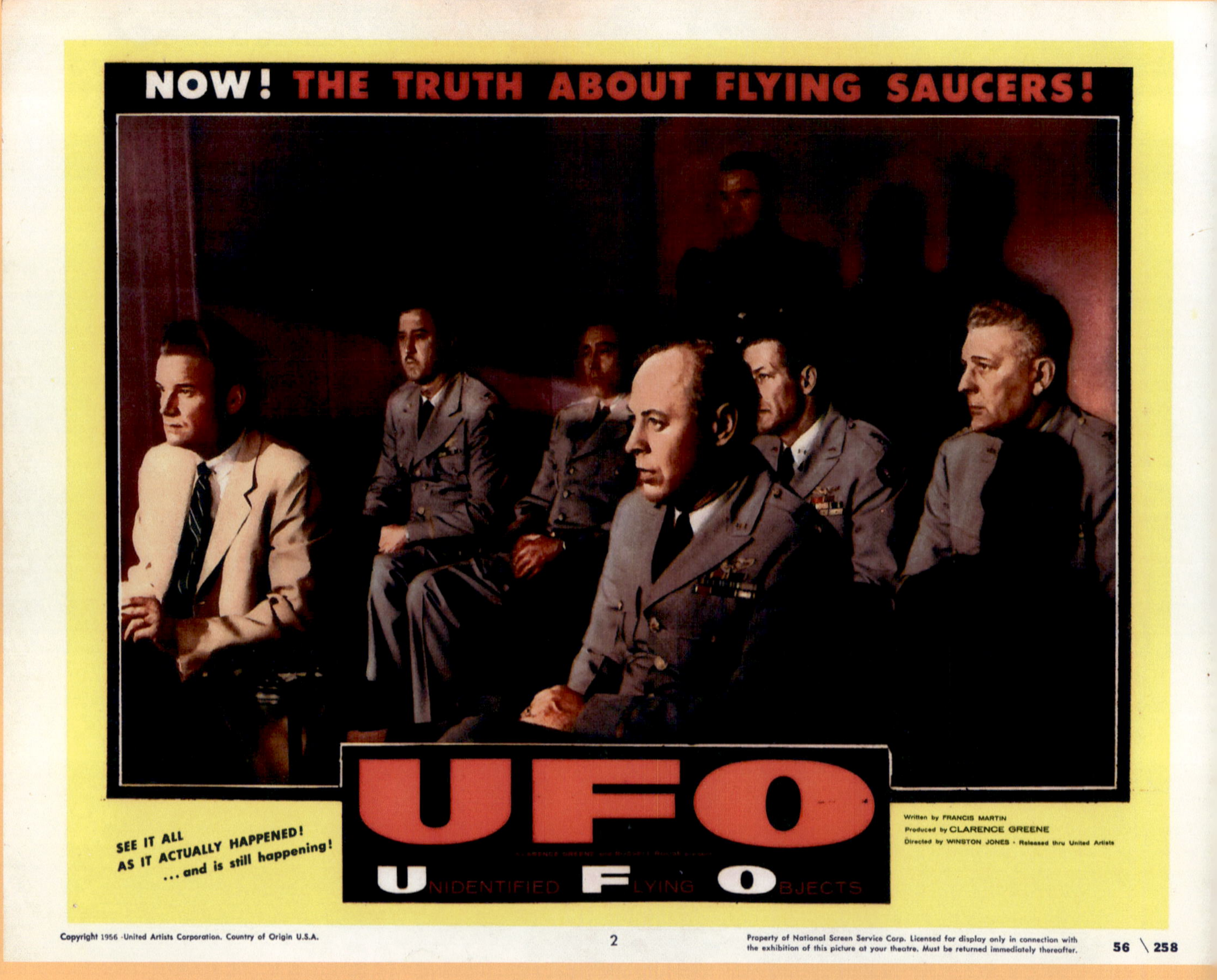
NOW! THE TRUTH ABOUT FLYING SAUCERS!
UFO
UNIDENTIFIED FLYING OBJECTS
SEE IT ALL
AS IT ACTUALLY HAPPENED!
... and is still happening!
Written by FRANCIS MARTIN
Produced by CLARENCE GREENE
Directed by WINSTON JONES · Released thru United Artists
Copyright 1956 -United Artists Corporation. Country of Origin U.S.A.
2
Property of National Screen Service Corp. Licensed for display only in connection with the exhibition of this picture at your theatre. Must be returned immediately thereafter.
56 \ 258

"The Motion Picture you are about to see is true. It is not fiction. Much of the information in it has never been told. You will see it here for the first time."

Rare footage. Real footage. Secret information made public. And once again, just you forget about that earlier word "enacts." This ain't fiction.

But it ain't a documentary either. Real footage, real interviews, faked footage, recreations, all hitting the feature-length running time of ninety-five minutes. Pretty weird, indeed.

Our producer is Clarence Greene, who had written the screenplay for *D.O.A.* (1951). Winston Jones directed *Unidentified Flying Objects*, this being one of his only two directorial credits. By contrast, writer Francis Martin and cinematographer Howard A. Anderson had long lists of films behind them, though Anderson was best known for his special effects work, including for sci-fi flicks like *Phantom from Space* (1953).

In all honesty, these guys weren't the first documentarians to tackle the subject of UFOs. In 1951, Hoffberg Productions and Telenews released the short subject *Mystery of the Flying Saucers* (a.k.a. *The Flying Saucer Mystery*), which featured "actual shots ... of the saucers and eye-witness accounts [from] people who have seen them."

But *Unidentified Flying Objects*—sometimes known as *UFO*—can take heart in being the first feature-length doc on the subject, one that was allegedly three years in the making. Our esteemed crew takes us through the most famous cases, beginning with Kenneth Arnold in 1947. After that incident, "saucer-shaped objects" become more and more common.

We get staged interviews and fake newspaper headlines. We also get actual interviews and press stories. We also see paperwork stamped "SECRET." Who am I to say if it's authentic or not? Maybe it's both.

That's certainly true of the issue of *Life* magazine dated April 7, 1952 that we see. The interior story about UFOs that we see is real, but the cover we're shown isn't, at least it isn't for that date. It features what looks to be Harry S. Truman; the April 7 cover featured Marilyn Monroe.

What we hear about that magazine issue is equally spurious. Our fake reporter Chop says, "The question, if anyone ever had a doubt about it, was forcefully answered." But the article didn't prove the existence of UFOs, instead suggesting a real case *could* be made for them. (Project Blue Book, or Project Screw Book?)

Of the legit interviewees, Captain Willis Sperry of American Airlines is probably the most compelling, even though it seems like he's reading off cue cards. He recalls what he saw in 1950:

> *The object was flying head-on at us. It was fifty times the magnitude of the brightest star. I immediately made an abrupt turn to avoid collision. As I looked to my left, the object appeared to come to a stop. ... It appeared as a perfectly streamlined object without wings or tail section, as it was silhouetted against the full moon. At all times it had a brilliant, shimmering blue light ... It was traveling at fantastic speed, and although it had passed off our left wing tip, it circled us in a manner of seconds and appeared off our right wing. There again it stopped, and we watched it for several seconds. When again it started, it reversed its direction, and we watched it for several more seconds until it disappeared in the east out of sight.*

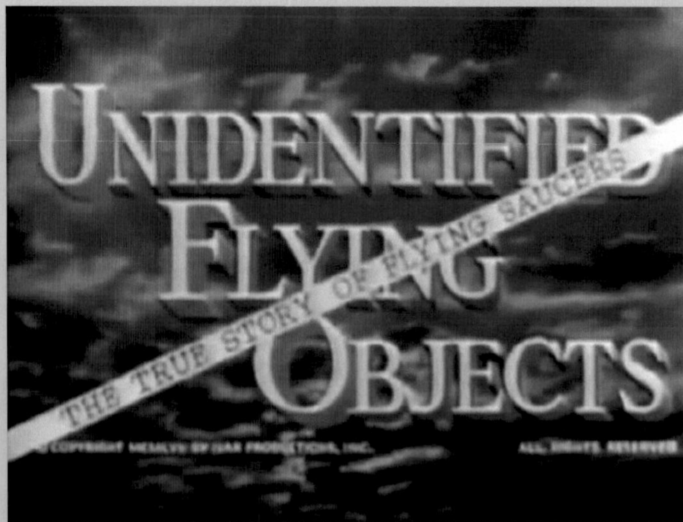
UNIDENTIFIED
FLYING
OBJECTS
THE TRUE STORY OF FLYING SAUCERS

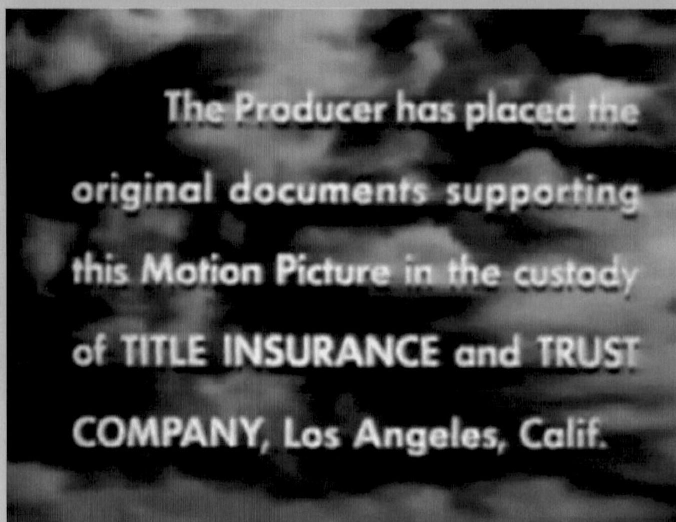
The Producer has placed the
original documents supporting
this Motion Picture in the custody
of TITLE INSURANCE and TRUST
COMPANY, Los Angeles, Calif.

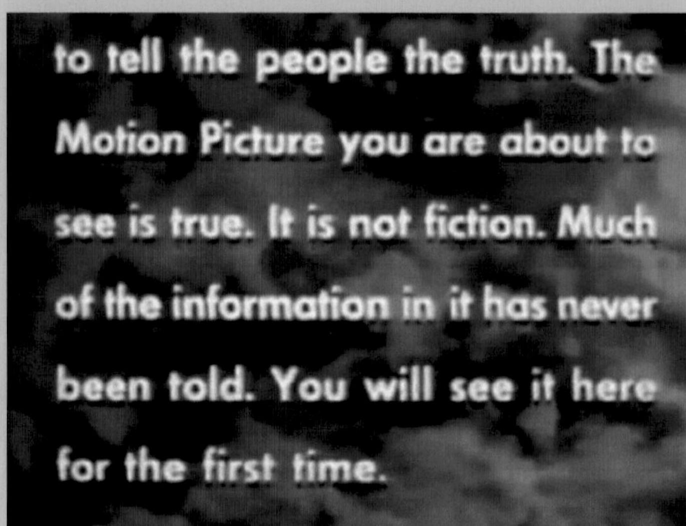
to tell the people the truth. The
Motion Picture you are about to
see is true. It is not fiction. Much
of the information in it has never
been told. You will see it here
for the first time.

After Sperry, the next most interesting is Lieutenant General John A. Samford of the U.S. Air Force, who appears via "Authentic Newsreel Film."

Other interviewees include the men who filmed this flick's most notable evidence, the UFO footage in Montana and Utah. Not only do we see their films, but we see them repeatedly.

Their images are fascinating, no doubt, not dissimilar to glimpses of alleged cryptids in later Weirdumentaries. And their footage is all the more striking because everything in this film is black-and-white, *except* for the Montana and Utah images, which are in color.

But most of *Unidentified Flying Objects* is dramatized footage of the fake reporter Chop. And while the actors might be jabbering about shiny metal objects, the best adjective to describe them is wooden.

Their conversations are generally dull, even when they watch radar of flying saucers over the nation's capital. *Variety* called the film "a bit overlong." Then I called *Variety* "a bit generous." Actually, "way more than a bit generous."

Anyhow, Chop—whose name is more interesting than probably anything else about the character—concludes the film by explaining:

> *The theories of the skeptics could not stand up to the actual experiences of high-ranking military personnel, radar experts, airline pilots, and other responsible witnesses referred to by General Samford as 'credible observers.'*
>
> *...Now, so far as I was concerned, it was no longer a question as to whether or not there were unknown objects flying in our atmosphere. For me, the only questions that remained were 'What are these objects? Where do they come from?' To me, the evidence indicated intelligence behind their control, and by now the belief that their source was interplanetary was no longer incredible.*

Boring though it may be, *Unidentified Flying Objects* has thus moved the Weird-O-Meter needle from the world of "nada" to "maybe."

The film ends with on-screen text that's so good a narrator reads it while we see it: "If they cannot be identified as objects known to man… *What are they?* If they are not man-made… *Who made them?* If they are not from this planet… *Where are they from?*"

Please move the Weird-O-Meter needle from "maybe" to "probably."

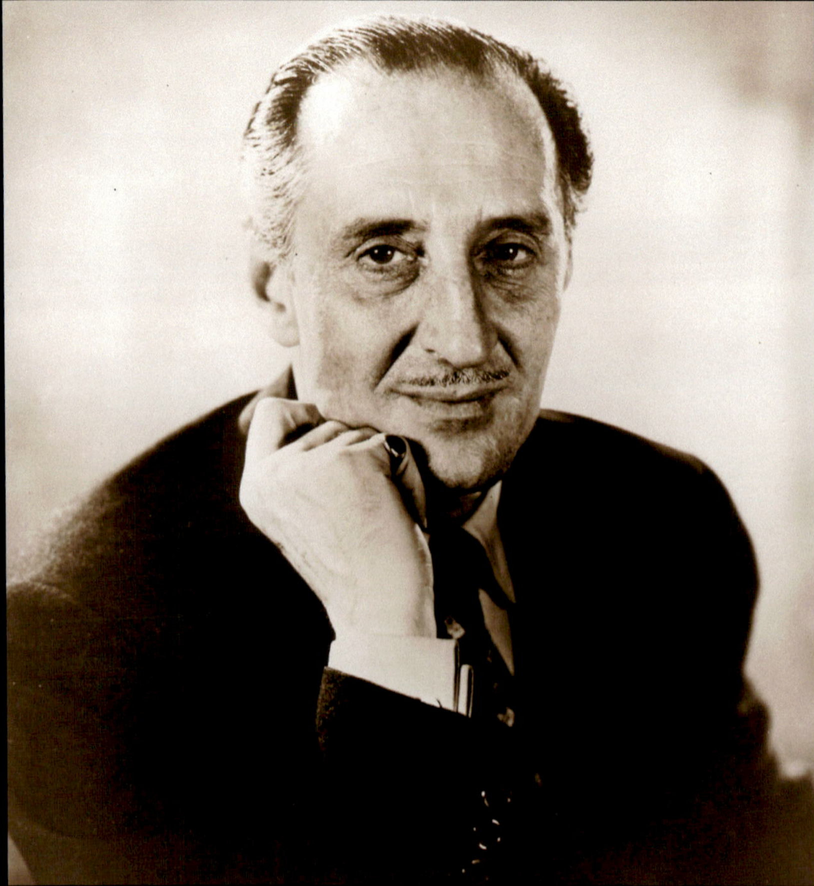

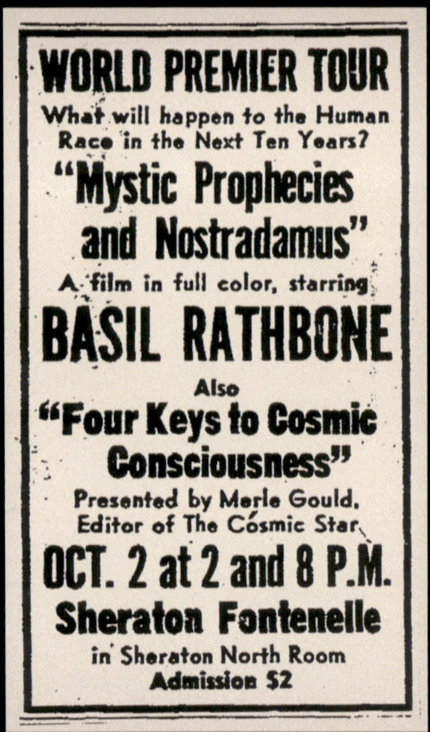
WORLD PREMIER TOUR
What will happen to the Human Race in the Next Ten Years?
"Mystic Prophecies and Nostradamus"
A film in full color, starring
BASIL RATHBONE
Also
"Four Keys to Cosmic Consciousness"
Presented by Merle Gould, Editor of The Cosmic Star
OCT. 2 at 2 and 8 P.M.
Sheraton Fontenelle
in Sheraton North Room
Admission $2

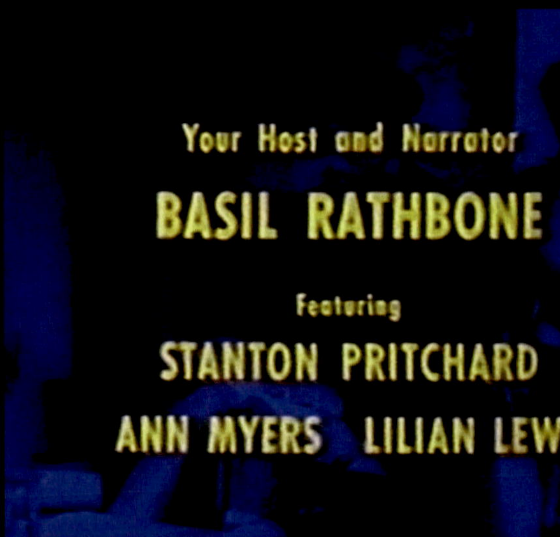
Your Host and Narrator
BASIL RATHBONE
Featuring
STANTON PRITCHARD
ANN MYERS LILIAN LEW

Mystic Prophecies and Nostradamus

(1961)

It was Carey D. Wilson who made Nostradamus into a silver screen star, his short subjects combining dramatized recreations with the veneer of historical documentary. *Mystic Prophecies and Nostradamus* is the next link in that prophetic chain.

But this new flick represents, well, something new. Basil Rathbone, famous for playing Sherlock Holmes and so many horror movie characters, is our "host and narrator." The thought process here was the same that would later guide Weirdumentaries, which opted for the likes of Rod Serling and William Shatner.

At fifty minutes, this filmed-in-color movie begins with Rathbone in an office talking about the meaning of "prophecy," which "has always existed." Perhaps even cave paintings and Egyptian hieroglyphics were predictions of Things to Come.

That was true of various religious texts, with Rathbone reading from the Bible. It foretold the return of Jews to Jerusalem, over 2,500 years before it came to pass.

That's in addition to tales told about the Oracle of Delphi and Cheiro and Edgar Cayce ... and liars and augurs and bears, oh my. In fact, approximately forty minutes of this hour-long flick covers soothsayers other than Nostradamus.

The spectacled Rathbone reads from a book that is big and old, two qualities suggestive of wisdom. We also see a wide range of historical footage, photographs, and paintings.

Having established that prophecy isn't intrinsically evil or bad, Rathbone turns his attentions to "the greatest prophet of the Middle Ages," meaning that we at long last get to Nostradamus.

Stanton Pritchard—whose two other credits are the exploitation movies *Revenge of the Virgins* (1959) and *Like Wow!* (1961)—plays Nostradamus in not-so-dramatic recreation footage. His fake beard deserves applause.

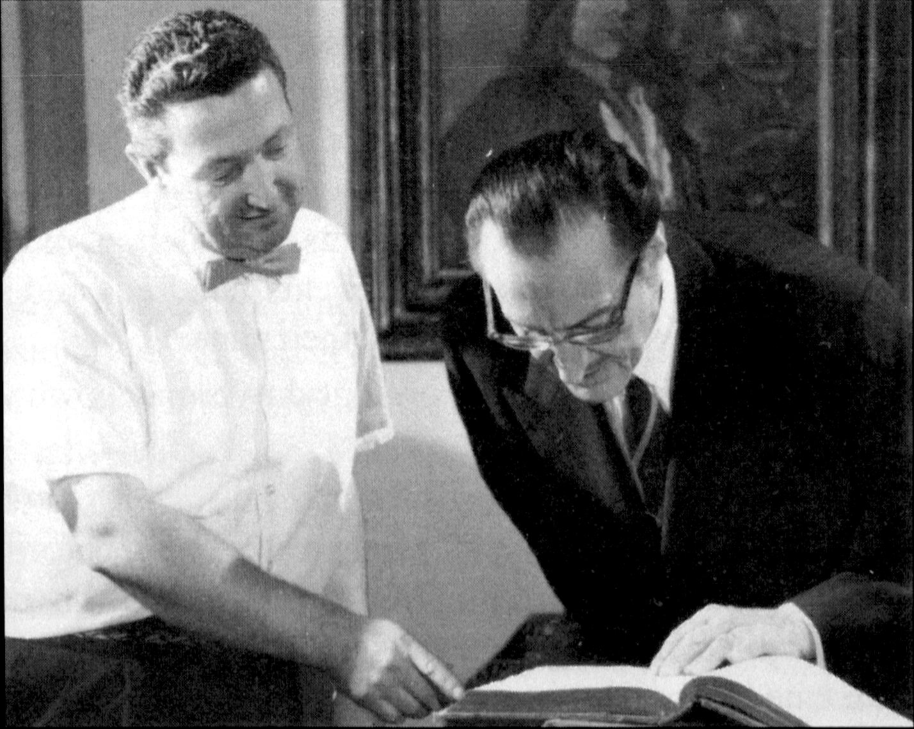

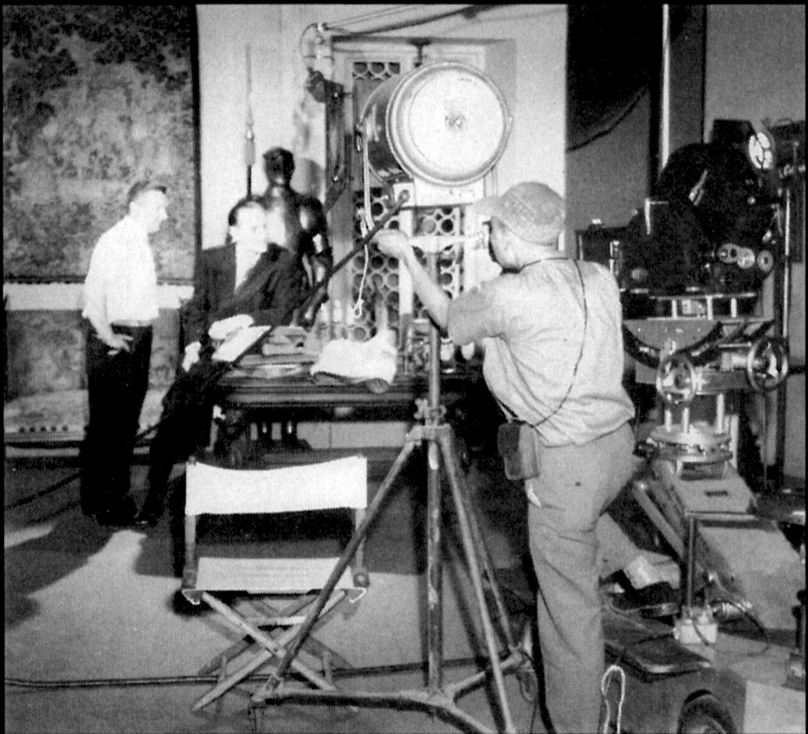

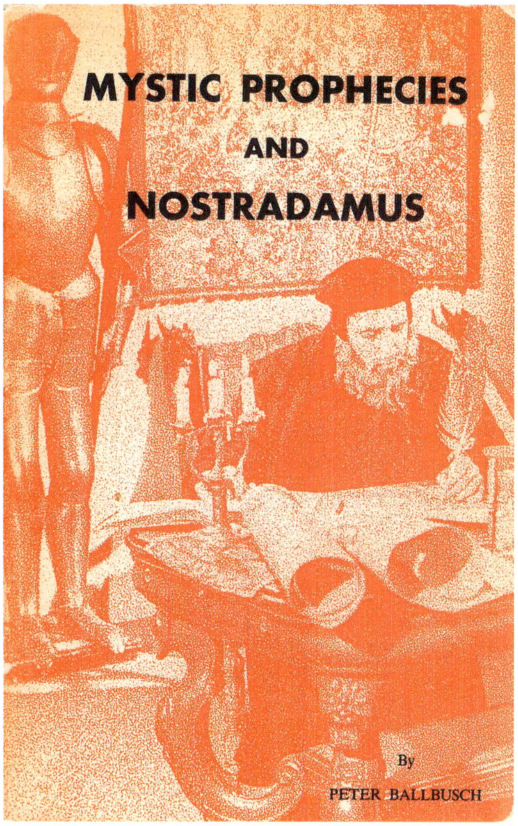

As with Carey Wilson's films, *Mystic Prophecies* presents the extremely vague quatrains of Nostradamus in starkly clear terms, unproblematically connecting his generalities to precise historical events. (And hey, that's cool. When I was a little kid, I loved jamming square pegs into round holes.)

Rathbone concludes the film by explaining that we have the power to change the future, that we hold fate in our hands. Then we see on-screen text that announces, "Not the End" and "Let Us Not Make It So!", to which a thinking person might inquire as to why we'd ever bother thinking about predictions, if the future is so easily subject to change.

Merle S. Gould directed *Mystic Prophecies*, and not too well, to be frank. Peter Ballbusch—who had directed Carey Wilson's *Nostradamus Says So!* (1953) and *Let's Ask Nostradamus* (1953)—wrote the script. Ballbusch was best known in Hollywood as a talented montage editor.

On the one hand, *Mystic Prophecies* is surprisingly dull toil and trouble. On the other hand, its bubble-bubble—a witch's brew of Rathbone, history, recreations, and nonfiction footage, all boiled down to feature length—makes it perhaps the most weird of any proto-Weirdumentary.

Come to think of it, *Mystic Prophecies* predicted the basic ingredients of the Weirdumentary with greater precision than probably anything Nostradamus ever wrote about anything.

Oh, and lest we forget: *Mystic Prophecies* had a companion book of the same name written by Peter Ballbusch. I will not even try to guess whether or not you'll buy it, but if you do, I confidently predict you won't finish reading it.

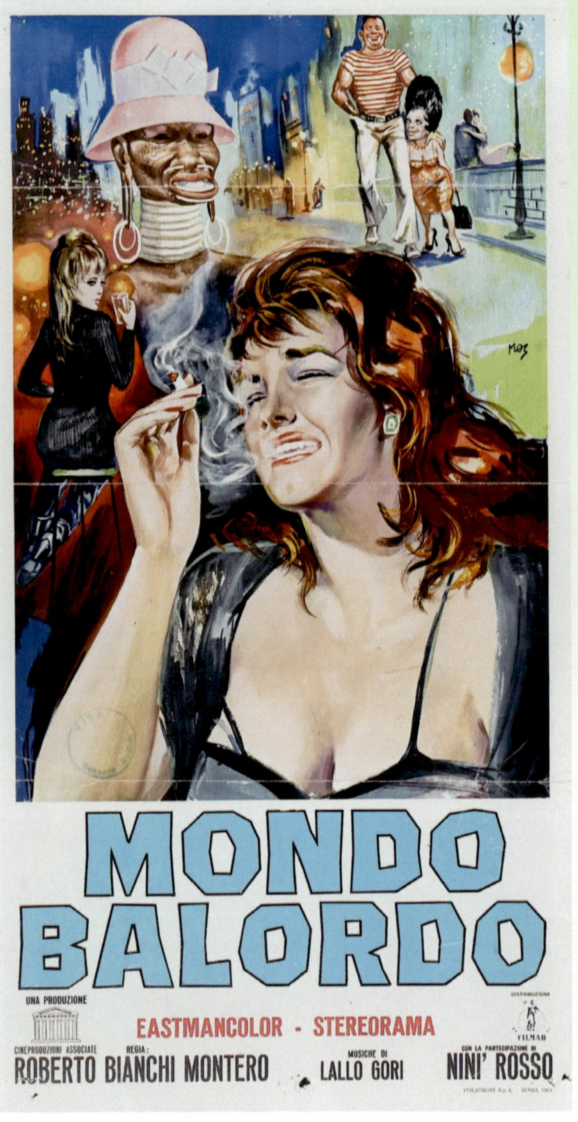
MONDO
BALORDO
UNA PRODUZIONE
EASTMANCOLOR - STEREORAMA
CINEPRODUZIONI ASSOCIATE
REGIA:
ROBERTO BIANCHI MONTERO
MUSICHE DI
LALLO GORI
CON LA PARTECIPAZIONE DI
NINI' ROSSO

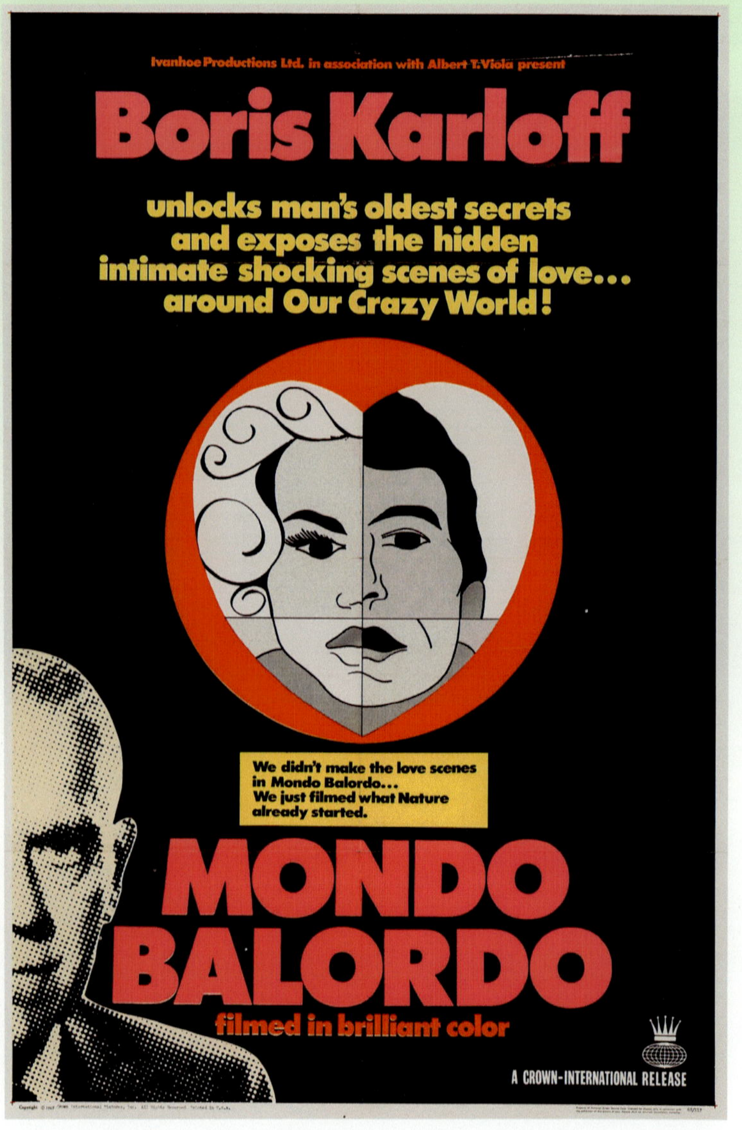
Ivanhoe Productions Ltd. in association with Albert T. Viola present
Boris Karloff
unlocks man's oldest secrets
and exposes the hidden
intimate shocking scenes of love...
around Our Crazy World!
We didn't make the love scenes
in Mondo Balordo...
We just filmed what Nature
already started.
MONDO
BALORDO
filmed in brilliant color
A CROWN-INTERNATIONAL RELEASE

Mondo Balordo

(1964)

"OUR WORLD… What a wild and fascinating place it is. Filled with love, hate, lust and all the hungers and driving passions by which the strange creature called man is possessed. MONDO BALORDO, throbbing and pulsating with love, in its infinite and unimaginable variety, from the jungle orgies of primitive native tribes to the sin-filled evenings of the London sophisticate. ... All of you who will watch the extraordinary scenes unfold on this screen have one thing in common. You are journeying together through the shadows and the sunshine of… OUR WORLD."

Crown International Pictures and Ivanhoe Productions Ltd., in association with Albert T. Viola, presented this Robert Bianchi Montero flick.

To hit the rewind button, I will repeat what I said in the Introduction: mondo movies aren't Weirdumentaries, even though they were pseudo-scientific. Instead, mondo movies deserve their other appellation, "shockumentaries," focusing as they did on sensational and disturbing footage and stories that were often racist, sexist, and ethnocentric.

Given all of that, and their somewhat random, collage-like structure, mondo movies exist in a universe closer to Walter Futter's *Curiosities* than they do to Weirdumentaries.

Thus the question: why include this entry? Well, like *Ingagi* (1930), but even more so, given their numbers and their later release dates, mondo movies proved that exploitation documentaries could get theatrical releases and make buckets of money.

Thus another question: if the reason to include a single mondo movie is to make that point, why choose this particular film? Why not feature the original and most successful of them all, Gualtiero Jacopetti, Paolo Cavara and Franco Prosperi's *Mondo Cane* (1962)?

The answer to those questions is important. *Mondo Balordo*'s narrator was Boris Karloff, the Frankenstein of the movies, one of the greatest horror stars of all time. The thought

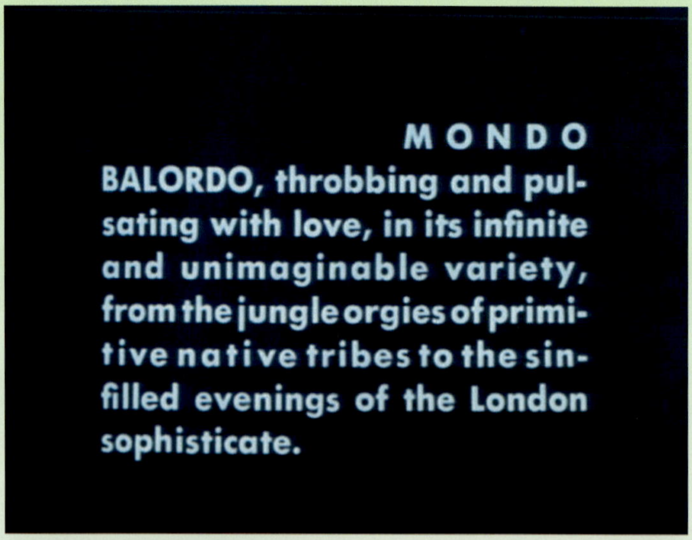
MONDO
BALORDO, throbbing and pulsating with love, in its infinite and unimaginable variety, from the jungle orgies of primitive native tribes to the sin-filled evenings of the London sophisticate.

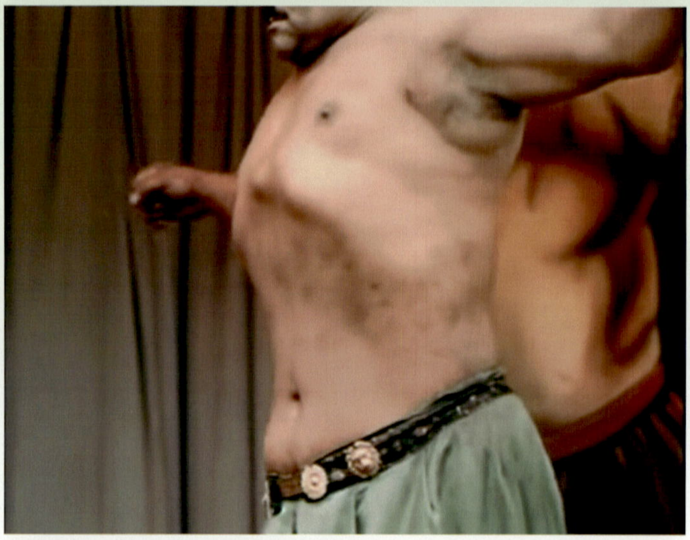

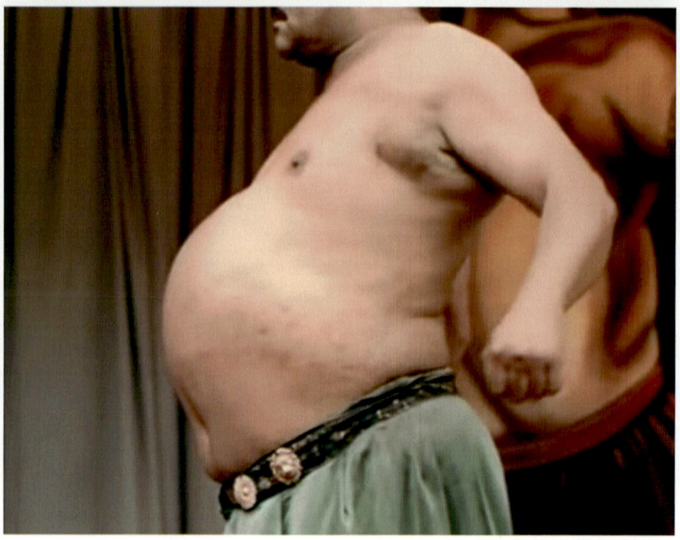

process here was similar to the choice of Basil Rathbone to host *Mystic Prophecies and Nostradamus* (1961, see entry).

To repeat myself, the use of famous narrators, specifically those whose careers were founded on the strange and unusual, became key to Weirdumentaries.

"In my career of nearly four decades in motion pictures, I've played every monstrous role it was possible for writers to create. But as you will see in the exciting film to follow, nothing invented by the human mind can be as macabre, grotesque, and thrilling as the behavior of people in so-called real life."

What does Boris show us? English women singing to improve their bosoms, Bedouins with harems, Hong Kong strippers, transvestites, models bound with ropes, peepshows, wrestling women, polyamorists, prostitutes, voyeurs, and Miss America contestants (with "well-filled sweaters"). Oh, and sunbathers "swinging their hips with every part moving in tip-top, or tip-bottom, condition."

But don't go thinking this is just a sexist sex romp. Nope, because now it's time to sing the Monster Mash-Up.

Other footage shows lions eating a zebra, a tribe killing an elephant, fishermen catching turtles, and natives conducting a "primitive" exorcism. We see a maharajah with the power to make the skies rain, Jehovah's Witnesses gathering in Northern Europe, and Arab hairstylists using camel urine as hair dye.

One of the longest scenes is of a little person wearing a zoot suit and singing "I Ain't Got Nobody" in the style of Louis Prima. (Which makes our friend here the historical link between Prima and David Lee Roth.)

And let's not forget the extensive montage of men staring lasciviously at women's behinds. "The eye demands its share," Boris explains.

Oh, and for some reason, we also glimpse the Berlin Wall, the marketplace in Naples, starving artists, animal surgeries, and dueling German swordsmen. (It's a graveyard smash-up.)

Most of the footage is real. Some of it is staged. And all of it has Boris' wonderful voice spouting some not-so-wonderful narration. (In fairness, nobody ever accused the Grinch of being a "nice one.")

That said, *Mondo Balordo* does feature a curious moment of introspection about its ethnocentrism when it cuts back and forth from dancers in Haiti and a rock singer: which is primitive and which is civilized, the film asks?

On-screen text tells us, "Life ebbs away in clouds of blue dream-smoke." And you know, about eighty minutes of mine did just that while watching this somewhat-interesting-but-still-overlong-and-ethnocentric mondo mélange.

If nothing else, though, you'll dig the theme song "Our World" as sung by Andy Badale. Be sure and add it to the next mixtape that you record on cassette. It's no "More," the theme from *Mondo Cane*, which was recorded by the likes of Frank Sinatra, Duke Ellington, and Glen Campbell, but hey, few songs are.

"There you have it. As they say in Italian, 'Mondo Balordo.' It's really a crazy world. Sincerely, Boris Karloff," the bad ole banana with a greasy black peel.

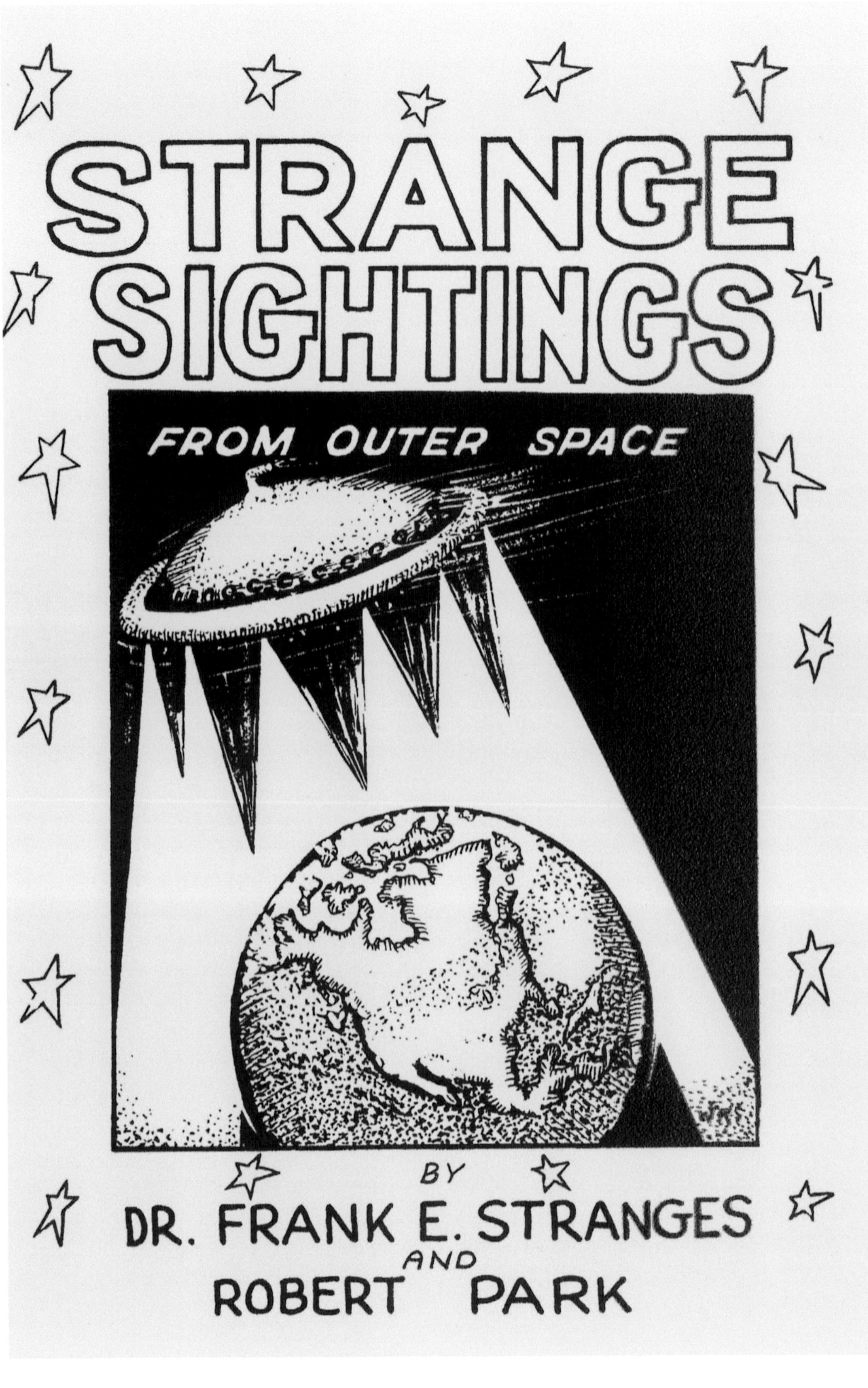
STRANGE SIGHTINGS
FROM OUTER SPACE
BY
DR. FRANK E. STRANGES
AND
ROBERT PARK

Strange Sightings

(1964)

Exactly how weird is this little number? Tough to tell. It's one of the most obscure in our journey into the unknown, in part because it's so very, very unknown.

Running approximately thirty-five minutes (or perhaps sixty-eight minutes, according to more than one 1964 newspaper), *Strange Sightings* was a "color documentary" that featured "actual photos of flying saucers." It had two producers, one being Merle S. Gould, who had directed *Mystic Prophecies and Nostradamus* (1961, see entry). A pilot in World War II, Gould also published *The Cosmic Star* each month, a publication that reported on "psychic phenomena, metaphysics, and allied subjects."

The other producer was Dr. Frank E. Stranges. Along with being president of the International Evangelism Crusades, he "worked as a special agent for a number of detective agencies, enabling him to gain an appreciation of sin firsthand." (I believe I know what this means, but the word "appreciation" does make me wonder.)

Stranges was also the author of *Flying Saucerama*, first published in 1959. By 1966, the book went into a fourth printing. (Not quite a best-seller, but still, good on ya, doc.)

A brochure for *Strange Sightings*—the culmination of Stranges' sixteen years of research—claimed that the film revealed the stories of "a selected group of men and women, UFO investigators, researchers, newsmen, school students, scientists, and others. The people are not fearful of willingly expressing their views on one of the greatest phenomena of all times."

The film apparently included dramatic recreations along with its "actual photos." Oh, and Peter Hurkos, the "Man with the Radar Mind," appears; he had gained "psychometric powers" after falling off a ladder. "When interviewed on the motion picture *Strange Sightings*, he not only revealed his own feeling on the matter of 'space people,' but opened the avenue of thought that has many to wonder just how many persons from other planets are walking among us." (Some of them need to take courses on how to write.)

A newspaper journalist added that Stranges' narration "takes the viewer back to 4,000 B.C. when strange objects in the skies were first reported," which sounds like he was not just proto-weird, but also proto-von Däniken.

Strange Sightings premiered on May 25, 1964, at the Hotel Continental on the Sunset Strip in La La Land. From there, it played hotels and civic venues in California, Colorado, Idaho, Utah, Washington, and probably other states.

Ads for screenings in 1964 usually publicized that Stranges would appear in person to give a talk and meet audience members. He even presented a lecture called *Unidentified Flying Objects and The Bible* at the Flamingo in Santa Rosa, California, in 1965.

All of this sounds cool for those in attendance, but probably not so cool for Stranges and Gould, as their film apparently didn't get theatrical distribution.

Unfortunately, sightings of *Strange Sightings* after the sixties have been much more rare than sightings of real UFOs.

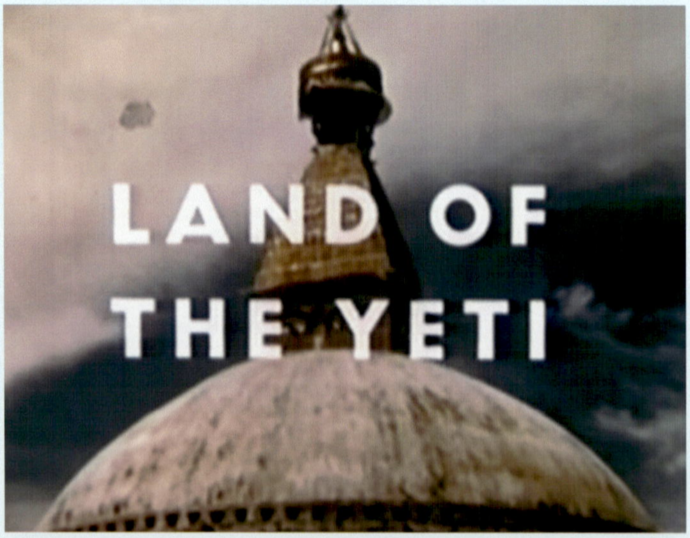
LAND OF
THE YETI

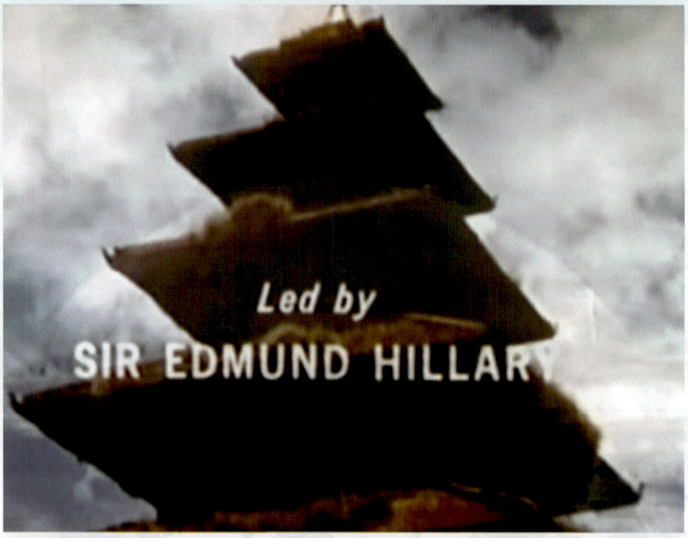
Led by
SIR EDMUND HILLARY

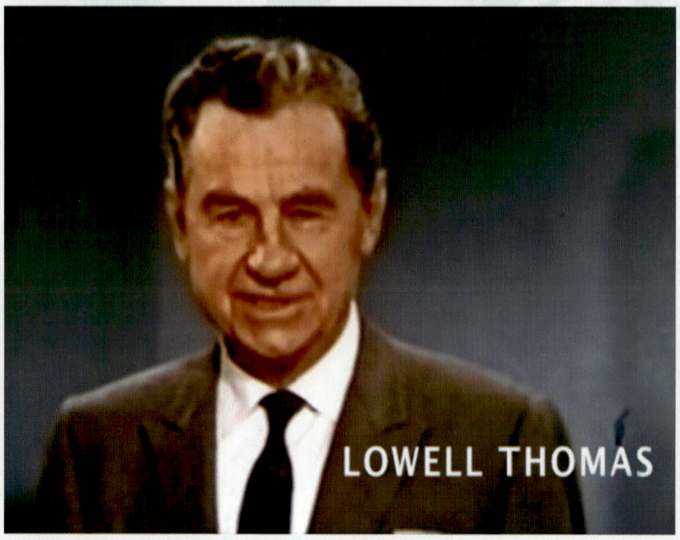
LOWELL THOMAS

Land of the Yeti

(1965)

Here's a curious little film, produced by Field Enterprises (owners of *World Book Encyclopedia*) and featuring narration from famed broadcaster and newsreel Voice-of-God Lowell Thomas. Its footage comes from Sir Edmund Hillary's 1960 expedition into the Himalayas. At the time, *Variety* told readers:

> *Not the scientific objectives which are actually motivating the expedition, but the remote chance that Hillary & Co. might encounter the Abominable Snowman who supposedly inhabits them thar hills, has turned an earnest research project (to study high altitude acclimatization) into a commercial bonanza. It entertains the imagination to ponder what the windfall will be—separate from what various communications media are guaranteeing for exclusivity—if the Snowman ... should be met vis-à-vis.*

To help capture the Yeti, or at least capture his image, various companies designed film equipment for Hillary that could withstand the extreme cold.

Land of the Yeti stars the Abominable Snowman, but only in absentia. Lowell Thomas explains:

> *The legend of the Yeti, the Abominable Snowman, has teased and intrigued the world. Many weird stories have come down to us from the high Himalayas about a giant anthropoid with a human face, human cunning, and superhuman ferocity. Some apelike being that prowls those mountains at heights of 18 to 20,000 feet. Many natives of [Eastern Himalayas] have claimed to have seen the Yeti, and finally an expedition was organized to make a business of clearing up the mystery of the elusive Yeti.*

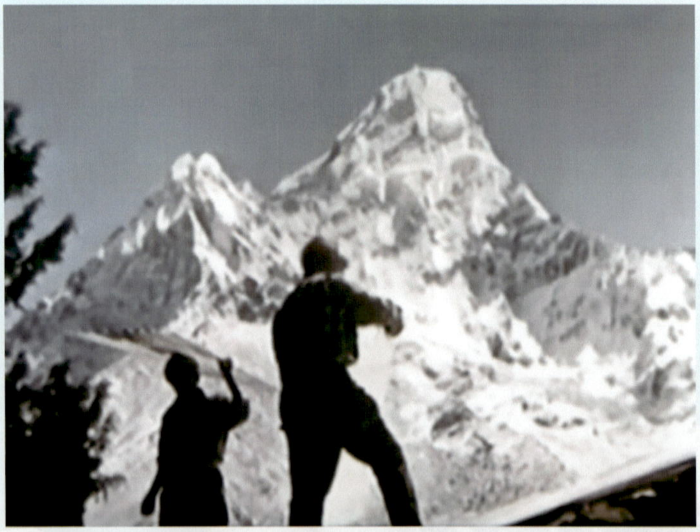

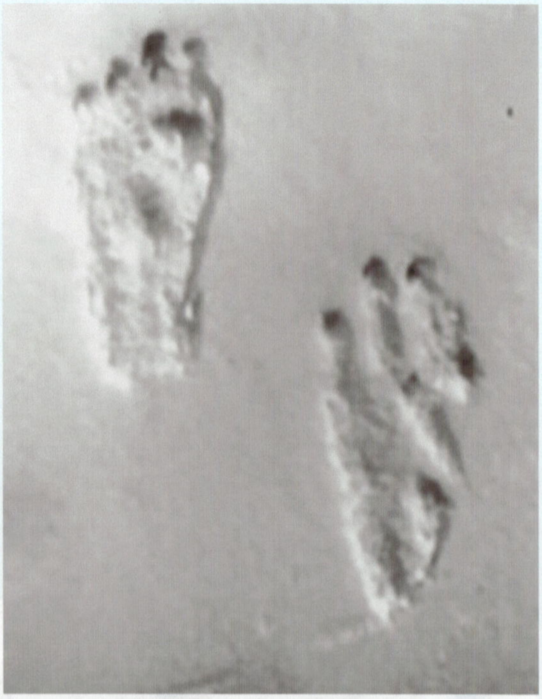

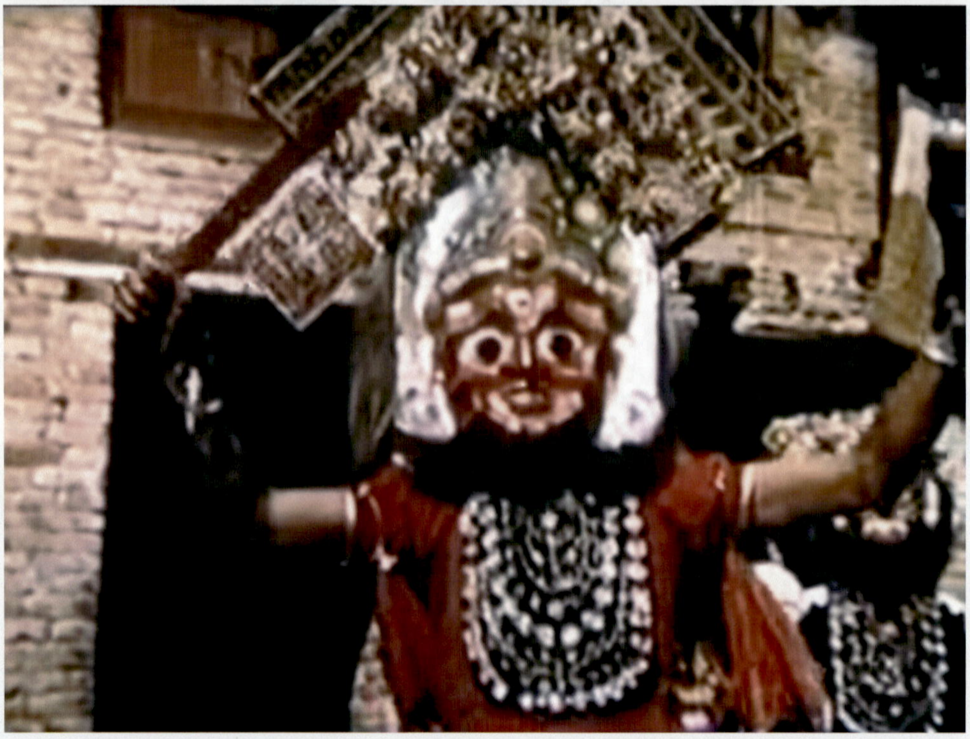

"I vant to be alone," the Yeti must have mumbled to everyone and no one when Hillary was hot on his cold trail. The mysterious monster is never seen, not even after nine months.

Refusing to give Mr. DeMille a close-up, the Snowman hardly commanded media interest. That may be why the 1960 expedition didn't even become a film until 1965.

Nevertheless, Hillary's Sherpa guides "were absolutely sure that, along with the mountain gods, supernatural animals and ice spirits, this frozen wilderness also housed the Yeti." And Hillary's group discover Yeti tracks, or some kind of tracks.

By the time of this fifty-two-minute film's release, the abominable snowman had inflicted abdominal pain on numerous explorers who had tried to find it. Marlin Perkins even briefly explored the subject on a 1962 episode of *Mutual of Omaha's Wild Kingdom*.

After the expedition, Thomas interviews Hillary on-camera. The famed New Zealand explorer admits that the footprints probably weren't from a snowman, whether abominable, angry, or just plain unfriendly.

Yeti wasn't on the Himalayan map, and Field Enterprises wasn't on the cinematic map. Everyone, including the audience, got left out in the cold.

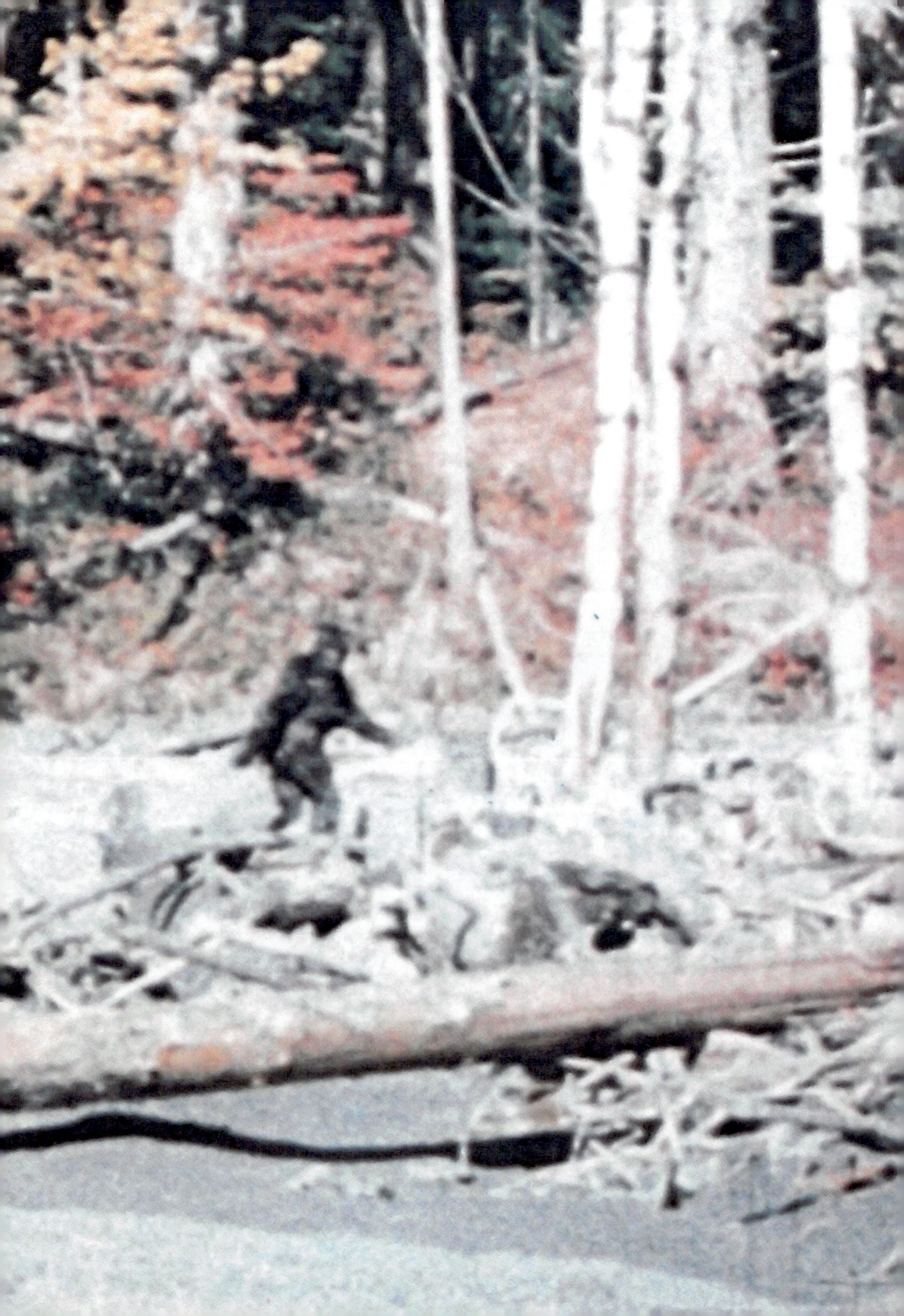

Bigfoot: America's Abominable Snowman

(1968)

Once upon a time, certainly before 1968, and along with his kinder cousin Frosty, the Abominable Snowman was far better known than Bigfoot, whether he was menacing Peter Cushing or making pets out of Bugs Bunny and Daffy Duck. Hence the subtitle of this early and wonderfully weird flick, which linked the new monster with the old.

To back up, further into the tall trees of the forest, Roger Patterson and Bob Gimlin were responsible for the biggest footprints of all in 1967. That was the year they shot their enigmatic and unforgettable 16mm color home movie at Bluff Creek in Northern California. They captured Bigfoot, or at least someone dressed as a Bigfoot, not in a cage, but on film, one in which the creature looks back at them, and at us, the viewers. Electric footage that became one of the most famous home movies ever filmed, second only to Zapruder.

Nine months later, their footage appeared in Producer Ronald Webster's *Bigfoot: America's Abominable Snowman*, which aired on the BBC in England in July 1968. After the on-screen title, we see the word "Fact?", followed by the word "Fraud?" The two question marks are larger than any of the letters, a fascinating point that I should like to make with an exclamation point!

Dr. John Napier, primatologist and paleoanthropologist for the Smithsonian Institution, acts as our host. Of Bigfoot, he explains:

> *It's a surprise for most people to learn that legends of the abominable snowmen and their kind occur all over the world, and, including, of all places, North America. Now perhaps it shouldn't really be a surprise, because wherever you get snowmen legends, you get areas of wilderness, particularly mountain wilderness, and mountain wilderness is something that North America has plenty of.*

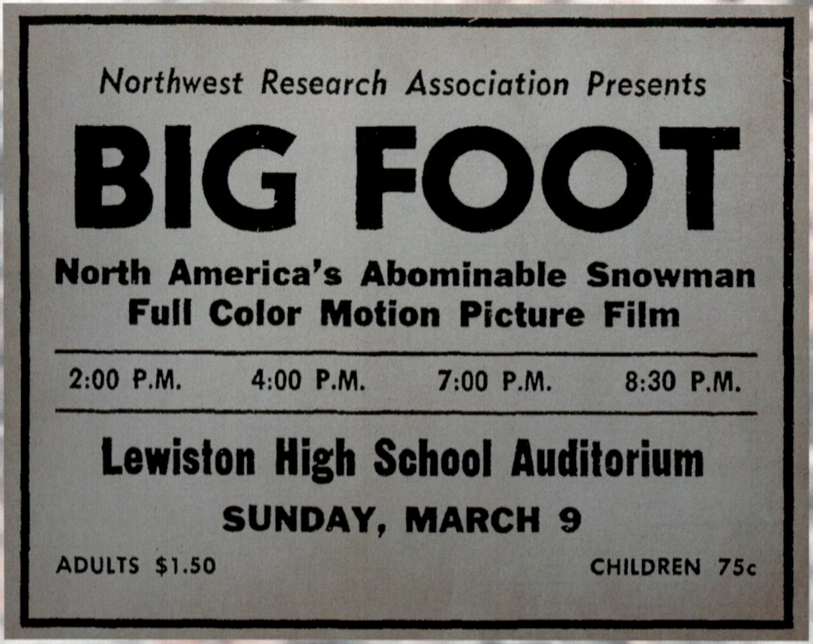
Northwest Research Association Presents
BIG FOOT
North America's Abominable Snowman
Full Color Motion Picture Film
2:00 P.M. 4:00 P.M. 7:00 P.M. 8:30 P.M.
Lewiston High School Auditorium
SUNDAY, MARCH 9
ADULTS $1.50
CHILDREN 75c

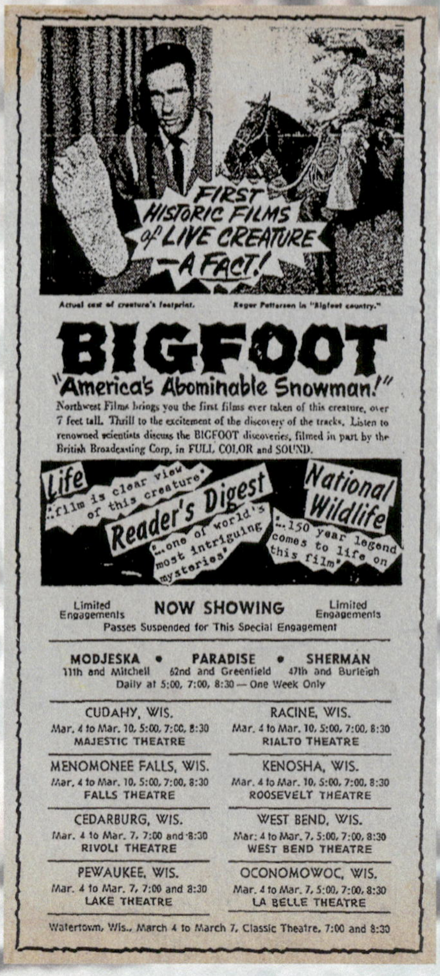
FIRST HISTORIC FILMS of LIVE CREATURE —A FACT!
Actual cast of creature's footprint.
Roger Patterson in "Bigfoot country."
BIGFOOT
"America's Abominable Snowman!"
Northwest Films brings you the first films ever taken of this creature, over 7 feet tall. Thrill to the excitement of the discovery of the tracks. Listen to renowned scientists discuss the BIGFOOT discoveries, filmed in part by the British Broadcasting Corp. in FULL COLOR and SOUND.
Life
"...film is clear view of this creature"
Reader's Digest
"...one of world's most intriguing mysteries"
National Wildlife
"...150 year legend comes to life on this film"
Limited Engagements
NOW SHOWING
Limited Engagements
Passes Suspended for This Special Engagement
MODJESKA • PARADISE • SHERMAN
11th and Mitchell 62nd and Greenfield 47th and Burleigh
Daily at 5:00, 7:00, 8:30 — One Week Only
CUDAHY, WIS.
Mar. 4 to Mar. 10, 5:00, 7:00, 8:30
MAJESTIC THEATRE
RACINE, WIS.
Mar. 4 to Mar. 10, 5:00, 7:00, 8:30
RIALTO THEATRE
MENOMONEE FALLS, WIS.
Mar. 4 to Mar. 10, 5:00, 7:00, 8:30
FALLS THEATRE
KENOSHA, WIS.
Mar. 4 to Mar. 10, 5:00, 7:00, 8:30
ROOSEVELT THEATRE
CEDARBURG, WIS.
Mar. 4 to Mar. 7, 7:00 and 8:30
RIVOLI THEATRE
WEST BEND, WIS.
Mar. 4 to Mar. 7, 5:00, 7:00, 8:30
WEST BEND THEATRE
PEWAUKEE, WIS.
Mar. 4 to Mar. 7, 7:00 and 8:30
LAKE THEATRE
OCONOMOWOC, WIS.
Mar. 4 to Mar. 7, 5:00, 7:00, 8:30
LA BELLE THEATRE
Watertown, Wis., March 4 to March 7, Classic Theatre, 7:00 and 8:30

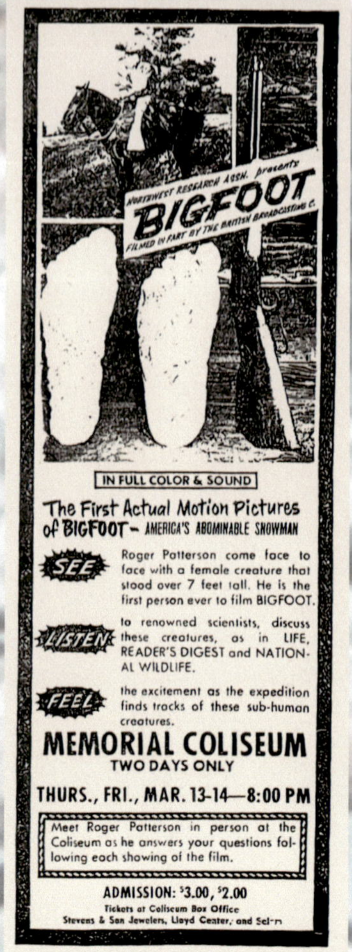
NORTHWEST RESEARCH ASSN. presents
BIGFOOT
FILMED IN PART BY THE BRITISH BROADCASTING C.
IN FULL COLOR & SOUND
The First Actual Motion Pictures of BIGFOOT – AMERICA'S ABOMINABLE SNOWMAN
SEE
Roger Patterson come face to face with a female creature that stood over 7 feet tall. He is the first person ever to film BIGFOOT.
LISTEN
to renowned scientists, discuss these creatures, as in LIFE, READER'S DIGEST and NATIONAL WILDLIFE.
FEEL
the excitement as the expedition finds tracks of these sub-human creatures.
MEMORIAL COLISEUM
TWO DAYS ONLY
THURS., FRI., MAR. 13-14—8:00 PM
Meet Roger Patterson in person at the Coliseum as he answers your questions following each showing of the film.
ADMISSION: $3.00, $2.00
Tickets at Coliseum Box Office
Stevens & Son Jewelers, Lloyd Center, and Sel-n

Napier draws attention to the vast, uninhabited regions of Northern California, Oregon, and Washington. It's "Bigfoot country, much of it unexplored and unmapped." Then he goes full-on Weirdumentarist:

> *It's not really difficult to accept the possibility that creatures unknown to science could live there in perfect solitude and safety. That the potential for even quite a sizeable population of Bigfeet is there nobody would deny. But of course this is not any sort of proof that such creatures exist.*

From there we get requisite soundbites from eyewitnesses, as well as one person who claims to have seen a man faking Bigfoot tracks.

Yeti expert Ivan T. Sanderson gets the most screen time, describing the history of Bigfoot sightings, ranging from Native American folklore to tales of the Gold Rush. He also shows off plaster casts of footprints.

The meat of the film is the Patterson-Gimlin footage, of course, which Patterson explains while we see it. Napier later replays with his own commentary.

Napier also takes the time to introduce a handful of experts who express "healthy skepticism" about Bigfoot. Consider Dr. Richard Van Gelder of the Museum of Natural History in New York, who states, "It is possible that such a creature exists. It is highly improbable that it does. I may be speaking to you from the moon today, but this is highly improbable. . . ."

Napier himself admits that many viewers may believe they have seen "rather a splendid hoax. ... Yet, talking to Roger Patterson, as I have done, it's very hard not to believe in him. It's also hard to entirely dismiss this film based on its rather unpromising face value."

In retrospect, it's hardly surprising that Napier was hopeful that Bigfoot existed, given that he ended up writing a book on the subject. The bigger mystery is whether he's serious when asking if a captured Bigfoot would be granted U.S. citizenship and the right to vote. (To the best of my knowledge, Napier was not speaking to us from the moon when he asked that question.)

Roger Patterson and his brother-in-law Albert DeAtley, Jr. saw an opportunity with this doc, obtaining the rights and adding some introductory footage. They released *Bigfoot: America's Abominable Snowman* in America, at least regionally.

In a few cities, *Bigfoot* stood tall thanks to heavy TV, radio, and newspaper promotion. That said, its brief running time (an hour at most with their added footage) kept it from attracting more theaters and audiences. Put another way, it was very weird, but little seen.

As for Patterson, he explains: "Now we have to capture one and prove this, and I might say that, if it takes me the rest of my life, I'm going to do it." Patterson died in 1972. Napier died in 1987. Bigfoot's date of death is unknown.

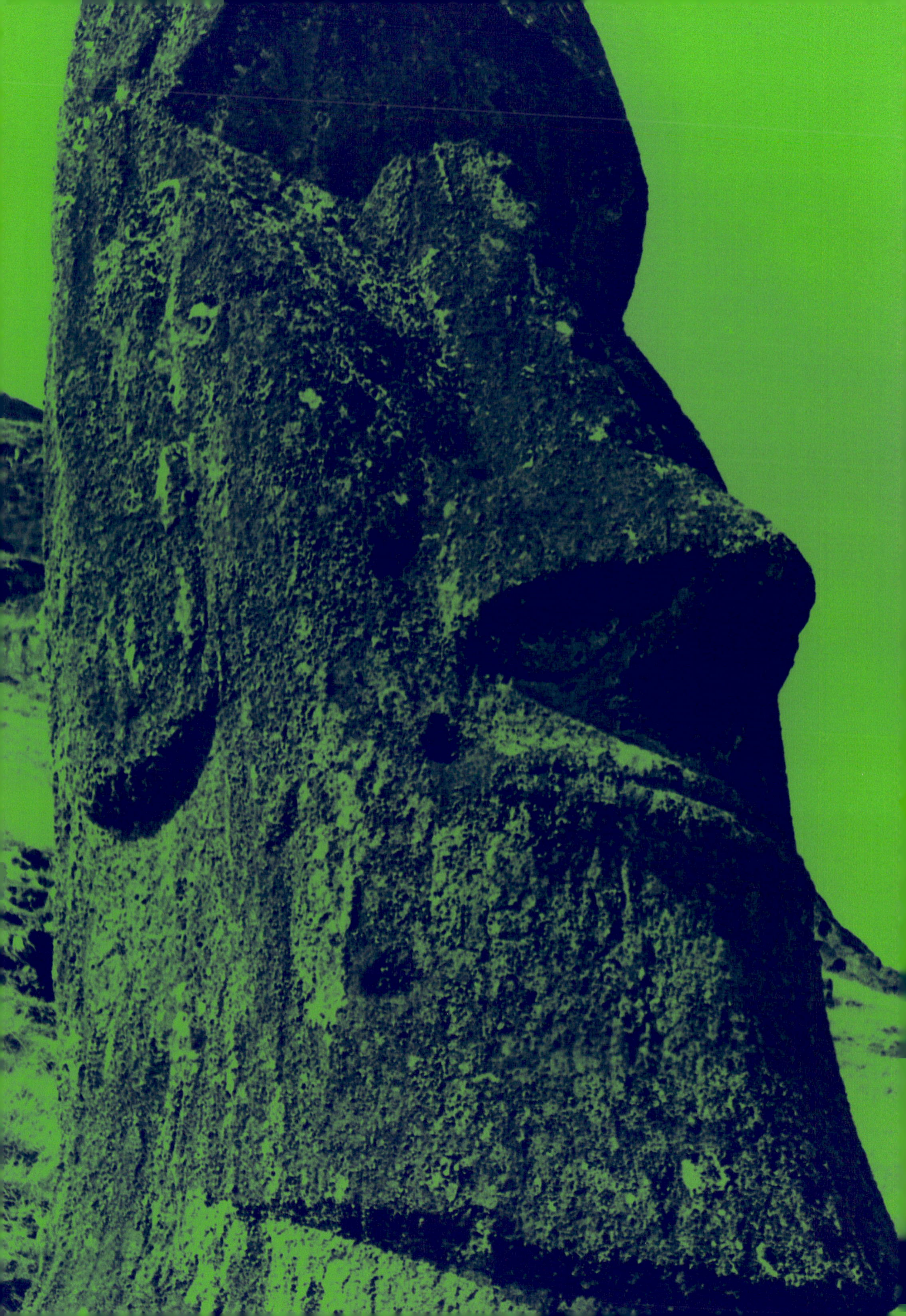

section 2: Ancient Aliens

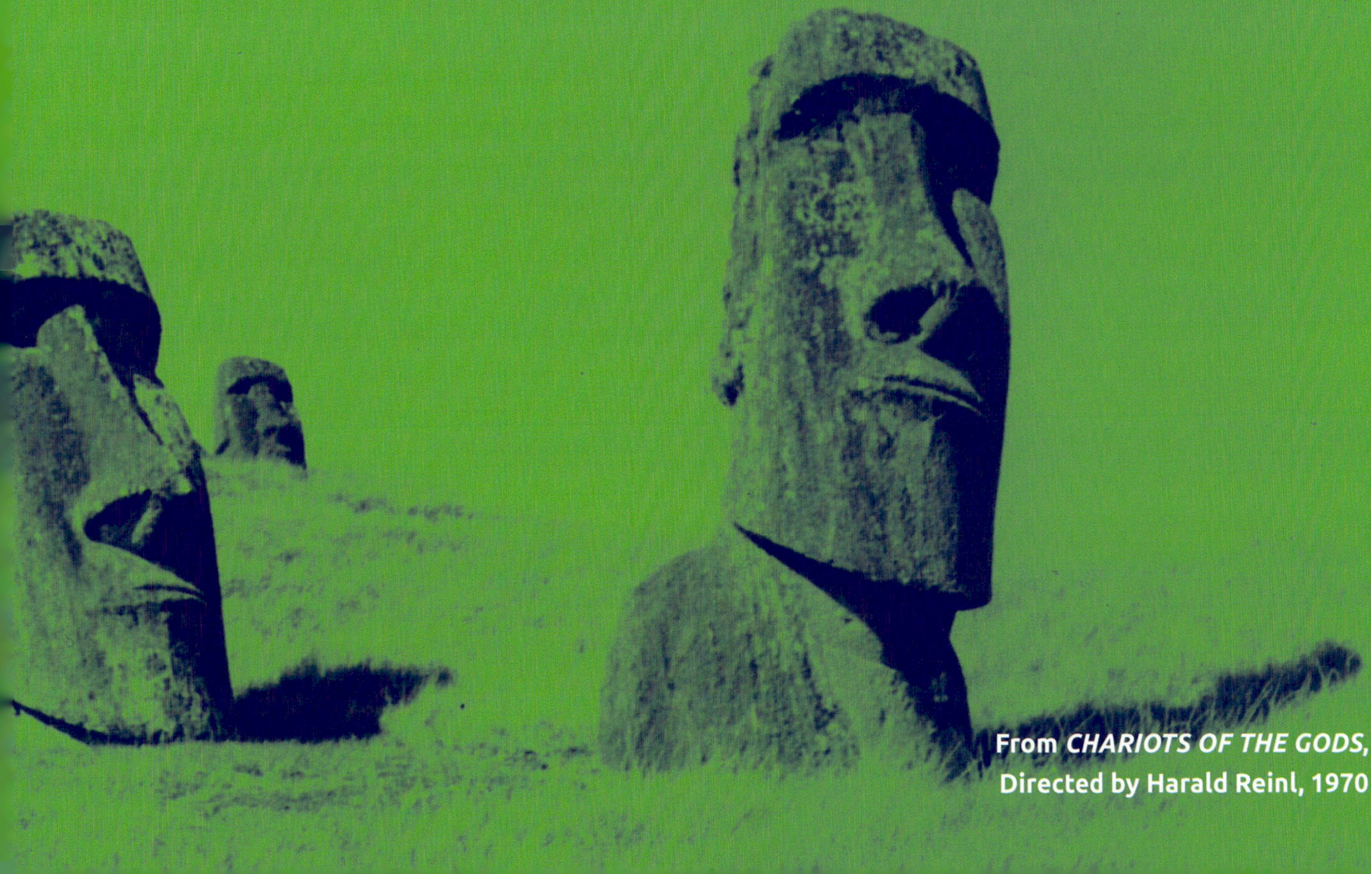

From *CHARIOTS OF THE GODS*, Directed by Harald Reinl, 1970

• SEPTEMBER 3, 1973
EASTERN EDITION
BOXOFFICE

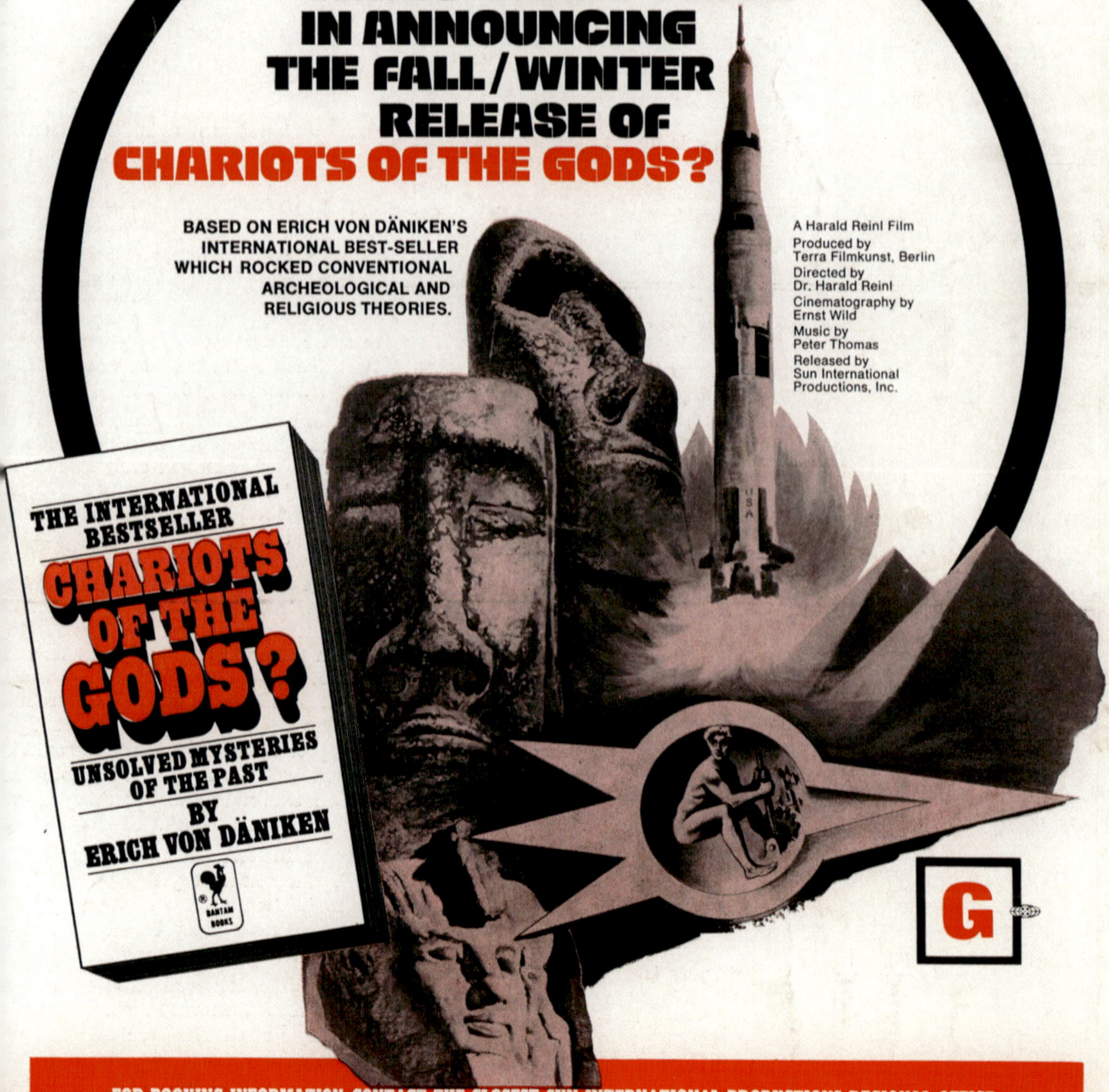

Chariots of the Gods

(1970)

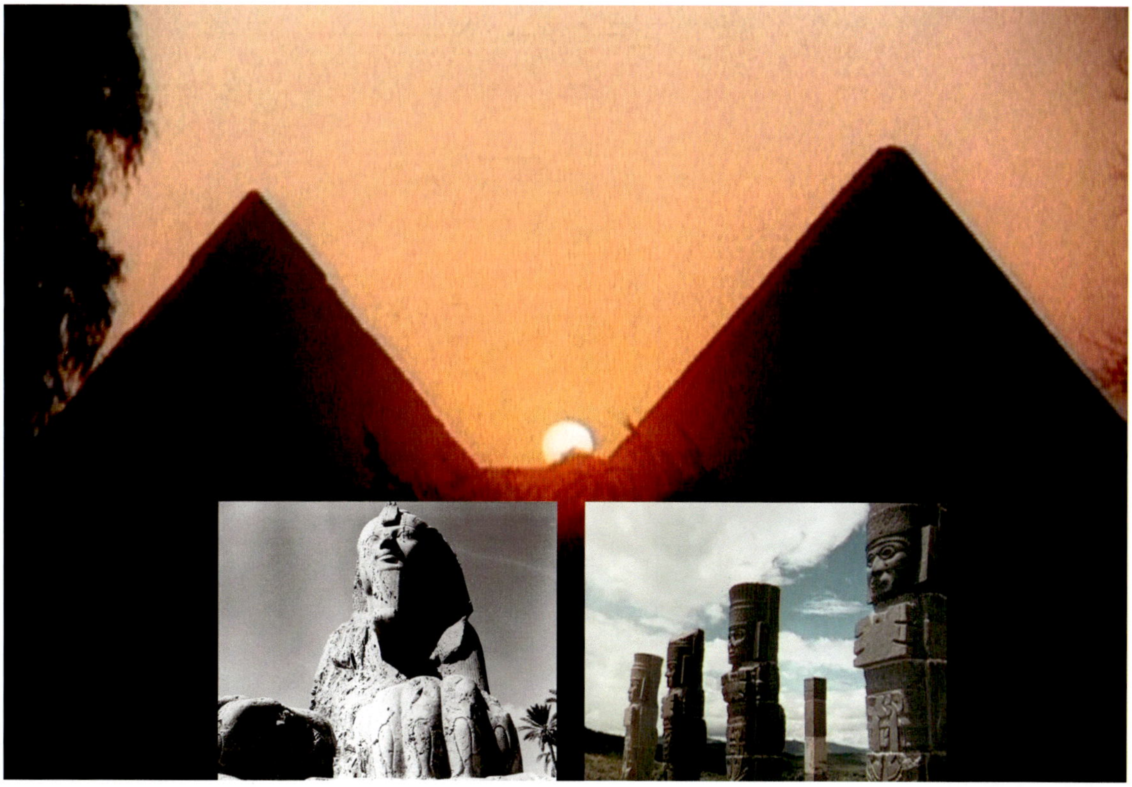

"Was Earth visited by gods from distant planets? Were the gods astronauts? We've accumulated a great deal of evidence to that effect around the world. We may still doubt the conclusion, but we dare not ignore the evidence, for as long as such ancient mysteries remain unexplained, our questions are valid ones."

In 1970, director Harald Reinl adapted two of Erich von Däniken's books for this ninety-minute gem: *Chariots of the Gods?* (1969) and *Return to the Stars* (1970). The film's opening credits describes both as being "novels." Even more curious is that von Däniken's name is never mentioned again while the running time runs.

Ernst Wild's cinematography is stunning, and Peter Thomas' music score is unforgettable, the best soundtrack of any Weirdumentary, which really is saying something. It deserved its LP and subsequent CD releases.

To overcome our resistance to the thesis of ancient astronauts, Reinl employs several tactics, one being the reliance on important scientists like Wernher von Braun and Hermann Oberth. Both men believed in the possibility of life on other planets.

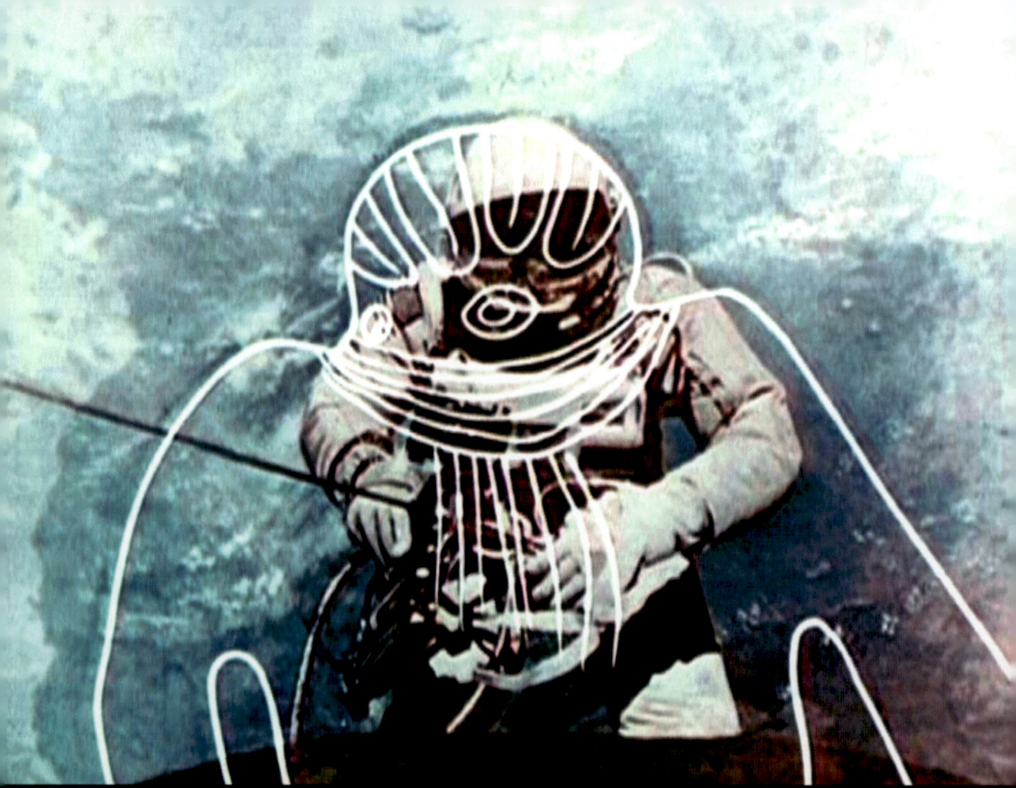

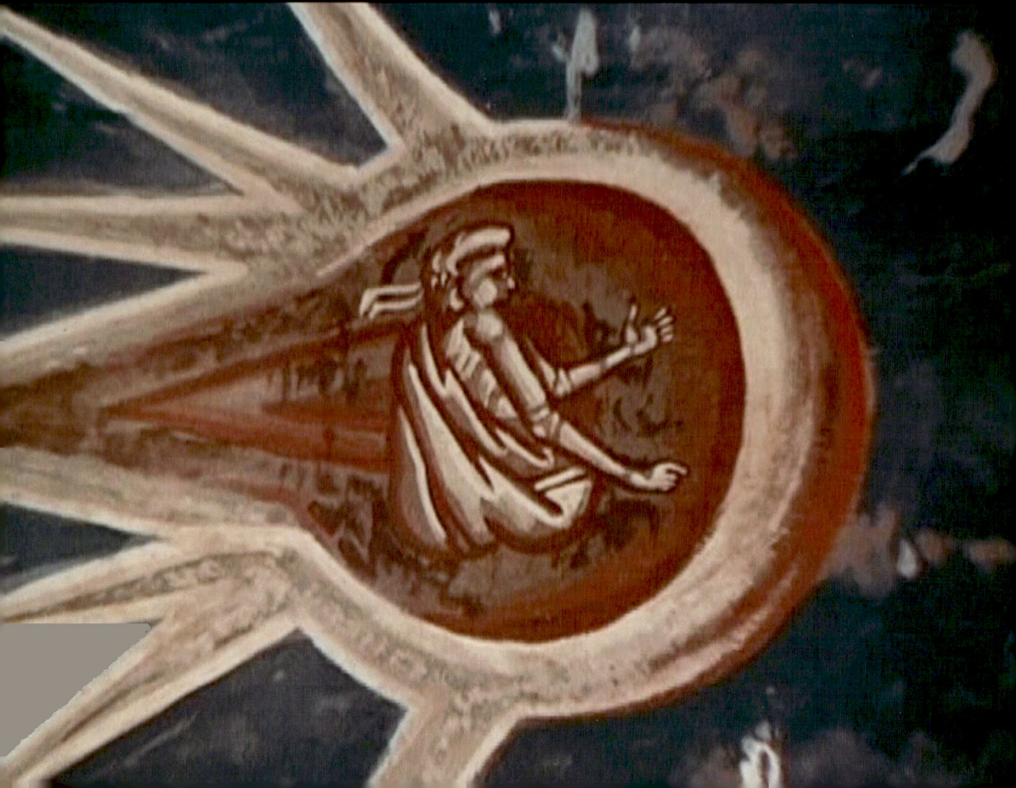

And then there's our own space travel. "The entire heavens" are "within our reach," we hear. But "how will our astronauts be welcomed" on other planets? Ergo, we can go to them, so they surely can come to us.

After all, mathematical probabilities suggest that life exists in our own galaxy. "It's quite possible that our own planet, at some remote moment in its past, had a visitor from one of these 50 million stars. And if they did, primitive humans would have regarded them as gods."

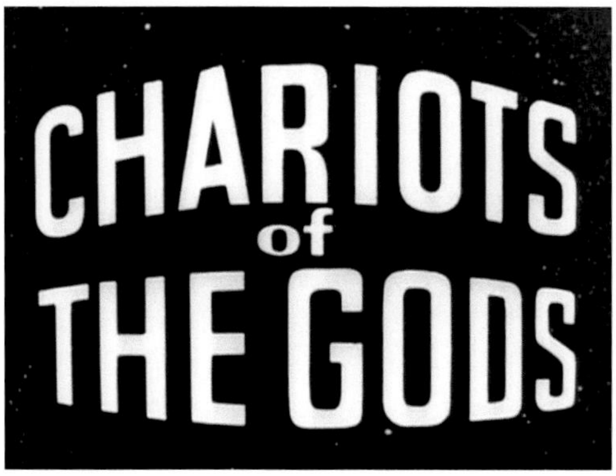

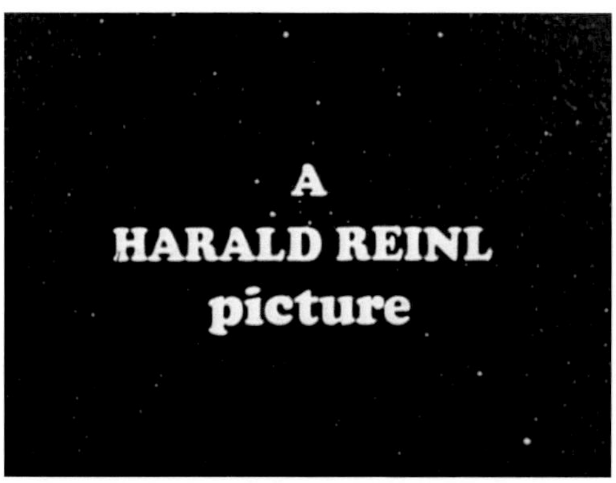

Another important piece of the puzzle are ancient sites that could not have been built by humans. Of Cheops, narrator Christian Marschall explains, "It's almost impossible to brush off the vast body of mathematical and astronomical values embodied in the pyramid's construction as just coincidence."

There's also the emphasis on the weight and distance of building supplies. "No one knows how" the stones to build Egyptian pyramids could have been moved. And on Easter Island, "the number of workmen is so small that it would have been impossible for them to create the more than six hundred gigantic stone figures found everywhere on the island." Maybe the inhabitants of Easter Island and Egypt were in fact "apprenticed" to the same "master builders." Maybe.

Alien influence even extended to mummies. "The theory has been advanced that embalming was a skillful imitation of a physical conservation method employed by extraterrestrial visitors, attempted unsuccessfully by the Egyptians." E.T. spent too much time moving rocks to convey the secret formula, apparently.

Chariots of the Gods depends heavily on ancient texts and drawings. The fiery chariot that took Elijah to heaven *might* have been a spaceship. One of the Dead Sea Scrolls mentions "strange sky vehicles." The author of the *Mahabharata* saw what *could* be called a "blast-off." And Quetzalcoatl helped the Aztecs before returning to the stars. All references to gods in the heavens speak to "space visitors." Perhaps.

As for artwork, "jets are clearly seen" in the frescoes of Dasani. Ancient images found in Europe, Australia, Africa, and South America seem to depict alien life forms. "Surely there were models, one is tempted to say *one* model, for these deities found on all continents."

Juxtaposition of specific images serve this argument well. At one point, Reinl

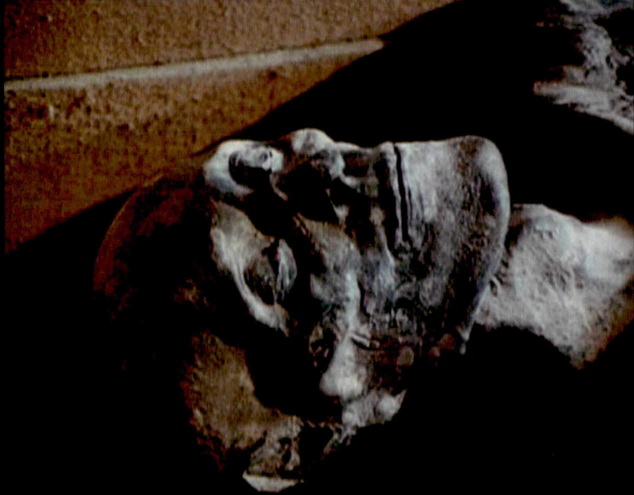

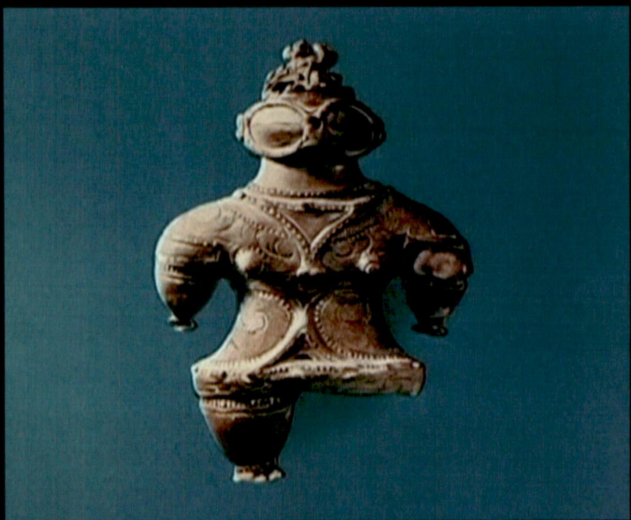

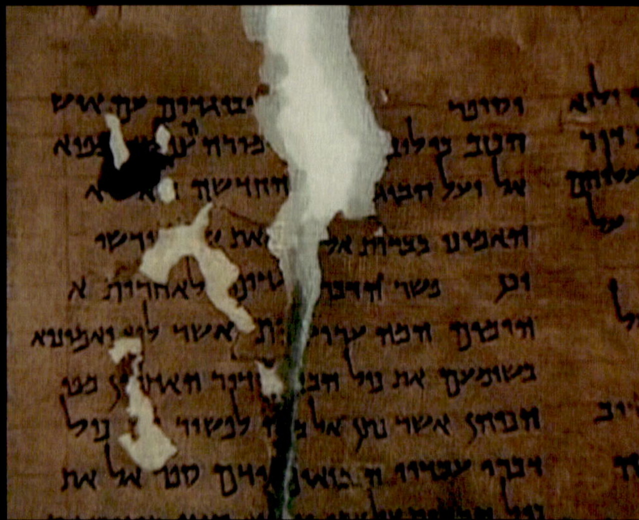

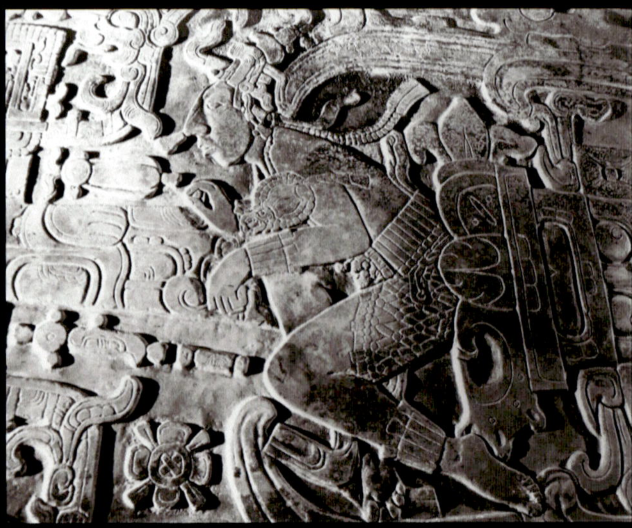

dissolves from an ancient drawing to a NASA astronaut. In other cases, he cuts back and forth repeatedly from age-old artwork to space-age technology. That makes sense, because aliens would of course traverse the star ways with equipment that looks just like ours. I can see it now ... thanks to Reinl showing me.

The language of *Chariots of the Gods* is also crucial, moving from infrequent skepticism ("To be sure, there are other explanations.") to rhetorical questions ("Is this the sketch of a space module?") to statements of absolute certainty ("There's no doubt. They are landing fields."). Nowhere is this more fascinating than in the film's U.S. title, which dropped the question mark at the end of the book's American name.

Lastly, we have to consider Herman Haller's editing. *Chariots of the Gods* rapidly moves from country to country, sometimes returning to locales already visited. But the film's narration often pauses, letting the images play with Thomas' music. The result slows down the whirlwind global tour, while still visually drawing links from disparate cultures.

Chariots of the Gods culminates with the Nazca lines in Peru, which "must have been made for someone arriving by air." The incredible images are nothing more or less than a "gigantic abandoned airport." Here is the theory's ace in the hole, or up its sleeve.

"The mysteries of the past manifest themselves on all continents." But they didn't at American movie theaters until Sun International released *Chariots of the Gods* with English narration and a G rating in 1974.

Boxoffice believed *Chariots* was "expertly produced, with excellent musical accompaniment." The *Los Angeles Times* called the film "astoundingly persuasive."

By contrast, the *New York Times* complained it was "questionable fare." "Director Harald Reinl is inept," the *Washington Post* carped. To which I reply, whatever you say cosmically bounces off of Reinl and sticks to you.

The *Independent Film Journal* went much further:

> *Sophomoric and repetitive documentary that attempts to prove outer space visits in the distant past. Lots of unexplained—and interesting—artifacts are made to fit a poorly developed theory. ... Could excite the imagination a bit but has little relation to fact as we currently know it. For quick playoff.*

Wrong on at least one count, my friends. *Chariots* became a major success at the U.S. box office. The playoff was slow, or long, or whatever the reverse of "quick" is.

Chariots was also a winner at the 1973 Atlanta Film Festival. The National Screen Council bequeathed its "Blue Ribbon Award" on the film in February 1974. And it was nominated for an Academy Award in 1971, the result of its 1970 release in Germany. Take that, puny Earthlings.

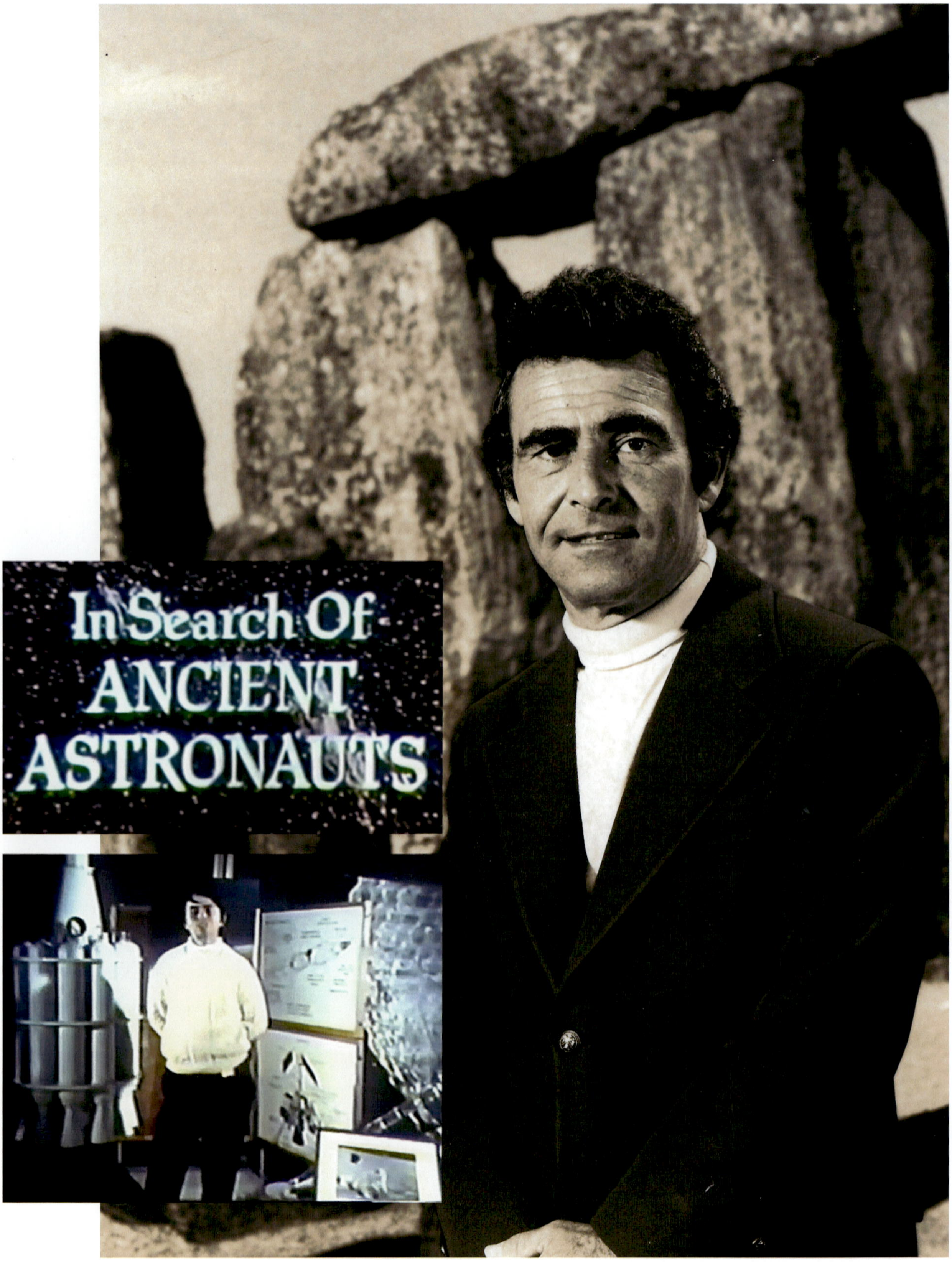
In Search Of
ANCIENT
ASTRONAUTS

In Search Of Ancient Astronauts

(1973)

Can it be? Is it possible that ancient astronauts landed in front of Americans *prior* to Harald Reinl's film *Chariots of the Gods* (1970)? Megaliths, hieroglyphics, and *TV Guide* all point to the same definitive answer: Yes. Sort of.

NBC broadcast *In Search of Ancient Astronauts* in January 1973, while Harald Reinl's film didn't get a theatrical release in the U.S. until 1974. But this fifty-two-minute Weirdumentary was largely comprised of footage from *Chariots of the Gods*, so much so that it credits Reinl as director. Even some of Peter Thomas' music is repurposed.

Alan Landsburg, famed pioneer in the TV documentary series, produced this American version of von Däniken's theory. Don Ringe directed additional footage and wrote dialogue spoken by Rod Serling of *Twilight Zone* fame.

Ringe's script largely follows von Däniken and Reinl. "Is it possible that this planet Earth has been visited by travelers from outer space?" Serling asks in his unforgettably enigmatic voice. And then there is Ringe's remarkably strange description of aliens traveling through "throbbing light years" to meet us. Along with teaching us the ways of the interstellar force, the aliens apparently lusted for our hot bods.

Unlike the narration in *Chariots of the Gods*, though, Ringe has Serling openly discuss the man of the hour: "Erich von Däniken, a German professor possessed of the mind of a scientist and the imagination of a romantic, wrote a book called *Chariots of the Gods?*" Of course von Däniken was no professor, but let's not get too technical with a film about technology. After all, the Baghdad battery works, so far as we know. And Serling does inform us that it was "impossible" for the men on Easter Island to construct those statues. To the bank, we may take that.

But Ringe also allows Serling to hedge their bets. Von Däniken has a theory. "Or is it a theory? Judge for yourself." Elsewhere, "The conclusion reached by von Däniken is that the [Nazca] lines represent a landing field." And sentences that begin, "All the evidence leads von Däniken to conclude. . . ." Credit Professor EvD, so *he* can take the rap.

Ringe's new footage features scientists Harold P. Klein and James G. Lawless on-camera. Best of all, though, is Carl Sagan, who ends the film by stating, "You can't exclude the possibility [of ancient astronauts], but there's not a smidgen of evidence that is compelling."

The *Los Angeles Times* believed much the same: "It works this way. You take a bunch of unrelated and unexplained incidents or phenomena, conjure up a possible common thread running through them all, and out of that thread you weave the whole cloth of a brand new fable. You ignore all contradictory evidence."

To which I respond, it also works another way. You take a German documentary, cut it down, add a famous American narrator, and broadcast it on a major TV network. Bookstores in many cities report "instant sellouts" of von Däniken's books. Sales of *Chariots of the Gods?* in paperback quickly soar from 200,000 to 4 million. That's evidence we can't ignore.

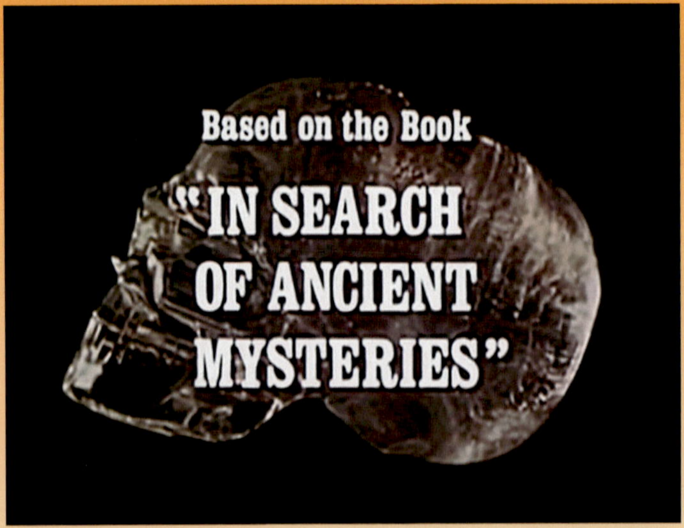
Based on the Book
"IN SEARCH
OF ANCIENT
MYSTERIES"

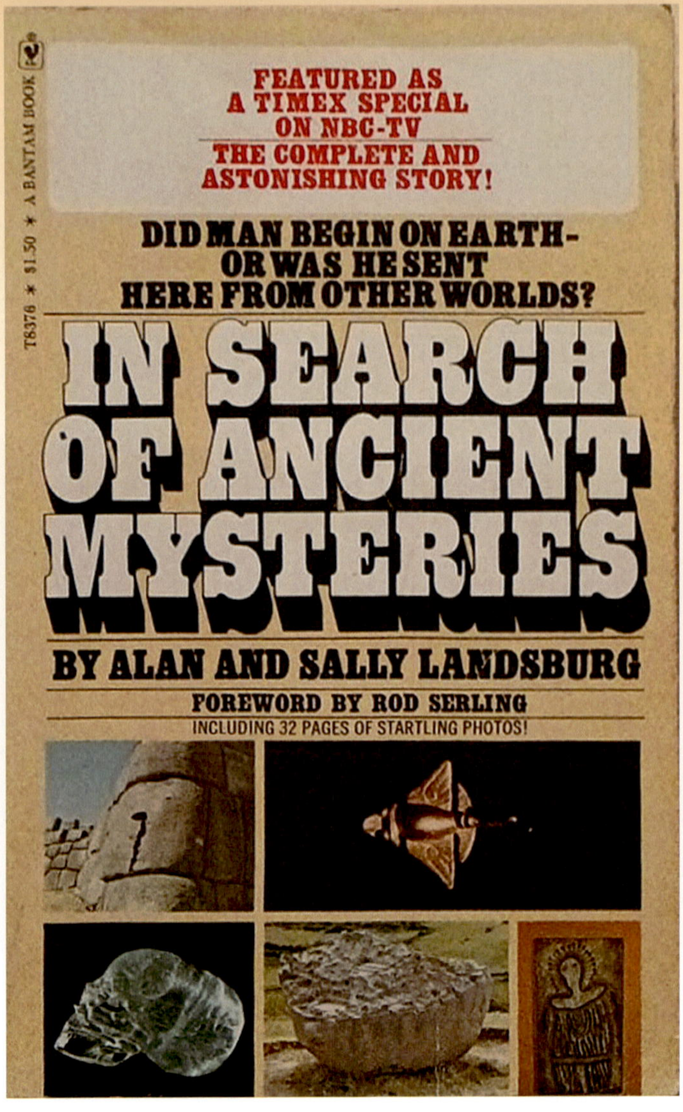
T8376 ★ $1.50 ★ A BANTAM BOOK
FEATURED AS
A TIMEX SPECIAL
ON NBC-TV
THE COMPLETE AND
ASTONISHING STORY!
DID MAN BEGIN ON EARTH-
OR WAS HE SENT
HERE FROM OTHER WORLDS?
IN SEARCH
OF ANCIENT
MYSTERIES
BY ALAN AND SALLY LANDSBURG
FOREWORD BY ROD SERLING
INCLUDING 32 PAGES OF STARTLING PHOTOS!

In Search Of Ancient Mysteries

(1974)

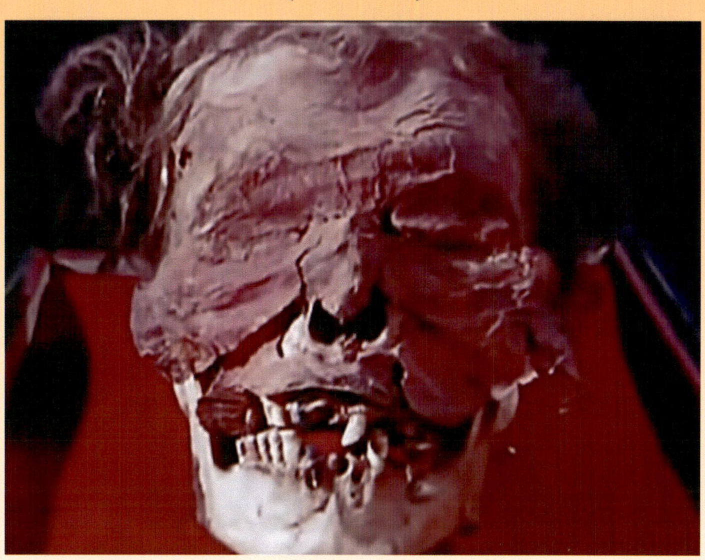

Variety called *In Search of Ancient Mysteries* a "sequel" to *In Search of Ancient Astronauts,* which was so popular that NBC rebroadcast it in September 1973.

In July 1973, producer Alan Landsburg assigned Fred Warshofsky to write and direct *In Search of Ancient Mysteries,* "filmed on location around the world." Timex served as sponsor. Rod Serling returned as narrator. Conspicuously absent is von Däniken, as this project adapted a book of the same name by Alan and Sally Landsburg. NBC aired the new film in January 1974.

In Search of Ancient Mysteries does feel like a sequel, so much so that it begins where its predecessor left off, at the Nazca lines, revealing new images of them as captured by survey satellites and Skylab astronauts.

It also extends the von Däniken thesis. The "Earth may not merely have been visited by ancient astronauts, it may in fact have been colonized by them." They might have "seeded the Earth." Panspermia, one might say, or Mars Needs Women.

Now, let's not go off half-cocked or half-baked. *In Search of Ancient Mysteries* "is based on established facts, but it is not a news report." The number of rhetorical questions makes that clear.

But the sheer weight of the monuments alone requires us to ask if Tiahuanaco could "have been built by colonists possessed of a technology far more advanced than that of man?" Perchance, I say, to speculate or to dream.

And if we prod our maybes down the interstellar trail, we can wonder if "our ancestors" were from space, and if early man "descended from the stars" to become our "founding colonists." I can almost picture it: they arrived in spacecraft in order to become Neanderthals. So very retro.

Ancient Mysteries also introduces a small number of locations that aren't found in its predecessor or Reinl's *Chariots of the Gods*: the Bermuda Triangle and its Bimini Wall, for example, as well as the Lost Continent of Atlantis. All the while, we get Roger Wagner's score. He's no Peter Thomas, but heck, who is?

The *Los Angeles Times* advised, "Even if you feel that our ancestors were neither apes nor god-like spacemen ... *In Search of Ancient Mysteries* should provide many brain-jobbing moments of pleasure."

Daily Variety unabashedly told readers, "Altogether it is an impressive doc, well-edited by Buck Speed, and of good quality. It does raise substantial questions." Indeed it does. Indeed it does.

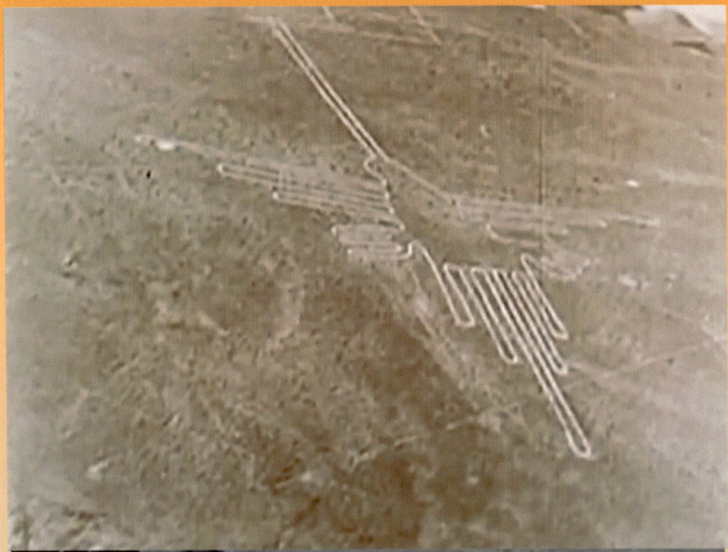

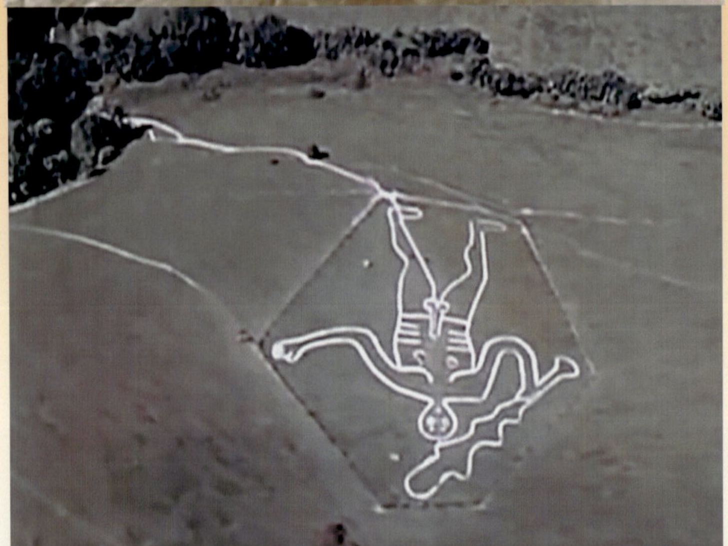

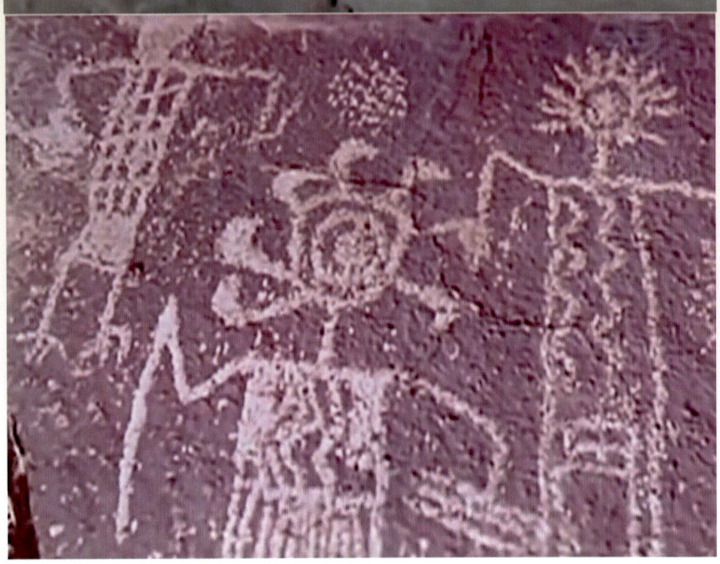

The Outer Space Connection

(1975)

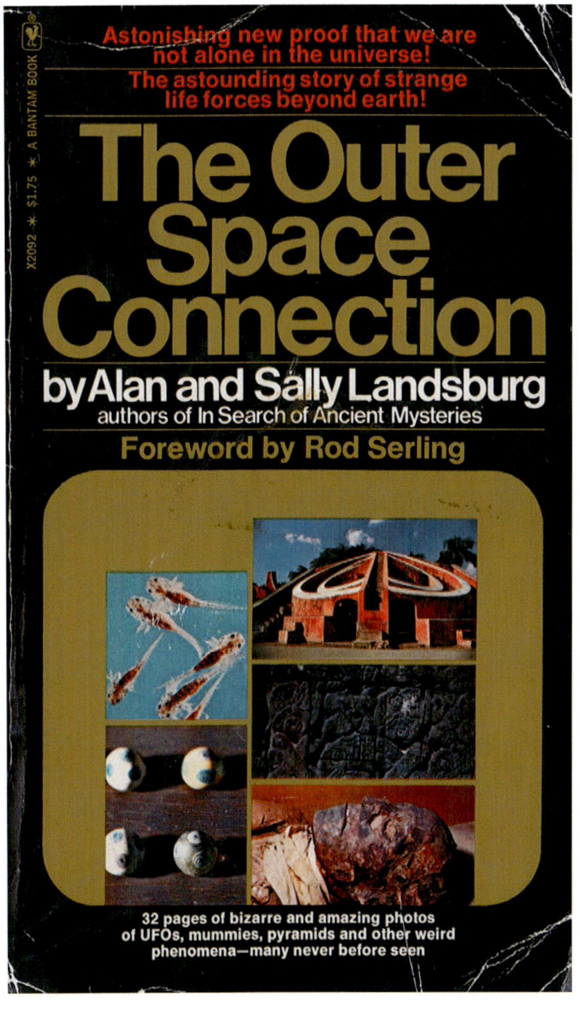

The team of Alan Landsburg, Rod Serling, and Ancient Astronauts are back, and they aren't taking prisoners, except for maybe a few yokels to probe.

Sunn Classic—the company having added the extra "n" to its original handle—distributed *The Outer Space Connection*, adapted from Landsburg's book of the same name. And it opts for the basic Reinl/*Chariots of the Gods* treatment. No dramatizations, in other words, and no Serling on-camera. It's the Voice of God, all the way, telling us about the Voices of the Gods.

Listen, one and all: "The motion picture you are about to see was filmed by four teams of cameramen at more than 120 locations around the world. Scientists representing more than forty museums and research centers took part in the explorations. There are no actors in the film. Every location is real. The facts that will be presented are true. This may be the most startling and controversial film you will ever see."

We get priceless soundbites from the likes of Duncan Lunan, who believes he has translated a radio message from aliens, and—better still—Patrick Flanagan, author of *Pyramid Power* (1975). His important discovery is that forces dwell inside the Mayan pyramid. It intercepts space particles and

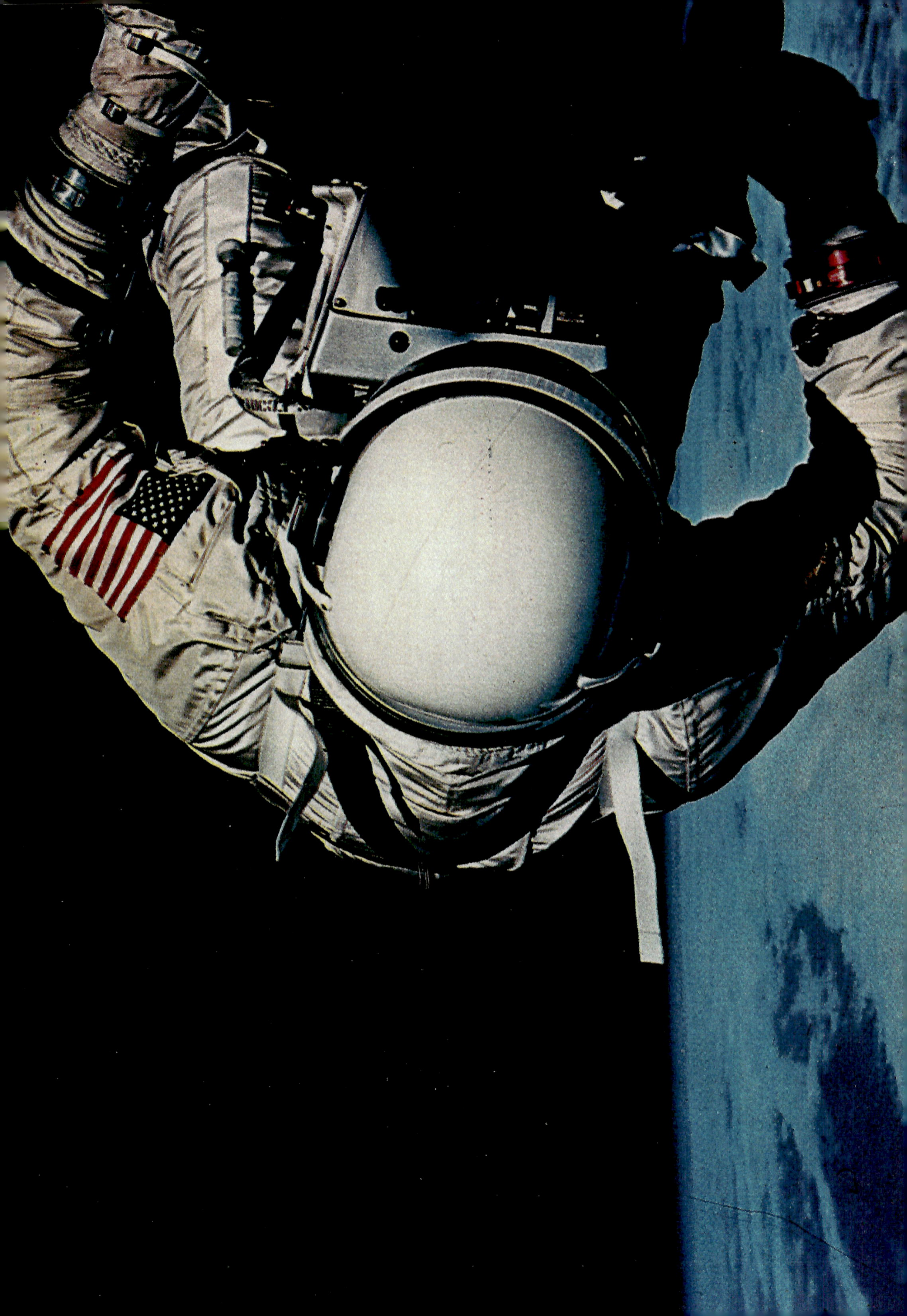

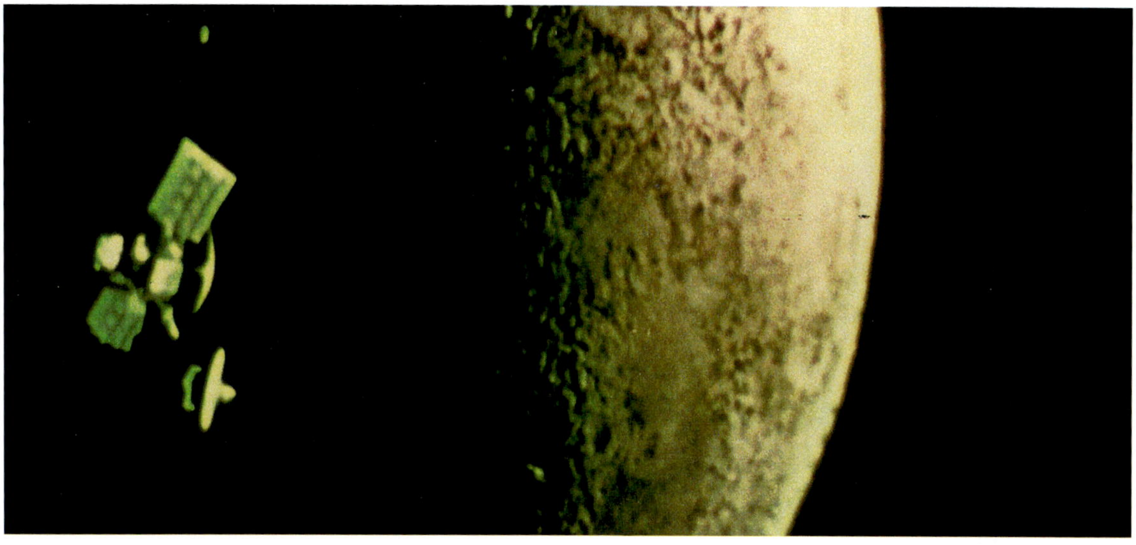

operates like a cosmic greenhouse. When not reaching for the stars, we should get these two guys together in Funky Town, where they already seem to reside.

At times, *The Outer Space Connection* drifts from its core topic, becoming a G-rated journey with scenic routes aplenty. The von Däniken premise becomes a launching pad for adventures into Kirlian photography, the Bermuda Triangle, crystal skulls, and cloning. Somehow it all meshes beautifully, thanks in large measure to screenwriter and director Fred Warshofsky.

As always, it is a joy to hear Serling speak with varying degrees of certainty. There is an "indication" that we are being "watched by a presence from somewhere else in the universe." They might have even mined rare minerals on the moon. Elsewhere, though, qualifiers are harder to spot than the Nazca lines from ground level. "The visitors have been here." No doubt about it. Don't believe him? Well, "they have been to Earth and left their mark in many ways in many places." And there can be no question that they are coming back.

When they do, I hope they take the time to dig on the film's soundtrack. Composer Roger Wagner's score is nearly the equal of Peter Thomas' for *Chariots of the Gods.* I'm as sure of that fact as Landsburg is about Tiahuanaco having served as "Earth Base One" for ancient astronauts.

During the early months of 1975, Sunn tested *The Outer Space Connection* in Phoenix and Tucson before sending prints to Kansas City, Wichita, Des Moines, and Omaha. They wanted to gauge audience reaction and plan their marketing strategy accordingly. But the film was already selling itself. Test runs quickly grossed $1 million.

Boxoffice called *The Outer Space Connection* an "intelligent documentary," one "worth seeing." And the *Los Angeles Times* rightly proclaimed, the film "goes pretty far out, but that's what makes it fun and stimulating."

What else is there to say? *The Outer Space Connection* became one of Rod Serling's last professional gigs before he stepped forever into the Twilight Zone. He is dearly missed, and always will be.

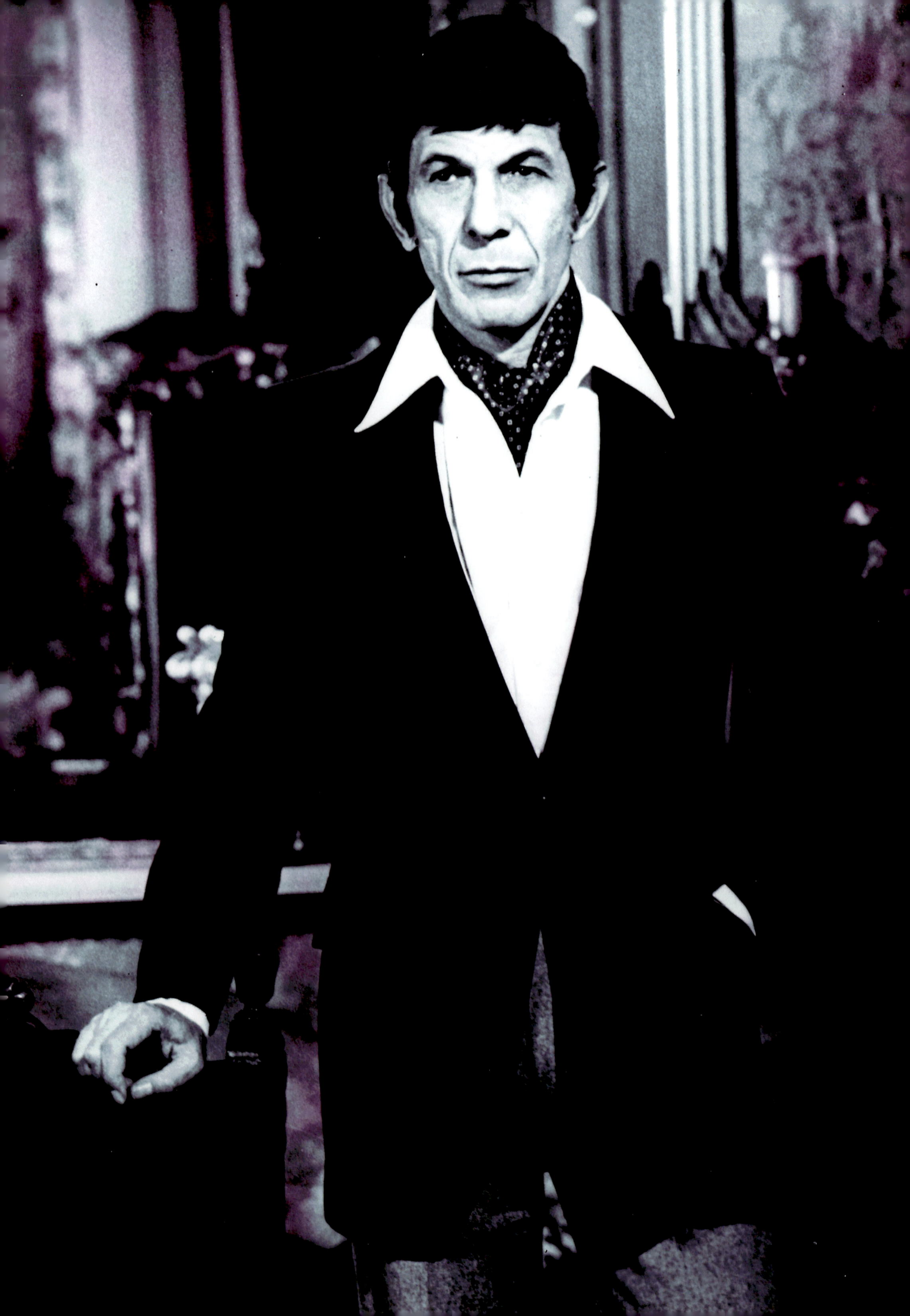

In Search Of... Ancient Aliens

(1976–1982)

In 1973, the trade publication *Broadcasting* published a fascinating advertisement touting "original programming for cable TV." The show's title was *The Unexplained,* a forthcoming series that would provide a "scientific look at famous mysteries, strange phenomena, ESP, UFOs, The Bermuda Triangle, etc." Next stop, Weirdumentary Central.

Wessex Communications of Whippany, New Jersey, owned *The Unexplained.* The ad was taking "reservations" for the pilot, *The Mystery of Oak Island.* Presumably the inaugural episode was filmed, given that the ad also promoted a *Behind the Scenes* documentary about "what went into making" it. But *The Unexplained* disappeared, without explanation.

Less than three years later, new ads appeared for a program called *The Unexplained,* a "half-hour series that explores those mysterious and dramatic events for which no rational explanations exist." Subjects included the Nazca Lines, UFOs, Haunted Houses, the Bermuda Triangle, the Loch Ness Monster, and our old pal Bigfoot.

"This list goes on. It is curiously long," the ad promised. And it curiously had nothing to do with Wessex Communications.

This 1976 program was a collaboration between Wolper Productions and Columbia Pictures. And Alan Landsburg, director of *In Search of Ancient Astronauts* (1973) and *In Search of Ancient Mysteries* (1974).

Bristol-Myers signed on as national sponsor for *The Unexplained,* which promised to "unravel the secret of good family entertainment and the riddle of high ratings."

But the new show had a new name before it ever aired. *The Unexplained* became *In Search of...* (Perhaps Wessex had made legal complaints?) And the show's narrator was not Rod Serling, as Landsburg originally wanted. (Serling died in 1975.)

While Robert Vaughn hosted the pilot, Leonard Nimoy signed on the dotted line for the series. Thanks to him, *In Search of...* would live long and prosper for six seasons after premiering in September 1976.

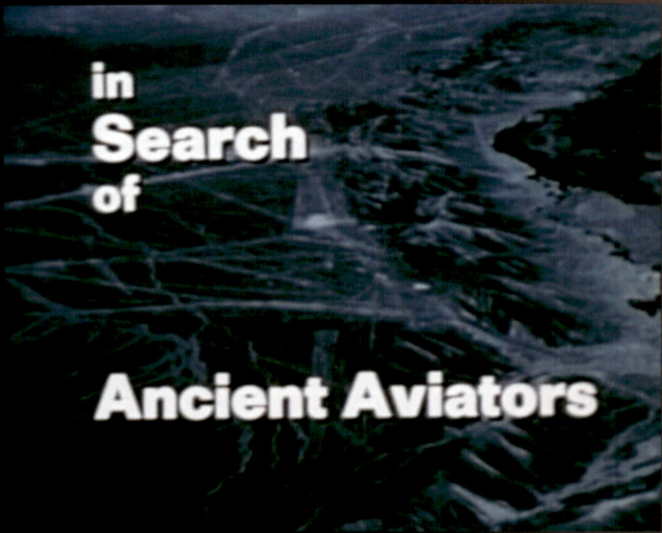
in
Search
of
Ancient Aviators

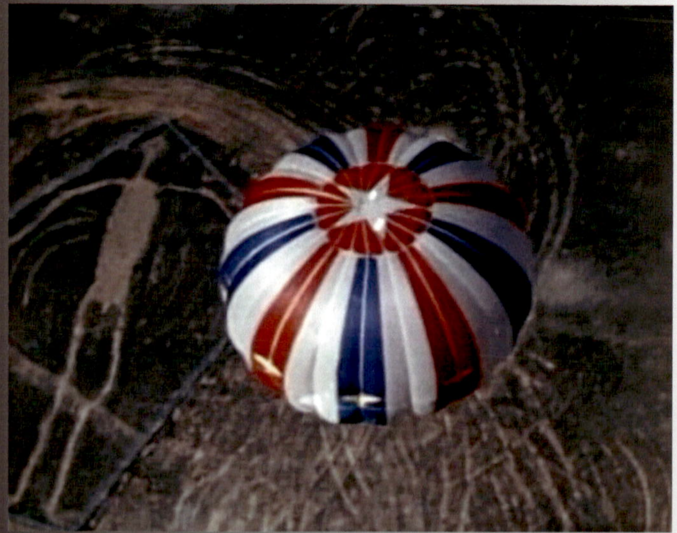

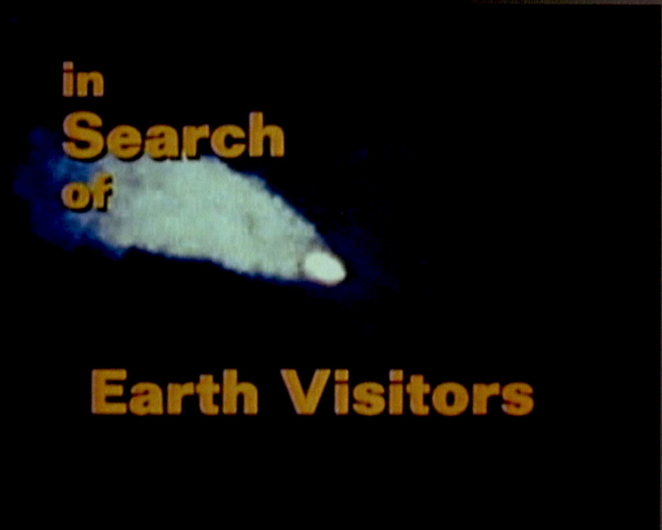
in
Search
of
Earth Visitors

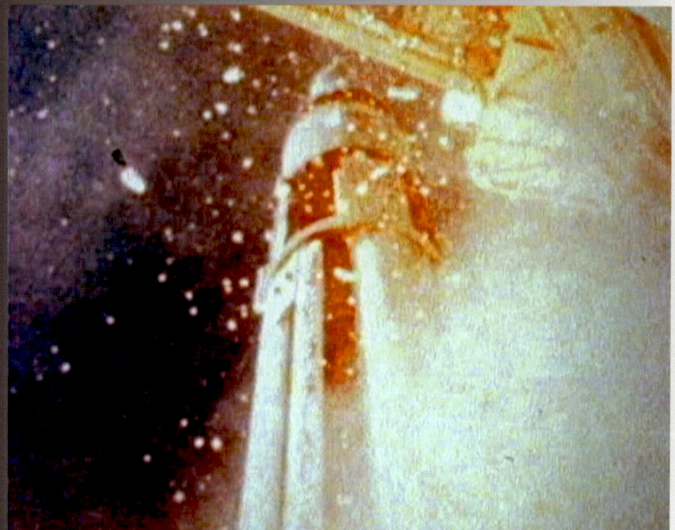

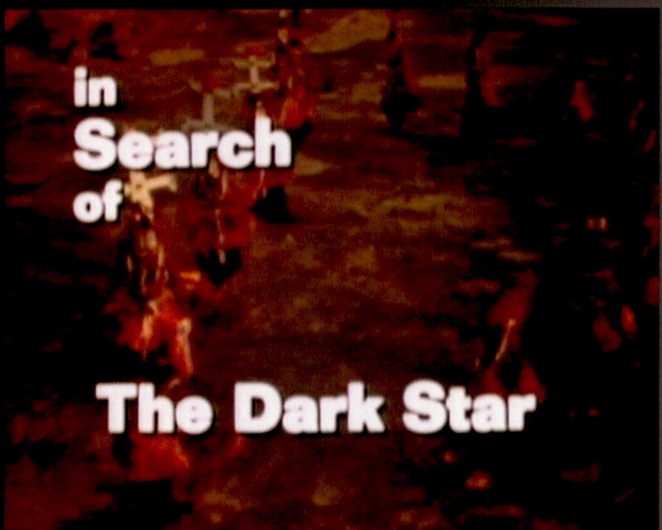
in
Search
of
The Dark Star

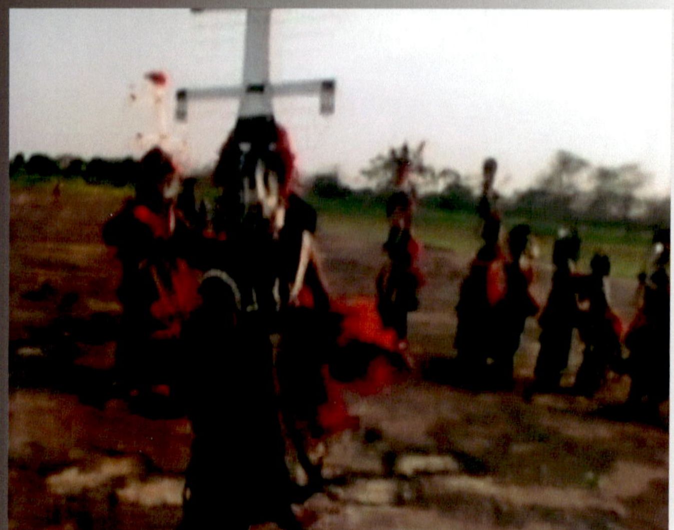

Each episode began with the following fantabulous disclaimer: "This series presents information based in part on theory and conjecture. The producers' purpose is to suggest some possible explanations, but not necessarily the only ones to the mysteries we will examine."

Surprisingly or not, *In Search of...* devoted only three episodes to ancient aliens, the subject that Alan Landsburg had introduced to Americans. Only three Chariots of the Nods, but they remain memorable enough to give a nod back to them.

Season 1, Episode 3, *Ancient Aviators*: It begins with footage of the Nazca lines. Nimoy explains, "They make sense only when viewed from a great height. Miles of what look like modern runways score the desert. If they were, what manner of craft landed here? Who were the pilots?"

When we see Nimoy on-screen, he wears a stylish white turtleneck while talking about the age-old human desire to fly. He describes the legends of Icarus, Osiris, and others. But the key question here is Nazca. Nimoy admits no one has solved their mysteries. But maybe, just maybe, peoples from above relied on them when visiting Earth. (Parking space ... the final frontier.)

Season 4, Episode 19, *Earth Visitors*: "We are familiar with rockets leaving the Earth to explore other worlds. What we are not familiar with are space explorers from other worlds coming to Earth. ... Is it possible that our planet was an early destination for Earth visitors?"

On that last question, I'll answer with a definite yes, if only for grammatical reasons. If they were indeed *Earth visitors*, then that does presuppose they visited Earth.

Maurice Chatelain, NASA scientist and author of the book *Our Ancestors Came from Outer Space* (1978), tells us about how aliens interbred with early man, as well as all kinds of other not-so-trivial trivia. By contrast, Erich von Däniken doesn't tell us anything, mainly because he isn't interviewed.

Season 4, Episode 13, *The Dark Star*: "Now we must ask, how did a primitive people, lacking instruments of any kind, discover a dark star hidden deep in space?" There is no choice, you understand. Along with Nimoy, we must ask this question.

A thousand years ago, you see, the Dogon people of Central Africa learned "ancient knowledge," including about a little star that doesn't twinkle, twinkle. It does have a voice, though, "calling initiates to a ceremony high in the cliffs." The Dogon have also known about planets that could not generally be understood without telescopes.

"Beings from the sacred star" descended and gave the Dogon many symbols to interpret. They revealed "an astonishing scope of astronomical knowledge, an infinite number of stars and spiraling worlds."

Incidentally, the Dark Star is what scientists now call Sirius B. For myself, I'll simply call it serious. And cool. Really, really, cool.

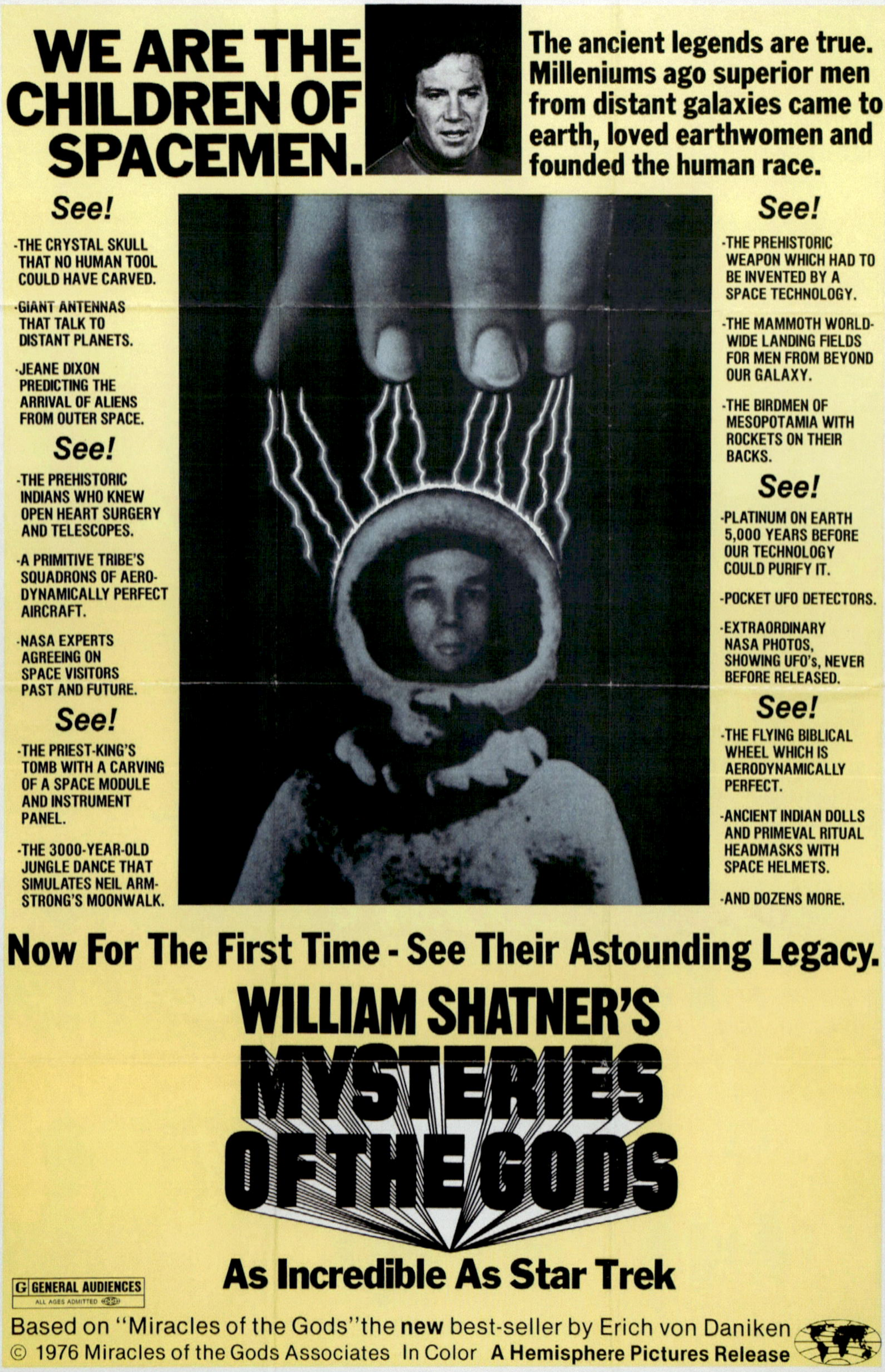
WE ARE THE CHILDREN OF SPACEMEN.
The ancient legends are true. Milleniums ago superior men from distant galaxies came to earth, loved earthwomen and founded the human race.
See!
-THE CRYSTAL SKULL THAT NO HUMAN TOOL COULD HAVE CARVED.
-GIANT ANTENNAS THAT TALK TO DISTANT PLANETS.
-JEANE DIXON PREDICTING THE ARRIVAL OF ALIENS FROM OUTER SPACE.
See!
-THE PREHISTORIC INDIANS WHO KNEW OPEN HEART SURGERY AND TELESCOPES.
-A PRIMITIVE TRIBE'S SQUADRONS OF AERO-DYNAMICALLY PERFECT AIRCRAFT.
-NASA EXPERTS AGREEING ON SPACE VISITORS PAST AND FUTURE.
See!
-THE PRIEST-KING'S TOMB WITH A CARVING OF A SPACE MODULE AND INSTRUMENT PANEL.
-THE 3000-YEAR-OLD JUNGLE DANCE THAT SIMULATES NEIL ARM-STRONG'S MOONWALK.
See!
-THE PREHISTORIC WEAPON WHICH HAD TO BE INVENTED BY A SPACE TECHNOLOGY.
-THE MAMMOTH WORLD-WIDE LANDING FIELDS FOR MEN FROM BEYOND OUR GALAXY.
-THE BIRDMEN OF MESOPOTAMIA WITH ROCKETS ON THEIR BACKS.
See!
-PLATINUM ON EARTH 5,000 YEARS BEFORE OUR TECHNOLOGY COULD PURIFY IT.
-POCKET UFO DETECTORS.
-EXTRAORDINARY NASA PHOTOS, SHOWING UFO's, NEVER BEFORE RELEASED.
See!
-THE FLYING BIBLICAL WHEEL WHICH IS AERODYNAMICALLY PERFECT.
-ANCIENT INDIAN DOLLS AND PRIMEVAL RITUAL HEADMASKS WITH SPACE HELMETS.
-AND DOZENS MORE.
Now For The First Time - See Their Astounding Legacy.
WILLIAM SHATNER'S
MYSTERIES OF THE GODS
As Incredible As Star Trek
G GENERAL AUDIENCES
ALL AGES ADMITTED
Based on "Miracles of the Gods" the new best-seller by Erich von Daniken
© 1976 Miracles of the Gods Associates In Color A Hemisphere Pictures Release

Mysteries of the Gods

(1976)

"We're going to look at the Earth and its mysteries from the past, long before recorded time. We're going to examine and perhaps question some widely held theories of what may have happened to this Earth of ours in that mysterious and murky dawn, of what we know as civilization. We're going to investigate some strange and bizarre events in the present, unbelievable happenings as fresh as today's headlines. And more important, perhaps, we're going to take a searching and scientific look into the future."

Words to the wise from on-screen host William Shatner, who promises to cover so much ground (and space) as to need warp drive to fulfill his mission in only eighty-seven minutes.

Based on Erich von Däniken's *Miracles of the Gods* ("A Dell Best Seller"), this Hemisphere Pictures Release originated as the 1975 German documentary *Phaenomene – die die Welt Erregen* (a.k.a. *Rätsel, die die Welt Erregen*). A.M. Schwarzer produced the original for Neue Emelka Films of Munich. Harald Reinel of *Chariots of the Gods* fame directed. Charles Romine adapted the Weirdumentary for English audiences, directing William Shatner and some other sequences. Roger Cahn and Ellis Eisenstein produced.

In some respects, *Mysteries of the Gods* echoes *Chariots of the Gods*, reusing old footage and doing some new globe-trotting that means we not only return to the Nazca lines, but we return to them *twice*. We revisit familiar worlds of the Mayans and of Easter Island. We bounce from South America to Europe to South America and back to Europe again. The film juxtaposes artwork and artifacts from eons ago with photos of twentieth-century astronauts.

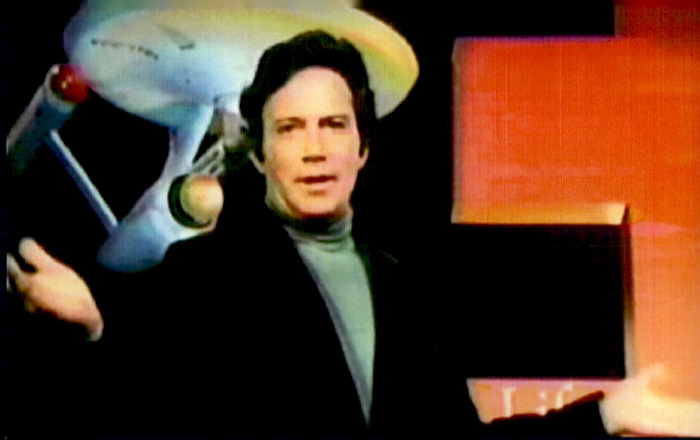

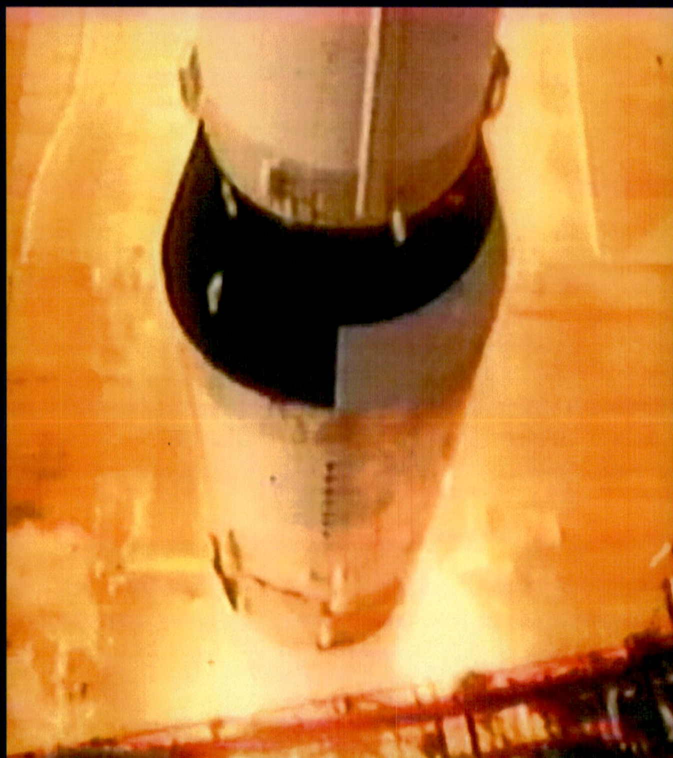

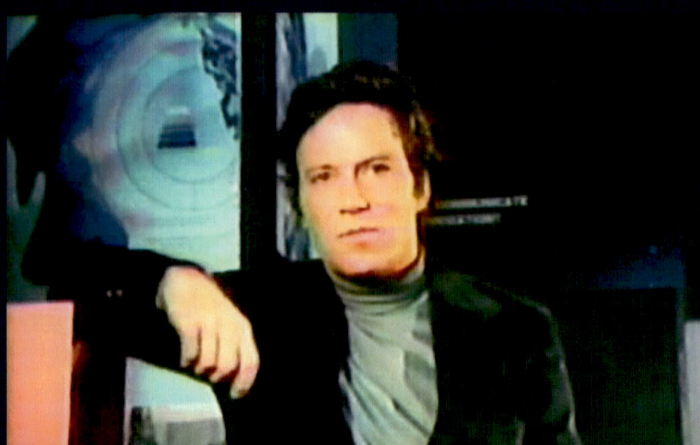

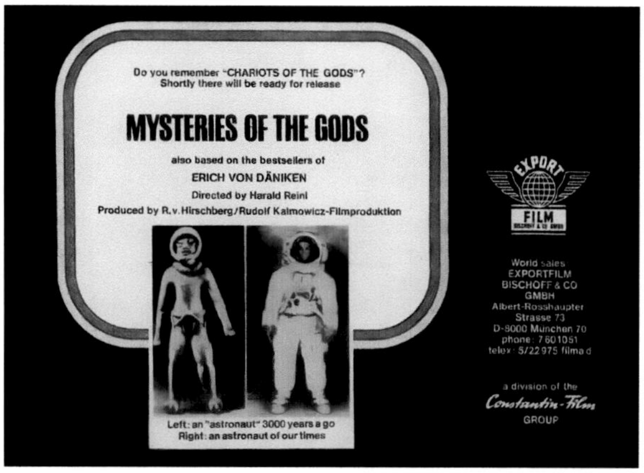

And then there is the overabundance of rhetorical questions. "Who are the ancient astronauts, if there were truly ancient astronauts who inspired these legends," Shatner asks. "Is there life out there?" (And if there is, does she have green skin?)

Rather than being a mere repeat of its predecessor, *Mysteries of the Gods* pushes the envelope. The spheres of Costa Rica, the mysterious structure on Nan Madol, the Carnac stones of Great Britain, and the meticulously illustrated stones of Peru's Ica River allow our imaginations to take flight. We hear von Däniken's name several times and even see footage of him. Feel free to applaud at your leisure.

Mysteries of the Gods unfolds differently than its predecessor in another respect. Shatner interviews several persons on-camera, so many that *Boxoffice* complained they were cumulatively "a bit dull." They range from Anna Mitchell-Hedges (who discusses the famed crystal skull she discovered), Daniel Cetrone (a parapsychologist who tracks UFO sightings), Jeane Dixon (who predicts that aliens will land on Earth in August 1977), and the delightfully strange exo-sociologist Richard Yinger. He tells Shatner that our efforts with space travel are nothing less than us "trying to find our way home," that "we, in fact, could be spacemen." Beam me up, Snotty.

Throughout the film, William Shatner proves his mettle, boldly going where von Däniken had gone before, but in his own stylish style. Consider dialogue like "These pictures are considered genuine by people who believe in UFOs." Lesser humans, or even Vulcans, could never read such dialogue with as much weight as the starship captain. Perhaps that's why the on-screen title actually reads *William Shatner's Mysteries of the Gods*.

The MPAA gave the film a G rating in November 1976. January 1977 marked its blast-off at American theaters. Throughout the spring, *Mysteries* did well in a number of cities. The head of Hemisphere Pictures later reported that it did best at those theaters where director Romine made personal appearances. All the cool kids wanted to meet the man himself, or at least the gods he represented.

Author's Log: Stardate, 2024: *Mysteries of the Gods* is a must-see entry in the other-worldly world of the Weirdumentary.

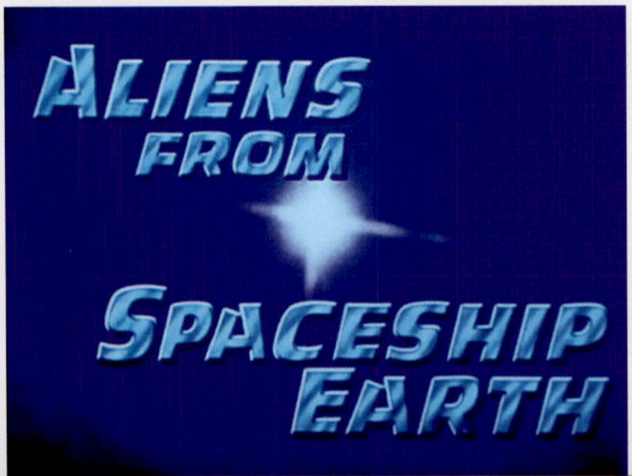
ALIENS
FROM
SPACESHIP
EARTH

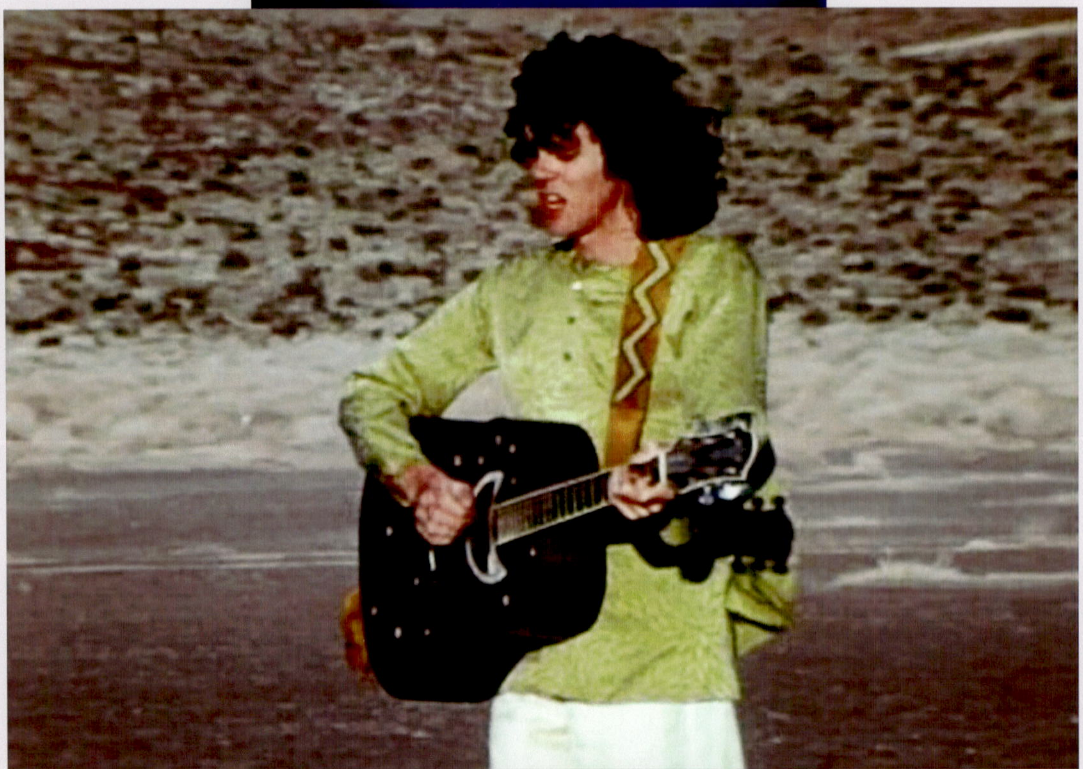

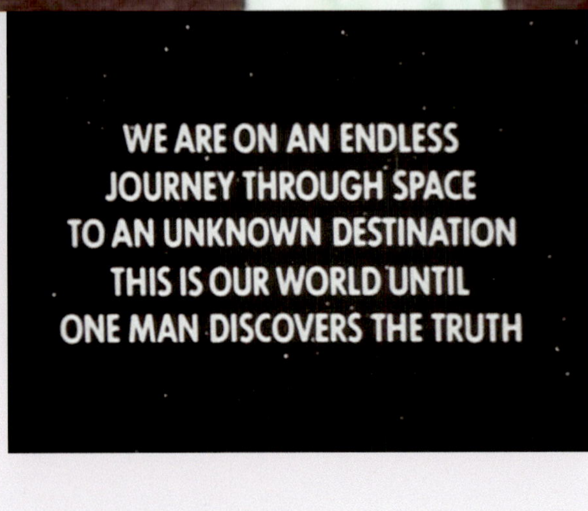
WE ARE ON AN ENDLESS
JOURNEY THROUGH SPACE
TO AN UNKNOWN DESTINATION
THIS IS OUR WORLD UNTIL
ONE MAN DISCOVERS THE TRUTH

Aliens from Spaceship Earth

(1977)

Some film titles are terrible, even if we come to accept them unquestioningly. If you stop and think about it, *Star Wars* (1977) is little more than serviceable.

Other film titles are unique, fascinating, tremendous. Such is the case with *Aliens from Spaceship Earth*, released the same year as *Star Wars*.

While titles label and represent films, they *aren't* films. George Lucas' space epic is wonderful, even if its title isn't. By contrast, *Aliens from Spaceship Earth* is a ninety-minute bore, despite its cool-sounding moniker.

The opening text of this Don Como-produced/directed Weirdumentary explains: "We are on an endless journey through space to an unknown destination. This is our world until one man discovers the truth."

So far, so good. But we soon learn this ain't a flick about ancient aliens having babies named Adam and Eve.

Footage of political activism in the sixties moves on to yoga in the seventies, from cultural revolution to a "threshold of a revolution in human consciousness." Meditation, we learn, might just be a "solution to the world's problems."

Our on-camera host is singer-songwriter Donovan, the Hurdy Gurdy Man himself. He explains how the Space Age and modern Western technology can merge with ancient Eastern philosophies. (Outer Trip, please let me introduce you to Inner Trip.)

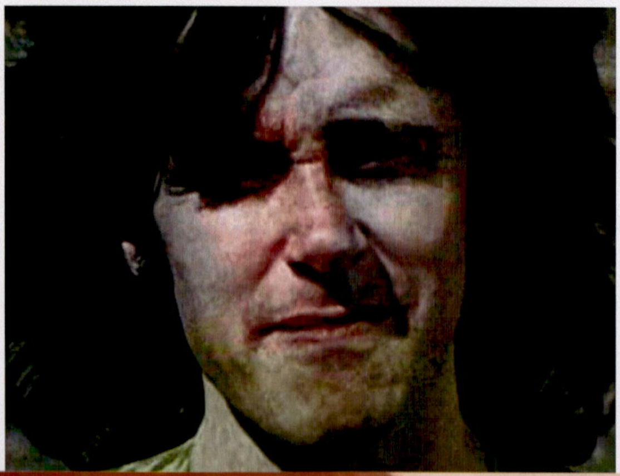

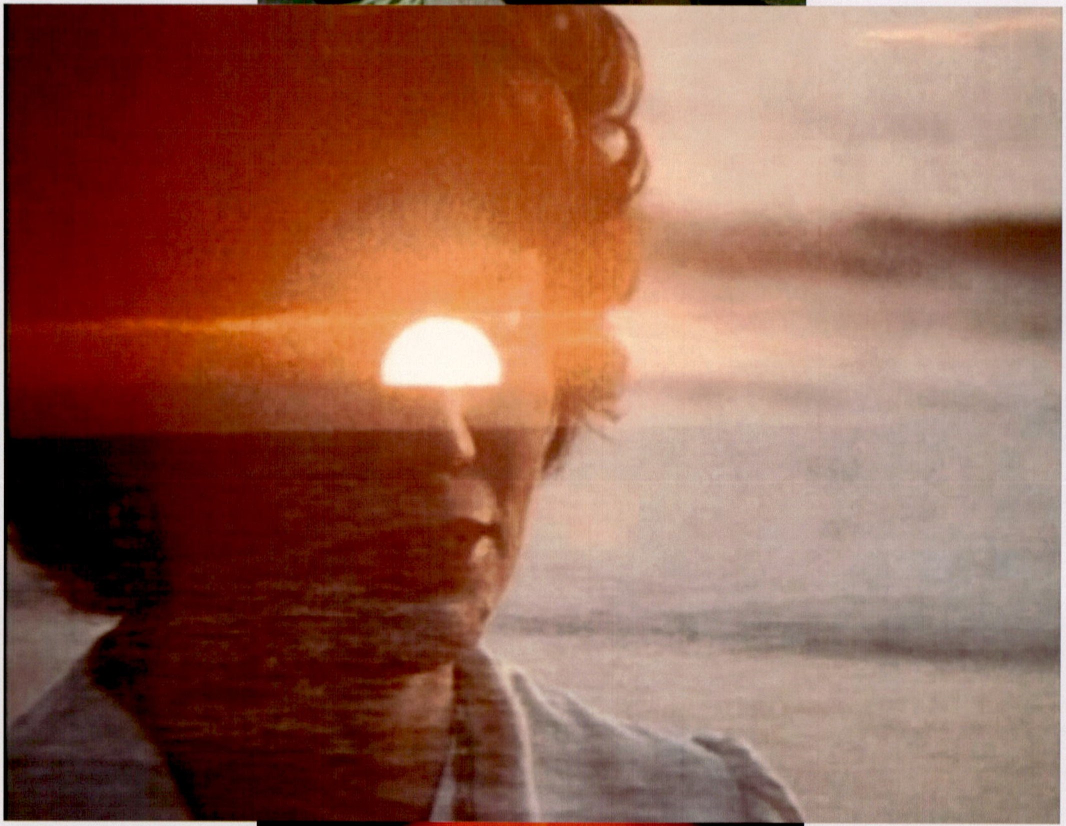

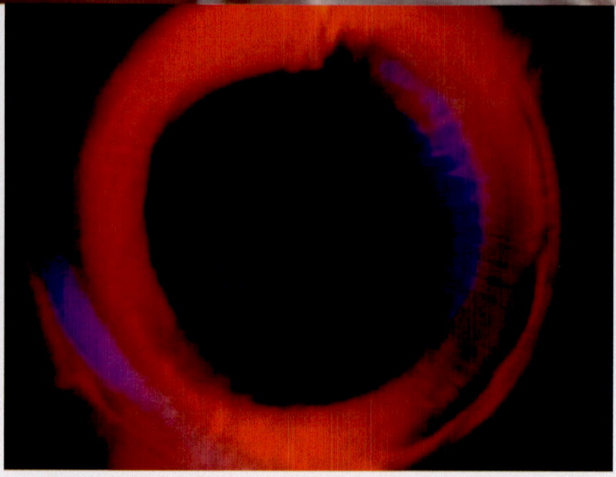

ALIENS FROM SPACESHIP EARTH — Filmed in 1979. Opinion, fair to good. Midnight. Channel 41. Lynda Day George, Donovan. Earth's defense systems are put to the ultimate test during an alien attack.

Donovan is certainly a sincere advocate for this discussion about "extraordinary powers and the wisdom of the universe." And he's the only Weirdumentary host who sings for us, repeatedly. Unfortunately, they're some fairly awful tunes composed for this dull overview of yogis, swamis, and gurus.

Flatteringly, we are part of the overview. We can all achieve a "higher level of awareness," apparently, which will eventually allow us to leave our bodies astrally.

Most of the film covers topics like Hare Krishna, Transcendental Meditation, and the "quest for higher consciousness." But never fear, things do take a detour down the Weirdumentary Road.

Footage of a firewalking ceremony shows us the possible powers to be gained. Step on the flames and you won't get burned. (Buy a DVD of this film, and you will be.)

Yogis buried alive without food or air survive for days at a time. We hear that while seeing footage of a man stretching.

The more enlightened one becomes, the more paranormal. "Many of the reports are extremely well documented," Donovan claims.

These include the controversial figure Sathya Sai Baba, thanks to footage repurposed from Como's movie *The Man of Miracles* (1975, see entry). Among other things, we see one of his alleged manifestations.

American followers of these spiritual leaders have found fulfillment, thanks to taking the Darjeeling Express instead of the Lipton Local.

It is only the Madonna Slavin case—in which a young lady's parents tried to free her from the clutches of a cult, or, depending on which side one takes, kidnap her and squash her free will—that the film gives a nod to the idea that all may not be perfect. (Age of Aquarius, or Age of Beware-of-Us?)

At any rate, the *Aliens from Spaceship Earth* are slow to take off. The narrative is slow-paced, and the structure loose. The running time seems padded, even though the film never fulfills its promise of describing how Western technology can merge with Hinduism. Nevertheless, Gold Key later released *Aliens* as part of the "Gamma Chronicles" package for television.

"Are there other worlds more highly evolved than our own?" Donovan asks. If so, they don't watch this movie.

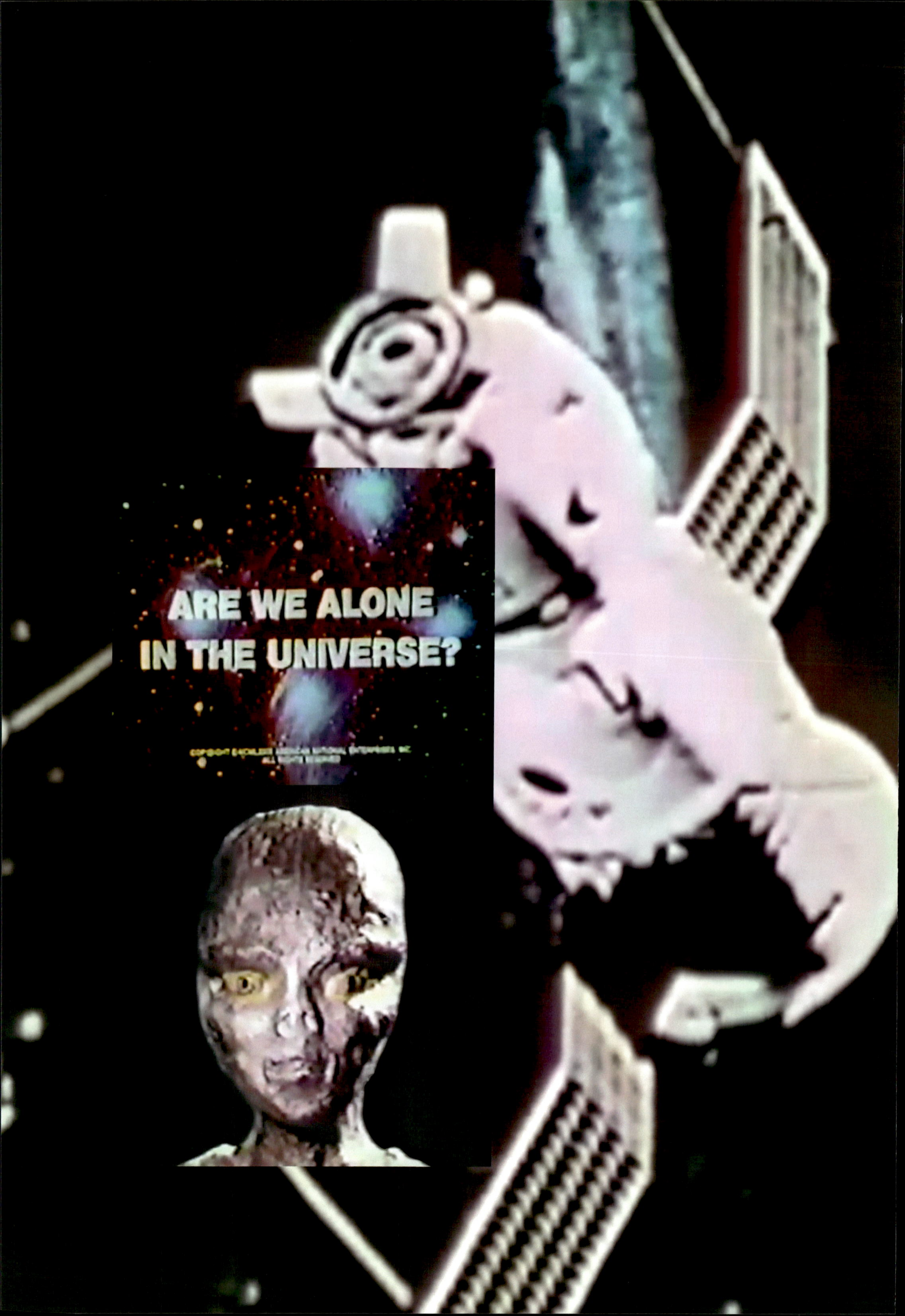
ARE WE ALONE
IN THE UNIVERSE?

Are We Alone in the Universe?

(1978)

"In the past quarter-century, mankind has made remarkable strides, reaching beyond the bounds of the planet Earth into the unexplored realms of space. Yesterday the moon was man's limit, but tomorrow it may be the stars. As yet no one knows what these missions may encounter, new worlds to explore, distant civilizations with which we may communicate. Or could it be that long ages ago, the cosmic connection was already forged, with the evidence preserved in the relics of ancient man?"

Good question, narrator Hugh Douglas, even though it had been asked repeatedly in prior Weirdumentaries. This Johnny-Come-Lately flick was produced and directed by George Gale for American National Enterprises. Kinda-sorta, anyhow.

You see, the good folks at Salt Lake City-based American National Enterprises produced and distributed family films after forming the company in the mid-sixties. In 1973, *Daily Variety* called ANE the "granddaddy of the recent four-wall upsurge," the distribution strategy that played such a role in Sunn Classics' success.

By 1975, George Gale became ANE's Vice President for Production. The following year, he formed his own production company, but continued to rely on ANE for distribution.

Fast-forward to July 1979. *Variety* announced that ANE "acquired" the rights to a "Question Pic" that Munich-based Horst Veit World Sales had exhibited at Cannes. The film was *Are We Alone in the Universe?*, which had been produced the prior year.

Then it seems that George Gale directed new English-language narration by Hugh Douglas, an actor who had previously appeared on such TV shows as *Batman* and *Ironside*.

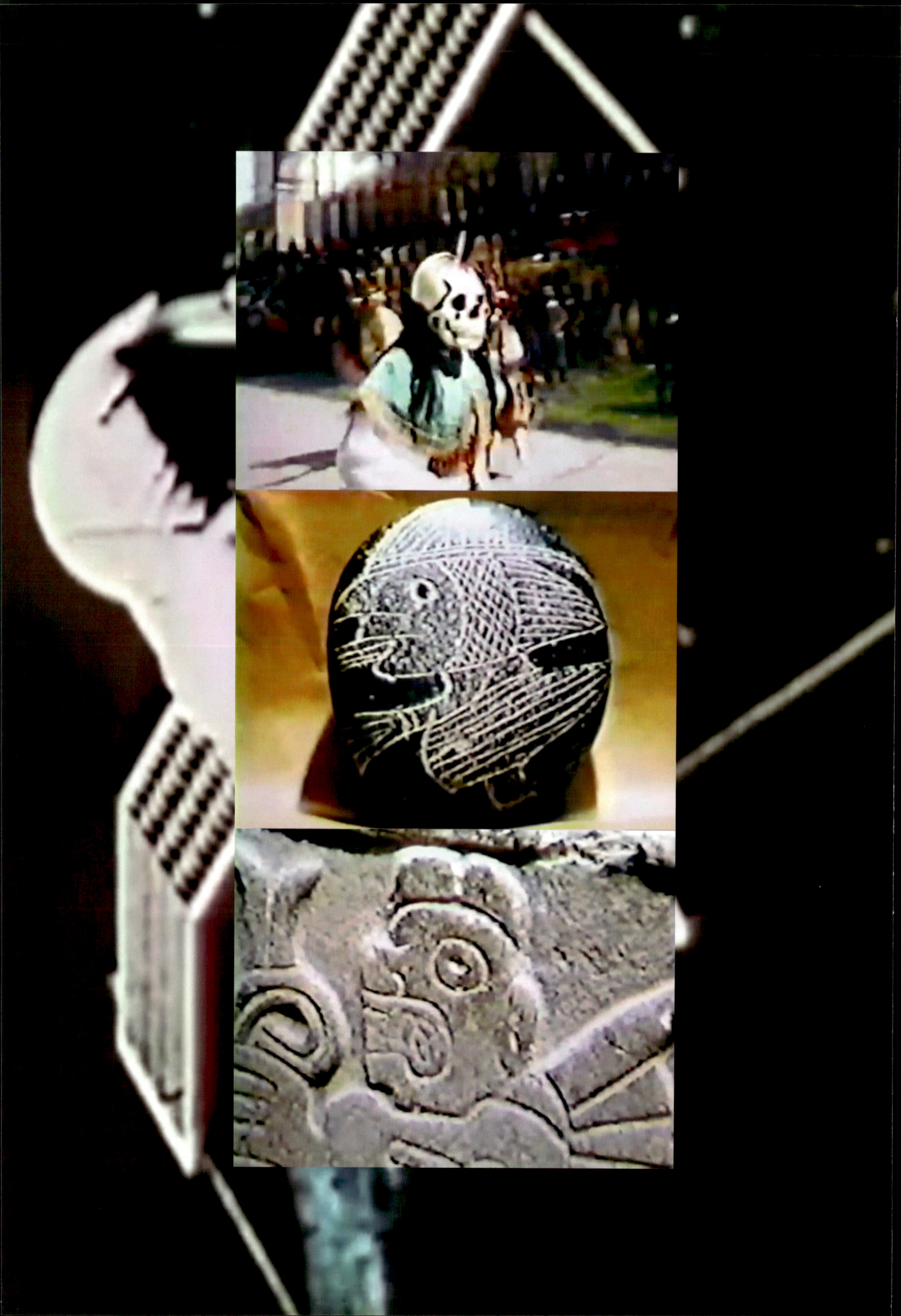

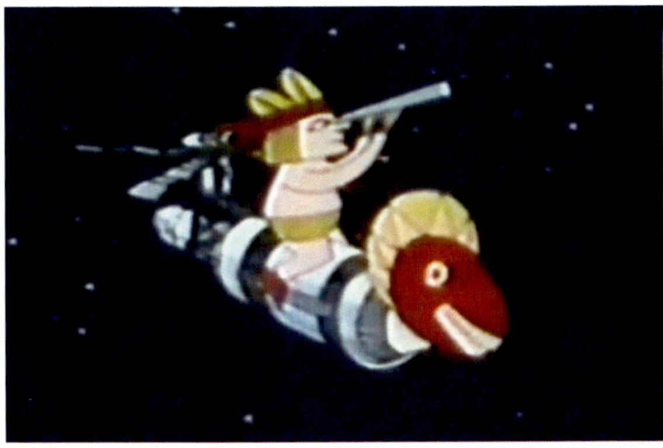 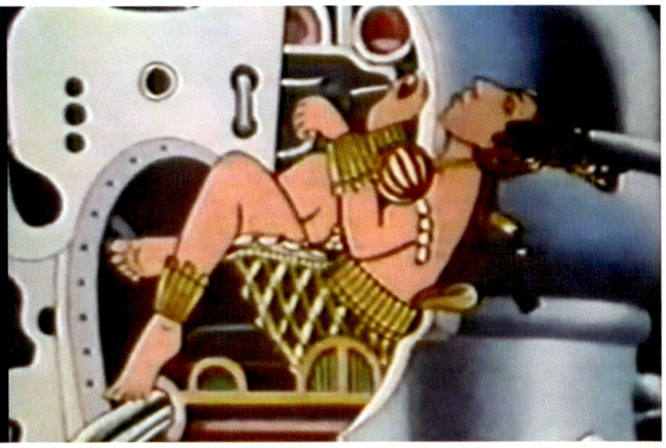

As for this Weirdumentary, we learn that investigators around the globe are "fascinated by the notion that extraterrestrial visitors may have left their mark on mankind's past." Yada, yada, yada.

With the exception of a brief (and by all appearances, pre-existing) interview with Dr. Christiann Barnard, who performed the world's first successful heart transplant, the entire film unfolds as voiceover. We do get plenty of questions, and counter-narratives from Those Who Don't Believe, sometimes in the same sentence. "Again we ask, are these the portraits of space travelers, or merely the stylized works of imaginative artisans of ancient times?"

Much of the story concentrates on South America, from Peru's Nazca Lines to Bolivia's Tiahuanaco. If all of this terrain sounds familiar, it should. "Celestial voyagers" have visited here before.

And so have we. Been there, done that. Carl Sagan's name comes up; von Däniken's doesn't. But it should have. This chariot belongs to his gods, even if it's last year's model.

The film most clearly reveals its budget limitations in discussions of genetic manipulation and underwater exploration. The sheer amount of time spent on these tangential topics has all the earmarks of relying on available stock footage to reach feature length.

Nevertheless, a bit of fun can be found in the far reaches of this universe. Simple animation of primitive heart surgeries is delightful. And the notion that mummification might not only have been taught to us by ancient aliens, but was also a way for them to preserve "bodies until the space travelers returned from their missions to awaken them at last to a new and glorious life" ... well, that gets the Weirdumentary seal of approval.

'Course it is worth asking if we're alone in the universe. "Are we just specks of cosmic dust, one planet in a billion, whirling in infinite space?"

The film doesn't tell us, but either way, rest assured that the "we" in question includes Hugh Douglas, who deserved a higher-profile career. To hear his voice and dig the film's music ... that keeps me from feeling too alone in this here universe.

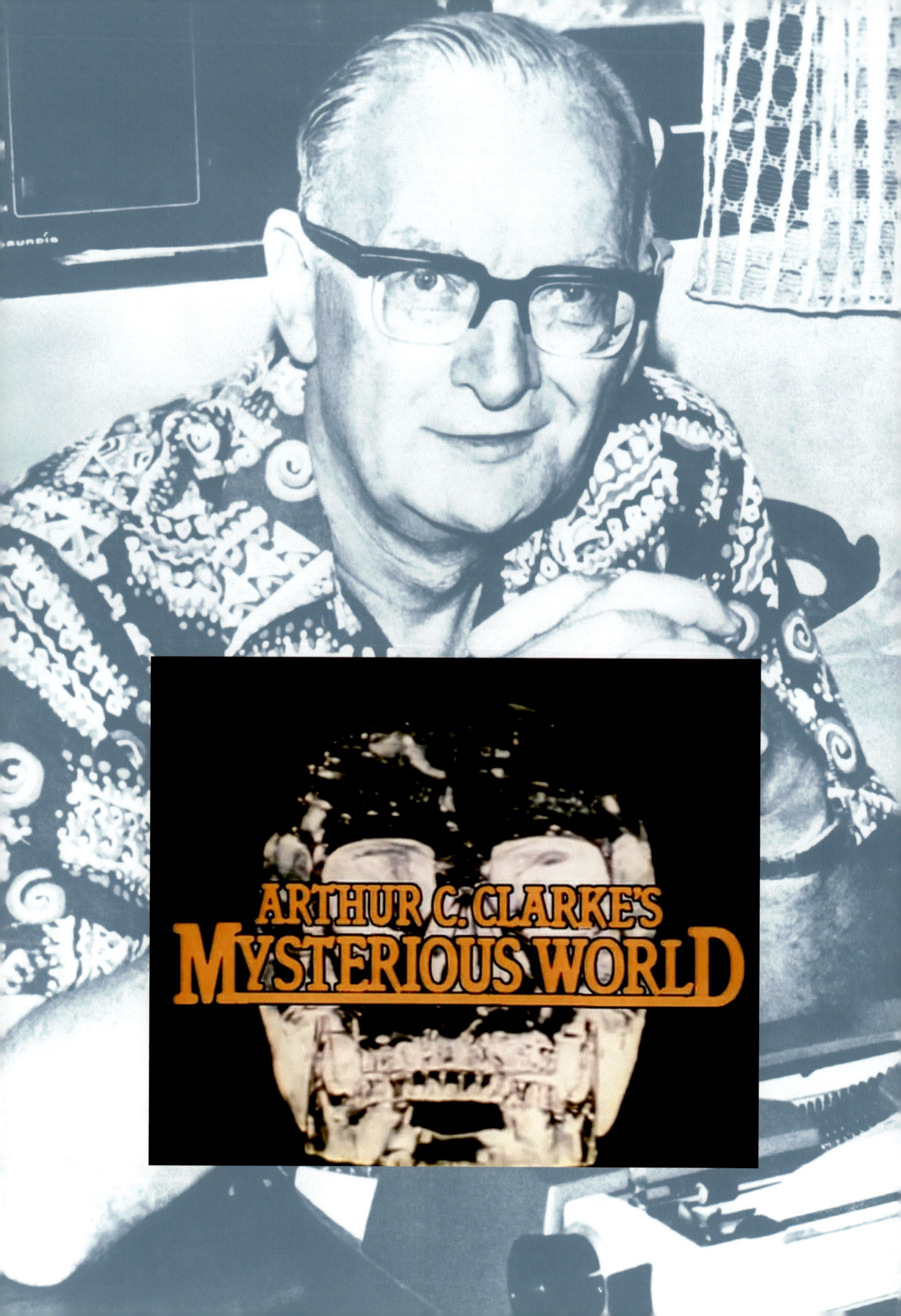
ARTHUR C. CLARKE'S
MYSTERIOUS WORLD

Arthur C. Clarke's Mysterious World: Ancient Aliens

(1980)

"Mysteries from the files of Arthur C. Clarke, author of *2001* and inventor of the communications satellite, now in retreat in Sri Lanka after a lifetime of science, space, and writing, he ponders the riddles of this and other worlds."

So explains the off-screen narrator of this TV series, which is distinct from other Weirdumentaries to the extent that the narrator (Gordon Honeycombe) is a different person than the on-screen host (Clarke).

Mysterious World was a "Yorkshire Television Colour Production" produced by John Fanshawe and John Fairley. The opening credits feature the Mitchell-Hedges crystal skull, long before Indiana Jones knew about it. Along with Clarke, the best thing about this wonderful program is its theme song, composed by Alan Hawkshaw.

Running thirteen episodes, *Mysterious World* premiered on ITV in the United Kingdom in 1980. Book Club Associates published a companion book that same year. By 1982, the series began to appear on American television.

Variety reviewed the program in 1980, calling Clarke a "somewhat awkward" presenter and stating that the half-hour format was "too limiting for an in-depth investigation." I beg to differ. Let the journey begin.

In Episode 1, *The Journey Begins,* which provides an overview of the entire series, Clarke tells us that mysteries of the "first kind" are those that baffled our forebears, but that we have solved. By contrast, mysteries of the "second kind" are those that remain unsolved, but we do have some clues. But mysteries of the "third kind" have no rational explanation whatsoever. Put another way, they're weird, damn weird, maybe weirder than the ancient sites that so fascinated Erich von Däniken.

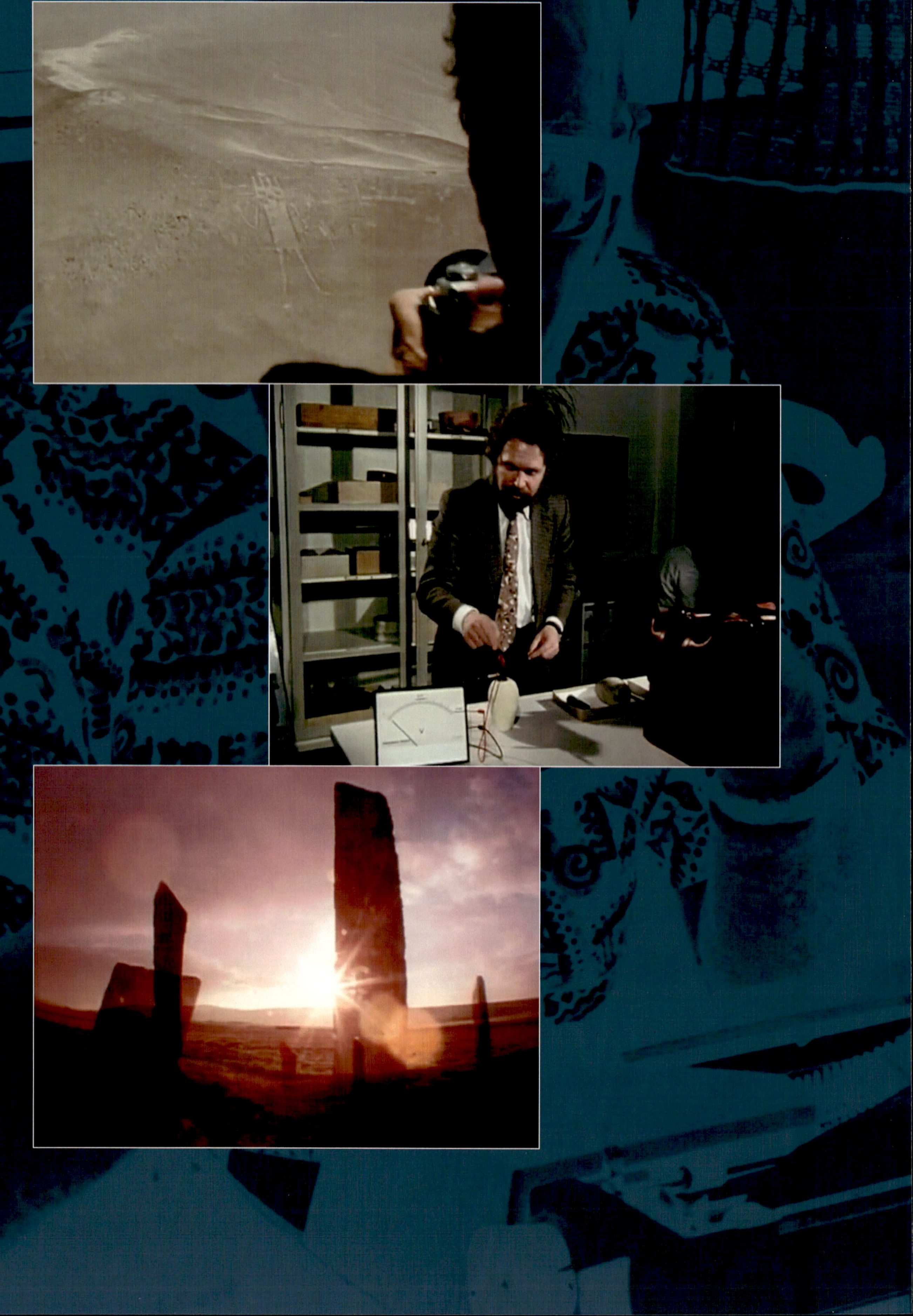

Episode 2, *Giants for the Gods*: "What strange compulsion made men etch vast designs on the face of the Earth, on downland and desert, on the slopes of solitary mountains? Why can so many be only seen from the air? What is their message from the distant past?"

Let's return to Nazca and other, similar sites across the globe, which constitute a "fantastic picture book of shapes and lines." Were they "built as an airport for ancient astronauts," or images designed to please the gods? Or could it be that some ancient peoples rose to the sky in primitive hot-air balloons, in order to see their artwork from above?

We also meet the Cerne Abbas Giant, the hill figure etched in Dorset, England, which is also known as the "Rude Man." He is apparently centuries old. One of the local women who wants a child sits on him—presumably near his enormous penis—and the following spring she is supremely pregnant. ("Baby Love, my baby love, I need your love...")

Despite the enigma of such designs, Clarke gives no quarter, or nickel or penny, to the notion that these geoglyphs were landing strips for aliens.

Episode 3, *Ancient Wisdom*: "How did man find the technology 2,500 years ago to melt rock and turn their hilltop fortresses into impregnable glass? Can this German scientist justify his astonishing claim that these relics are an electric battery invented long before the birth of Christ? In Athens, has this distinguished professor found irrefutable evidence of ancient wisdom? Can it be that in the heart of this fragment, lost from a ship 2,000 years ago, lie hidden the cogwheels of the world's first computer?"

Perhaps some these eggheads are on to something, but as for von Däniken, all the king's horses and men can't put his theory back together again after Arthur C. explodes it without even mentioning his name. "A lot of rubbish has been written about mysterious knowledge possessed by the ancients. They didn't need any help from visitors from outer space..." (No mysteries of the third kind here, and certainly not close encounters of that same number, says he.)

As for that ancient computer, which is known officially as the Antikythera Mechanism, its story is much more engaging and convincing than the so-called Baghdad battery. (Henceforth, the first computer shall be known as the HAL 1000.)

Episode 8, *Riddle of the Stones*: "Why did the people of prehistoric Britain set up this great stone circle on Salisbury Plain? What is the meaning of Stonehenge? Were Britain's other rings of stone centers of an unknown pagan cult? Were they places of sacrifice and death? Were they observatories, where, 4,000 years ago, astronomers plotted the courses of the sun, moon and stars?"

Once again Clarke gives us the goods, describing the "awe" that we rightly feel when visiting the likes of Stonehenge in England and Newgrange in Ireland. But once again, he turns down the dial of the Weird-o-Meter, still refusing to join von Däniken on a chariot ride. No one on *Mysterious World* argues that ancient aliens helped move these stones, even though Clarke's most famous fictional tale—*2001: A Space Odyssey*—features alien monoliths that help to guide humans on their evolutionary journey.

All that said, don't go thinking Clarke isn't open to a good dose of the weird. After all, during the series he declared, "Our universe is not only more mysterious than we imagine, it is more mysterious than we *can* imagine."

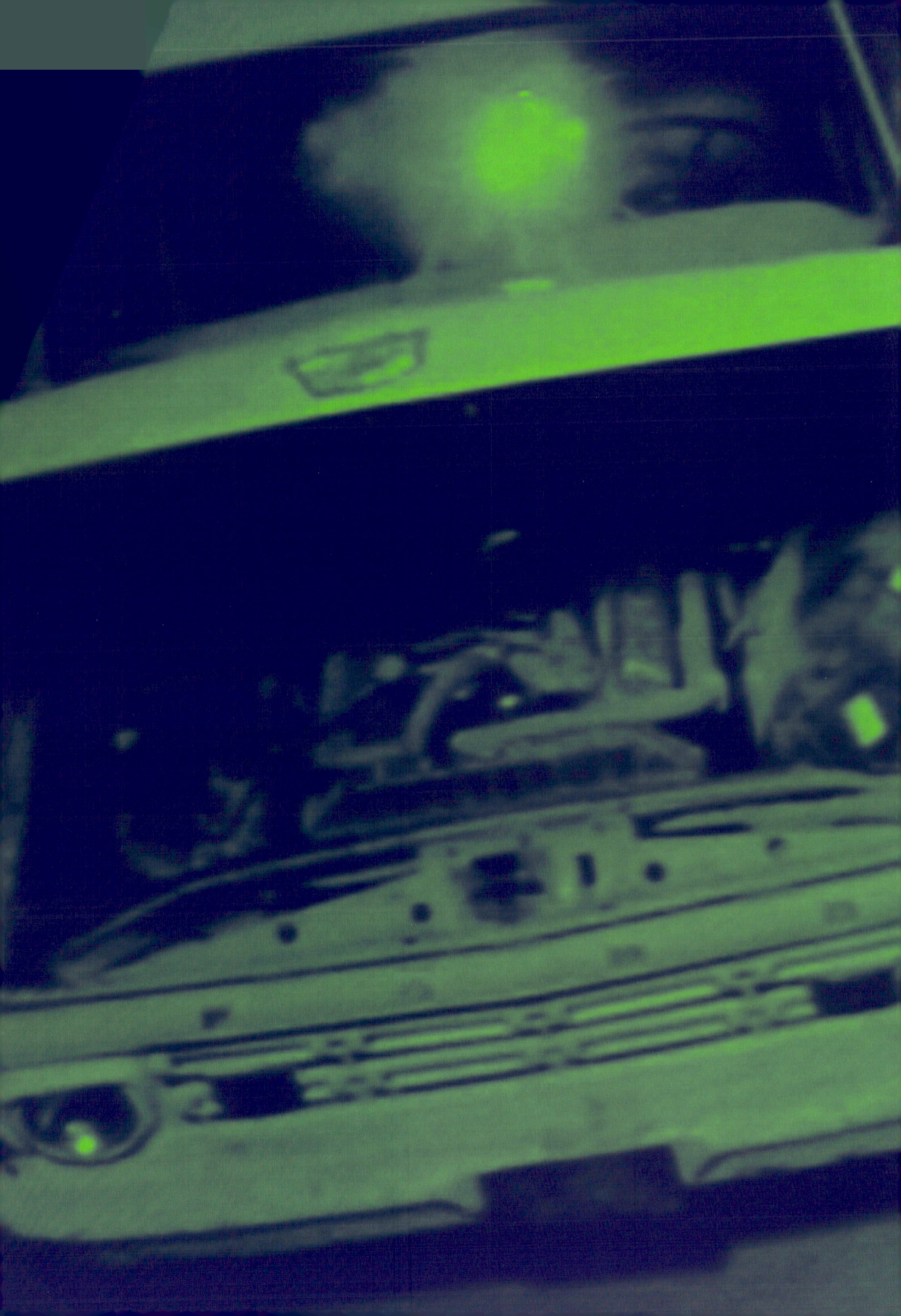

section 3:
UFOs

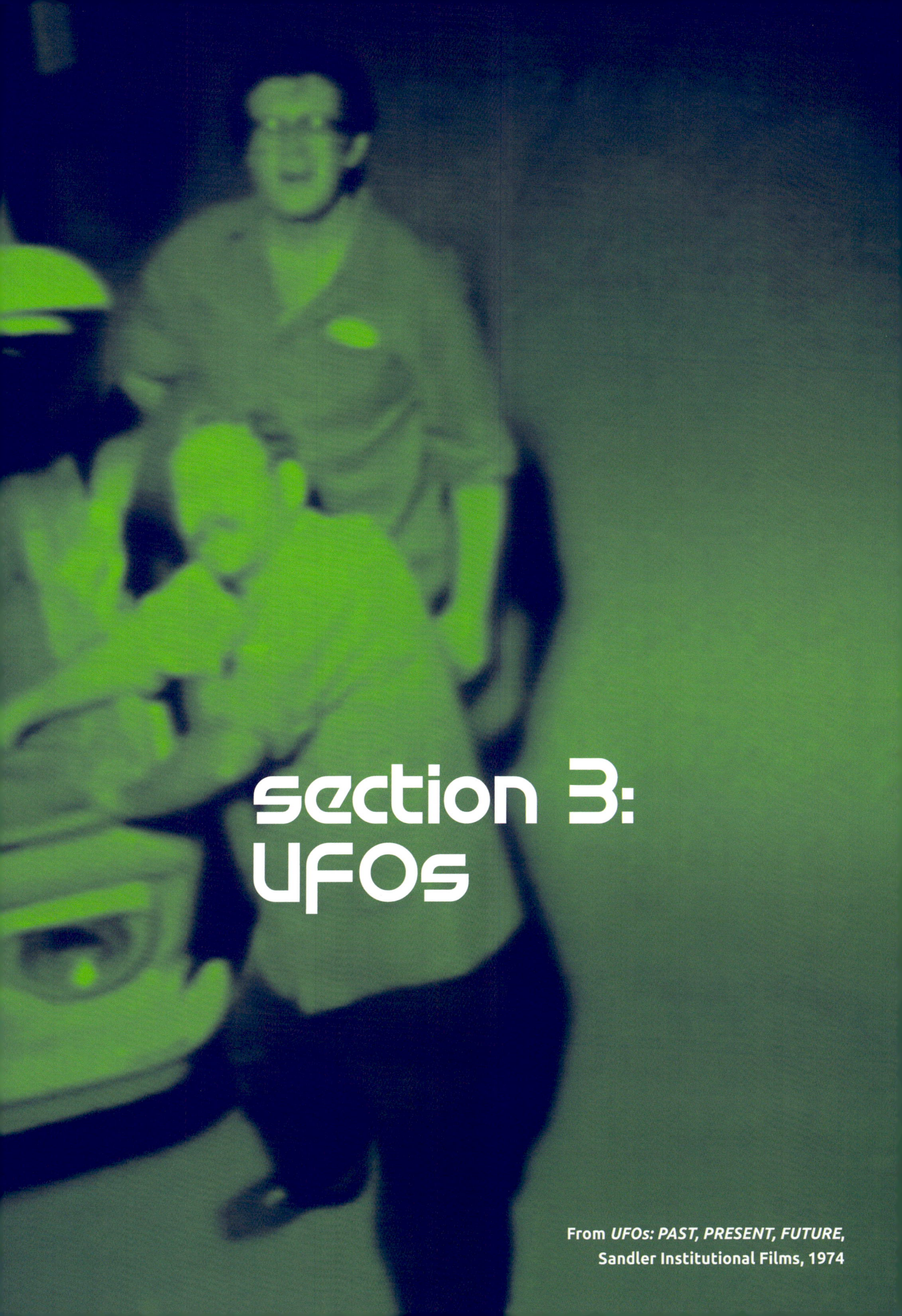

From *UFOs: PAST, PRESENT, FUTURE*,
Sandler Institutional Films, 1974

The Unexplained

(1970)

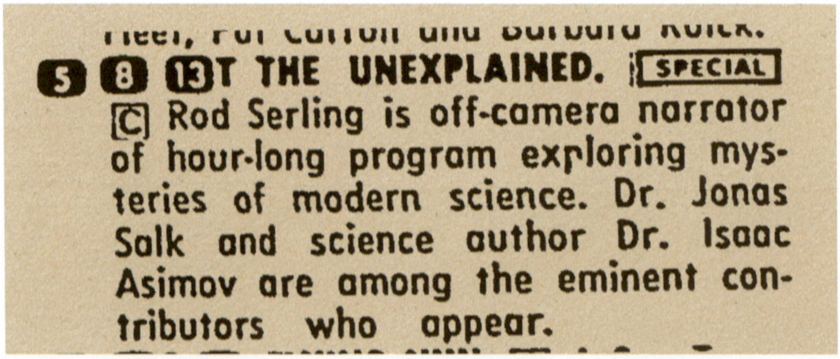

5 8 13 T THE UNEXPLAINED. SPECIAL
C Rod Serling is off-camera narrator of hour-long program exploring mysteries of modern science. Dr. Jonas Salk and science author Dr. Isaac Asimov are among the eminent contributors who appear.

Narration by Rod Serling and starring Arthur C. Clarke: how's that for a starting lineup in one of the earliest of all Weirdumentaries?

Here was also the "First Encyclopedia Britannica" television special, filmed in color and produced by Lee Mendelson, the man best remembered for so many Charlie Brown and Snoopy cartoon specials. Lest anyone doubt, though, *The Unexplained* is not peanuts.

If anything, it's a racehorse in full gallop, all hooves off the ground, Muybridge-style. That's because it covers, in the words of the *Chicago Tribune*:

> *...mysteries that lie in the baboon generation gap, the language of dolphins, the genetic something or other, computer art, UFOs, E.S.P., anxiety control, a pre-Columbian civilization uncovered in New Hampshire, a walking erector set that moves railroad ties and 'feels,' men on the moon, and the possibility of extraterrestrials within and beyond our solar system.*

But this description still wasn't enough to encapsulate the entire show. Here's a few choice words from the *Indianapolis Star*:

> *Jumping off the deep end, Serling next threw in 'ghost lights,' which have never been resolved, and the Devil's Triangle, a stretch of ocean in which 2,000 lives have been mysteriously lost since 1918. The Triangle once swallowed up a whole squadron of Navy planes.*

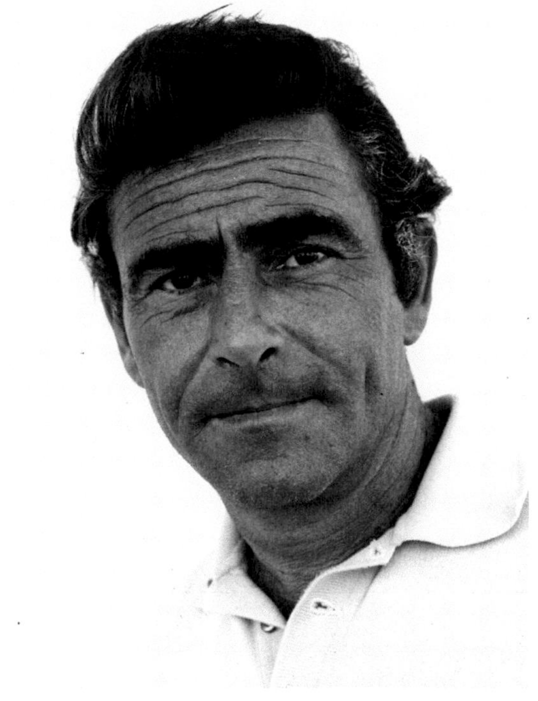

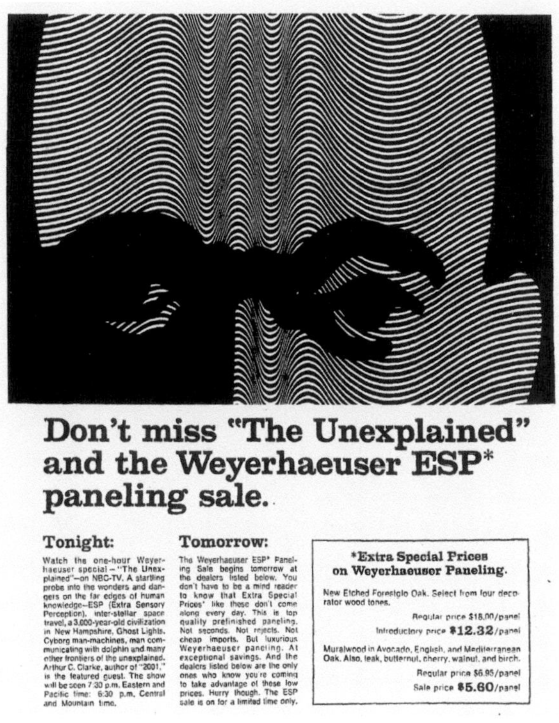

For that journalist, *The Unexplained* possessed the "consistency of a grasshopper." And all of its mysteries unfold in the span of a mere hour, less really, given breaks for station identification.

How was such speed accomplished? A couple of reasons, one being two dozen experts who hurriedly talked about their individual research, among them Jonas Salk and Isaac Asimov.

The other was what Mendelson referred to as a "giant question mark," actually a set of question marks. Overall, the program didn't try to answer the questions it raised, certainly not in any depth. Invoke one mystery and then race on to the next, and the next, and the next. (Keep 'em guessing.)

As Serling told the press, "The show doesn't even try to give answers. It simply defines some of the questions and reports on current scientific inquiries which someday may answer those questions."

Some reviewers were impressed. The *Indianapolis Star* wrote, "It is doubtful that [Serling's] most extravagant horror tale was as eerie as some of the unanswered questions that now face white-coated scientists."

And *Variety* thought the show did a "masterful job of compressing a mixed bag of perplexities into one coherent package ... tightly edited and paced into a non-pedantic entertainment form, a mind-stimulating experience that rates a quick reprise on the tube."

The *Chicago Tribune* critic believed much the same: "I hope they use this program as a kind of sampler and go on to bite more deeply into the mysteries we get only a taste of here. There is at least an hour's worth of good television in every topic."

Sounds to me like a call to arms, and to questions: we need Weirdumentaries. Oh, and Snoopy and Woodstock and Vince Guaraldi, too.

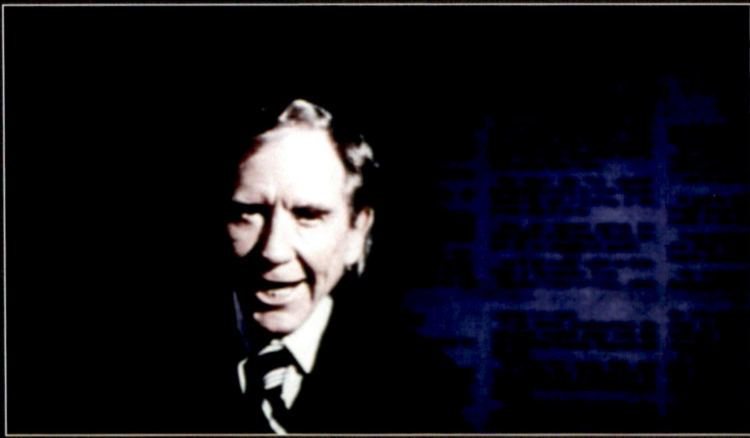

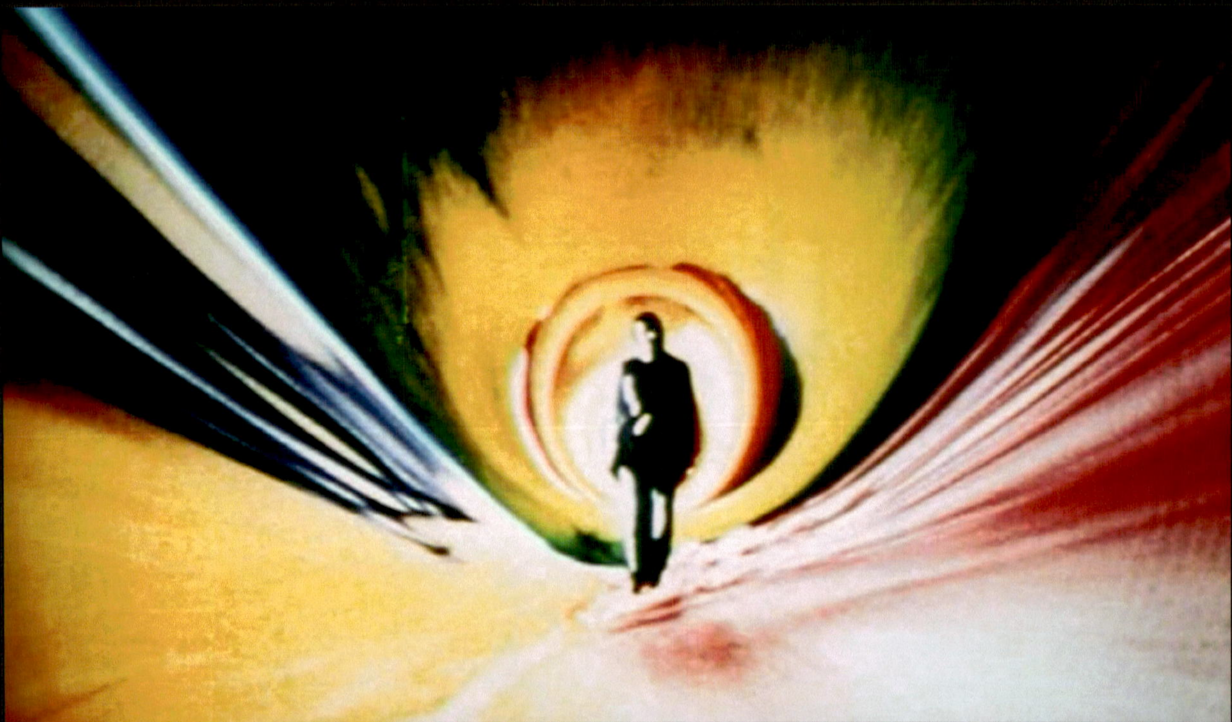

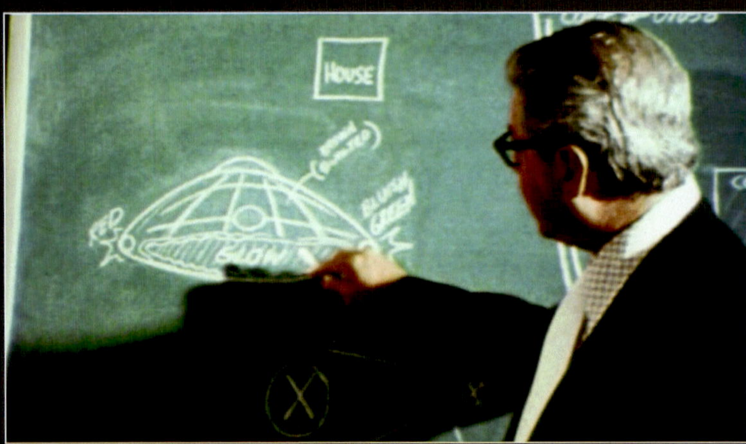
HOUSE

UFOs: Past, Present and Future

(1974)

We see Rod Serling walking toward us. Thanks to special effects, he glows, as do we, in the reflected light of his great presence. He speaks philosophically.

"Occupied by his daily affairs, [man] finds little time to contemplate such questions [as UFOs], except for those moments on a clear night when man pauses and looks to the star-filled heavens, and in his mind stirs an unanswered question. He searches his thoughts for an explanation, a key to the faint forgotten memory of his past, and perhaps at that moment somewhere else in the universe, on a distant planet similar to his own, somewhere on the other side of our galaxy, other intelligent beings wondered too, and set out in airships on an adventure through space, to search for their answers."

Based on the book of the same name by Robert Emenegger, *UFOs: Past, Present, and Future* became the first Weirdumentary to focus on modern UFO visitations. Emenegger was on board to write the script and to compose the music. Allan F. Sandler produced; Ray Rivas directed. The result was a Sandler Institutional Films documentary.

The project allegedly began with cooperation from the U.S. Department of Defense, which promised the filmmakers access to footage of an actual flying saucer landing at Holloman Air Force base in New Mexico in 1971. Men in black nixed the agreement, leaving *UFOs: Past, Present, and Future* to its own devices.

Burgess Meredith and José Ferrer join Serling on-camera to become, in effect, a trio of hosts, one sometimes finishing a story that another began. Shot in a darkened room, Meredith reads from Ezekiel, and Ferrer recounts an incident in the era of Charlemagne. Here we do visit the "past" briefly, but without allusion to aliens building ancient structures.

Most of the film is devoted to recent stories, such as the Lonnie Zamora incident of 1964, in which a policeman saw aliens ascending in a UFO. Much time is also dedicated to the subject of Visitors mutilating cattle. We get numerous interviews, photos and footage, as well as a few recreations featuring competent cinematography and special effects. "What you're witnessing is based on fact," Serling helpfully reminds us.

Nominated for Best Documentary Film at the Golden Globe Awards in 1976, *UFOs: Past, Present, and Future* lost to Max B. Miller's *Youthquake!*

The future of *UFOs: Past, Present, and Future* involved a change of title. It appeared on television stations in 1980 as *UFOs: It Has Begun*, featuring new footage of Dr. Jacques Vallée, the inspiration for the character Lacombe (François Truffaut) in Spielberg's *Close Encounters of the Third Kind* (1977). VCI Entertainment issued the revised version on DVD in 2007.

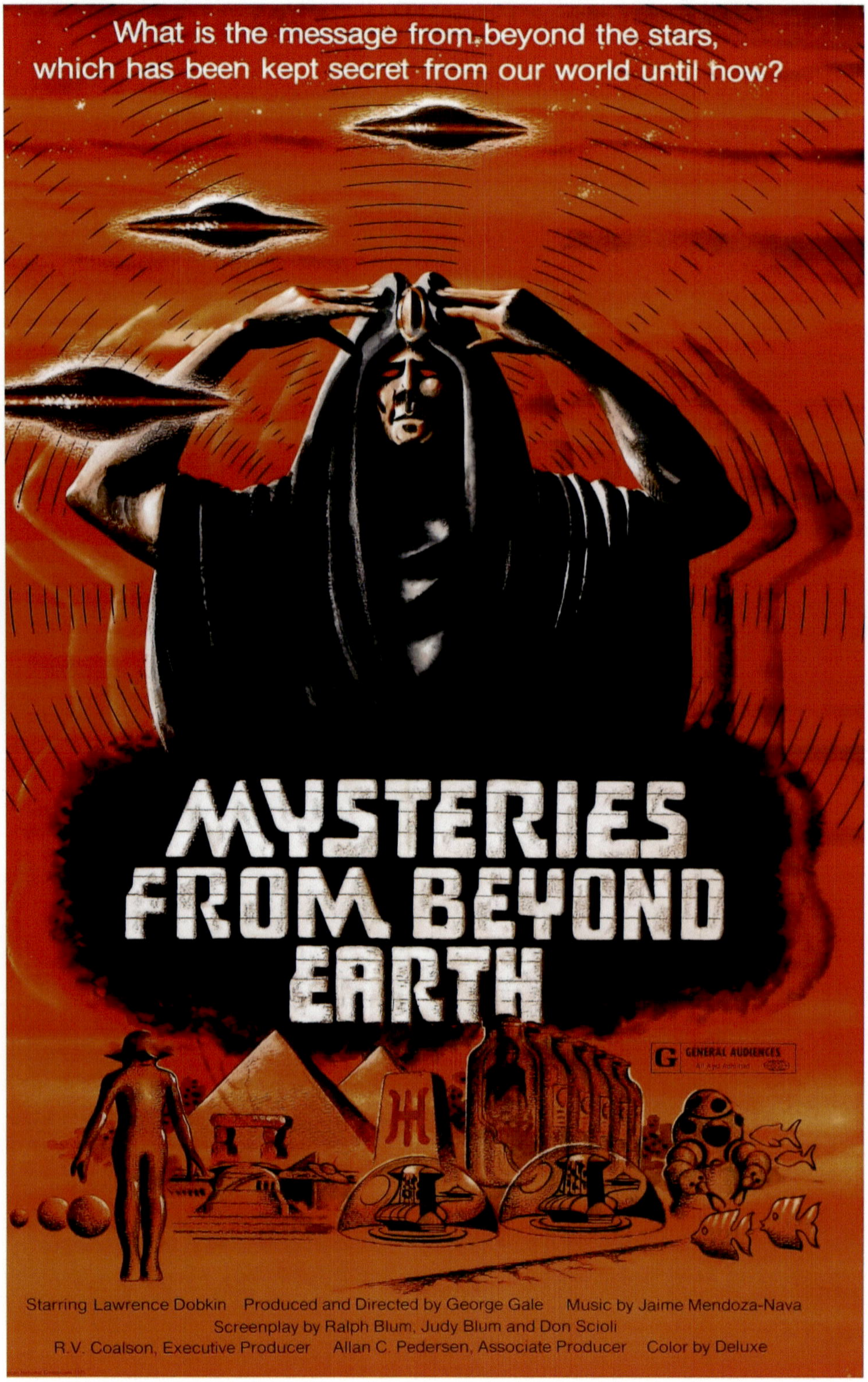
What is the message from beyond the stars,
which has been kept secret from our world until now?
MYSTERIES
FROM BEYOND
EARTH
G GENERAL AUDIENCES
Starring Lawrence Dobkin Produced and Directed by George Gale Music by Jaime Mendoza-Nava
Screenplay by Ralph Blum, Judy Blum and Don Scioli
R.V. Coalson, Executive Producer Allan C. Pedersen, Associate Producer Color by Deluxe

Mysteries from Beyond Earth

(1975)

"American National Enterprises presents... A Rainbow Adventure Film." It sounds sweet, and during the first of the two titles we see a majestic eagle. All very nice and safe and sound, until a Doctor Who-style tunnel appears on-screen. Through it we must go. That or leave the theater, change the channel, eject our VHS tape, or do whatever the cool kids are doing nowadays.

For the brave among us who do stick around, the narrator quotes from H.G. Wells' *The War of the Worlds* (1897): "We know now that in the early years of the twentieth century this world was being watched by intelligences greater than man's, and yet as mortal as his own. We know now, that as human beings busy themselves about their various concerns, they were scrutinized and studied, perhaps almost as narrowly as a man with a microscope might scrutinize the trenchant creatures that swarm and multiply in a drop of water."

The voice belongs to Lawrence Dobkin, longtime TV actor who also had small parts in films like *The Day the Earth Stood Still* (1951) and *Them!* (1954). Writer Don Scioli worked with UFOlogists Ralph and Judy Blum to craft a script that traverses more ground (and air, water, and space) than any other single Weirdumentary.

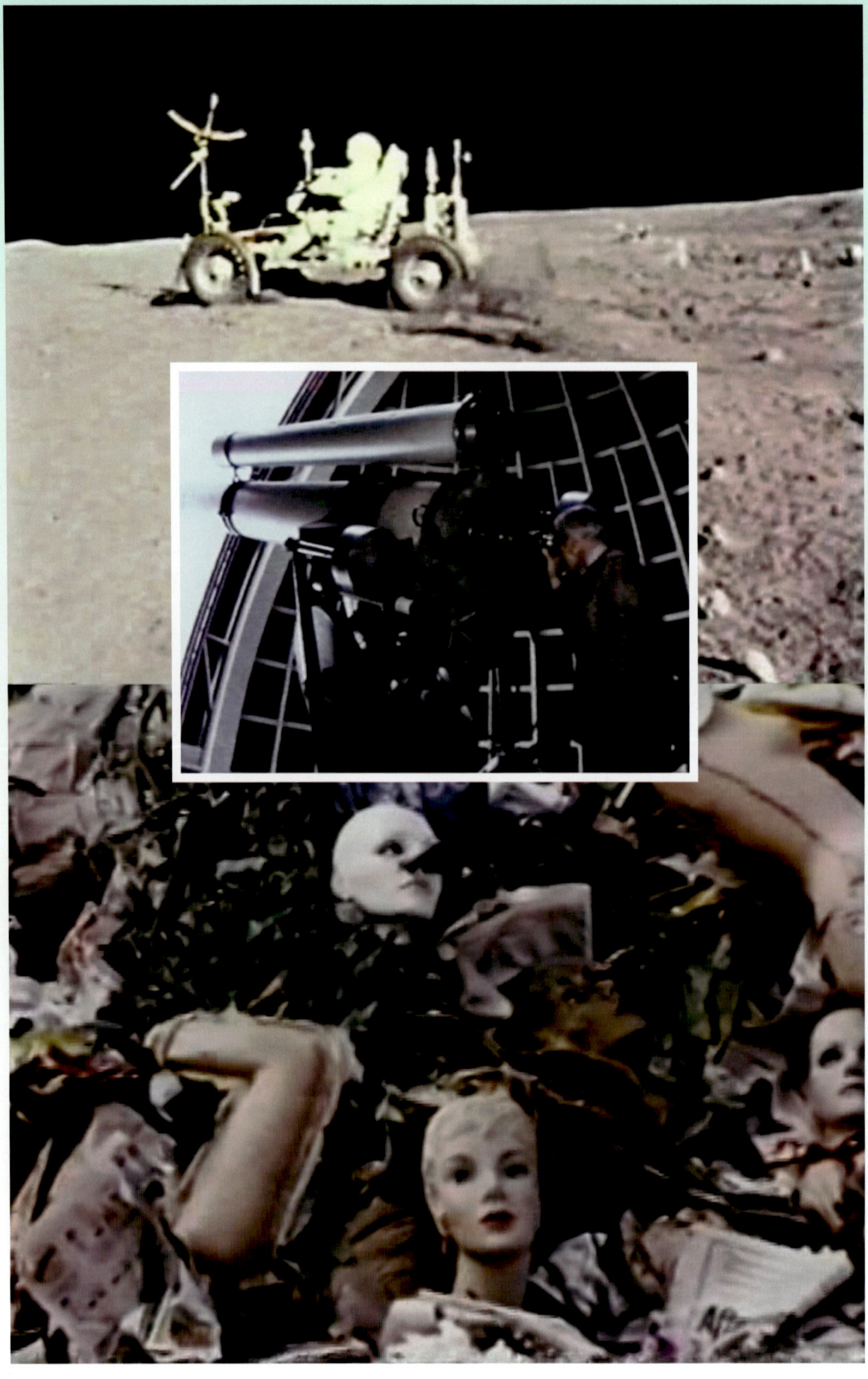

The film does concentrate on the "overwhelming" evidence for UFOs, because, after all, "our planet is indeed being visited by intelligences greater than man's." And it was in the past as well, with nods to unnamed scholars (insert Erich von Däniken). They apparently helped our ancestors build pyramids, the statues on Easter Island, and Stonehenge (which is nothing less than a "Neolithic computer"). Perhaps a "master set of blueprints" once existed for all of these sites.

But what is the relevance of clairvoyance, telepathy, and psychokinesis in the film? Uri Geller, we learn, believes extraterrestrials channel through him. They came in peace so he could leave spoons in pieces.

Of the Bermuda Triangle story, Dobkin asks, "Is this area controlled by some unknown intelligence?" And our excursion into Bigfoot country? UFOs have been spotted near him, and may have even dropped him and his brethren from the sky, hopefully with parachutes.

Elsewhere the film doesn't bother with tenuous connections to aliens. The line between editor and schizoid blurs. We journey expediently into the worlds of Kirlian photography, cloning, psychic surgeons, haunted houses, firewalkers, witchcraft, voodoo, Satanism, and the secret lives of plants. Why? Well, why not? As Dobkin explains, "people want to know more about them." Outer space and inner space both have value. After all, the whale that swallowed Jonah might actually have been an underwater craft.

Dobkin appears on-camera throughout, whether in a comfy chair or at an observatory. He even stands in the darkness beside a small projection screen, allowing us to see him and the evidence simultaneously. And his performance is competent. If we do cringe when he refers to cryonics as a "chilling development," shift the blame to producer-director George Gale, who should have told the aliens to reprogram the puns.

Mysteries from Beyond Earth opened in late 1975, becoming a hit at a number of theaters before moving on to TV as part of Gold Key International's "Alpha Chronicles," a group of fifteen films that also included *The Legend of Loch Ness* (1976) and *The UFO Journals* (1978).

Boxoffice called *Mysteries from Beyond Earth* "provocative." I call it cinemaphrenic. And yes, that is a compliment.

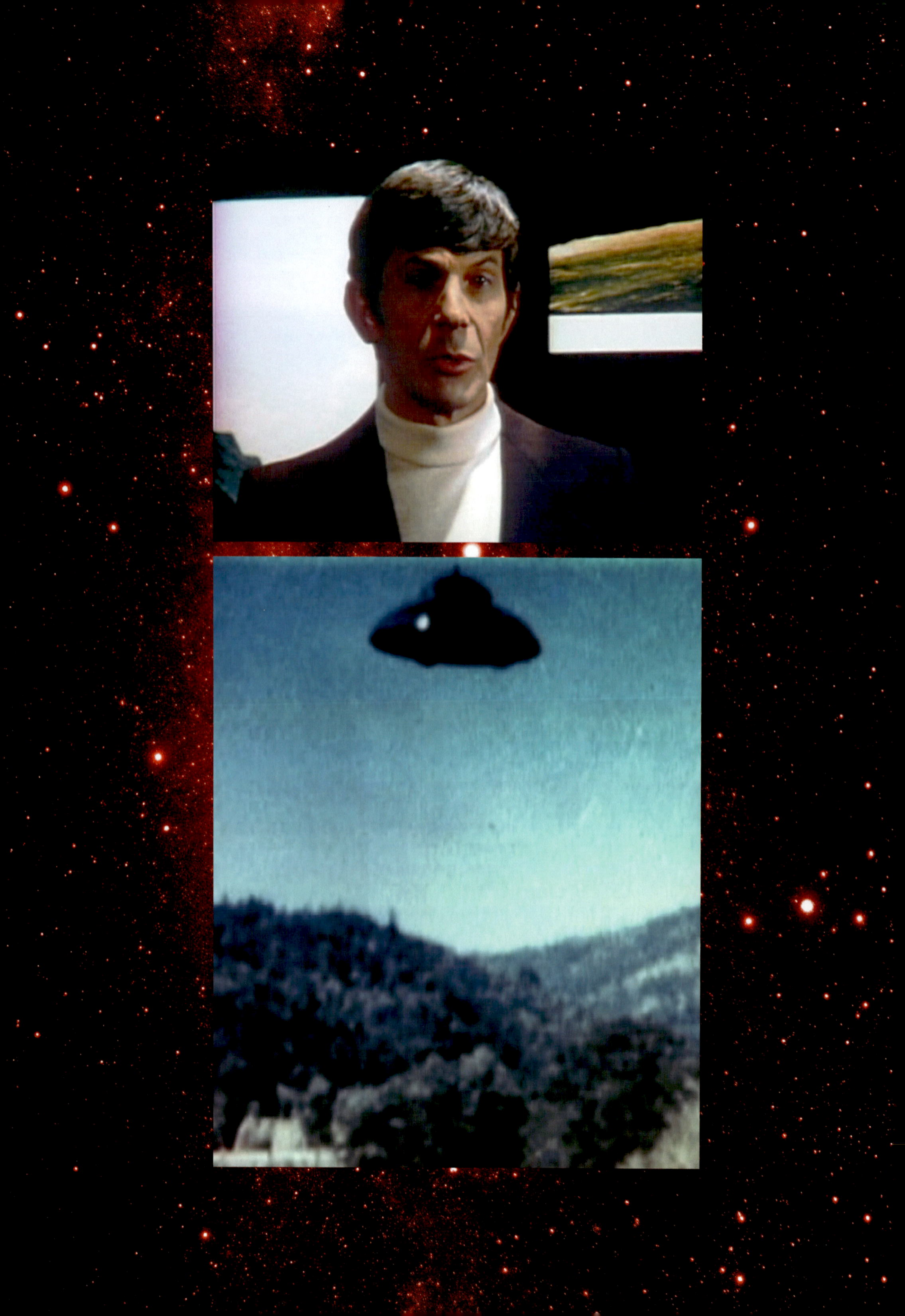

In Search of... UFOs

(1976-1982)

On June 22, 1977, the *Hollywood Reporter* reported. And it reported fantastic news. Alan Landsburg Productions was going into production on Season 2 of *In Search of...*, with Leonard Nimoy continuing his role as host-narrator.

The Vulcan was back on planet Earth, an alien in our midst. And of course aliens and UFOs were important subjects during the whole of the series.

Season 1, Episode 12, *A Call from Space*: So, we're trying to contact aliens and hope that they're trying to contact us, and that we can understand them if they do.

Nimoy tells us, "We have always dreamed of talking with celestial beings. Discoveries in deep space have revealed that the same chemistry that created earthly life operates elsewhere. Perhaps we are not accidents of creation. Perhaps we are not alone."

Perhaps. "Who or what will answer our call?" Maybe aliens. And our research on communicating with dolphins might help us talk to them.

Or maybe we will even answer our own call, at least if we're Trekkies. In this episode, Carl Sagan talks about Pioneer 10, which featured a message to aliens. In *Star Trek: The Motion Picture* (1979), a similar spacecraft named Voyager 6 returns to Earth as V'ger, a sentient robotic entity with a bad temper.

Our search for extraterrestrial intelligence also involves radio waves. Galactic tunes and interstellar talk shows: the possibilities are truly infinite.

Season 1, Episode 21, *UFOs*: "They've been reported at dusk or in the dead of night, in clearings, amid still woods, and fields in lonely farm country. Sometimes they come in silence; sometimes with quiet thunder. Often, they leave marks in the earth, signals of their passing. They've been seen, but fleetingly, and their extraordinary presence creates a frightening mystery."

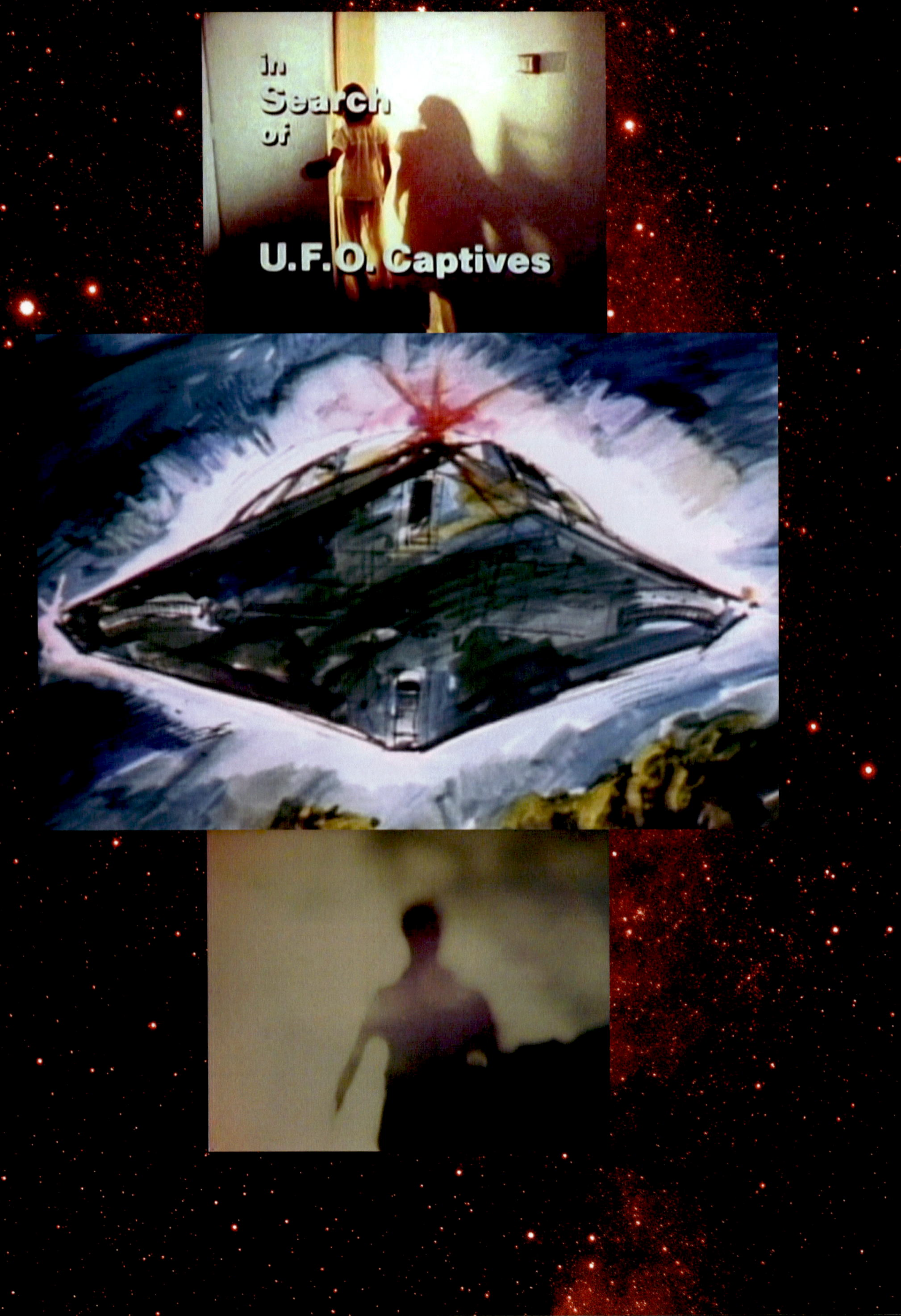
In
Search
of
U.F.O. Captives

Flying saucers, man, and lots of people saw them, "up in the sky," hailing from "some outer space place." One eyewitness passes a lie detector test, so you know, that's a game-changer.

Nimoy concludes by suggesting, "Perhaps it's time to approach the question of UFOs again, without bias. For we can only hope that if we are being studied by aliens, it is with more thoroughness and care than we have focused on them."

Season 3, Episode 1, *UFO Captives*: Mr. Spock knew well of what he spoke when he told us that we should focus on UFOs again, because now they've moved on to abducting us.

Dramatized recreations begin this episode, which tells us just how often this phenomenon happens. These are "close encounters of the fourth kind," having one-upped Spielberg.

"What makes their testimony difficult to dismiss is that it comes from average Americans," Nimoy explains, a statement needing further explanation in order for me to understand why it makes sense.

Anyhow, the abductees are held prisoner for at least enough time to be probed and prodded. Then they are returned home, unable to remember what happened, and sometimes unable to sit down comfortably.

So how can these people recall what they can't recall? Hypnosis is the key to unlocking whatever happened, or whatever they think or even hope might have happened. (With such low-budget recreations, it's hard to be sure.)

Variety reviewed *UFO Captives* and condemned it as a "pointless exercise." I disagree heartily, having appreciated its pointedness.

Season 4, Episode 4, *U.F.O. Australia*: Why focus on Australia? Nimoy presents some engrossing stories and footage, so that makes perfect sense. But why use periods in the abbreviation "UFO," when previous episodes didn't? Like so many questions in Weirdumentaries, there's no satisfactory answer.

More cheap dramatizations in this episode, but also more great "authentic" photos and footage. And there's a psychic who holds a séance to get in touch with a pilot whose plane vanished after a UFO encounter.

If that scene doesn't make you love *In Search of...*, you should go in search of a new personality, or undergo hypnosis to reclaim the one you forgot.

Overlords of the U.F.O.

(1976)

"Tower Films Presents... A Scientific News Documentary." The Overlords of the UFO have landed, but with little to no pomp, let alone circumstance.

Producer-writer W. Gordon Allen acts as on-screen host. We learn he had been a radio and television reporter in the Pacific Northwest and has long written about UFOs. He even saw one. All of this makes him a proper Saucerian, a man on a mission that NASA won't consider. Of alien visitations, Allen asks, "Is a Watergate-type scientific cover involved?" (Hint, hint: There is.)

After all, Allen explains that 15 million persons have witnessed them, some up-close-and-personal. So, "Who are the overlords of the UFO, and why are they here right now, at this time?"

Answers come fast, but not furious. Allen intrigues us with notions that the visitors are from other dimensions. Places of origin might include Zeta Reticuli and Ummo. Two, three, even four levels of alien intelligence might be involved. And though he doesn't broach the subject of ancient astronauts, Allen briefly suggests the angel that Joseph Smith encountered might have been an E.T. (No mention is made of whether he brought Reese's Pieces, or condoned polygamy.)

Of course, UFOs regularly visit Earth, whether in the air, as completely believable film footage and photographs show, or beneath the sea, causing underwater "disturbances." If they land, aliens might abduct us, usually returning us safely home. We rate higher than cattle, in their eyes, it would seem, as they are hardly Hindu in their belief system. Allen explains, "There seems no other explanation of what has happened to the thousands of mutilated animals."

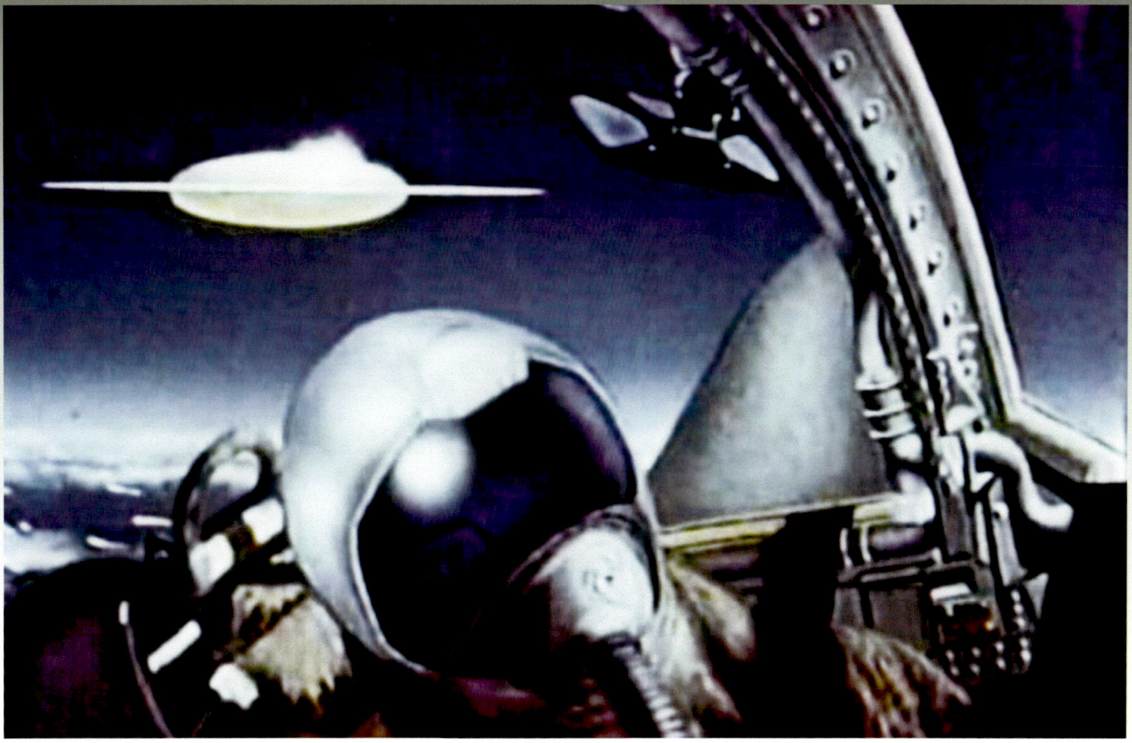

All of this is a "secret that couldn't be kept, that can no longer be covered up." Here is why Allen lobbies for astronauts, the military, and the FAA to receive proper training to deal with the Visitors.

Produced in 1976, *Overlords of the U.F.O.* might well be the cheapest Weirdumentary of them all.

Stock footage abounds, including in the interviews we see. A good part of the budget probably went to licensing Uri Geller's key-bending demonstration.

Animation hardly deserves the word, given that artwork of a plane flying near a UFO features a large image of a pilot who doesn't move in the slightest. And props like a "large circulation newspaper" headlining a $1 million reward for information on aliens are so cheap and obviously fake that the film would be better off without them.

Two recreations feature actors reciting dialogue over stock footage, so they didn't have to be filmed. Clever? Not really. Fun? Probably the best segments in the film. The lines spoken by "high public affairs administrators of NASA" are worthy of being sampled.

Though it bears a 1976 copyright date, *Overlords of the U.F.O.* didn't get a release deal until the fall of 1977. Key International Film Distributors secured worldwide rights to the film, leading to test screenings in October "backed with extensive TV campaigns, plus possible appearances of some of the alleged recent captives of visiting UFOs that are depicted in the film." In other words, there were more than enough saucers if you were already in your cups.

Overlords of the U.F.O. reaches its peak when it concludes. For one, we see an atomic blast, not with the words "The End," but rather "The Beginning." Secondly, and more importantly, is the fact the film commits the ultimate cinematic sin. Overlords of the Weirdumentary unanimously deem it boring.

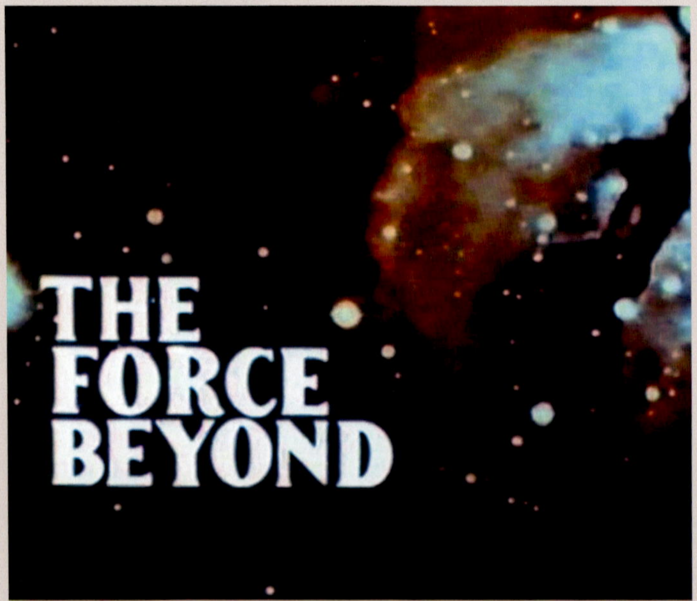
THE
FORCE
BEYOND

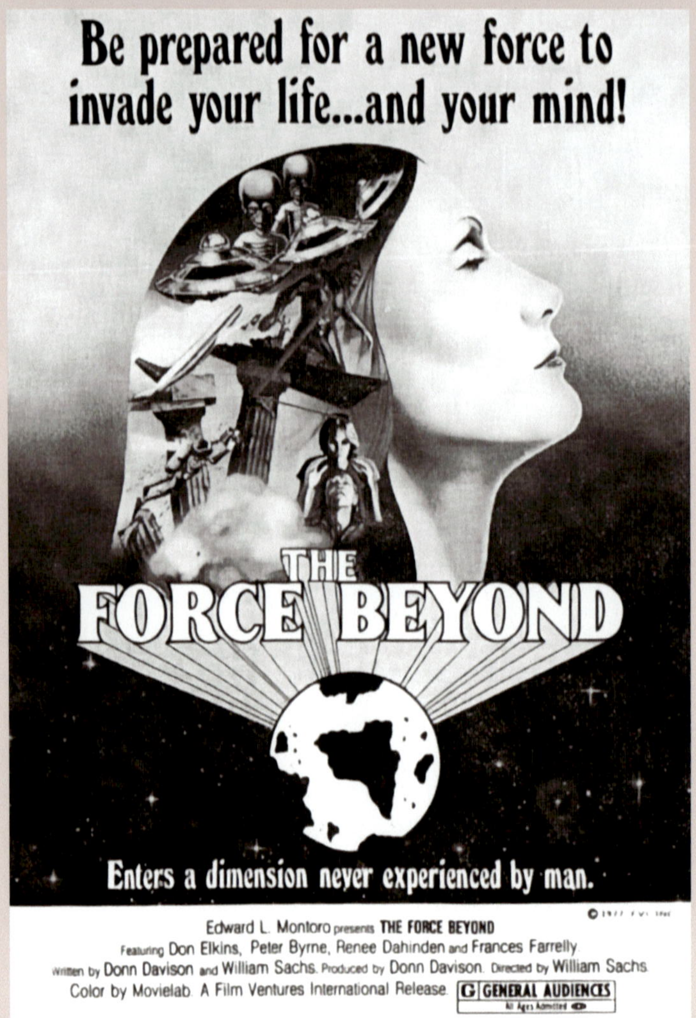
Be prepared for a new force to invade your life...and your mind!
THE
FORCE BEYOND
Enters a dimension never experienced by man.
Edward L. Montoro presents THE FORCE BEYOND
Featuring Don Elkins, Peter Byrne, Renee Dahinden and Frances Farrelly.
Written by Donn Davison and William Sachs. Produced by Donn Davison. Directed by William Sachs.
Color by Movielab. A Film Ventures International Release.
G GENERAL AUDIENCES
All Ages Admitted

The Force Beyond

(1977)

A small abstract object spins in the darkness while a scream echoes in our ears. The object? A newspaper, which gets larger and larger. The scream? A response to Orson Welles' 1938 broadcast of *The War of the Worlds*.

"The terror you have just seen was caused by science fiction," voiceover explains. "Everything else in this motion picture that you will see is science fact. The phenomena you are about to witness could well revolutionize your way of thinking. ... The producers accept no responsibility for any mental trauma caused by the contents of this motion picture." We have been warned.

Released by Film Ventures International with a G rating, *The Force Beyond* was the brainchild of Donn Davison and William Sachs. They co-wrote the script, with Sachs also acting as director and editor. Davison produced and appeared as an on-screen host. By contrast, the narrator was the mysterious "Rosko." *The Force Beyond* is so out there that we apparently need two Virgils to guide us through its Stygian darkness.

The sheer scope of our universe makes it unlikely we are alone. UFO sightings are common because aliens are "here today." Davison's experts, who are "truly amazing people," tell us so. Aliens have built megaliths on the moon, and they are responsible in varying degrees for Atlantis, the Bermuda Triangle, major power outages, and a number of instances in which people have simply vanished off the face of the Earth, "never to be seen again." "Linked together," we learn, these various phenomena "play a strategic part" in, well, something. Us being watched, apparently, and if we're (un)lucky, snatched, even diddled.

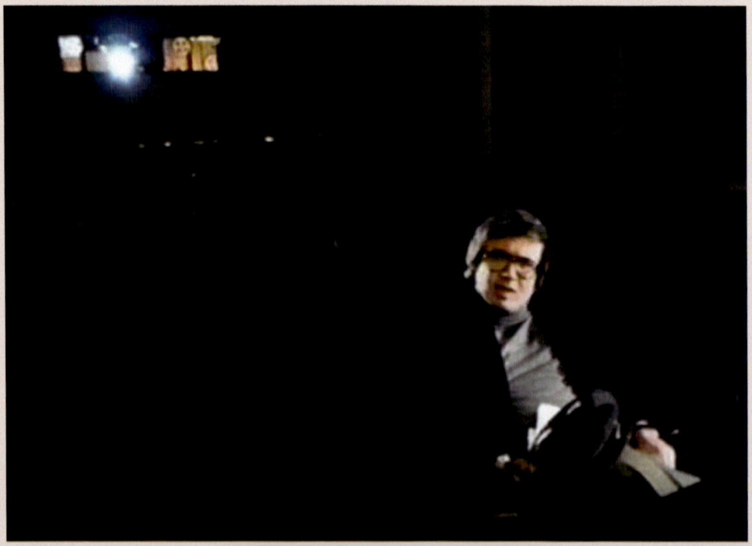

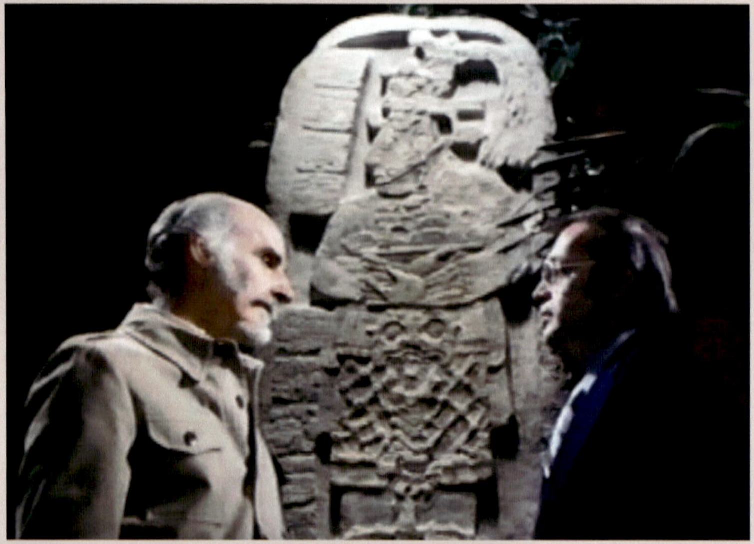

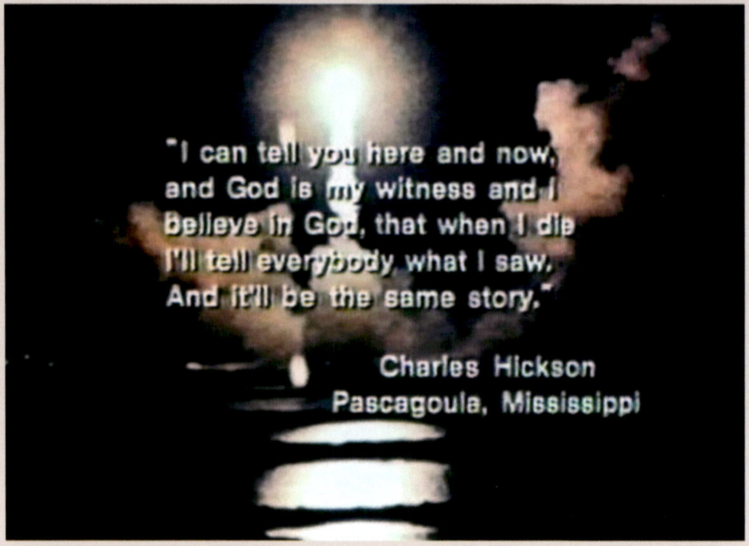
"I can tell you here and now,
and God is my witness and I
believe in God, that when I die
I'll tell everybody what I saw.
And it'll be the same story."
Charles Hickson
Pascagoula, Mississippi

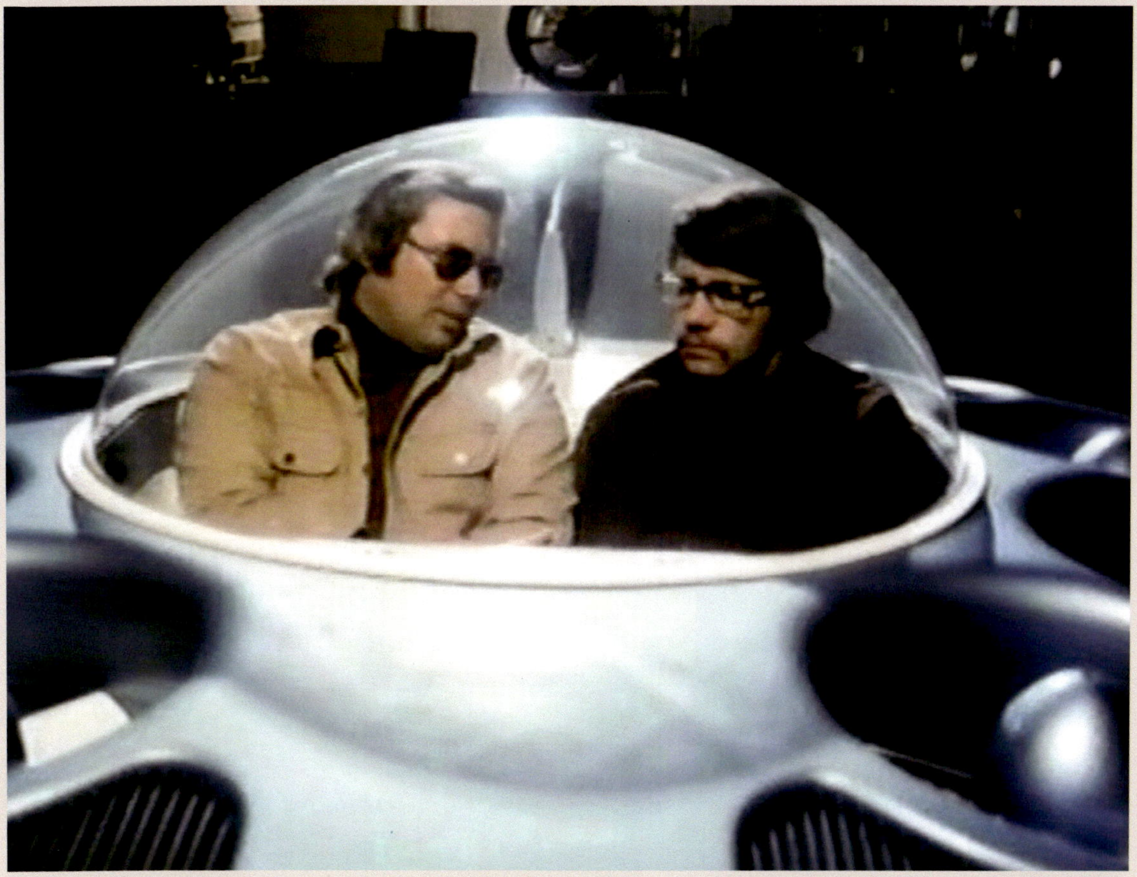

Evidence assaults us: photos and footage and eyewitness accounts. Good old newsreel footage shows the Nazca lines and the early days of the flying saucer craze. We even see a bit of metal from a flying saucer that, for proper preservation purposes, has been encased in plastic. Thrusting the film beyond the general confines of its predecessors, Davison visits a man who tries to make his own flying saucers, a bookstore in New York specializing in UFOlogy, and a UFO convention in Arkansas, a state where the rocks are little, but the tales are tall.

All the while, Davison is an amiable host. He's at his best when standing next to an alien costume and mask that he introduces as our new "neighbor." But do we believe his "incredible proof"? Maybe, maybe not. Let's just note that *The Force Beyond* is itself proof of something, tenacity perhaps, having arisen phoenix-like out of the ashes of *The Secrets of the Gods*, an ill-fated Davison-Sachs film from 1975–76.

As we watch the film closely we can see incredible proof the duo left behind, as *Secrets of the Gods* appears as an on-screen graphic during the closing credits. More obviously, we get an extremely abrupt and otherwise illogical foray into the story of Bigfoot (including previously unseen footage!). And then there's a psychic investigator trying to find the location of Atlantis, in part by rubbing her hands on a table that may or may not be dirty.

The greatest impact of *The Force Beyond*? Hard to say, but it might be the fact it caused a horror movie with the same name to get retitled as *The Evil* (1978). That film opted for Richard Crenna over "Rosko."

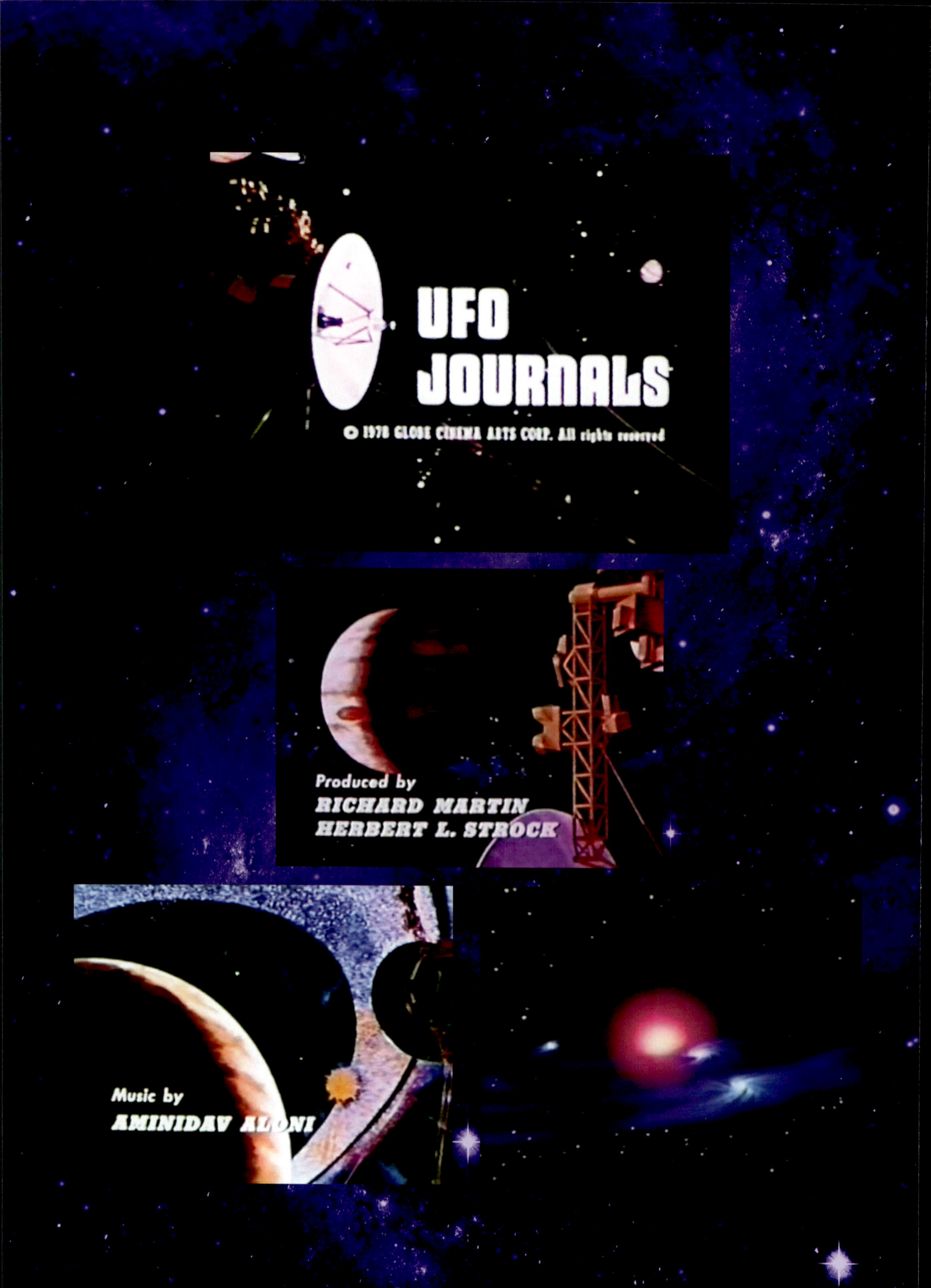
UFO
JOURNALS
© 1978 GLOBE CINEMA ARTS CORP. All rights reserved
Produced by
RICHARD MARTIN
HERBERT L. STROCK
Music by
AMINIDAV ALONI

The UFO Journals

(1978)

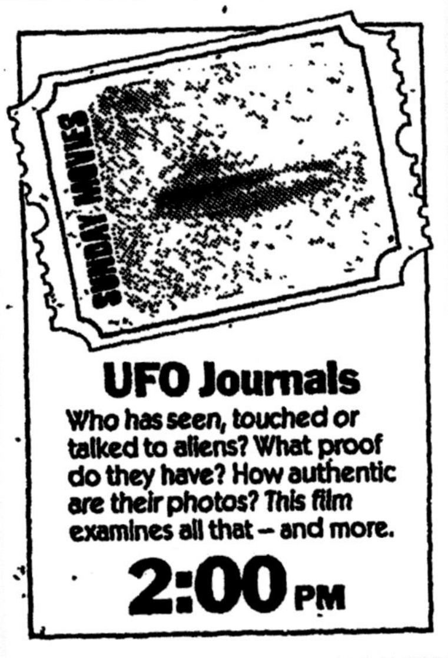

Here is one of the best Weirdumentaries, sadly overlooked in its day and forever after.

Director Richard Martin, who had already helmed *The Legend of Loch Ness* (1976), begins *The UFO Journals* by posing the standard questions: "Why are they here? … How long have they been coming here? … Why do world governments continue to deny their existence when photos like these continue to appear in newspapers the world over?"

Then we quickly get answers, as concrete as the foundation of any good alien landing pad. "This Earth, indeed this solar system, has been invaded several times in the past twenty years." With enough reverb to cause an earthquake, those words come to us from a talk given in the hallowed grounds of L.A.'s Shrine Exhibition Hall. The speaker? Dr. George King, of the Aetherius Society.

It gets better, much better. Our narrator asks, "Are they trying to contact [us?] physically as well as psychically?" Both, it seems, with much emphasis on the latter. After all, Dr. King (George, not Martin Luther) received his religious calling from outer space, when the Cosmic Masters invited him to join the Interplanetary Parliament. King had not studied UFOs at the time, but he knew all was copacetic because he does yoga. You see, he was open to aliens. (Stop snickering, you kids in the back row.)

One lady explains she is the psychic messenger of many alien races, their herald. All of them will be landing soon to lead us into a "higher way of life." Awaiting that day, the lady has constructed a welcome sign. She's ready to take them to our leader.

Best yet is the man who undergoes a "dangerous experiment" to contact the alien

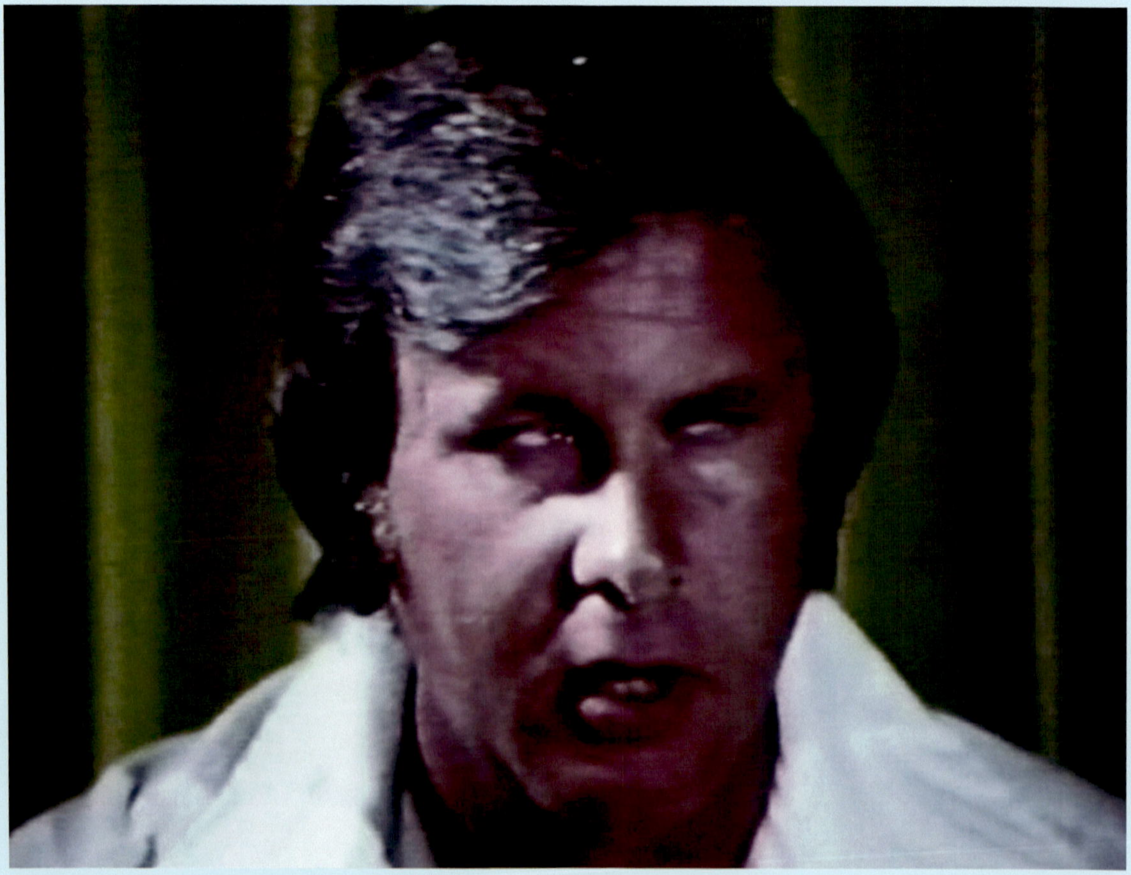

Voltar, who visited Tiahuanaco in days gone by. Once in a trance, the man speaks in an alien voice, one that belongs to an interstellar intermediary. After being connected with no long-distance fees, the man shifts into Voltar's voice. And what a voice it is. Wonderful nonsense that must be seen and heard to be believed, or not believed, as the case may be.

The narrator's subdued, methodical, and dry intonations provide a wonderful contrast to the interviewees, and even the outrageous tales he offers.

Consider one of the many UFO photographs we see on-screen. The narrator explains: "This one, unlike many of the UFO sightings, gave off a high-pitched whining sound above Tulsa, Oklahoma, about one o'clock in the morning. Many witnesses were frightened, and some petrified with their mouths open. As it departed, the whine changed to a high screeching pitch, sending dogs scurrying for cover." What a great story, made all the more special because the accompanying photograph looks like someone hurled Milton Bradley's Simon high into an evening sky.

But some of the best moments come when no one is speaking. Several minutes are devoted to Apollo 11 footage, during which the narrator often pauses. Aminadav Aloni's music accompanies the majesty of the first moon landing. His compositions are transcendent, far more than on-screen jokers jabbering about ancient civilizations and Kirlian photography.

Produced by Richard Martin and Herbert L. Strock for the Globe Cinema Arts Corporation, *The UFO Journals* deserves your time and attention. Voltar out.

UFO—Exclusive!

(1978)

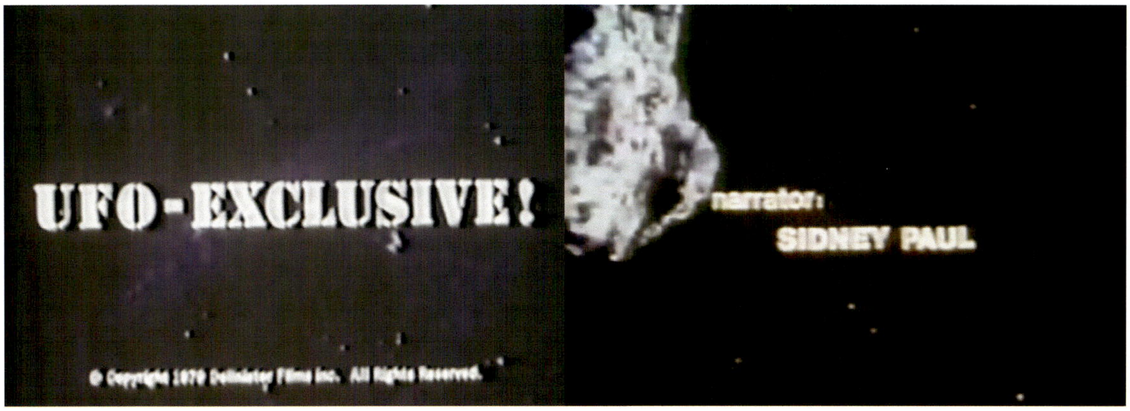

What do *Viva Zapata!* (1952), *Them!* (1954), *Oklahoma!* (1955), *Oliver!* (1968), *Hello, Dolly!* (1969), *Oh, God!* (1977), *Airplane!* (1980), and *Moulin Rouge!* (2001) have in common with *UFO – Exclusive!*, directed by Wheeler Dixon? They all belong to the elite club of movie titles ending with exclamation marks, as if we should shout their names to the heavens on high.

UFO – Exclusive! also holds membership in the majestic and time-honored guild of the Weirdumentary. Undeservedly forgotten, it is distinctive in various respects, not least of which is that its running time is one hour, forty-five minutes, making it the longest Weirdumentary on record.

"Welcome to the world of outer space, a world still little known and understood even in our nuclear age. What you are about to see is the beginning of a voyage through space and time, a voyage which reaches from a launching pad in Cape Canaveral to the most distant star in the heavens. This is a world of unexplained mysteries and visitations, a world of flying saucers and monsters from other worlds. It is a world of science, of fact, and fiction, a world of reality and incredible fantasy."

Dixon's cards are thus on the table, explaining that all we see and hear won't necessarily be truthful. And if we don't initially understand the import of those words, voiceover during the end credits states in no uncertain terms, "The producers bear no responsibility of any kind for inaccuracies, irregularities, or other errors in the claims and cases discussed herein." So lawyer down, not up, and enjoy the intergalactic ride.

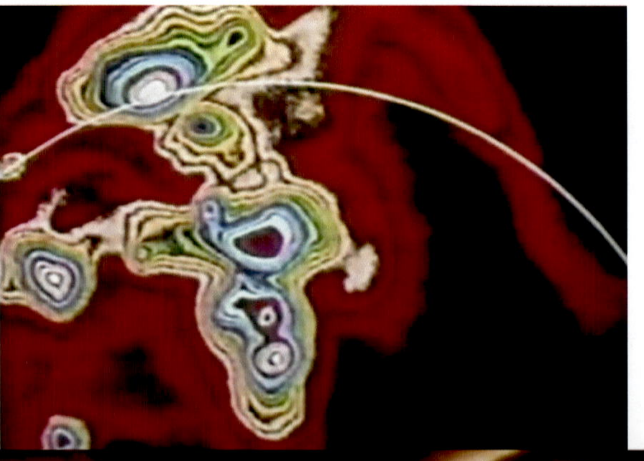

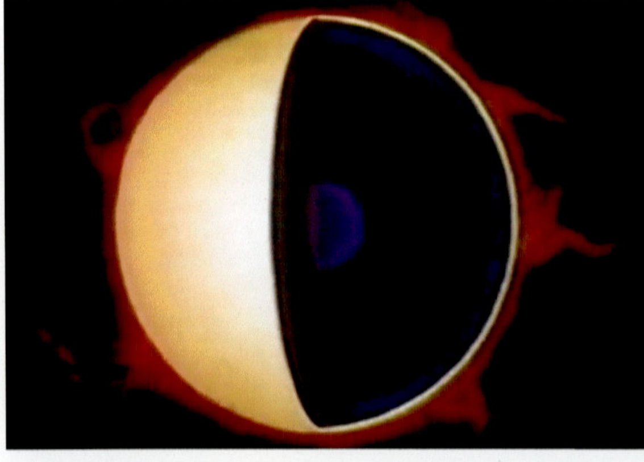

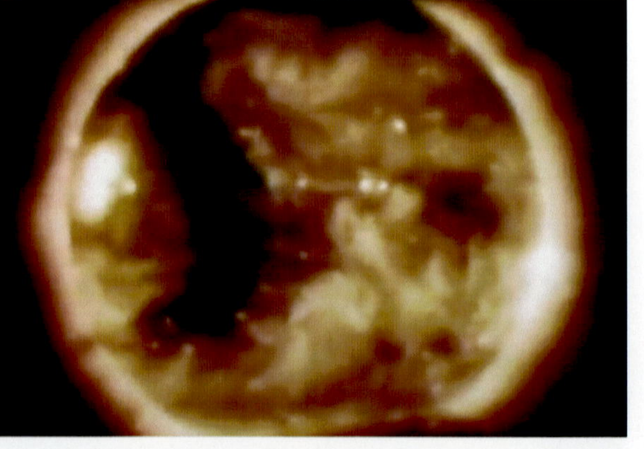

Produced by Delineator Films, *UFO – Exclusive!* features no interviews and no dramatizations. Instead, the lengthy film relies solely on Sidney Paul's narration, edited against everything from NASA stock footage to simple artwork and animation.

The script—by Christopher Sereni (apparently Dixon's pseudonym)—keeps things moving with the twin stories of UFOs visiting us and us visiting them, or at least the farthest reaches of space. We get, for example, speculative questions like, "Could not UFOs ... live at the center of the sun and venture forth to explore the Earth? Although there is no basis in fact for this theory, notions and beliefs that UFOs may come from the sun persist." I can dig it. Hopefully my shovel can withstand the heat.

Then Paul guides us through our own solar system, as if we're inside a planetarium, with or without James Dean seated nearby. "If we are still uncertain of something as mundane as the rings of Saturn, then what *are* we sure of?" What, indeed.

We see flying saucer photos, hear about the space shuttle, and learn that invading aliens could be microscopic, resulting in a plague from outer space.

The music score, supervised by Jim Cookman, is a delight from beginning to end. At times it is reminiscent of Ligeti, at times it is space-age electronica. In other places, the soundtrack flat-out rocks. Most of it is underscore, but the film's wonderful pacing allows plenty of time for the narrator to go silent and for us to enjoy the sights and sounds, the penultimate trip, so to speak, with proper deference to Kubrick's *2001: A Space Odyssey* (1968).

And if all that doesn't thrill you, get this: our friendly neighborhood narrator promises us that we'll be visiting Mars in the 1980s. I hope a good time was had by all.

UFO: Top Secret

(1978)

Here is another project from Delineator Films. Director Wheeler Dixon returns, as does narrator Sidney Paul. We thank our lucky stars.

The new film is quite similar to *UFO – Exclusive!*, but that's no bad thing. No interviews, no dramatized recreations, just wall-to-wall voiceover with music supervised by Jim Cookman.

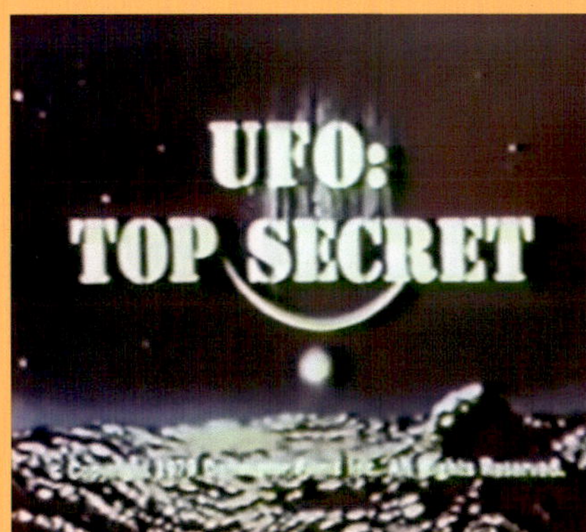

Come and see, and interpret, with Paul as escort: "Looking out over this vast alien landscape, we cannot help but wonder what creatures might be waiting out there in the vast void of space, waiting patiently for man to contact them. What kind of world is it? It looks completely inhospitable, and yet we cannot be certain. Who knows what creatures, what monsters might be lurking in the vast depths of this planet, living in vast subterranean cities, with a culture far in advance of ours."

Do aliens hover near us, as all of the saucer photographs seem to suggest? Did they visit ancient civilizations? Did one of them trail President Carter's helicopter? Might solar flares from the sun signal their visitations? What do they want? Do they see us as primitive barbarians? The files are "ever-expanding." But hard evidence is not.

Paul calmly explains, "These alien civilizations might bring peace, knowledge, and understanding, but they might also bring death, destruction, and evil, as they spread a red glow of carnage through our Earth, reducing it to nothing but a slaughterhouse, an alien food breeding ground."

In the meantime, the aliens are somewhere else, waiting and maybe watching. They might even be hiding in our solar system, plotting an attack or just enjoying the reality show that is planet Earth.

"The rings of Saturn have many possible explanations. Most likely, the rings are an accumulation of cosmic dust and debris, and the rings are also probably composed of poisonous gases, but it is possible that the rings are really alien command posts, functioning as space stations in disguise, for the vanguard of an alien invasion from outer space." Preach it, brother Paul, preach it.

To a large extent, Christopher Sereni's script for *UFO: Top Secret* opts for the structure of *UFO – Exclusive!* Our journeys into space, depicted through NASA file footage and some animation, form a

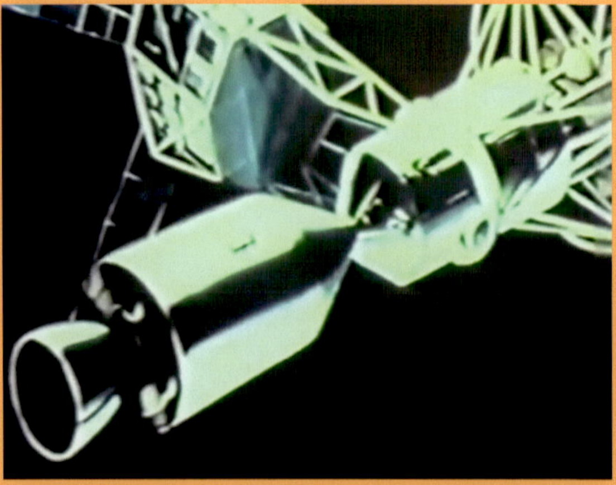

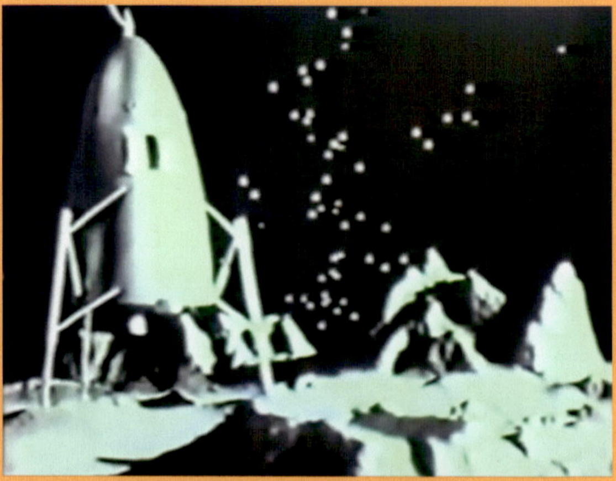

second narrative. Aliens travel here; we travel out there, at least with our "baby steps."

But the narratives in the new film seem more elliptical and even random, given a few detours. On two different occasions, *UFO: Top Secret* recounts humankind's "bungling" efforts at flight, using early film footage to show all those early planes that didn't fly. Kitty Balk, not Kitty Hawk.

We witness footage of natural disasters like tornadoes, all for the purpose of illustrating that the "affairs of man are of little consequence." We also hear that Idi Amin used computers to torture innocent victims. At these moments, the writing seems to justify available stock footage, rather than the other way around.

In any event, the film is a joy in some measure due to its peculiar, non-linear narrative. Cookman's musical choices are more subdued than in *UFO – Exclusive!* Flute with occasional electronic sounds seems to evoke a kind of interstellar loneliness, us being "prisoners" on Earth, not yet having "conquered" the stars.

Later we hear harmonica, as well as plenty of other galactic funk. When Dixon lets the music play without narration, as he often does, the film becomes almost trance-like.

While some of the shots are trite stock footage and repetitions from other Delineator projects, Dixon does experiment here with two, three, and even four different images on-screen at the same time.

Far out, man. Way far out.

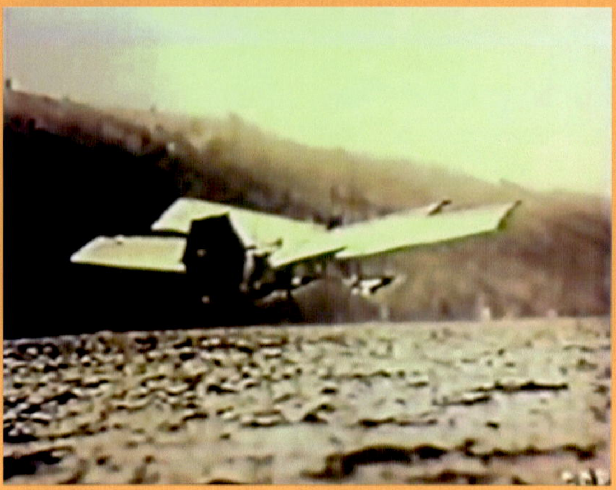

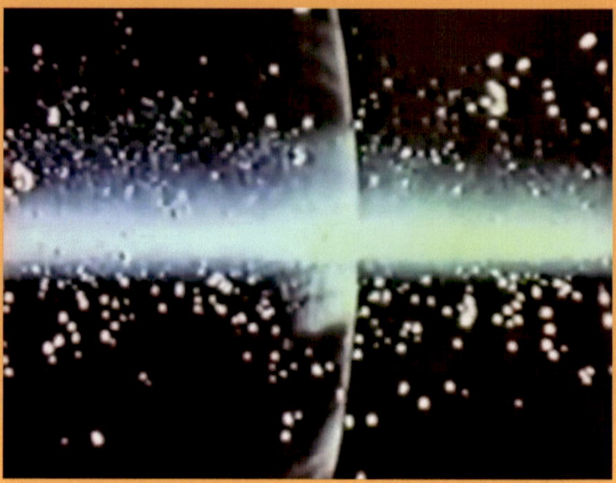

Attack From Outer Space

(1979)

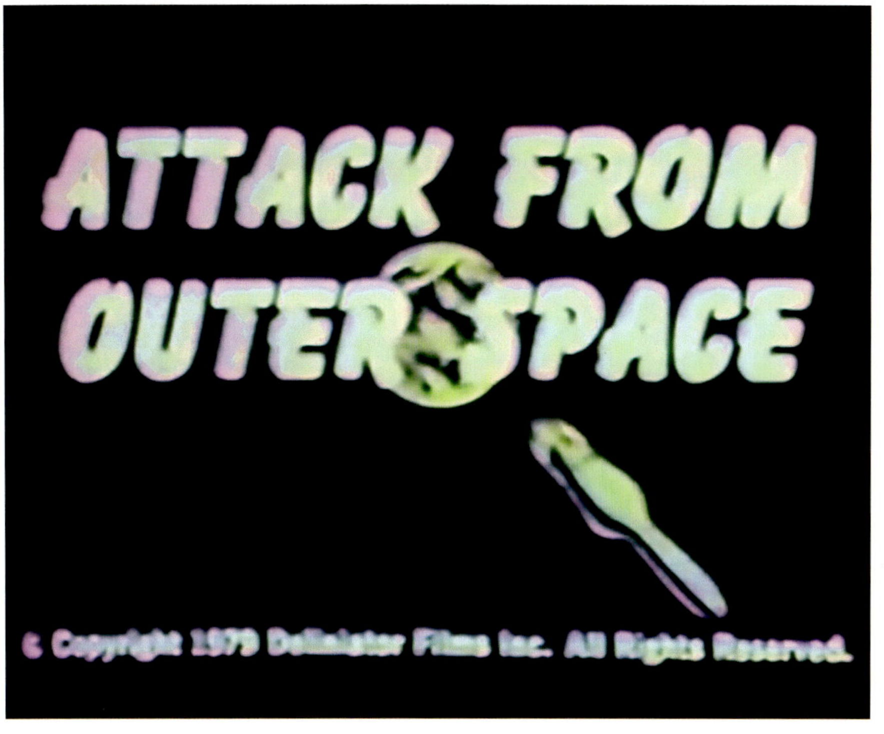

The same team at Delineator Films unleashed *UFO – Exclusive!*, *UFO: Top Secret*, and *Attack from Outer Space*. But all things considered, even with its provocative title, *Attack from Outer Space* remains the bronze medalist.

Sidney Paul's delivery of voiceover narration is much the same as in the prior films, as is Christopher Sereni's script. Plenty of "astounding questions," but few answers. Right after Paul tells us that UFOs have been linked to natural phenomena and disasters, as well as to the natural cycle of the planet and animal world, he asks, "Do UFOs really exist?" Inept logic? Not at all. In the world of the Weirdumentary, it's ept. Totally freakin' ept.

Anyhow, perhaps aliens are mapping our planet, and scrutinizing our military installations. Or perhaps they won't attack because they've already destroyed themselves with nuclear power. Who knows? *Attack* floats in a most peculiar way, which is probably why the stars look so very different today.

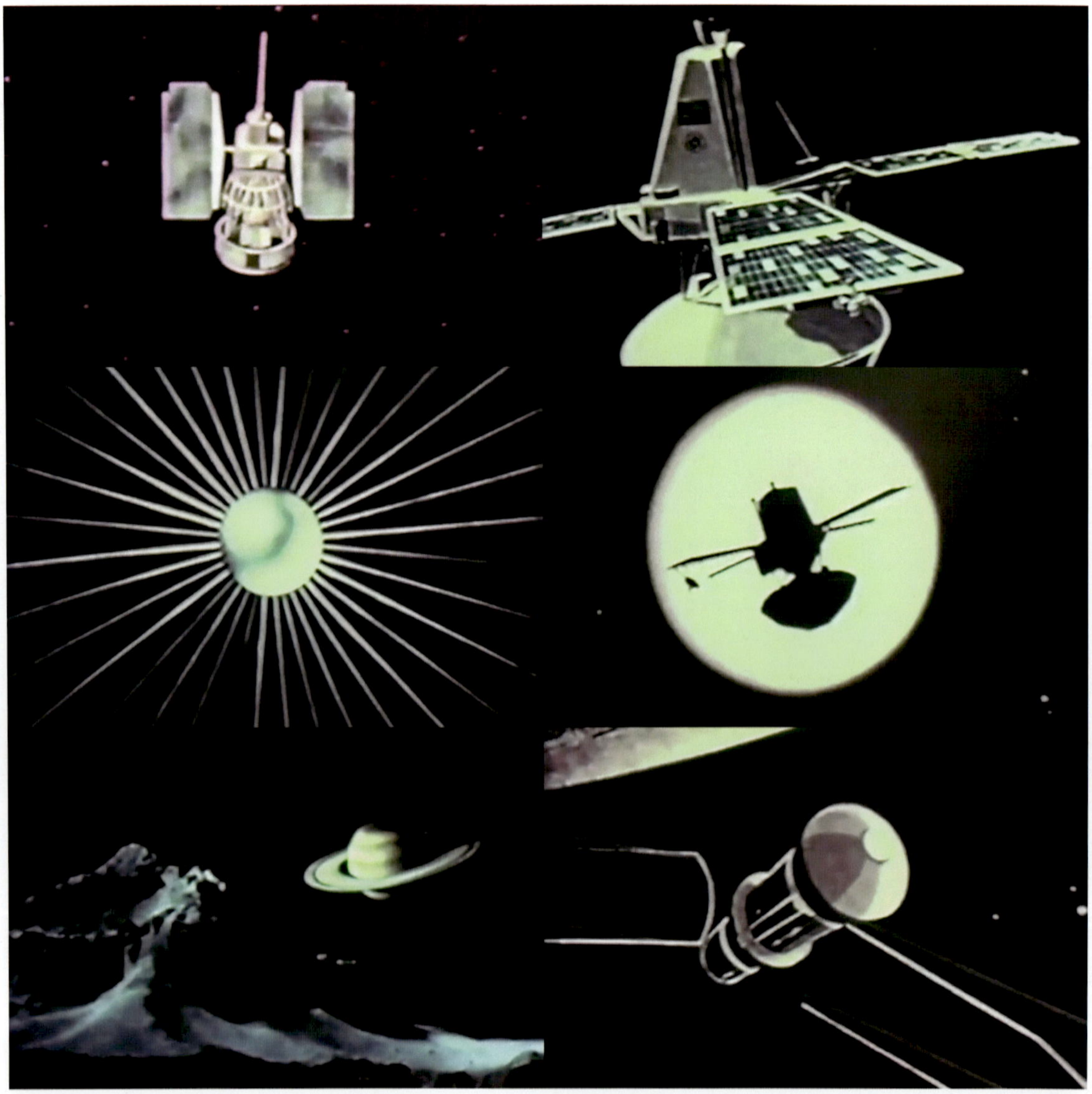

Director Wheeler Dixon relies on minor aesthetic choices not seen in the previous films, using swish pans as transitions between some images, and offering new special effects, some nearly qualifying as avant-garde.

But the biggest difference from the prior Delineator projects is that we get three interviews in addition to Paul's voiceover: These eyewitnesses to UFO phenomena are not seen, but heard. And they detract rather than add to the film, taking away from the otherwise wonderful rhythm of Paul's narration and the soundtrack.

When the music's cranked, Dixon gives us eye candy, like eerie winds blowing across an alien terrain, bizarre starscapes from a more civilized era, pre-CGI. In other cases, the images are mundane and unfold without explanation. A man uses a pencil to point at a map. What's he pointing at, and why? We never learn, but then, well, why ask why, as a wise man once asked.

After all, only part of the film has to do with alien invasion, with much of the running time devoted to our journey into the stars.

Nevertheless, Paul warns us to "Keep watching the skies." And so we shall.

UFO's Are Real

(1979)

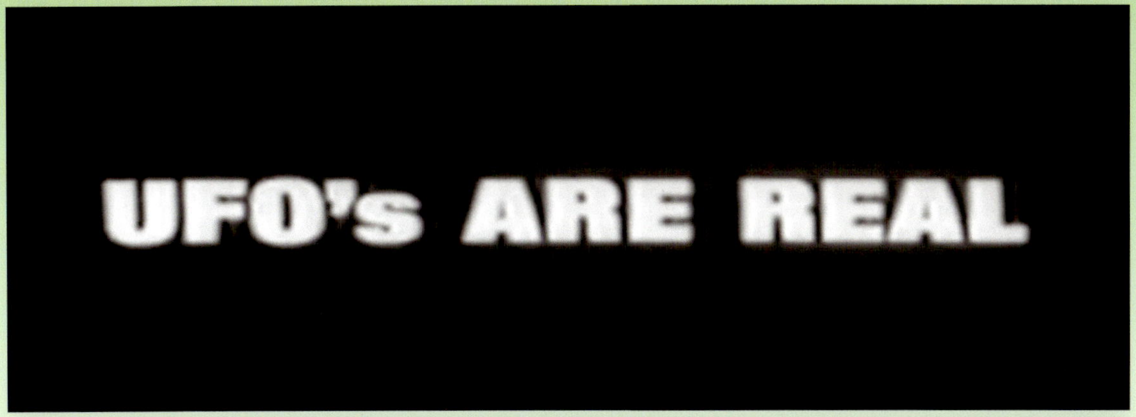

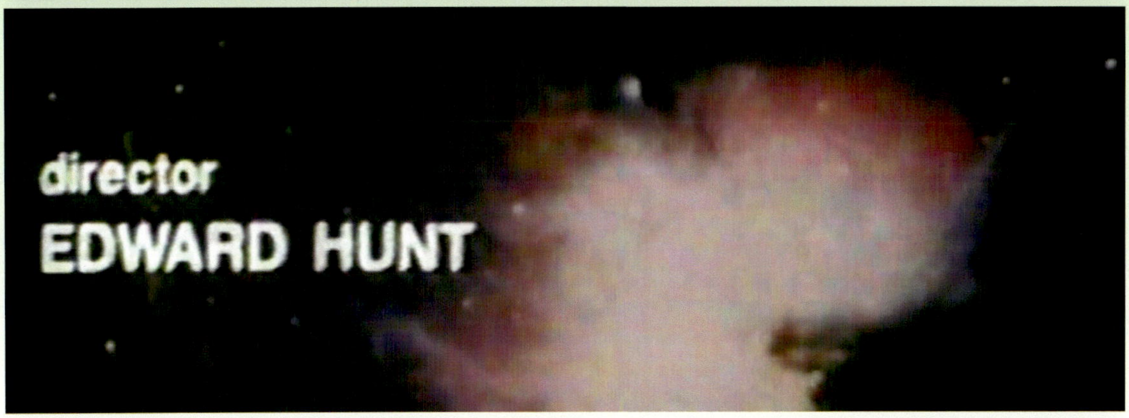

Okay, English teachers. You got us. There's no denying it. The title *UFO's Are Real* is grammatically challenged. But what's an incorrect apostrophe among friends? (Or should I say "friend's" - ?)

Edward Hunt directed this film for the company Group 1. Executive producer Brandon Chase served as off-screen narrator. His voice and delivery seem eminently credible. And most of the photographs and footage we see of UFOs feature on-screen titles that indicate the location and year they were taken, varnishing the film's magic cabinet with an "authentic" veneer.

In 1979, *Screen International* told readers, "the list of witnesses in the film is very impressive." Here again, *UFO's Are Real* often feels like a real documentary, with on-screen testimony coming from a number of retired military personnel. UFO expert Stanton T. Friedman, who co-authored the film's script with Edward Hunt, also appears. His beard and glasses look appropriately professorial. As for his words, Friedman claimed the U.S. government was involved in a "cosmic Watergate."

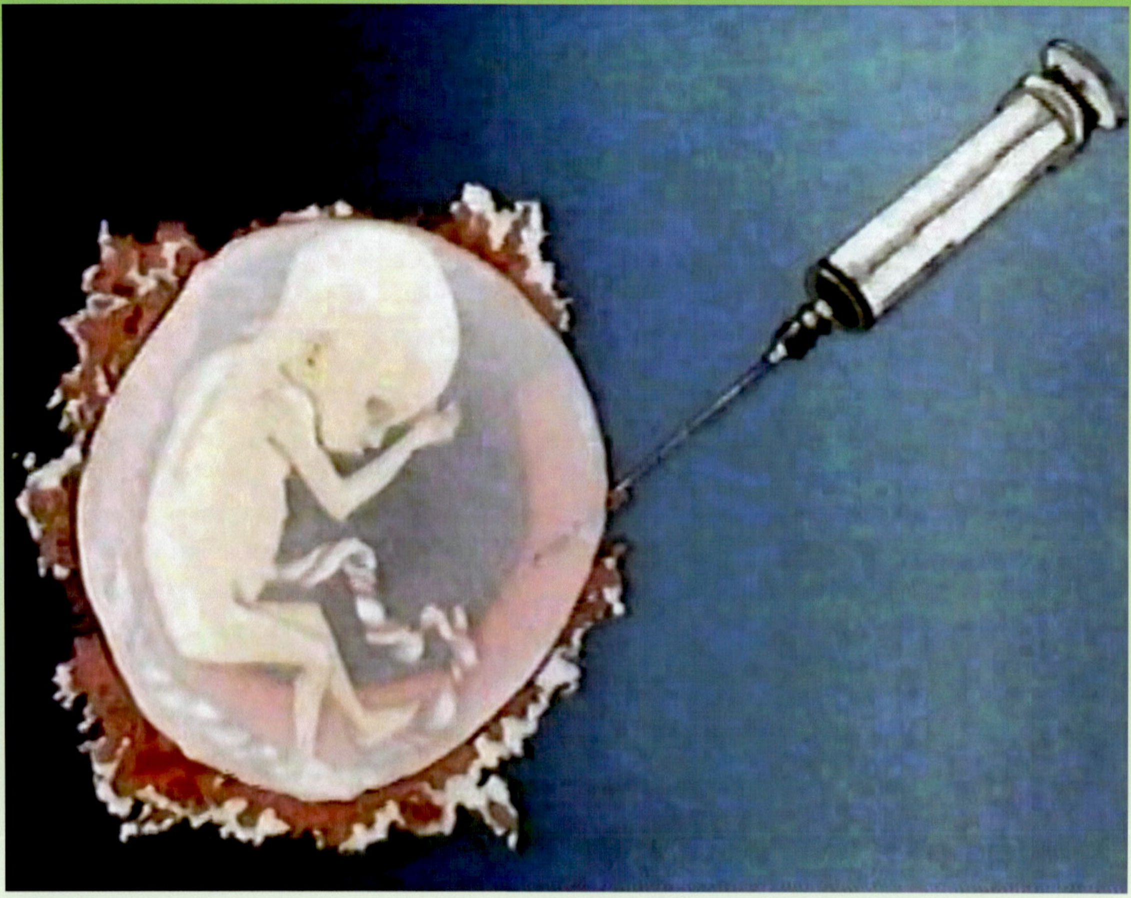

And then there are the stories we hear. Unlike its predecessors, *UFO's Are Real* addresses the Roswell incident of 1947 at length. The film also spends much time on the Travis Walton alien abduction of 1975, which was later adapted into the movie *Fire in the Sky* (1993). What's more, we get an interview with Ted Phillips, who tests soil samples from alien landing ground. Contact with extraterrestrials apparently leaves the soil extremely dehydrated, unable to absorb water or support seed germination.

But before Chase's voiceover lulls us into thinking this is an objective documentary, let's return to the title, which shoves the film's bias right in our face. From there, Chase explains, "The evidence we have presented establishes well beyond a reasonable doubt that alien beings are visiting the Earth in extraterrestrial spacecraft." Paintings of alleged incidents helps to convince us, either of verified alien encounters, or at least that *UFO's Are Real* is indeed a Weirdumentary.

Group 1 had moved from Scarsdale, New York, to Hollywood in 1975, making most of its money that decade from sexploitation. They also released horror movies, mainly imports, but also some they produced themselves, like *The Clonus Horror* (1979) with Peter Graves and Dick Sargent. *UFO's Are Real* was their sole venture into the outer limits of the Weirdumentary.

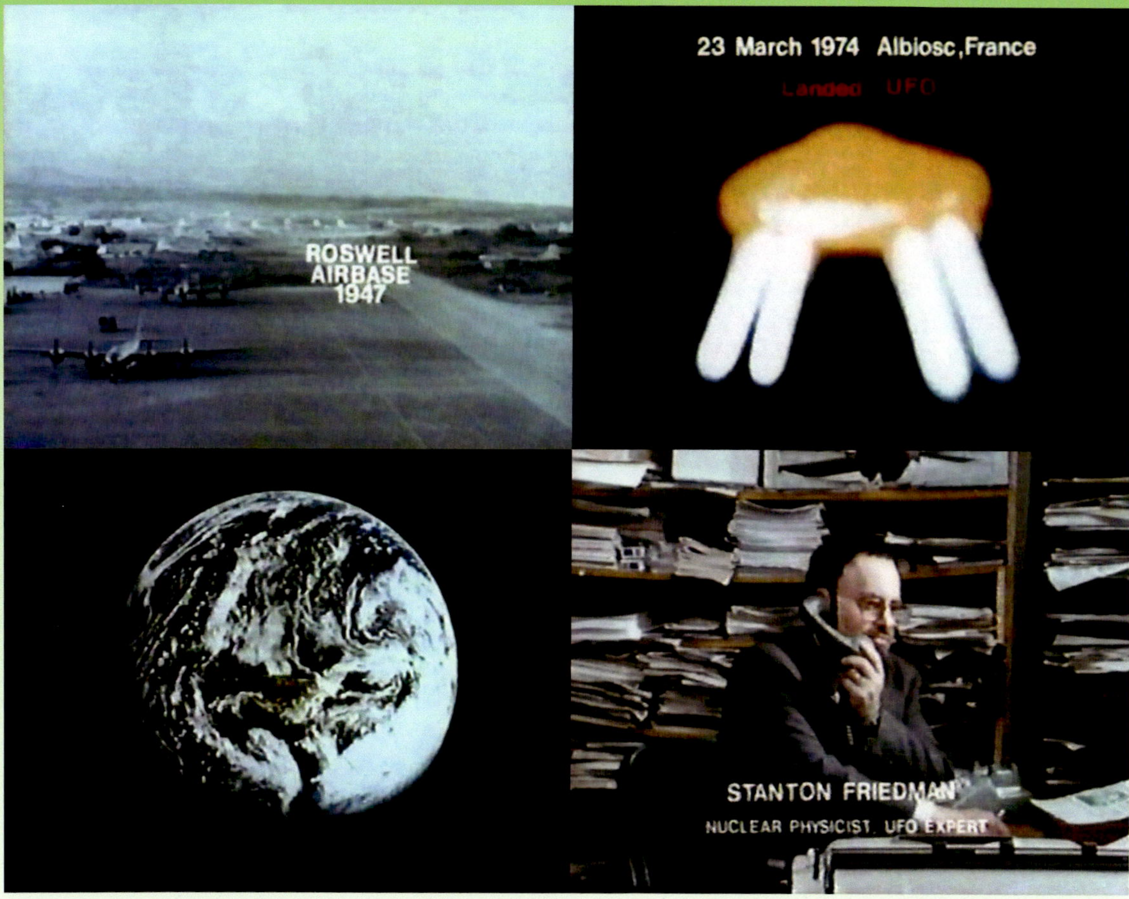

The trade press announced the production of *UFO's Are Real* in May 1979. *The Hollywood Reporter* wrote:

> *Because [Chase] thinks the CIA may try to interfere with the picture's four-wall openings, market by market, Chase said he has applied for an insurance policy to protect the company should there be any delays in the scheduled openings.*
>
> *Chase admitted that he was skeptical about UFOs, but now believes they are real, thanks to computer-authenticated photo sightings, computer scannings, lie detector tests, and 'other information.'*

By December 1979, the MPAA granted the film a G rating. Group 1 distributed the movie with a saturation ad campaign.

By and large, the public did not notice or care. In fairness, some of them might have been abducted at the time.

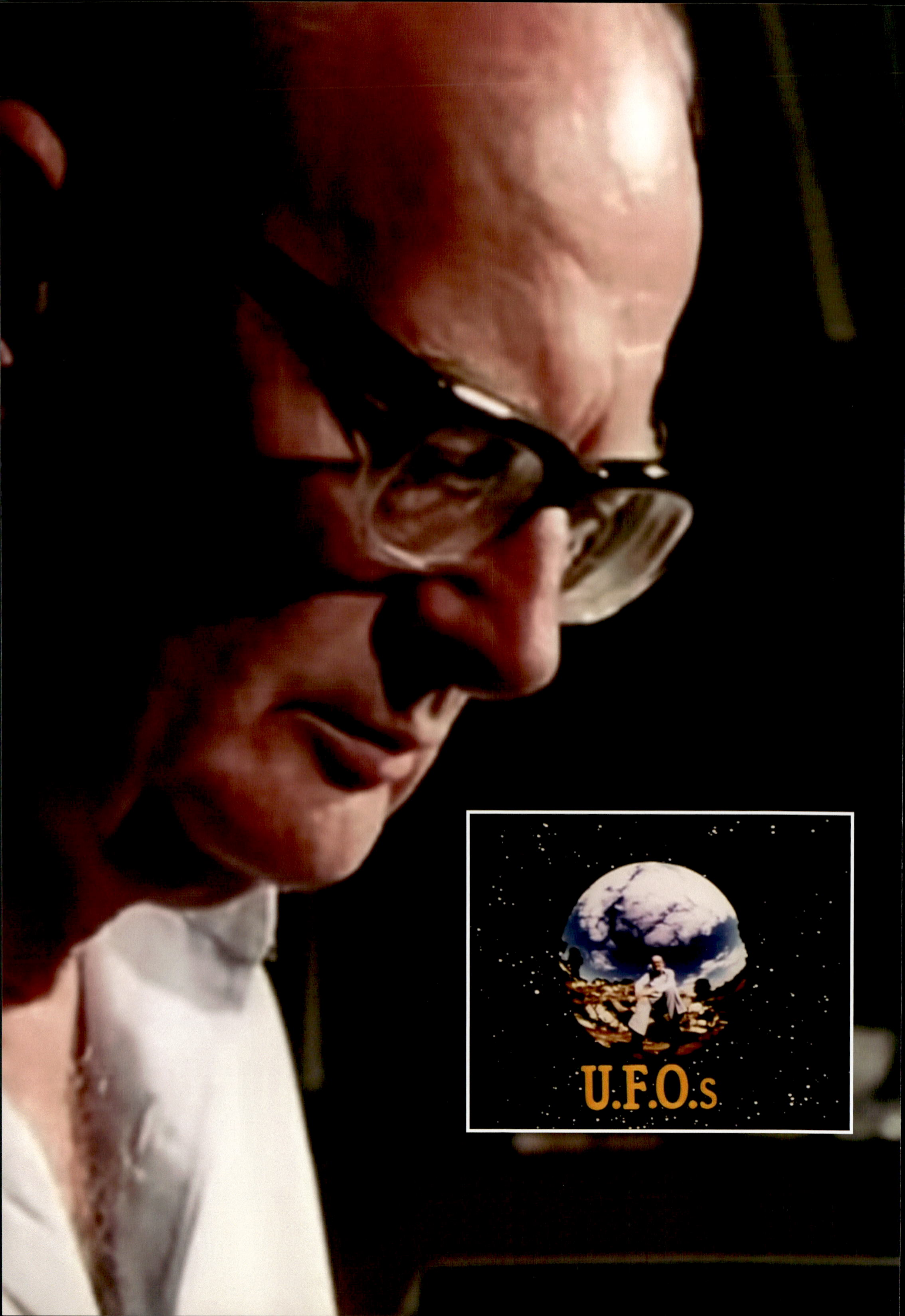
U.F.O.s

Arthur C. Clarke's Mysterious World: UFOs

(1980)

"Are we being watched by aliens from outer space? Are these the craft that they're using to visit us? Did this Scottish forester really have a closer encounter in this lonely glade? And what does this classic UFO film show? A flying saucer or something more down to earth?"

The narrator of the *Mysterious World* episode entitled *U.F.O.s* asks all the right questions, and so Arthur C. tries to see about answering them.

"I think I can claim to be a reluctant expert on UFOs. I've been interested in them for almost fifty years, long before the phrase 'flying saucers' was invented. UFOs are very common. If you've never seen one, you're either unobservant or live in a cloudy area. I've seen half a dozen good ones, and now I have some very definite opinions on the subject."

We get fascinating footage of a UFO filmed in New Zealand, bright lights "bouncing" around the sky. The film features a "luminous base with a transparent top." A single frame shows an "extraordinary trail," which really does appear extraordinary. There is "no known explanation."

Then we meet Ray Stanford of Texas, head of Project Starlight, a company that has nothing to do with after-dinner mints and everything to do with watching the skies.

Stanford doesn't believe these unknown craft originate from Earth, but he admits they could be secret government stuff: "If the Soviet Union has that kind of technology, God help the free world, and if the free world has it, God help the Soviets." (Men in Black thus get a bit of flack.)

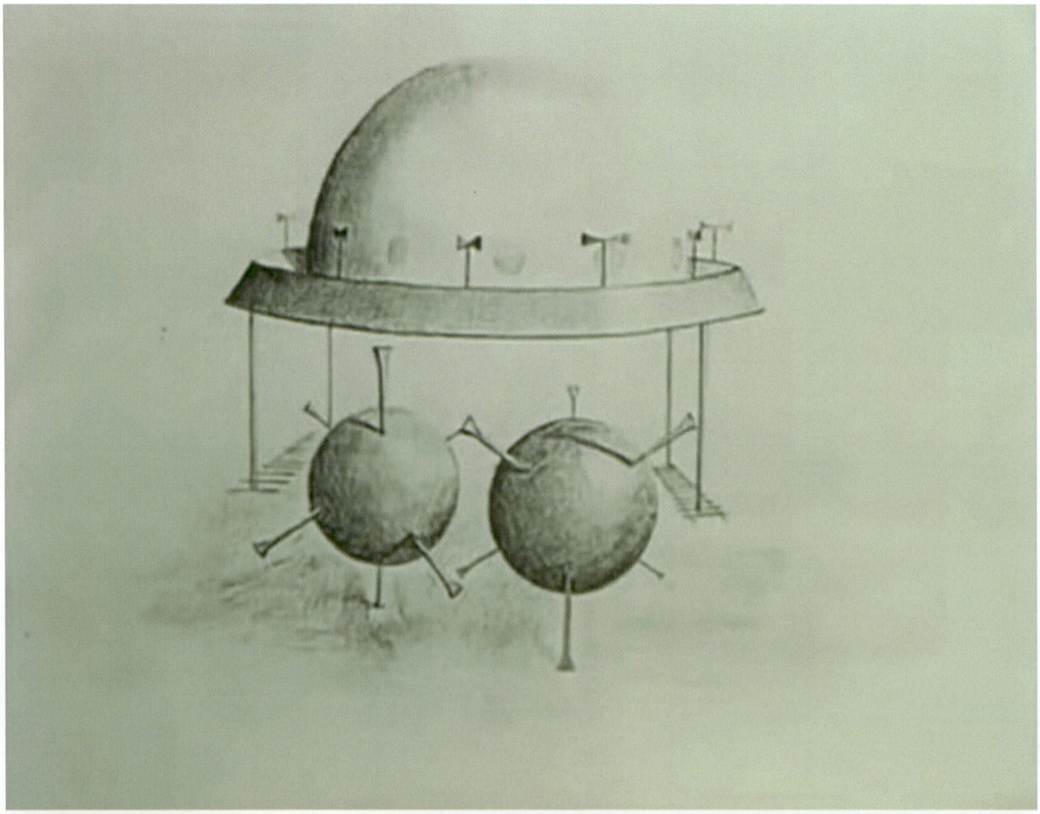

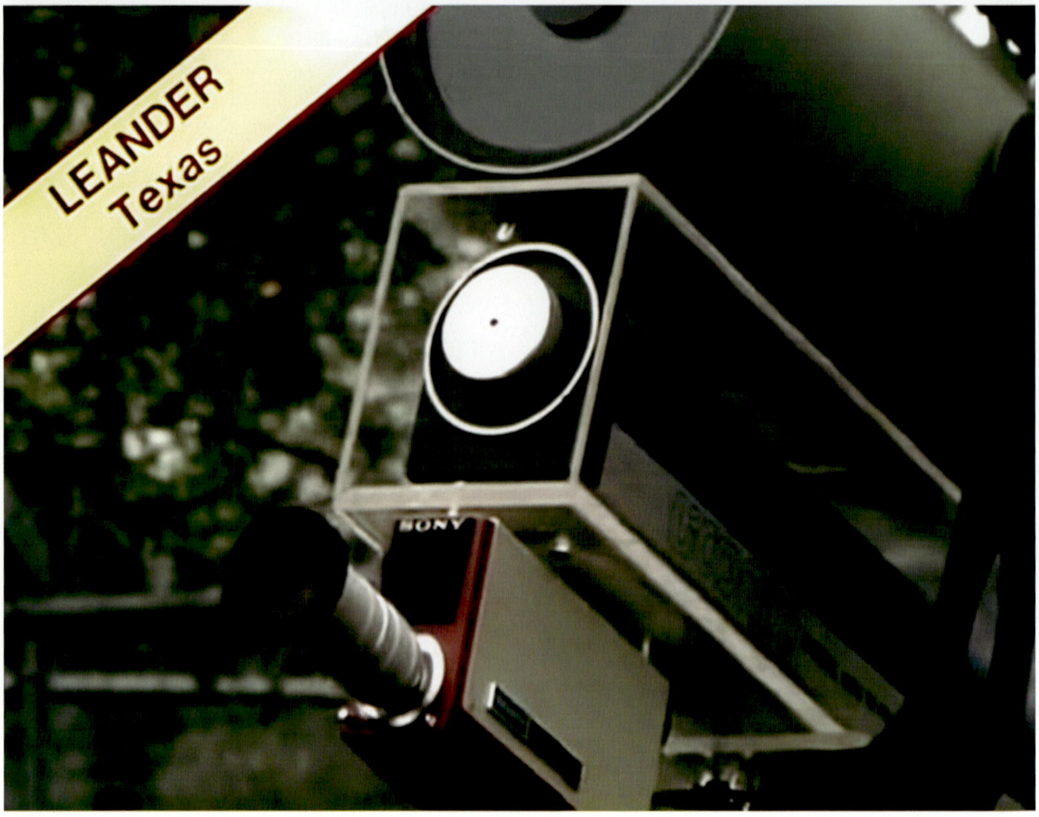
LEANDER
Texas
SONY

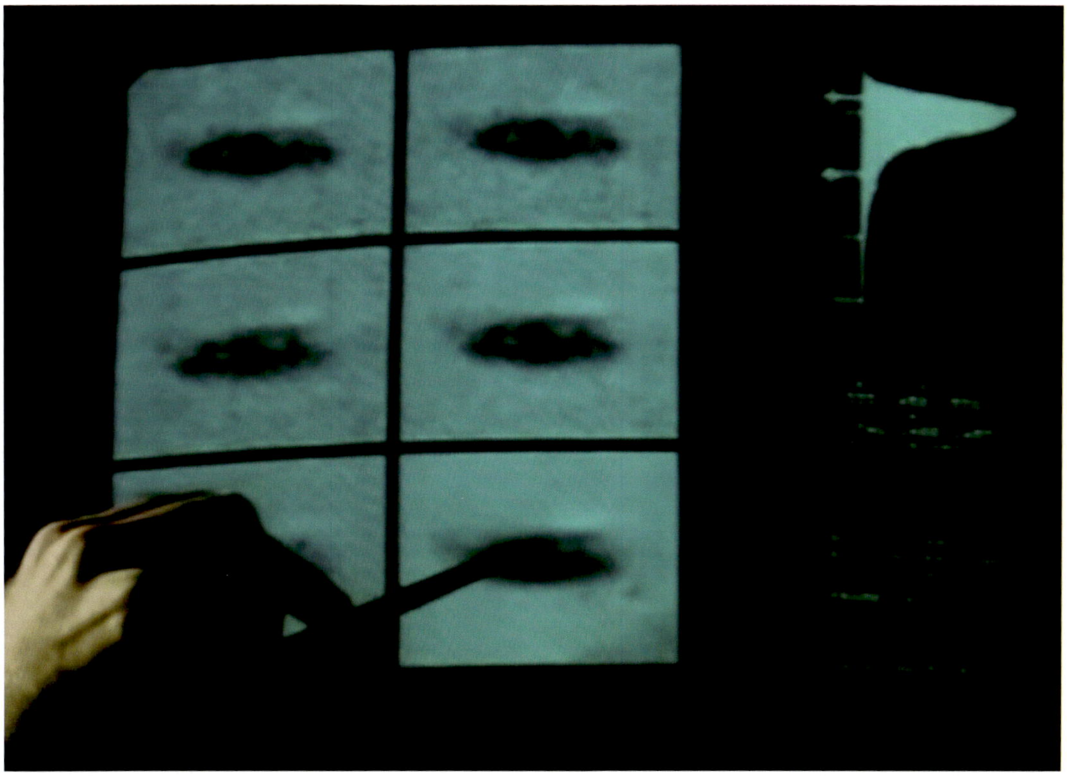

Mysterious World proves that the mysteries of the world need not always be mysterious. We see 1972 footage from Wyoming state. Eyewitnesses believed that a speedy object in the sky was a spaceship. "In fact, it was a large meteorite which grazed the Earth's atmosphere forty miles up and then bounced off forever into space."

Clarke himself attends the launch of weather balloon to explain how he was fooled once upon a time, mistaking the same type of object for the planet Venus.

But "mistaken identities" don't explain all of the bizarre footage we see, which was filmed across the globe. Some of the objects are strange, curious, inexplicable. Whether or not they contain little green men visiting our big blue world, well, I'll ask my own question: Who knows?

Then we hear from those persons who have allegedly seen aliens close-up and personal, tales that fascinate Clarke more than distant objects on grainy films. Some of these eyewitnesses are people of "high integrity," so, you know, there's that.

Nevertheless, Clarke remains skeptical, particularly given the amount of radar networks and tracking devices that exist. He concludes, "I feel that when there really is a visitation from space, it'll be something spectacular, rather like the end of the movie *Close Encounters of the Third Kind* [1978]. We'll be certain of it within about five minutes."

Close encounters with *Mysterious World* are, in their own way, spectacular. I was certain of that within about five minutes.

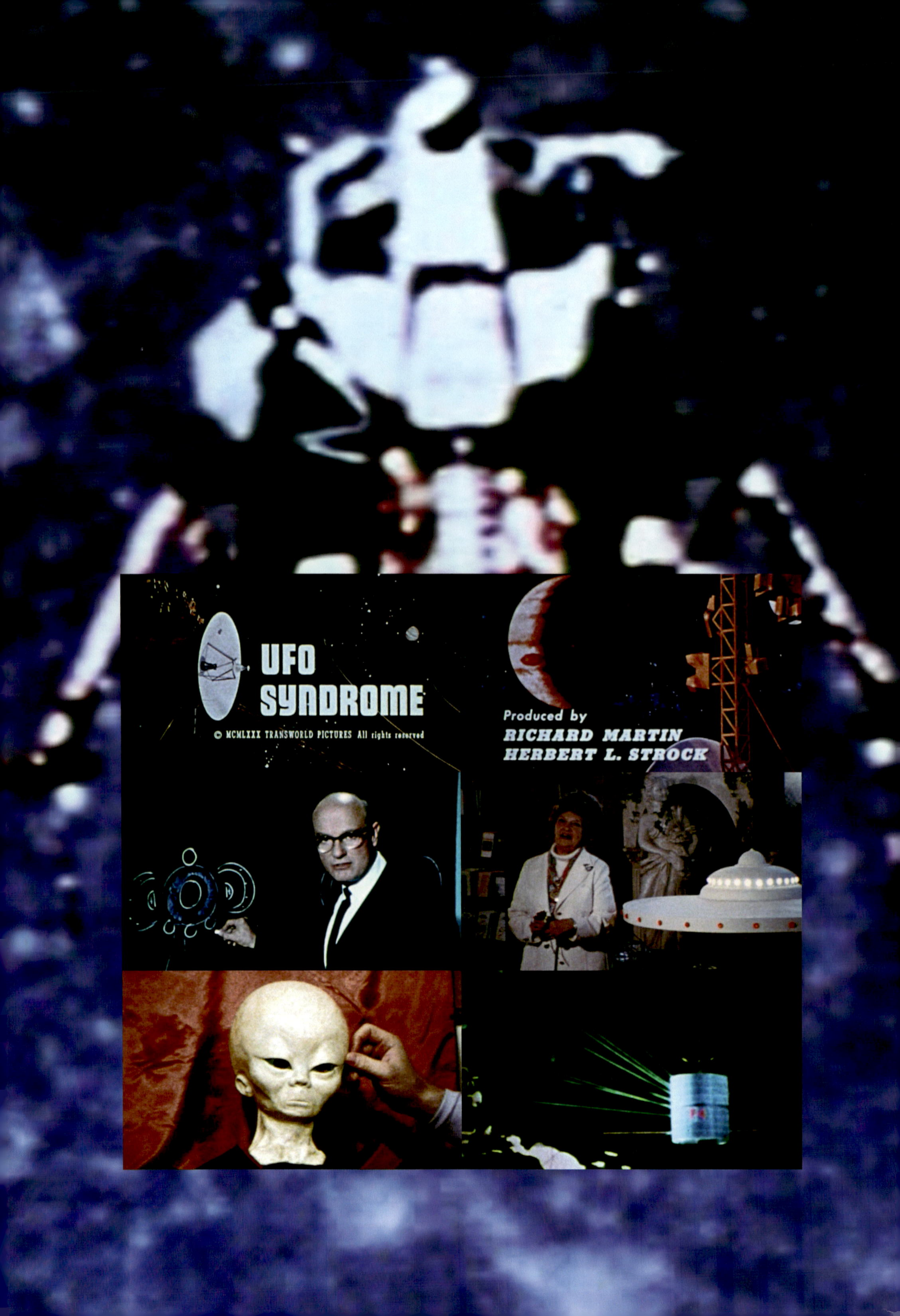
UFO
SYNDROME
© MCMLXXX TRANSWORLD PICTURES All rights reserved
Produced by
RICHARD MARTIN
HERBERT L. STROCK

UFO Syndrome
(1980)

"Unidentified flying objects are spying on our planet. Extraterrestrials are observing us on Earth. Flying saucers have land bases here. Aliens continue abductions of Earthlings. These shocking statements are being made by space scientists all over the world. No matter what the language, the message is the same. We are being watched by beings from outer space."

They're back! The great team of director Richard Martin, producer/writer Herbert L. Strock, and composer Aminadav Aloni return in a follow-up to *The UFO Journals* (1978). The result is memorable, but more of a *Godfather III* than a *II*. Not a bad accomplishment, especially when you don't have the money to cast George Hamilton.

UFO Syndrome presents a few unique stories, including news of Visitors in New Zealand in 1979. And we learn about an Italian who has been abducted four times, to which the only reasonable response is "Quattro Formaggi!"

But most of the time the film revisits the distant past. It re-roasts such cinematic chestnuts as the Nazca lines and Stonehenge. In voiceover, Tony Eisley discusses how much of the evidence has been "censored or completely suppressed." Funny that, given how most of it had already appeared in earlier Weirdumentaries.

Worse still is that on-camera testimony from Brian Scott of Voltar fame and Dr. George King of the Aetherius Society is simply repurposed footage from *The UFO Journals*. Here we learn that one can have too much of Voltar. To Ground Control, Major Tom jokes, "Send me up a drink."

Nevertheless, to hear Aloni's music and to see some quite special special effects helps keep us on board this space oddity. After all, "Too many hard facts lead to the conclusion that we are not alone."

So, required viewing? Absolutely. Second viewing? Magic 8-Ball says head back to *The UFO Journals* instead. The countdown's on.

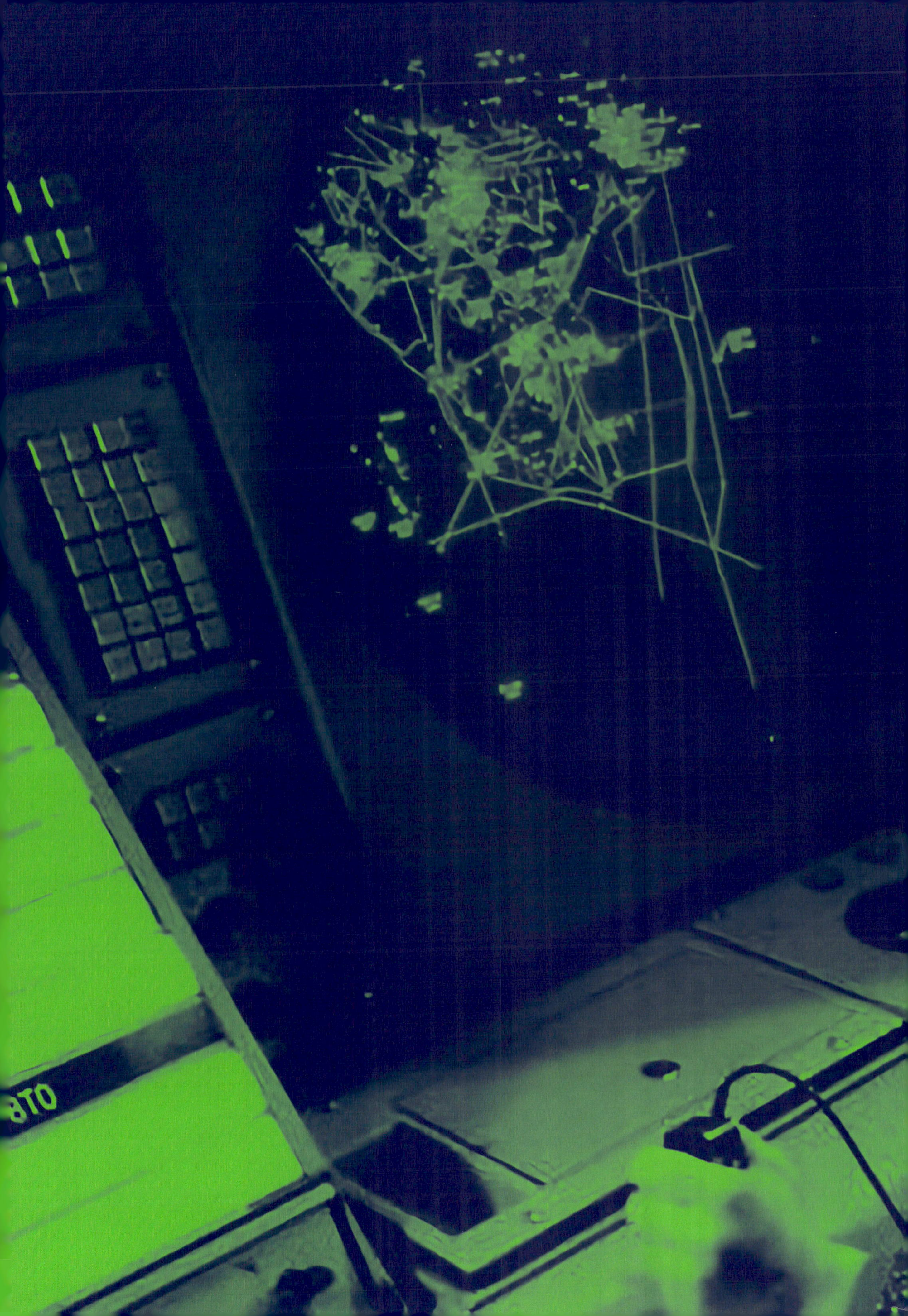

section 4: The Bermuda Triangle

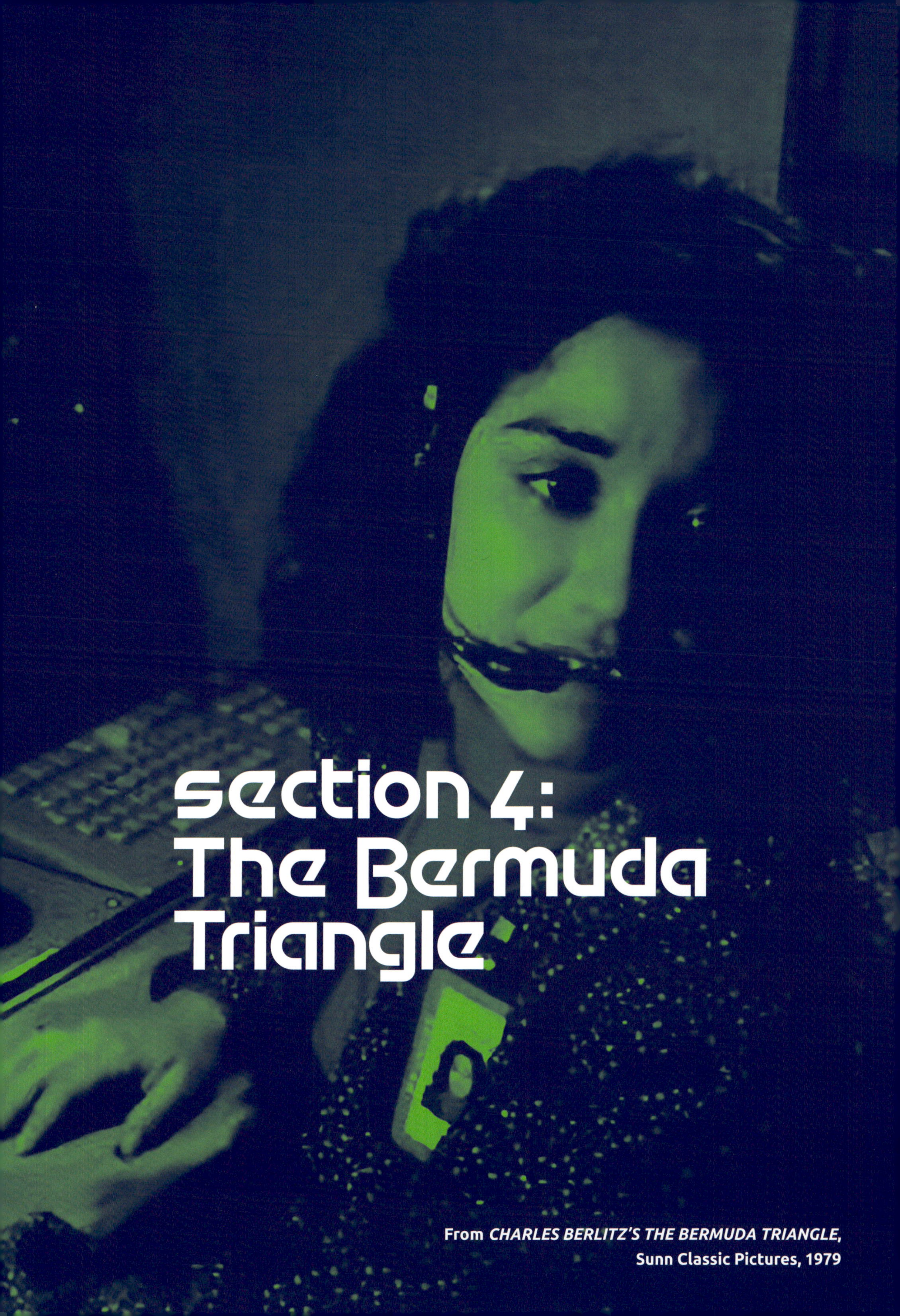

From *CHARLES BERLITZ'S THE BERMUDA TRIANGLE*, Sunn Classic Pictures, 1979

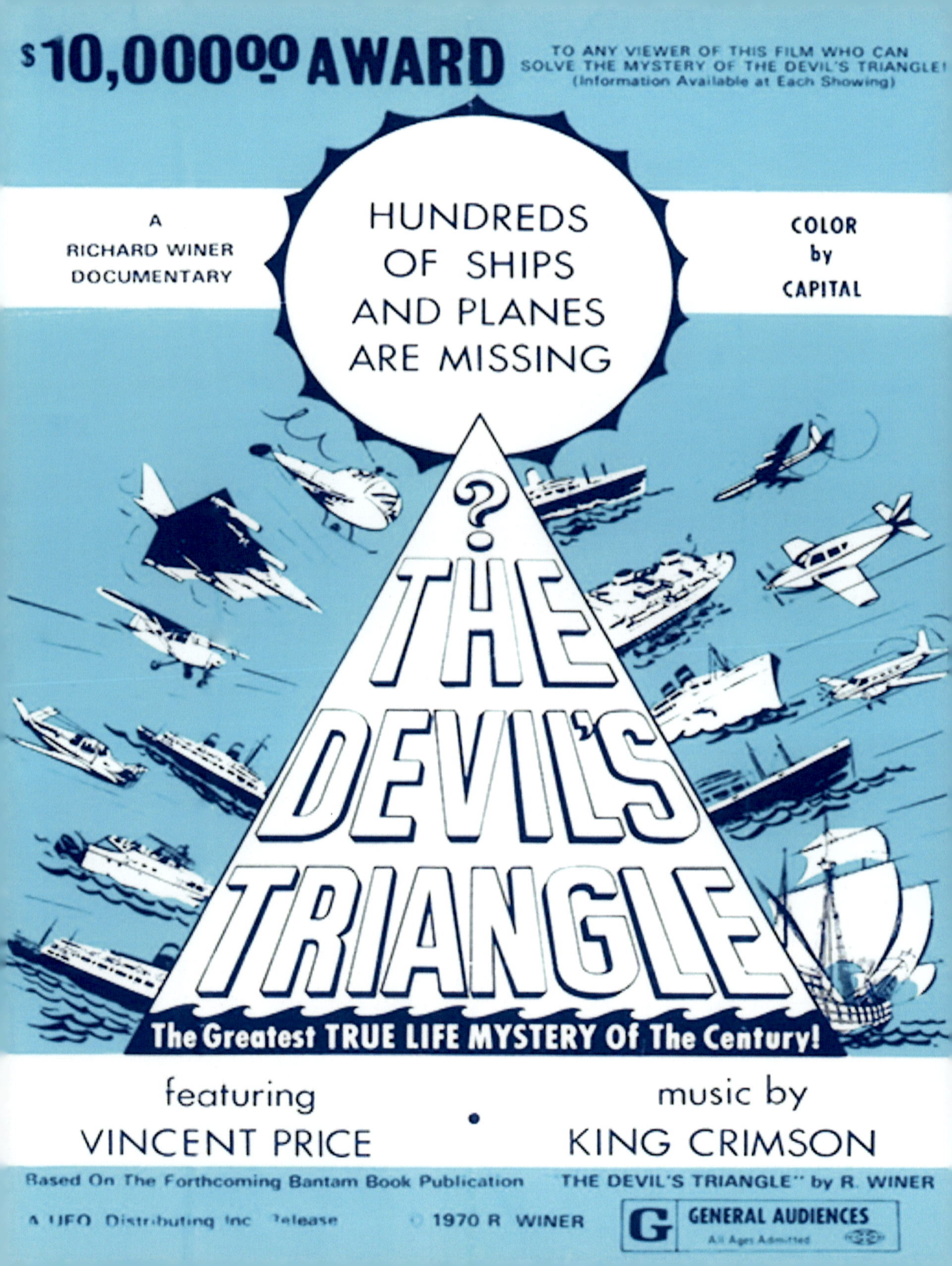

$10,000.00 AWARD
TO ANY VIEWER OF THIS FILM WHO CAN SOLVE THE MYSTERY OF THE DEVIL'S TRIANGLE!
(Information Available at Each Showing)
A RICHARD WINER DOCUMENTARY
HUNDREDS OF SHIPS AND PLANES ARE MISSING
COLOR by CAPITAL
?
THE DEVIL'S TRIANGLE
The Greatest TRUE LIFE MYSTERY Of The Century!
featuring VINCENT PRICE
music by KING CRIMSON
Based On The Forthcoming Bantam Book Publication "THE DEVIL'S TRIANGLE" by R. WINER
A UFO Distributing Inc. Release
© 1970 R. WINER
G GENERAL AUDIENCES
All Ages Admitted

The Devil's Triangle

(1972)

"The Devil's Deep Blue Hokum." That's how a critic at the *Washington Post* labeled this TV documentary on the Bermuda Triangle. In fact, the critic subsequently jammed the phrases "sheerest hokum" and "sheer hokum" into a single sentence, so much did the hokum cup overfloweth. But riddle me this: when did hokum become a bad thing?

Variety was not much kinder, complaining about the "pastiche" of stock footage, as well as Vincent Price's narration. "It played up the sensationalism of the events at great length with little attempt at explanation." To which I respond, if *that's* bad, I don't wanna be good.

Running approximately fifty-two minutes, producer-director-writer Richard Winer's *The Devil's Triangle* has the distinction of being the first Weirdumentary on the subject. Winer, best known at the time as a cinematographer in Florida, began working on the film in 1968 and hired Vincent Price in 1970. By the time Price arrived in Fort Lauderdale to cut the voiceover, *Variety* referred to the project as an "imaginative documentary."

The master of horror is heard, but never seen. The words Price speaks wonderfully describe those unholy waters, "where numerous ships vanish off the face of the earth, where countless planes never reach their destinations, and where hundreds of yachts never return to port."

The film depends on a number of ingredients, from on-camera interviews with experts and eyewitnesses to some decent recreations that aren't properly identified as such. The cinematography is quite good, even if the acting is marginal. Better still is the music and editing, the latter achieving its fever pitch during fast-paced montages that depict the maelstrom that is the Devil's Triangle.

The waters heat to a boil when a clairvoyant explains that the dreaded locale is where the "sea opens." That's what happens to the planes and ships. "Exactly the same" events will keep happening, over and over again, he warns us. Thank-you cards can be mailed to this sage in care of your local network affiliate.

"What is this wraith-flinging, horrifying curse that prevails in the Devil's Triangle?", Price demands to know, having already damned its mysteries as "blasphemous." A skeptic responds that there is a "basic scientific explanation." Boo on you, sir. Heed instead the words of the anthropologist who jabbers about a magnetic field "produced by a flying spacecraft."

The Bermuda Triangle is cool, and Vincent Price is cool. Even the *Washington Post*'s critic had to admit, "Actually, *The Devil's Triangle* is so bad it's really almost good." Easy on that "almost," fella. ▲

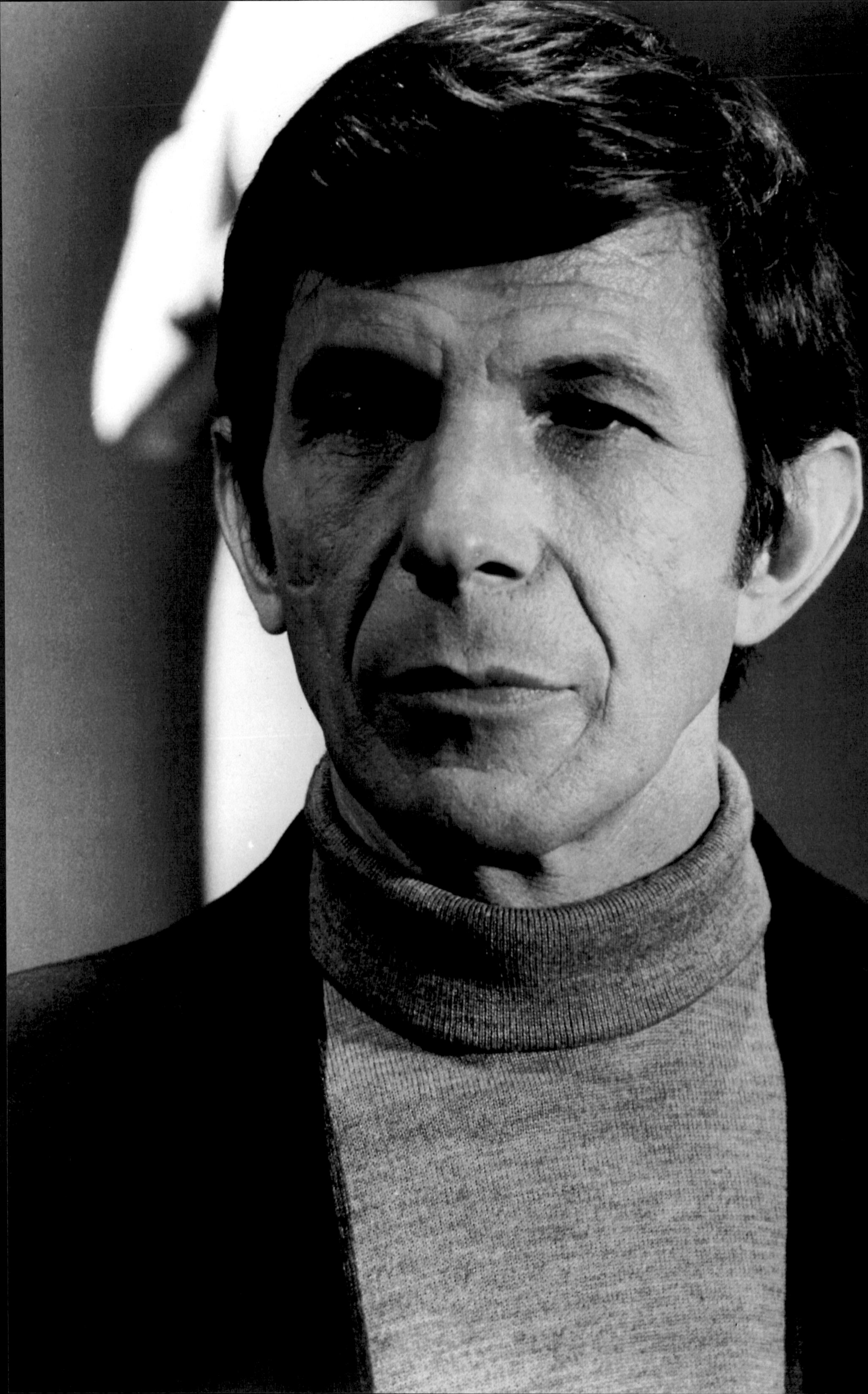

In Search Of... The Bermuda Triangle

(1976–1982)

In 1978, Landsburg Productions—headed by our old pal Alan—was very busy. It had become an "autonomous" unit within the Reeves Teletape Corporation. It was making four projects for television, one of which was a mini-series. Oh, and it was also producing the third season of *In Search of...*

Speaks of threes, there are three points on a triangle, and three episodes of *In Search of...* devoted to the triangle named Bermuda.

Season 1, Episode 4, *The Bermuda Triangle*: Leonard Nimoy tells us, "In the open waters of the Atlantic Ocean, there abides a phenomenon that is difficult to explain, a danger zone that seems to swallow ships and planes. No one has found a satisfactory answer, but somewhere in this region, between the sea and the sky, lurks the solution to the mystery of the Bermuda Triangle."

So many disappearances that "cannot be explained." And it is a mystery, mind you, despite skeptical scientists who don't believe there's any mystery at all. They have not done their homework, obviously. Nimoy explains that they didn't interview the eyewitnesses.

Most of what we hear in this episode is same-old, same-old, but oldies are indeed goodies. "The unknown force, it appears, is there, in the Bermuda Triangle, begging for investigation." And the investigation would indeed continue.

Season 3, Episode 10, *The Bermuda Triangle Pirates*: "A ghost ship is discovered adrift on the Caribbean. Another mystery for the men who patrol those waters of dreadful fascination, the infamous Bermuda Triangle."

This time we get dramatic recreations of some of those who vanished in the "now-legendary body of water."

Pirate's Lady, a luxury yacht, is among the vessels that disappeared. Its owner (who wasn't aboard at the time) is convinced it's still afloat somewhere. He offers a big, fat reward, which results in a big, fat nothing.

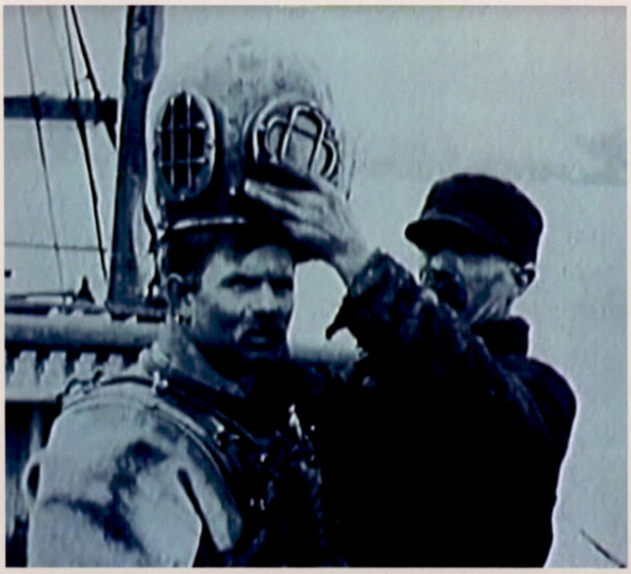

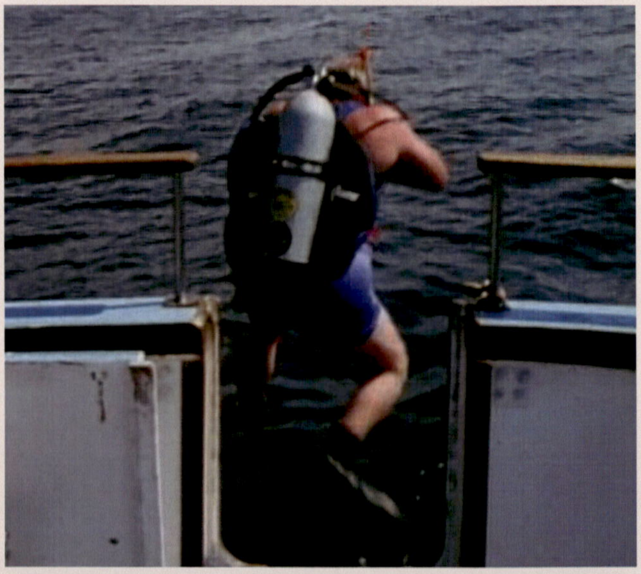

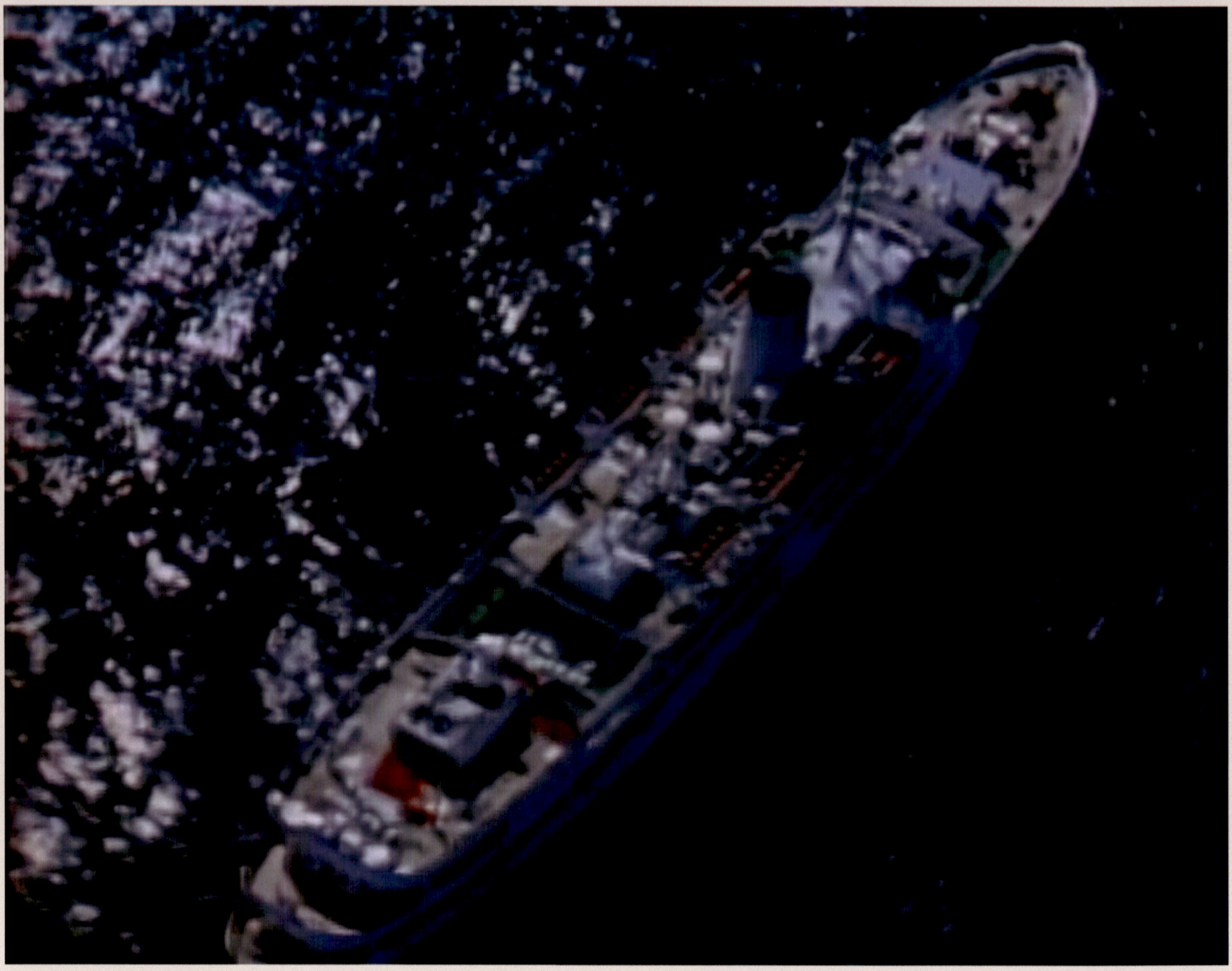

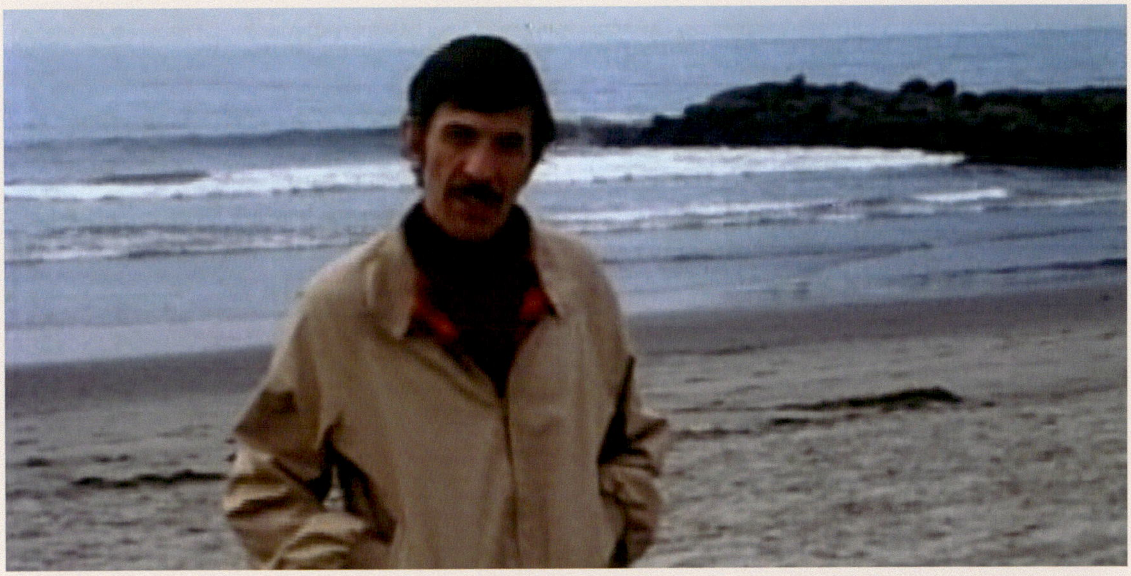

Maybe, just maybe, *some* of the missing ships were hijacked by pirates, modern buccaneers: personable, smart, cold-blooded, and connected to the drug trade. Here's a fascinating addition to the Triangle lore. (Let's take time to give Nimoy the Vulcan salute.)

Season 4, Episode 22, *The Bimini Wall*: It is "a long stone structure that scientists have yet to explain." A road? A wall? A remnant of Atlantis? Or an entirely natural phenomenon? We've heard all of this before, making this episode just another brick in the… well, you know. At least we get one unexpected interviewee, Ernest Hemingway's brother. Death in the afternoon in the Triangle.

Season 3, Episode 8, *The Great Lakes Triangle*: "There is the body of water from which the cry of distress comes more often per square mile than any other body of water in the world. ... Not the Bermuda Triangle, but another triangle, a triangle formed by the Great Lakes, locked in the heart of industrial North America."

Here's one of the best curveballs that *In Search of…* threw us, exploring a different triangle. Rescue teams from Canada and the United States regularly search for missing ships and planes, as well as recovering the remains of those destroyed "by forces no one can explain." A third of all American sea and air disasters happen in this particularly devilish but little-known triangle. (Like the Great Pumpkin, I suspect it just needs more publicity.)

"High government officials" seem not to understand the import of the Great Lakes Triangle. And the mysteries here are particularly, well, mysterious, because the geographical area is so small, especially as compared to the Bermuda Triangle.

Eyewitnesses "describe their bewilderment" at vanishing craft. Sometimes the evidence is contradictory; sometimes it is nonexistent. As Nimoy explains, "there is no apparent reason for sudden death," but it happens all the same.

Of the third season, *Variety* told readers that *In Search of…* was successful because its episodes "steer clear of controversy [by] covering topics that most thinking people put in the category of pseudo-science, anti-intellectualism, superstition and old wives' tales."

Yes, indeed. Steer clear of controversy. And also of watery triangles. ▲

Mysteries From Beyond the Triangle

(1978)

The Bermuda Triangle deserves, or at least has earned, the plural word "mysteries." Boats and planes go missing; the Bimini Wall remains, as do our questions.

But this specific Weirdumentary has at least one mystery of its own, and that would be its year of release. Internet sources variously cite 1976, 1977, 1978, and 1979.

It's easy to understand the confusion. It doesn't seem that William F. Miller's *Mysteries from Beyond the Triangle* was ever copyrighted. And then there's the fact that the film quickly sank into oblivion, like deeper than 20,000 leagues.

That's not to say that there wasn't room for Bermuda Triangles, or, for that matter, Quadrangles or Pentangles. In 1977, even Wonder Woman investigated the subject on prime-time television, in an episode called "The Bermuda Triangle Crisis."

For Miller's film, the crisis came in the form of *Secrets of the Bermuda Triangle* (1978) and *Charles Berlitz's The Bermuda Triangle* (1979), the former being an Alan Landsburg film and the latter being a Sunn Classic. Those two effectively docked at the Weirdumentary marina, leaving Miller's unmoored.

At any rate, boats against the current are borne back in the past. So, before we go further, let's go backwards.

A "group in the Washington, D.C. area" contracted Miller and his Bostonia Films to film an expedition of "scientists, researchers, psychics, oceanographers, [and] divers ... all aboard a luxury liner ... some 300 strong heading into the Graveyard of the Atlantic to challenge the devil." But the expedition didn't happen.

Undaunted, Miller chartered his own expedition, one involving about a dozen people. He later recalled:

> *Finding a ship to take us into the Triangle area presented more problems than finding financing. ... It was unbelievable how many captains and ship owners turned us down. ... Surely someone would be willing to sail*

(40) **Movie** "Mysteries From Beyond The Triangle" (1977) Documentary. The mysteries of space from beyond our universe are revealed as never before. (2 hrs) ★★

(10) **MOVIE -(DOCUMENTARY)** ••½ **"Mysteries From Beyond the Triangle" 1977** An intriguing look at some of the possible answers to the murderous puzzle of the Bermuda Triangle Just what does happen to all those ships and planes that vanish from the Earth? (60 mins.)

1:30 (2) THE LATE SHOW: "Mysteries from Beyond the Triangle" — Taking off in fact from where Star Wars left off in fiction, the mysteries of space far outside our universe are revealed as never before.

> *us into the unknown. That somebody turned out to be a young British captain who was just starting a new career as a charter boat captain... His ship,* The New Freedom, *seemed perfect.*

And so, Miller and Co. set sail not for a three-hour tour, but for a two-week voyage, the group consisting of two camera operators, a sound engineer, a production assistant, two psychics, two physicists, a diver, and an oceanographer.

Problems were plentiful, from hot weather and seasickness to unsteady camera shots. Miller also said:

> *The trip was not without its lighter moments. One of the more comical ones came only a few hours out to sea when we first rolled the cameras. Not thinking of its double meaning, we shouted 'syncing' as the cameras rolled for a take. Captain Fincham thought we had shouted 'sinking' and was prepared to haul out the rafts. We quickly changed the phrase to 'slating.'*

With all of the ups and downs, ups and downs, and ups and downs of the waves, Miller's ship returned to shore with 35,000 feet of 16mm footage. The result became a ninety-minute film.

Mysteries from Beyond the Triangle made its television debut in August 1978, with some television listings claiming it was copyrighted the year before. Rebroadcasts occurred occasionally over the next several years. One TV listing promised, "Taking off in fact from where *Star Wars* left off in fiction, the mysteries of space far outside [of] our universe are revealed as never before."

Maybe, but not nearly enough viewers ever saw those revelations for themselves. This is one of the hardest to find of all Weirdumentaries. (Like the song said about another fateful trip, the minnow would be lost, the minnow would be lost.) ▲

SECRETS OF THE BERMUDA TRIANGLE

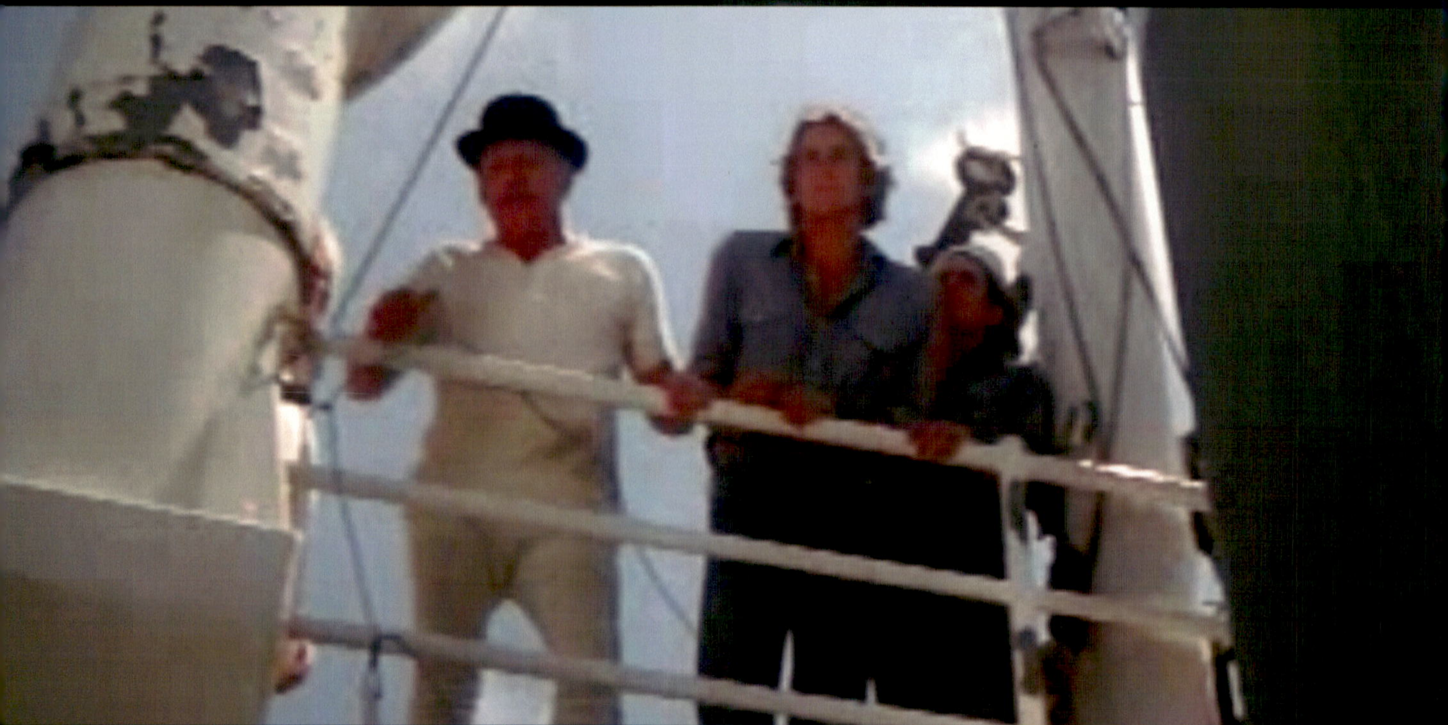

The Investigator

PETER TOMPKINS

Secrets of the Bermuda Triangle

(1978)

And now, at long last, we encounter what appears to be the biggest-budget Weirdumentary of them all.

Peter Tompkins is our on-screen host, "The Investigator." Genteel and believable, this best-selling author of *Secrets of the Great Pyramid* (1972) explains, "I spent a lifetime trying to crack some of the mysteries of this universe." But the Bermuda Triangle baffles even him. The "essence of its dark powers" remains obscure. We have been notified: it's time to go land-lover.

Our old pal Alan Landsburg penned the story for *Secrets of the Bermuda Triangle.* He co-produced it with Donald Brittain, who wrote the screenplay and directed. J. Barry Herron's aerial and underwater cinematography is superb, and Director of Photography Brianne Murphy brilliantly captures all else.

Thanks to more-than-adequate sets and actors, the recreations easily best those seen in most other Weirdumentaries. Consider the infamous tale of Commander Worley of the S.S. *Cyclops.* He went crazy when helming his Navy vessel through the Triangle, appearing on deck in long underwear and a bowler hat, predating the Alex look of *A Clockwork Orange* (1971) by a half-century. Worley's final journey through the Triangle ended in oblivion. Worley and his crew of over three hundred disappeared. Brittain directs the sequence excellently, far exceeding other Triangle films dramatizing the same event.

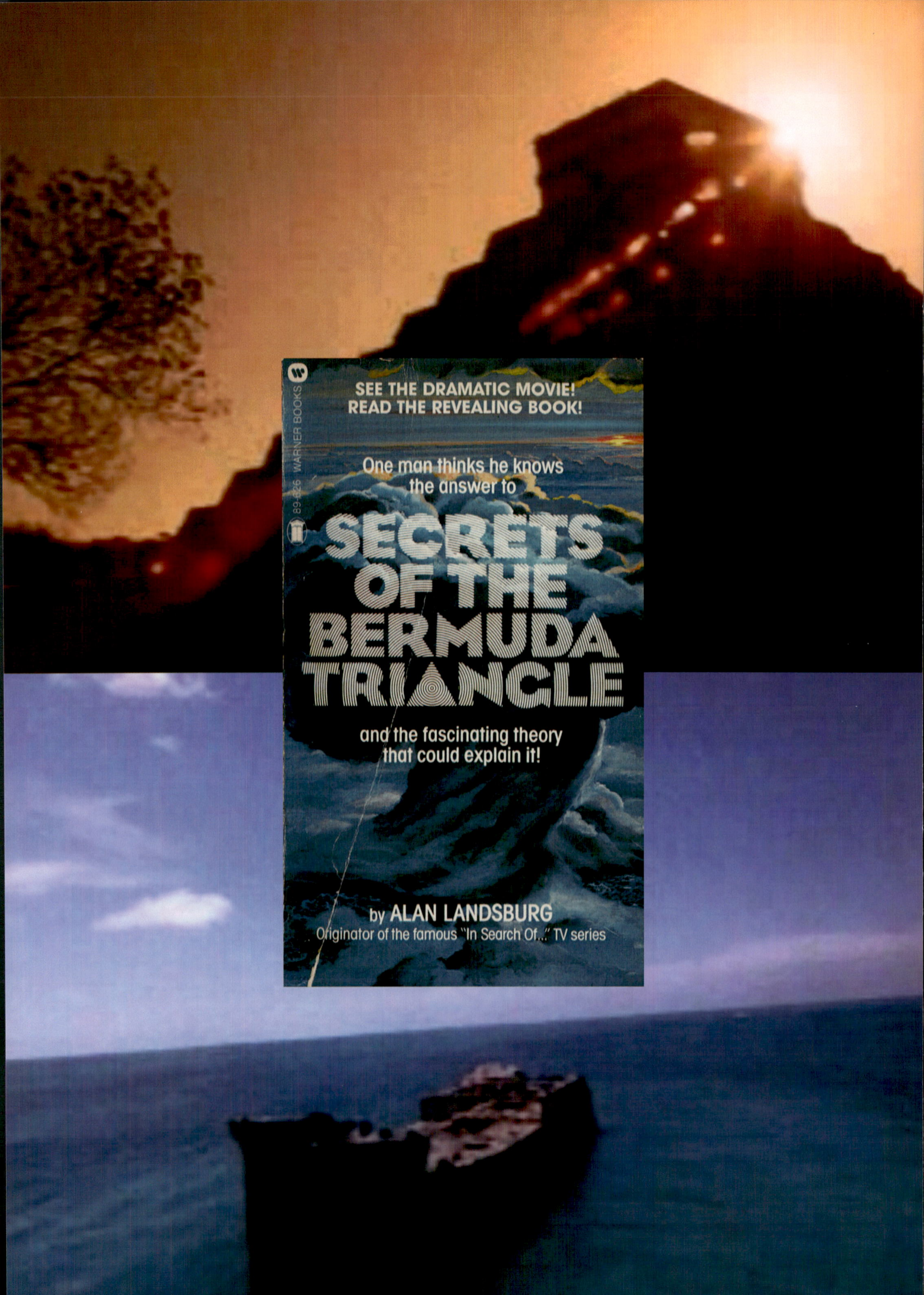
WARNER BOOKS
SEE THE DRAMATIC MOVIE!
READ THE REVEALING BOOK!
One man thinks he knows the answer to
SECRETS OF THE BERMUDA TRIANGLE
and the fascinating theory that could explain it!
by ALAN LANDSBURG
Originator of the famous "In Search Of..." TV series

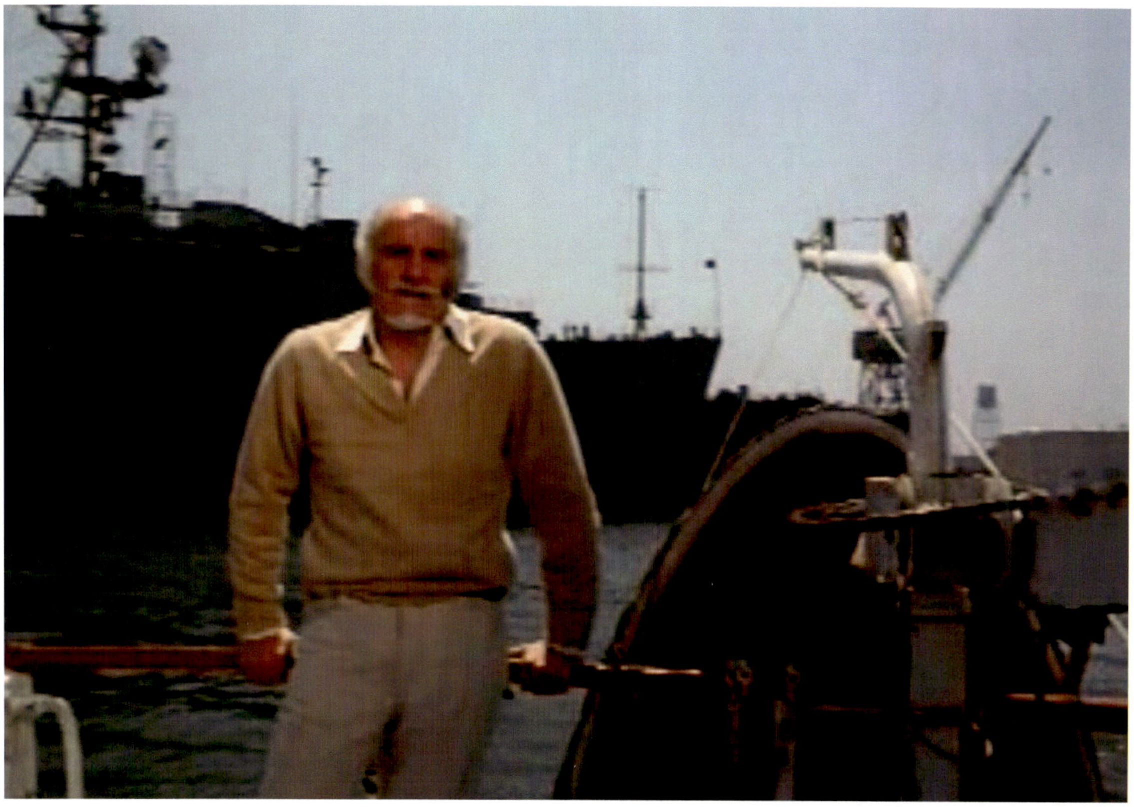

What does all of this mean? At times, it feels as if we are adrift in shallow Weirdumentary waters, including when Tompkins pronounces some tales as being the work of "liars, fools, and charlatans." But never fear, true believers. This triangle does not go square on us.

Tompkins asks if these events might be proof of UFOs, which have "plucked" the missing vessels into "outer or inner space" in order to guinea-pig them.

A radio show takes a caller who claims the Triangle is the "aura" of planet Earth, a "timeless void" that allows the "Millionth Council" to communicate with us, or at least with those who disappear. Tests of the caller's voice prove he's not a prankster. He's telling the truth, as I'm sure the Millionth Council will testify.

We also get a lengthy "ghost story" about lead coffins in a crypt that repeatedly rearranged themselves. It has nothing to do with the Triangle, save for electromagnetism being the potential cause of the strange events in both places. After all, Tompkins has studied electromagnetism at the Cheops pyramid in Egypt, and knows well of what he speaks.

The explanations culminate with Edgar Cayce's belief that Atlantis would be rediscovered in the 1960s. The infamous Bimini wall in the Triangle is apparent proof of its existence. "Here may lie the secrets of the Triangle," Tompkins suggests, "even the secrets of existence." And now you know the rest of the story.

Though it bears a copyright date of 1977, *Secrets of the Bermuda Triangle* didn't appear in theaters until 1978. Warner Bros. distributed the film, and Warner Books published Landsburg's tie-in tome of the same name. Such was the synergy of dark energy. ▲

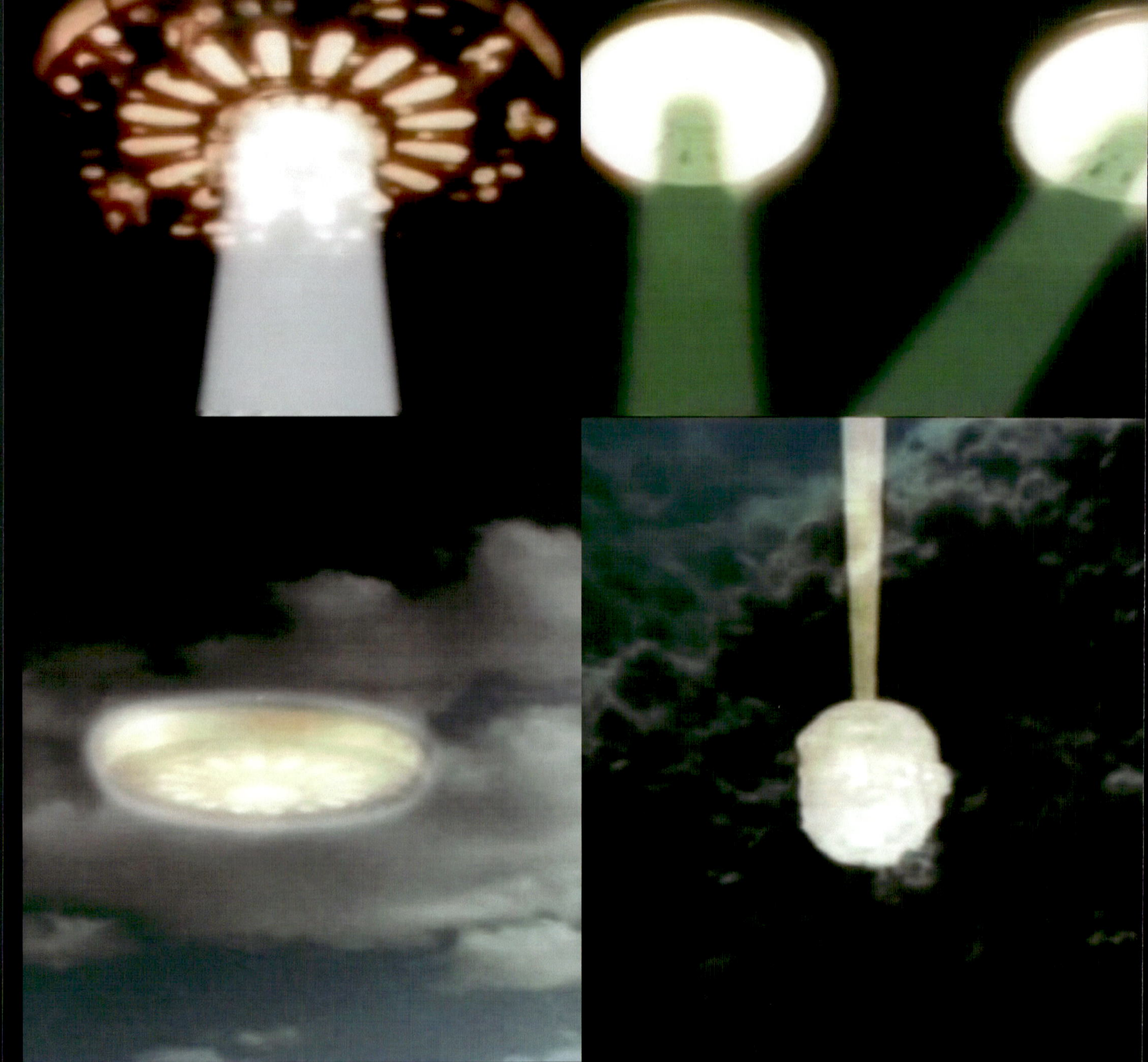

Charles Berlitz's The Bermuda Triangle

(1979)

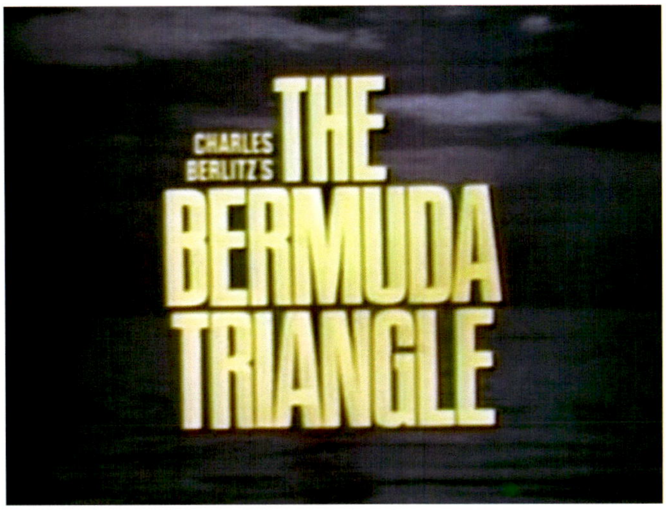

Paradoxes abound in the Weirdumentary universe. Being last can sometimes mean being first.

Charles Berlitz's The Bermuda Triangle was the final Weirdumentary on the subject to hit theaters, but it was certainly the best of them, or at least the most fun.

A dark night in 1492: Columbus is off the coast of Bimini, his crew alarmed by the appearance of bright lights in the sky. We realize what the great explorer could not: the lights are flying saucers, soaring over their beloved Triangle.

Years before helming *A River Runs Through It* (1992), director Richard Friedenberg pushes us into those deep waters immediately, not even waiting for the opening credits to roll.

Enter our on-screen host, the great Brad Crandall. He informs us that the film is based on Berlitz's book, plus a "staggering file of verified incidents, official records, and new evidence never before available. ... Much of the dialogue is word-for-word, as taken from flight recorders, and the testimony of some of the people who were actually involved." (And from those who weren't involved, too, it seems. The closing credits give thanks to *The National Enquirer*.)

Recreations come fast and furious, the longest being a seventeen-minute dramatization of six military planes that went missing in 1945. It's well-directed, and does bring to life one of the most bizarre Triangle stories. But some of the other re-enactments are more entertaining, including one about a small boat's towline that leads into oblivion.

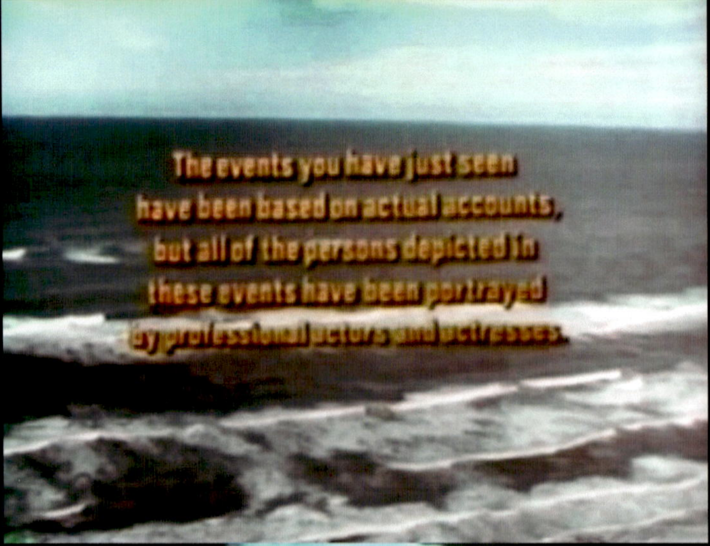
The events you have just seen
have been based on actual accounts,
but all of the persons depicted in
these events have been portrayed
by professional actors and actresses.

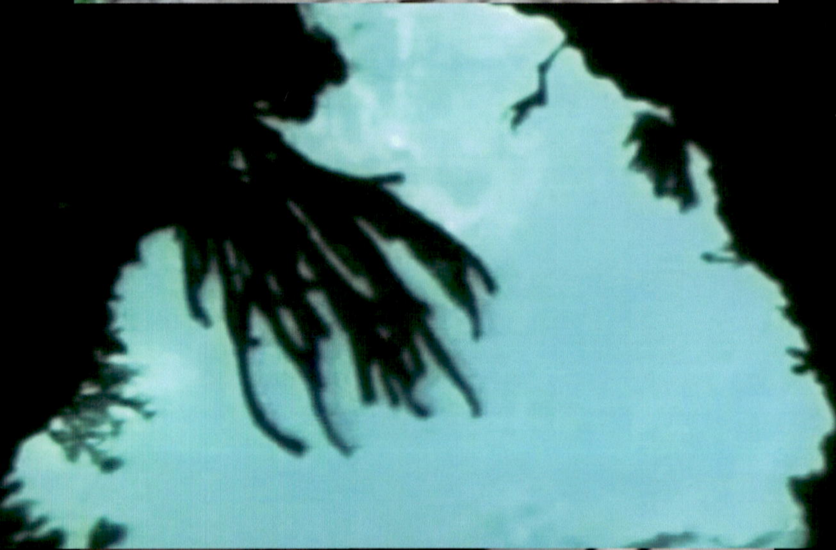

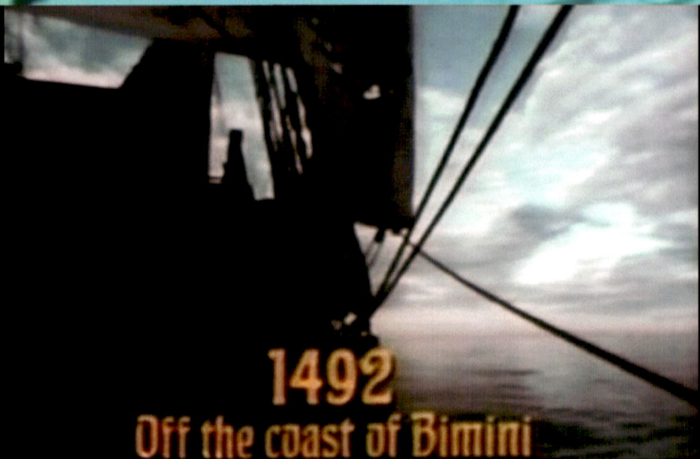
1492
Off the coast of Bimini

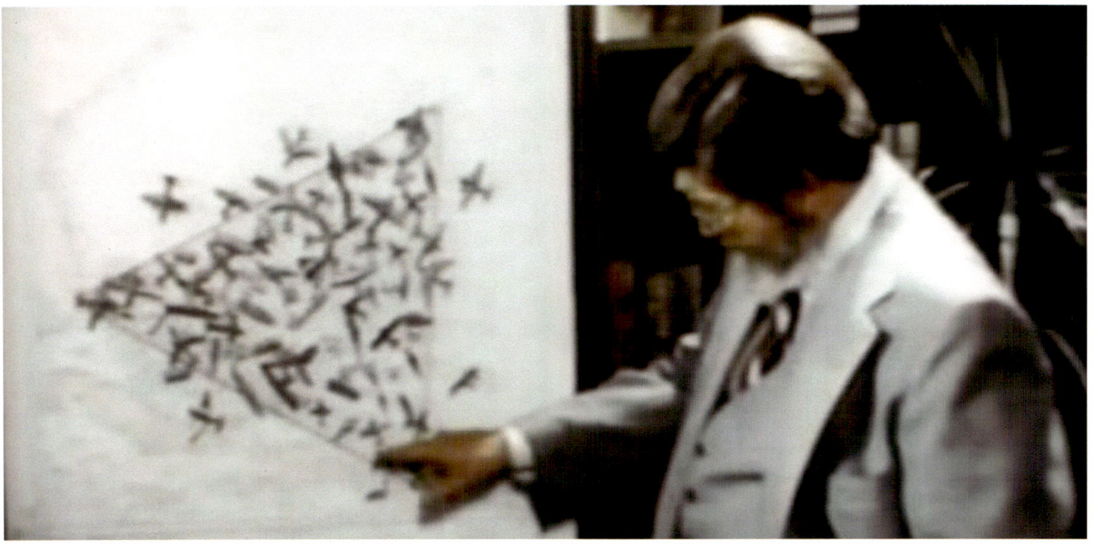

Better yet is the discussion of Plato and the Egyptians and Edgar Cayce. All of them agreed that Atlantis crumbled into the sea some 12,000 years ago. The Atlanteans had great knowledge, but were buried after a "sudden calamity." The cause? A "force crystal," a prism-like device that looked like a satellite dish mounted atop a pyramid. It "harnessed the awesome power of the stars," but brought eventual doom to Atlantis. And perhaps it's still active, shooting up rays that show no mercy, be ye man, woman, or child.

Or maybe instead the Triangle is an anti-gravity tunnel, a vortex visible only as a whirlpool that causes ships to dissolve away into "another dimension," or at least to the cutting room floor. Or maybe it's E.T., given the sheer number of UFO sightings at the Triangle and also, of course, Doug Hubbard's excellent special effects. (Hubbard would go on to work on the likes of *Weird Science* in 1985, *Starship Troopers* in 1998, *Magnolia* in 1999, and *Bruce Almighty* in 2003.) Whatever the precise cause, Brad Crandall explains, "Somewhere out here, something or someone is swallowing up ships and planes and people, at the rate of one ship or plane a month."

For those popcorn-holders among us, *Charles Berlitz's Bermuda Triangle* is one of the highlights of the Weirdumentary era. Here we bask in the warm rays of the Sunn.

Are there limitations? Sure. Henning Schellerup's cinematography has nothing on the camerawork in *Secrets of the Bermuda Triangle* (1978). And budget limitations force us to sit through an abundance of stock footage.

The *Los Angeles Times* argued *Charles Berlitz's Bermuda Triangle* was "unimaginatively conceived." *Variety* moaned it was "so bad it's beyond criticism." But I dare say that neither of the critics in question ever wrote anything half so wondrous as the following words that Crandall speaks: "Has some highly intelligent aquatic race found its way up from the depths of the ocean? Is the Triangle a base of sorts for aliens from outer space? Is lost Atlantis below these waters, and just who or what is collecting human specimens?"

At the end of the film, while we see footage of the United Nations, Crandall warns us, "Together the nations of the world must find the answers before it's too late. Our very survival may well depend on knowing what is going on here in the Bermuda Triangle."

And so to anyone who doesn't dig this flick, I retort: "Yo-ho-ho and a bottle of dumb." ▲

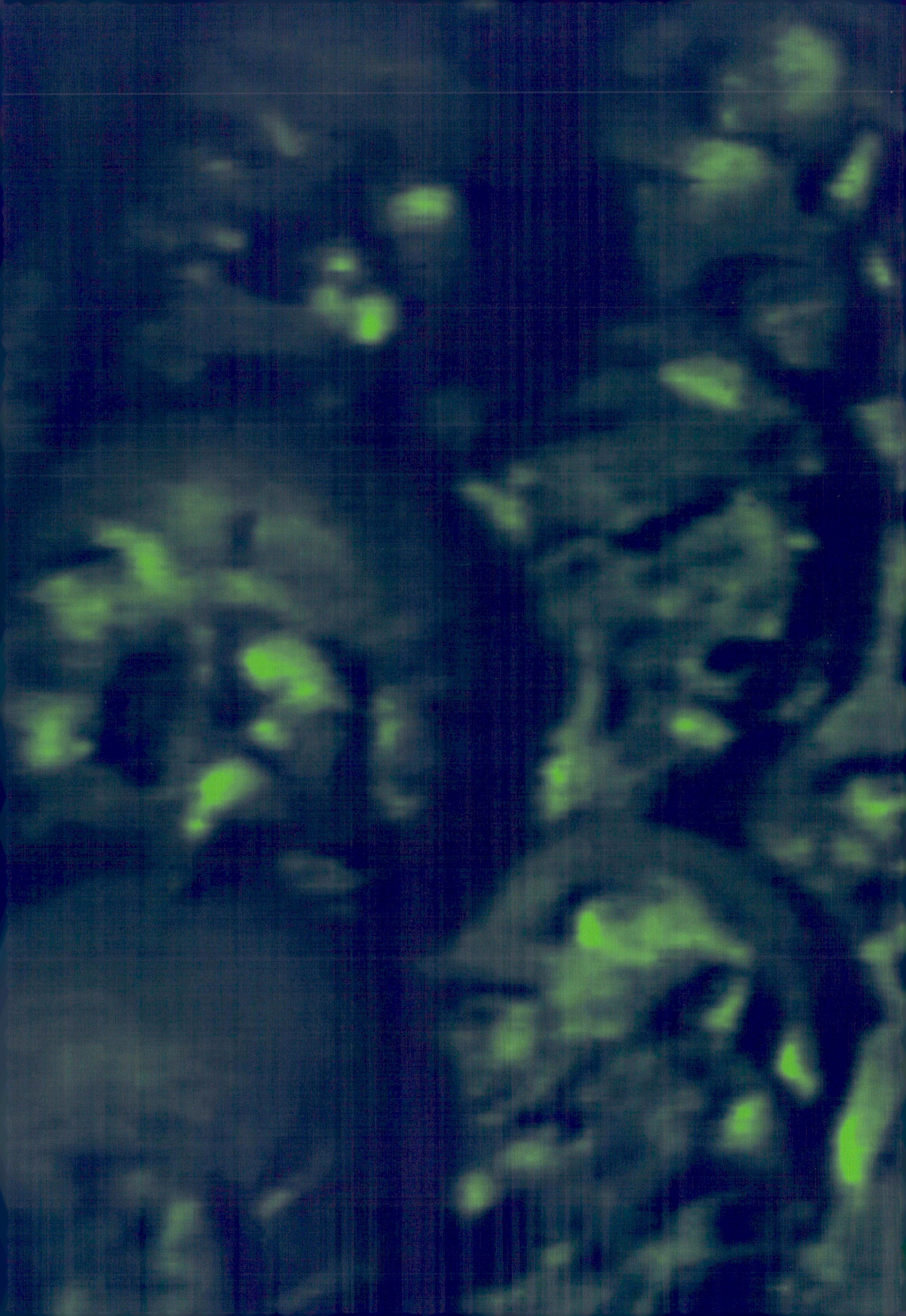

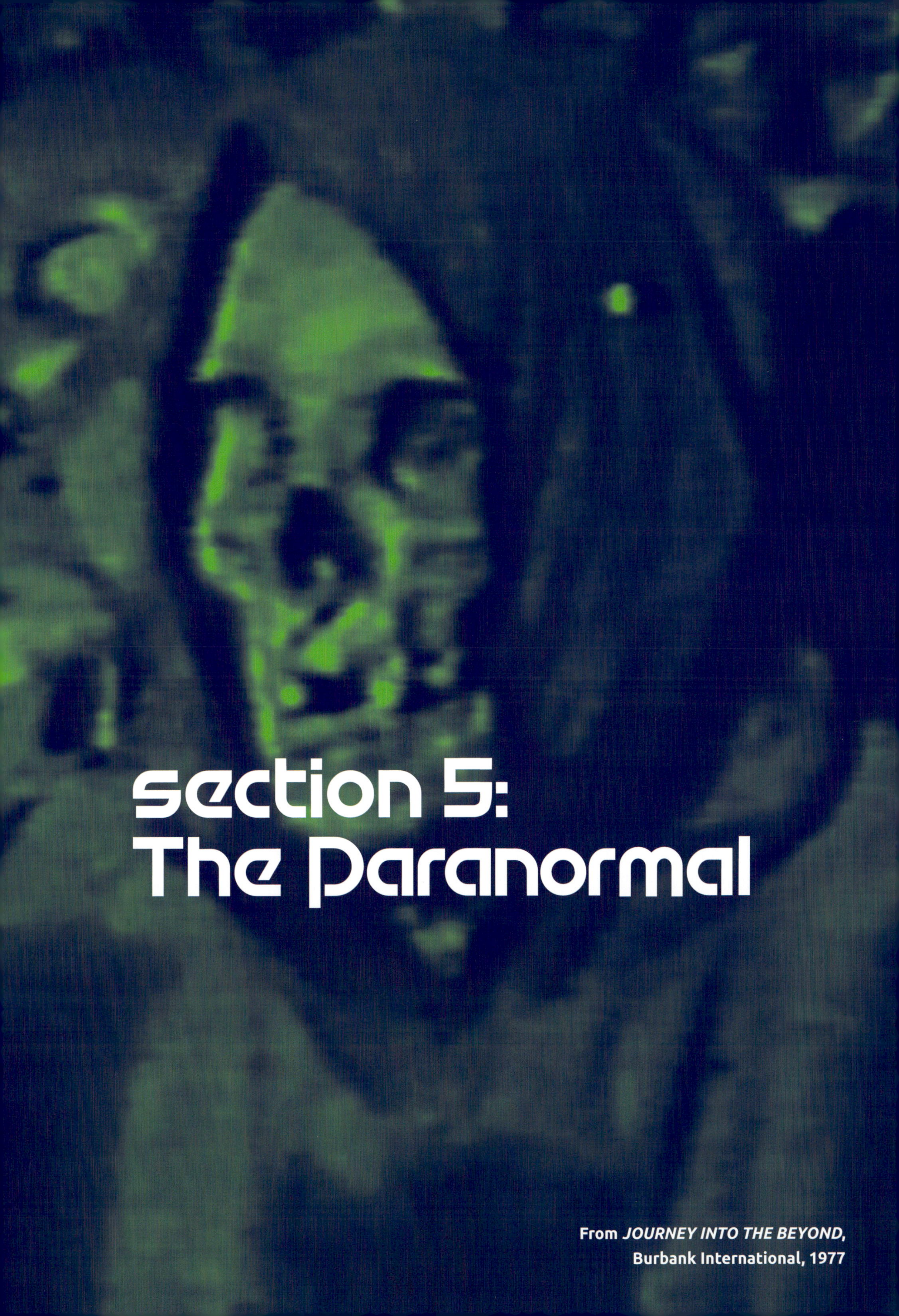

section 5: The Paranormal

From *JOURNEY INTO THE BEYOND*, Burbank International, 1977

The Legendary Curse of the Hope Diamond

(1975)

Exactly why the Smithsonian Institution became involved with this film is hard to understand. Yes, the Hope Diamond is housed at the Smithsonian Museum of Natural History, which means no, it is not housed at the Smithsonian Museum of Unnatural History.

And unnatural history is what we get in this hour-long, made-for-TV Weirdumentary. A newspaper article explained:

> *Waving the august imprimatur of the institution, this is a dramatization based on a book by Evelyn Walsh McLean, who acquired the famous stone in 1912 and then proceeded to stumble through a life of personal tragedies, including the untimely deaths of her two children and the mental deterioration of her alcoholic husband.*

Diamonds are a girl's best fiend, it would appear, so do please talk to us, Harry Winston, and tell us all about it. Give us the low-down on the down-low.

Evelyn, played by Samantha Eggar, finally had to take the cursed gem to a priest, who performed an exorcism on all facets of it. (Evelyn doesn't vomit pea soup, nor does the diamond.)

Flashbacks from Evelyn's problems take us on a dark ride through the history of the "French Blue," as the stone was known. It seems that possibly, maybe, perhaps, the 44.5-carat diamond once weighed an impressive 68 or even 112.5 carats, and—more impressively—it was "torn from the eye of a Hindu god in India in the seventeenth century." (Forget Harry Winston. Wilkie Collins needs to tell us all about it.)

From there, actor Robert Clary pops up, not from a *Hogan's Heroes* hole in the ground,

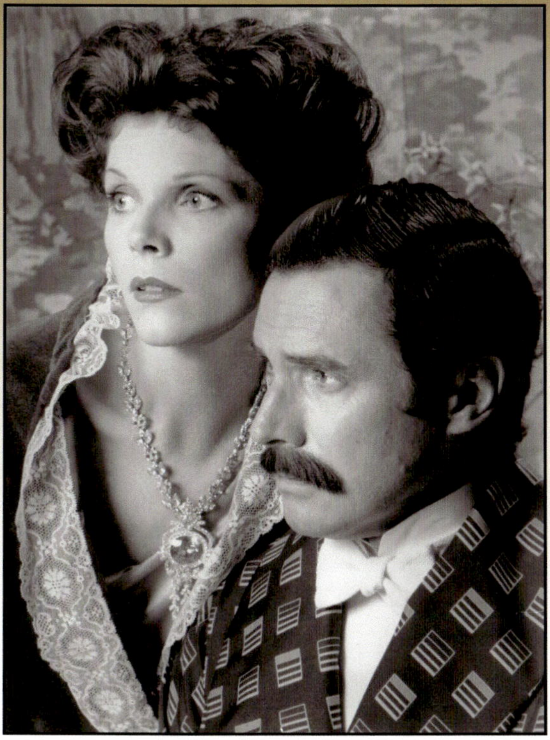 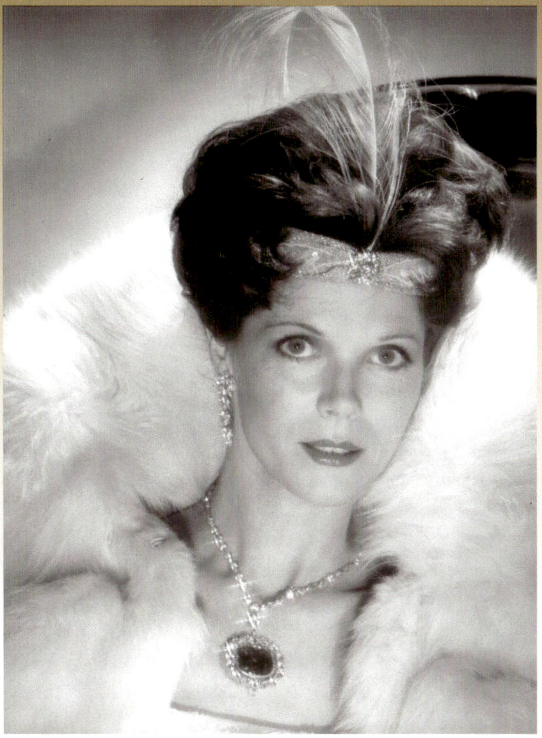

but in the royal garb of Louis XVI, opposite Claudine Longet's Marie Antoinette. The two women who wore it after Marie dropped dead inside of a year.

Let them eat cake, all of those who touched the unholiest of stones, including President Warren G. Harding, who drank from a teapot dome while eating his slice.

Delbert Mann—who helmed many a television movie—directed this Wolper Productions flick, which is largely comprised of recreations, along with some choice narration by—yes, you guessed it—Rod Serling.

After all the blood and thunder, the death and lightning, the dramatizations finally give way to experts. One review explained:

> *At the end of the hour, a couple of Smithsonian officials appear in an attempt to bring a touch of scientific rationality to the proceedings. The 'legendary curse' is treated as little more than an interesting myth. The gem is merely a magnificent example of man's instinct for collecting. At this point, though, science and reason have been completely overwhelmed by the titillating demand of schlock entertainment.*

That, even though S. Dillon Ripley, longtime secretary of the Smithsonian, appeared in an epilogue to announce, "Contrary to the myth of the so-called curse, we regard it as a stroke of very good luck that the Hope Diamond is here, and that it belongs with priceless treasures to the American people."

You see, we can rest assured that the Hope Diamond curse hasn't bothered anyone in many years. Neither has this film.

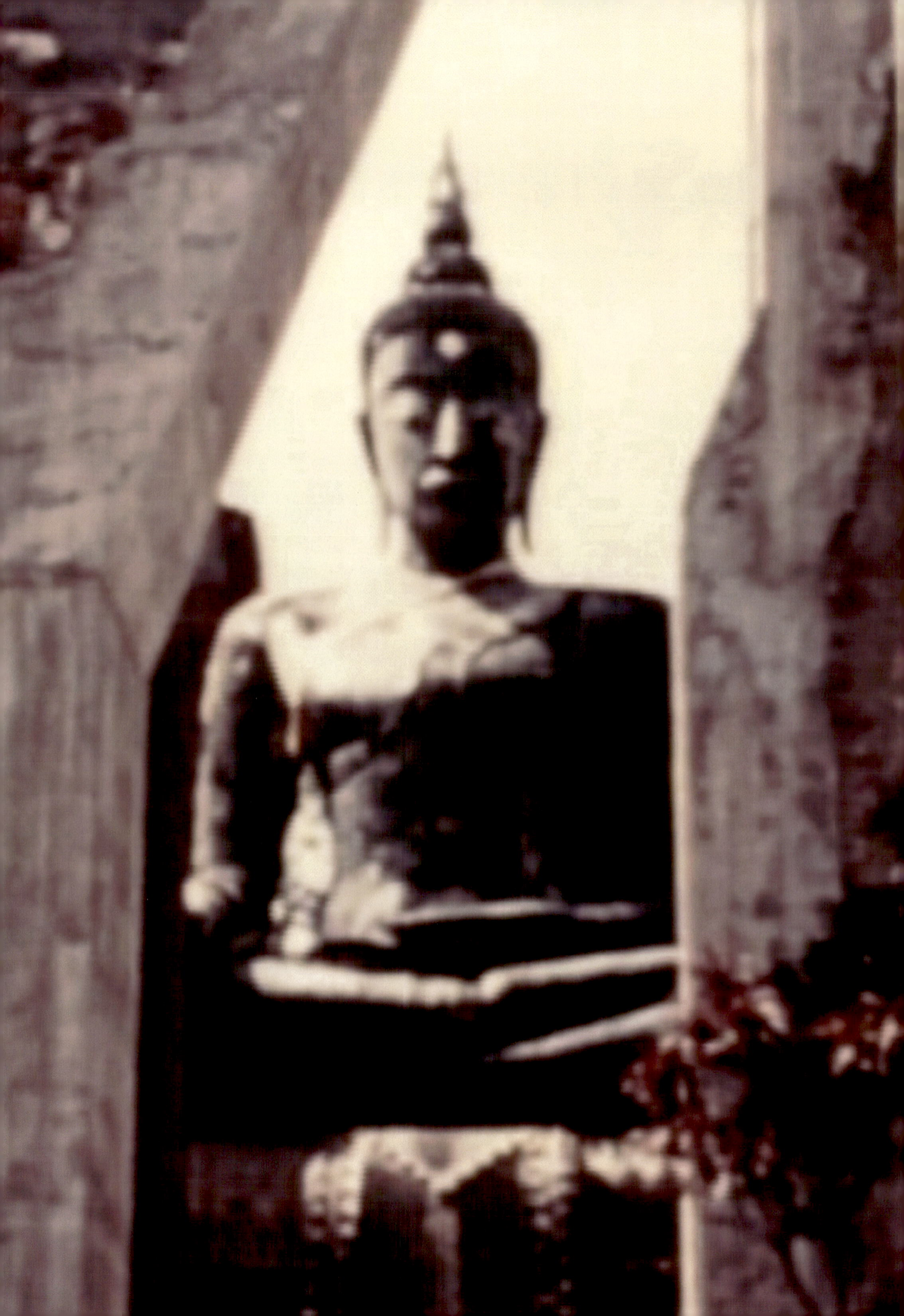

The Man of Miracles

(1975)

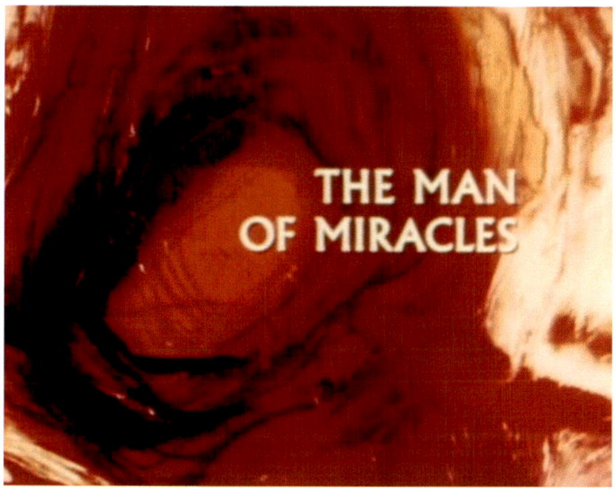

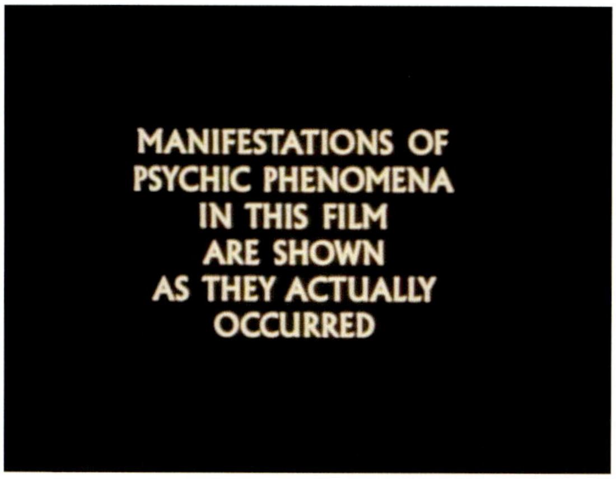

"Manifestations of psychic phenomena in this film are shown as they actually occurred." That's what we read on screen. Then we hear Rod Serling's unmistakable voice while seeing the close-up of a man's palm.

"You are about to witness the apparently spontaneous manifestation of amrita, a nectar said by those who've tasted to be unique in all the world for its exquisite taste and aroma. The origin of amrita is mysterious. Those most familiar with it compare it to the legendary 'nectar of the gods' and claim that it is materialized from another dimension. This peculiar phenomenon is only a very ordinary one among those attributed to a man believed by his followers to possess extraordinary psychic powers, an Indian mystic and guru self-named Sathya Sai Baba."

Two small pendants are held in the palm we see. Sure enough, a bit of liquid emerges from them. From *under* them, rolling downwards, probably because the palm is at an angle. Only drops, droplets really, hardly enough nectar for one god, let alone a number of them.

So begins producer/director Don Como's Weirdumentary, which concentrates on the parapsychological powers of one man.

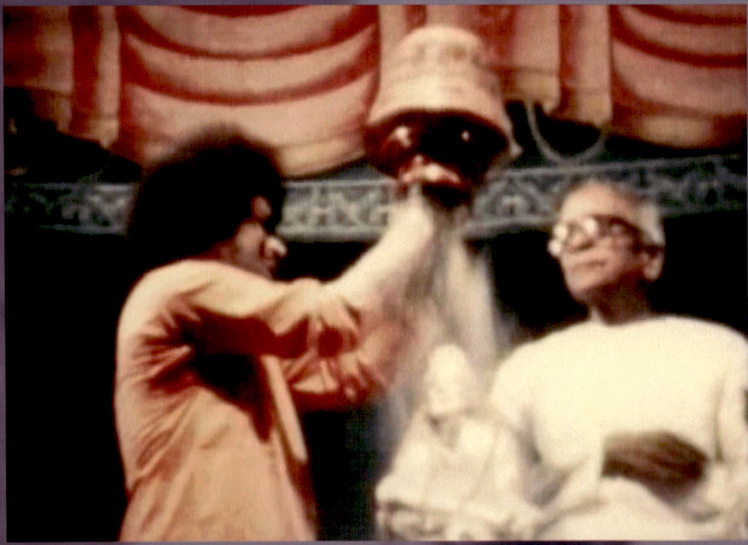
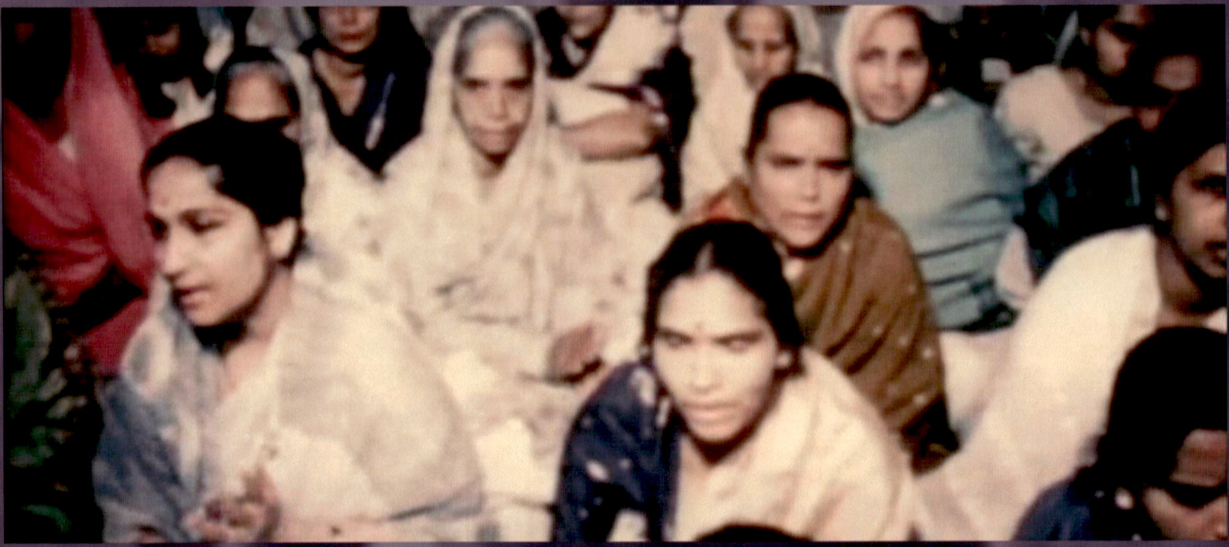
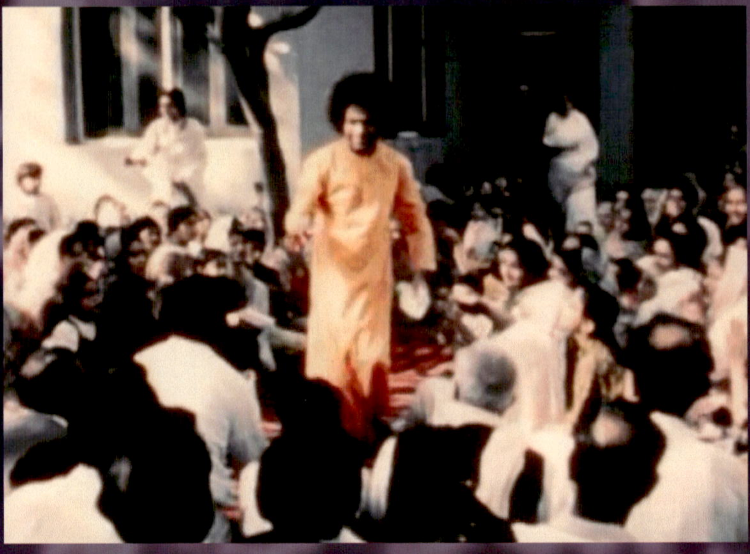

"What you are about to see are occurrences which may be unacceptable to you in the context of our rational conception of a reality framed by mathematical logic and physical laws. Try to keep an open mind, however, for some of the feats of this man of mystery have been captured on film, and you will see them now, actually happening."

Serling next tells us about the history of Hindus and Hinduism. Such context explains how Baba reaches "beyond the veil," from reading minds and curing diseases to predicting the future and materializing objects out of "thin air." He can project his astral body, "adopt other human and animal forms," and "in some cases ... bring one back from the dead." (In *some* cases, hmmm, yes, I see.)

Baba's belief system suggested that everything is God, or part of God. He just gets to be a bit more a part of it than the rest of us, at least insofar as performing "supernormal" miracles.

Evidence of his abilities includes a shot of him dumping sand (or something like it) from a pot on top of a statuette. Allegedly it shows the manifestation of someone or something.

Anyhow, it turns out that Baba's powers became apparent at age thirteen, possibly after he was stung by a scorpion, or more likely from being reincarnated, or possibly being the reincarnation of a scorpion. Soon he was able to manifest sugared candy from nowhere. Thus the Man of Miracles, because, like the song says, "the Candy Man can."

Baba's followers grew in number to the point that he established an ashram where they could visit him or even live on the grounds. But maybe not run cameras very often, because we don't see footage that looks particularly miraculous.

In fairness, Baba does draw a picture in the sand and then pulls a three-dimensional object from it, all in glorious semi-darkness. He also seems to manifest a necklace, which I'm certain was not hidden up one of his long sleeves. (Give me David Copperfield—the magician or the Charles Dickens character—any day of the week.)

The most unique thing about this film isn't Sathya Sai Baba, who ended life with a laundry list of fraud, sexual abuse, and other charges long enough to keep a chain of laundries busy. (Baba didn't opt to bring himself back to life, apparently.)

Instead, the fascinating thing is that this Weirdumentary focuses on a single individual. That was rare, and curious enough to make me wonder why there weren't more films focusing on the likes of, say, Jeane L. Dixon or Uri Geller.

Then again, I suppose there really can be too much of a good thing.

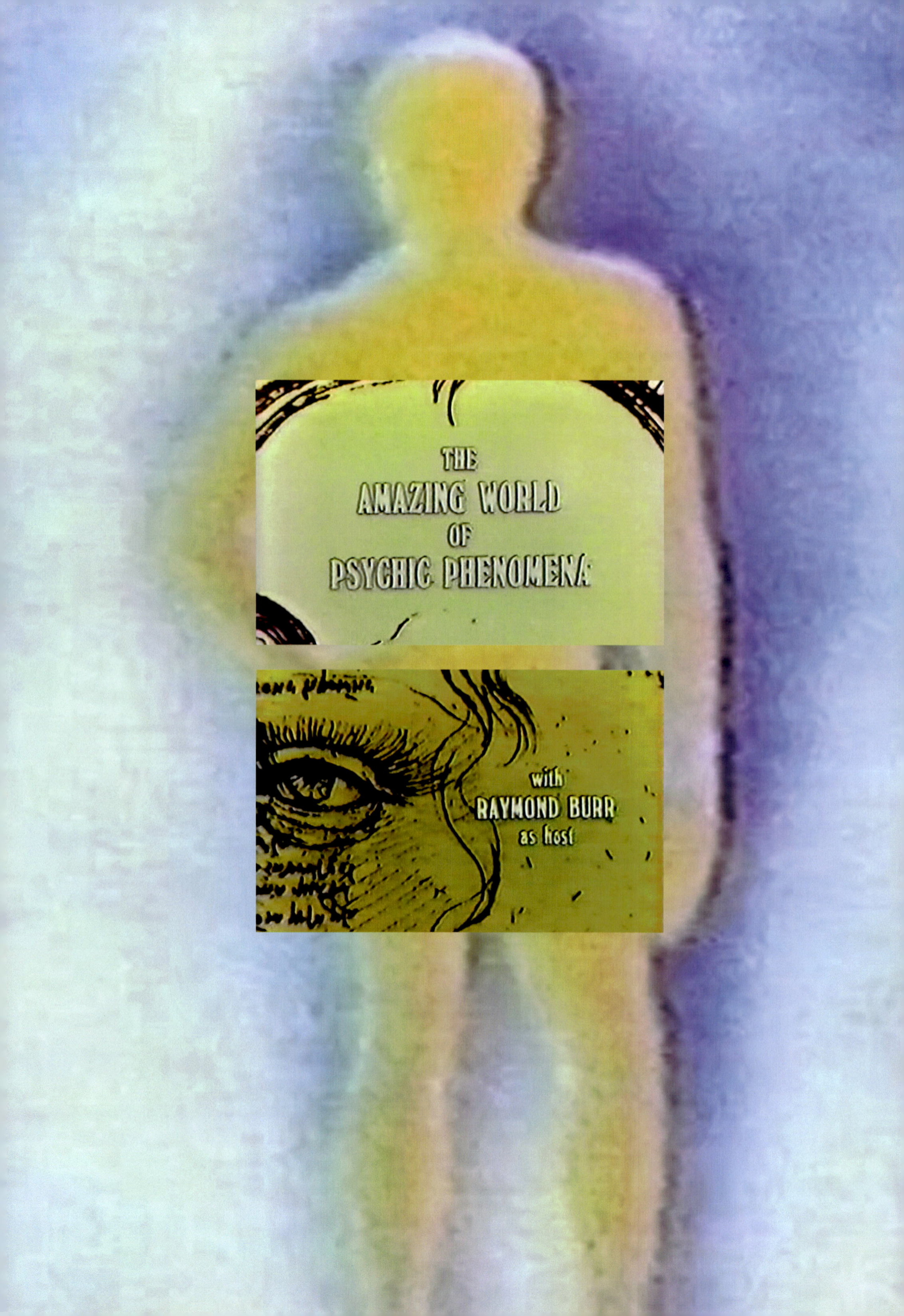
THE
AMAZING WORLD
OF
PSYCHIC PHENOMENA
with
RAYMOND BURR
as host

The Amazing World of Psychic Phenomena

(1976)

Here is a film about psychic powers and related mysteries that range from ghosts to reincarnation. On-camera host Raymond Burr explains, "We've heard about these things, and some have been skeptical ... skeptical but tantalized, intrigued by the possibilities. In this motion picture, we're going to examine these possibilities. Our camera teams have traveled around the world collecting the evidence. Great effort has been made to scrutinize this evidence, to assure authenticity. We're going to examine, firsthand, if these phenomena are fact or fiction."

Thank goodness for the trustworthy star of TV's *Perry Mason* and *Ironside*. He and the team have vetted everything to the extent that the second scene immediately jumps into the "evidence," meaning an actor portraying Nostradamus, the prophet who very definitely predicted Hitler and the atomic bomb.

The producer was Charles E. Sellier, Jr. The writer and director was Robert Guenette. He had been a news producer during the Vietnam War, a documentary filmmaker who had embraced the cinéma vérité style, and an innovator in docudramas thanks to such programs as *Appointment with Destiny* (1971–73). A perfect guy for the Weirdumentary multiverse.

The Amazing World of Psychic Phenomena offers a steady diet of experts who "seemingly point to one conclusion, that telepathy does exist." Thanks to these "reputable scientists," Burr goes so far as to say, "We've proven, partly at least, that we all have such powers."

If you don't trust the scholars, trust the practitioners. We meet those who control these powers. Old footage of faith healer Kathryn Kuhlman, thought-ographer Ted Serios, psychokinetic Nina Kulagina, and spoon-bender Uri Geller add age if not weight to on-screen interviews with the likes of psychics Peter Hurkos and Jeane Dixon (the woman who later gave sage advice to Nancy Reagan). Medium Dorothy Vallas performs a séance for the cameras. And then there's Jerry Turmell, who "has proven that he can successfully use [telekinesis] sixty percent of the time," by making dice roll his number on average "more than double that of chance."

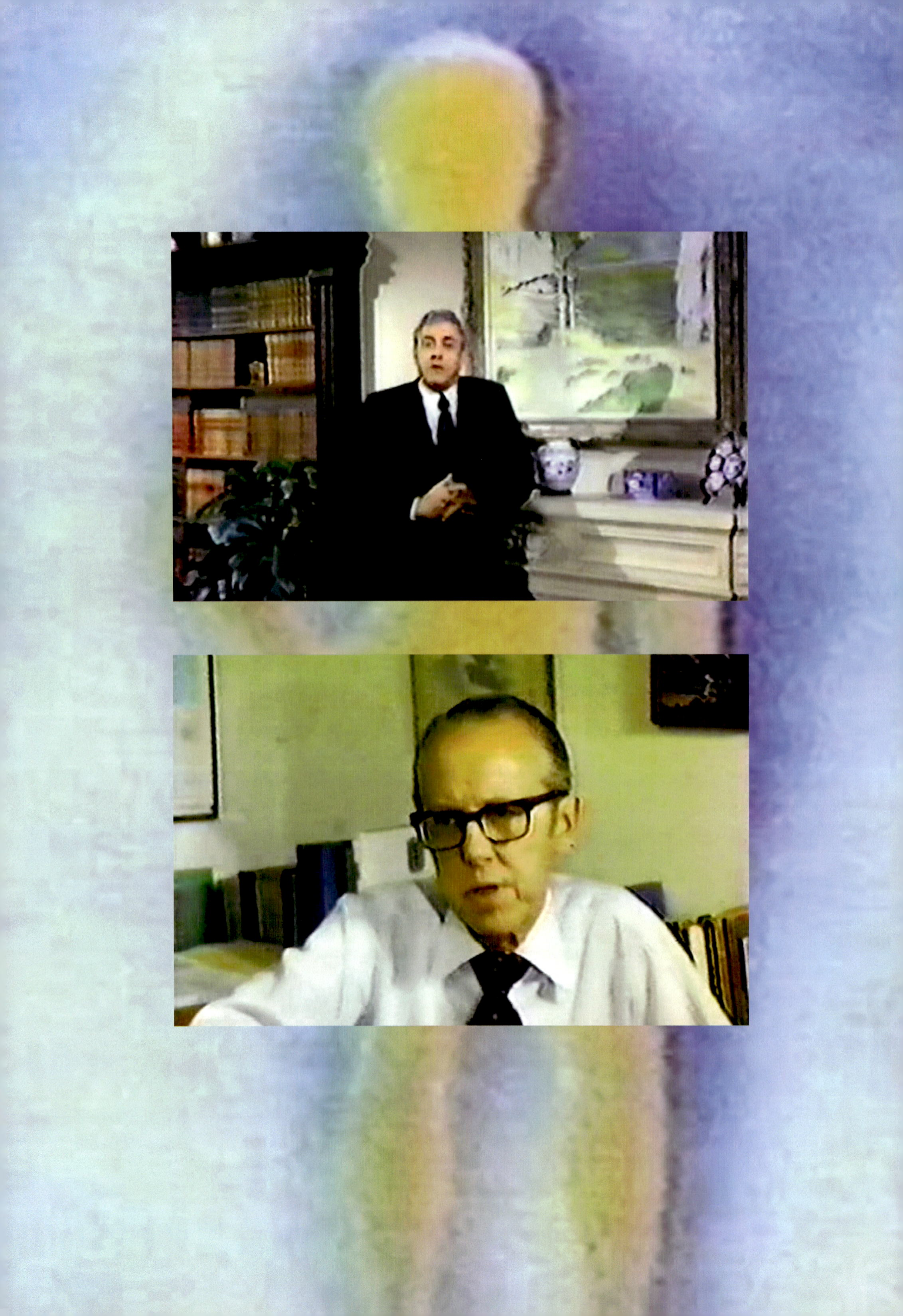

If you don't trust the practitioners, then place your bets on the recreations. Abraham Lincoln, Mark Twain, Harry Houdini, and the great psychic Edgar Cayce all appear thanks to Guenette's cast, and all of them upstaged, incidentally, by other actors playing unknown characters. Linda Gray, still two years away from becoming famous as Sue Ellen Ewing on *Dallas*, portrays a housewife who unintentionally causes objects to fly around her house.

And Kiss Me, Fate if that isn't Kathryn Grayson playing an unnamed psychic detective who helps the police solve a crime, to the extent that she not only finds a murderer, but also knocks a gun out of his hand. You go, girl.

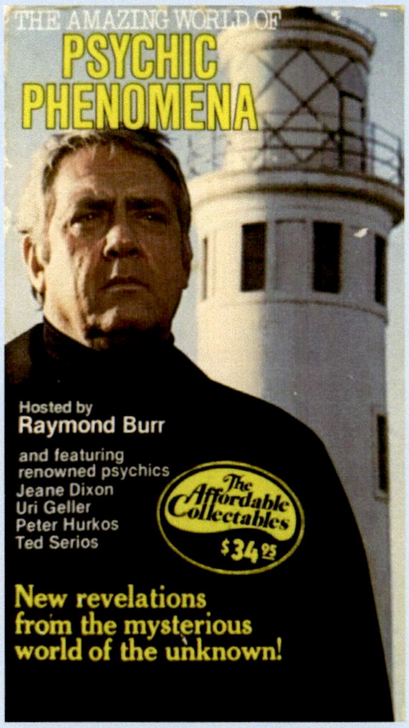

Equally surprising to see is Olan Soule, the ubiquitous character actor of the 1960s, perhaps best remembered for playing the choir director on *The Andy Griffith Show*. He appeared in everything from prune juice commercials to *Perry Mason*. And here? Well, here is Roger Doyle, so Burr tells us. Except the credits claim he is Roger Hawkins. Either way, he has lived many previous lives, all thanks to reincarnation. Roger, that is, not Olan, but it's hard to tell, really, given Guenette's wonderful ability to move from real people being interviewed to fakes without revealing which is which.

The film is at its best when it invites audience participation. Along with Raymond Burr, we get to take part in a psychic test, making choices between cards, race cars, fish, and women. Which is the *correct* one? The on-screen doctor knows, but with just a little effort, we can focus our mind to determine the answer. Burr scores 3 out of 5, not bad, but of course the odds are either 50-50 or 1 in 3, more the stuff of Las Vegas than psychic breakthroughs.

The MPAA granted *The Amazing World of Psychic Phenomena* a G rating in June 1976. At the time of its completion, Guenette-Asselin Productions ran a full-page ad in *Daily Variety*, proudly announcing that, in its first five months, the company had produced a television drama and a feature film (meaning *The Amazing World*). They had also acquired a "major book, set an international co-production deal on a second feature, and put into development scores of projects." We wait with breath that was bated and baited.

In mid-July 1976, KBSC launched a weekly series hosted by Damien Simpson called *Psychic Phenomena: The World Beyond*. The following month, Vancouver Film Production announced plans to produce a half-hour series called *The Unexpected* for broadcasters in Canada and the U.S. Its topic? "True stories of psychic and spiritual phenomena."

But Guenette's film bested them all. The Film Advisory Board gave *The Amazing World* an Award of Excellence at the end of 1976. Amazing, indeed.

Or not, maybe. As Burr concludes the film, "We are energy and we are forever." Long live Robert Guenette!

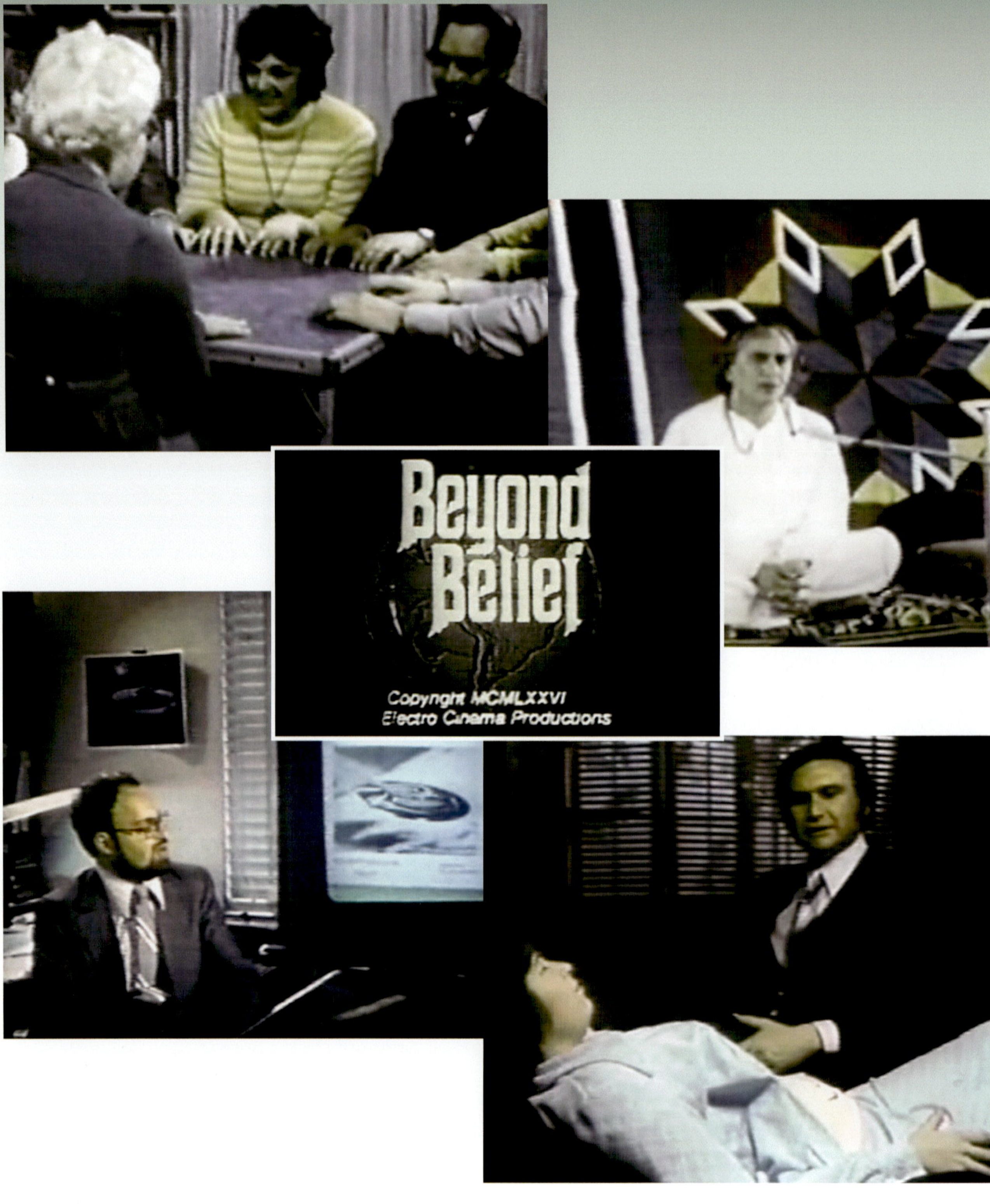
Beyond
Belief
Copyright MCMLXXVI
Electro Cinema Productions

Beyond Belief

(1976)

"Everything that your eyes will witness in this film is real. Nothing has been staged. There are no actors, only real people." Except of course for the man speaking these words, actor Richard Mathews, who plays the on-camera host, sans the Office of Knowledge.

An Electro Cinema Production, *Beyond Belief* was co-produced and directed by Alan Baker. It chronicles "ghosts, ESP, psychokinesis, [and] faith healing," placing it squarely onto the terra firma of *The Amazing World of Psychic Phenomena*. Squarely, indeed.

Does yogurt have emotions? This question is actually addressed, then everything begins to cinematically melt.

What isn't present is the classic Sunn Classic formula, with all of its fervent and fevered dramatizations. At best, we get Mathews inviting us to undertake a psychic examination not unlike the one Guenette had us take with Raymond Burr. Then a hypnotist causes a woman to regress through a dark tunnel into an earlier life, Bridey Murphy-style. After that, a parapsychologist works with a test group of ordinary people and—in the film's most wonderfully imprecise language—"proves the powers that *may* lie within us all."

That's all in addition to dream telepathy, poltergeists, automatic writing, and psychokinetic metal bending.

At some point, perhaps when it began appearing on TV in 1978, *Beyond Belief* was expanded to include extraterrestrials and UFOs, but with a different narrator, and with mediocre special effects that gives lie to the promise all that we see is "real." (This version concludes with credits that name Charles E. Sellier, Jr. as producer and George Gale as director.) The abrupt transition to the new footage is perhaps the most exciting moment in the film.

At its worst, *Beyond Belief* offers interviews with sincere persons and dedicated scholars who are exceedingly boring, despite their tales of wonder. The worst of these is Stanton T. Friedman, who literally presents a dull slide show on-camera. We can only pray that momma will take his Kodachrome away.

"What you have just seen is part of an astounding collection of psychic phenomena, demonstrations of the powers of the mind." Maybe, but somehow, I have my doubts.

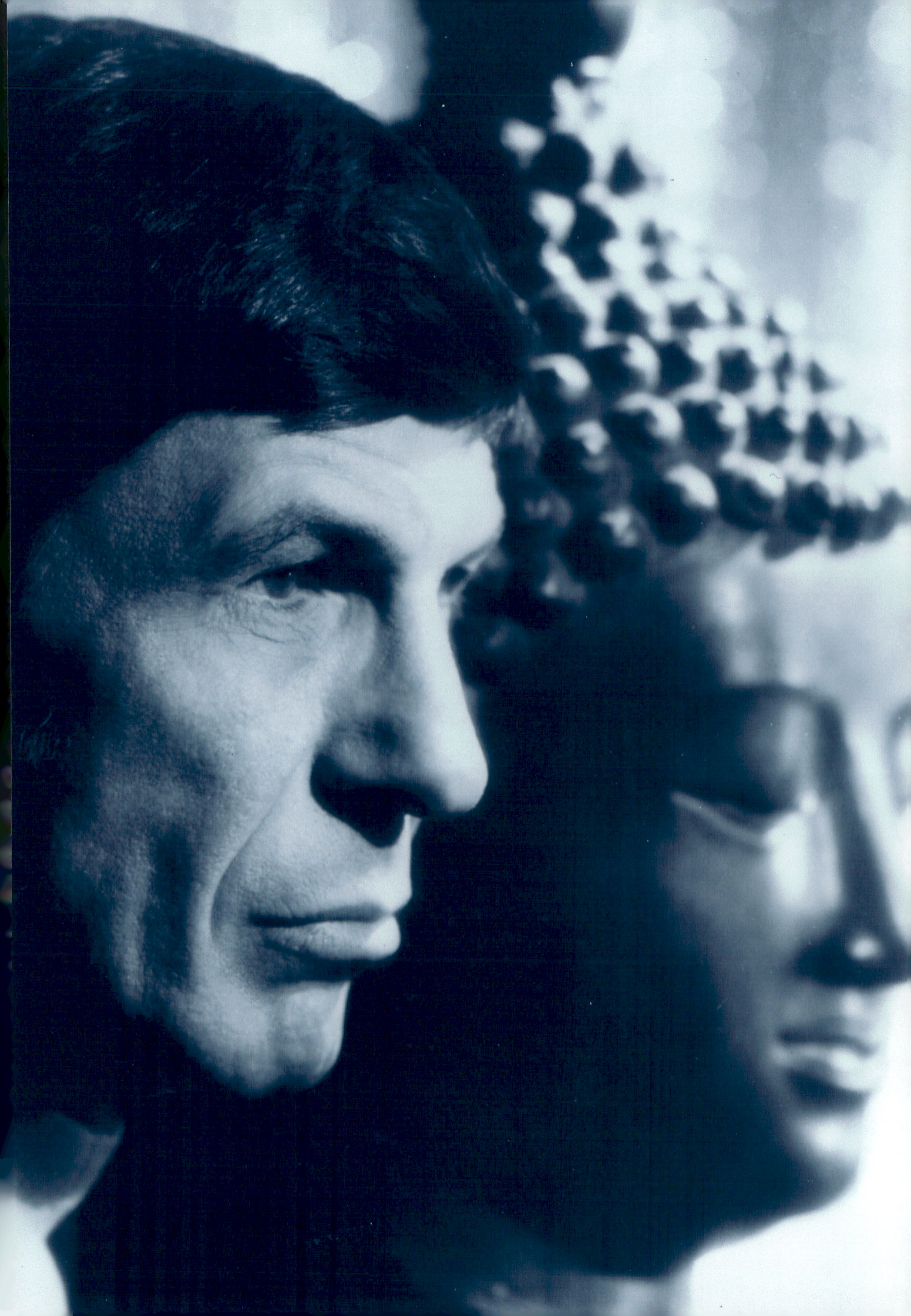

In Search Of... The Paranormal

(1976-1982)

On August 29, 1979, *Variety* announced, "Bristol-Myers and Alan Landsburg Productions will do a fourth year of the syndicated barter series *I Search of...* with Leonard Nimoy returning as host." It would boldly go where it had thrice gone before.

And for that I'm eternally grateful. As I am for Nimoy's unexpected moustache, which he sports in Seasons 4 and 5. How very un-Vulcanlike, and thus—from my perspective—how very weird.

I am also grateful for Casey Kasem, the great American disc jockey. He wasn't weird, though the cartoon character he famously voiced—Shaggy on *Scooby Doo*—got caught up a lot of weird situations. (Shaggy also ate Scooby snacks, which may or may not have been dog food.)

Anyhow, I bring up Casey Kasem because he famously counted down the Top 40 songs each week on the radio during the Weirdumentary era (and even after it, for that matter).

That's what I get to do now, offering up the top paranormal episodes of *In Search of...* There's less than twenty-five of them, and they fall into the basic categories of psychic phenomena, curses, supernatural powers, life after death and reincarnation, and—of course—ghosts. Let the countdown begin!

Season 1, Episode 11, *Psychic Detectives*: "He touches an object belonging to a victim of a crime. He claims that suddenly he is transported beyond time and space. A crime is re-enacted before his eyes. He says he is reliving a moment in the past, in a place he's never seen before with people he does not know."

Peter Hurkos is the person in question, helping to solve murders by providing important keys to the Keystone Kops. Hurkos also appeared in *The Amazing World of Psychic Phenomena* (1976, see entry) and *The Mysterious Monsters* (1976, see entry).

As for ESP, Nimoy explains, "Scientists acknowledge that it exists, but don't understand how it works."

There was good reason to title this episode in the plural, as we see several psychics at work. One of them is a "licensed private detective." (Whereas I am an unlicensed private skeptic.)

Nimoy concludes that, in the future, psychic detectives might play a larger and larger role in policework. ESP "may become a deterrent to anyone contemplating a criminal act."

Season 1, Episode 13, *Learning ESP*: "There are newer, more sophisticated ways of testing ESP, tests that seem to confirm some ability in people beyond what is considered to be the normal range. Investigators are beginning to find ways to perfect those abilities. ESP is real, they believe, and it can be taught to almost anyone who is willing to learn."

Here is a rare episode. Usually Nimoy speaks on-camera or off, but in both cases by himself. This time we see him sitting around a table with a group of fourth graders, testing their ESP powers.

The results? Not particularly instructive or conclusive. (None of them even ask Nimoy for an autograph.)

From there, we learn that some ancient peoples could use ESP, but they "turned their minds against each other. Hopefully we will not be so foolish."

Season 3, Episode 15, *Animal E.S.P.*: "Throughout history, man has felt a unique kinship with animals. The special relationship between pet and master may be based upon an unexpected link. Only recently has science begun to investigate the possibility of a psychic, extrasensory connection."

Dogs sometimes find their former masters by traveling hundreds of miles. "There is no explanation other than ESP." (So don't even go thinking of other possibilities.)

Pet owners concentrate on given images; do their pets understand what they're thinking or share their emotions? (Red Rover, Red Rover, send your intimate thoughts right over.)

Proof is "difficult" to find, alas, though one woman allegedly has out-of-body experiences and visits her distressed cat to calm it down. It seems to work, time and again. "We don't know what that means," an expert admits. (Neither do I.)

But maybe, just maybe, the secret life of pets includes paranormal activity and supernormal abilities.

Season 3, Episode 17, *Psychic Sea Hunt*: "Twenty-six miles off the coast of southern California lies the island of Santa Catalina. A unique team of psychics and scientists has gathered here. Aided by the world's most advanced, deep ocean technology, they will attempt history's first experiment in undersea psychic archaeology."

Finding things below sea level is difficult and dangerous. "Man was not made to recover history underwater," Nimoy explains.

"Perhaps the answer lies not with machines, but within ourselves. Can some strange and as yet unexplained psychic ability help us to see that which is concealed from ordinary vision?" Put another way, maybe psychic predictions can direct explorers to specific locations way down in the depths.

This awesome episode unfolds before our eyes, with cameras capturing the progress of the Catalina expedition while it was underway.

Season 2, Episode 3, *Firewalkers*: "Around the world, a bizarre ritual persists. Man knowingly and willingly matches himself against the flames. Practiced in diverse cultures, embodied in several religions, the mysterious and ancient custom of firewalking has intrigued observers for hundreds of years. Two puzzling questions remain unanswered through the centuries. How did the custom originate, and what protects the firewalkers from being hurt?"

A third puzzling question: did the script writer intend for the word "matches" in the fiery text above to be a joke?

Whatever the case, we see one "perilous walk" after another, bare feet on hot coals. Some get burned; some do not. "Although some skeptics may claim there's a trick involved, a more convincing argument comes from experts investigating the powers of the mind."

Nimoy is at his best in this episode, sitting in the dark, surrounded by candles, offering us a "radical new explanation": the historic cultures that practiced firewalking were located in volcanic zones.

(There's more than one hot foot joke here, but I'll leave them to the pranksters and fetishists.)

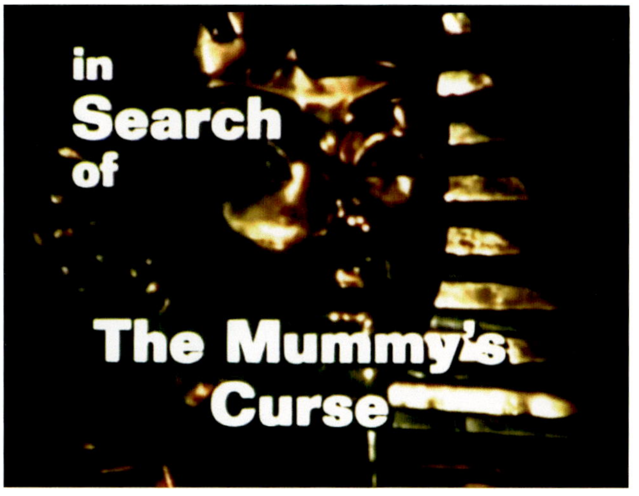

Season 1, Episode 8, *The Mummy's Curse*: Is there really a curse on King Tutankhamen's tomb, "working its evil way after nearly 4,000 years?"

Howard Carter's discovery of King Tut's tomb in 1922 remains one of the greatest archaeological finds of all time. Along with the valuable gold, there was Tut's mummified body, as well as a tablet that bore the following warning: "Death will slay with his wings whoever disturbs the rest of the Pharaoh."

Lord Carnarvon bankrolled the expedition, and his son appears on-camera, one of this episode's highlights.

The real story here is the unreal story of the curse, and the twenty-two deaths associated with it. But as Nimoy observes, Carter himself lived out "a long and happy life."

Season 3, Episode 20, *The Diamond Curse*: "Throughout the ages, diamonds have inspired poets and smugglers, gentlemen and thieves. The diamond is the most precious of all gems, and maybe the most dangerous to possess, for many diamonds are said to carry a curse."

Nimoy's describes how "mysterious powers" have long been attributed to diamonds, from warding off disease to casting unbreakable spells. But they have also been responsible for tragedy after tragedy.

The Hope Diamond occupies the bulk of the story. As so often the case, the historical recreations we get range from the good to the bad to the ugly.

Nevertheless, *In Search of...* once again proves that less is more. This episode is dramatically more engaging than *The Legendary Curse of the Hope Diamond* (1975, see entry).

Season 1, Episode 22, *Voodoo*: "The ceremony mingles the demons of humanity's oldest fears with elements of a young religion. The result is a faith filled with the spirits of good and evil and tinged with magic. For priest and practitioner alike, the cares of the real world disappear in the ecstasy of celebration. They transport themselves into a domain rich in legend, dark curses, and mystery."

This is also a "world haunted by the specter of the zombie." Because, you see, "this is voodoo."

Voodoo in Haiti was a popular proto-weird topic on-screen, including in Walter Futter's *Curiosities* (1930, see entry). And it's back again, in a fascinating array of new footage shot on location.

Voodoo, we learn, "holds the key to good fortune and good health," as well as curses and death. (To Voodoo, or Voo-don't?)

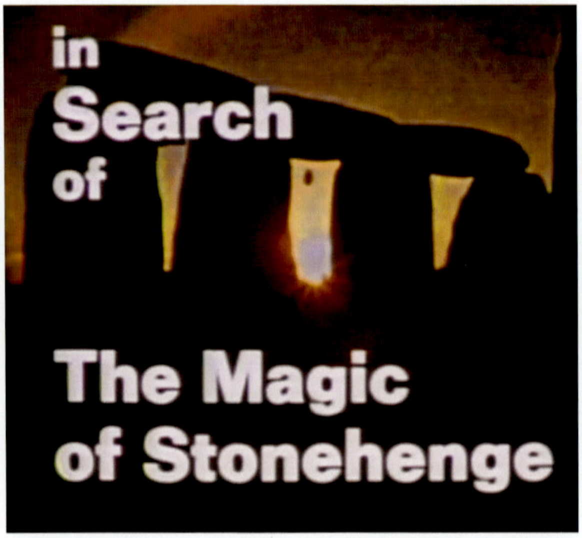

At ceremonies, "the drums will speak, and the spirits will enter the sanctuary." Rare footage here of actual ceremonies. A possession takes place at one of them, making this one of the best episodes. If you go in search of *In Search of...*, be sure to find it, particularly this episode.

Season 2, Episode 19, *Witch Doctors*: "With the magic powers believed to dwell inside cloud of smoke, a Mayan healer performs an ancient cure. The rising smoke will lift away the patient's evil spirits ... To us, this kind of medicine may seem primitive and strange, for it is the work of people we call witch doctors."

The Mayan healer is just one of many indigenous doctors we meet from around the world. "Though ancient forms of healing may appear bizarre, they are often successful, even today."

In Search of... could definitely be ethnocentric, but this episode is surprisingly respectful to its subjects, to the extent that it explains that Europeans wrongly applied the term "witch doctor" to cultures they didn't understand. (Thus phrases like "Ting, tang, walla walla bing bang" remain thankfully and mercifully unheard.)

Season 5, Episode 2, *Faith Healing*: "Faith healing is a part of modern life. Are the cures it claims to accomplish real? ... Between religion and medicine, the laying on of hands remains a subject of intense controversy."

Now we come to a topic that producer/director Don Como covered in more than one of his Weirdumentary features. First Nimoy gives us an overview of faith healing through the ages, including voodoo in Haiti.

Then we meet the likes of Aimee Semple McPherson, Kathryn Kuhlman, and Morris Cerullo, the latter appearing in extensive interview footage.

Some faith healers are charlatans. Others might spur humans into a mind-over-body triumph. At least one expert argues that's the case.

My research tells me that Nimoy wears a brown shirt with a sporty white sports coat, which looks almost like a lab coat. Hip threads by any standards, and certainly those of the seventies.

Season 1, Episode 24, *The Magic of Stonehenge*: "A complex machine stood in the middle of no place. ... a strange power still seems to linger over the stones. It beckons some men to worship, others to search for the magic of Stonehenge."

Such an enigmatic structure, such an unknown origin: it's difficult to understand why Stonehenge didn't loom larger during the Weirdumentary era than it did. But that's what makes this episode welcome.

And it's even more exciting because we learn that Stonehenge and other unique stones in Great Britain might be magical. One expert tells us that "a certain kind of power existed in them and was known to the people at that time."

"How were the stones [for Stonehenge] moved?" Supernatural powers, perhaps, or maybe just lots of blood, sweat, and fears.

"Time has no limits," Nimoy explains. But *In Search of...* did. About twenty-two minutes per episode, *The Magic of Stonehenge* being among the most enjoyable.

Season 5, Episode 13, *Salem Witches*: "The woman calls herself a witch. She claims to be performing an ancient ceremony of candle magic. The power of the planets has been petitioned, and as the paper burns, a spell is cast. This rite of witchcraft is being practiced in Salem, Massachusetts, a place where people believed to be witches were once put to death."

Salem, 1692: Such a sad and tragic story, so much so that clichéd phrases like "sad and tragic" don't seem strong enough. There were no witches. None.

By the fifth season of *In Search of...*, that had changed. "Witchcraft now thrives in Salem." Nimoy introduces us to the "city's official witch." She explains that witches aren't what people think, meaning old hags that cavort with the devil.

We also get an official tour of the official witches' store, full of tourists and local coven members.

Ancient rites guide the initiation of a new witch. Nimoy shows us what happens at the rarely filmed ceremony. One witch has a hand extended with fingers arranged quite similar to the Vulcan salute. (The needs of many witches outweigh the needs of the few, or the one.)

So, do these modern witches have powers? At least enough that I watched this episode four times.

Season 1, Episode 19, *Life After Death*: Code Blue, an emergency call used at the hospital. A patient has died. "A resuscitation attempt will be made. If it is successful, the patient is brought back to life. In some cases, they have amazing stories to tell about what it is like on the other side."

This episode features the important disclaimer, "Some of the hospital sequences in this program are recreations of real events." Most recreations in the series never get such identification.

What is death? What is the exact moment of death? What is it like to die? Fascinating questions all, but then there's more, much more. Tales beyond the veils, with souls detached, freed from their bodies, "overcome with peace and tranquility." Bright lights and big heavenly cities.

"Is there life after death?" Nimoy asks. Maybe death "is not an ending, but a beginning." That's what he tells us at the ending of this episode.

Season 5, Episode 5, *Life After Life*: I shall now ask, is there life after *Life After Death*? The answer is yes, of course, because this episode from Season 5 takes us back to an episode from Season 1, with a cooler, more enigmatic title. Upbeat too, for the normally downbeat topic of death.

Tommy, a Vietnam War veteran, gives us an emotional account of his near-death experience. Here is one of the most compelling stories in all of *In Search of...*'s six seasons.

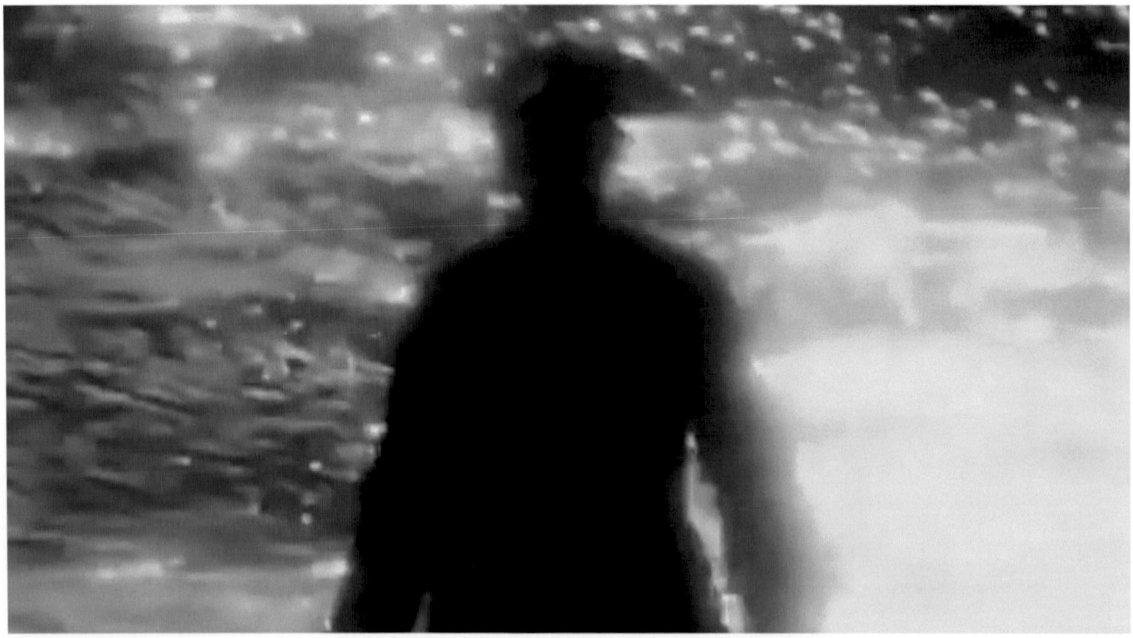

He experienced "pure peace" until waking up in a military hospital eleven days later. "Was Tommy indeed dead? How can we explain his profound and mysterious experience?"

Some slow-motion ghostly figures beckon someone during a near-death experience. The recreation, while brief, is worthy of mention. It's simple, but wonderfully effective.

Out-of-body experiences are intriguing. But perhaps *In Search of...* experienced an out-of-topic experience. That might explain two episodes on the same subject.

Season 2, Episode 11, *Reincarnation*: "There are people who claim to remember events that happened in a former lifetime."

One modern woman remembers being a little girl named Maria in another life. Maria could cure others, but the townspeople tried to burn her as a witch. The woman recalls Maria's terror, and the fact that Maria jumped off a cliff rather than go up in flames.

We meet a clinical psychologist who acts as a guide for research subjects who undergo hypnotic regression and then "float" backwards. Over the span of five years, she has "regressed more than 2,000 persons in her search for scientifically valid data on the reincarnation experience." (By my count, that works out to regressing more than one person a day.)

Some subjects offer up little more than fantasies. Others present compelling stories. For example, a retired stockbroker writes in Egyptian hieroglyphics while under hypnosis.

"How many pasts can a person have?" Nimoy asks. (If there's a limit, he doesn't tell us. All I know is that I only get three when playing Pac-Man.)

Season 4, Episode 24, *Past Lives*: "How do we explain the feeling when we know we've been somewhere before? Is this feeling coincidence, or is it possible that we have lived past lives?"

Perhaps we have even lived past episodes, as Nimoy once again covers the subject of reincarnation. The stories here are similar, as are the skills used to obtain them, specifically hypnotic regression.

One of the women believes she's the reincarnation of a king. (I believe I'm the reincarnation of someone who didn't have to watch two episodes on the very same topic.)

Season 1, Episode 18, *Ghosts*: "A sudden draft from a window that was supposed to have been closed. A chill at the back of the neck. Groans, creaks, and bumps in the night. Man has always been frightened by the dark, troubled by noises just beyond the reach of lights, occurrences just beyond the reach of understanding."

We don't meet ghostbusters, but we are introduced to ghosthunters, among them the famed parapsychologist Hans Holzer, who authored dozens of books on supernatural topics. (I'm confident that he ain't 'fraid of no ghosts.)

Eyewitnesses are witnesses with eyes, and eyeball they do, strange things, mostly ghostly, sometimes evil, sometimes not. But thankfully Holzer can sometimes put the restless spirits to rest. (Give up the ghost, they finally do.)

Season 2, Episode 20, *Haunted Castles*: "Strange apparitions haunt the countryside of England. Spirits, it is said, lurk in the meadows which once rang with the sound of life. There are those who swear that the dead have risen. Some hear the sounds of ghostly horses, hurdling up the stone stairs of a castle. Others bear witness to the cries of an African prince outraged because he was buried on English soil. The ancient ghosts of England, it would seem, are the scariest spirits of all."

Dramatizations in this episode range from one of the best in the history of the series (a ghostly figure in eighteenth-century garb who emerges from the shimmering waters of the lake where he drowned) to one of the worst (an actor with ridiculous red-and-white face makeup meant to look *s-p-o-o-k-y*).

The episode ends more humorously than most, showing us a skull while we hear a not-so-serious scream. (Those who are hungry should take that corn and pop it.)

Season 3, Episode 21, *Ghostly Stakeout*: "Ghosthunters believe they can communicate with spirits of the dead. They believe they can transcend the barriers of space and time, and see into the past, and actually make contact with the ghost of a tormented person, and relive the trauma of some long-forgotten tragedy. Can a ghost be set free to move on to another world?"

It is a joy that *In Search of...* attended a séance, and not just any séance, but one attempting to exorcise an old house of a malevolent presence. The film footage shows something, but whether it's supernormal or just plain normal, we don't know.

Sylvia Browne is among the psychics who appear. Time and again, she famously made incorrect predictions. (The Amazing Randi repeatedly proved just how unamazing Browne was.)

In the end, the stakeouts strike out, not capturing a ghost, but that doesn't prevent us viewers from having a lot of fun.

Season 4, Episode 3, *The Amityville Horror*: "A recent motion picture has mystified and frightened thousands of moviegoers. Most people think *The Amityville Horror* [1979] is a good scary ghost story. What is not commonly known is that the film is actually based on fact. It's a true story. Was there an evil presence living inside this house?"

Let's just review the last two sentences that Nimoy read, because they bring into sharp relief the lay of the Weirdumentary Land: At first pronounce a bizarre tale to be true, but then immediately proceed to question it.

Combining actual photos and footage with clips from *The Amityville Horror* and *In*

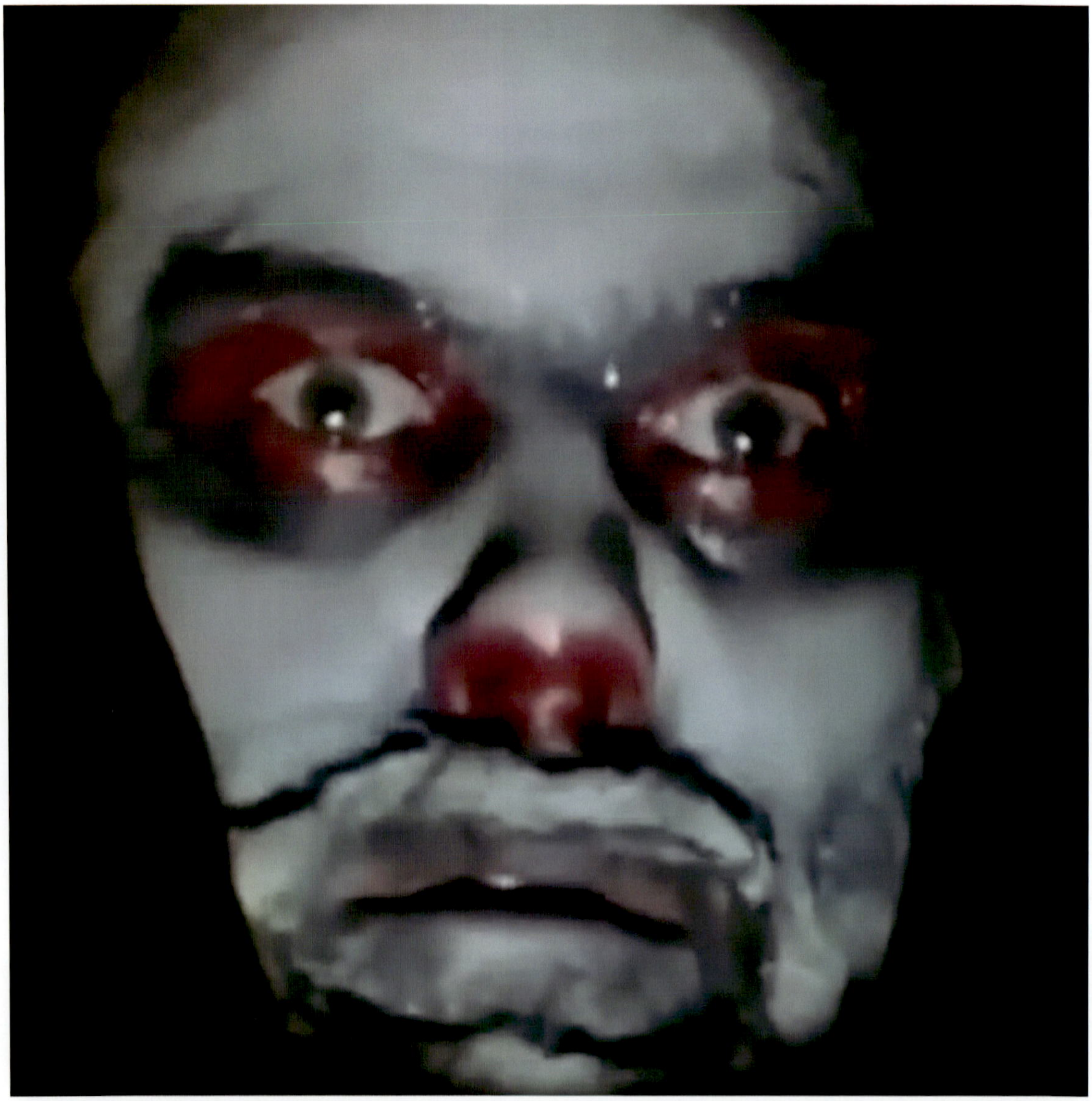

Search of...'s own recreations, this is a dark ride into an even darker house. Among the interviewees are Ed Warren, still famous thanks to being portrayed by Patrick Wilson in *The Conjuring* universe.

At the time, this now-old episode was extremely topical, coming right on the heels of the Hollywood film's release. (As Rodgers and Hammerstein wrote, "Everything's up-to-date in Evil City; they've gone about as vile as they can go.")

Nimoy even gives his on-camera narration from the real Amityville house. Five stars and two ghostly thumbs up.

Season 4, Episode 18, *The Ghost Ship*: "It appears to be unmanned and steering wild. The only reply is an eerie creaking. No one appears on deck. The ship is completely forsaken. What happened to the crew of the *Mary Celeste* is one of the enduring mysteries of the sea."

Modern derelict ships generally mean one thing, we learn: the illegal drug trade. But not so of the nineteenth century. Let's set sail for the Weirdumentary Bay.

"Theories abound as to why the *Mary Celeste* was abandoned. It might have been the result of a prearranged salvage fraud, pirates, mutiny, a burst of deadly marine gas, or even a homicidal maniac, killing the rest of the crew, one by one, dumping their bodies, and then committing suicide."

Like *The Amityville Horror* episode, this one is a dream (or nightmare) come true. Perfect Weirdumentary fare, with a sharp narrative focus and some very strong recreations.

If only the ghost ship had reappeared in the Bermuda Triangle. But we can't have everything, I suppose, even when riding the waves of the weird.

Season 6, Episode 3, *Ghosts in Photography*: "Once in the developing room, something unusual happened. At first, [William Hope] wondered if he had forgotten to clean the photographic plates, but it soon became clear what had taken place. The image of a woman had appeared on the photograph. Hope's friend recognized her immediately. It was his sister, who had died twelve years before. Mr. Hope believed he had photographed a ghost."

Are these ghost photos real? Or do they show the results of psychic power? Or—and this will be controversial in some circles, especially séance circles—are the photo bogies bogus? (In those circles, I'm known as a square.)

We see footage of Ted Serios, who allegedly used "thought-ography" to make mysterious images appear on photos, all thanks to the power of his mind. The Amazing Randi later exposed how Serios really created them.

And then there are the Cottingley Fairies, which were captured on film in 1917 and 1920. Conan Doyle believed in them. I do not, largely because one of the women who took the photos later admitted to faking them.

"Experts will continue to disagree on a phenomenon that theoretically records the presence of entities that are invisible to the naked eye." (And sometimes visible to the clothed eye.)

Season 6, Episode 16, *Spirit Voices*: "For centuries psychics and mediums have attempted to pull back the dark curtain of mystery that separates the land of the living from the realm of the dead. Some claim to have successfully recorded spirit voices on electronic equipment."

Edison tried to record sounds of "those beyond the grave." So have many others, which raises the question, "Are we ready to establish direct communication with the spirit world?"

Yes, we are. I hate to knock them, but spirit raps aren't enough in the twentieth century. Words, talking, even singing are what we need, or at least desire.

D. Scott Rogo, the author of *Phone Calls from the Dead* (1979), tells us about—guess what—phone calls from the dead: speaking spooks with enough quarters to dial the living, hoping not to get busy signals.

Then some folks make recordings in an old cemetery. One of their microphones is attached to an antique phone. When played back, the tapes feature strange sounds, and perhaps a voice. (Even without my shovel, I dig that graveyard.)

Science Officer Spock suggests that these kinds of experiments yield "possible scientific significance." What an amazing phrase. It encapsulates the results of all Weirdumentaries, where anything and everything is possible, even if forever remaining unproven.

Time for that Scooby snack.

The Miracle Healers

(1976)

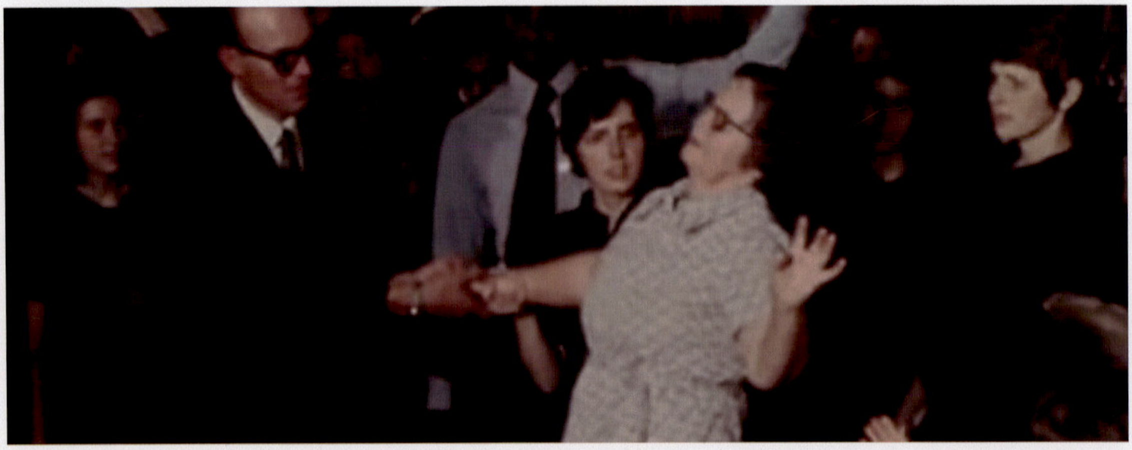

So many great actors, and yet so little time and mental space inside the average moviegoer's mind to appreciate them, let alone to learn all their names.

Roscoe Lee Browne was certainly one of the greats. An amazing actor, distinguished and poised, with a flair for drama and comedy. Yes, he won Emmys, and yes, he was a regular on the TV show *Soap* (1977–1981), but he deserves to be better known, better remembered for his many great performances.

Hosting *The Miracle Healers* wouldn't be near the top of Browne's accomplishments, but he's still the best thing about this flick, healing its deficiencies with his own magnificent voice.

"What is the mysterious force called healing? Western science and medicine have traditionally looked for the answer in the laboratory. Startling and sophisticated methods of healing predating the beginning of science by thousands of years have generally been ignored or ridiculed. The scientific method demands controlled experimental conditions and results which can be measured and duplicated for verification. But today we may be on the threshold of balancing the scientific side of our nature with its non-rational counterpart: the vast world of human knowledge and belief ranging from orthodox religion to the occult."

Produced and directed by Don Como, *The Miracle Healers*—which won an award at the Miami Film Festival—brings into focus the world of mystics and psychics, as well as the scientists studying them.

And then there's Kundalini. "Supposedly, the rare individual who can learn to tap this natural force will attain an increasingly higher level of consciousness, as symbolized by

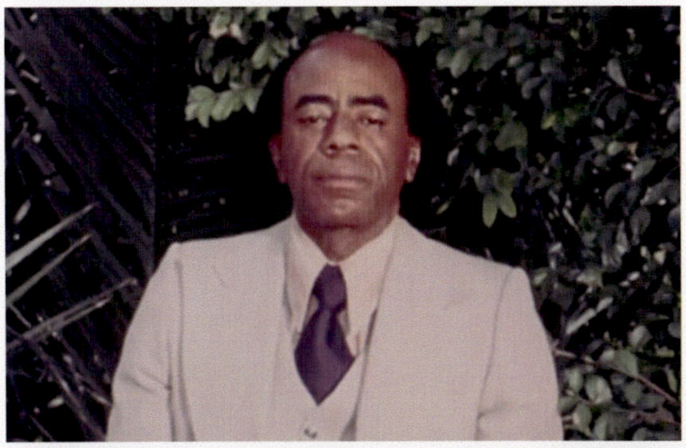
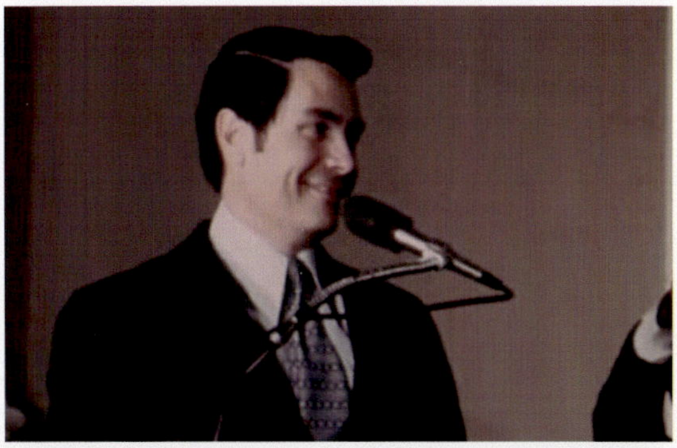
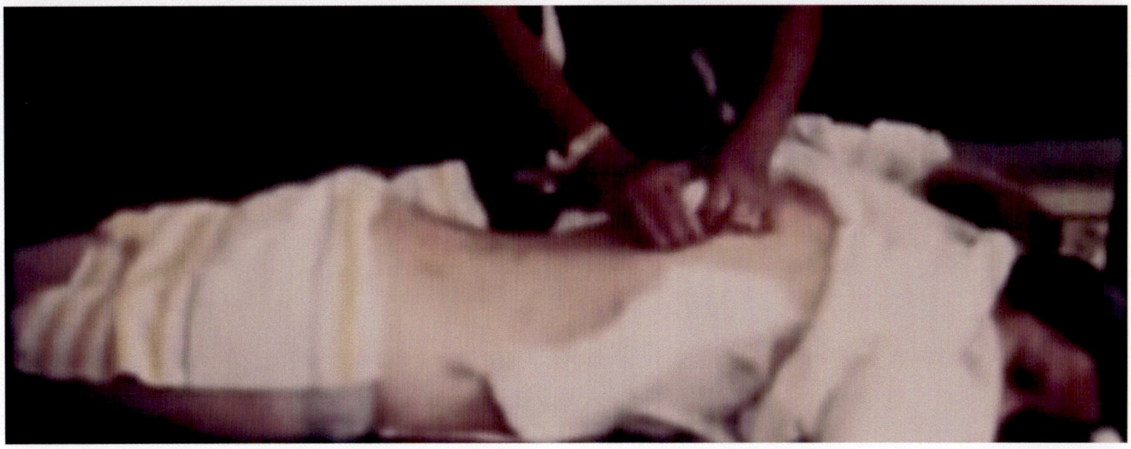

the wings of the caduceus, even eventually being able to leave the body at will."

Browne's investigation also examines psychic surgery, a subject that would resurface in Como's film *The Underground Doctors* (1977, see entry). Quackery? Not according to an interviewee who underwent such procedures, one of which didn't even involve the doctor physically touching her. (Look, Ma, no hands!)

Much of Browne's time is devoted to a couple of controversial faith healers. "To some Kathryn Kuhlman was a saint. To others she was sort of a superstar of the bizarre, a possessed-looking woman in a flowing gown whose temple of healing was the TV tube. One thing fairly certain about the charismatic woman who liked to call herself the 'Handmaiden of the Lord' was her ability to transfer a strange power to those with whom she came in contact."

The film features extensive interview footage with Kuhlman. She claims that two million people had been healed through her television appearances. As Marshall McLuhan said, "the medium is the message." (Of course, McLuhan also said "the medium is the massage.")

But then the message becomes not medium, but large, overwhelming, and tragic. *The Miracle Healers* presents extensive footage of the Reverend Jim Jones healing members of his flock in Los Angeles, some time before founding a town in Guyana and relying on Kool-Aid as a cure for it.

Don Como made eight Weirdumentaries. Even though it isn't great, this is one of the most enjoyable. I actually feel much better after watching it.

As Roscoe Lee Browne says, "nothing strikes so strong a chord as the voice crying 'I am healed.'"

World Beyond Death

(1976)

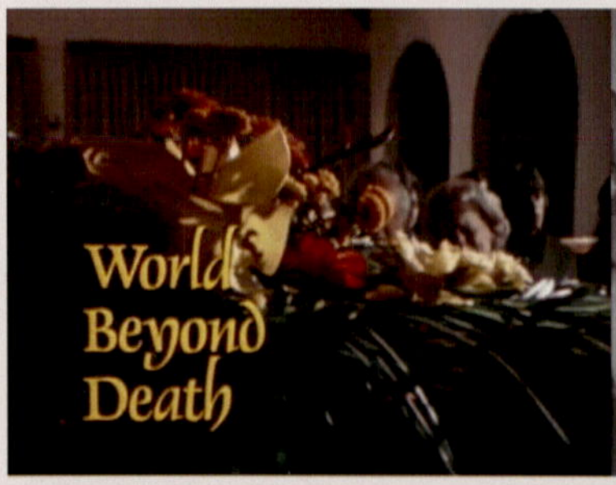

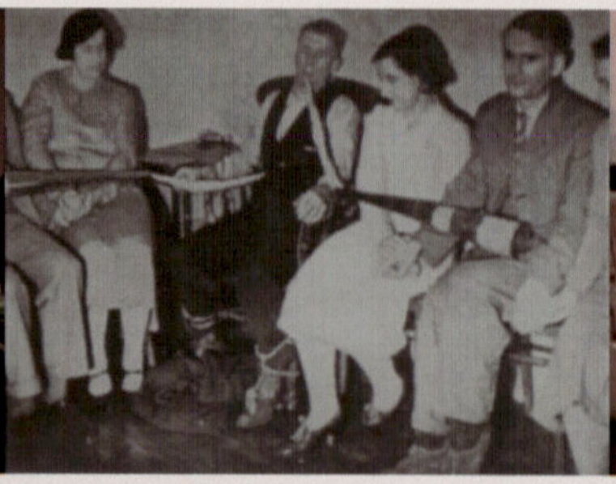
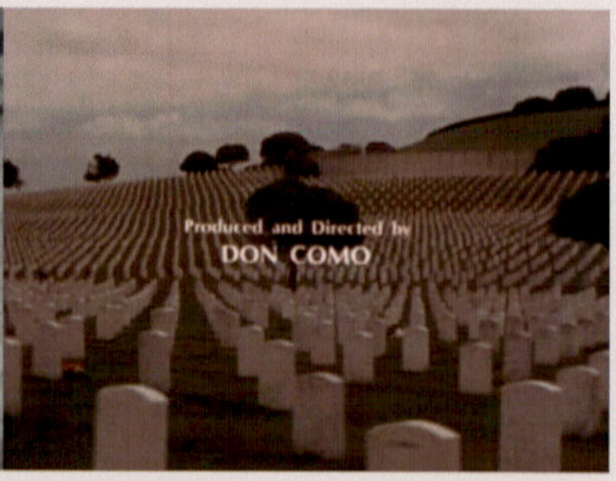

Heaven or hell? Live in a coffin forever? Return to Earth in spirit form? Or just fall into oblivion? Those are some of the possibilities that we hear at the beginning of this fifty-minute flick directed by Don Como.

On-screen host Will Geer acted in films from the thirties to the seventies. He speaks to us—initially from a cemetery near a working gravedigger—about the riddles of life after death, about the worlds (plural) that might await.

At times Geer speaks in the form of questions. When discussing spirit photography, he asks, "Are these apparitions the products of fakery, or is photography somehow capable of recording what the naked eye cannot see?

He also keeps an open mind on the afterlife. "Whether spiritualist-inspired, biophysically produced, or ingeniously hoaxed, ectoplasm has become part of the dramatic trappings of the séance."

Most of the time, though, the *World Beyond Death* relies on experts. For example, a psychiatrist speaks about those who are revived after having been pronounced dead. Some met Jesus. One man thought he traveled the cosmos before returning to his body.

Then a swami—who "understands what death means"—uses willpower to stop his own heart from pumping blood. As a doctor explains:

> *At the appointed time, the swami made a sudden movement, and the tracing in the laboratory showed a rapid change. The technicians were somewhat puzzled since the heart didn't actually stop. Instead, the tracing increased to three hundred beats per minute.*

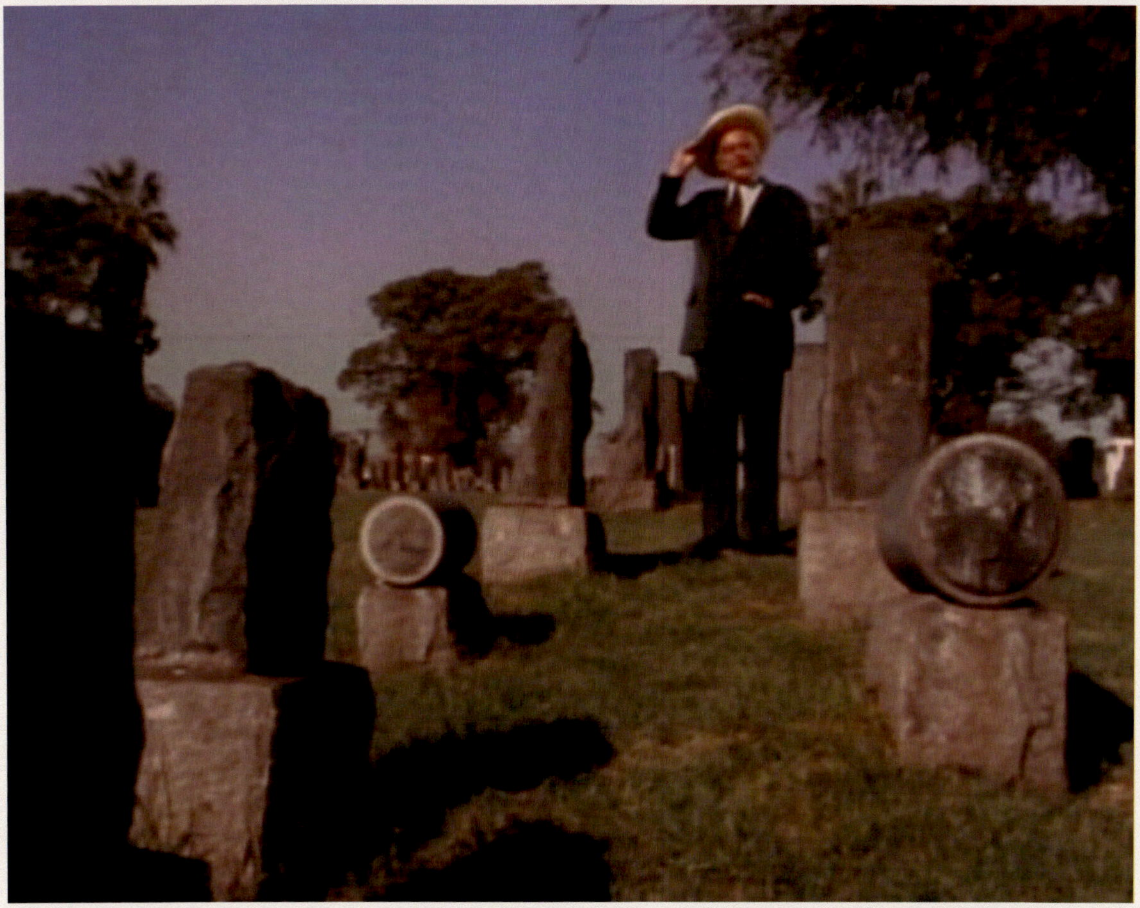

The swami had succeeded and survived, even though—the doctor adds, helpfully—"this is a condition that's usually fatal." (Words to the unwise.)

We also hear about thanatology and regression therapy, the latter allowing scientists and psychics to study reincarnation. Naturally we see sessions where people talk about who they once were. One of them can even feel the pain of an arrow that pierced his skin in a prior life.

'Course, if there is life after death, that might mean—hold your breath—we can communicate with the dead. We see a séance in which a medium allows adherents to speak to their loved ones, or—as it appears—with himself, as the dearly departed talk through him. In one instance, he affects a horrible and racist Asian accent.

And then there's the psychic who plays the piano with great aplomb, even though she's "untrained" in music. Songwriters are working through her. They have ever since she was a child. And curiously enough, these aren't unknown composers. We're talking Chopin, Brahms, and Haydn. This "proves that there's life after death."

The most interesting segment presents Bill Welch, a man who sits in silence at the same hour each night while recording audio. Playing back the tapes, he hears "discarnate voices" under the "background sound." The examples he plays for us are fascinating, certainly eerie enough for a good B-movie. Then we learn Bill died, and his friend captured Bill's own voice on reel-to-reel.

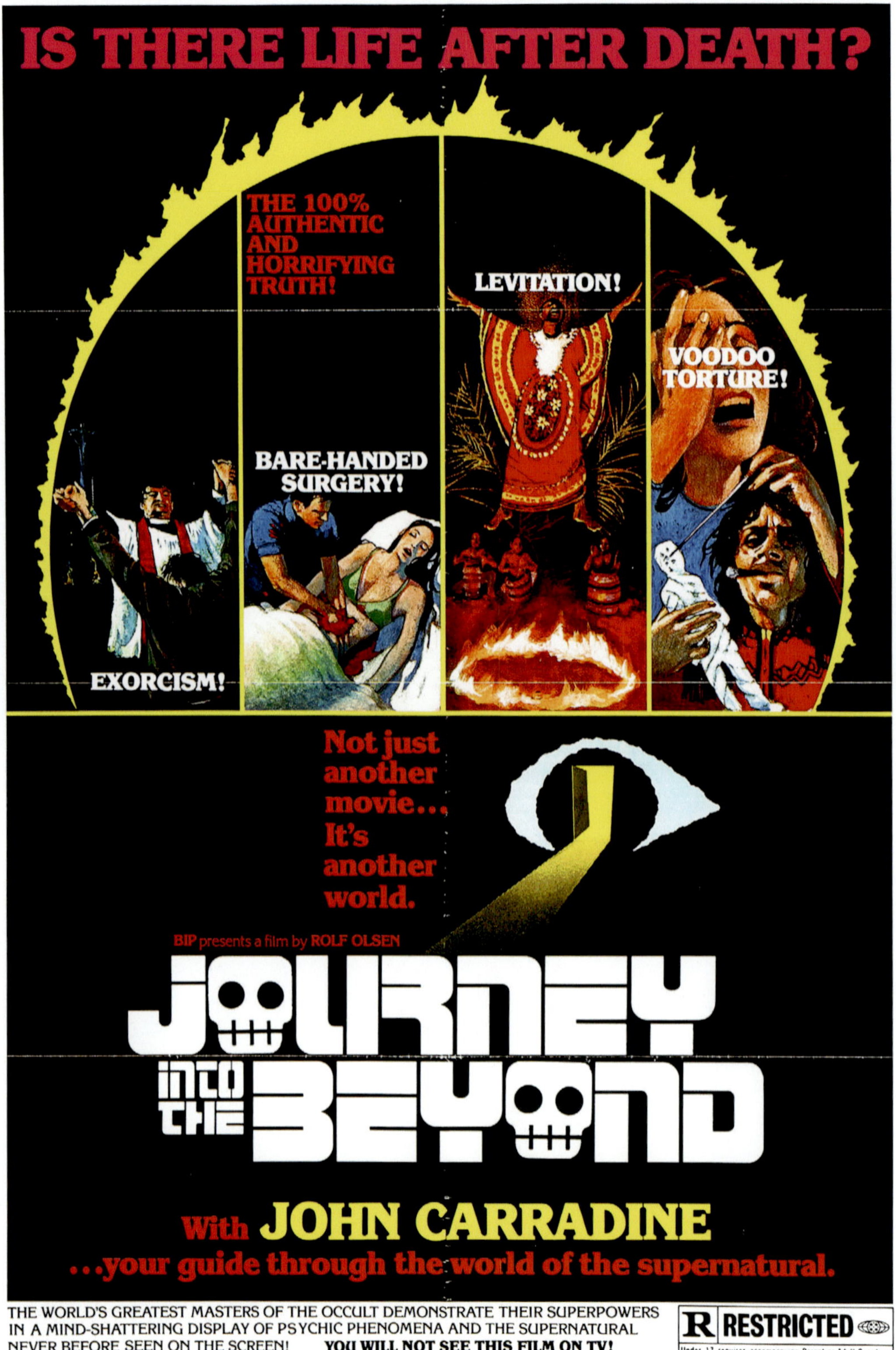
IS THERE LIFE AFTER DEATH?
THE 100% AUTHENTIC AND HORRIFYING TRUTH!
LEVITATION!
VOODOO TORTURE!
BARE-HANDED SURGERY!
EXORCISM!
Not just another movie... It's another world.
BIP presents a film by ROLF OLSEN
JOURNEY into the BEYOND
With JOHN CARRADINE
...your guide through the world of the supernatural.
THE WORLD'S GREATEST MASTERS OF THE OCCULT DEMONSTRATE THEIR SUPERPOWERS IN A MIND-SHATTERING DISPLAY OF PSYCHIC PHENOMENA AND THE SUPERNATURAL NEVER BEFORE SEEN ON THE SCREEN!
YOU WILL NOT SEE THIS FILM ON TV!
R RESTRICTED
Under 17 requires accompanying Parent or Adult Guardian

Journey into the Beyond

(1977)

After Orson Welles, the greatest American voice of the twentieth century belonged to one man. "This is John Carradine. Please join me on an adventure that will raise questions and provide many answers, a journey that will test your sanity, an expedition as bizarre as the edge of the universe."

The journey traverses much ground, ranging from firewalkers and astral projection to levitation and Immaculate Conception. And it features so much grisly footage that Carradine informs us from the onset of the film's gimmick. The moviegoer will hear an audio signal "before each highly graphic scene." You should, of course, "look away, if you are squeamish." More calming musical notes then cue us to look back again, once it's safe.

Here then is the film's signal achievement: it successfully married the Weirdumentary with the mondo films of the sixties, those pseudo-documentaries that—after the fashion of *Mondo Cane* (1962)—displayed shocking footage of taboo subjects. Cue applause for director Rolf Olsen.

Here is also the film's greatest setback, at least in the United States. Olsen made *Journey into the Beyond* as a German documentary, *Reis ins Jenseits – Die Welt des Übernatürlichen* (1975). Carradine's English-language narration destined the film for American eyes in 1977. Its graphic violence destined it for an R rating, a far cry from the general audiences that Weirdumentaries normally enjoyed. Though distributor Burbank International lodged a challenge, the MPAA appeals board upheld the earlier decision. That damned *Journey into the Beyond* to remain beyond the architecture of most movie theaters.

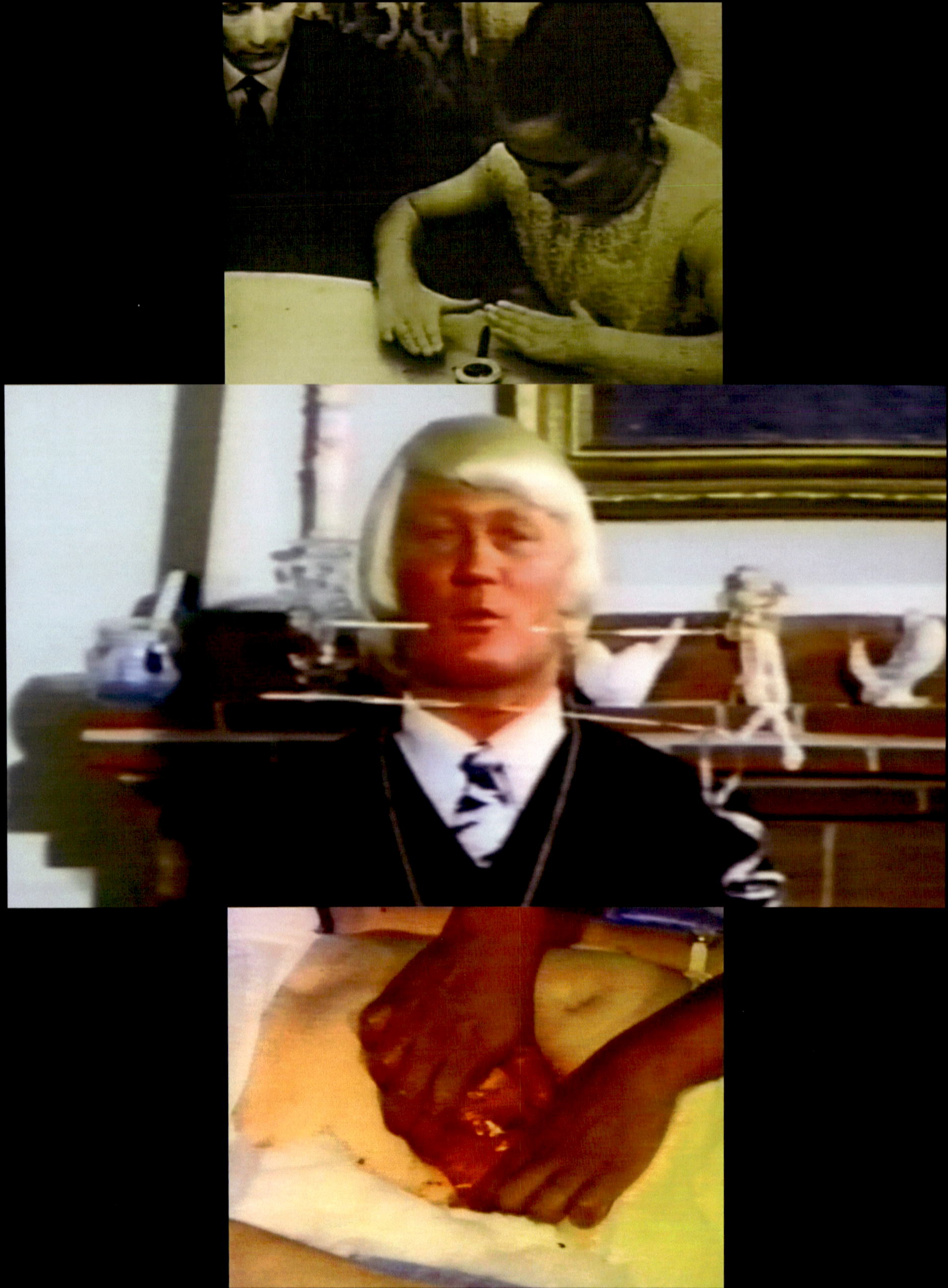

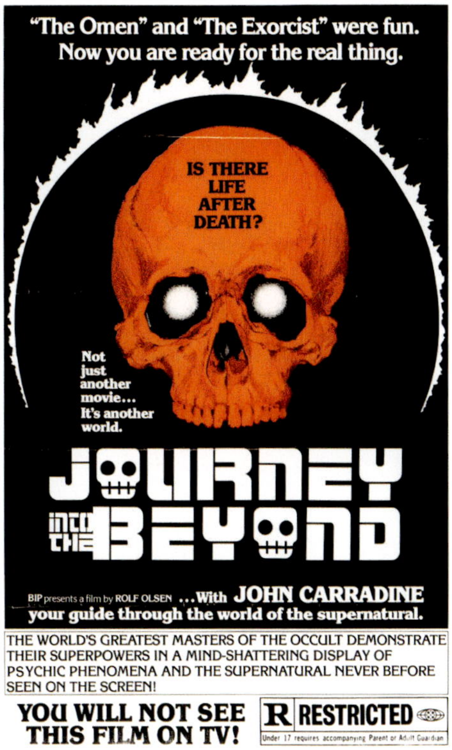

Nevertheless, those who did get to see it were in for a treat. In general, Paul Ross' script is crafty, using enough careful language, occasional skepticism, and rhetorical questions to allow for crazier notions to surface with the greatest of ease. Universities are being "forced" to take notice of parapsychology, we learn. And Kirlian photography is assuredly "proof of the aura surrounding the human body."

Various on-camera experts help us to understand the phenomena. Some are German scholars, but others include the likes of Dr. Edgar Mitchell, the American astronaut who walked on the moon and later pursued such subjects as remote healing and UFOlogy. And then there are the keepers of the flame, practitioners like spiritual healer Harry Edwards and the Reverend Christopher Neil-Smith, England's most famous exorcist.

Where the script fails us, by accident or design, is its meandering narrative. We spend time with a spiritual healer before moving on to other subjects, only to return to spiritual healing again. The film's structure is held together more by the power of Carradine's voice than anything else.

Maybe that doesn't matter, given the amount of time devoted to bizarre sights, from a stigmatist to a rainmaker. There's telekinesis (with the most extensive footage of Nina Kulagina seen in any Weirdumentary), demonic possession (in the form of a victim writhing on the floor), and a bloody surgery conducted with fingers but no instruments (thus giving new meaning to the term "hands-on").

The highlight is extensive footage of a séance conducted by an Italian spiritualist. The table rocks. A spirit materializes. And ectoplasm secretes from the medium, falls onto the floor, and burns. All before our very eyes, of course.

Burbank International promised to pay $25,000 to the "first person in the U.S. to who can achieve authentic self-levitation" and thus duplicate footage of the same in the film. "Trickery, fakery, or any earthbound technological magic" would result in disqualification. There's no evidence that anyone even tried to claim the prize money, but hope floats, even if people don't.

The critic at *Boxoffice* understood this, or at least understood something good, calling the film a "fascinating exploration" that leaves its viewers "with an eerie feeling."

When the film ends, Carradine explains, "The world we know is only a small stone in the sky, only a point of origin from which we should continue on our *Journey into the Beyond*." To emphasize his invocation of the film's title, the last four words feature an echo effect.

It reverberates still. Danke, Rolf, danke.

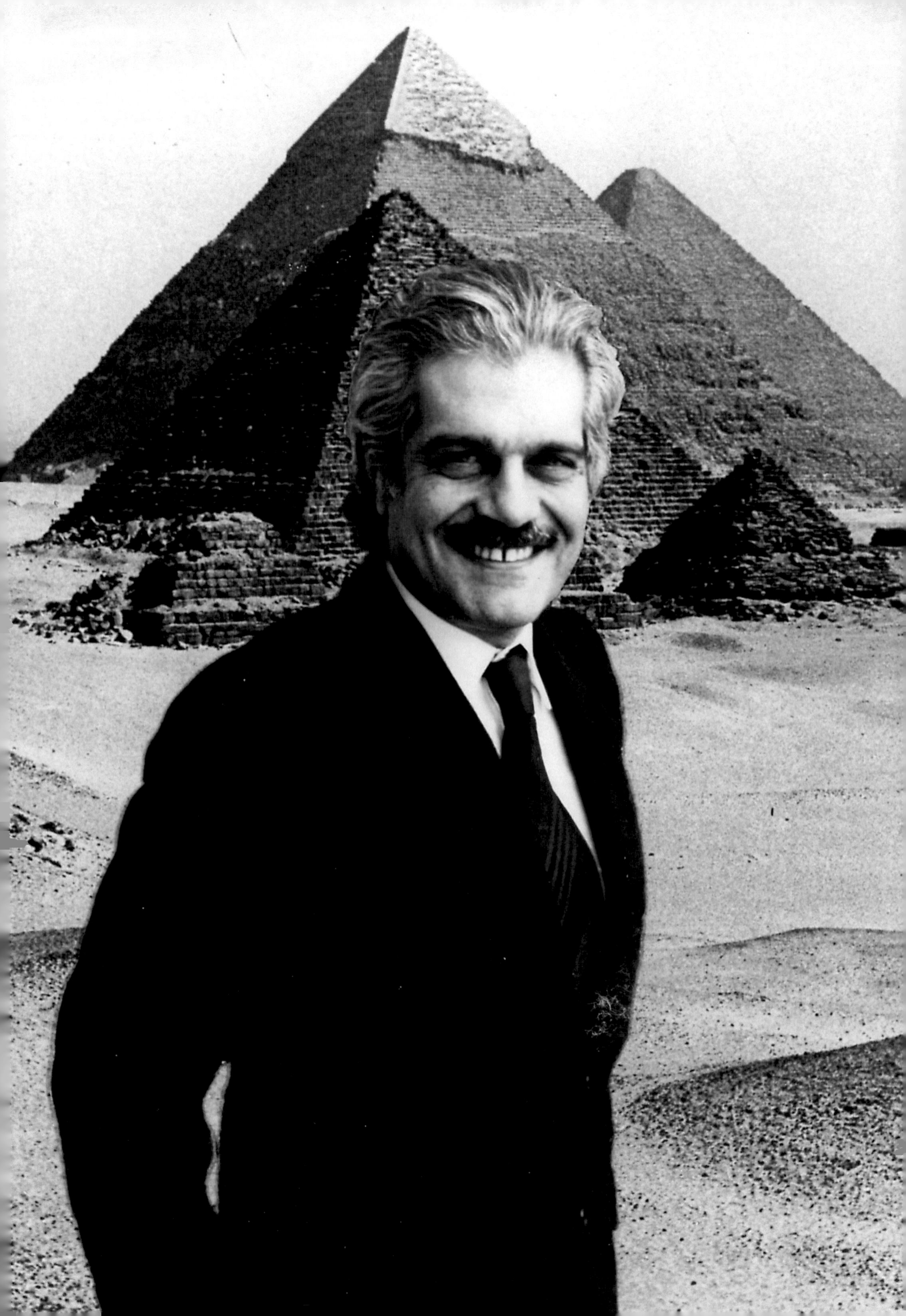

Mysteries of the Great Pyramid

(1977)

'The word 'documentary' ... leads people to believe reality is represented. But that's seldom true because seldom are both sides of the issue given equal representation."

William Kronick, producer/director/writer of *Mysteries of the Great Pyramid*, spoke those words, quickly adding that his film was different, because it wasn't possible to take a side on the subject of Egyptian pyramids. If I were to speak up, I'd have to say that he not only can, but that he definitely does.

The on-screen narrator of this sixty-minute made-for-TV Wolper movie is Omar Sharif. Yes, indeed, we see and hear Egypt's most famous actor, star of *Lawrence of Arabia* (1962) and *Doctor Zhivago* (1965).

And a superb job he does, explaining that we don't know how and why the Great Pyramid was built:

> *Thus we find ourselves confronted with theories ranging from outer space influence to prophecies of the future. And so in this area of the unknown into which are about to plunge, we will attempt to see logic prevail, but not at the expense of free thought and imagination.*

I do not believe that anyone has ever described the Weirdumentary philosophy better than he does.

When production began in 1976, Kronick's crew filmed in Los Angeles, England, and, of course, Egypt. They faced various challenges, including how to properly light the pyramid's tomb. Co-producer Jeffrey Pill recalled:

> *In addition to the 'normal' problems of cramped space, little air, and fluorescent lights (that we killed when actually filming), the situation was further complicated by having to close off the pyramid to all tourists.*

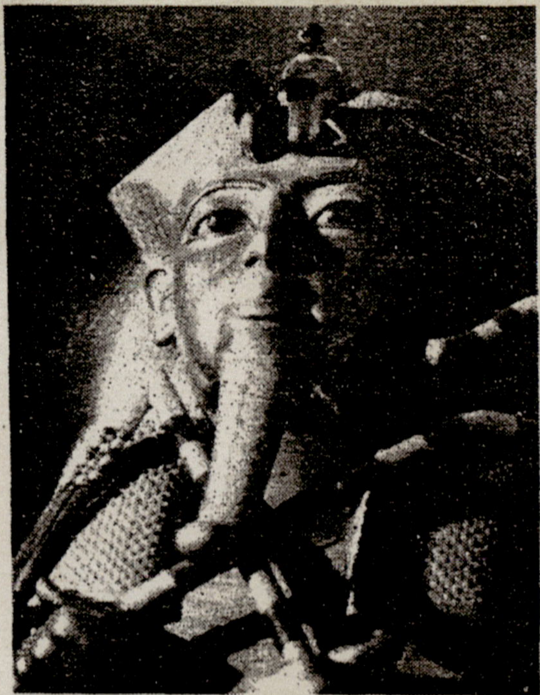

PHARAOH'S EFFIGY – The discovery of King Tutankhamen's tomb is reenacted in "Mysteries of the Great Pyramid," a special that explores the enigmas of the Great Pyramid of Giza in Egypt on Wednesday from 8 to 9 on CBS.

FOR CENTURIES mankind has been fascinated by the mysteries surrounding the Pyramid of Cheops at Giza in Egypt and tonight at 8 p.m. on Channel 5 television will seriously explore that ancient puzzle. Omar Sharif will host the program.

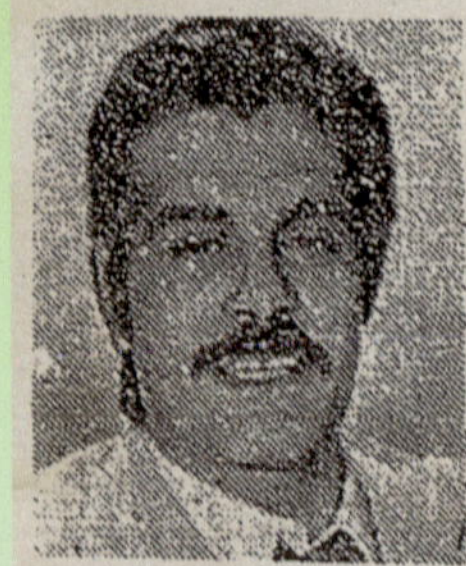

Omar Sharif

"Mysteries of the Great Pyramid" doesn't solve anything but it represents the first time an entire hour has been devoted to the only one of the seven wonders of the ancient world still standing.

Apparently the oth-

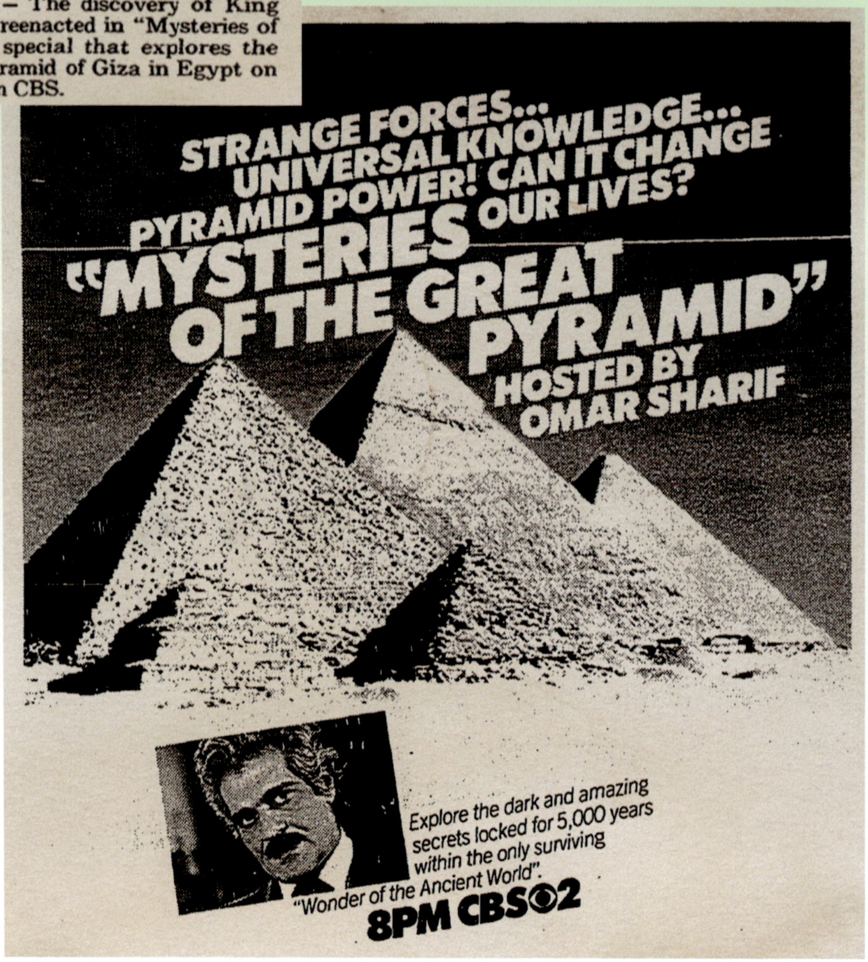

...When we were ready to shoot, our Egyptian would light his torch, we would make the shot, and then we would tell him to put out the torch. This proved more difficult than we anticipated. The torch would not want to go out, especially after we had used gasoline on it to make it burn brightly.

...Being that the passageways are not very large, by the end of the two hours of work, there was very little air left inside the Great Pyramid and quite a bit of smoke.

Pill also spoke about the difficulties the crew had in obtaining aerial footage of the Valley of the Kings, mainly due to military security.

After a journalist watched *Mysteries of the Great Pyramid*, he wrote about the sheer number of questions that it poses:

Were the pyramids merely tombs for kings, or did they represent a complicated use of knowledge in geography, geology, and astronomy? Were the ancient Egyptians perhaps on a mental wavelength which we are yet to comprehend? Numerous experts, most of them disagreeing with one another, are brought before the cameras to present a dizzying collection of theories, propounding anything from powers of levitation to an interpretation of the Great Pyramid at Giza as the Bible in stone.

...The Great Pyramid is subjected to the observations of sensible scholars and improvising amateurs. Rational explanations are mixed with speculations about clairvoyant wizards. As usual in this type of project, the overall question is simply answered with another question.

To this discussion, I would simply add my own view that one does not have to be "in stone" to be stoned. And I am not alone. *The Hollywood Reporter*'s review said much the same:

If you have ever placed a razor blade under a pyramid and expected it to get sharper, then you should enjoy this hour of speculation over the mystery surrounding the pyramids at Giza. ... the legends and theories appear to be endless, and this hour explores some of the more fanciful speculations.

I doubt that *Hollywood Reporter* meant those words to be laudatory. For me, they represent high praise, which should also extend to the part of the film that deals with "pyramid energy," Olden Times thus impacting the New Age.

Special shout-outs to the cinematography team and Lyn Murray's music are in order. There's also some tremendous archival footage, and even an appearance by Peter Tompkins, the host of *Secrets of the Bermuda Triangle* (1978, see entry).

"We should and shall explore further," Omar suggests. Hands up, all who agree.

Don't like pyramids, you say? Tut tut, I retort.

The Underground Doctors

(1977)

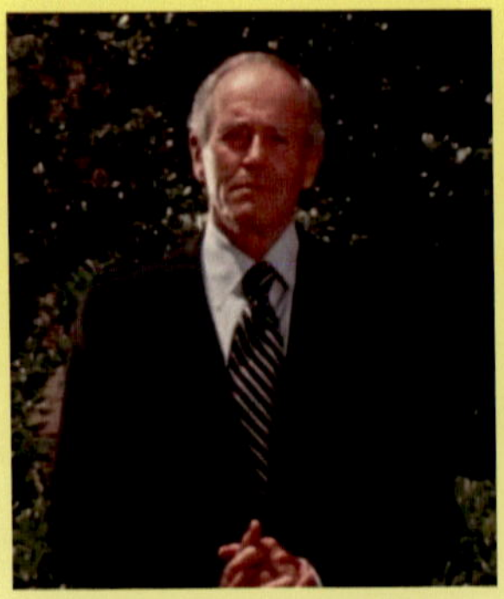

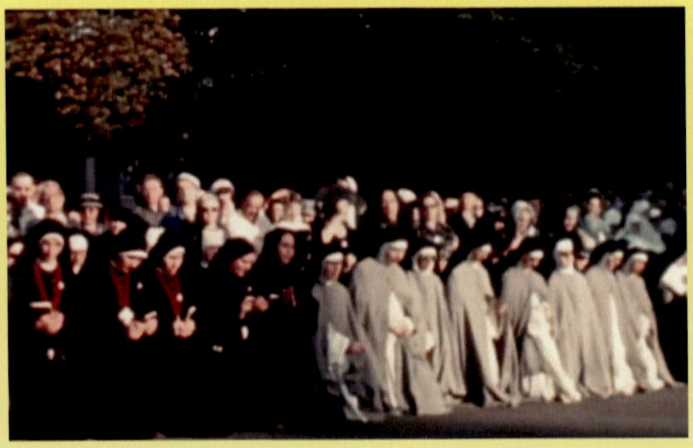

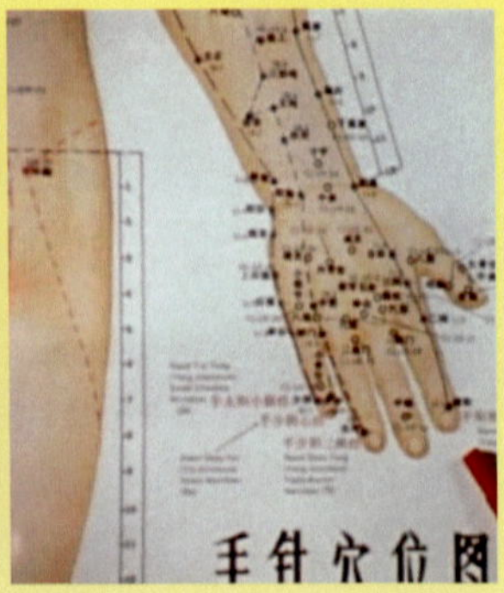

Henry Fonda, one of the greatest of all film actors, made his single foray into Weirdumentary cinema with this Don Como-directed gem.

"From the beginning of time, there has been an urgent need to heal the sick. Once disease was blamed on evil spirits, and the cure was to frighten the demons away ... and sometimes the patient went with them."

Nevertheless, "many still look to unorthodox means for achieving and maintaining physical and spiritual health. Some of these methods—often shocking, bizarre, and just downright amazing—are explored here as we meet *The Underground Doctors.*"

While hiding out in the "remote Himalayas," a hitman for the mafia "learned amazing ancient healing techniques from a Tibetan lama." He was something of a criminal version of Dr. Strange. And our Dr. Stranger spent over eleven months in total darkness, eating only one meal every three days, part of a training exercise to bring medical secrets from the East to the West.

He performs a ceremony for the cameras, chanting before grabbing a woman's feet, head, and chest. Something happens, but I'm not really sure what.

Another doctor explains, "Maybe there are things in other societies that have been known for thousands of years that we are unable to comprehend." (Maybe, baby, I'll have you ... and your secrets.)

Fonda also introduces Wayne Cook, a dowsing expert in Southern California. His divining rods allow him to, well, divine the location of underground water. The old boy's successful, too. (Don't trust me. Just go on and ask him.)

Cook even uses the dowsing rods on people, and not just any people, but no less than a young Martin Sheen. Cook explains:

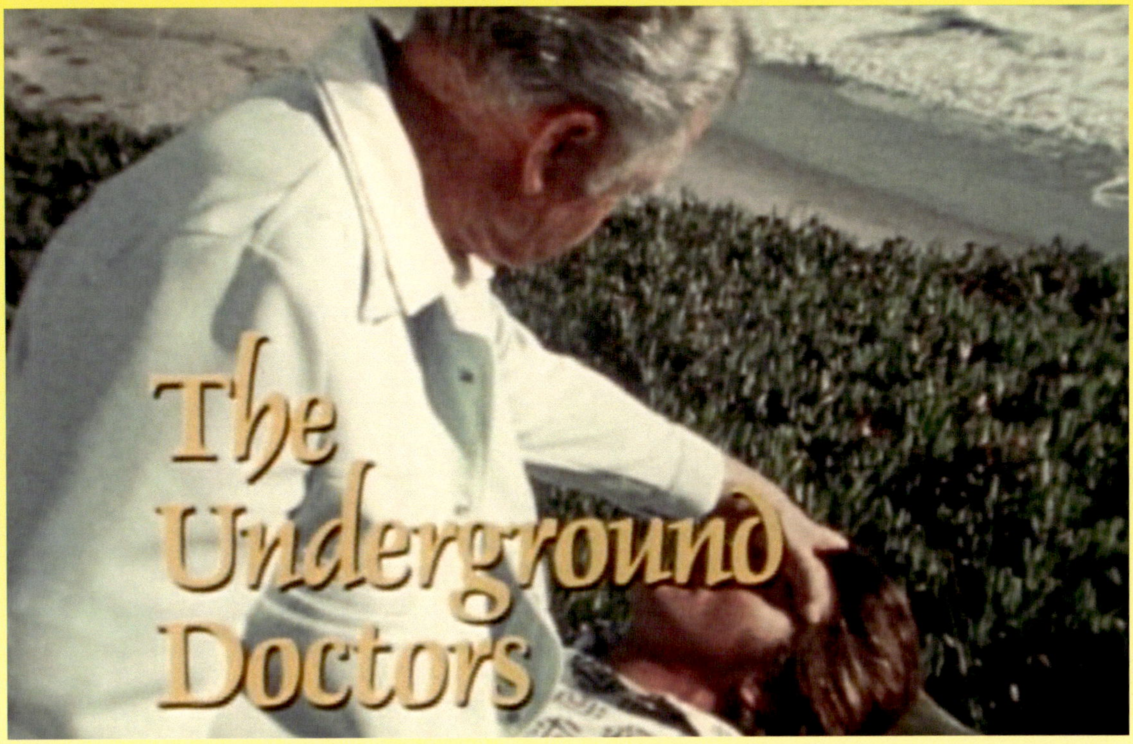

Now what we have to find is what is making that energy blockage. Somewhere in your system there's a blockage of the vital essence of life that flows through the meridians of your body. You see, Martin, everything in the universe has either a bipolar polarity, a positive polarity, a negative polarity, or an oscillating polarity.

Cook proceeds to discuss vortices and the "river of life," as well as his system for releasing people's energy and making them feel better. Sheen's response is that he "feels different," but "can't really verbalize it." (Apocalypse Maybe?)

Acupuncture, acupressure, and muscle manipulation for energy flow get their due as well. One doctor claims that acupuncture can make people feel high and horny, which makes it surprising that more people don't partake.

"Now, this is not replacing the skills of a medical doctor," another practitioner explains, "but it is supporting a medical doctor who is a channel for this healing energy." (The fine print writ large: don't sue us.)

From there we meet healers like the "Modern Edgar Cayce" and another guy who specializes in "energy transference."

And Father Yod at the "Brotherhood of the Source." Yes, if it looks like a cult and sounds like a cult, it's a cult. Yod was a fraud, who abused women and was terrible to his followers.

The Underground Doctors features great cinematography, strong pacing, and appropriately enigmatic music. Two healthy thumbs up for this Weirdumentary.

As a doctor myself, I prescribe it to all viewers. (But please, don't call me in the morning if you dislike it.)

The Unknown Force

(1977)

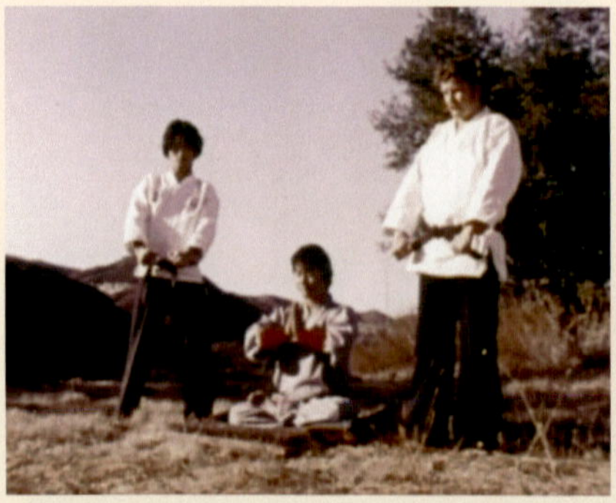

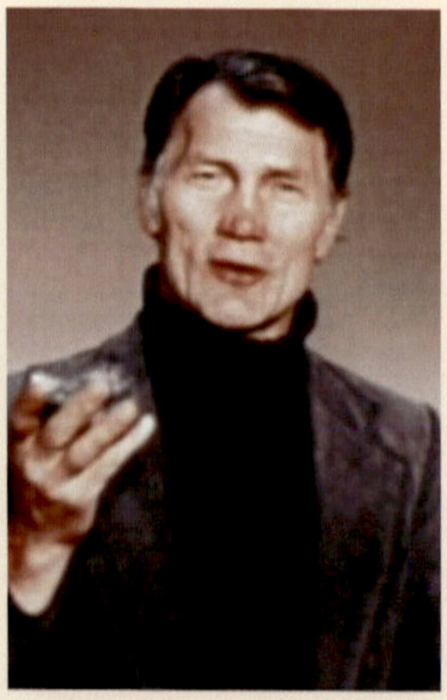

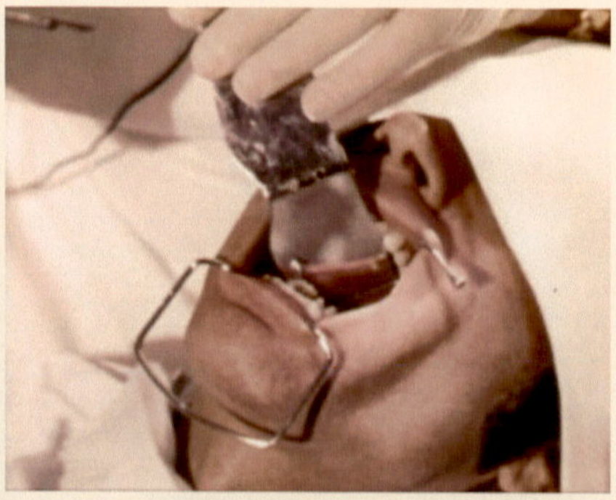

Mysterious flute music. Even more mysterious figures in the desert at sunset. Are they actors? Are they shamans?

"The oldest literature known to man tells of an all-powerful force underlying everything in nature and occurring throughout the universe. This mysterious force was called prana, and those who learned how to tap it and channel it through themselves were said to become like gods. But the world was barbarian, and plunder and brute easier to understand..."

The unforgettable voice of Jack Palance speaks those words, prior to the great thespian appearing on-camera and bringing things up to date.

"It remained for the dawning of the space age to prompt us to re-examine our skeptical dismissal of these Indian writings. Twentieth-century science has finally developed instruments sensitive enough to measure what a handful of mystics and psychics down through the ages have claimed to be able to perceive all along."

Some of Palance's dialogue begins with beautiful phrases like "Could it be?" His questions involve human auras, psychokinesis, and "astonishing feats" of mind over matter.

"Every culture in the history of man has had individuals claiming to possess extraordinary powers. Will we be the first to prove that such powers actually exist?"

Producer Don Como's film coincided neatly with the release of George Lucas' *Star Wars* (1977) and its exploration of "The Force."

Why are some people extraordinary? Palance asks, "Is it possible that they are able to tap some sort of force which is generally unavailable to the average person?"

After all, martial artists can "push their bodies seemingly beyond human endurance without injury." We see one of them run over by the wheel of a truck without wincing. And a blindfolded swordsman uses his blade to cut a zucchini on a man's stomach without

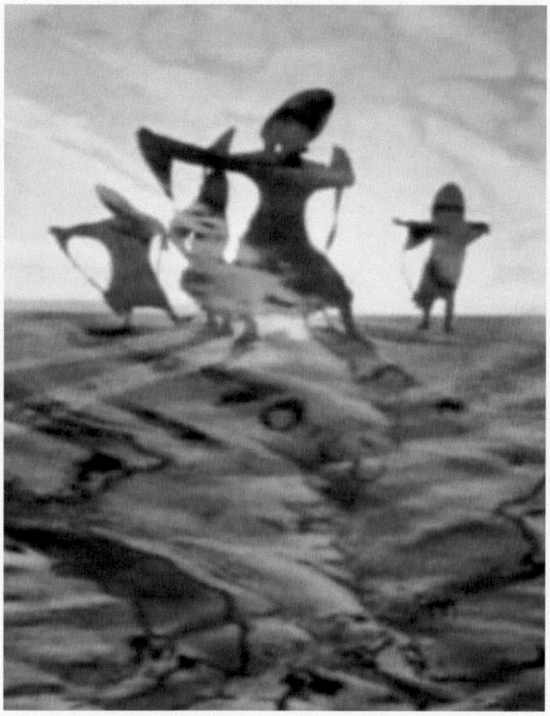

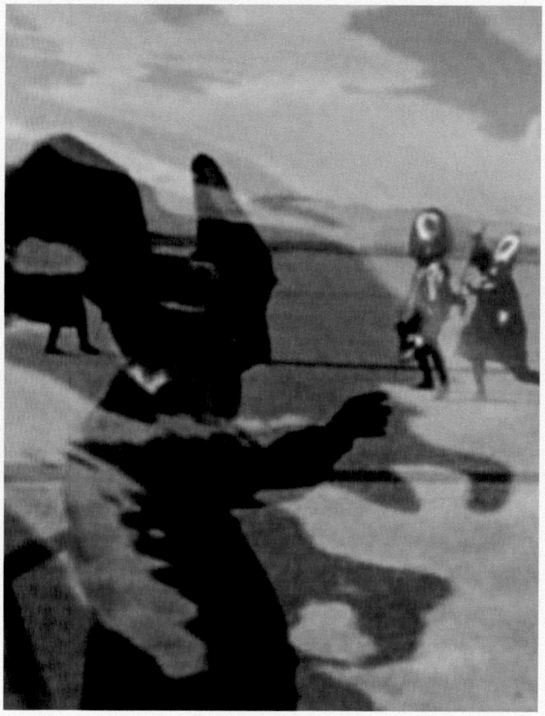

cutting into his skin. (Use the Force, Luke, rather than that Veg-o-Matic you got last Christmas.)

Next up is Nina Kulagina and her "still unexplained" ability to move objects just by thought alone. The black-and-white footage proves two things: the Soviets might be ahead of us in ESP, but behind us in the use of color film stock.

Dr. Thelma Moss also appears, as does footage of her Kirlian movies. Kirlian photography was so cool and colorful as to make me wonder why it isn't still a thing, or if it is still a thing, why is it a thing that we stopped caring about?

From there it's pyramid energy, including a "pyramid grid system" made of metal that hangs over a married couple's bed. It gives them more energy and causes their sex to be more "pleasurable." It even helps them to conceive a child, thus resulting in the biological version of a pyramid scheme.

Perhaps the most unique scene is the one where avant-garde music—not unlike Ligeti's *Lux Aeterna*—plays while various people sway in bizarre, undulating movements.

But there's so much more in this flick, which was written and directed by Dick Croy. For example, an expert believes that we could or at least *should* be able to look into and through each other's bodies. (Sales of X-ray specs will plummet, I fear.)

"We are energy," another expert claims. We just need it to flow. We need to channel it. Or maybe, just maybe, we need to change the channel to another program.

I won't change channels, though. Jack Palance and the cool music are more than enough to keep my attention for a single viewing. As for a second, you ask? Even with a pyramid on my head, I'll admit that I don't have the energy for that.

In conclusion, I shall defer to my childhood hero, Han Solo: "Kid, I've flown from one side of this galaxy to the other. I've seen a lot of strange stuff, but I've never seen anything to make me believe there's one all-powerful Force controlling everything."

The Amazing World of Ghosts

(1978)

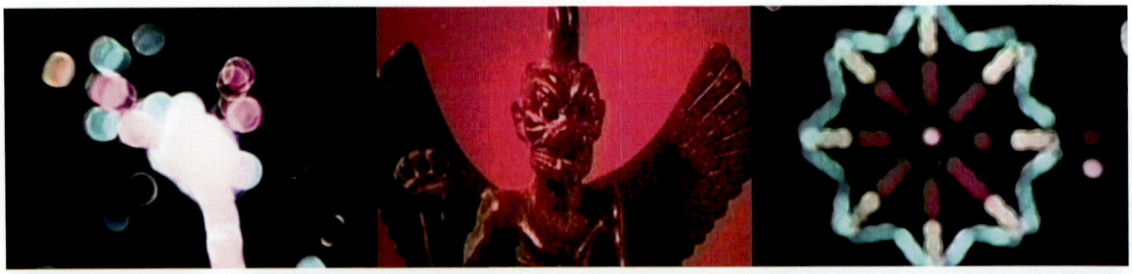

Blurred lights shine out of the darkness, moving eerily thanks to a pan. The camera zooms outward slowly to reveal a city. "It is night and there are only the sounds of the city to keep us company. Who or what is out there in the vast blackness of night?"

Thanks to our old pals at Delineator Films, actor Sidney Paul invites us to consider that question for ninety-six minutes. Following in the footsteps of Reinl's *Chariots of the Gods* (1970), this documentary features no interviews or on-camera commentary of any kind. Paul is heard, but never seen. And nearly ten minutes pass before any historical photograph appears on-screen.

True to its title, the film asks questions like "Do you believe in ghosts?" and "Is there life after death?" Near the beginning, Paul suggests that we will "perhaps arrive at a few conclusions."

Most of the time, *The Amazing World of Ghosts* accepts the evidence it presents unquestioningly. "Real ghosts are very hard to find," Paul admits, but they *can* be found, over and over again, at least in this film, as well as in the typical American home, which can be "haunted by creatures of the night, haunted by monsters from beyond the grave, who return from the realm of the dead to haunt the living and exact their terrible revenge on those who would disturb their rest."

While we hear about poltergeists and mediums and automatic writing and spirit photography, as well as the literary history of ghostly intercession, Paul also describes creatures like vampires, werewolves, goblins, and screaming skulls, meaning boneheads who can shriek without the assistance of vocal cords.

As the film moves at a slow, trance-like pace, we are likewise treated to discussions of Bigfoot, the Loch Ness monster, hypnotism, voodoo, earthquakes, satanic rituals, the phases of the moon, and—thanks be to the gods—aliens.

Paul asks, "Are we being visited even now by creatures from beyond space?", which inevitably (?) leads him to the questions, "Are ghosts really the living dead from outer

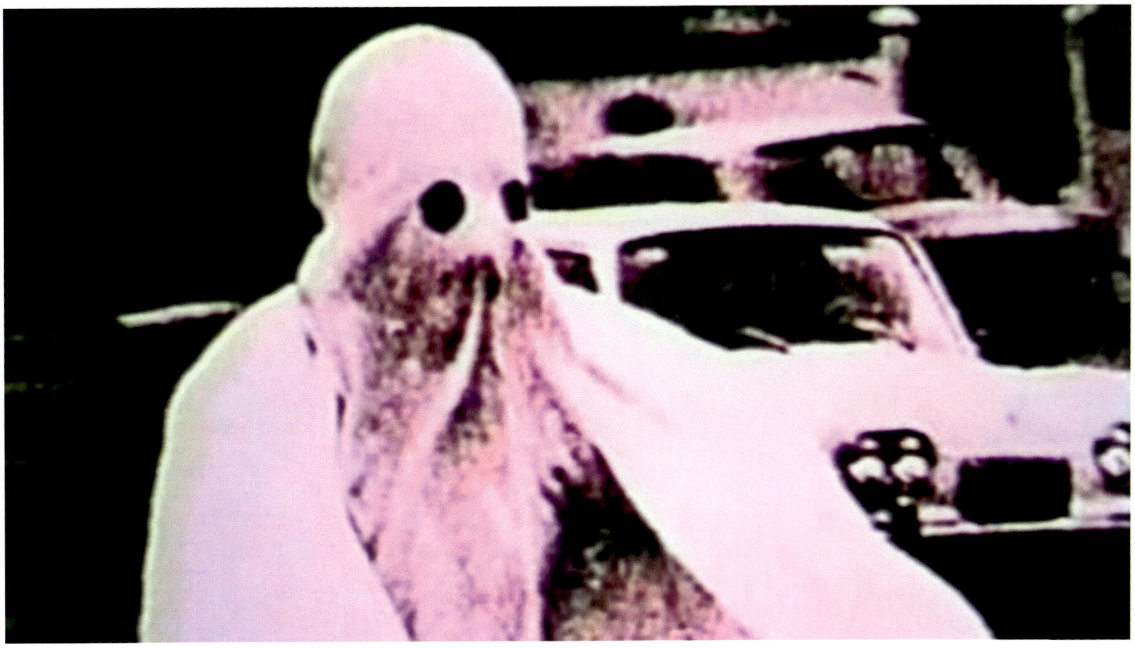

space?" and "Is there actually a connection between the phases of the planets and the world of ghostly and supernatural phenomena?" That's in addition to rightful concern that a sneak attack on Earth might well be mounted from aliens hiding on a nearby planet. Our solar system, it seems, is not ours, at least not exclusively.

By the time this Weirdumentary ends, Paul says, "We leave the final answer up to you," while simultaneously declaring, "These forces of darkness are real." Perhaps the contradiction isn't entirely surprising for a film that implies witchcraft really *was* present in Salem in 1692. Fear not, though, for the fine print at the conclusion maintains, "the producers bear no responsibility of any kind for inaccuracies, irregularities, or other errors or omissions in the claims and cases discussed herein." Lawsuits need be aborted before they begin.

Christopher Sereni's script is wonderfully relentless, not only barraging us with facts, but also returning to the same subjects over and over again, even after we thought them dead and gone. After the initial introduction of aliens, for example, we abruptly see a ghostly tapestry, a spiritualist photograph, the statue of a gargoyle, and the exterior of an American "spook house." Then, in short order, it's back to aliens again, then again, and then again. Even particular phrases like things that "go bump in the night" are repeated.

Repeated, but in a way that feels less repetitious than like a nightmarish lecture from which we can't—and generally don't want to—escape. It's déjà voodoo, all over again. Like a wheel within a wheel, or a circle in a spiral, or a carousel turning rings around the moon. And on and on, anon anon. Jim Cookman's eerie and at times downright groovy musical supervision helps us swirl around the cosmos, joyously so.

Even the credits are crazy. It was "Produced and Directed by Delineator Films, Inc.," we learn, right before learning the "Director" was Wheeler Dixon.

Here is a marvelous film. If it had been edited down to sixty minutes, it would be sublime.

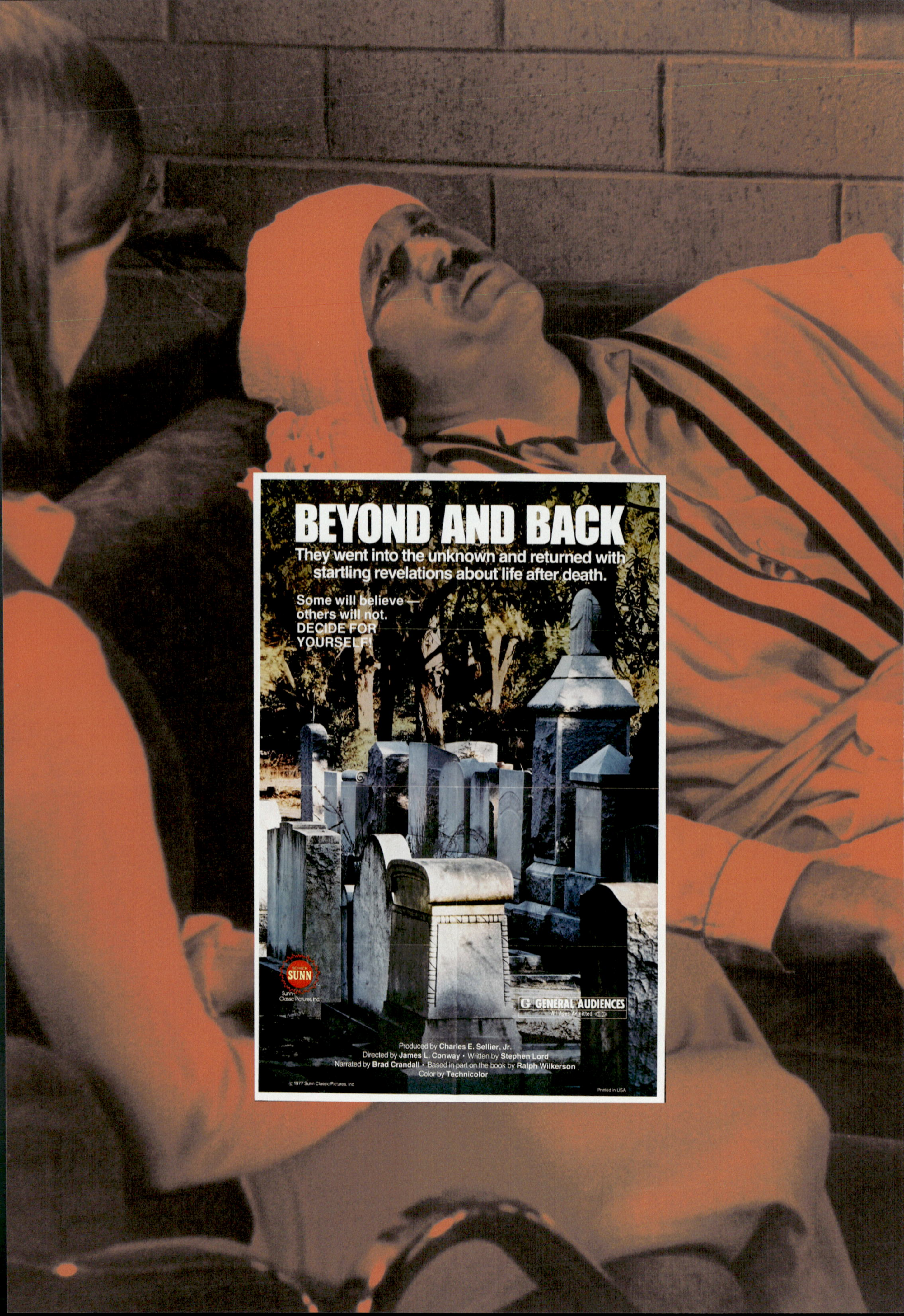
BEYOND AND BACK
They went into the unknown and returned with startling revelations about life after death.
Some will believe — others will not. DECIDE FOR YOURSELF!
SCHICK SUNN
Sunn Classic Pictures, Inc
G GENERAL AUDIENCES
All Ages Admitted
Produced by Charles E. Sellier, Jr.
Directed by James L. Conway • Written by Stephen Lord
Narrated by Brad Crandall • Based in part on the book by Ralph Wilkerson
Color by Technicolor
© 1977 Sunn Classic Pictures, Inc
Printed in USA

Beyond and Back

(1978)

"You are about to see one of the most extraordinary films of our time, a movie that dares to investigate the possibility of life after death." So sayeth Brad Crandall while walking through a cemetery full of fog. All of this is thanks to the hard work of parapsychologists and doctors, as well as the testimony of real people, people whose names have been changed to protect the innocent and guilty alike.

And then there are recreations featuring such historical characters as Plato, Benjamin Franklin, Elizabeth Barrett Browning, Louisa May Alcott, Thomas Edison, Ernest Hemingway, and Harry Houdini (who is also seen in archival footage).

Sunn Classic hired Stephen Lord to script *Beyond and Back*, which was based upon Ralph Wilkerson's book *Beyond and Back: Those Who Died and Live to Tell It* (1977). The studio was perhaps inspired by Howard B. Kreitsek's plans to produce *Life After Death* for MGM in 1977. It was never made, which left near-death experiences lying in the street, the power of the afterlife waiting to be grabbed.

Charles E. Sellier, Jr. produced, James L. Conway directed, with *Beyond and Back* filmed "entirely on location in Utah," ranging from Salt Lake City to a ski resort. The MPAA bequeathed a G rating in December 1977, with the film released onto more than one hundred screens in New York in February 1978. Sunn blitzed local TV stations with trailers.

The *Los Angeles Times* thumped *Beyond and Back* for being "slipshod" and "banal." After damning it as "amateurish in every way," *Daily Variety* declared, "The only element of this dramatized documentary that rightly could be described as incredible is that Sunn Classic is able to sell it ... so successfully." The public politely disagreed. In the L.A. area, the film generated "enormous" and even "heavenly" profits. Cue the bright lights, and the angelic harp music.

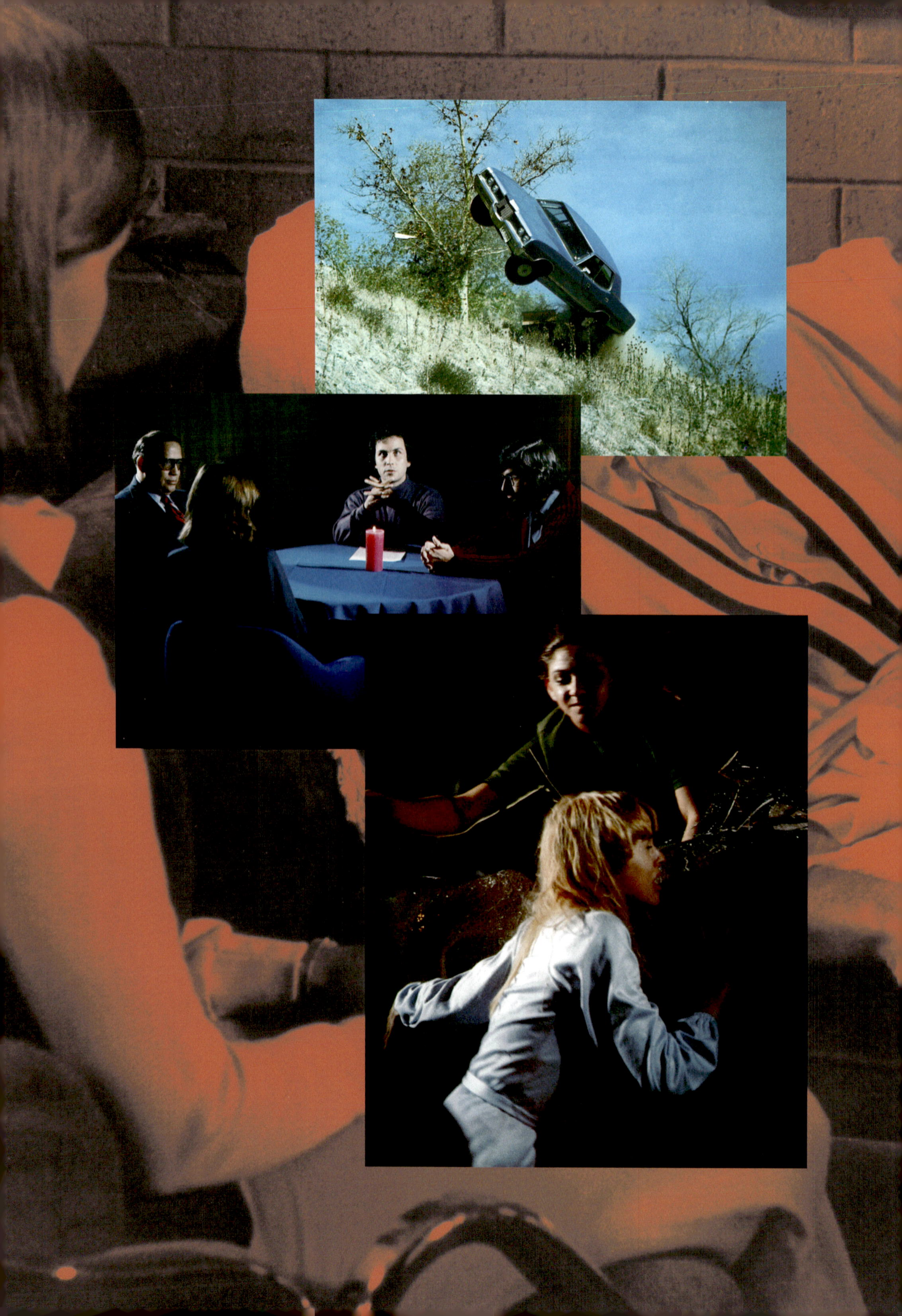

Unlike so many Sunn Classic projects, *Beyond and Back* features high action, ranging from a car flying off a cliff and crashing onto the rocks below to a small airplane exploding when it nose-dives back to the ground. "These are some of the most incredible scenes we've ever filmed for one of our movies," Sellier enthused. The near-death experience of suicidal folk also allows for a brief visit to Hell, in which condemned humans with no eyes cannot see the tortures that surround them.

Cinematographer Henning Schellerup explained his excitement over putting into practice an experiment that he had been "dreaming of for a long time." It involved images of a soul passing through solid objects. He positioned a fifty-percent mirror at a right angle to the actor, who was against a blue screen. He then achieved the desired effect by placing his lens on the same axis as the light beam.

The film's standout is Doug Hubbard's special effects. The similarities between near-death experiences include the sensation of leaving and hovering above one's own body, as well as seeing bright lights and even images of Jesus. That's where Hubbard comes in, creating light "tunnels" influenced by *2001: A Space Odyssey* (1968). These effects are repeated, saving money and visually reinforcing the sameness in witness testimony. You see, repetition means evidence in the world of the Weirdumentary.

But it doesn't mean ninety minutes of running time, and so Crandall also takes us on forays into reincarnation (including a brief recap of the Bridey Murphy case), psychokinesis (complete with Uri Geller footage), spiritualism (featuring Houdini's widow), and the research of Duncan MacDougall, who measured the weight of the soul as it left the body. Twenty-one grams, so he wrote. We also learn the term "thanatology," thanks to the work of Dr. Eleanor Stevens (actress Maxilyn Capell), a nonexistent researcher based on Dr. Elisabeth Kübler-Ross.

All the while, Crandall asks us questions that begin with such phrases as "Is it possible?" and "How can you explain?" The answers come so easily that Crandall ends the film by pronouncing, "We've presented you with the facts."

Beyond and Back is at its best when Crandall invites us, the moviegoer, to undergo a near-death experience. POV shots place us on the hospital table. We leave our body, float above it, experience a divine presence, and observe a gateway to the other side before returning to our body. Oh, and we get to see the *2001*-style lights again.

The Sunn doth shineth bright, so let us quaff a cup to the dead already, and give a hurrah for the next who dies ... and comes back to tell the tale.

P.S. Like all good near-death stories, *Beyond and Back* deserves a postscript. In 1979, Sellier produced another film for Sunn Classic, *Beyond Death's Door*. Based upon a book by Dr. Maurice Rawlings, the film featured Tom Hallick as a physician who investigates those who saw the afterlife and lived to tell the tale. Though based on "actual accounts," *Beyond Death's Door* unfolds as a mainstream fictional film narrative, not as a Weirdumentary. And its special effects were not nearly so special as those of Doug Hubbard.

Curse of the Mayan Temple

(1978)

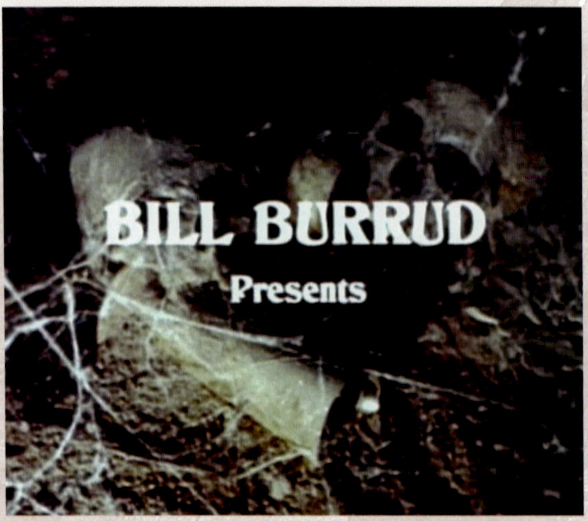

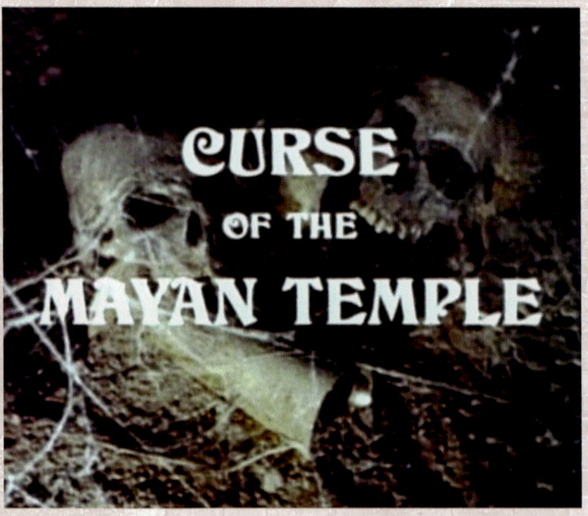

Yucatán, 200 A.D. Footage at the actual location, even if not the actual year. The Mayans sacrifice someone in a ceremony, a recreation with a camera shadow on a wall.

Bill Burrud, our producer and our narrator explains, "For a thousand years, the jungles of Yucatán had concealed the dark mysteries of the Mayan people. The Mayans' isolated civilization—intensely intellectual, profoundly religious, and terrifyingly bloodthirsty—had flourished most abundantly during Europe's dark medieval period. Until the late eighteenth century, the monuments of the Mayans lay undisturbed and all but forgotten."

Yucatán, 1937 A.D. Two German explorers in Mexico (or rather two actors in another dramatization), search for lost cities in the jungle, this time with no camera shadow. It takes them months (the Germans, not the actors), but finally they uncover ruins of the Mayan civilization. "This could be the find of the century," Burrud tells us. (Sa-fari, so-good.)

One of the explorers discovers a sealed door. On it is a small stone bearing the image of a Mayan god. The explorer takes the stone with him. (Not a good idea, IMHO.)

They pass their looted treasures on to the captain of a small boat, who will have them shipped to Germany. Then the explorers return to the jungle, never to be seen again. (Told ya.)

Yucatán, A.D. 1977 or thereabouts. Bill Burrud, his son John, and his son's friend Brian go south of the border, planning to find the same lost city. None of the locals will talk to John and Brian about the captain of the small boat. Perhaps it's because they're scared.

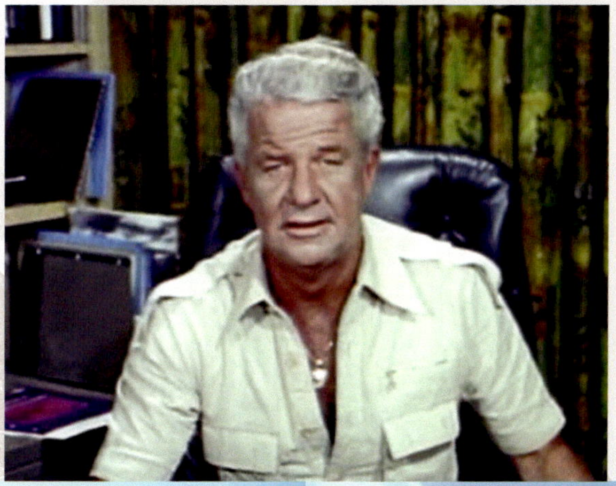

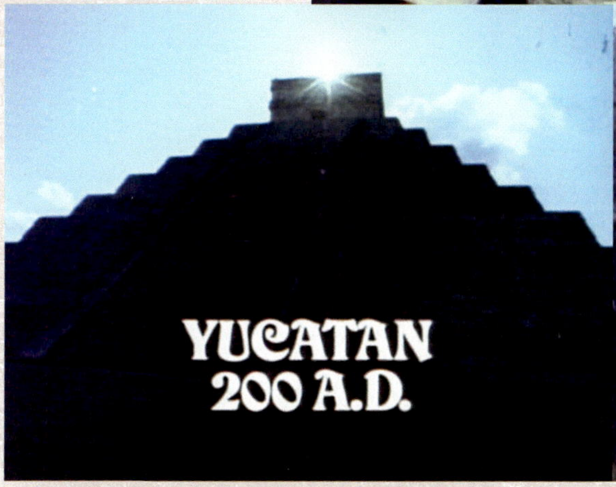

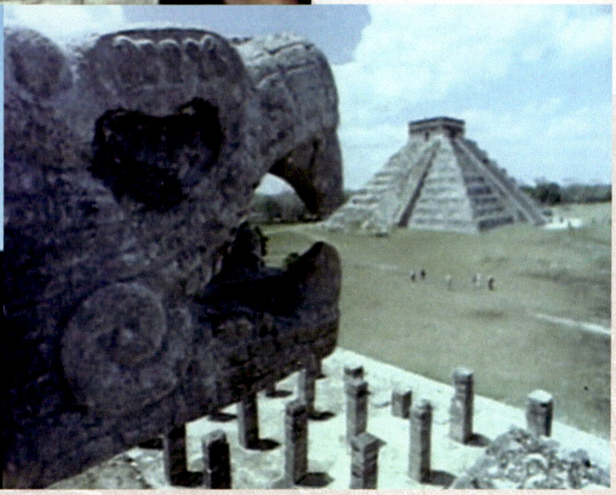

Perhaps it's because they have something to hide. Or perhaps it's because they don't know anything and don't really give much of a damn.

Someone finally points John and Brian in the right direction. They find the old captain. He even has the small stone of the Mayan god, which he lets them borrow. (Probably not a good idea, given curses and all, but I'm not as worried this time. After all, their film did get finished.)

A dangerous voyage by sea and land unfolds. In between drinking coconut juice and eating bananas, the trio finally reaches the same locations where the dramatizations were staged. But they don't find the remains of the German explorers, or even of the actors who portrayed them earlier in this film.

Curse of the Mayan Temple struggles to reach its ninety-minute running time, just as I struggle to watch it. (Headache-inducing, right in the, um, temple.)

To be fair, some of the cinematography—including underwater footage—is quite good, and the locations are wonderful.

The real issue—as much for me as for the film—is that *Curse of the Mayan Temple* has more Weirdumentary in its title and initial dramatizations than it does during the bulk of its running time. Put another way, this Mayan curse is so lame that it'd need a miracle to walk, let alone to stalk.

Anyhow, Gold Key Entertainment included *Curse of the Mayan Temple* in the "Beta Chronicles" TV collection. Earlier plans to four-wall it theatrically had come to naught.

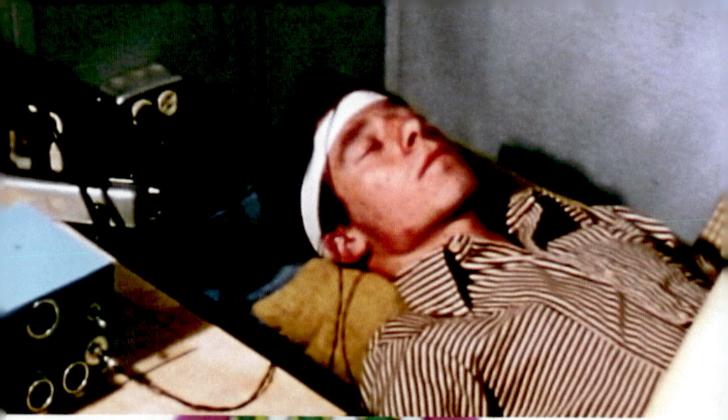
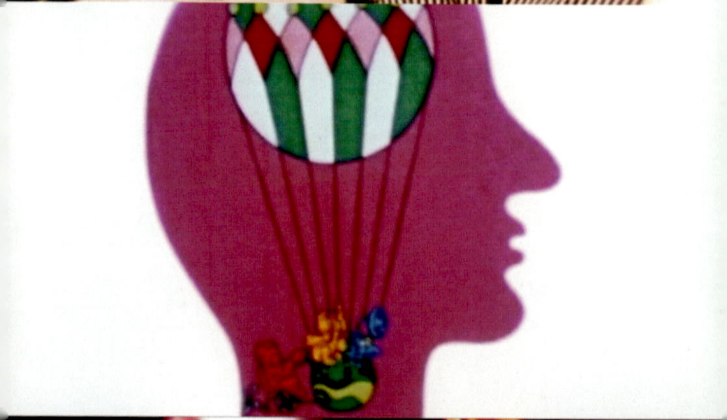
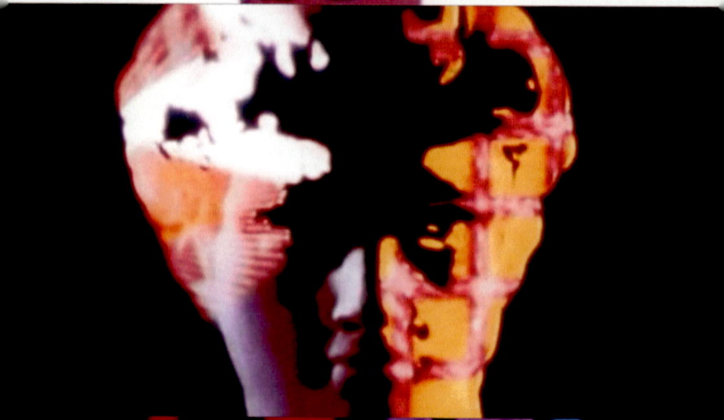
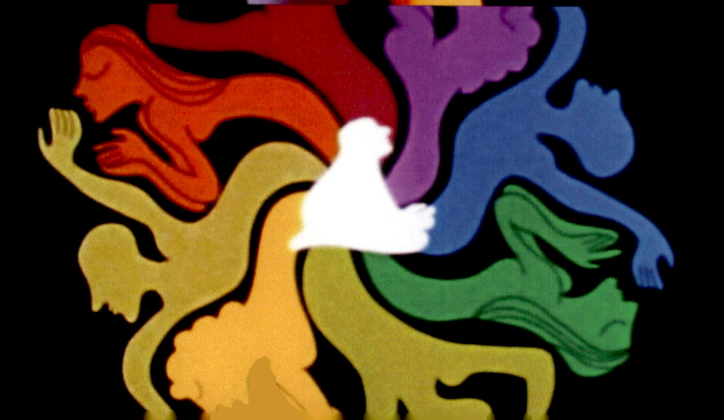

Mysteries of the Mind

(1978)

"There are more things in heaven and earth, Horatio, than are dreamt of in your philosophy." So said Hamlet after seeing his father's ghost in Shakespeare's immortal play, written in 1603. Well, today, over four centuries later, people are still in awe of the supernatural. Indeed, there seem to be more kinds of unexplained psychic phenomena in our supposedly modern age. Telepathy, telekinesis, ESP, astro travel: these are but a few of the many *Mysteries of the Mind.*American National Enterprises presents a film produced by Irving and Elda Hartley. Irving had shot the Hindenburg disaster in 1937; Elda had acted in Hollywood movies in the early thirties. Once married in 1940, they made documentaries together, many of them about religion and spirituality.

"There's a vast terrain of inner space only partially mapped within each of us, a realm as great as the universe outside," narrator Hugh Douglas explains. "Mapping this terrain is the great adventure of the Aquarian Age." Break on through to the other side, sayeth Douglas, like Aldous Huxley and Jim Morrison before him.

Douglas doesn't get to say much else, though, because astronaut Captain Edgar D. Mitchell acts as the film's "commentator." After walking on the moon, Mitchell walks in our mind. Don't blast off, man. Blast in. In-*ward.*

Though she doesn't get credited at the film's opening, parapsychologist Thelma Moss presents almost as many ideas as Mitchell. And she was no stranger to the silver screen. Along with being interviewed for *The Outer Space Connection* (1975), Moss had written the script for *The Colossus of New York* (1958).

Here is why *Mysteries of the Mind* seems a bit disjointed. In 1971, Irving and Elda Hartley made a short documentary called *Psychics, Saints and Scientists.* All of the Moss footage first appeared in it, before being repurposed into this Weirdumentary.

As the running time trudges forward, we also get to meet Olga Worrall (faith healer), Paul Solomon (the modern-day Edgar Cayce), Cleve Backster (polygraph expert who believed plants could feel pain), and Christopher Hills (founder of the University of the Trees).

And we learn important stuff. Mung beans will actually grow better if you tell 'em you love them, dude. And "ASC" doesn't stand for "American Society of Cinematographers," but instead for "Altered States of Consciousness."

Mysteries of the Mind is an uneven exploration of its subject. Highlights include Kirlian photography and some simple but very, very, *very* groovy animation.

Anyhow, the farthest reaches of the mind are within your grasp. All it takes is the power of the brain, and—for at least one of these cool cats—a divining rod. You can pick up your own in the backyard, or perhaps at the University of the Trees.

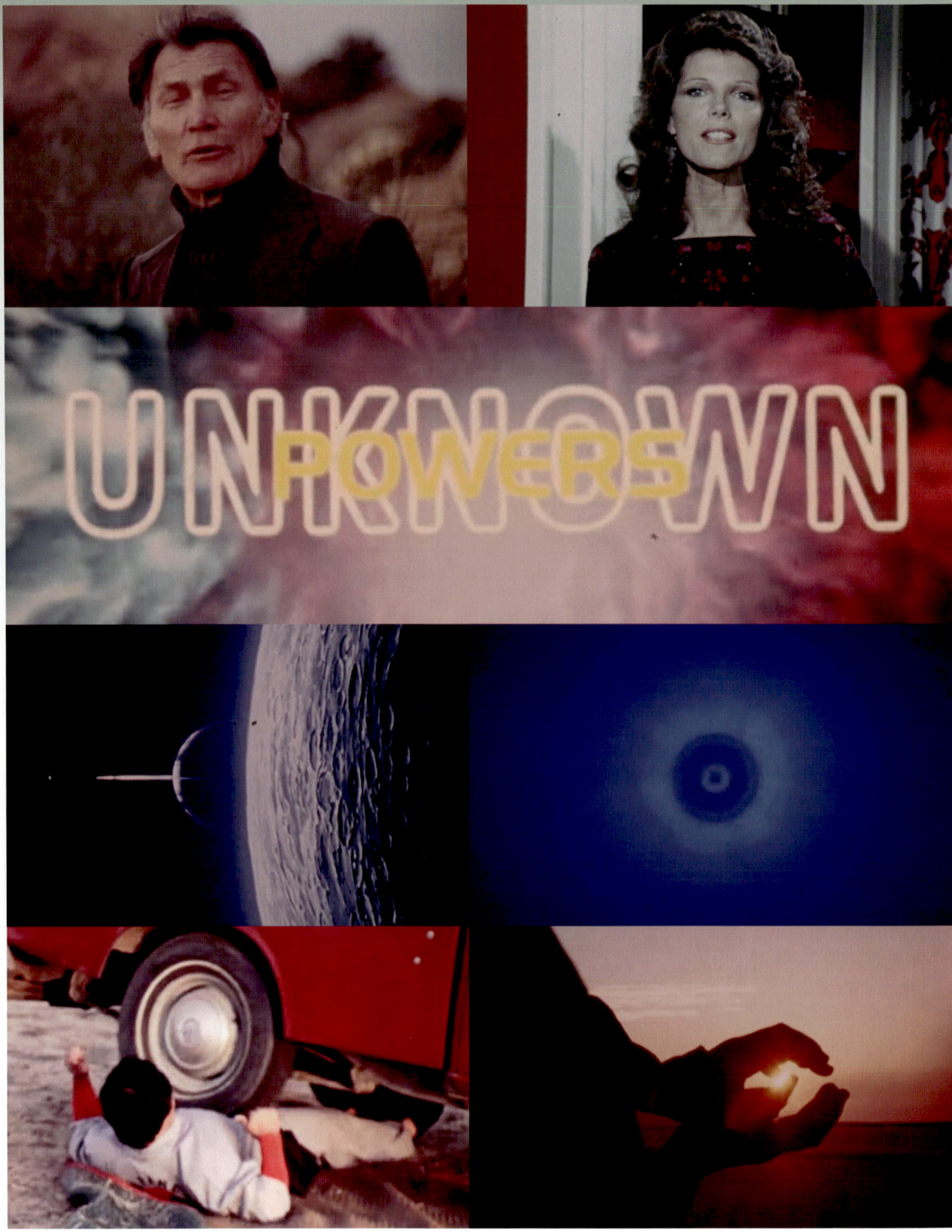
UNKNOWN
POWERS

Unknown Powers

(1978)

Here's a Frankensteinian monster produced and directed by Don Como, stitched-together footage from his prior films into a single, ninety-minute Weirdumentary.

For those of us who either live on Planet Weirdumentary or at least vacation there on occasion, the first quarter of this project is by far the most enjoyable.

Here, you see, is the one new segment, hosted by Samantha Eggar. She informs us: "What you are about to see may be quite different than anything you've ever witnessed before. There are no actors involved, and events have been filmed as they actually occurred. You will meet some of the people who claim extraordinary powers, and experience their world yourself."

Eggar's dialogue helps to set up and tie together, as best it can, the various old footage. And she also takes us into the world of the mind, from the use of astrology in World War II to psychics assisting the police in criminal investigations.

One of those psychics helped the police find twenty-four missing children and solve six murders. (Want proof? You got it! She tells us so, right there on-camera.)

Another psychic explains how lonely her life is because she spends so much time in seclusion. She also tells us that she has seven children, three sons and four daughters. (Not quite all of her time is spent alone, apparently.)

Eggar then introduces us to a woman who talks to animals and—guess what—they talk back to her. Real conversations. Really. (Dr. Doolittle, please allow me to introduce you to Ms. Do-More.)

After about twenty-three minutes, we shift to Jack Palance in a shortened version of Como's *The Unknown Force* (1977). See the entry on that flick for more info.

The third section of this hodgepodge is an abbreviated version of Como's *World Beyond Death* (1976). To learn about that world, see its entry.

Four of four? Footage from Como's *The Miracle Healers* (1976). See the entry? You betcha.

It was footage originally seen in *The Miracle Healers*, specifically of the Reverend Jim Jones, and directly excerpted from *Unknown Powers*, that led Como's distributor to file a $25 million lawsuit against CBS for using clips without permission when reporting on the Jonestown mass suicide.

As Eggar explains, "More and more scientists have come to recognize that the real meaning of [the word] 'occult' is not 'weird' or 'bizarre,' but 'hidden.' They have begun to realize that it is not just the dark side of the moon that needs exploration, but the unknown side of our own natures as well."

On that I hope we can all agree. Or at least agree to disagree.

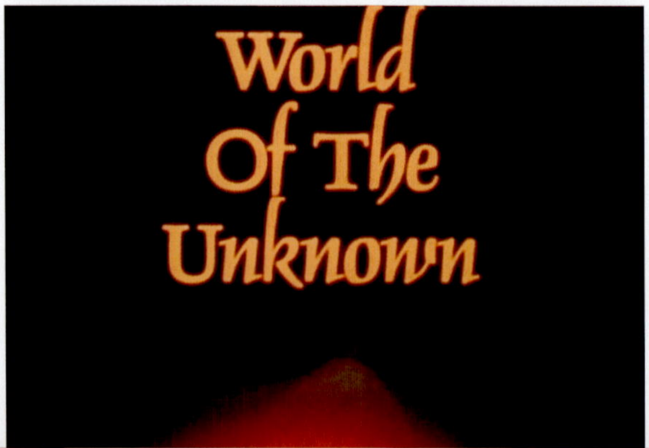
World
Of The
Unknown

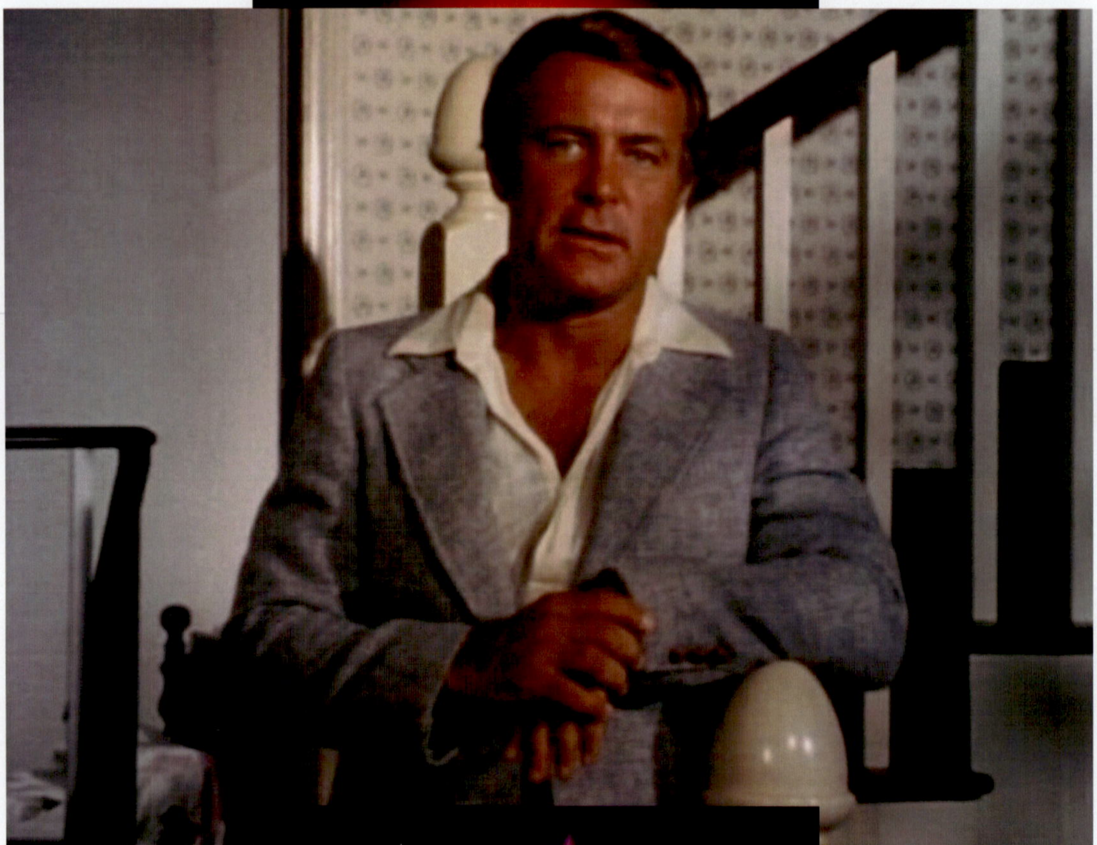

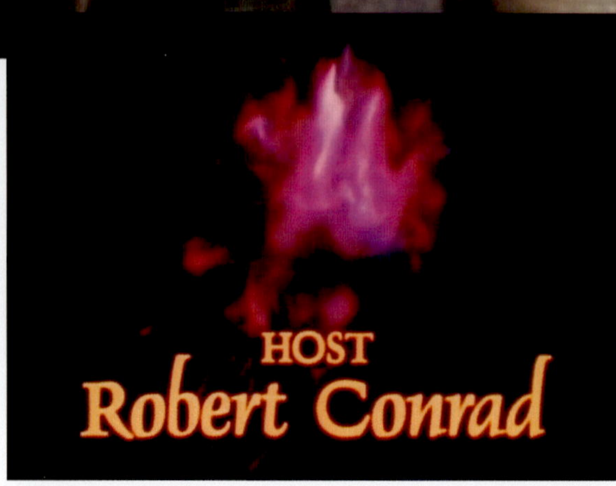
HOST
Robert Conrad

World of the Unknown

(1978)

"As difficult as it may be for us to accept, the war between good and evil, darkness and light, God and the devil, continues. The horrifying rite of exorcism still takes place, often with shocking brutality. For thousands of years, different forms of madness, abnormal behavior, and even physical disease have been explained in terms of demonic possession of a living body by a disincarnate spirit. Accounts of possession have many traits in common, and may occur in any place in the world and to anyone."

Robert Conrad, star of television's *The Wild, Wild West* (1965–69), speaks those words about the wild, wild demons, because writer-director Don Como's film begins in Georgetown and offers numerous clips from *The Exorcist* (1973).

Hysteria? Invasive spirits? Either way, Conrad explains, "There is only one cure: driving the demon out."

The unknown world mentioned in Como's title is one of demonic possession. We see Shia Muslims undergoing self-flagellation and skull bloodletting in order "to beat the devil out of one's own body."

But soon the devil takes a backseat to other weird tales. Conrad explores psychic surgery as it is performed in the Philippines and in Brazil. The performing doctors really do give a performance, one in which the patients' "tissue appears to part" thanks to hands charged with magnetism and electricity. An M.D. tells us that she is "utterly convinced" by the authenticity of these doctors. After all, they work while in a "higher state of consciousness."

One of them says, "I do not usually have a recollection or memory of what I did during the healing session." (To which I must ask, "How then do you even remember that you are a psychic surgeon?")

Nevertheless, some of these folks get results, and nobody has ever so much as reported a case of infection from unwashed hands plunging deep inside their innards.

We see black hair pulled from the chest cavity of a woman who is "possessed by an evil spirit." Even after burning the hair, the mop pulsates "as if it had a life of its own."

Next up is Giza. Dr. Patrick Flanagan explains that pyramids are capable of "cosmic rays," and that there is a "force at work within [the Great Pyramid] that defies the laws of science as we know them."

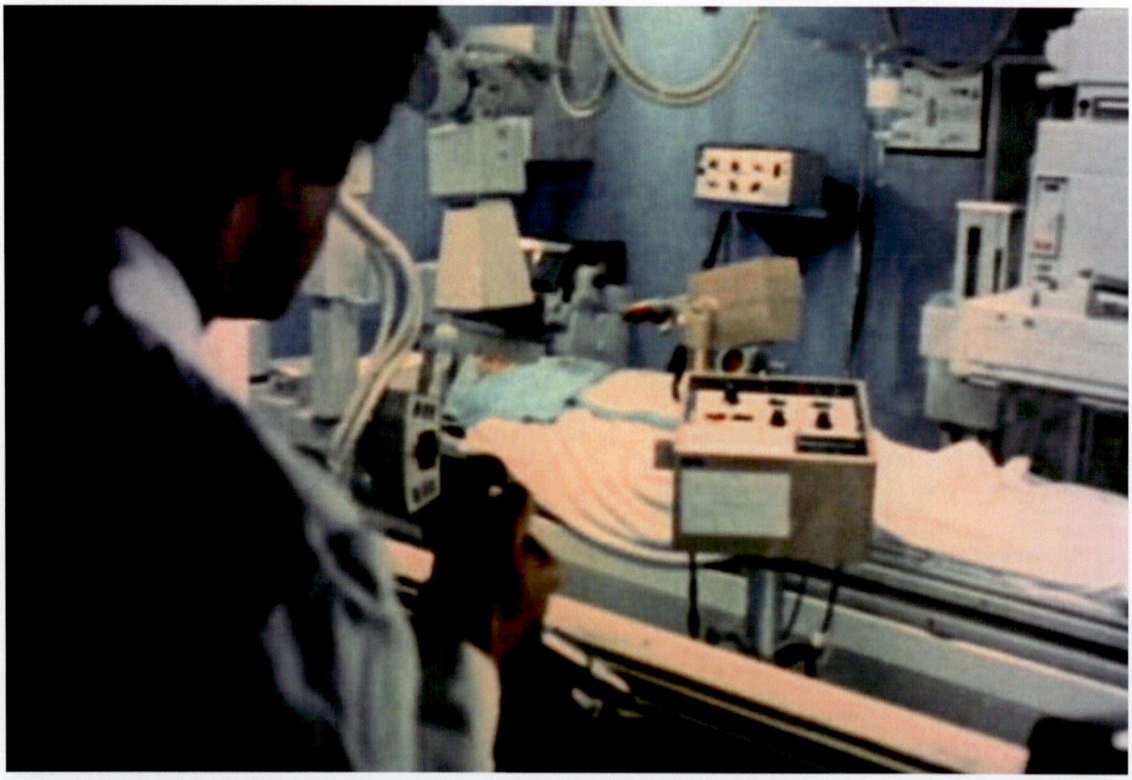

This force is etheric energy, which is similar to static electricity, but it isn't static electricity. Flanagan knows this to be true, all thanks to the Etheric Energy Detector that he devised. (The fact that his clothes stick to it occasionally is mere coincidence. Nothing to see here.)

Flanagan explains that an Arab guide told him, "Anyone who has ever spent the night in the Great Pyramid either was found dead the next morning, or they were found insane." So, of course, Flanagan slept inside it.

And then a thing happened. Actually, a "very strange thing happened." His "body started vibrating and shaking." He "went into a cataleptic state," his body becoming "rigid," but not fully stiff. He survived, thanks be to Isis, and possibly Osiris.

About a month later, a thirteenth-century Persian began to speak through Flanagan.

This Persian gives a press conference on film, one of the best scenes in Weirdumentary history. Questions come from a reporter, doctor, psychologist, movie director, and even the Associate Editor of *Esquire* magazine. Their answers are heard in Flanagan's voice, but with an affected accent. (Needless to say, the 700-year-old Persian speaks English.)

And he's happy to be of help to modern humans. He repositions a baby in a woman's pregnant body, because it is "slightly in the wrong position." And he tells a guy to shave his head to achieve a higher state of being. As a result, that guy gets possessed by a different Persian.

From there, it's time for a little bit of Edgar Cayce and the Bermuda Triangle. Dr. Ray Brown appears on-camera to describe the pyramid he discovered underwater at Bimini. Inside it was a rectangular-shaped room, and inside it was a pedestal and a golden rod bearing a red stone.

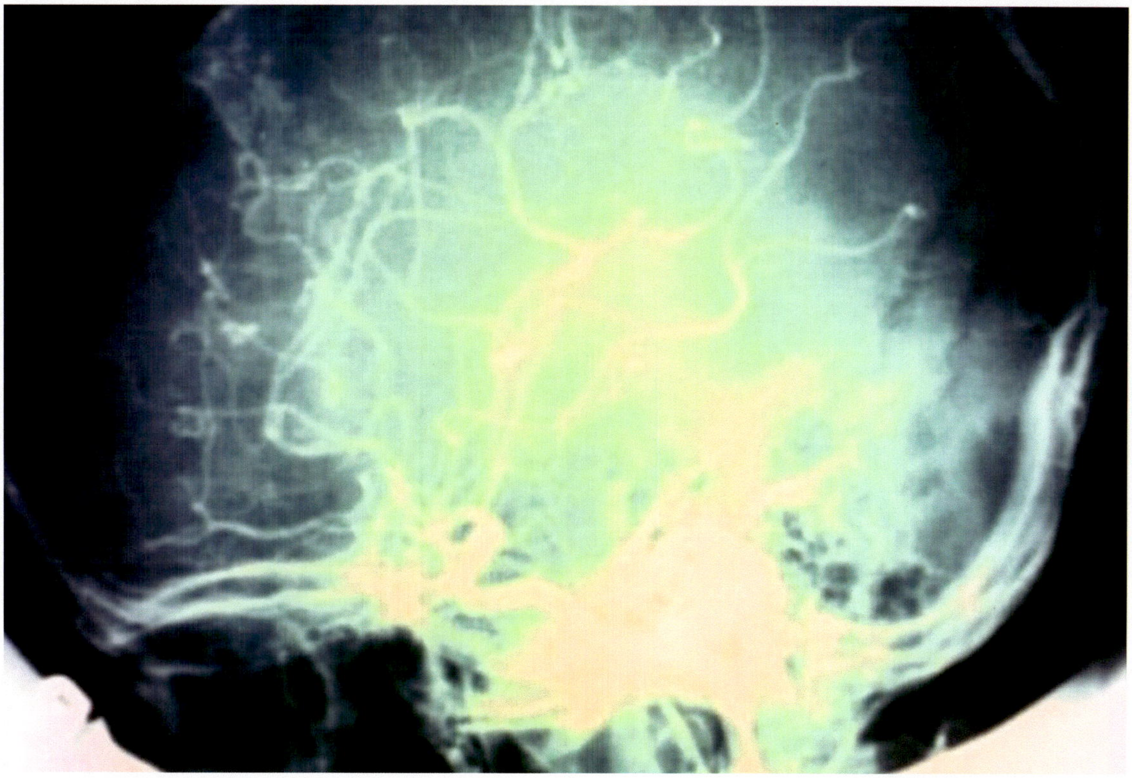

"I felt the past talking to me," Brown explains. An ominous voice told him to leave and not come back. He did, but not without palming a crystal as a keepsake. It allegedly gives off radiation and even causes some people to pass out.

Oh, and before I forget, all of the other divers on Brown's expedition died, may they rest in peace.

Then we hear the tale of a prospector named Larry Forman, who met an alien in the desert, and not just any old alien, mind you, but the "head of the Supreme Court in outer space." Larry learns that the Earth is "nothing more than a penal colony."

Our time in jail is nearly over, thankfully, so much so that the alien allows his robot to cure Forman of heart trouble. The recreation footage of the android and Forman himself is good enough to be worth a prison sentence, at least a short one.

World of the Unknown culminates with accounts of young men who can bend spoons, because—as we all know—spoons are important. (Chopsticks and forks aren't worth a damn when it comes to supping soup.)

And the father of one spoon-bender assures us that his boy's telekinesis will only be used for the "betterment of everybody concerned." (Soup's on, kids.)

Conrad ends the film by declaring, "Whatever is manifesting within us is something we possess rather than something that possesses us. This increased awareness may lead to a new age of self-discovery, and perhaps someday, deep within this world of the unknown, we may finally come face to face with the greatest mystery and phenomenon of all: ourselves."

I'll end this review by saying, "Whatever manifested in Don Como when he made this Weirdumentary, I offer my sincere and humble thanks."

Death: The Ultimate Mystery

(1979)

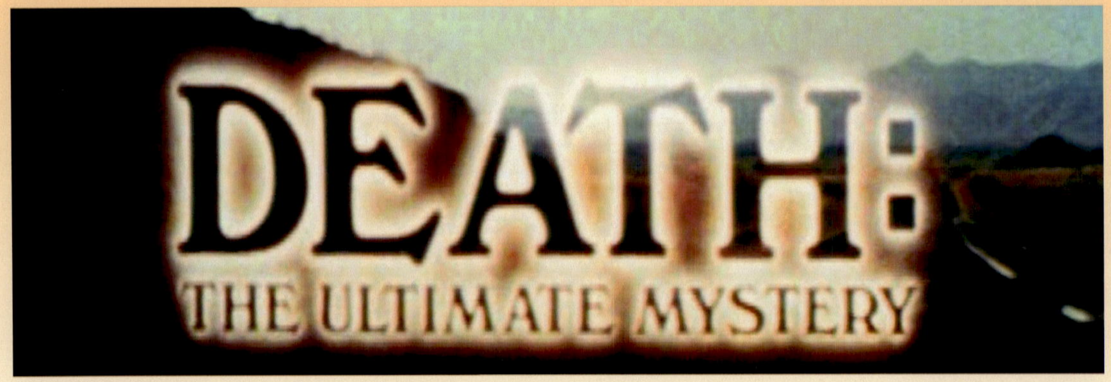

"In the time it takes to watch this program, 20,640 new lives will begin, and 6,960 lives will reach their end. And as much as we wish to deny it, each of us will in our measured time know the end called death."

Actor Cameron Mitchell—remembered not only for his turn on Broadway in *Death of a Salesman* (1949), but also for a spate of horror films like *Nightmare in Wax* (1969) and *The Toolbox Murders* (1978)—speaks those ominous words. Out of the void of space, we see star child after star child, tumbling toward us. Each is terminal from the moment of its birth.

"This is a most unusual but factual account of my attempt to uncover the deepest mysteries that surround . . . *Death: The Ultimate Mystery*."

Robert Emenegger and Allan Sandler, of *UFOs: Past, Present, and Future* (1975) fame, are back, and I couldn't be more grateful. Both get credited here as producer, writer, and director.

Emenegger composed the score, which meshes wonderfully with Mitchell's voice and the film's unhurried pace. It all feels like descending slowly into a warm bathtub while gently opening your veins.

Death: The Ultimate Mystery unfolds in first person, with our on-screen host surviving a car wreck and becoming obsessed with the subject of dying and the afterlife. In wonderful Weirdumentary style, the identity of the narrator is more of a question than an answer. We hear Cameron Mitchell's voice speaking in first person, and the frame often assumes the point-of-view of the host, achieving the old camera Eye/I effect.

At other times, though, we see the host, who is definitely *not* Cameron Mitchell. He is regularly filmed at a distance, either from the back or his face obscured. Whoever he is,

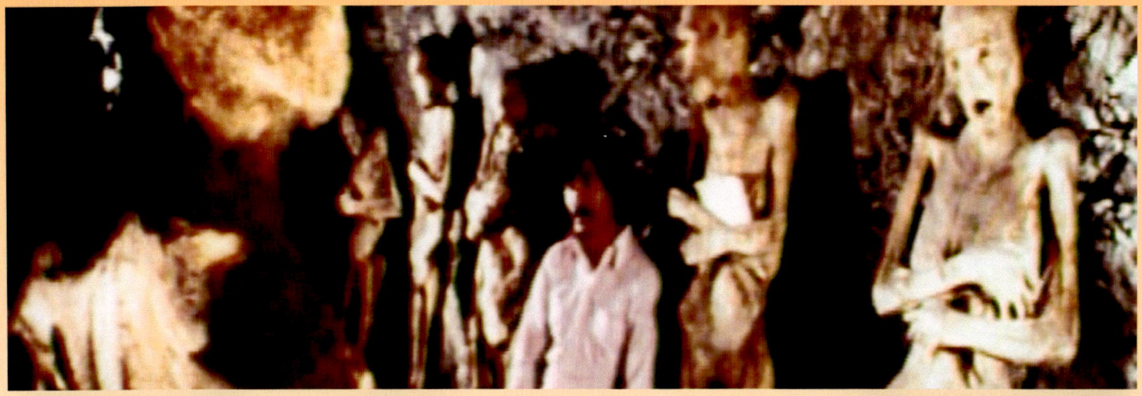

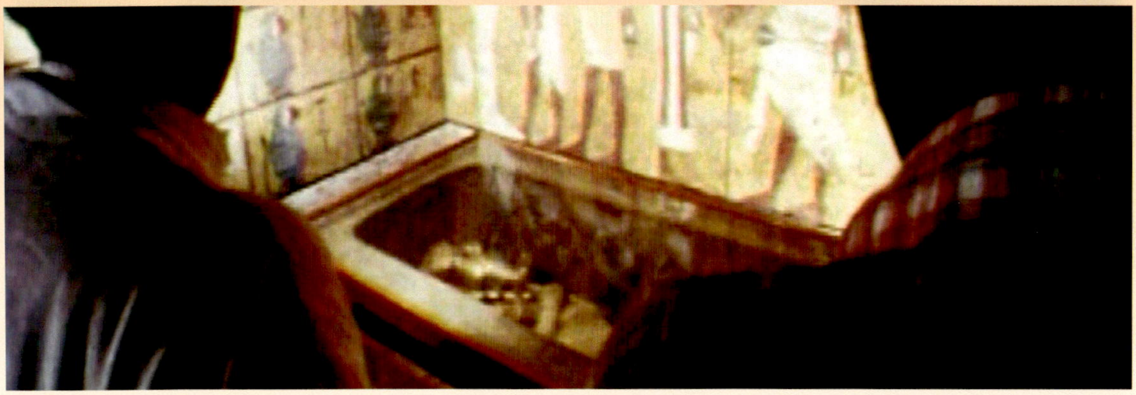

though, be sure to dig on his groovy bell bottoms. They are to die for.

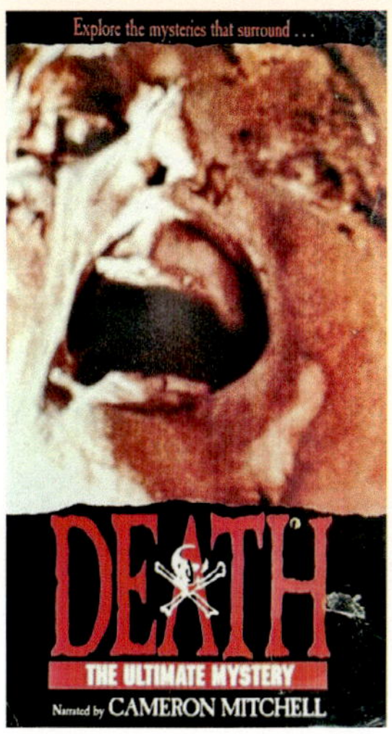

This stylish dude traverses the globe to determine whether or not "something exists after death." He visits the mummies of Guanajuato, the Sphinx in Egypt, and a Swami in India, as well as a group of experts in America, among them Dr. Maurice Rawlings, author of the book *Beyond Death's Door* (1978).

The film's breakthrough comes with hypno-regression therapy. One patient describes a past life she lived in Corning, Ohio, giving enough details that the host makes his way to that little town and verifies all that she recalls. The story "checks out," which should give us all a bit of solace when we check out.

Emenegger and Sandler save the best for last, though, with the host undergoing hypnosis that will take him into the future, to see his forthcoming demise. POV camerawork puts us right on the table, the hypnotist staring down into our eyes. For this scene, and for the entire film, I give two rigor mortis thumbs up.

Copyrighted in 1979, *Death: The Ultimate Mystery* first appeared on television in late 1980. The film never seems to have found its audience, even in the DVD age when released by VCI Entertainment in 2007. Alas, death is not a growth business.

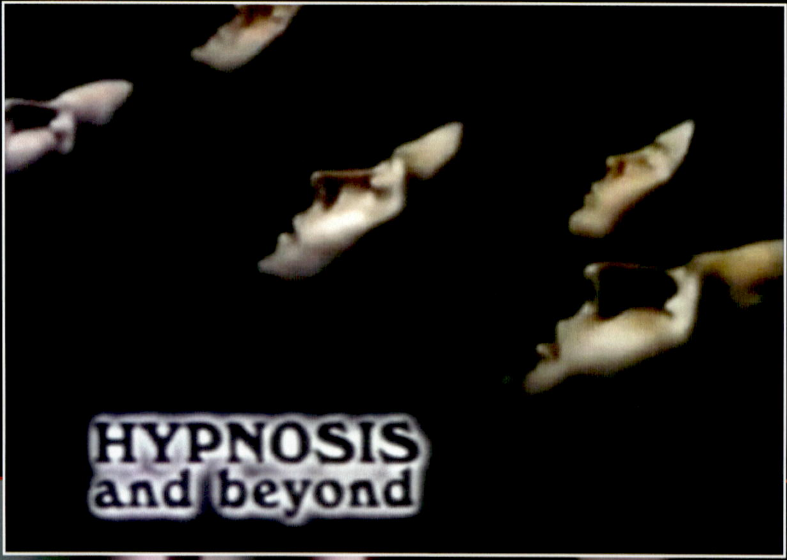
HYPNOSIS
and beyond

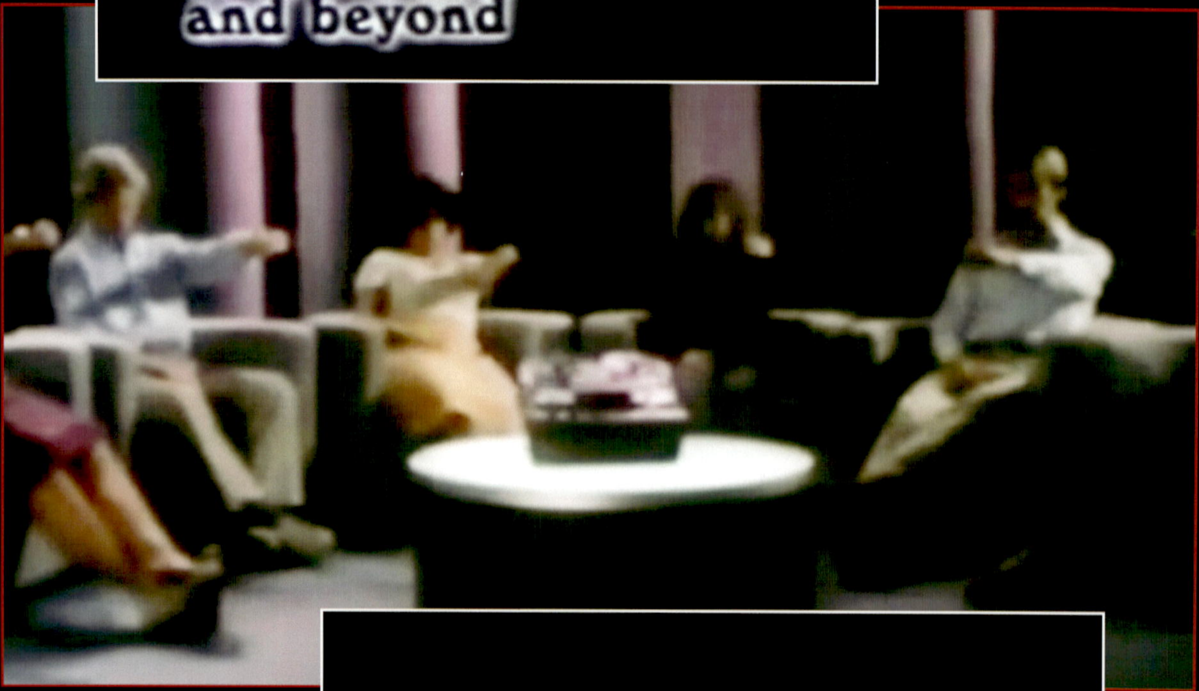

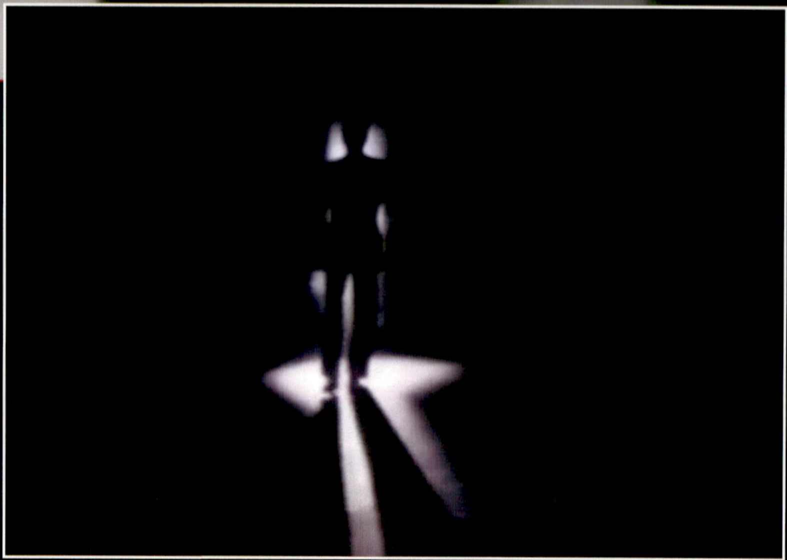

Hypnosis and Beyond

(1979)

Though copyrighted in 1979, *Hypnosis and Beyond* doesn't seem to have been broadcast until 1980. According to one *TV Guide* listing, "Host William Shatner explores the mysteries of mind control through dramatic recreations and live demonstrations of hypnotic trance." Accurate enough, but it hardly does justice to a film written and directed by Allan Sandler and Robert Emenegger, the dynamic duo who brought us *UFOs: Past, Present, and Future* (1975) and *Death: The Ultimate Mystery* (1979).

This Weirdumentary opens with Shatner emerging out of the darkness to explain: "Man, perceiving himself as a unique creature in all of creation ... has been led to believe that he alone has been given a mind to think, to invent, to create. In just this century, man's growing curiosity has led him to make more discoveries than ever before in history."

These discoveries include space travel, nuclear power, genetics, and "the greatest mystery of all" ... the human mind, "that very source from which all ideas, thoughts, behavior, desires, and creativity arise. The mind, looking into itself..."

Then *Hypnosis and Beyond* delves into trances and hypnosis, discoveries that of course predate the twentieth century, but hey, who am I to question a Starfleet captain, even if he is out of uniform?

In fairness to all concerned, we do learn about the history of mental powers in ancient Egypt, China, and elsewhere. The film treats us to a brief bio of Franz Anton Mesmer, the father of Mesmerism. And historic footage depicts the sway that Adolf Hitler and Jim Jones held over their followers.

But the heart of this Weirdumentary arrives in the form of "laboratory" experiments with volunteers undergoing hypnosis. They're actually on a film set that features appropriately mysterious lighting.

Can you make a hypnotized person perform an act against his or her will? A test subject proves you can. Might a person under hypnosis regress to a former life, or even to a future life? You betcha. As Shatner explains, "by using this power ourselves, no longer can others keep us from our destiny."

The Power of Suggestion suggests you exercise your power in pushing play on the nearest VCR and watch *Hypnosis and Beyond*, which last surfaced on a VHS tape in 1989.

World of Mystery

(1979)

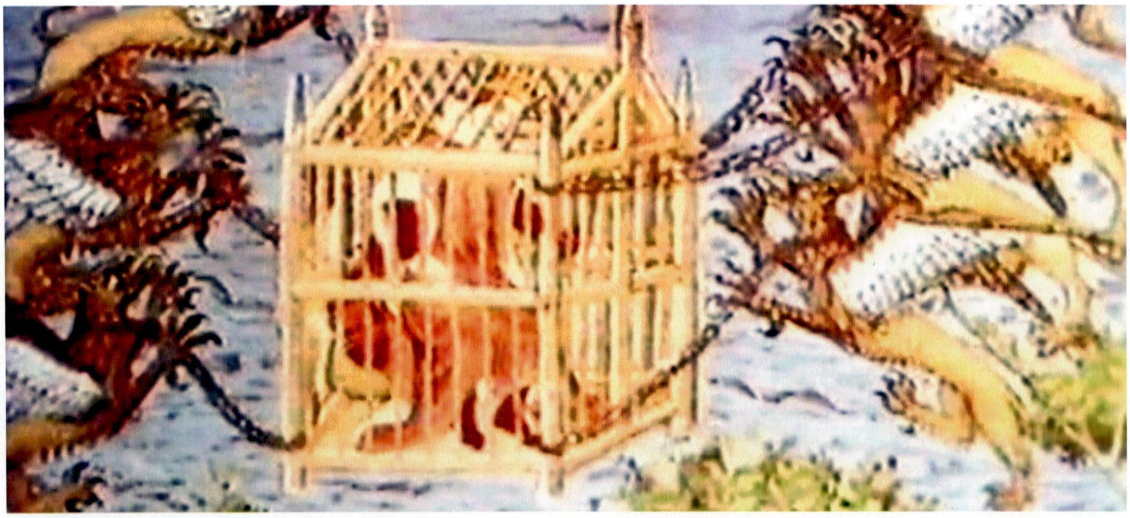

"Welcome to the World of Mystery, a world of strange sights and sounds, a world of unexplained mysteries and visitation from other planets. It is a world of ghosts, of monsters from outer space, of demons and sorcery, of monsters from the depths of the seas, of werewolves and satanic ceremonies, of despotic rulers and wars, in short, a world of contradictions, continual conflicts, and unexplained phenomena that scientists are only now beginning to unravel."

If this is indeed the "short" version, I'd hate to hear narrator Sidney Paul take the long way around the Weirdumentary Bend. It might have been quicker if'n he'd just told us what *ain't* in this here movie.

After all, we get Conan Doyle, Houdini, and Mesmer. Earthquakes and volcanoes and hurricanes. DNA and electron microscopes and mermaids. Voodoo and psychics and ghosts. Aleister Crowley and Uri Geller and Charlie Manson. Lions and tigers and bears, *oh why?*

Delineator Films is hard not to love, but *World of Mystery* places a little bit of pressure on our relationship. Whereas their other films have wonderfully elliptical and repetitive structures, this one seems more like potluck minus the luck.

"How long must man wait to learn the secrets of the universe? How long must man wait to understand the mysterious world about him?"

A lot longer than director Wheeler Dixon's ninety-five-minute film, which is more than long enough, methinks. Paul's opening narration tries to justify why everything that's anything will be covered, but with these broad horizons ironically comes a less-than-panoramic vision.

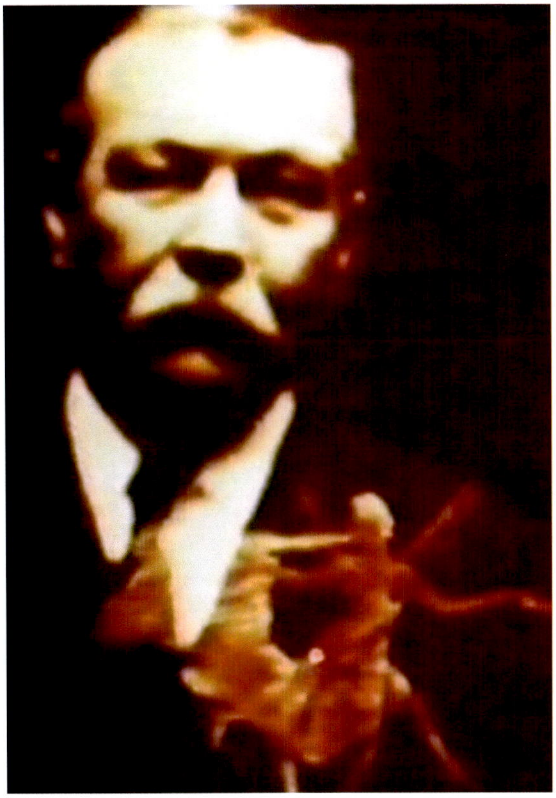 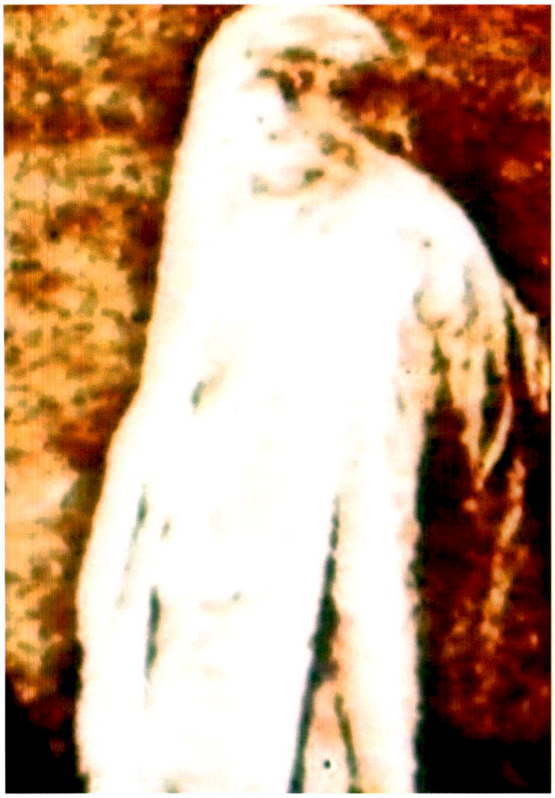

Rather than a brisk pace through all that's unholy and unknown, our feet get bogged down in whatever footage was near at hand. For example, nineteen minutes is spent on Hitler, presumably because that was how long the cheap stock footage lasted.

Most of the rest of the film launches us into space, with talk of rockets and aliens and Martian canals. That leads us to more a universe of mystery than one mere world, as the title suggests.

Music supervision by Jim Cookman gets an A+, for sure. But we've been here before, those of us that enjoy the far-out space nuts that Dixon cracked open in his other Weirdumentaries.

Even the credits are kooky, which is saying a fair bit for Delineator. At the beginning, we see the copyright date "1979/80," but at the end we see "1978." Not a world of mystery, but a mystery nonetheless.

World of Mystery might well have made its biggest splash in 1983, when it was released on VHS in the United Kingdom as part of the "Gamma Chronicles," a series that also included Dixon's *Amazing World of Ghosts* (1978) and *UFO—Exclusive!* (1978).

Despite its faults, never let it be said that *World of Mystery* doesn't have some charm. How can we not feel joy when Sidney Paul asks, "Do we really own the moon, or is it the domain of a hidden race which watched our faltering steps onto their planet with amusement and dismay?" My own personal favorite, though, is a question about another faraway world: "What sort of life might exist here, in the volcanic sea-washed bosom of an emerging planet?" The answer is obvious, of course. Rock people. And no, you aren't stoned. Sidney Paul really does suggest there could be "Rock People."

WE'VE LOOKED INTO THE MOST POWERFUL FORCE ON EARTH. AND BROUGHT BACK PICTURES.

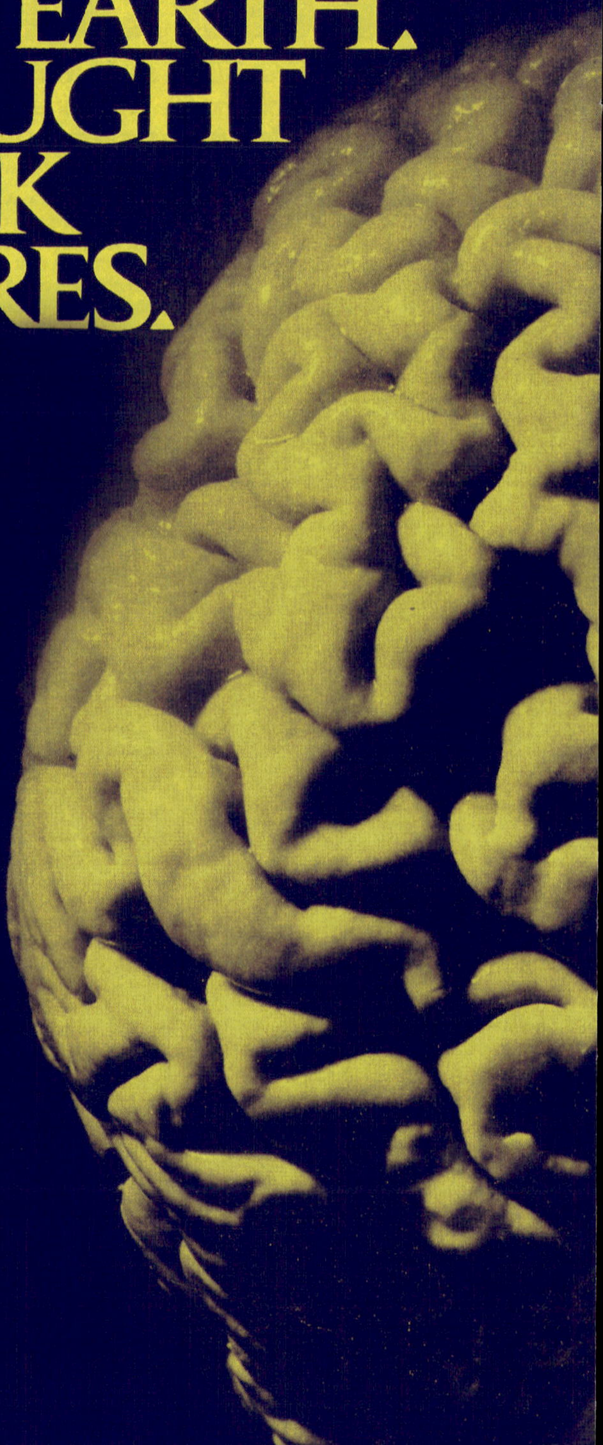

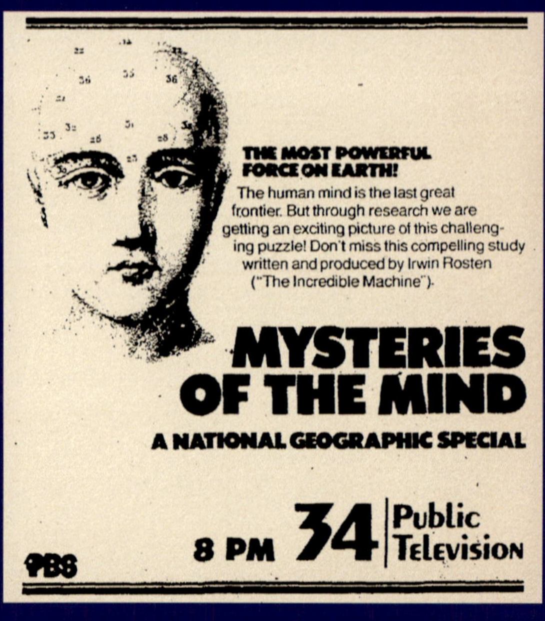

Mysteries of the Mind

(1980)

"This is a film about the most powerful force on Earth—the human mind. To explore it is to embark on an endless journey, awesome in dimension and complexity."

So sayeth E.G. Marshall, in a documentary created by the National Geographic Society. Money from Gulf Oil greased producer-director-writer Irwin Rosten's budget. And the title, well, for whatever reason, Rosten used the same title as Irving and Elda Hartley had in 1978 (see entry).

Like so many great Weirdumentaries, this film begins with an enigmatic scene, one hard to believe, and hard not to believe. Vernon Craig, known professionally as Komar, lies on a bed of nails. Another man places a concrete block on his chest and strikes it with a sledgehammer. Komar stands up, showing no signs of pain, despite the indentations pressed into his back.

"What is the mind and where is it located?" Marshall asks in a far nicer tone than he ever used in *12 Angry Men* (1957):

> *To mystics, the mind is the universe; the universe is the mind. To science, mind and brain are one. Either way, it is a matter of wonder and mystery, and a paradox, too, that the most powerful force on Earth lacks the power to understand itself.*

For example, how does someone write a symphony, or have the talent to play in an orchestra? So many neurons firing at the same time, drawing on training and talent, while also helping the same person to sit upright, maintain equilibrium, and perform in front of an audience. ("Look Ma, no hands… all brain!")

Photographs, models, and some early computer-generated animation explore the physical brain:

> *Behold a human brain. Its appearance tells us nothing of its functions, nothing about the individual whose personality it once contained. Nowhere in this wrinkled, jelly-like mass is there even a clue to race, nationality, or religion. It could be the brain of a genius or a cretin, a killer or a saint.*

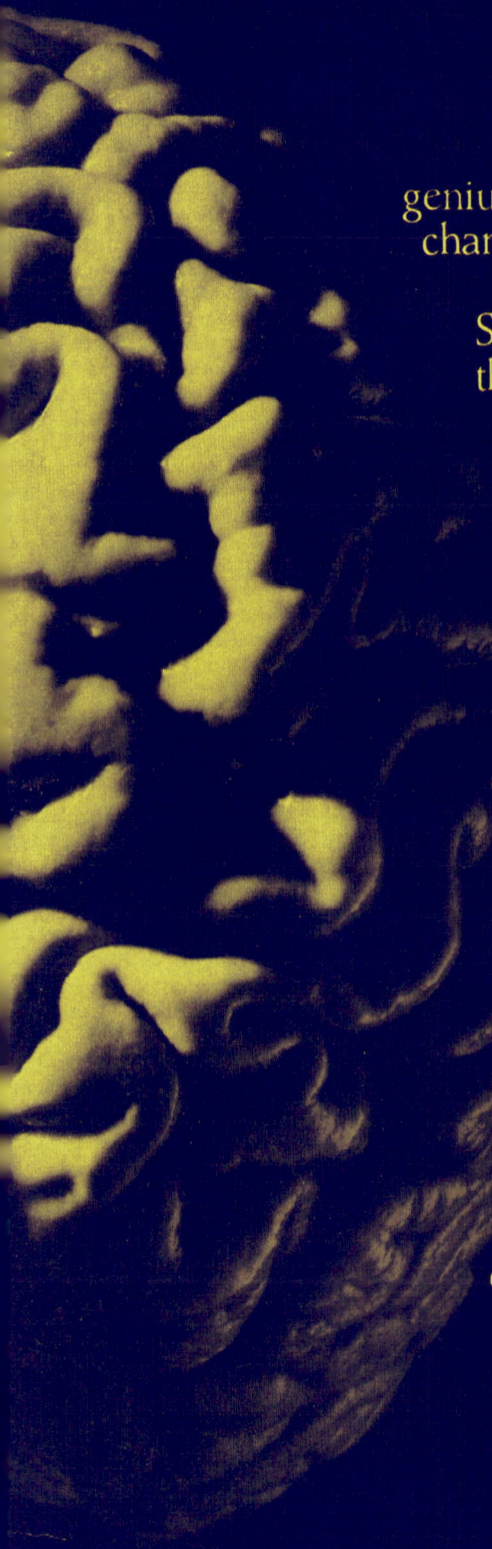

Is it the brain of a killer or a saint? The mind of a genius or a cretin? Is there any way to tell? Any way to change it?

Mysteries of the Mind, a new National Geographic Special, explores the most powerful force on earth, the human brain.

This mind-expanding hour for the entire family, produced by the National Geographic Society and WQED/Pittsburgh with a grant from Gulf Oil Corporation, looks at pain control, sleep, and hypnosis research in America, as well as yogis in India, and acupuncture in China.

Gulf made a commitment with the National Geographic Society and the Public Broadcasting Service five years ago to American-made Public Television.

Together, we've set Public Television viewing records.

In fact, the shows are consistently the highest-rated specials on PBS.

For an hour of discovery television, remember the first Monday of January, February, March, and April in 1980.

And enjoy great television that has sent film crews around the world, diving to the depths of the ocean, digging into new worlds, and exploring the most powerful force on earth.

GULF OIL CORPORATION
NATIONAL GEOGRAPHIC SOCIETY
PUBLIC TELEVISION

Partners in Discovery

Gulf

Words to the wise, Frankenstein. And to all of us, because the brain and mind might well be two different things. Thus, Marshall starts thinking about thinking:

> *Through the brain, we know what we are. We know we're alive. But how do we know? That's the mystery that plagues us still. The last few decades have seen enormous progress in mapping the brain, and learning how it functions—with powerful tools like computers and electronic microscopes, science has compiled vast amounts of data, but each new gateway leads to a new horizon. The brain remains the ultimate frontier.*

To boldly go where so many have gone before, including in prior Weirdumentaries, into the depths of inner space.

Carl Sagan appears on-camera, closing instead of opening our minds, explaining that the mind-body dualism is really nothing more than chemical and electrical aspects of the brain. No mystical goings-on.

Nevertheless, Marshall guides us into the dark recesses of the mind's underworld, telling us: "If all the nerve cells and fibers in one human brain were stretched end to end, they would reach at least to the moon and back." One giant step for brainkind, I'd say.

Things go from kinda-sorta cool to full-on weird during the final third of this film, where we learn about the content of dreams and the powers of meditation, acupuncture, faith healing and mysticism. (Mind over matter, no; mind over pain, yes.)

One nice guy is hypnotized and then his hand is placed in ice water. It doesn't hurt. He requires no glove, let alone coat. As Marshall tells us, "We know [hypnotism] works, but we do not know how it works."

And so it does, including on a woman riding a stationary bicycle. A doctor asks her to hold a pencil and tells her it is getting hotter and hotter, which causes her to drop it. This proves something, apparently.

The weirdest of all, though, is a yogi (not named Bear or Berra) placed inside a chamber without enough oxygen. He survives, thanks to a meditative state. (Cue up the Air Supply.)

"It would seem there are many interesting areas that are neglected by [*Mysteries of the Mind*]," *The Hollywood Reporter* wrote. That would be true, true believers. Mesmerism isn't mentioned, and there's nary a Kirlian photograph to be found.

Nevertheless, as one newspaper article told readers, *Mysteries of the Mind* "demonstrate[s] that as we discover more about the limitless capabilities of the mind, we can harness that knowledge to help realize the glorious human potential." And hey, it won an Emmy. Left and right brain, please applaud in unison.

Arthur C. Clarke's Mysterious World: The Paranormal

(1980)

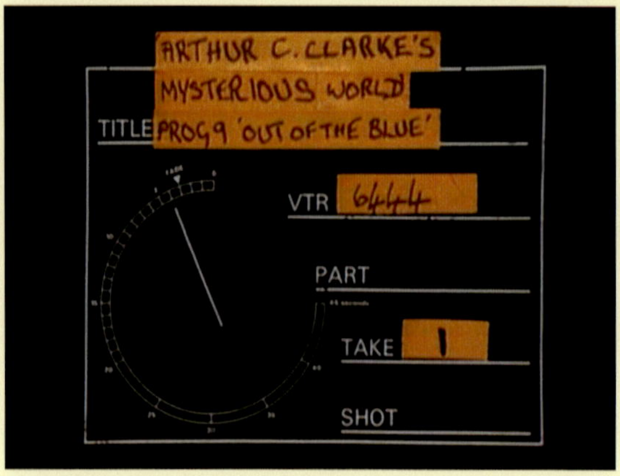

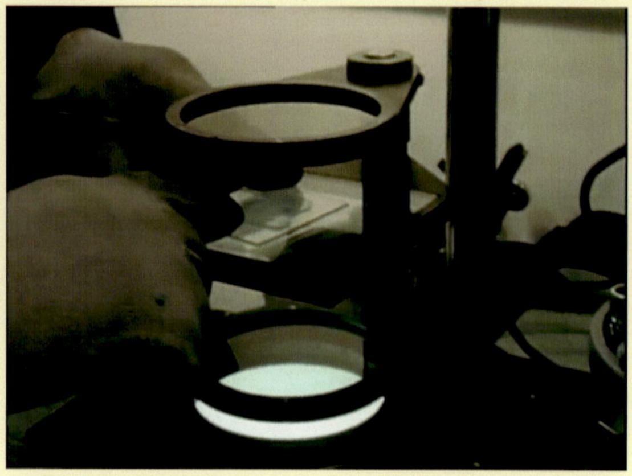

Mysterious World paid little heed to the world of the paranormal, but just enough to merit some choice words.

Out of the Blue, Episode 9: Did freshwater perch fall from the sky in Australia?

Or in Sri Lanka? "What an extraordinary thing! Fish falling from the sky!"

Even stranger (or would it be less strange, after the 1999 film *Magnolia*?), "millions of frogs" fell from the sky in England during World War II. "It rained frogs for at least an hour and a quarter," one eyewitness reports.

Clarke tells us that tales like these first provoked his interest in the mysteries of this and other worlds. He invokes the name Charles Fort, who chronicled such oddities during the teens and twenties.

We hear about strange chunks of ice falling from the sky. "Now, there may be something of real scientific importance beyond this," Clarke advises us, especially given accounts recorded before the advent of aviation. Could this be "cosmic ice" from outer space?

Maybe, but what about the inexplicable shower of hazelnuts in England in 1977? Clarke explains that there is no "rational explanation," adding "your guess is as good as mine." (We don't hear if the nuts were shelled.)

Clarke's Cabinet of Curiosities, Episode 13: "Why do stones move all by themselves in California's Death Valley? Can frogs and toads really live for centuries entombed in solid

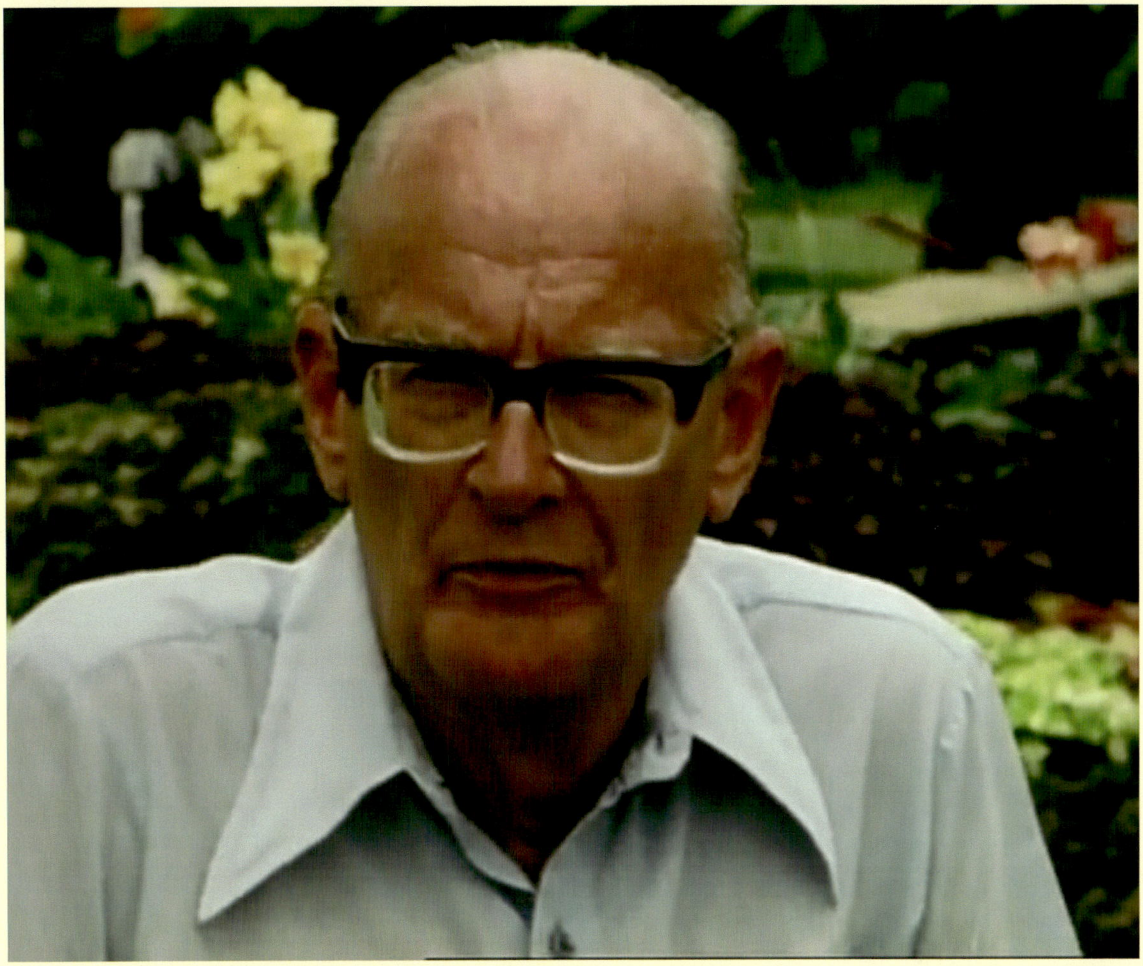

rock? … This man helped build the world's first atom bomb. Has he also found the key to the age-old puzzle of ball lightning?"

And, to add to the narrator's collection of questions, let me ask: How many Fortean stories can you fit into a single episode of *Mysterious World*? Are they here together simply because none of them had enough oomph for individual episodes?

Now let me answer my own question. Yes, these topics are here together in the season finale as leftovers that weren't enough to make a meal of their own. Thus, mysterious gumbo, some ingredients possibly paranormal.

As for Clarke, his final take is as follows: "In this series, we've scanned an entire spectrum of mysteries. Some are amusing, some are trivial, some are complete enigmas, some we may even have solved, but they vary wildly in significance. Some, though fascinating, are probably quite unimportant. Others, if we could fathom them, might change our entire understanding of the universe."

What I cannot fathom is why *Mysterious World* avoided ghosts, poltergeists, spirit photographs, and other supernatural topics. I do not know, and so any answer I might give shouldn't be trusted. "I believe nothing of my own that I have ever written," Charles Fort once declared.

Land of Celtic Ghosts

(1980)

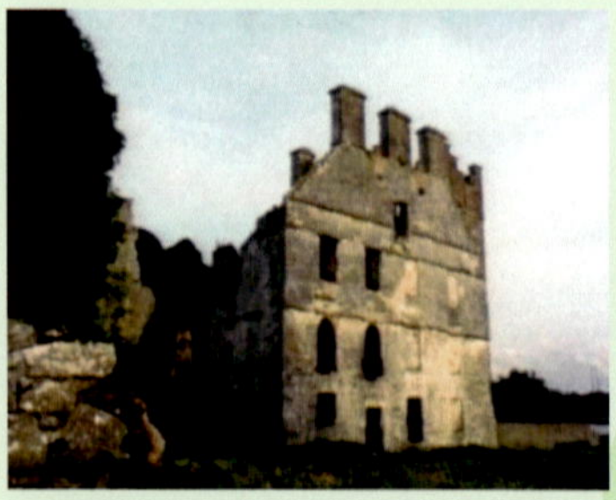 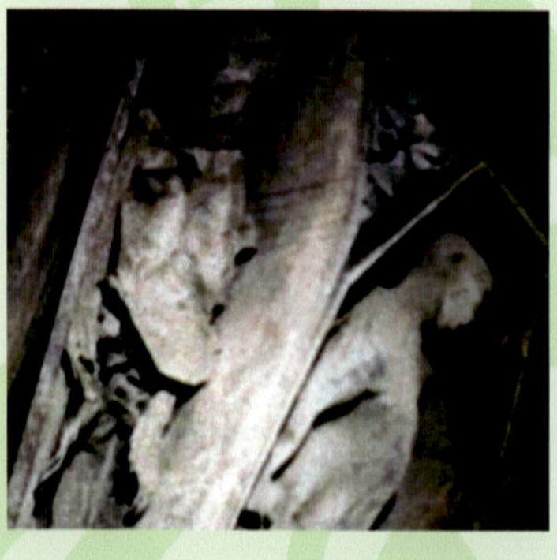 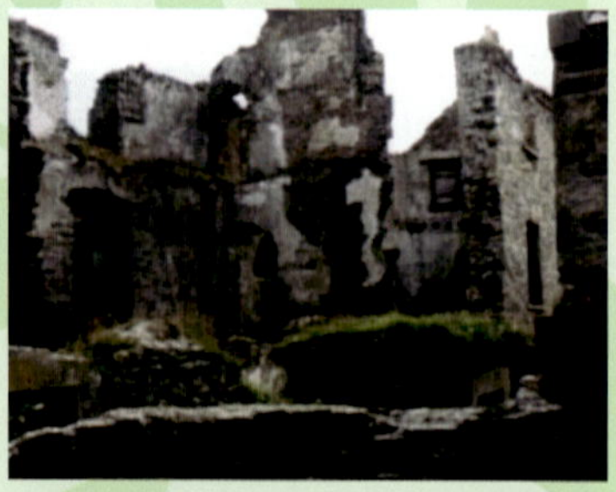

"Ireland: The very name evokes romance, but in the clouded twilight of Irish/Celtic history, there are countless references to unexplained phenomena. Spirits of another time, another place, from the other world, dwell in this ancient land. Even today, tales abound of ancestral spirits who still haunt the halls of Irish castles. And sacrificial altars stand as mute evidence of a dark, once-flourishing civilization, whose origins are lost in the mists of time."

Richard Basehart was a great actor, and a great narrator, too, whether voicing the opening for TV's *Knight Rider* or this wonderful introduction to *Land of Celtic Ghosts*.

The Irish, we learn, are more "sensitive" than most people to the supernatural, which results in so many ghostly encounters. The script by Maureen Curtis presents tales from centuries ago, through the Great Famine and World War II, and all the way up to the television age.

The stories unfold throughout the island: Dublin, Kerry, Limerick, Tara, Wicklow, and beyond. Some ghosts live in homes; others in churches. Some are friendly; some are not. Some are famous; some are not.

Particular ghosts are visible to those lucky enough to see them, like the "Lady in White." Others are audible, like the recurrent screams of a murdered woman. One spirit even caused a horrible stench in a home until it was exorcised.

The great Jerry Johnson produced, directed, shot, and edited *Land of Celtic Ghosts*, which is usually dated as 1980, but its closing credits note a copyright year of 1979.

The film is a gem. Its pacing is wonderfully and methodically slow. It features beautiful and eerie cinematography, which is often marked by expert moving camera. And music supervision by Don Great is, well, great, with a capital "G."

It's easy to see why so many people have fond memories of watching *Land of Celtic Ghosts*, which subtly creates an unsettling mood. On-camera interviewees

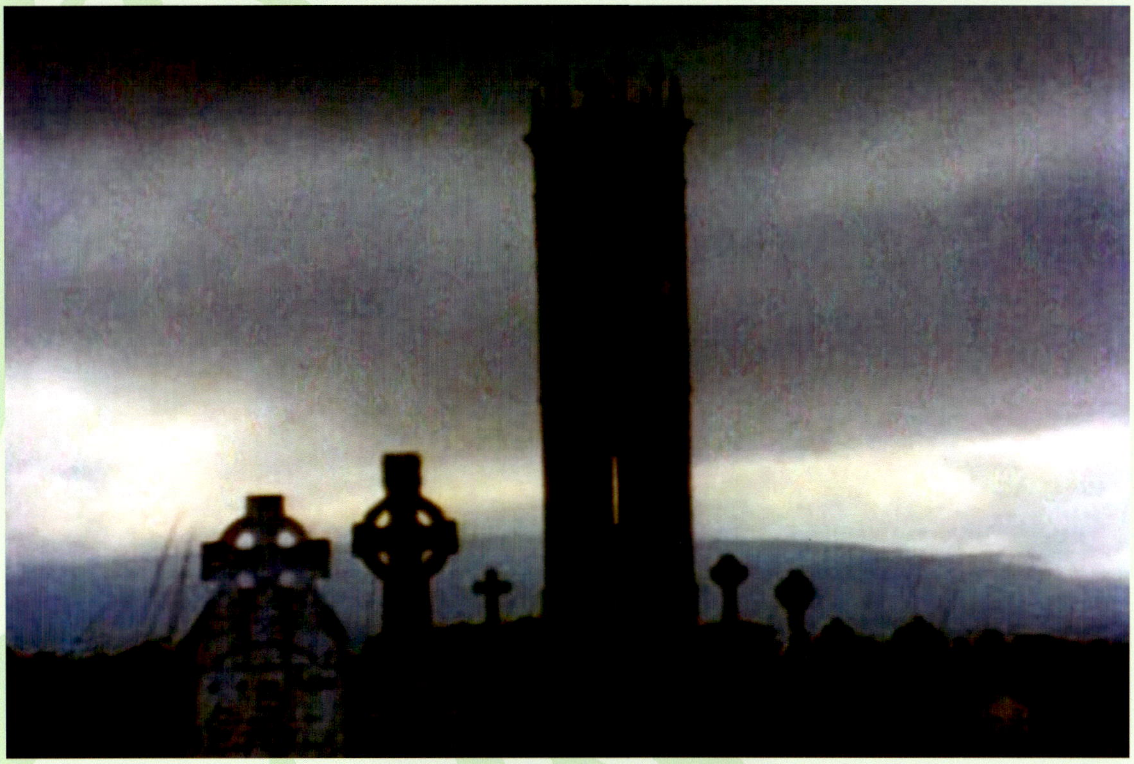

seem perfectly sane and credible. And the recreations are expertly filmed, not with actors and costumes, but with POV camerawork on location, accompanied by a soundtrack that vies with the best horror movies of the period.

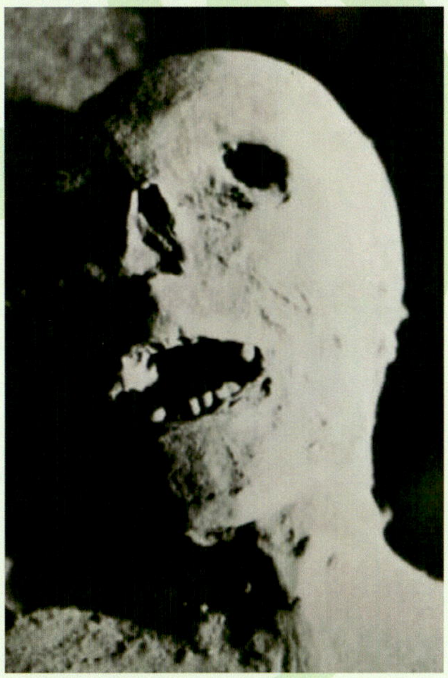

The film thus resides in a fantastical borderland, and I'm not talking about life and afterlife. What I mean is that in many respects it doesn't qualify as a Weirdumentary.

But *Land of Celtic Ghosts* must be included, if only because it so completely believes in the ghost stories it tells. Even before the title credits, we read text that gives us to know where it's coming from: "This motion picture is dedicated to those unbelievers who think there are no such things as ghosts."

From there, we learn about "documented" cases, like the "true story" of the Curse of Grace O'Malley, a "Sea Queen Pirate."

"Who are these ghosts of times past, and why do these souls of the dead still haunt the living?" Basehart asks that question, but he does not ask if Irish ghosts are a bunch of hooey and if those who believe in them are touched in the head. This is the land of Celtic ghosts, not Celtic skeptics.

"Beneath the veil of Celtic twilight there is another land, a land where restless souls that once sought peace and pardon in the shadows of these ruins now mourn their passing."

I do too. To honor them, I will happily rewatch *Land of Celtic Ghosts*.

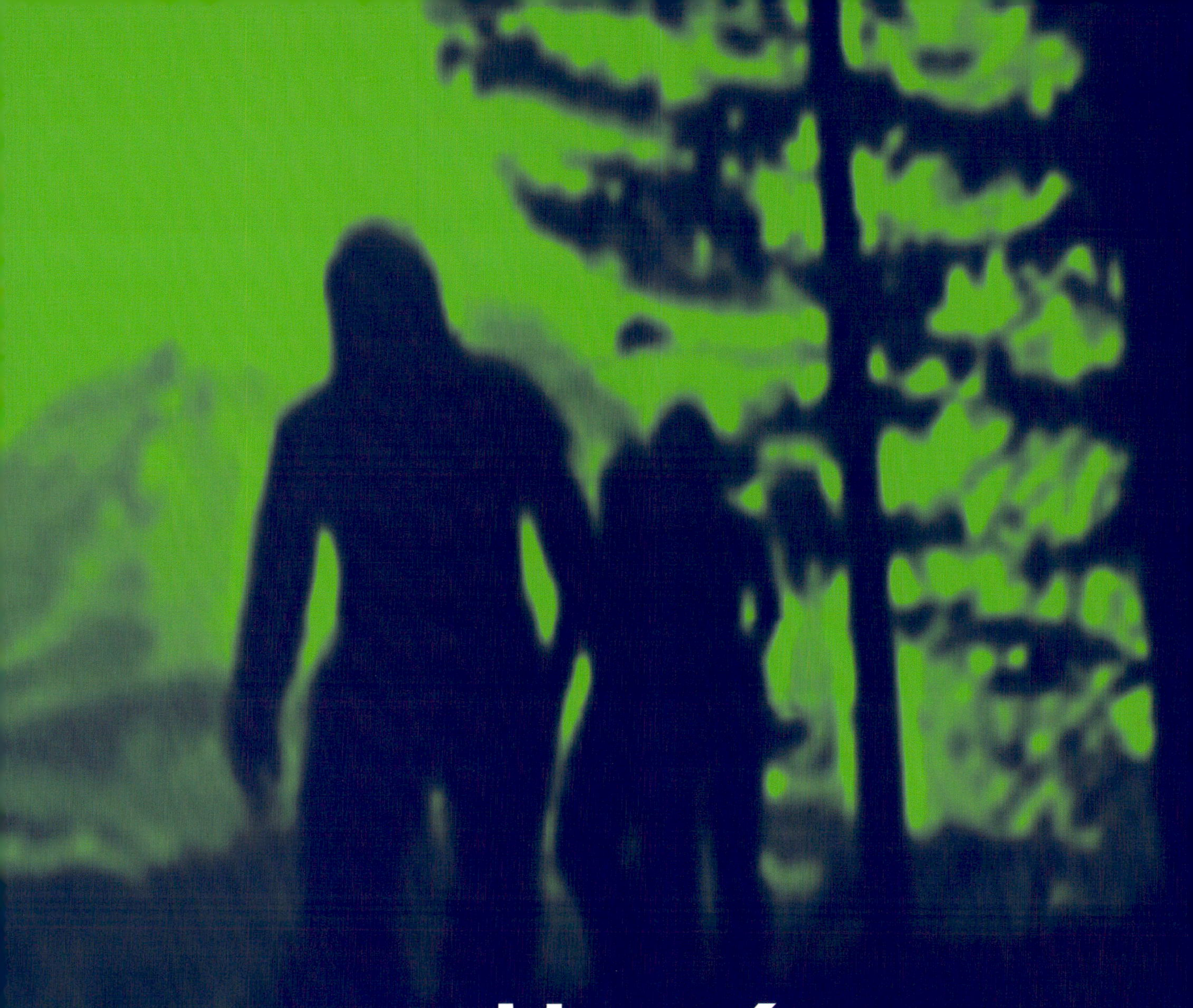

section 6: Mysterious Monsters

From *IN SEARCH OF ... BIGFOOT*,
Alan Landsburg Productions, 1976

Bigfoot Man or Beast

(1972)

"We are now flying over some of the wilderness areas of [the] northwestern United States and Canada. Here there are thousands of square miles of uninhabited wilderness that is still unexplored. It is in these vast, unexplored wilderness areas of North America that a nine-foot-tall, humanlike creature is reported to live. This is the home of the Bigfoot, or Sasquatch, as the Indians call him."

J. English Smith speaks these words at the beginning of the first Bigfoot Weirdumentary. Big foot, short subject, one might say of writer-director Lawrence Crowley's film. In its original form, *Bigfoot Man or Beast* was twenty minutes long. And its on-screen titles do in fact forego the otherwise expected colon and question mark, à la *Bigfoot: Man or Beast?*

During the film, Smith appears on-camera in "Bigfoot country" to interview investigators like Grover Kranz, Ronald D. Olson, and Rene Dahinden, as well as "people who have had some firsthand experiences."

For example, we hear two stories from 1924, the first about some miners in Washington who were harassed by four or five creatures that threw rocks at their cabin. Damned if they weren't hairy. And then there is the family of Sasquatch that kidnapped a man. He escaped after "getting them sick on a box of snuff." In fairness to all concerned, that was decades before the Surgeon General's warning.

Other evidence includes plaster casts of large footprints. "Here now is physical evidence of something that made tracks," Smith wonderfully declares. My personal favorite is a dramatized audio recording, and Smith's explanation of the same: "Here is an approximation to the sound that they reported hearing that evening."

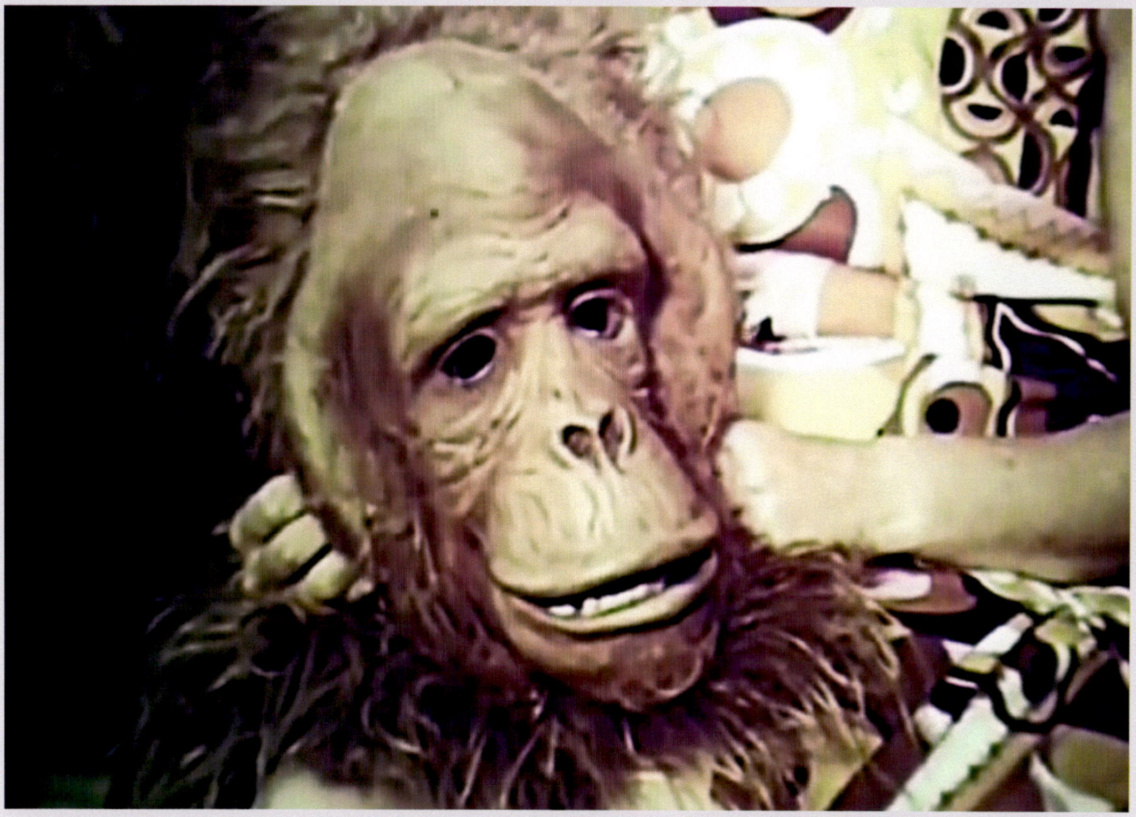

All that said, the highlight is the (in)famous Roger Patterson-Bob Gimlin film of Bigfoot of 1967. When *Bigfoot Man or Beast* first appeared, viewers had not generally seen the "PGF," as it would become known. It remains the most famous Bigfoot footage of them all, of course.

The film culminates with Smith repeating as many words as possible in a single paragraph: "In the past, many sightings went unreported for fear of ridicule. Law enforcement officers got most of these reported sightings, and most of the people that did the reporting were considered some kind of a nut. Now a central reporting system has been developed, and all sightings can now be reported to our Portland headquarters, by simply dialing Bigfoot, Portland, Oregon. Other information can be obtained by writing, Bigfoot, Portland, Oregon."

Though copyrighted in 1971, *Bigfoot Man or Beast* does not seem to have played movie theaters until 1972. Distribution seems to have been sparse, though the Bigfoot office allegedly received over 20,000 letters and 17,000 phone calls from impressed viewers.

Then, in 1977, *Bigfoot Man or Beast* was reborn as a ninety-three-minute feature with the same title. The short Bigfoot film became a big Bigfoot film. How, you ask? After a pregnant pause, I birth my answer. Producers quickly edited a later film, *In Search of Bigfoot* (1976), onto the end of this short subject, and then peddled it to television stations. (*In Search of Bigfoot* is covered in a subsequent chapter.)

Oh, and in case you have any concerns about Bigfoot encounters, take heart in J. English Smith's helpful words: "Procedures have been worked out to cover every aspect of a capture."

HOWCO INTERNATIONAL PICTURES

presents

A PIERCE-LEDWELL PRODUCTION

PRESS BOOK

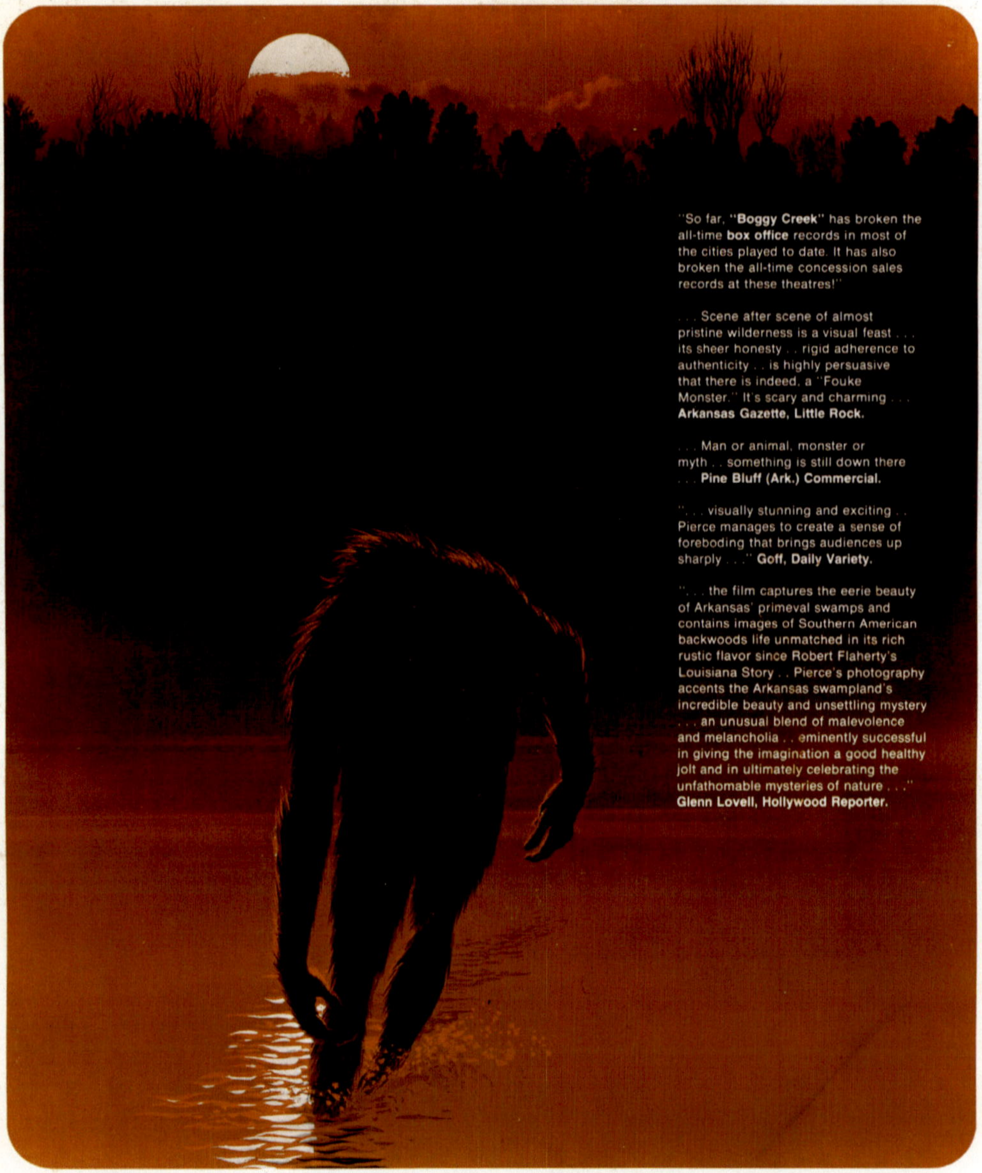

The Legend of Boggy Creek

A TRUE STORY

A PIERCE-LEDWELL PRODUCTION

G ALL AGES ADMITTED

Produced and Directed by CHARLES PIERCE · Written by EARL E. SMITH · Music by JAMIE MENDOZA-NAVA · Executive Producers L. W. LEDWELL/CHARLES PIERCE
Color by TECHNICOLOR · Filmed in TECHNISCOPE

The Legend of Boggy Creek

(1972)

It's amazing that one of the most famous Bigfoot films isn't actually about Bigfoot. The creature in question is the "Fouke Monster," a wild man-beast that hides in the woods of Arkansas. While we hear about Sasquatch, the fearsome Fouke fiend is not him, in part because its tracks leave three toes, not five. In other words, he has a less-than-big-foot.

Set decorator Charles B. Pierce made *Boggy Creek* on a budget of only $160,000. For his first feature, he served as writer, director, and—auteur alert—cinematographer. Pierce was also promoter, taking his film "from town to town" until New Orleans-based Howco International got involved. The company distributed *Boggy Creek*, which launched Pierce's career into the big time.

"THIS IS A TRUE STORY," the opening credits announce. "Some of the people in this motion picture portray themselves—in many cases on actual locations." Most of the time, these persons are heard in voiceover, edited against MOS footage of themselves in the Fouke countryside. As first-person narrator Verne Stierman informs us, it's a "right pleasant place to live, until the sun goes down." After dark, well, he doubts if we "could find a lonelier, spookier place in this country than down around Boggy Creek."

That's because of the monster, of course, one that Pierce effectively keeps at a distant remove from his camera, thus making the ape-suited actor appropriately threatening and generally believable. And Pierce effectively casts the monster's shadow on a besieged home during the intense fifteen-minute conclusion scene.

If the ending offers the biggest shocks and the fastest editing, the rest of the film is appropriately slow-paced, methodical and atmospheric. This is particularly true for the

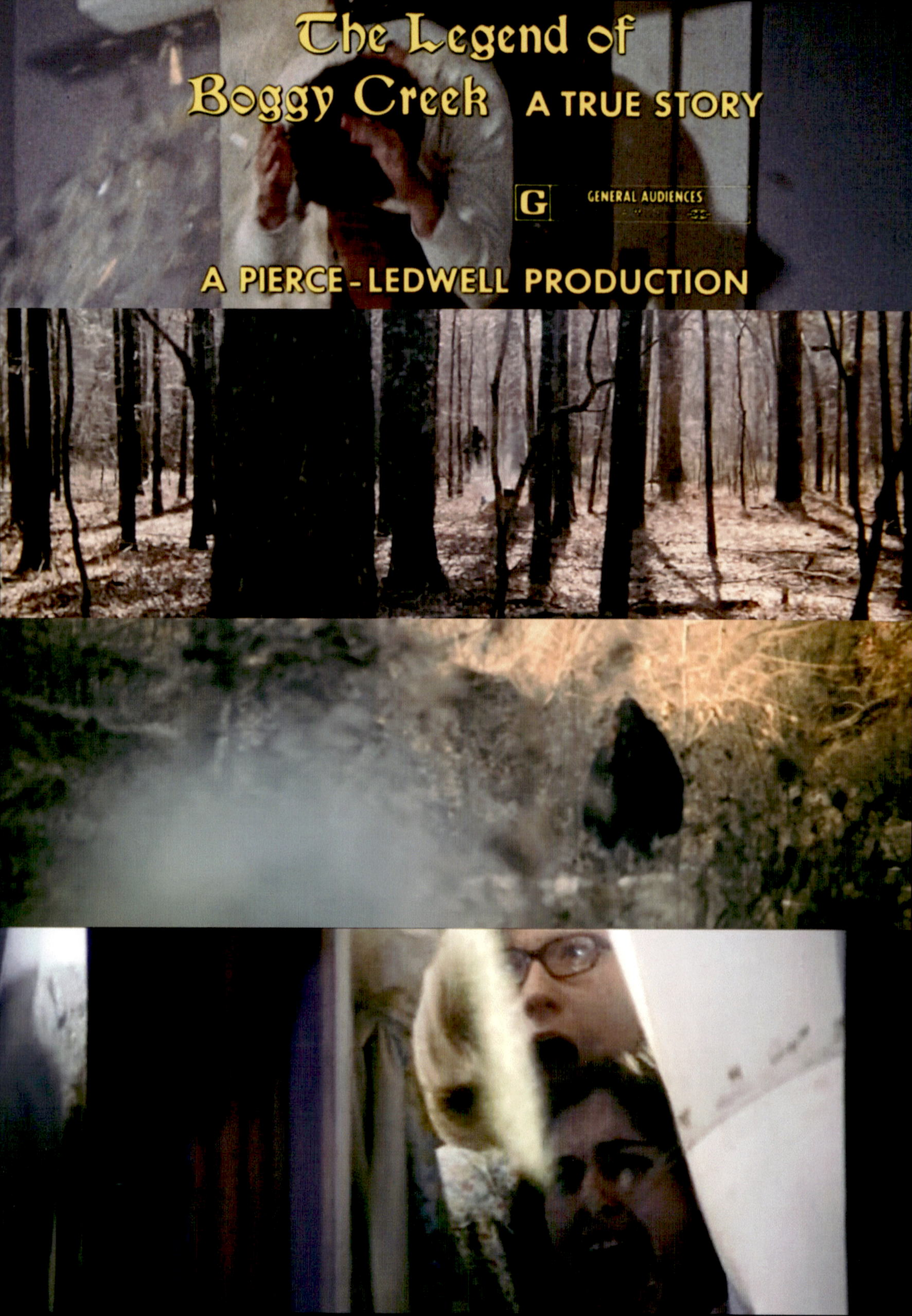
The Legend of
Boggy Creek A TRUE STORY
G GENERAL AUDIENCES
A PIERCE-LEDWELL PRODUCTION

opening, which merges beautiful cinematography (the camera slowly moving down the creek) with natural sounds. Later, Pierce treats us to some handheld camerawork that adds to the documentary veneer.

The instrumental music is appropriately eerie, as opposed to two vocal ditties we hear. The first, "The Legend of Boggy Creek," evokes sympathy for the monster, melancholia for being the only one of his kind, one forced into exile. By contrast, the second song, "Nobody Sees the Flowers but Me," seems gratuitous, an effort to either please someone putting money into the film and/or to push its running time to eighty-five minutes.

To insulate this "true story" against skeptics, one of the first recreations features old men laughing at tales of the monster. A hermit living near Boggy Creek explains he's never seen or heard anything of it. And our amiable narrator concludes the film by announcing, "You may think the whole thing is a hoax, and that's your privilege." 'Course you'd be a dad-blamed fool to do so, but that's your own prerogative, ya cityfied fool.

During the rest of the film, needless to say, the monster is as real as can be. Interviewees describe their encounters with it. Famous hunting dogs are too scared to track it. All of this results in nationwide publicity, save for an eight-year period when the monster went into hiding. But eventually he can no longer resist the "lure of civilization," even if his intent is to smash a few of its inhabitants.

Fredric Milstein of the *Los Angeles Times* believed *The Legend of Boggy Creek* was "unsubtle" and "ludicrous." He bemoaned, "those hicks are really hicks, insulting stereotypes, unbelievably stupid hillbillies, many of them, alas, playing themselves." Put another way, it was too real for his delicate sensibilities.

By contrast, the *Hollywood Reporter* praised the movie's "menacing immediacy and rustic authenticity." The *Independent Film Journal* went so far as to liken its style to Val Lewton, the horror maestro of RKO during World War II. And *Boxoffice* believed that Pierce was on his way to becoming "King of the Cheapies," a compliment in this case, given comparisons of him to the creators of *Easy Rider* (1969).

Audiences fell in love with *The Legend of Boggy Creek. Boxoffice* claimed the flick was a "sleeper" hit. It racked up $4.8 million in North America, becoming the tenth high-grossing release of 1972. It even broke some box-office records in Dallas, Houston, New Orleans, and—holy of holies—Los Angeles. Take that, Fredric Milstein.

Aside from being a hit, what exactly is *The Legend of Boggy Creek*? The *Independent Film Journal* called it a "semi-documentary, semi-True-Life-Adventure study." The lengthy moniker fits, much better than, say, "docudrama" or "mockumentary." After all, it's far more than anything those terms connote.

As the introductory chapter to this book notes, *The Legend of Boggy Creek* was instrumental in the formation of the Weirdumentary, augmenting the narrative and aesthetic approach of Reinl's *Chariots of the Gods* (1970) with the use of on-camera interviews and recreations.

For Charles B. Pierce, *The Legend of Boggy Creek* flowed into the seas of feature filmmaking, his later credits including *The Town That Dreaded Sundown* (1976) and *Boggy Creek II: And the Legend Continues* (1985).

For the rest of us, *The Legend of Boggy Creek* roils across the oceans of time, a reminder of turbulent nightmares we delightedly endured as children.

Monsters! Mysteries or Myths?

(1974)

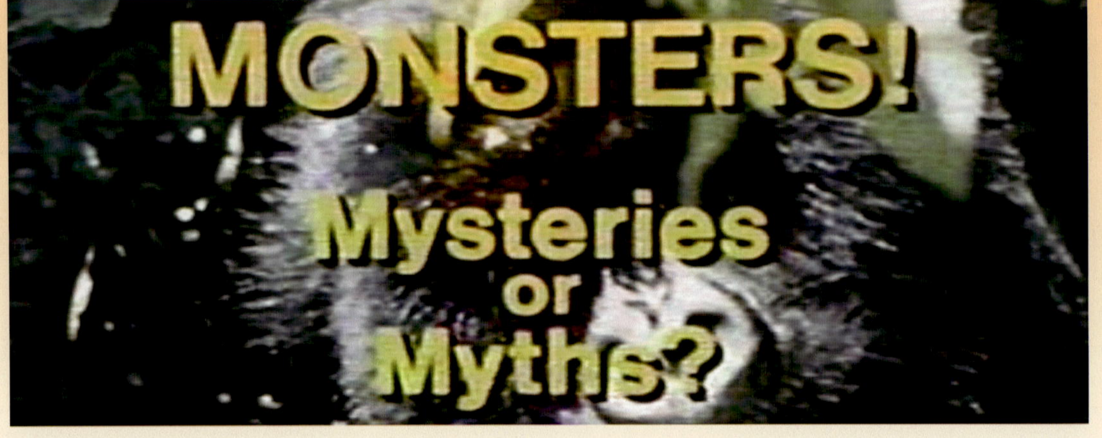

Rod Serling, the horror host with the most, guides us into a different kind of twilight zone, a world in which questions must be asked, questions of the highest order. "Do Monsters dwell among us, or are they only apparitions walking in the landscape of our minds? Are they subjects for zoologists or psychologists?"

Monsters! Mysteries or Myths? has a lot going for it, not least of which is the ability to use two of the coolest punctuation marks in a single film title. Along with Serling, its cast features Bigfoot, the Yeti, and the Loch Ness Monster. Here is the Weirdumentary equivalent of throwing Dracula, Frankenstein, and the Wolf Man into the same monster rally.

Monsters! was one of three Smithsonian Institution specials to air on CBS in the 1974–75 season, the other two covering the Hope Diamond and the history of aviation. Robert Guenette acted as writer, director, and producer, thus becoming the first Weirdumentary auteur.

Given the Smithsonian connection, we meet a number of real scholars, but thank goodness the film has a greater number of eyewitnesses. That's along with images that allegedly capture the creatures, from Ivan Marx's Bigfoot film to Tim Dinsdale's famous Nessie footage. That's along with historic photos aplenty.

Perhaps at the behest of the Smithsonian, Guenette's script carefully explains that these are "intriguing, but unsolved" mysteries. Some of the evidence for them is spurious, and pranksters are clearly at work, faking photos and even footprints.

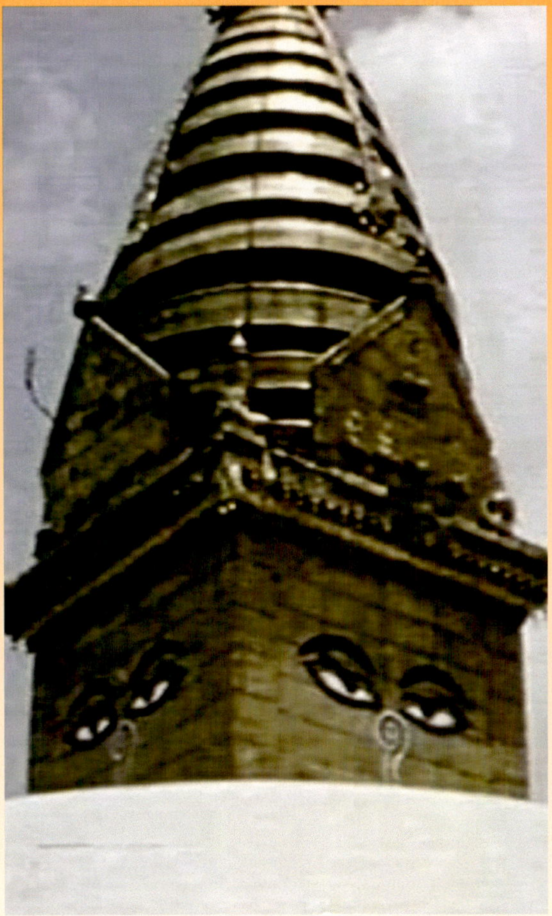
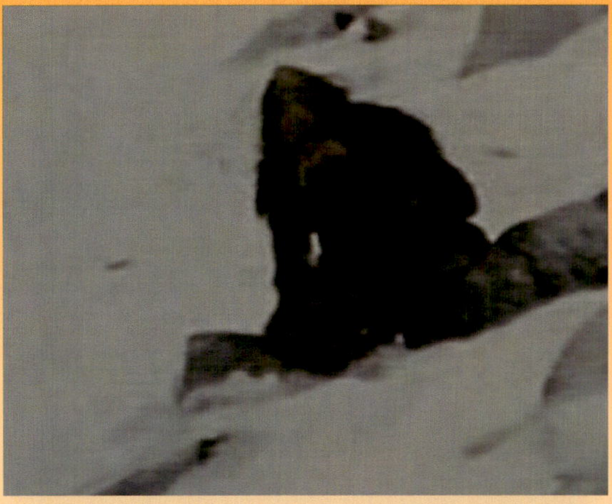
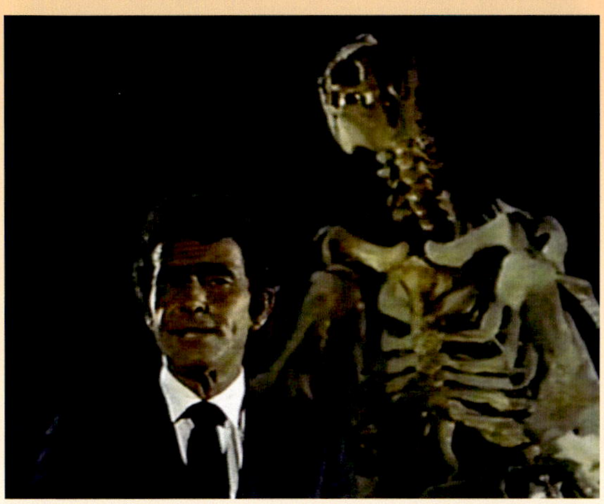

Thankfully, the kibosh is not put down on all our fun. We see a clergyman literally exorcising Nessie, casting holy water onto the loch in order to expel the demon. And, better yet, we get recreation scenes of Bigfoot and the Yeti. Performed with more-than-adequate costumes, these dramatizations are clearly indicated as such thanks to on-screen notes, thus separating them from all the other potentially "real" reels.

But declaring re-enactments on-screen does not deter our man Guenette. He does sneak in a wonderfully fictional moment that is not undercut by such academic niceties. The image is of the Himalayas. The sound we hear is a Yeti howling in the distance ... that, or it's an actor screaming under Guenette's expert direction. And there's no disclaimer.

Serling's concluding narration (which is the only time we see him on-screen) also contains a gem. He suggests that scientists will one day discover new species, either on Earth or—thank our lucky stars—"outer space."

The film's premiere telecast came in November 1974. *The Hollywood Reporter* said, "The end result was both informative and entertaining." *Daily Variety* called it "fascinating," with "suspension of disbelief" (including in the dramatizations) being "half the fun."

Audiences agreed. *Monsters! Mysteries or Myths?* was one of the three top-rated shows for the week it aired, the other two being episodes of *Maude* and *Sanford and Son.* Yeti's coming to join you, Elizabeth!

The Legend of Bigfoot

(1976)

"My name is Ivan Marx. The film you are about to see is authentic. It records the last ten years, which has changed my life."

Ivan goes on to explain, "You see, I'm a tracker. And believe me, I'm the last of a vanishing breed. I know tracks like the FBI knows fingerprints." He had also spent time as a game warden, and allegedly had the "largest collection of bear film in the world."

The title of course makes clear his biggest game: the bushman, the Oh-Mah, the Sasquatch. "Let's just call him Bigfoot," Ivan says in his relaxed, genial narration.

Initially he pronounces his skepticism. "I couldn't believe a grown man would tell me a Bigfoot was killing his cattle. What a bunch of hogwash!" Later, his brother-in-law advises him, "Don't be so quick to make judgments."

Thus the expedition begins. "I had to figure out what was fact, and what was fiction," he explains. First Ivan discovers eighteen-inch footprints and hair. The lab couldn't match them with "any known animal." Then, at roughly sixteen minutes into the film, the initial sighting happens: Bigfoot in the distance, obscured by trees. Wonderful POV shots of Ivan, handheld and shaky, allow us to see through his eyes as he chases the creature. Though he smells a "nauseating, musky odor," the object of his desire escapes.

At least for another nine minutes. The next Bigfoot sighting shows the creature at length, slowly lumbering along, far enough in the distance to keep the costume's zipper at bay. Ivan exclaims that he has finally come "face to face with Bigfoot," even though the creature's back is to the camera.

That causes the tables of skepticism to turn. Ivan is now a true believer, and his footage stands up to "under every conceivable test." By contrast, the scientists challenged him. His "documented evidence wasn't good enough for the experts," even though some of them had allegedly profited by screening the footage on "lecture circuits." Of academia, we are not fans, and rightly so.

To stay focused, Ivan and his wife Peggy keep on Bigfoot's trail, being certain the migratory animal is heading north. At sixty-one minutes, we glimpse a younger Bigfoot in

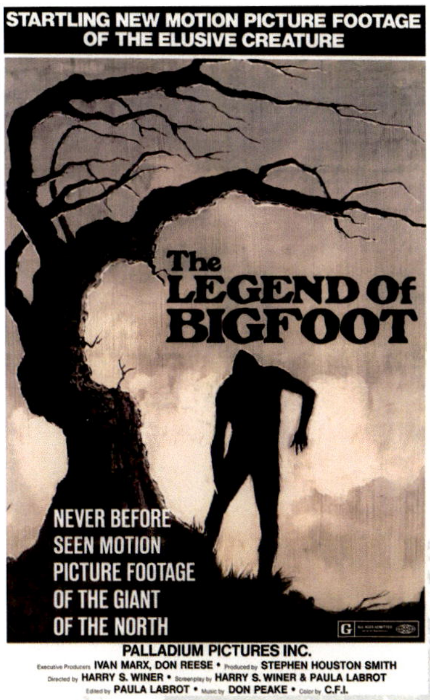

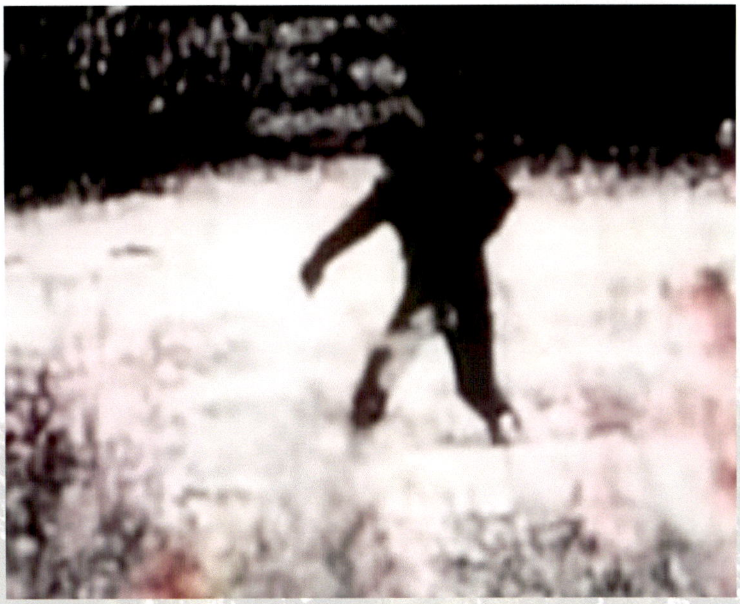

the distance. He splits as Ivan approaches. Then, to keep us engaged, we see two Bigfoot (Bigfeet?) at sixty-seven minutes, one in front of Ivan, and another, smaller one behind him. Though surrounded, Ivan is safe, though. The creatures are benevolent. And they're vegetarians, except for the occasional filet o' fish.

The seventy-five minute film ends with penultimate footage of Bigfoot that freeze-frames on the arm-swinging creature looking back at us, clearly reminiscent of the Patterson-Gimlin Bigfoot film of 1967. The we see the final image: the lumbering creature disappears over the horizon, his blocking beautifully staged. Here is a legend indeed.

Ivan called his Weirdumentary "unchallengeable proof." *Boxoffice* believed the film was "remarkable" and contained "some startling new motion picture footage of the elusive creature." Those who would debate the subject proceeded to do so.

What is certain is that *The Legend of Bigfoot*, though directed by Harry Winer, is Ivan's show all the way. Not only does he narrate and occasionally appear on camera, but he also shot most of the footage. The result is beautiful and striking, with much time and attention given to locations and other animals in order to pad the running time. Few would complain, though, because Ivan's narration and Don Peake's wonderful score work towards a composite that deserves to be seen in its entirety.

In October 1975, the MPAA gave the film a G rating. As early as Thanksgiving weekend 1975, a trio of screenings occurred in St. Louis. Ivan and Peggy attended, receiving big crowds despite a severe snowstorm. Ivan also began making the interview rounds, including on a Minneapolis TV show, where he appeared side-by-side with Bobby Bare, best known for such hit records as *Detroit City*. From there, *The Legend of Bigfoot* slowly moved across parts of the United States and into our hearts.

Ivan and Peggy Marx forever maintained their footage to be genuine. In some ways, it's easier to believe that claim than Ivan's declaration that he spent *ten years* filming his pursuit. Either he wore makeup or had plastic surgery. Or maybe he too was wearing a costume.

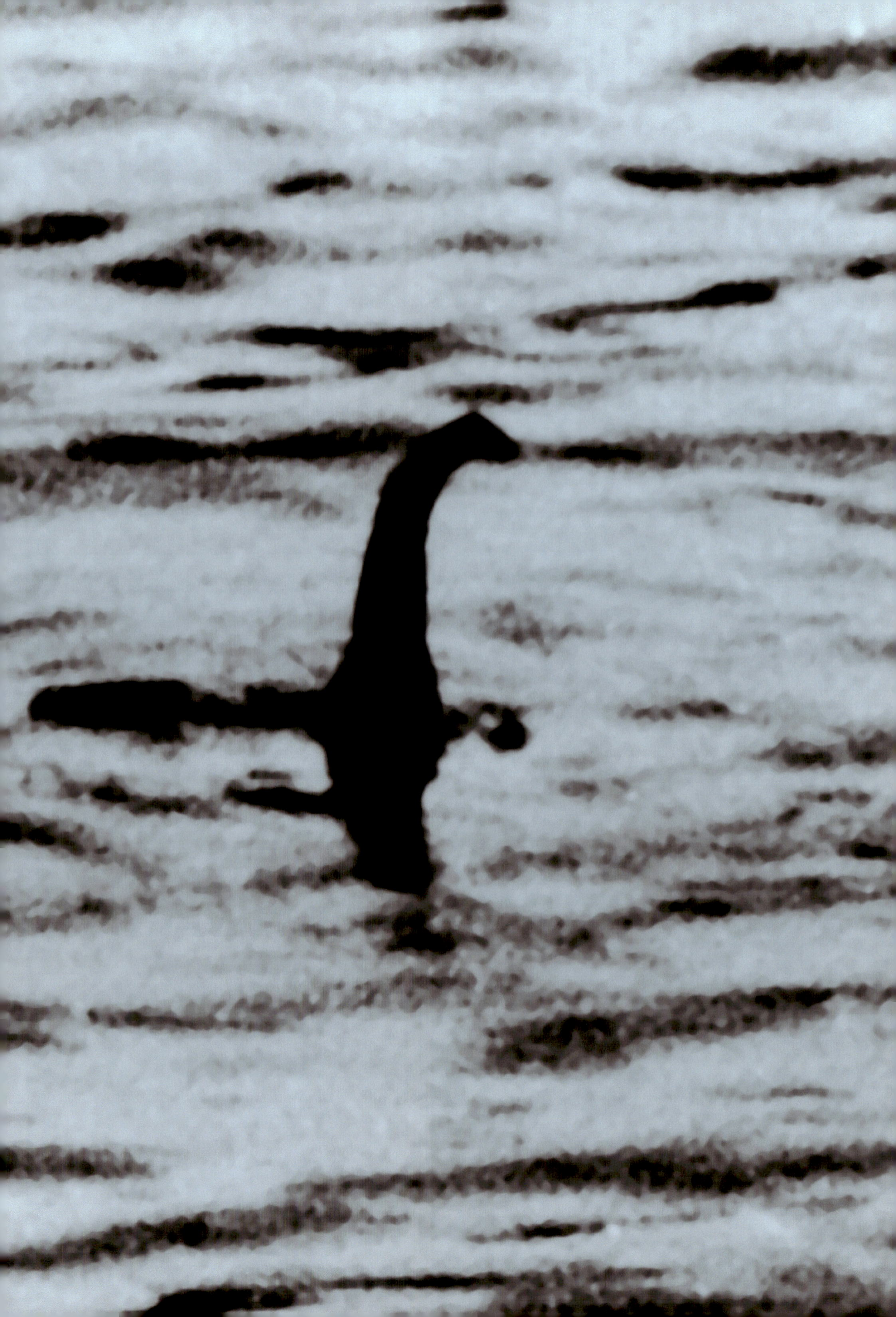

In Search Of... Mysterious Monsters

(1976–1982)

When talking about *In Search of...*, Leonard Nimoy admitted, "I don't know if I've ever had any genuine psychic experiences myself, but I've read quite a bit on the subject and it intrigues me." He hastened to add, "We're in a time when people are finding out things we once thought were so weird ... aren't so bizarre after all. There are a lot of phenomena we need to explore, and maybe find new kinds of knowledge."

Mysterious monsters need not be mysterious, or daffy, in other words, if we just take the initiative to explore them. (Cue Bugs and Daffy: "On with the show, this is it!")

Season 1, Episode 5, *Bigfoot*: "A giant hairy creature, part ape, part man. Indians call him Sasquatch. They believe he is as gentle as he is powerful and mysterious. He's been seen many times in the rugged mountains and deep woods of the Pacific Northwest. The encounters have not always been peaceful." (Big-footloose, kicked off his Sunday shoes.)

While the tales are familiar, some nice handheld camerawork adds real drama to the dramatic recreations. And as always, the brevity of these episodes makes them hard to dislike.

Nimoy tells us, "There is persuasive evidence that men may be closing in on Bigfoot." I am still awaiting his imminent capture.

Season 1, Episode 20, *The Loch Ness Monster*: "What is beneath the surface of the loch? We will be closer to knowing the answer, closer for having discovered new evidence."

After going through the standard stuff, we learn about a major National Geographic expedition that got underway shortly before this episode was filmed. Underwater cameras, sonar, and so forth. Bob Ballard, who later rediscovered the *Titanic*, appears on-camera as part of the NatGeo group.

As for new evidence, we see footage of a "long trail of bubbles" on the surface water. Thus Nessie. Possibly. Nimoy tells us, "intensive effort may soon turn up the monster of the lake." (Know what? To save time, I'll keep waiting on Nessie while I'm waiting on Bigfoot.)

Variety reviewed *The Loch Ness Monster*, praising Nimoy for being a "smooth host-narrator," and calling the episode "fairly elaborate."

Season 4, Episode 9, *The Abominable Snowman*: "From the beginning of his time on Earth, man has always been fascinated by monsters, real or imagined."

As inevitable as he was abominable, Yeti eventually just had to co-star with Mr. Spock.

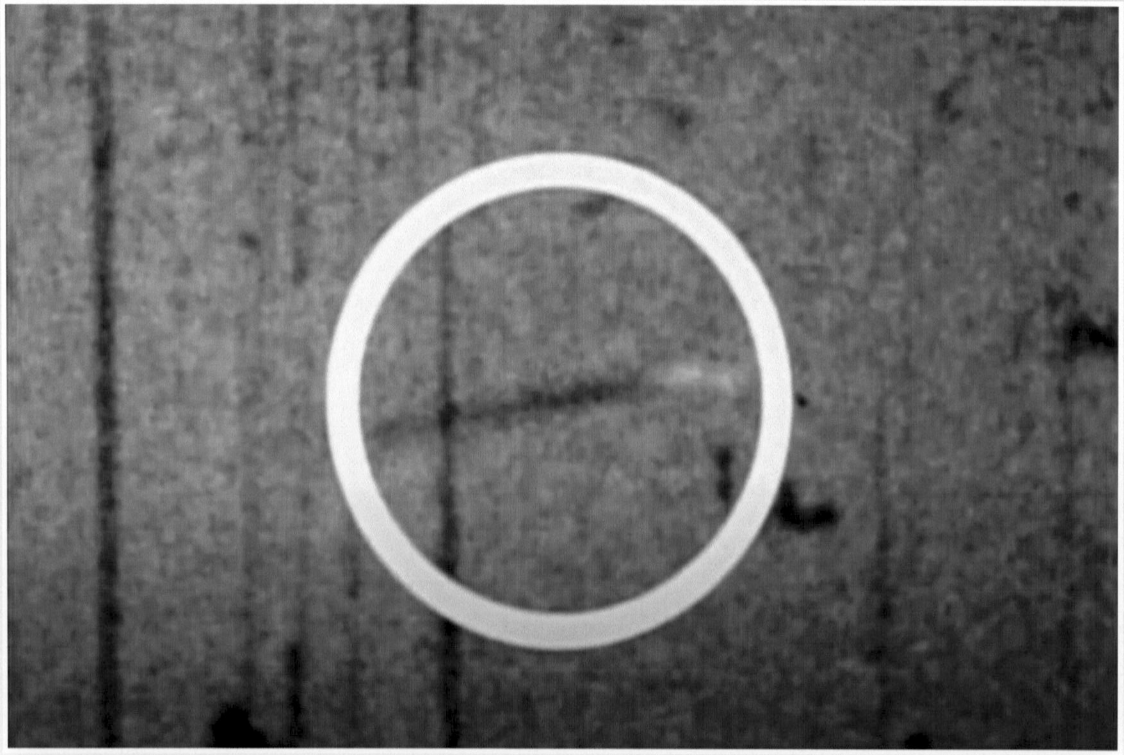

Like the *Bigfoot* episode, *The Abominable Snowman* is a nice romp through tracks left by others, and I'm referring to other filmmakers, not man-apes. There's nothing new, but hearing Nimoy's voice venture into Weirdumentary-land is never unwelcome, not at my house. And hey, Yeti authority Peter Byrne is back, which is no bad thing either.

Season 3, Episode 9, *Monster Hunters*: Turnabout is fair play, so they tell me. This time Nimoy returns to the likes of Bigfoot and Nessie, but he focuses on the explorers chasing them.

Loch Ness expert Tim Dinsdale and Sasquatch/Yeti expert Peter Byrne appear on-camera to give us updates on their respective areas of expertise. Alas, they don't really have any new news.

Not all of these monster hunters follow in the footsteps of Clyde Beatty, Frank Buck, and Elmer Fudd. One of the Bigfoot chasers is filled with love and believes that which he pursues shares the same disposition. (Whether this is all about brotherly love or big foot fetish, he does not say.)

Season 2, Episode 8, *The Ogopogo Monster*: What a welcome episode. *In Search of…* sought out a mysterious monster that had been generally ignored by other filmmakers. Forty feet long with a snake-like head, living in the depths of Okanagan Lake in British Columbia, Canada.

Ogopogo is a serpent with a silly name. Or it is a "snake in the lake." Or maybe it is the descendant of some ancient sea creature. Or maybe nothing at all.

Eyewitnesses are plentiful, though. And then there are photographs that are either compelling images of its humps, or not-compelling images of choppy water and waves. Far more intriguing is film footage shot by Arthur Folden. In it, something is in the water. (Ogo or no-go?)

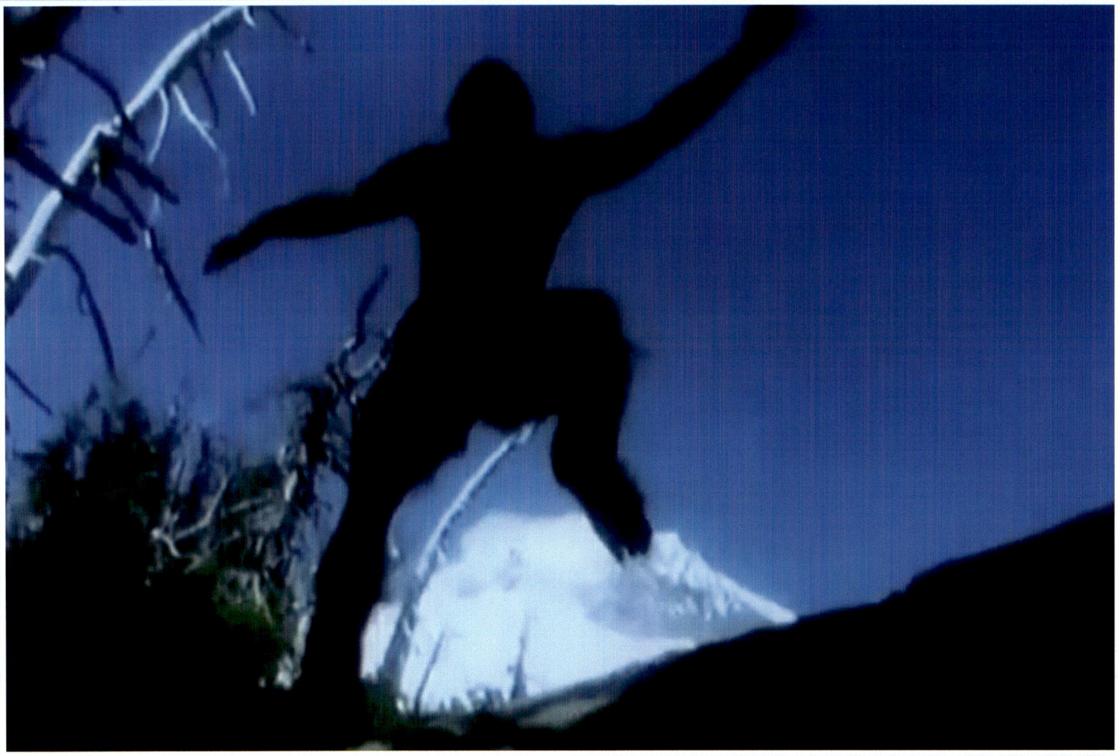

What's fascinating about this episode is that *In Search of...* hired its own exploratory crew to investigate the Okanagan Lake and search under its mysterious waters. "After a long and careful search, no monster." (Guess that means no-go.)

Season 2, Episode 16, *The Swamp Monster*: "Swamps inspire fear in many minds. Dark and damp, they are full of mystery and creatures that slither in the mud. An experienced guide entered Louisiana's Honey Island swamp one fall day in 1973. The outing would become the stuff nightmares are made of."

Once again, I'm wowed by this series. First Ogopogo, and now "something else," something other than the famous monsters of filmland.

"Is it possible that an unknown creature lives on the edge of man's civilized world?" Yes, I say. Well, yes, I hope so, I say. Well, yes, it is true that I am hopeful, but it is also true that I am uncertain, and it is also true that I am doubtful.

As for this swamp monster, it stands on two feet and looks like a seven-foot-tall man or man-ape, with amber-colored eyes and hands hanging below its knees. This swamp thing—sometimes called the Cajun Sasquatch—has been seen repeatedly, but never captured or killed.

"If finally cornered, what will the creature do?" Nimoy asks. Get mad, I should expect, or remove its costume and announce that it's a fraud. ("Trick or treat!")

A makeup man devises a costume based upon eyewitness accounts. It looks something like a gray Chewbacca with no laser gun, no *Millennium Falcon*.

In these episodes, Nimoy and many experts get their say. Now it's time for my five cents at the nickelodeon: Forget Klingons, Romulans, and even the Gorn. *Star Trek* has nothing on the mysterious monsters chronicled by *In Search of....*

BETTER THAN "King Kong" BECAUSE IT'S TRUE!

A Full-Length Motion Picture

IN SEARCH OF BIGFOOT

© 1975

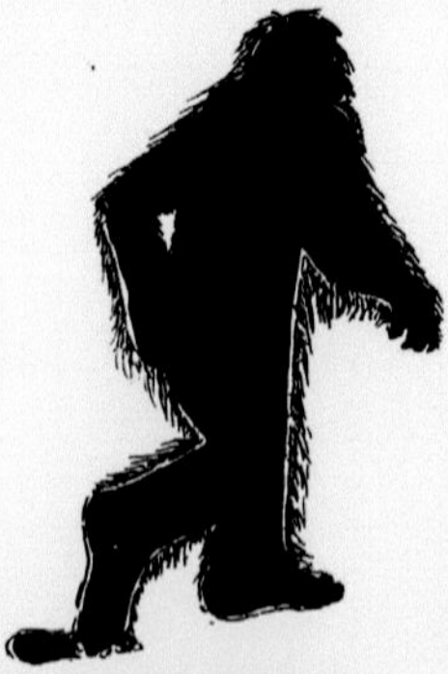

RATED G Raymond W. Hardy 4-21-07

TRUE EXCITING ADVENTURE STORY OF SCIENTISTS AND CONSERVATIONISTS OF THE AMERICAN YETI EXPEDITION AS THEY UNRAVEL THE MYSTERY OF THE AMERICAN ABOMINABLE SNOWMAN.

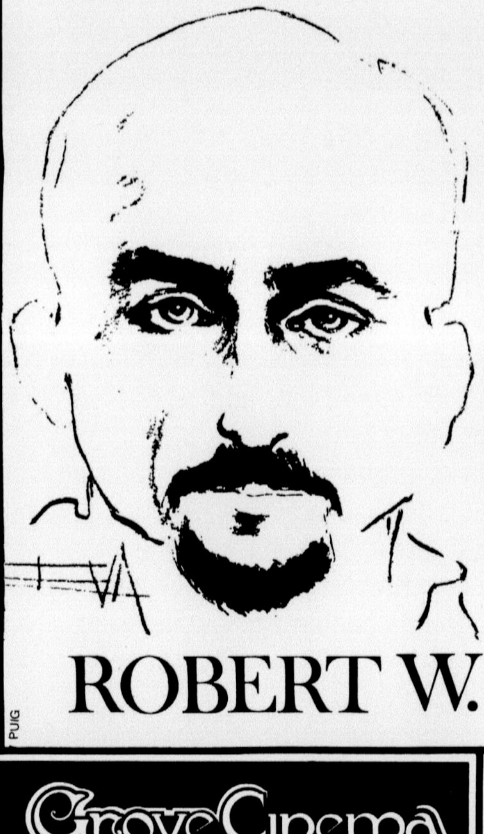

IN PERSON!

EXPEDITION DIRECTOR

You read about him:

Tropic, National Wildlife Magazine, newspapers and Best selling books.

You saw him on T.V.:

Smithsonian Special: Monsters: Myth or Mystery?
NBC's Tomorrow

ROBERT W. MORGAN

PUIG

Grove Cinema
3199 Grand Ave.
Coconut Grove
(301) 446-5352

ONE SHOWING ONLY!

SUNDAY JAN. 9 2:00 pm

ADULTS: 2.50
CHILDREN: 1.50

G

In Search Of Bigfoot

(1976)

When is a Weirdumentary not a Weirdumentary? The borderland, the between the genre and its (not so?) near relative the documentary is best understood by examining Lawrence Crowley and William F. Miller's *In Search of Bigfoot*, which edges closer than most films herein to the world of nonfiction.

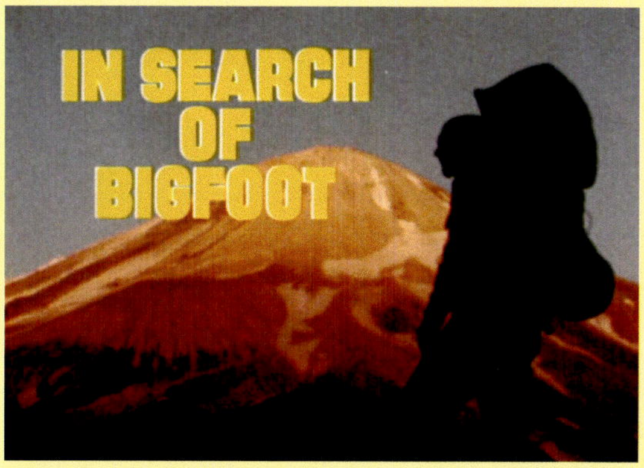

Robert W. Morgan leads a carefully chosen group into the wildness of the Pacific Northwest to find the creature he encountered as a child, one that he firmly believes is alive and well. His fellow experts include an anthropologist, a biologist, a microbiologist, a botanist, a naturalist, a sociologist, and a Sasquatchologist. For their three-and-a-half-month expedition, Morgan is a taskmaster, "tough because he has to be."

One movie poster for the film proclaimed it was "Better than *King Kong* because it's true!"

Unfolding in cinéma vérité style, *In Search of Bigfoot* features no dramatizations and only a few specific anecdotes from eyewitnesses. Here the film's title fulfills its promise: the quest takes up the bulk of the running time. And the major conflict is not with Bigfoot, but rather between the sincere Morgan and two hunters who are hoping to kill the creature.

Morgan's crew discovers "evidence Sasquatch has left behind," mainly in the form of tracks and a hair. But they don't discover Sasquatch, leaving them to other diversions, like playing harmonica and taking swims.

Undeterred, even by a fire that forces an end to his expedition, Morgan retains the strength of his convictions. At its most Weirdumentary moment, the film explains there are just "too many reports from too many people for a hoax to be considered." Bigfoot's out there; we just have to find him.

Produced by Bostonia Films and carrying a 1975 copyright date, though not released until 1976, *In Search of Bigfoot* strangely didn't get the traction it should have. It's a well-directed film with Morgan a compelling figure, but, alas, its cinematic footprint was no bigger than a size 6 at Kinney Shoes.

The Legend of Loch Ness

(1976)

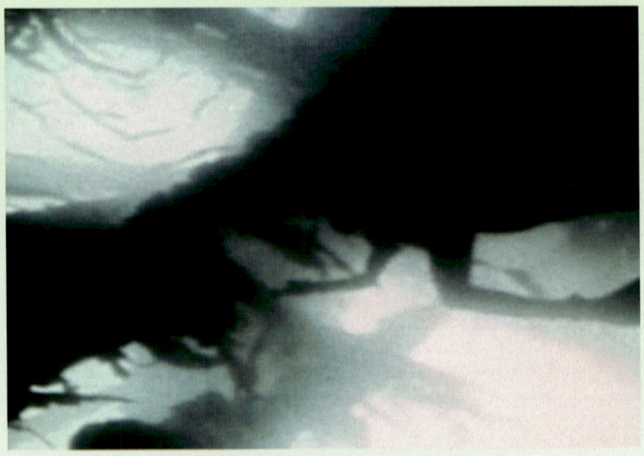

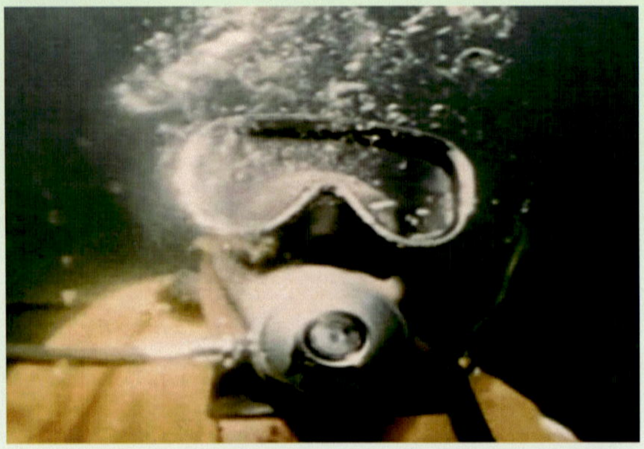

Not unlike *In Search of Bigfoot* (1976), *The Legend of Loch Ness* largely operates as a standard documentary film. Hollywood character actor Arthur Franz provides stately narration. Director Richard Martin carefully presents historical footage and photographs with a variety of interviews. Experts include a scholar working at the Los Angeles Museum of Natural History.

Opening voiceover describes Nessie love as being a "fervor that knows no bounds," but we are then cast into the deep waters of the dull. Several minutes of running time are devoured by land-based creatures, not just experts, but also bears and reptiles, both allegedly offering insight into what Nessie really is.

Mercifully, though, screenwriter Christian Davis manages to throw us an occasional life jacket. We learn that Nessie eyewitnesses date back to Saint Columba in the sixth century. And that there are "undisputed photographs" of the monster. And that "the authenticity of [Tim Dinsdale's 1960 footage of Nessie] has been absolutely established." Lest there be any doubt, of course.

A Scottish woman claims not only to know where Nessie lives in the loch, but also to have a psychic connection to the water. And thank God (?) if Aleister Crowley doesn't materialize, at least in name, if not deed. The Great Beast, we learn, was in league(s) with Nessie, who was perhaps his alter ego. A trek into a house on the loch where Crowley once lived gives Franz his best chance to deliver a line with zest: "In his strange life, might not [Crowley] have communed with the monster itself, as he claimed to do so often with the raised souls of the dead hovering over the silent stones of the ancient crypts?" Attaboy, Artie.

Near the end of our long journey to the 90-minute mark, *The Legend of Loch Ness* finally comes across with the money shot. Underwater photography catches a scuba diver as

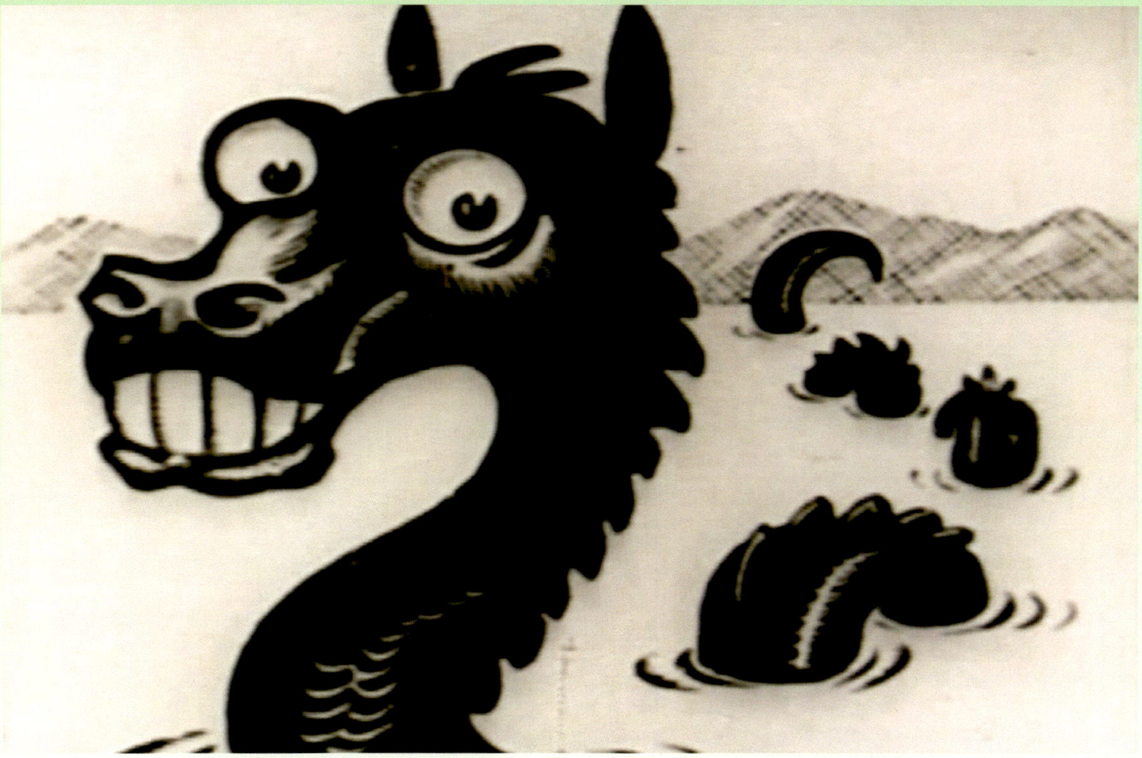

dramatic music plays on the soundtrack. The audiovisuals remind us of *Jaws* (1975). Other underwater troupers are inside a mini-submarine, listening to microphones. First there is noise. And then ... and then ... an image that doesn't make much of an impact until we see it again, thanks to the editor, this time in slow motion. Some dark aquatic creature passes over the camera. It is "five times as big as the submarine."

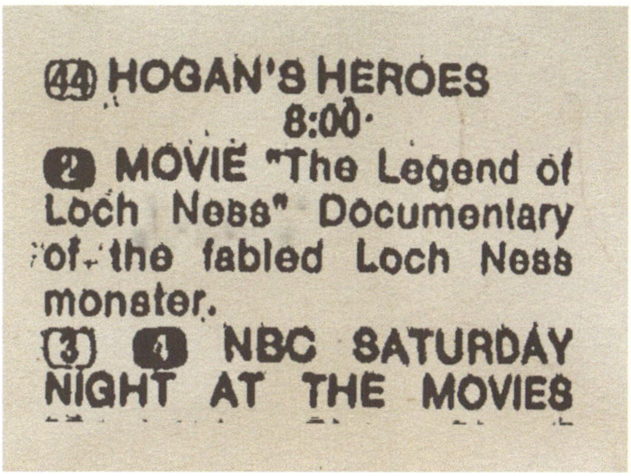

44 HOGAN'S HEROES
8:00
2 MOVIE "The Legend of Loch Ness" Documentary of the fabled Loch Ness monster.
3 4 NBC SATURDAY NIGHT AT THE MOVIES

And it is "the first known motion picture of its kind." We don't hear the word "undisputed," though. Maybe that went without saying.

Martin's film definitely tried to ride a wave of popular interest. To be sure, Nessie was getting almost as much play as Bigfoot in the mid-seventies. Hollywood was planning a few big-budget features, one to be helmed by Ken Russell. The Old Country Theme Park in Virginia constructed a Loch Ness Monster ride. And cans of fresh "Monster Water" from Loch Ness were being exported to America. Regrettably, the product test-marketed to little success.

The same seems to have been true of *The Legend of Loch Ness*. Trade publications largely ignored it. By October of 1977, *Broadcasting* listed it as one of the "Alpha Chronicles," a package of films available for TV that also included *Mysteries from Beyond Earth* (1975) and *Overlords of the U.F.O.* (1976).

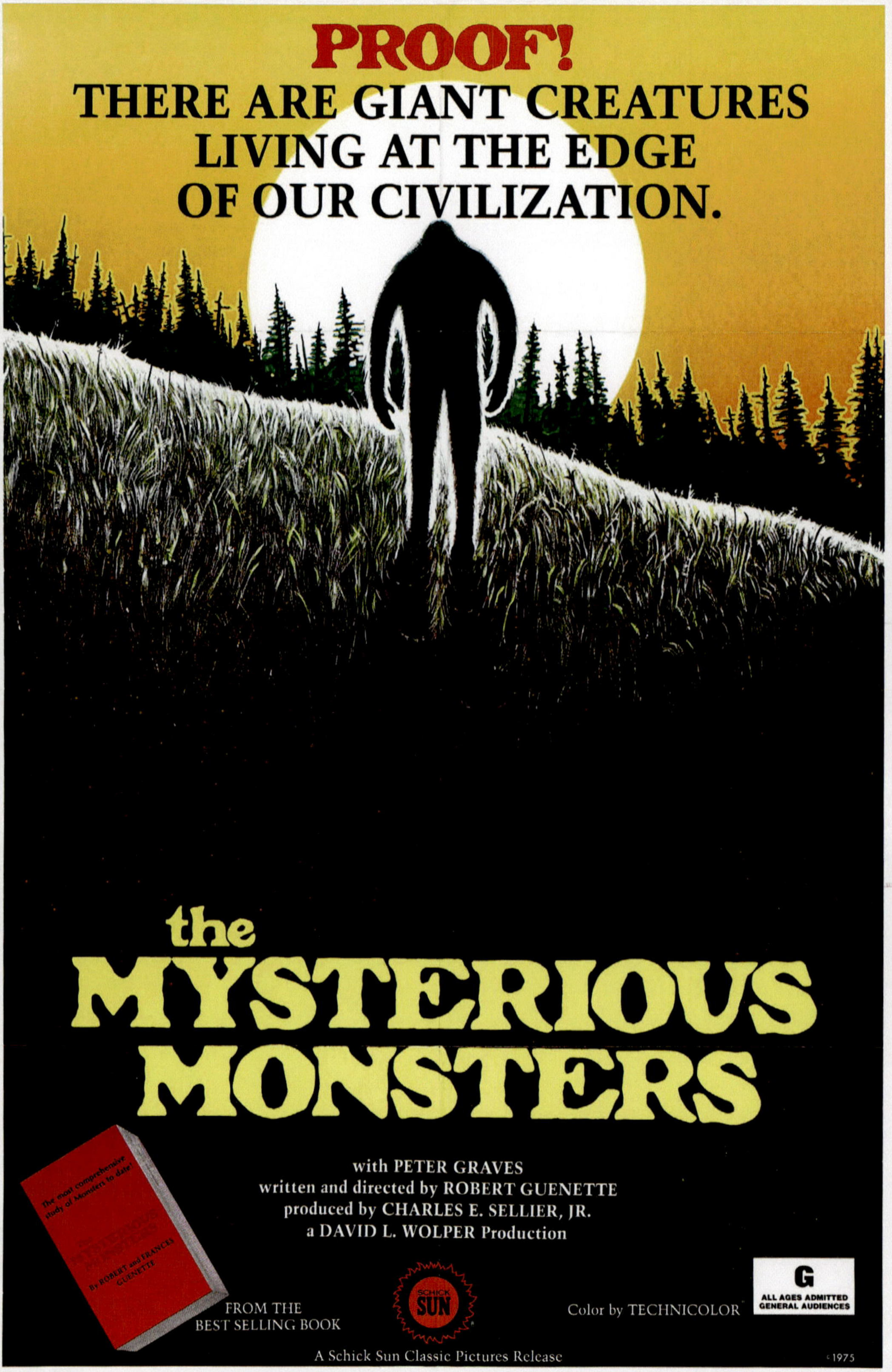
PROOF!
THERE ARE GIANT CREATURES
LIVING AT THE EDGE
OF OUR CIVILIZATION.
the
MYSTERIOUS
MONSTERS
The most comprehensive study of Monsters to date!
By ROBERT and FRANCES GUENETTE
with PETER GRAVES
written and directed by ROBERT GUENETTE
produced by CHARLES E. SELLIER, JR.
a DAVID L. WOLPER Production
FROM THE
BEST SELLING BOOK
SCHICK SUN
Color by TECHNICOLOR
G
ALL AGES ADMITTED
GENERAL AUDIENCES
A Schick Sun Classic Pictures Release
©1975

The Mysterious Monsters

(1976)

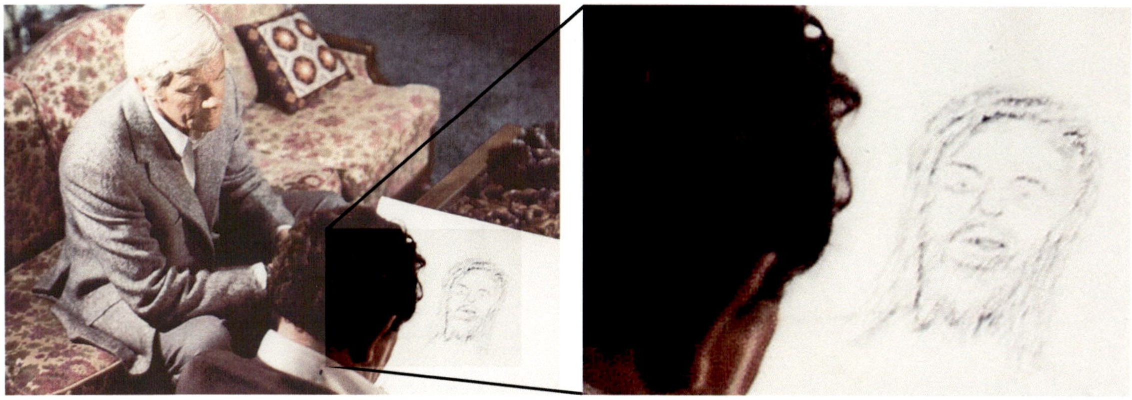

Rarely had such a wonderful advertisement appeared in the pages of *Daily Variety*. It was in the March 12, 1975 edition. "SCRIPT WANTED: Nation's leading 4-Wall distributor is searching for a very good documentary style or pseudo-documentary script about the North American Bigfoot beast. Scripts for consideration should be mailed to: Charles E. Sellier, Jr."

Enter Robert Guenette, the writer-director-producer of *Monsters! Mysteries or Myths?* (1974). Not only did he have a script, but he also had footage, all thanks to his earlier TV movie. And meeting Sellier was the equivalent of playing a Weirdmentary board game and drawing a card from the deck that read, "Get Out of [Scholarly] Jail Free."

They originally titled their joint project *Bigfoot: The Mysterious Monster*, with ads in the fall of 1975 guaranteeing it "proves the giant creatures live at the edge of our civilization, and contains actual footage never before seen." Of course most films do contain actual footage never before seen, but I digress.

Bigfoot fever, which was even raising the temperature on a couple of episodes of *The Six Million Dollar Man*, made concentrating on the creature logical. But something changed, perhaps the pending distribution of *The Legend of Bigfoot* (1976). A day late, but a dollar long, Sellier and Guenette broadened their horizons to add the Yeti and Loch Ness into the mix, thus making plural these "Mysterious Monsters."

With a G rating in hand, the film (bearing a copyright date of 1975) began to make the rounds at successful test screenings beginning in January 1976 before playing the Egyptian in Hollywood in July of that year. With a distinct lack of charity, the *Los Angeles Times* dubbed it a "mishmash," a "fascinating example of failed documentary film-making." The reviewer's name, incidentally, was "Gross."

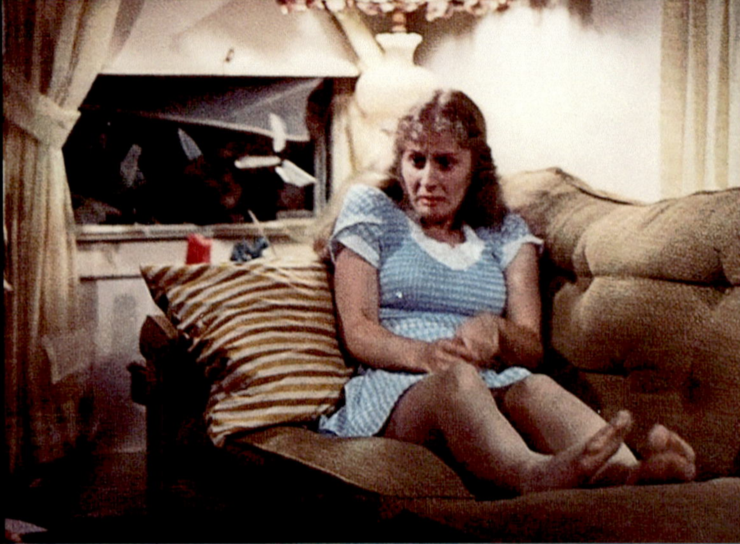

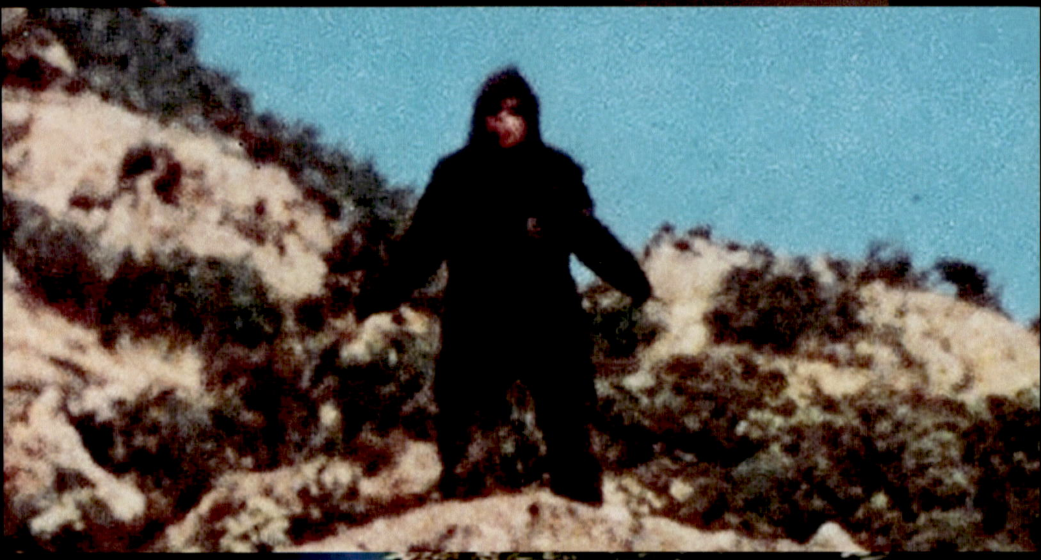

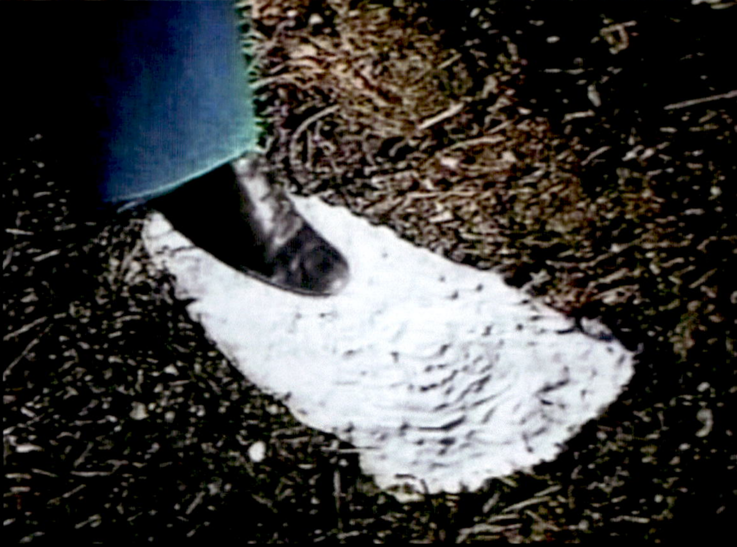

By contrast, *Variety* called *The Mysterious Monsters* a "marketable blend of documentary footage, pseudoscientific speculation, and hokey dramaturgy … pitched at the less discriminating audience." And the trade added, "one must admire the cleverness with which writer-director Robert Guenette mimics docu-veracity while dealing with outlandish subject matter."

On-screen host Peter Graves, of *Mission Impossible* fame, admits that he began as a skeptic of mysterious monsters, but "What I found out I will now show you, a body of evidence difficult to ignore." He also declares, "The facts that will be presented are true. This may be the most startling film you'll ever see."

While we see Graves in Office of Knowledge for one scene, he spends most of the time on location, speaking with experts and eyewitnesses. Of the film's "Exhibit G," Graves tells us: "Using hypnosis as a tool to help us establish the truth, we have verified an actual eyewitness account of an encounter with Bigfoot."

And then comes "Exhibit H," in which we hear about the famous Patterson-Gilm footage of Bigfoot: "If this film is legitimate, then there can no longer be any question about Bigfoot's existence." Such writing secures Guenette in the Weirdumentary Hall of Fame.

All kinds of other evidence come to life as well, ranging from a polygraph test that proves an eyewitness saw "something" to an interview with psychic investigator Peter Hurkos. Graves visits Hurkos' home with a briefcase secretly containing a plaster cast of a Bigfoot's big foot. Please do "psychometrize" on its contents, asks Graves. Hurkos envisions a Bigfoot, and draws his portrait. It's Mission Possible, even Mission Effortless.

The devotee of Weirdumentaries will notice eyewitnesses who appeared in *Monsters! Mysteries or Myths?* It isn't just the same people, it's the same footage, whether of Bigfoot tracker Peter Byrne or others who saw and lived to tell the tale. And that leads us to what's conspicuously absent. The notable scientists from the earlier documentary are nowhere to be found. In this film, the skeptics are the outliers, the outcasts.

Guenette is at his best in *The Mysterious Monsters* when he blurs the lines between fact and fiction. Unlike his earlier film, which clearly indicated when we were watching recreations, the new documentary feels no such obligation, whether its repurposing his earlier shots of the Yeti or filming new images with costumed actors playing Sasquatch. We even see POV footage of Bigfoot rustling through the trees.

Despite the time spent on Nessie, which is considerable, *The Mysterious Monsters* concentrates on Bigfoot. Graves asks whether the creature is "Man or beast?" It must be one of the two, of course, as the third option would be "non-existent," and no thinking person would consider such balderdash.

Graves concludes by confidently announcing, "Whatever it is, the volume of evidence seems conclusive. Our Earth *is* host to such giant creatures as the bigfoot." I sleep the better for it, and hope all of you do as well.

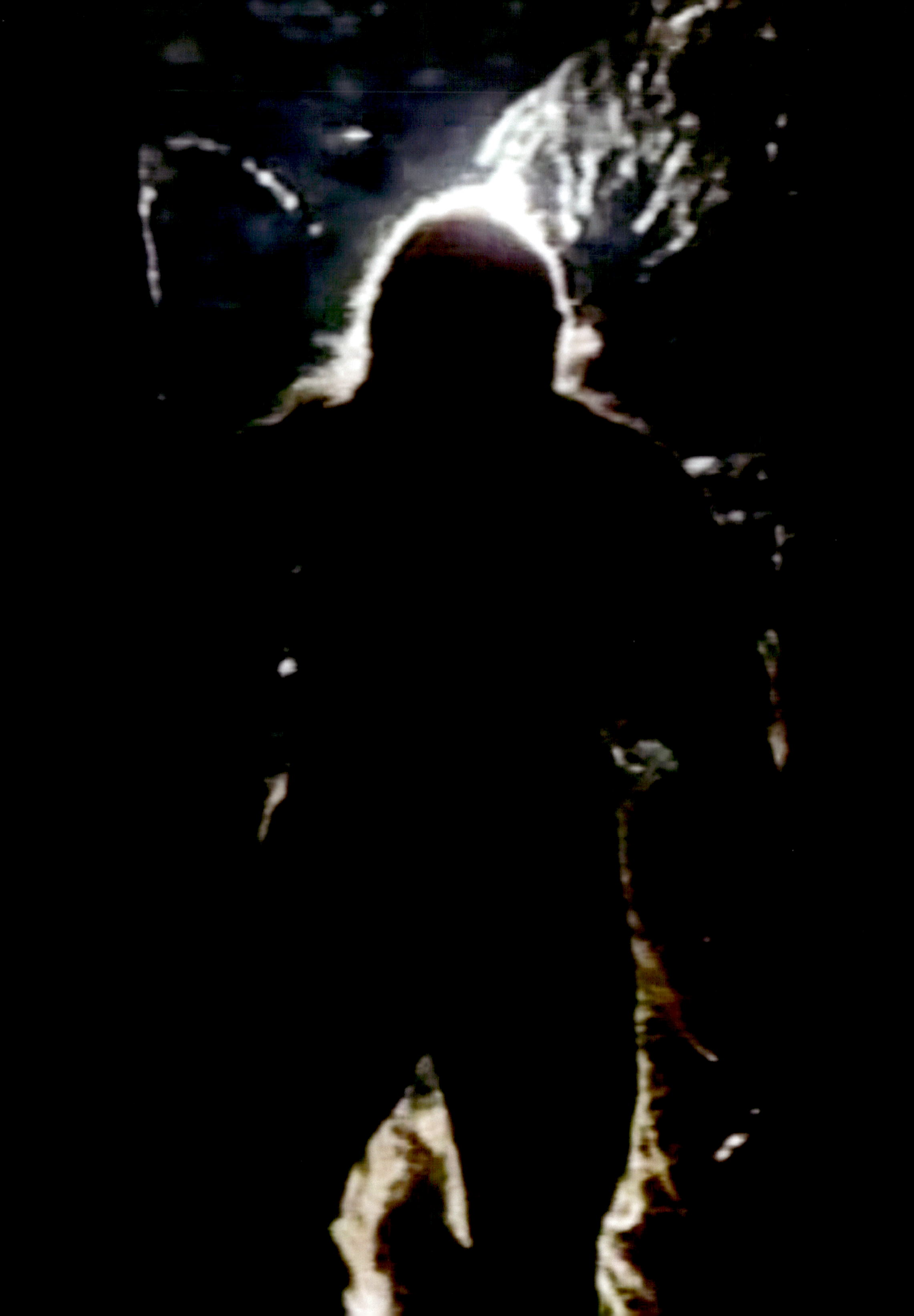

Manbeast! Myth or Monster

(1978)

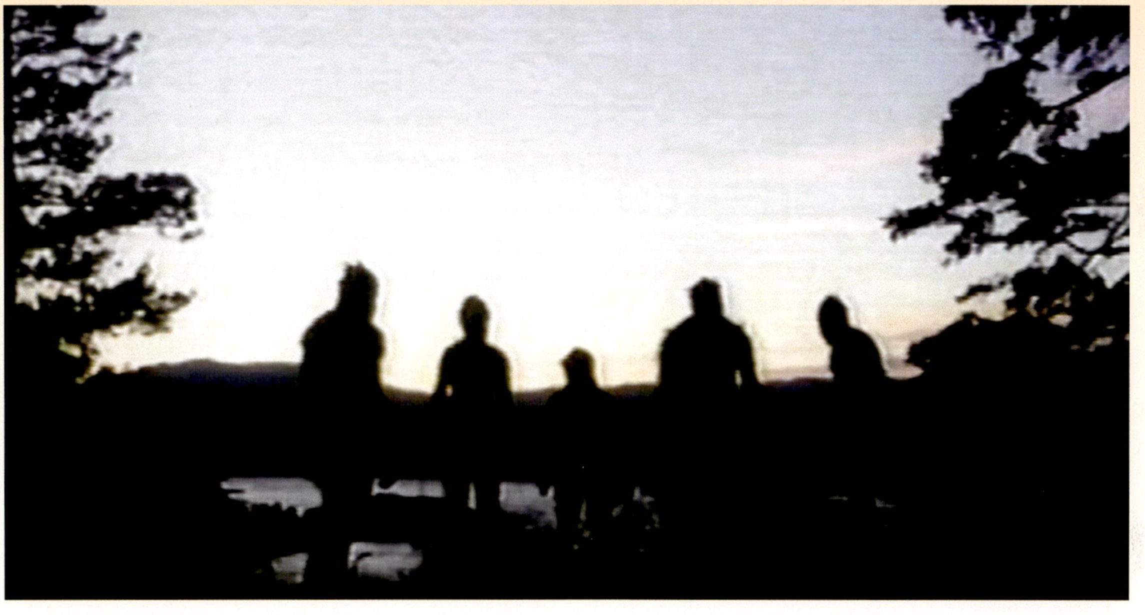

"The Earth is four billion years old. Modern man has been around for only 35,000 years. His beast-like forefathers are supposed to have died out. But is it possible that an ancestor from the distant past still roams the earth?" As these words are spoken, a silhouetted family of Bigfoot creatures appears on-screen: a father, mother, and their children.

Not unlike *The Legend of Bigfoot* (1976), *Manbeast!* concentrates on a single character's pursuit for the creature. This time it is former wild game hunter Peter C. Byrne, "The Investigator," whose killing streak ended in 1968. He became a conservationist, as well as a new kind of nice hunter, one who hopes to find Bigfoot in order to communicate with him, even to help him as much as possible. (The in-crowd had already met Byrne thanks to his appearance in *Monsters! Mysteries or Myth*? in 1974.)

This made-for-TV movie was the brainchild of Alan Landsburg, a Weirdumentary all-star dating to *In Search of Ancient Astronauts* (1973). Though credits claim the film is based on Landsburg's book *In Search of Myths and Monsters* (1977), what unfolds is Byrne's story, the self-proclaimed Ahab whose new "quest" is the "ultimate hunt."

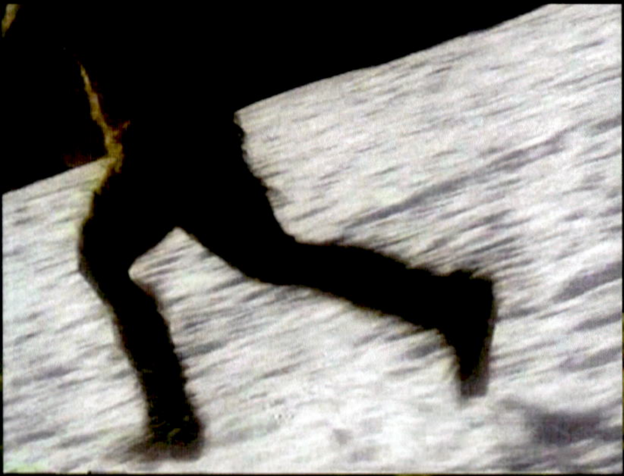
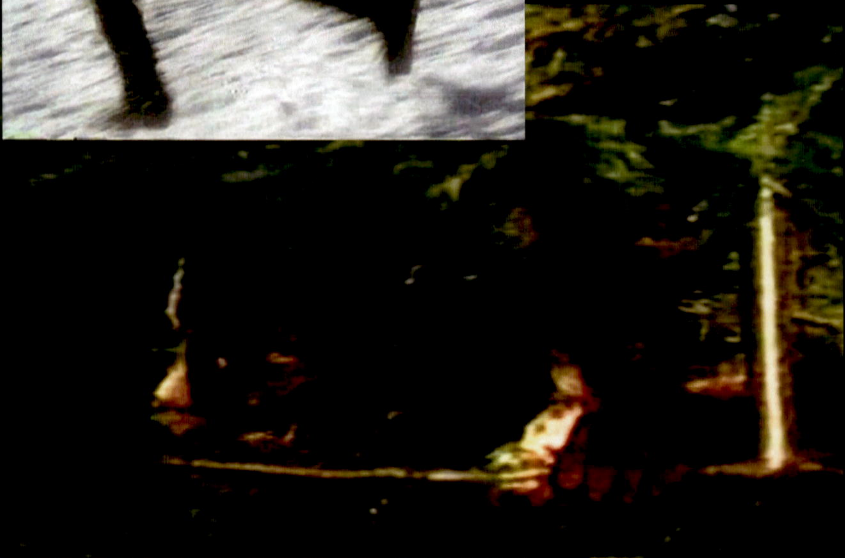
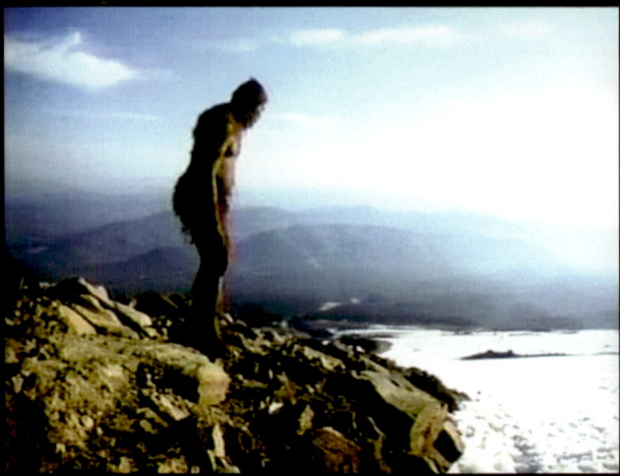

Byrne—who had himself written the book *The Search for Bigfoot* (Acropolis, 1975)—has never seen Bigfoot, and admits he might never find him. The creature is a "needle in a haystack." But Byrne fervently believes there exists "a man or an ape, a creature somehow left behind or a remnant that evolution passed by." His faith results from the footprints he has discovered, a journalist's (un?) sound recording of Bigfoot's yell, and a plethora of first-person anecdotes.

Most of Byrne's story finds him exploring Oregon and Washington, but he also travels to Nepal in search of the Yeti, even showing us a bone belonging to a snowman that was not at all abominable. That's in addition to a British woman's story about a hairy savage caught in Russia in 1921, one who had at least two babies thereafter. Whether the father was man or beast, we cannot say.

Byrne asks, "Could the Sherpas of the Himalayas, the Russian peasants of Siberia, and the American Indians of the Pacific Northwest all have invented the same prehistoric creature?" Or did the manbeast originate in China and then migrate to these other countries?

Either way, "credible witnesses [tell] incredible stories," which are brought to life in dramatizations. The best chronicles a skier who went forever missing. Footage shows Bigfoot chasing him through the snow. The skier falls, as all good victims on the run must. He regains his wintry footing and continues at a high speed, but Bigfoot the Olympiad catches up. The skier's friends believe something unusual and violent happened to him, which automatically means Sasquatch, even though they didn't see a monster or even his tracks. This is but one of "hundreds of actual stories," as opposed to all those un-actual stories that screenwriters Nicholas and Diana Webster didn't use.

For better or worse, Peter Byrne's demeanor is far more believable than Ivan Marx's, whether he's speaking to tourists at the Information Center & Exhibition in Oregon or attending a Sasquatch Conference at the University of British Columbia. While his conviction is strong, his occasional skepticism seems sincere. And when he says "manbeast," it's gentle, sounding not at all like he's using the exclamation mark in the film's title.

Though not nearly as fun as *The Legend of Bigfoot*, this sixty-minute film has two key attributes that make it worthwhile, the first being William B. Hartigan's beautiful cinematography, which ranges from aerial footage to nature scenes.

Another peak as high as the Himalayas are Rob Bottin's "Monster Creations." Despite the film's low budget, they best more ape costumes in Hollywood history than most of us can count. In fact, their triumph allows Hartigan to shoot them at times up close and personal, which not only evokes the sympathy that director Nicholas Webster hoped to achieve, but also makes them seem lifelike. Even if you don't believe, you want to. And so did Hollywood, which kept Bottin busy on big-budget fare ranging from *The Thing* (1982) and *RoboCop* (1987) to *Se7en* (1995) and *Fear and Loathing in Las Vegas* (1998).

Manbeast! concludes with Peter Byrne's sentiment that legislation needs to be passed to protect Bigfoot. It's still sitting there on Capitol Hill, that bill.

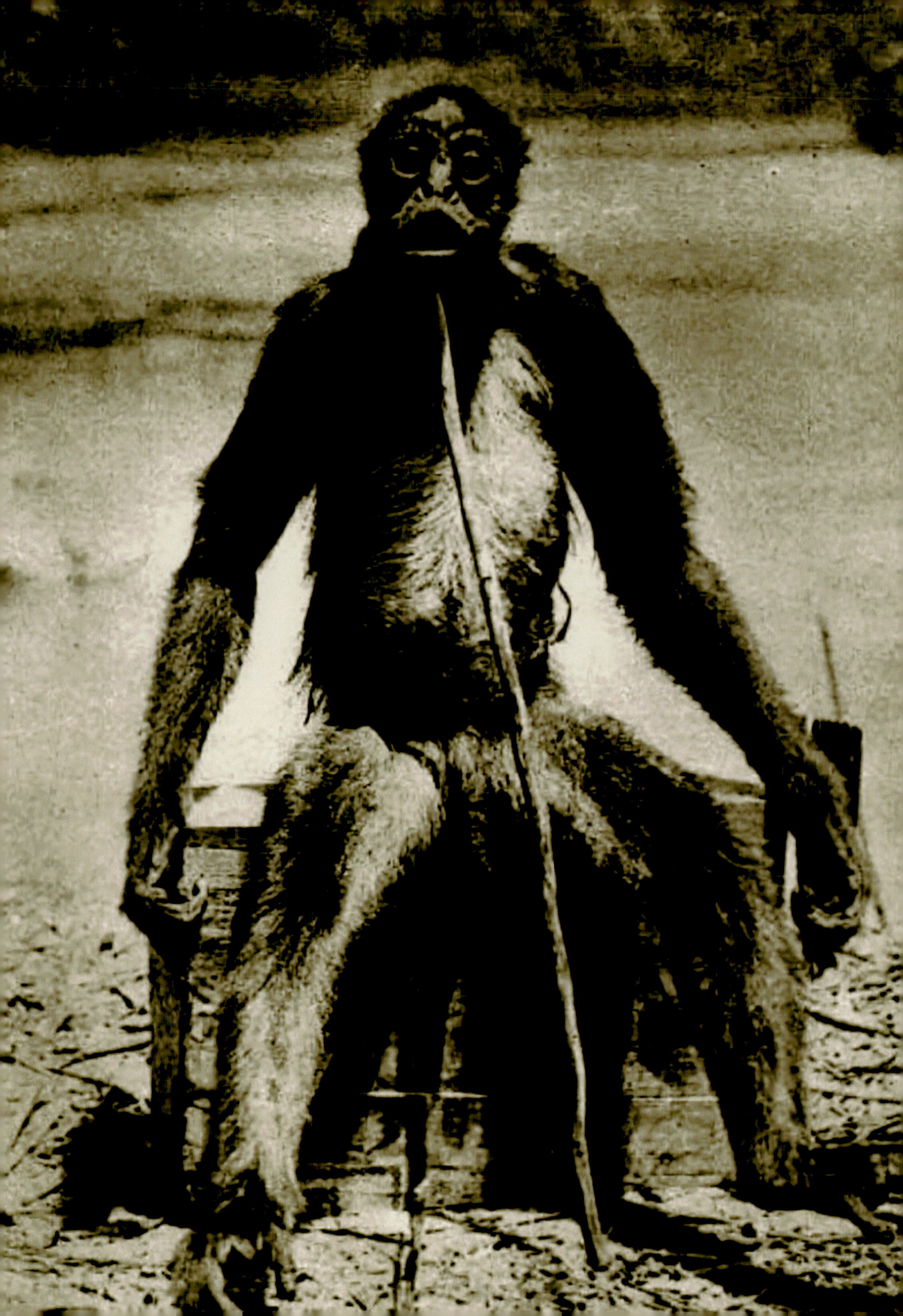

Arthur C. Clarke's Mysterious World: Mysterious Monsters

(1980)

While Arthur C. Clarke doesn't believe in ancient aliens, he does allow for the possibility of unknown bodies living in bodies of water, and maybe even prowling in secluded forests and snowy mountains. While we don't get to go beyond the infinite with *Mysterious World*, the show does ponder a few monsters that aren't discussed in other Weirdumentaries.

Episode 2, *Monsters of the Deep*: "What was the sea monster that attacked and mauled this American warship? Did a giant octopus as big as Piccadilly Circus come ashore on this beach? Did the legendary serpent of the sea appear to this Cornish fisherman?"

Between the devil and the deep blue sea is a weird place to be. Who knows what might be lurking in the ocean depths or even in black lagoons? No "full-grown giant squid has ever been caught," but we certainly hear stories about them. And even weirder stories about sea serpents of enormous size and ill temper.

"The evidence for still-unknown sea monsters is almost overwhelming," Clarke believes.

Episode 6, *Monster of the Lakes*: "Is there a really a monster in Loch Ness? Does this film, shot in 1936 but lost until today, really show the creature? And does this film, shot forty-one years later, mean the monster is still lurking there today?"

Forget extra-large calamari in the Atlantic or Pacific. Nessie is the real deal, even if he's unreal. And Nessie's pals in a few other lakes, though not as famous, are also worth a look, even if they can't be seen.

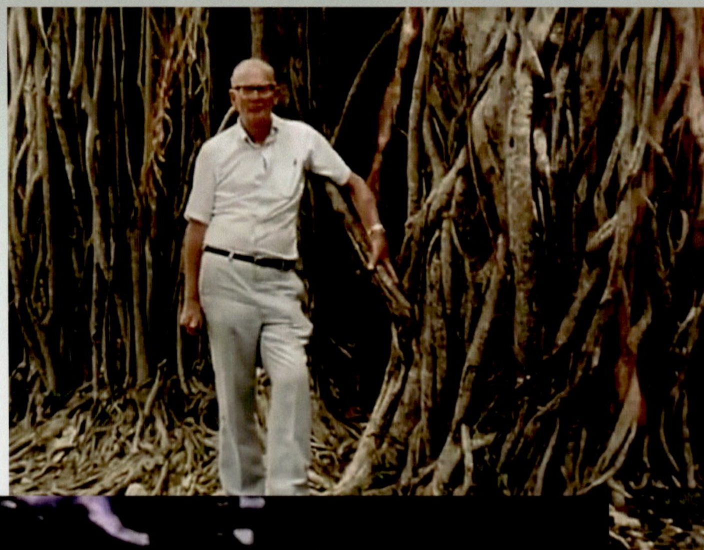

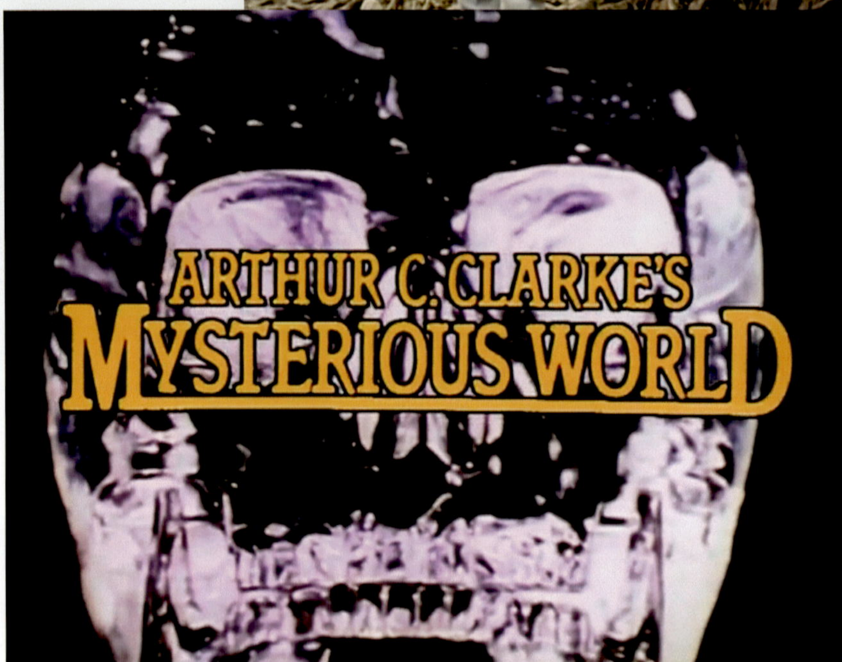
ARTHUR C. CLARKE'S
MYSTERIOUS WORLD

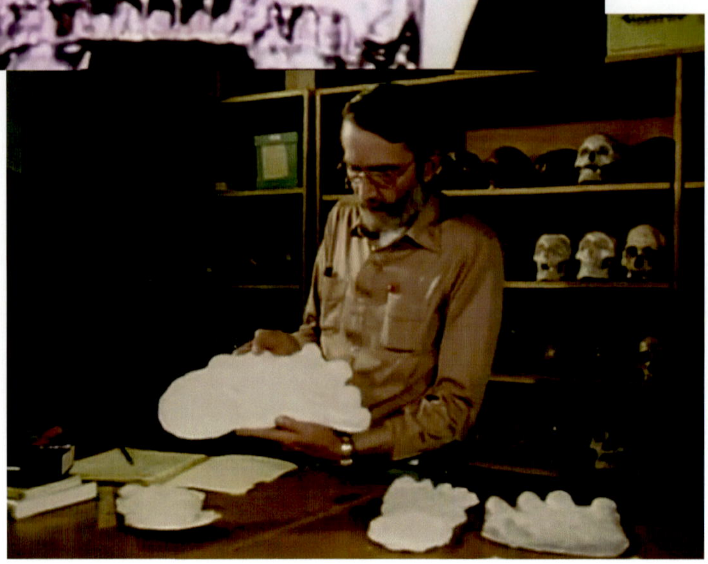

This episode takes us on an expedition for Ogopogo, the monster in Lake Okanagan in British Columbia, Canada, as well as others in such locales as Ireland and Japan. And, of course, we go back to the unsolved mess in Loch Ness. Clarke explains that he's more skeptical of lake monsters than sea monsters. Fair enough, say I, but what of terrestrial monsters? (There is a Land Shark; *Saturday Night Live* taught us that.)

Episode 4, *Missing Ape-Men*: "In the wild tracks of the Pacific Northwest of America, men are now out to try to kill the ape man. Indeed, is this unique film of Bigfoot, the Yeti of the United States? Is this the footprint of the Abominable Snowman of the Himalayas?"

Clarke seems willing to believe the answers could be yes. He explains, "It may seem incredible that creatures like large man-apes can still exist in the modern world. Yet the evidence for this is now quite considerable." Now that's full-on weird Arthur, or at least it's Art for Art's sake.

One woman in Nepal tells us that a Yeti attacked her and threw her in the river. The same creature killed some yaks. And then a woman in America tells us she didn't want to look at Bigfoot but couldn't look away, because "you want to see what you're going to see, but yet you don't." (Pure poetry, the makings of song lyrics, even.)

One Nepali man imitates the yell that the Yeti makes; one American man plays a recording of what might be Bigfoot's yell. (Bigfoot sounds angrier, even though he isn't the one out in the cold.)

Clarke isn't convinced by the Patterson-Gimlin footage, noting that the film *2001: A Space Odyssey* (1968) proved just how convincing mimes in costumes could be.

He ends the episode by saying that if someone gave him $100 to bet on their existence, he'd put forty bucks on Yeti, ten on Bigfoot, and keep the other fifty for himself. (Which reminds me, Arthur, could you loan me fifty bucks?)

Episode 11, *Dragons, Dinosaurs, and Giant Snakes*: "From the jungles of South America, is this an unknown ape? In the forests of the Congo, how huge was this snake, which rose up and menaced a helicopter? In Mozambique, could this be an unknown species of big cat? In the Pacific, did this man see the legendary dragon of New Guinea? Did the mammoth, and supposedly extinct creatures of the ice age, really all die out?"

One argument is that numerous "legendary" or "extinct" animals have been discovered in the twentieth century, so perhaps some of these other creatures also exist, particularly in faraway places.

Clarke readily admits, 'There's room for a whole zoo full of unknown animals [in the forests of Africa and South America]."

But then there have been apparent fakes and frauds, too, like "De Loys' Ape," the subject of controversy after it was photographed in 1920.

We meet explorers seeking dinosaurs, as well as one chasing dragons. (No one is searching for dungeons, or if they are, it's in a very different type of film.)

At any rate, Clarke concludes, "I think we've given enough evidence to suggest that very large, strange, and possibly amazing creatures may still exist in the remotest places of this world."

Thank goodness for that.

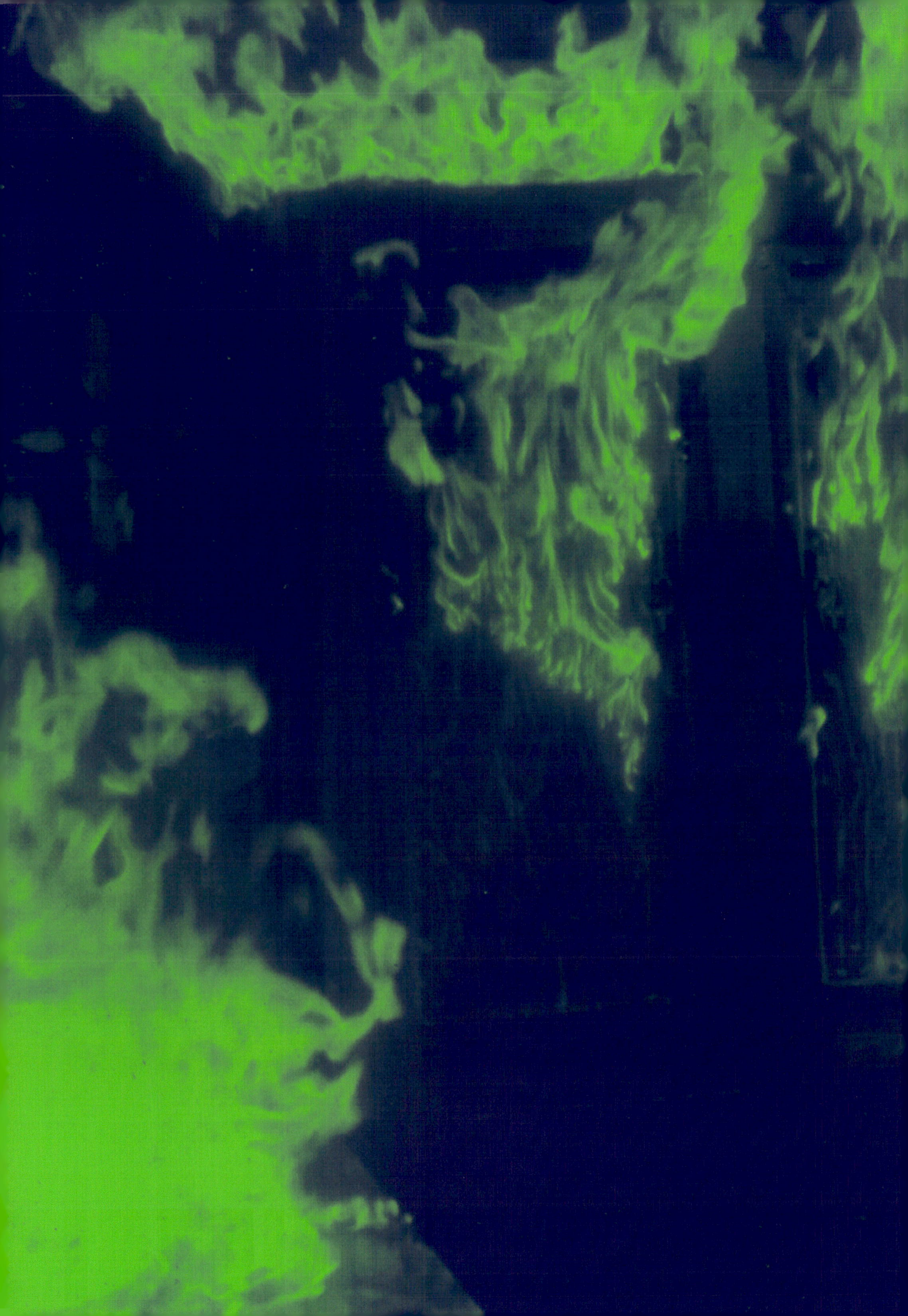

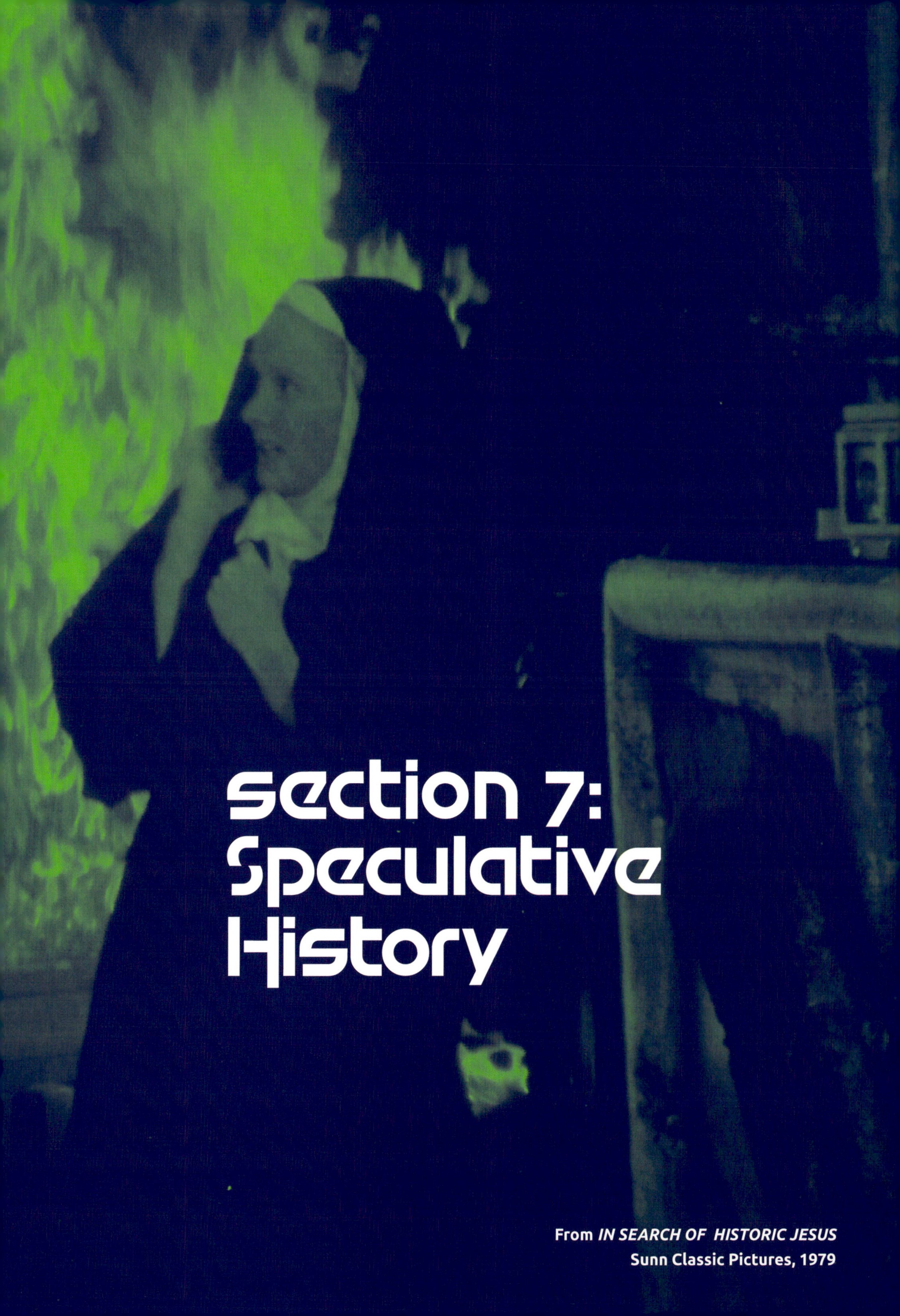

section 7: Speculative History

From *IN SEARCH OF HISTORIC JESUS*
Sunn Classic Pictures, 1979

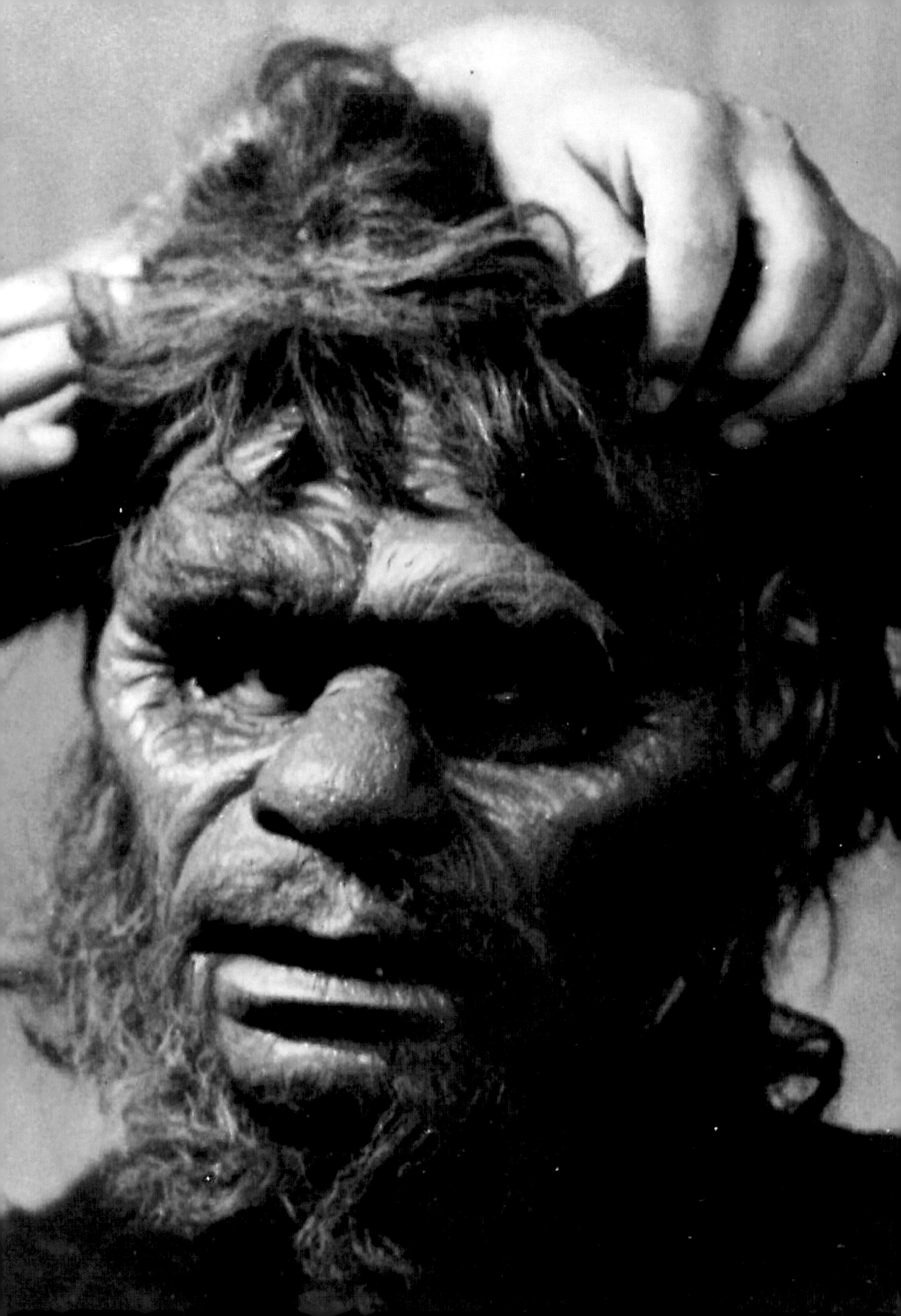

Primal Man

(1973–1974)

So, we can jabber about Darwin if we want. Or we can argue about the pronunciation of "Neanderthal." Or—best yet—we can talk about the one, the only, Weirdumentary mini-series, which was brought to us by David L. Wolper Productions.

The history lesson here may have been less about the Scopes Monkey Trials than about films like Stanley Kubrick's *2001: A Space Odyssey* (1968). Early humans were popular, and Wolper's crew were ready to take advantage of them.

Ready? Set? Let's go ... backwards, to the ancient past, one directed by Dennis Azzarella and narrated by Alexander Scourby. Four episodes, one hour each. Oh, and with makeup by John Chambers, who won an Academy Award for his work on *Planet of the Apes* (1968).

Though the recreations were meant to look like they had been filmed in Africa, they were actually shot in Bronson Canyon and the Vasquez Rocks in California. The police even showed up when the crew was shooting in Palm Springs, thanks to residents who saw "weird-looking people" running around. They were, of course, actors in makeup.

Before *Primal Man* premiered, producer Jack Kaufman told the press, "I hope that people who watch the series ... will come out feeling a little better about their predecessors. If they end thinking we're not all a bunch of brutal apes, we've done something worthwhile."

Episode 1, *The Killer Instinct*, aired in November 1973: Here was a "probe of man's basic instinct for aggression." Is our behavior rooted 10,000 years in the past? *Variety* reported:

> *The first humanoids shown (in an excellent job of makeup) were man's predecessors, including Neanderthal. They were successively more intelligent, and even the lowest was much more so than any other animals. Culmination was Cro-Magnon man, himself and yourself.*
>
> *The show had a fascinating ability to carry the viewer back into the distant past and easily forced identity with the hairy, befurred creatures who first existed on the leavings of other hunting animals and later learned to hunt their own prey and guard it from their greatest enemies—other men.*

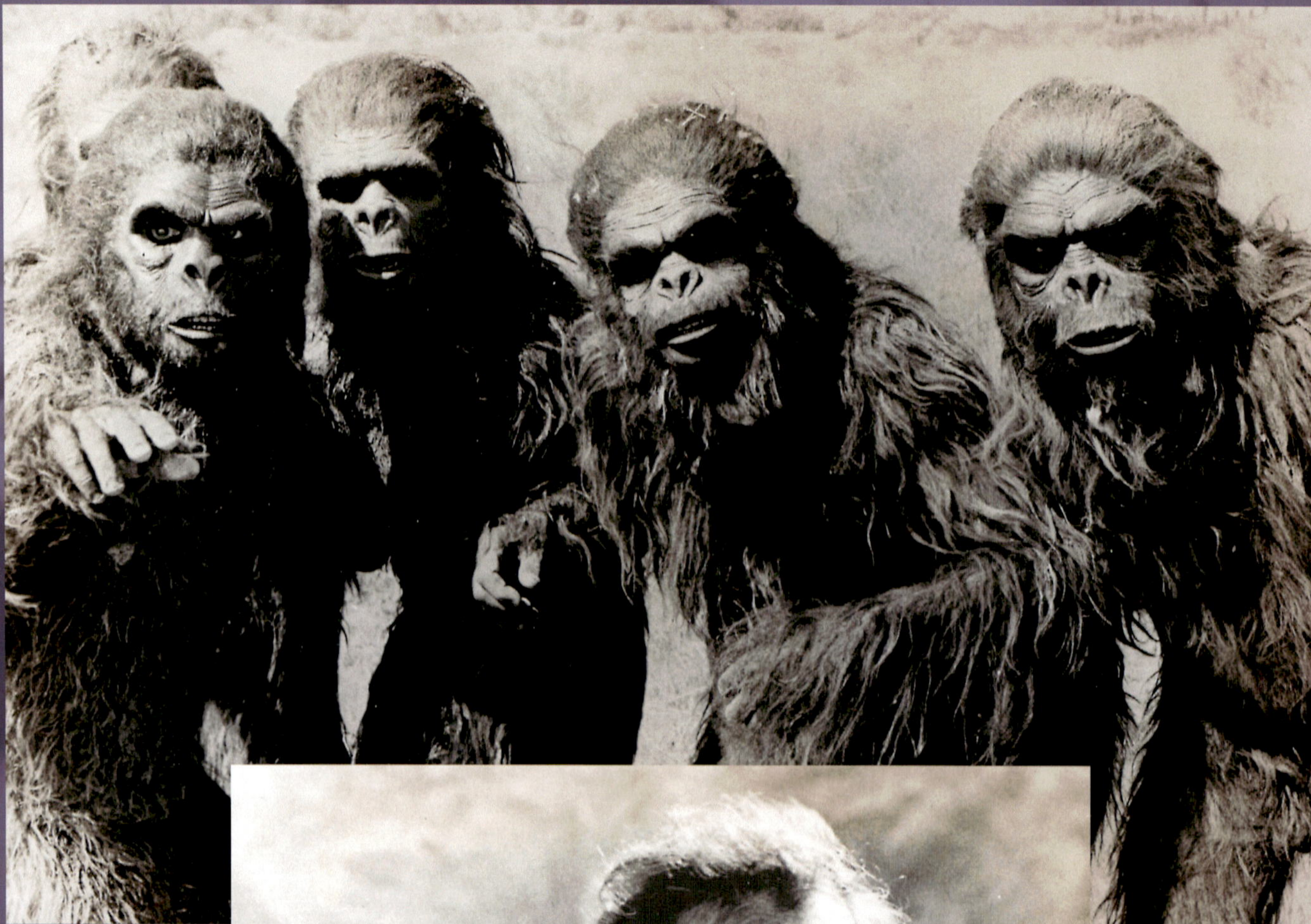
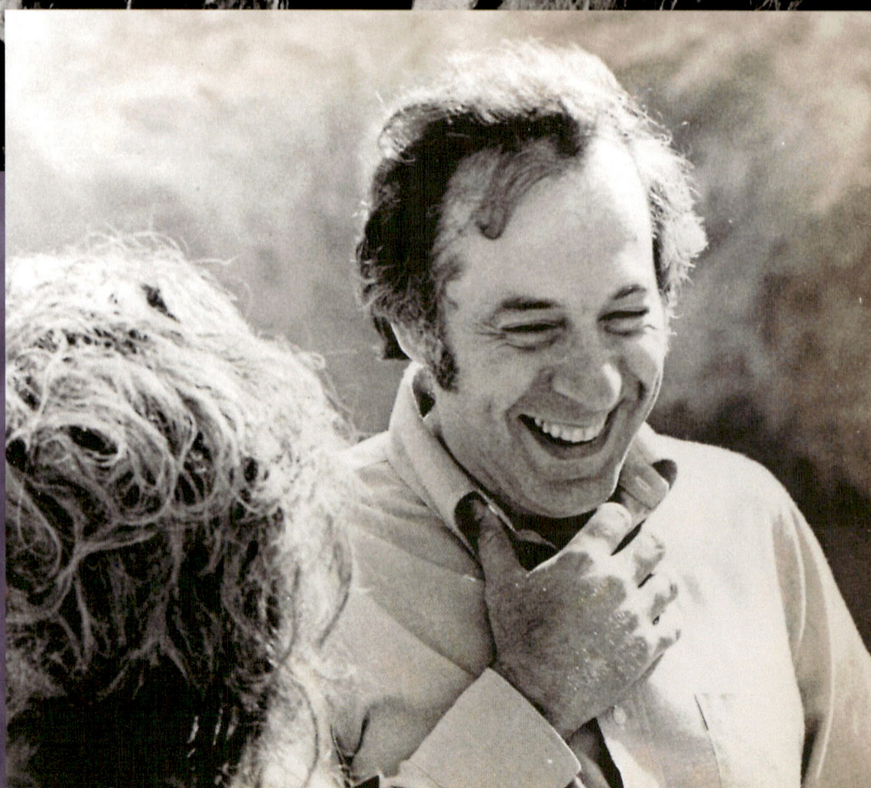

Despite the praise, *Variety* didn't really see the link between Them and Us. But such is the joy of the Weirdumentary. It's okay to intercut two ape men clubbing each other with footage of modern man kicking a vending machine. No science degree needed.

Episode 2, *The Battle for Dominance*, aired in January 1974: Here was a recreation of early humans "to focus on what makes some men leaders and others followers, from prehistoric times to modern-day human behavior." Oh, and more makeup, lots more makeup.

Episode 3, *The Struggle for Survival*, aired in June 1974: Now we get to the domination of animals and the origins of farming. The episode ended with footage taken at the La Brea Tar Pits, asking the question "Are we going the same route?" Oh, and there was even more makeup.

Variety complained, "It's difficult to make actors in ape outfits look like anything but actors in ape outfits, especially on a TV documentary budget...." Truer words never spoken.

Episode 4, *The Human Factor*, aired in May 1975: The *Los Angeles Times* declared that it had "most of the virtues and only a few of the flaws of its predecessors," adding:

> *Chief among its many qualities is a visual richness rarely seen in even the best documentaries—a blending of imagination and intuition which occasionally hits the level of art. The hunting sequence under the main title, wherein a band of our early ancestors turn into a frieze on a cave wall, is one example. And another is the short but very effective montage which ends tonight's hour—a journey through history by the same band of warriors.*
>
> *This concluding chapter explores the origins of those elements in our nature which separate us from the animals—art, language, religion, writing, play, superstition, and laughter.*
>
> *... The whole series can stand as a tribute to the people, living and dead, who worked on it—and to the rest of us for getting as far along the road as we have in spite of everything.*

The meaning of that last sentence is poignant, because of the terrible accident that had occurred during the filming of *The Struggle for Survival*.

A staggering thirty-one crew members died in a plane crash on their way to a shoot. It was the worst tragedy in Weirdumentary history. It was one of the greatest tragedies in film history. All of them were working on *Primal Man*. Dennis Azzarella was among them, which required Alex Grasshoff to finish directorial duties on *The Human Factor*. The loss was genuinely profound.

As for the overall series, *Variety* called it "an exercise in pop anthropology." Another critic said, "I have a feeling I'm seeing a sort of academic *Planet of the Apes*." Pseudo-academic, more likely.

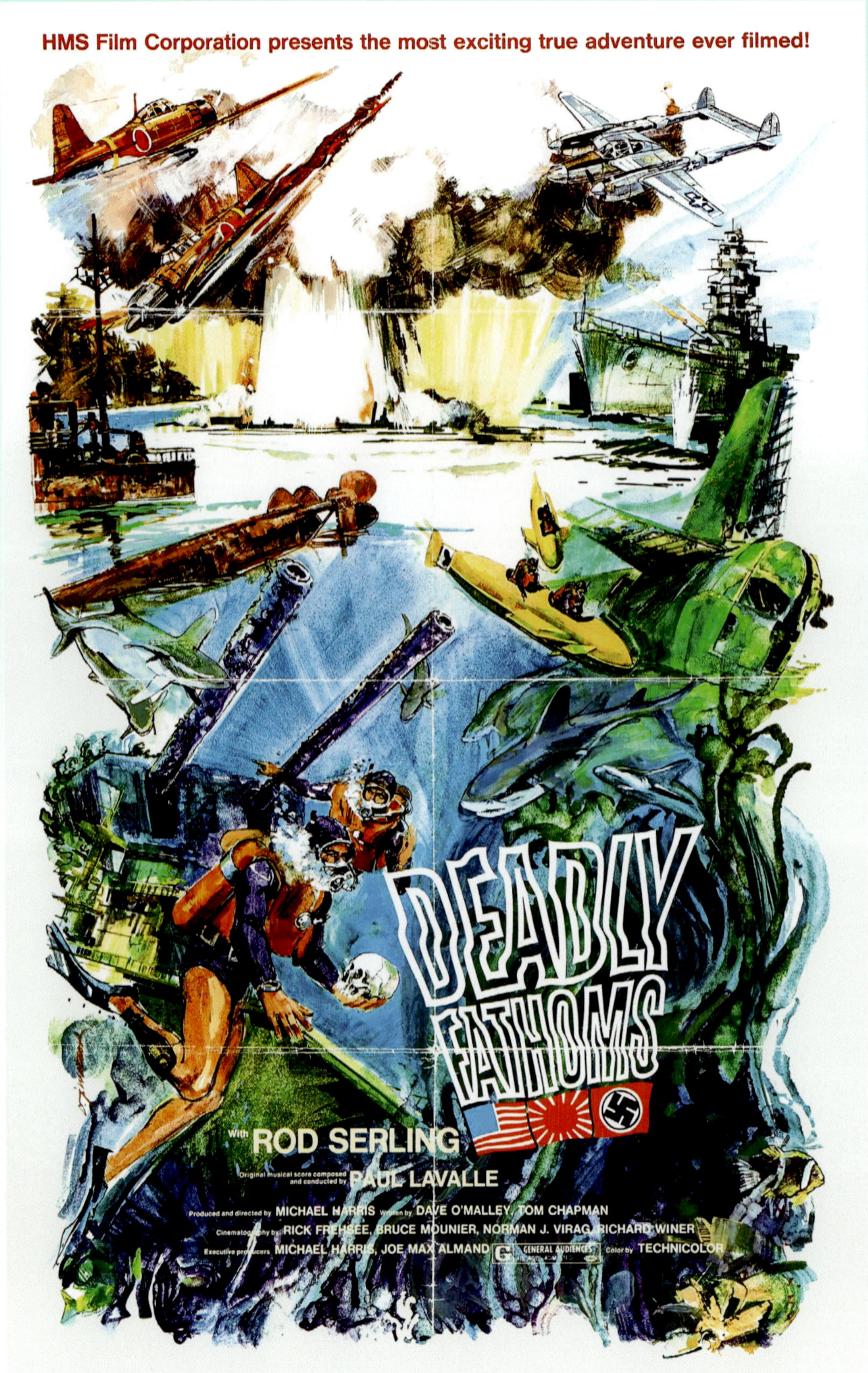
HMS Film Corporation presents the most exciting true adventure ever filmed!
DEADLY FATHOMS
with ROD SERLING
Original musical score composed and conducted by PAUL LAVALLE
Produced and directed by MICHAEL HARRIS Written by DAVE O'MALLEY, TOM CHAPMAN
Cinematography by RICK FREHSEE, BRUCE MOUNIER, NORMAN J. VIRAG, RICHARD WINER
Executive producers MICHAEL HARRIS, JOE MAX ALMAND
G GENERAL AUDIENCES
Color by TECHNICOLOR

Deadly Fathoms

(1974)

"Twelve daring men challenge sharks, deadly radiation and crushing ocean depths to film the atomic graveyard of Bikini Lagoon!" A thirteenth man, Rod Serling, serves as our trusted narrator.

American National Enterprises, Inc. released many Weirdumentaries, and *Deadly Fathoms* qualifies as one of them, at least to a degree. *Boxoffice* gave potential exhibitors the lowdown:

> *Ten years after the U.S. government concluded exhaustive testing of atom and hydrogen bombs in Bikini Atoll in the Marshall Islands of the Pacific, producer-director Michael Harris took a filming crew, headed by cinematographer Eric Frehsee, into the area for an in-depth photographic study of lingering effects of the massive bombing. A 12-man dive team swam among sharks and still radioactive ships.*

One catchline touted this movie as being "The Most Exciting True Adventure Ever Filmed!"

Mike Harris had to obtain permission from the federal government to shoot at Bikini Atoll, knowing all the while that the production would be anything but easy:

> *The dangers would be extreme: infestation of man-eating sharks was reportedly the highest in the world, hazardous radiation still lingered on in many places, and the sunken wrecks were filled with live explosives.*
>
> *...We would be giving the world its first glimpse of the infamous atomic graveyard at Bikini and a close-up view of what man and his more than twenty nuclear bombs had done to Mother Earth.*

Three of the film's cameramen wrote separate articles for *American Cinematographer*, one being Eric "Rick" Frehsee:

> *It's difficult to comprehend the photographic problems in filming shipwrecks, many of them 600 feet long in 180–200 feet of water. There are photographic problems, logistical problems, problems in communicating with models and light men, diving and environmental problems, not to mention limited bottom time and decompression. Fortunately, we have been able to find at least partial solutions to many of these problems.*

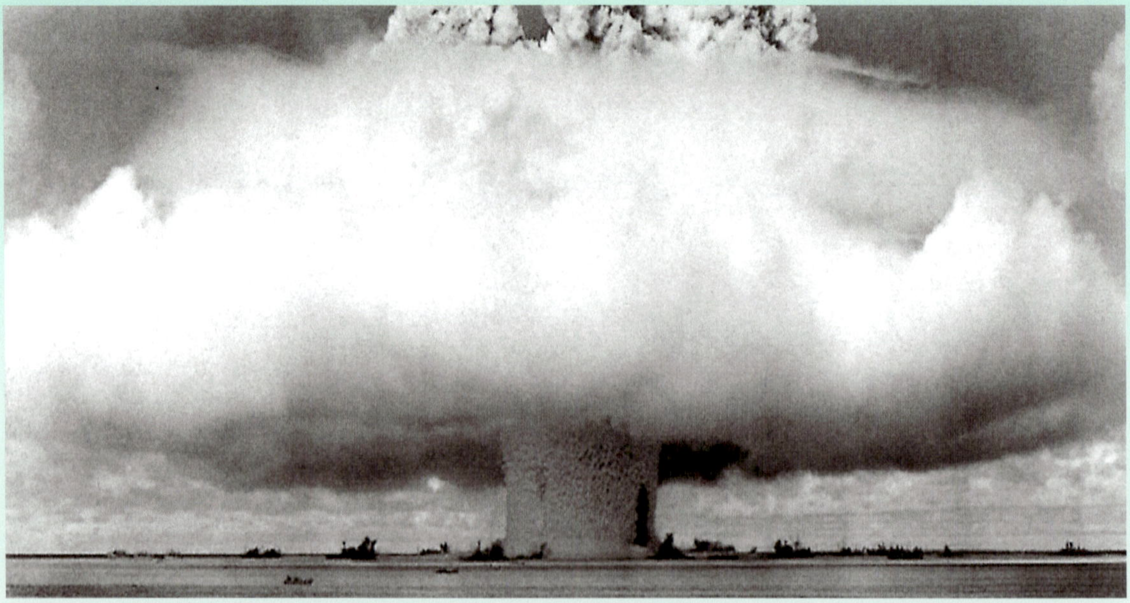

> *...By the end of six weeks we had actually spent more time decompressing than we had filming, the average depths of our dives being more than 150 feet. But we also had more than 30,000 feet of film in the can.*

Camera operator Norman J. Virag admitted, "This was a grueling assignment for both men and machines, testing their strength, courage, and reliability." And cinematog Bruce Mournier added, "It was an eerie experience, swimming through a darkened tomb laden with aircraft, live bombs and deadly torpedoes—all in battle-ready condition."

Nearly four decades after making the film, Mike Harris wrote the book *Deadly Fathoms*, recounting the many challenges he faced. From initially trying to produce a movie with Mickey Rooney to riding in Rod Serling's Bugatti, from contaminated crabs to tiger sharks: an amazing story, perhaps more fascinating than the resulting flick.

Deadly Fathoms did win a silver medal at the Atlanta International Film Festival, but not all critics were in its thrall. *Variety* praised the underwater cinematography, but condemned the project as "lackluster" and "dull," adding:

> *The filmmakers appear to have missed the boat even before they got on it. Other films of this genre usually present some scientific (or pseudo-scientific) reason for existing with the resulting film appearing to be a by-product. This doesn't happen here.*

Harris' Bikini bombshell wasn't speculative enough, in other words. Nevertheless, another trade publication predicted, "This spells top box-office money."

Exactly how much profit *Deadly Fathoms* generated is unknown. But more weird, it definitely could have been. Even before the release of Spielberg's *Jaws* (1975), man-eating sharks just weren't mysterious enough. Whither the three-eyed fish or a sponge wearing pants?

In Search Of Dracula

(1974)

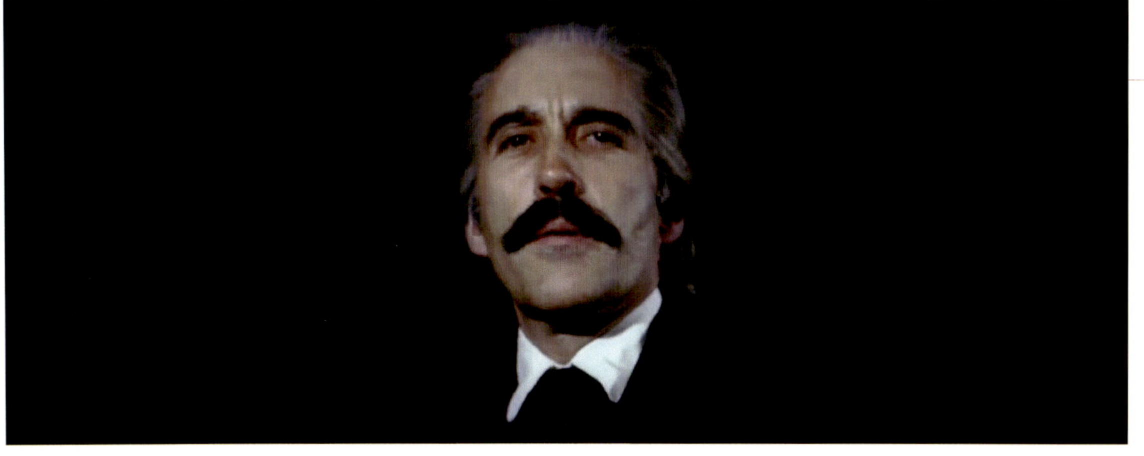

"There are more things in heaven and earth than are dreamt of in your philosophy." Those words—with Horatio's name being noticeably absent—belong to Hamlet, of course. Never were they spoken on-screen with more aplomb than by John Barrymore in *Svengali* (1931). But Christopher Lee gives the same dialogue real gusto at the beginning of *In Search of Dracula*.

Independent-International Pictures released this documentary, which was written by Yvonne Floyd and directed by Calvin Floyd. Never heard of them? Well, you probably have heard of Raymond T. McNally and Radu Florescu, who wrote the 1972 book *In Search of Dracula*.

Okay, so most folks haven't heard of them either, but that book became critical in vampire studies. McNally and Florescu's on-the-ground research in Communist-era Romania drew a definite link between Vlad the Impaler (a.k.a. the historic Dracula) and Bram Stoker's neck-biter. The Famous and the Infamous, together again.

For whatever reason, Ray and Radu don't appear in the film version. Apparently this flick began as a serious production, but the Floyds arrived to pad it with a bit of the Weirdumentary treatment.

The result is Christopher Lee's show, all the way. He narrates, he shows up in recycled footage from the movie *Scars of Dracula* (1970), he appears in new footage dressed as Stoker's Dracula, and he performs in new footage dressed as Vlad the Impaler.

Opening credits reassure us, "All film locations are authentic and historically accurate." And that ain't no lie. *In Search of Dracula* was probably the first movie to show off Vlad the Impaler's actual stomping grounds, staking grounds, and impaling grounds.

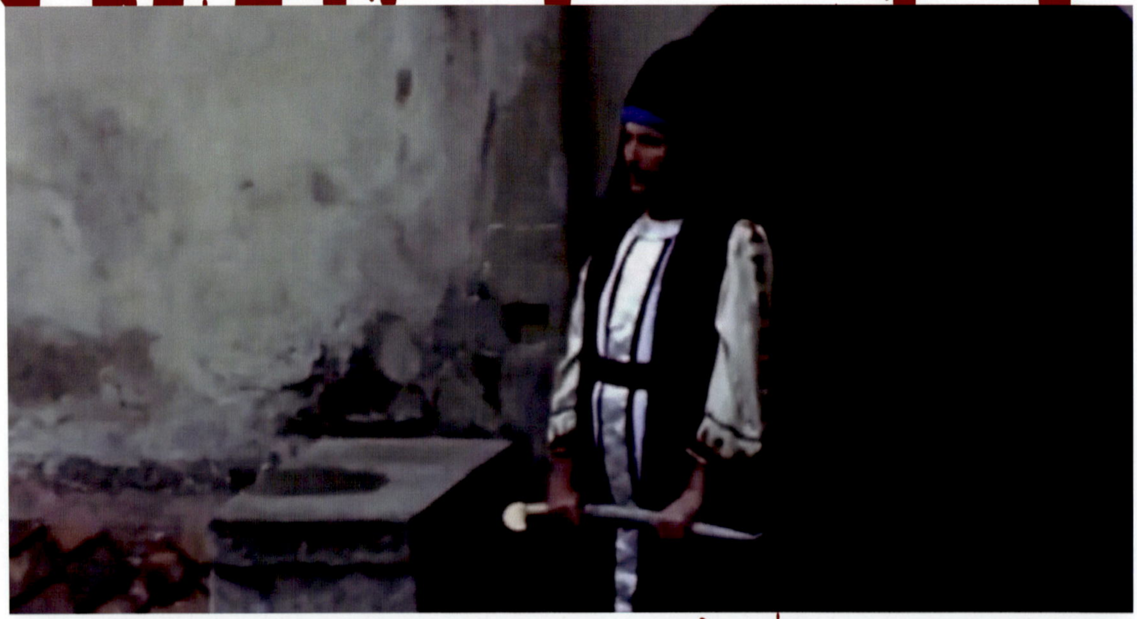

The history lesson we get comes in the form of many lessons. We hear vampire legends from around the world. Who gets to be a vampire? What do they do? How do you destroy them? Some of these tales are familiar; some aren't.

For example, Lee explains that vampires allegedly gather on St. Andrew's Eve, meeting in graveyards "to decide on their programs for the coming year: who is to be killed and by whom." (We don't learn if they take a vote, draw straws, or play rock-paper-scissors.)

And then there's this rare tidbit about tid-biting: "One common method of locating a vampire was to choose a boy or girl young enough to be a virgin and seek [vampires] naked on a horse of a solid color, which was also a virgin and had never stumbled." (Lady Godiva that cemetery, and the vampire will be found.)

Some info is folkloric, some psychological, some historical. Countess Elizabeth Bathory bathing in blood, for example, and Peter Kürten murdering victims in Düsseldorf.

There's a bit of zoology, with vampire bats on parade. There's a bunch of literature, starting with Lord Byron and John Polidori, proceeding through *Varney the Vampire* (1845–1847) and *Carmilla* (1872), and ending with Bram Stoker himself.

As so many critics have noted, this movie loses steam once it starts chronicling vampire cinema. Footage from F.W. Murnau's *Nosferatu* (1922) is welcome, but extensive clips of a vamp from the teens and of Bela Lugosi in a pre-*Dracula* (1931) role seem to be padding, part of a vain and vein effort to reach feature length.

That said, there's plenty of lifeblood in the old flick. Lee rightly declares, "Seventy-five years have passed since Bram Stoker created his sinister Transylvanian count. However, he still fascinates vast numbers of people and will no doubt continue to do so, for there has yet to be another fictional character quite like Count Dracula."

Ads for *In Search of Dracula* proclaimed it was "Not a horror movie, Not a documentary—But a living vampire experience!"

The *Independent Film Journal* believed the experience was "tame and sleepy." *Variety* was less kind, claiming that the Floyds relied on:

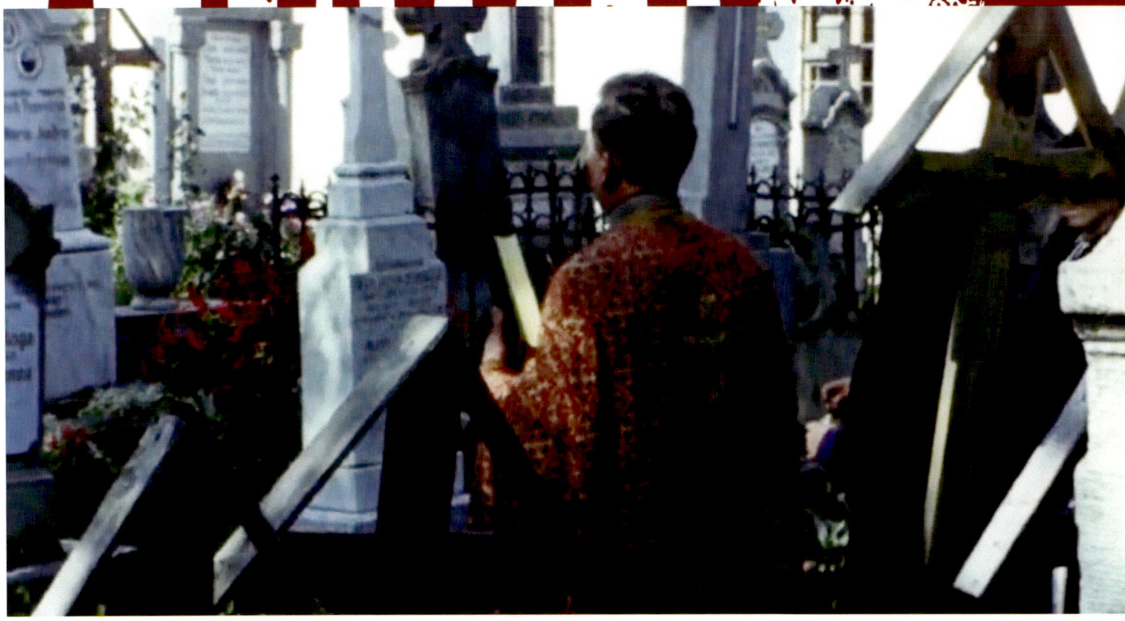

...the same cheapie metaphysics that crops up regularly to sell books and pix. To wit: the abominable snowman who eats people, the Bermuda Triangle that eats aircraft, the chariots of the Gods whose garbage became humanity, or for that matter, the devil, who stoops to such theatrics as writing messages on little girls' stomachs in Georgetown.

All that said, is this Drac Attack a full-on Weirdumentary? Okay, it isn't full-on, but it is on. Certainly we get some exaggerations, including this gem: "In reality, peasant life in the more remote villages of Transylvania has not changed much for centuries, and belief in vampires and other superstitions is still strong, though such things are now rarely spoken of."

And the connection between Vlad the Impaler and Dracula is a wee bit less than the film—and the book on which it's based—argues. Vlad counts in stories about the Count, to be sure, but he was just one of many influences on Bram Stoker.

Best of all, we get this wonderfully weird final speech by Lee, which he delivers on-camera with fangs in:

Just a word, ladies and gentlemen, a word of reassurance. When you go to bed tonight, and the lights have all been turned out, and you're afraid to look behind the curtain, and you dread to see the face appearing at the window, just remember, there are such things.

Tongue-in-cheek, yes. In fact, it's based on a speech that Bela Lugosi gave onstage at the end of *Dracula—The Vampire Play*. (Mercifully, Lee doesn't say, "Fangs for the Memories.")

What I must add, with equal parts joy and puzzlement, is that I don't understand why Lee pronounces the word "archetype" with only two syllables: "arch-type." Please don't get cross (or crucifix) when I openly judge that to be weird.

In Search Of... Speculative History

(1976–1982)

"We're not trying to sell anything," Leonard Nimoy once said of his television program. "We're merely exploring various questions and offering some theories ... What the show is trying to say is that there are ways of perceiving things in new ways."

Well put, my green-blooded friend. And the ongoing speculation became as true in the series' sixth and final season as in those that came before.

Throughout its run, *In Search of…* particularly enjoyed reaching into the past, discussing strange and bizarre historical tales, perhaps because there are so very many of them.

Jack the Ripper (Season 3, Episode 5), *The Elephant Man* (Season 6, Episode 5), and *Jim Jones* (Season 6, Episode 7) serve as great examples.

The historical basis for Biblical stories was also popular: *The Garden of Eden* (Season 2, Episode 24), *Noah's Flood* (Season 3, Episode 19), *Sodom and Gomorrah* (Season 3, Episode 23), *John the Baptist* (Season 4, Episode 20), *The Holy Grail* (Season 5, Episode 18), and *The Walls of Jericho* (Season 6, Episode 21).

There was a great deal of wonderfully speculative history. Could there have been a real Sherlock Holmes (Season 3, Episode 12)? Was Van Gogh mad (Season 4, Episode 16)? Might Richard III have been responsible for the death of his nephews (Season 6, Episode 9)? Did Oswald act alone (Season 5, Episode 3)? Tried-and-true (or not so true) topics all.

Ahh yes, speculative history, where amateur and professional historians stand as tall (or as short) as one another. Opinions and facts are equally heralded. Let's go back to that simpler time, shall we, even if it never existed.

For those of us without enough spare time to read books or watch feature-length Weirdumentaries, there were a few episodes that trod the very same ground covered elsewhere, but with brevity: expeditious expeditions.

Season 1, Episode 16, *Dracula*: Okay, for starters, we should make clear that *In Search of… Dracula* is totally different than the feature film *In Search of Dracula* (1974, see entry).

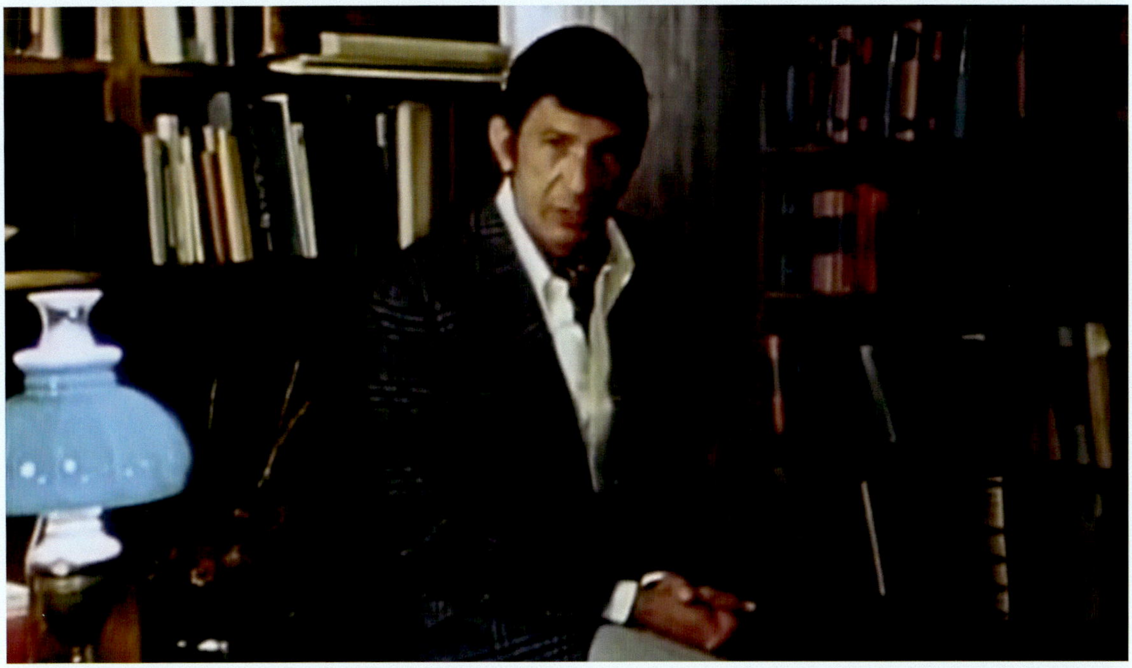

Secondly, we should make clear that they're the same ... kind of. Different projects, same subject, and same theory. "Dracula ... fiction or reality?" Vlad the Impaler became Bram Stoker's Dracula. "What of the truth behind the legend?" Well, the truth is that Vlad was an influence on Stoker, but only one of many.

It must be said that herein are some great images of Romania, as well as attention paid to Bran Castle, which certainly wasn't one of Vlad's, or any vampire's, for that matter. (I would add that Vlad didn't wear a cape, or—so far as I can determine—a shroud.)

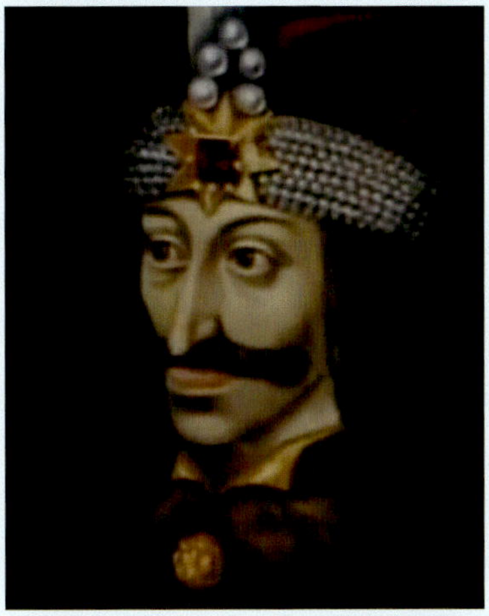

Season 4, Episode 7, *The Shroud of Turin*: "Today scientists are using modern technology to investigate the authenticity of this ancient relic. A young skeptic, however, has come forward with the claim he can prove the shroud is a fraud. Is [the image on the shroud] the face of Christ, or a forgery perpetrated by some unknown genius?"

In Search of... didn't have to search far for this topic. Harry Mastrogeorge's *Mystery of the Sacred Shroud* (1978, see entry) had already covered the relic at length, of course.

But in an unusual move, Nimoy and friends interview a rather intelligent skeptic, who demonstrates one plausible way to create a shroud image. Not surprisingly, a shroud proponent makes the skeptic's process seem implausible.

Season 6, Episode 6, *The Lincoln Conspiracy*. After the assassination, "was justice done?" The machinations of John Wilkes Booth and his confederates receive careful review, from initial plans to kidnap Honest Abe to the eventual assassination.

Of course, Sunn Classic and James L. Conway had

already given us *The Lincoln Conspiracy* (1977, see entry). So, is this Nimoy episode déjà vu, or déjà new?

Nimoy does introduce some fascinating information, and he does rightly suggest that a couple of folks might have been wrongly convicted. But *In Search of...* proves, once again, the more historical the setting, the less convincing its cheap recreations.

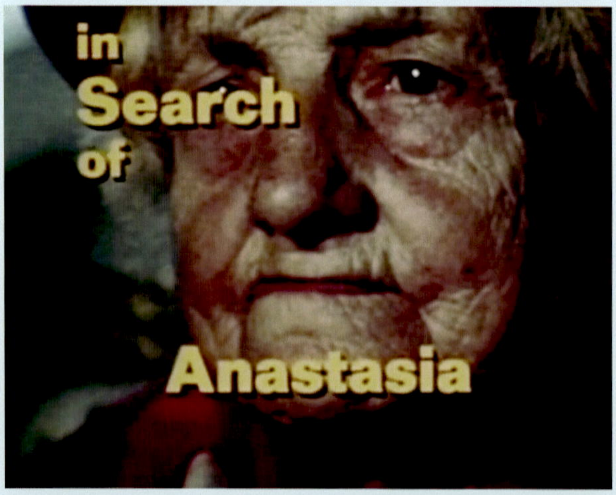

Okay, let's say you're ready for something new about something old, rather than slinging rehash at the Weirdumentary diner. Fair enough. We won't worry about Potent Potables. Instead, we'll choose People, then Places, then Things.

Season 1, Episode 15, *Amelia Earhart*: "Now, nearly forty years after Amelia Earhart's disappearance, there are surprising new theories to explore." Requisite biographical details of the aviator's accomplishments precede not-so-requisite speculation.

Was Earhart an American spy captured by the Japanese? Maybe she was later spirited out of Japan by wearing a nun's habit and then changing her habits back stateside, taking on a new identity.

Or maybe her plane just ran out of fuel? Or maybe I ran out of fuel, after hearing a variety of other What-Ifs about her fate.

Season 2, Episode 13, *Anastasia*: "A legend endures ... that the Czar's youngest daughter, Anastasia, escaped the massacre and is still alive today." Nimoy tells us that a woman named Anna Anderson claimed to be Anastasia for fifty years, and she "has never been disproved." One expert confidently tells us, "We will never know." (Hmmm. How does one spell the sound that a wrong answer receives on *Family Feud*? You see, that expert was wrong. Some years after this episode first aired, DNA proved Anderson was not a Romanov.)

Season 2, Episode 21, *Butch Cassidy*: "South America, 1909. According to this famous film [with Paul Newman], a gun battle claims the life of Butch Cassidy. If the film version is right, who was the mysterious stranger who appeared on a Wyoming road fifteen years later? A mysterious stranger who bore a strong resemblance to Butch Cassidy."

Nimoy continues by confidently announcing, "Now, those who have kept their silence for years are ready to reveal the true ending to this remarkable story."

What do those folks tell us? Son of a Butch if Cassidy didn't survive, having returned from Bolivia to America, where he reconnected with old friends and family. Don't believe 'em? Well, now, just watch those recreations of him riding in a Model T, and you'll come to learn the truth of it.

Season 6, Episode 1, *Jesse James*: "Most historians maintain that Jesse was killed six years after his doomed Northfield, Minnesota, raid. Yet in 1948, J. Frank Dalton claimed he was Jesse James. Is it possible that Jesse James could have perpetrated a hoax on the entire country for over sixty years?"

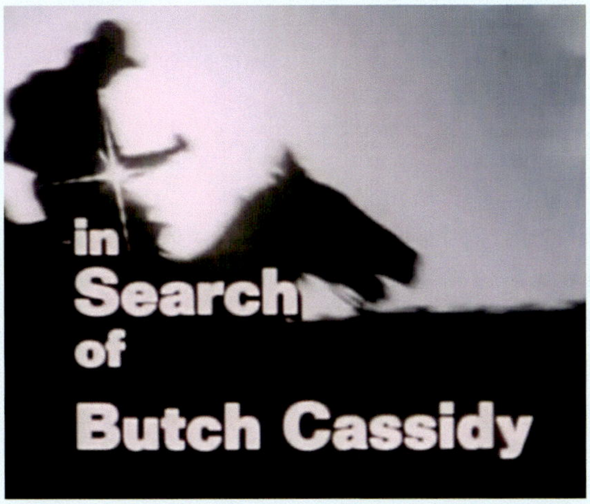

Certainly, someone died at the hands of the Coward Robert Ford. And certainly someone claimed to be Jesse James decades later. (Either way, eventually poor Jesse was laid in his grave.)

Season 6, Episode 20, *Eva Braun*: "Recent scientific findings indicate that the woman's body the Russians claim to have found beside Hitler's may not have been that of Eva Braun. ... Did she escape, as persistent rumors claim? Is it possible that Eva Braun is alive today?"

So much time has been spent speculating about Hitler's alleged escape to South America, that many of us weren't even aware of the "persistent rumors" about Eva.

One anonymous, silhouetted interviewee declares that she saw Eva Braun in Tibet. (We don't hear if Eva was traveling with the Abominable Hitler or the Abominable Snowman at the time.)

Quick recap? *Amelia Earhart*, *Anastasia*, *Butch Cassidy*, *Jesse James*, and *Eva Braun* are all the same episode, or at least they all share the same weird theory. Those that we thought had died did not. They lived to fight and love and wear a nun's clothing another day.

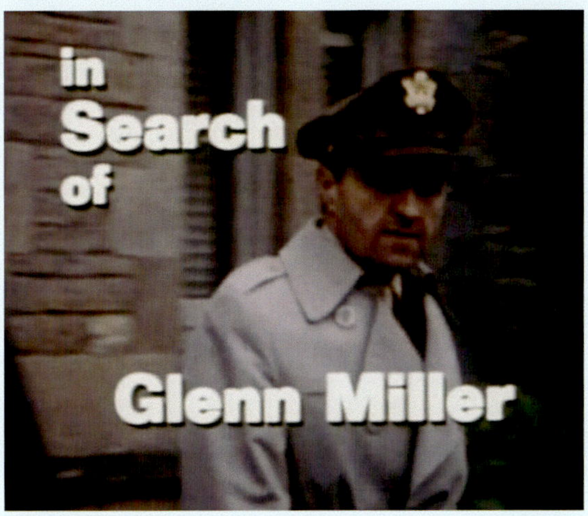

But then are stories where we share the belief that somebody did die at the stated time and place, but then—as in the JFK assassination—things get weird when we argue about *how* they died.

Season 2, Episode 6, *Michael Rockefeller*. In 1961, explorer Michael Rockefeller disappeared "in the midst" of New Guinea. Here was a famous event, given that Mike was the son of New York Governor Nelson Rockefeller. But what happened to Mike? Drowned? Killed by a shark? Or murdered and even eaten by the Asmat tribe? The mind wanders and wonders. Nimoy concludes that the mystery "may never be solved."

Season 4, Episode 23, *Glenn Miller*. The famed bandleader and trombonist serves in the military, and travels on a small plane from England to France in December 1944. "Glenn Miller will never be seen again. It has long been believed the plane iced up and went down in the English Channel. Yet recent information raises some disturbing questions. What were the circumstances around the disappearance, and why was there never a search made for the aircraft?"

Why risk the flight given the poor weather? Nimoy explains that some believe the official story to be incorrect. Did the plane crash on British soil, instead of in the water?

Or did something else happen? (While watching this episode in bed, my blanket whispered about a cover-up.)

Season 5, Episode 19, *The Death of Marilyn Monroe*: "Was [Monroe's death in 1962] really a suicide, as her millions of fans were led to believe?" Suicide, accident, murder, or even the victim of a "political" assassination?

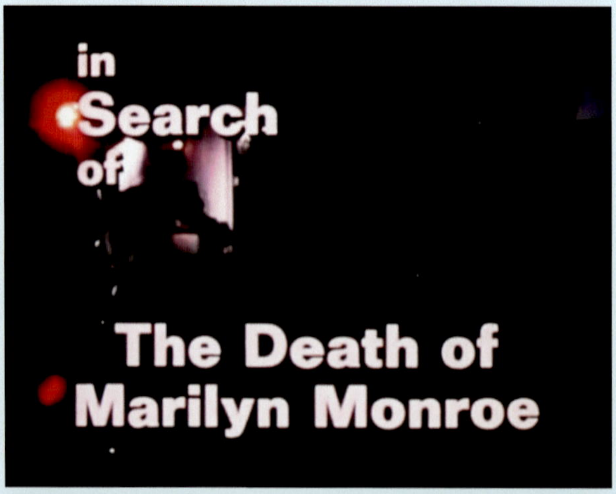

Nimoy describes "inconsistencies" in the record regarding the night Marilyn died. Experts disagree, which means the inconsistences lead to inconsistent interpretations.

Anyhow, one expert says it was "unquestionably a murder." That's when we hear about wiretaps, blackmail, and the "alleged existence" of Marilyn's diary. What we *don't* hear are names like JFK and RFK. "Will we ever really know what happened…?" Possibly not, but time's a-wasting, so let's move onto our next category, Places.

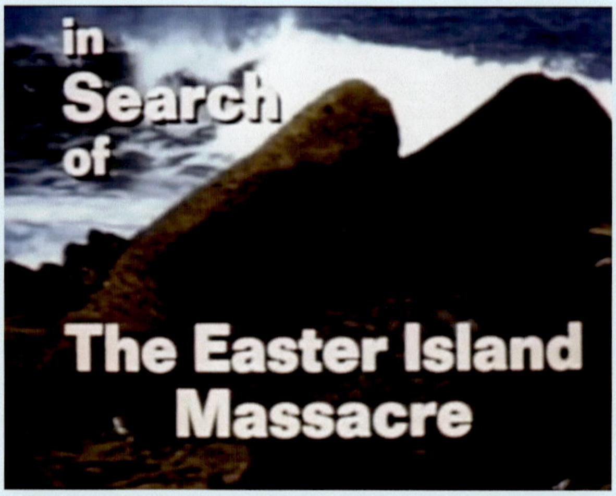

Season 1, Episode 10, *Atlantis*: For this episode, *In Search of…* was ahead of the other searchers; *Atlantis* aired a couple of years before Richard Martin made his Weirdumentary feature *The Lost City of Atlantis* (1978, see entry).

"Never before have explorers been so close to finding Atlantis. Never have we possessed as many clues, nor have we been able to bring the detection equipment of modern science to the search … until now."

"Was it a real city, a wondrous land, or a myth, a tale created by someone's wild imagination?"

And how do you lose such a great place? According to Plato, earthquakes and floods caused Atlantis to sink into the sea quickly. Explorers have sought it ever since.

Nimoy introduces us to a handful of possible locations. We are particularly thankful that Peter Tompkins is part of the investigation at Bimini. He would later appear in *Mysteries of the Great Pyramid* (1977, see entry) and *Secrets of the Bermuda Triangle* (1978, see entry).

Season 1, Episode 17, *The Easter Island Massacre*: "On a remote island in the Pacific Ocean, a frightening and mysterious massacre took place. A race of stone giants carved a thousand years ago guard the shore in silence, as if unable to endure what they have witnessed. The clues to the mystery remain locked behind mute lips. There is no voice to tell who carved the giants and why hundreds of them were destroyed in the Easter Island massacre."

If that isn't tremendous opening dialogue, I don't know what is. The statues of Easter Island are enigmatic, wonderful, and bizarre. To add a massacre, well, now, that's the stuff dreams and nightmares are made of.

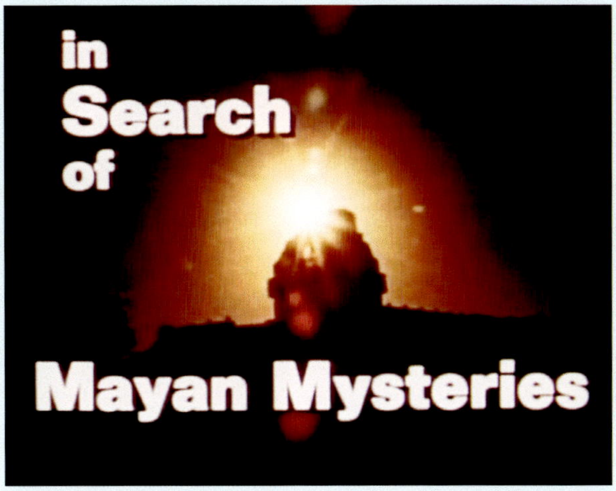

"A ritual murder seems to have taken place. No one knows who did it or why." (Count me among that group. I have no knowledge of the event, but I can confidently attest that I was somewhere else at the time.)

Most of this episode is devoted to how the statues were moved. Hard to tell. Perhaps the original inhabitants had "gifts that have been lost to us."

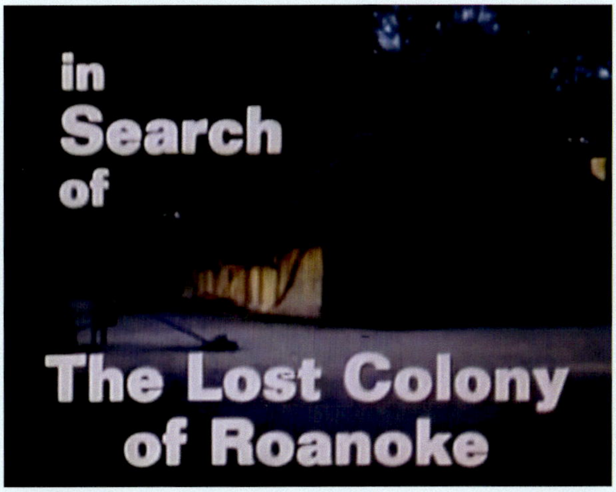

Season 2, Episode 4, *Mayan Mysteries*: "Where did they come from? Why did their civilization flourish and then disappear?" And how, one thousand years ago, could they have had a knowledge of astronomy that "rivals" our own?

Nimoy tells us that most human civilizations developed slowly, save for the Mayans, who progressed rapidly, becoming the oldest culture in the world. And they were really good at math, at devising calendars, and at building pyramids. (Oh, and at sacrificing humans, which seems to undercut their civilized civilization a wee bit, or am I being unkind?)

Then the Mayans up and left, abandoning their sacred cities for parts unknown and reasons unknown. "It is a strange and fascinating puzzle." Perhaps a natural disaster or changing climate caused them to flee? Or perhaps they traveled across the Atlantic to start a new society in another land?

Nimoy suggests that the end of the Mayan calendar in 2012 could reveal the "answers to some of the ancient mysteries." (Thinking back, I guess I missed the news that day.)

Season 4, Episode 6, *The Lost Colony of Roanoke*: Before the thirteen colonies, before the Pilgrims at Plymouth Rock, there was Roanoke in 1587. But the fate of its 100-plus inhabitants is unknown.

"What did happen to them?" *In Search of*… provides numerous possible answers.

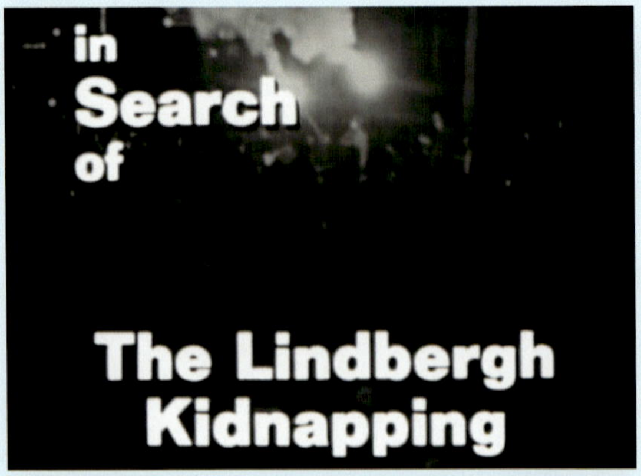

Did Spaniards kill them? Did they become absorbed into a Native American tribe? Did they die at sea during an unsuccessful return trip to England? The riddle remains, as do the low-budget dramatic recreations. "It would seem that fate definitely was against the unfortunate lost colony of Roanoke." (And the actors hired to play them.)

Final category on the board is Things, but I shall now use personal privilege to rename it "Events." Like the *Titanic*, what went down, went down. But it went down differently than we've been told.

Season 5, Episode 8: *The Lindbergh Kidnapping*: "A death watch outside Trenton State Prison awaits the execution of Bruno Richard Hauptmann. He has been convicted of kidnapping and murdering this child, the first-born son of Charles Lindbergh. On the night of April 3, 1936, Bruno Hauptmann is put to death."

New evidence suggests Hauptmann may not have been the murderer, but was instead the victim of a frame-up. "Justice may have faltered," Nimoy suggests. Worse still, evidence might have been planted, distorted, and even manufactured. (Hauptmann or Haupt-pigeon?)

Season 5, Episode 21, *The Hindenburg Mystery*: We all know about the dirigible tragedy of 1937, but just what is the mystery surrounding it? "Was it an accident or sabotage?" So asks Leonard Nimoy. "The reason why the fire started has been the source of controversy to this day."

The official verdict laid blame on St. Elmo's Fire. But some men in motion believed it was indeed sabotage. (Another mystery: when did that little red Elmo achieve sainthood?)

Some great war footage and some great re-enactments in this episode. And of course, Nimoy delights in admitting that the real answer to this question may "never be known."

Season 5, Episode 23, *The Lusitania*: "Was the sinking of the *Lusitania* an unprovoked act of war? Why did the unsinkable ship go down so quickly? Public opinion ran high, as the blame was laid squarely on Germany. But was the Germany navy solely responsible?"

Good questions all. Answers are pretty good, too. The torpedo hit a hull containing explosives, which were in fact contraband munitions. One expert calls it a "monumental Anglo-American coverup." And so, the *Lusitania*'s captain was unfairly blamed. Perhaps.

Anyhow, as Nimoy says in one episode, "We usually believe what we want to believe." Good times, I say, even if they didn't happen the way we think they did.

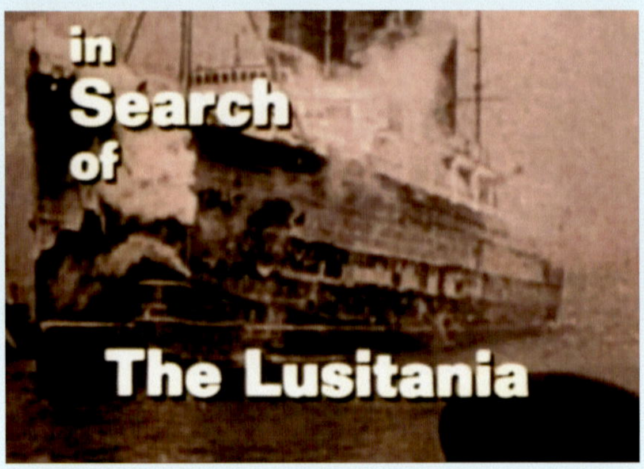

In Search Of Noah's Ark

(1976)

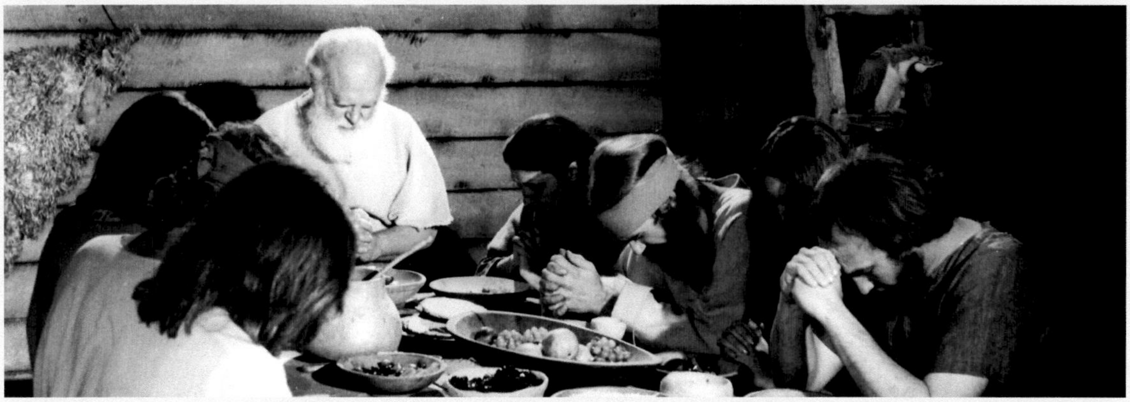

Brad Crandall, the man of the hour (ninety minutes, actually), declares *In Search of Noah's Ark* to be a "new" type of "disaster movie." With expected hyperbole, he advises us, "This may be the most incredible film you will ever see, but the facts that will be presented are true."

In short order, we learn about archaeology's ability to prove the Biblical stories. "There seems no doubt that at one time the Earth was engulfed in a great deluge." Them's the deep waters, sure enough.

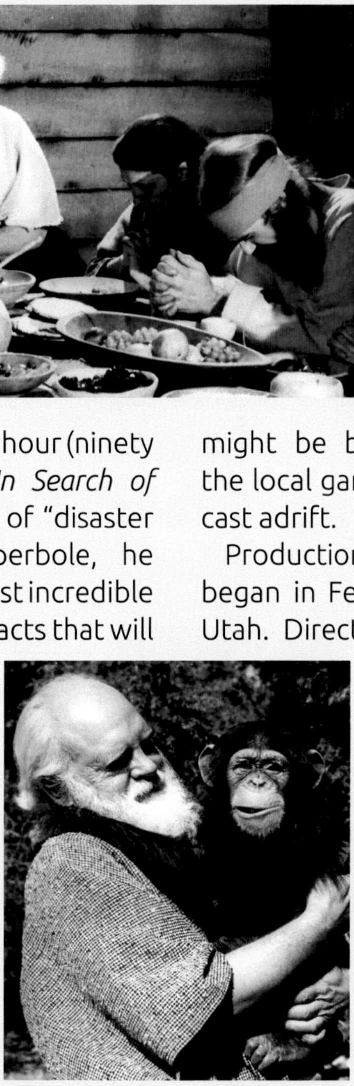

Crandall explains all of this from various locations, ranging from an observatory to a scientific lab. At one point, he stands in front of a table that holds various, well, things. They look old to the eye, but we never hear *what* they are. They might be precious finds from antiquity, or they might be broken pottery purchased at the local garden store. That boat is simply cast adrift.

Production of *In Search of Noah's Ark* began in February 1976, "on location" in Utah. Director James L. Conway sails us into a nice dramatization of the Noah story, certainly within the constraints of a low budget. In publicity materials, producer Charles E. Sellier, Jr. claimed their aim was to shoot recreations that looked like newsreels. Vern Adix plays Noah. Two years later, he'd star in *Teen Alien* (1978), though not as the title character.

Conway wisely devotes most of the running time to the search for the Ark at one particular location, Mount Ararat in Eastern Turkey. Here we learn many historical accounts of the Ark's

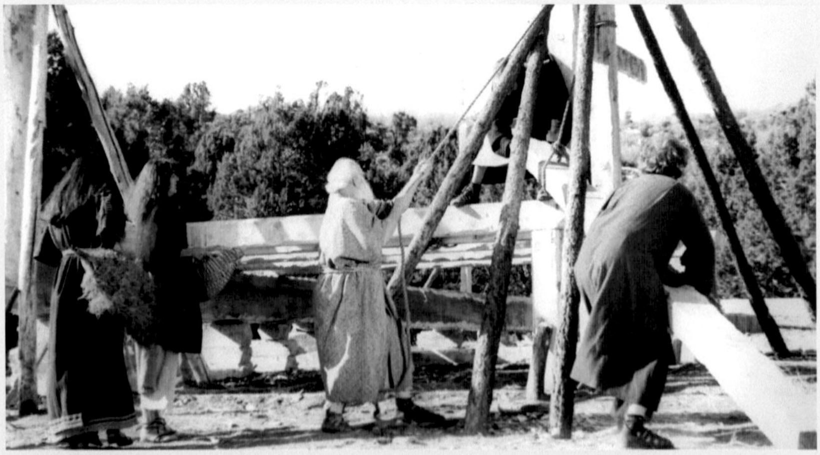

final resting place, which date to at least the age of Marco Polo. Dramatizations as well as actual photographs and archival footage depict various attempts to scale the treacherous mountain.

French explorer Fernand Navarra succeeded. Twice. In 1955 and 1969, he returned with wood from a crevasse. Tests reveal it is 5,000 years old, except for the radio carbon dating, which Crandall dismisses in short order. And then there is "computerized, electronic analysis" of satellite imagery that reveals a single pixel on Ararat. No one can yet prove it *isn't* the Ark. Of course, we can prove that only one letter separates the word "deluge" from "delude."

Favorite moments abound, not least of which is the inclusion of Utah Senator Frank Moss amid the various experts and scholars, all relevant in their own way, it seems. And then there's Crandall placing tiny little Arks on a scale model of Ararat. But, like all great things, the film comes to an end, with Crandall emphasizing that the evidence for Ark's location is "overwhelming." A tidal wave's worth, even.

Fourteen months after its initial screening, Sunn Classic announced the film's domestic box-office gross was $23 million. Sellier claimed it was Sunn's most successful film.

In September 1976, the Film Advisory Board presented *In Search of Noah's Ark* with an Award of Excellence. Brad Crandall accepted. To this day, I still applaud, but I'm too reverent to shout, "Atta boy!"

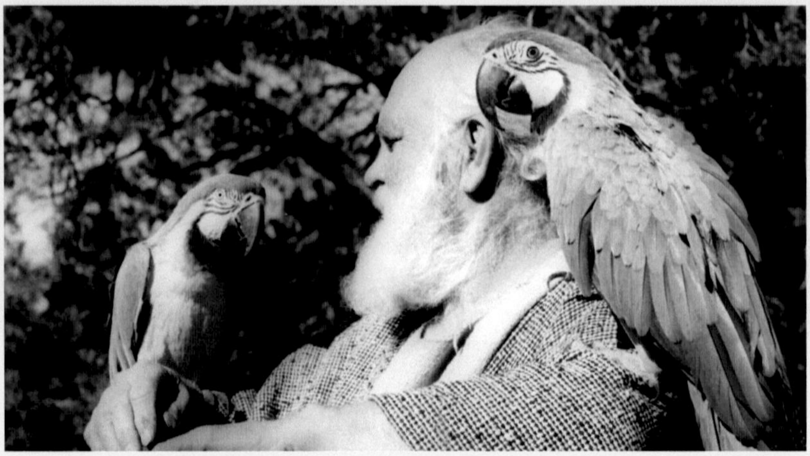

The Lincoln Conspiracy

(1977)

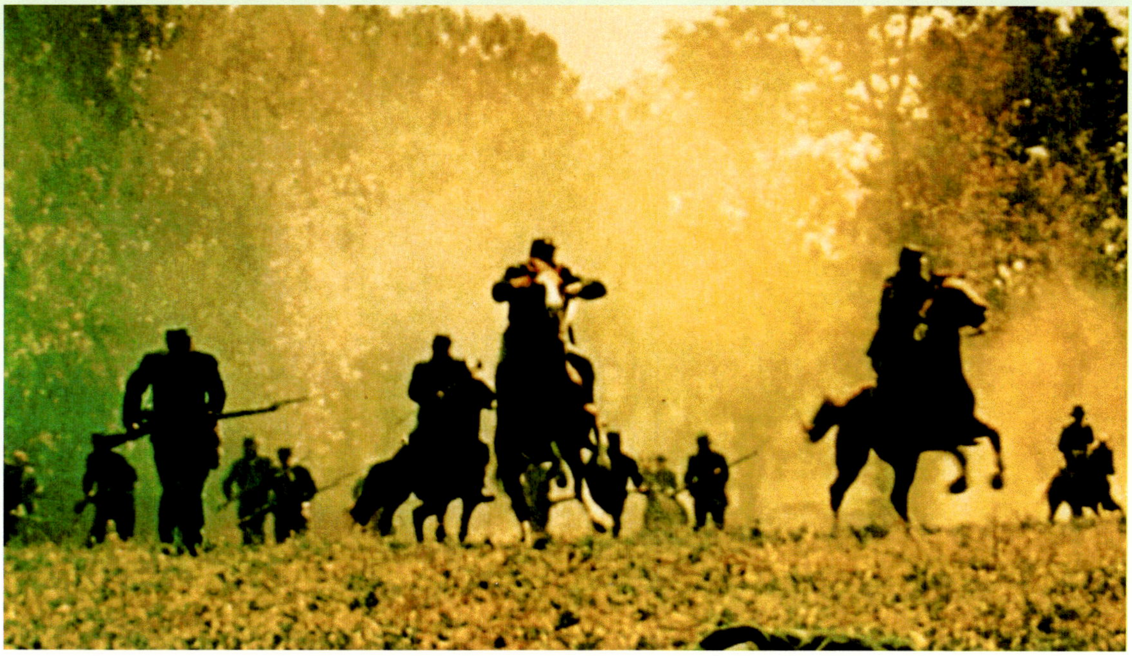

"The motion picture you are about to see will shock you. Because the true story of President Lincoln's assassination cannot be found in any history book. It is a story of corruption, treachery and cover-up. It is a story every American has a right to know."

Thank you, Brad Crandall, who is heard but never seen in this gem produced by Charles E. Sellier, Jr. and directed by James L. Conway.

A hitherto-unknown coup d'état was underway in 1865, involving some of the highest officials in government. Leading culprits included Secretary of War Edwin Stanton, Senator John Conness, and Colonel Lafayette C. Baker. The reason? Lincoln was planning to be too nice to the South during Reconstruction, so they wanted to kidnap him. The group knew about John Wilkes Booth, and for a time even conspired with him. Allegedly.

As Crandall explains, "The truth would be concealed for more than a century after Lincoln's death." The *Los Angeles Times* told readers, "In an era when mistrust of government is rampant, the film capitalizes on the audience's cynicism and on obvious parallels between historical and contemporary coverups." Sellier went further, claiming the Lincoln conspiracy "makes Watergate look like kindergarten plotting."

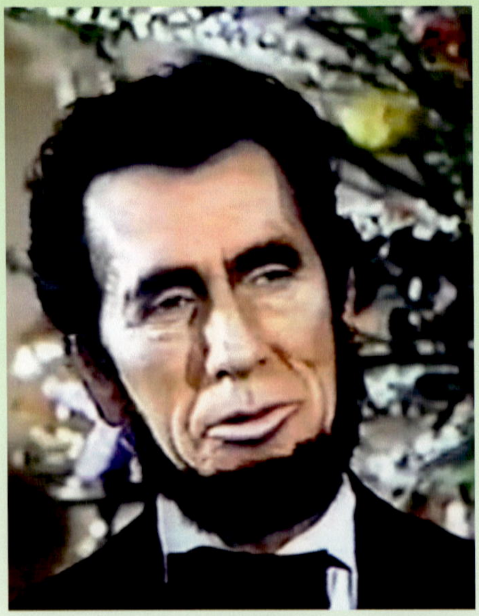 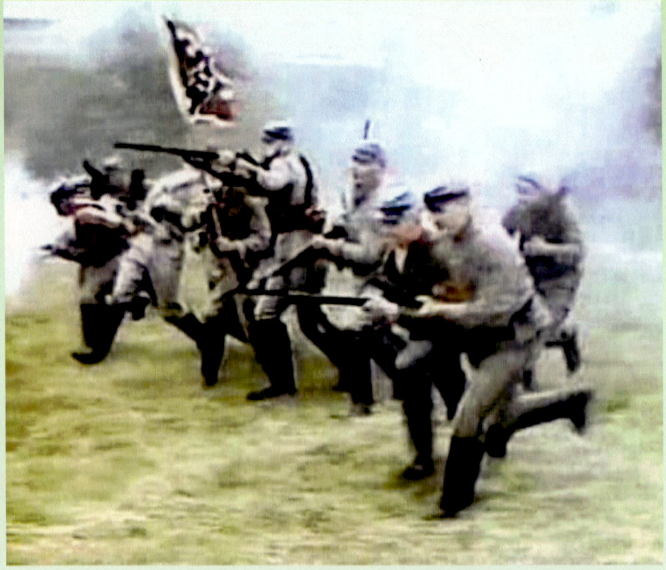

Sunn Classic "spent more than $100,000 and 10,000 man-hours on research in order find and bring together information and new evidence from recently discovered unpublished Secret Service documents, congressmen's diaries, old letters, manuscripts, deathbed confessions and secret cipher-coded messages." The company shot the film, originally titled *The Conspiracy to Kill President Lincoln*, in and around Savannah, Georgia.

Sellier announced *The Lincoln Conspiracy* to be Sunn's biggest-budget film to date. Money for marketing alone was in "excess of $5 million." According to advance publicity, the "sensational Sunn film ... will change history." And for those among us who couldn't get enough, Sunn's book of the film answered all of our remaining questions.

No doubt about it, *The Lincoln Conspiracy* features some of the best historical recreations Sunn ever produced. The battlefield recreations are credible, and the cast features such luminaries as Bradford Dillman (as Booth), John Dehner (Baker), Robert Middleton (Stanton), and Whit Bissell (Conness). John Anderson turns in a particularly impressive performance as Lincoln; he had already played the president in *The Fortune Cookie* (1966) and would again on the TV show *Voyagers!* (1982).

The *New York Times* called *The Lincoln Conspiracy* a "competent enough piece of work." *Variety* believed it was "a kind of travesty of truth in the name of supposed truth-telling." By contrast, the film's credits explain, "The story you have just seen is true. It has been authenticated. . . ." Those disparate views sound like the very recipe for a Weirdumentary. Honest Abe meets Dishonest Film.

But in all fairness, *The Lincoln Conspiracy* barely qualifies as a Weirdumentary. It unfolds almost exclusively as a docudrama punctuated with occasional exposition from the unseen Brad Crandall. Alas. If only we could see Crandall in the Office of Knowledge, overflowing with historic memorabilia and paraphernalia. And maybe one or two interviews with hack, would-be scholars. Or even spurious connections to ancient astronauts or the Bermuda Triangle. Alas, indeed.

Put another way, not every coup d'état results in a coup de théâtre. Put even another way, *ehh*.

The Lost City of Atlantis

(1978)

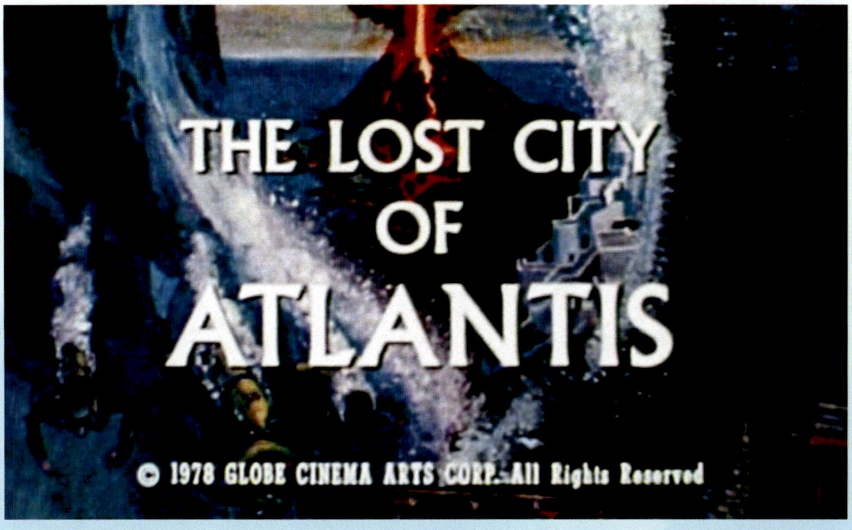

"Legends tell of a magnificent civilization which flourished on the island continent of Atlantis. Were the citizens natives or were they alien refugees from some distance galaxy? Maybe Atlantis never did exist, except in the minds of men, who created fables about the rise and fall of empires."

Or maybe, just maybe, quite likely, even probably, Atlantis is complete and total fact. So runs (amok?) the argument of Richard Martin's follow-up to *The Legend of Loch Ness* (1976). What does not run is the film's pacing, which slowly and laboriously mopes along for ninety minutes.

The Lost City of Atlantis clearly tries to capture the style of Reinl's *Chariots of the Gods*, to the extent that von Däniken is mentioned twice. "Perhaps Atlantis was involved with powers from outer space and its citizens were victims of an intergalactic war," we hear, before being asked, "Could man have escaped to another planet?" A plausible theory, of course: those who drowned to death in the "Atlantean Holocaust" left their submerged graves for the cosmos. And they left us behind.

In fairness, the film offers little on the subject of outer space, drawing its influence from *Chariots* more in terms of structure, with Steve Shuttack's cinematography (and a boatload of stock footage) whirling us around the globe repeatedly, presenting images of many sites that *could* have been Atlantis, or influenced by it, or even home to its survivors. All of this begs the question of how Atlantis can be lost, since it seems to be found, everywhere, even by a moviegoing wretch like me.

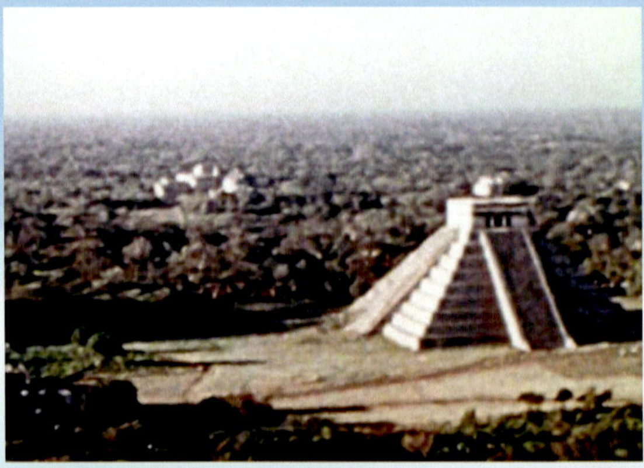
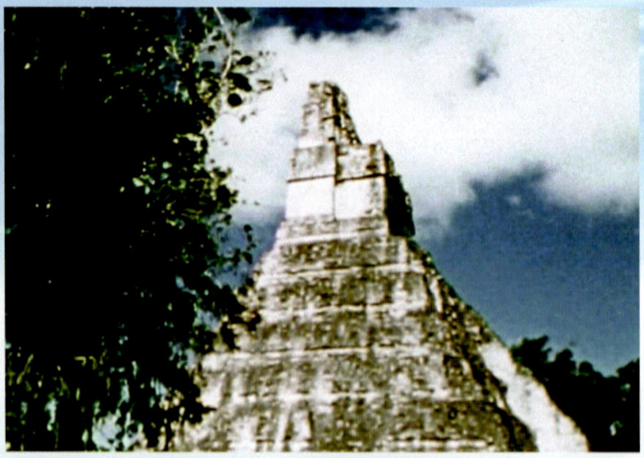
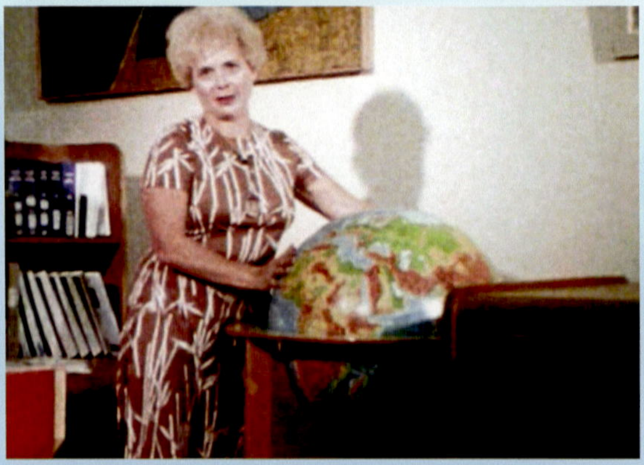
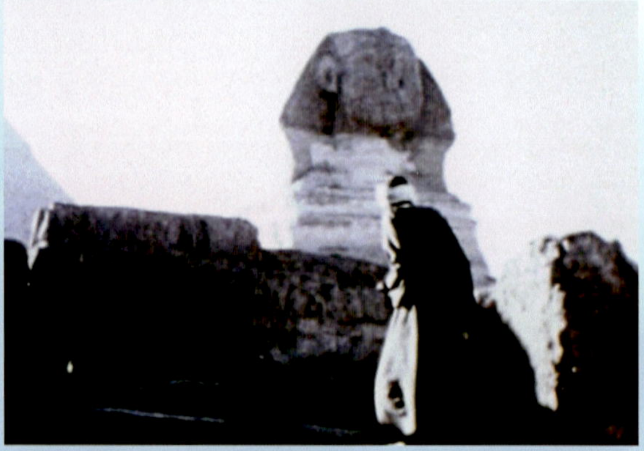
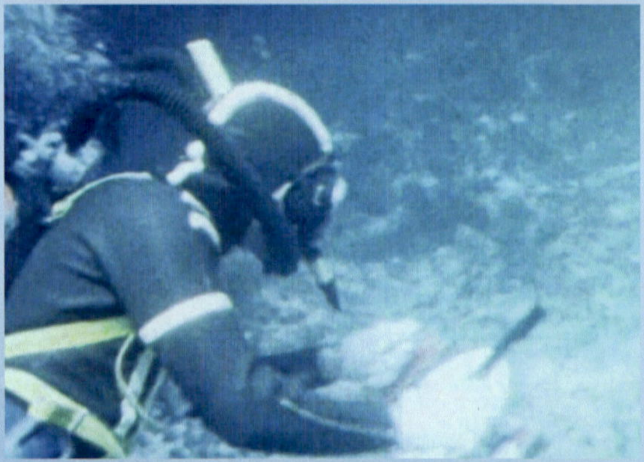
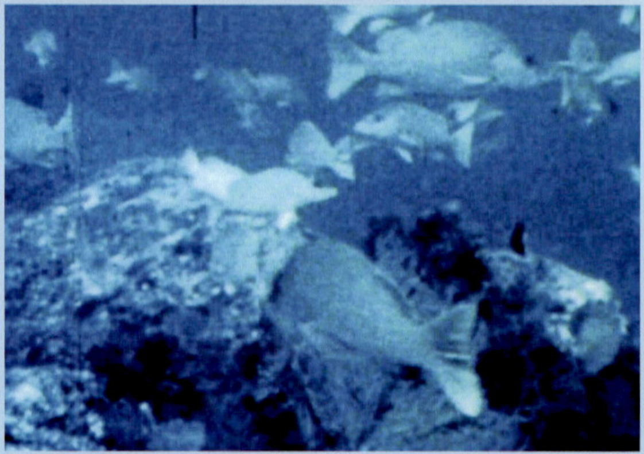
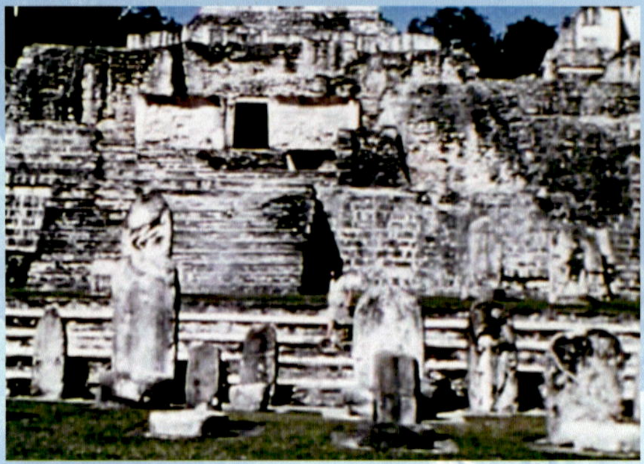
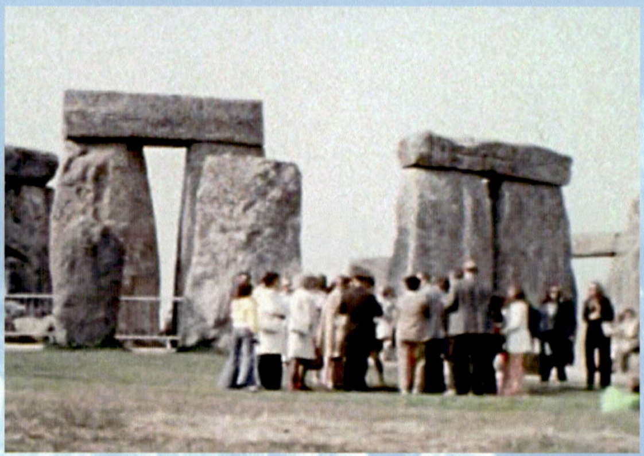

And then there is the barrage of possibilities and questions. "Perhaps the Atlanteans were men that could live under water, and the dolphins were his pets and companions." Does Atlantis "haunt our subconscious minds"? Do its ghosts "still perform their mystical rights and ceremonies"? And of its mythical crystals, "were they used as an energy source or in communication"? To this list, I'll add a question of my own: wasn't Atlantis a continent, not just a city, as the film's title suggests?

On-camera interviews are infrequent, the first not appearing until twenty minutes in. Among them is Lowell Ponte, then famous for his work on ice ages, old and (allegedly) new. His eyes regularly dart to a mysterious place off-camera. Methinks it is inhabited by cue cards, given his stilted speaking style.

But Dr. Maxine Asher is tops. She is best remembered now for founding American World University in 1990, a diploma mill not accredited by any organization on the planet, save for the World Association of Universities and Colleges, also operated by—guess who—Maxine Asher.

In the 1970s, Asher devoted herself to finding Atlantis. In Martin's film, she talks about her trips to various sites, including all the time she spent in Spain, and the assistance the government there gave her. In actual fact, Asher's group had to leave that country after officials suspected they were spies. They escaped to Ireland, where (wouldn't you know it) the ancient megaliths turned out to be the handiwork of the Atlanteans.

Such expertise led Asher to become a "Technical Adviser" on *The Lost City of Atlantis*, as well as a talking head who is incomparable at being incomprehensible. She touts scientific knowledge, but also insists on the import of "psychic data," meaning the "intuition" and "dreams" and "hunches" that everyday people have about Atlantis. These even led Asher to discover archaeological finds. Funny, but, you know, I have a hunch about all of that palaver.

Not surprisingly, *The Lost City of Atlantis* relies to some degree on Plato, who wrote about the continent, and Edgar Cayce, who made predictions about it. The mysterious Bimini Road is also a major player.

To be sure, there is some fun in Sara Nickerson's bizarre script. The monuments at Stonehenge might have been radioactive, we learn, which accounts for the magic that Merlin used to place them where they now reside, Merlin of course being a genuine historical figure. To make things delightfully confusing, we even learn a little bit about the pre-Atlantean creature known as Yeti, whose cameo is memorable due to its complete irrelevance.

Theme music by Bill Reddie is strong, as is music from the library of Aminadov Aloni. As for the film's special effects, the best moment comes when a wooden stick points to particular locations on a map of the world.

Gold Key Entertainment released *The Lost City of Atlantis* to TV as part of its "Beta Chronicles" package of Weirdumentaries in 1978. From there, it sank into further depths than Atlantis itself.

Mystery of the Sacred Shroud

(1978)

Produced by Andros Films, *Mystery of the Sacred Shroud* begins with Secondo Pia's son, who shares memories of his papa's 1898 photograph of the holy relic. "The photographic process was legitimate," we hear, "and not due to tricks or chemical manipulations."

Then Richard Burton, our off-screen narrator, tells us about Giuseppe Enrie, the shroud's second photographer: "Like Pia, his negative plates have mysteriously taken on the properties of positive images."

Why the use of present tense? Probably because we get some wonderfully low-budget recreations of those photographers, as well as of the suffering and crucifixion of Christ, the latter presented with rapid-fire editing. The Biblical history explains the origins of the linen cloth. It also helps this flick reach its eighty-five-minute running time.

"Is it truly the burial cloth of Jesus Christ?" Burton asks of "Christendom's most holy relic." Whether the question is rhetorical or whether we are meant to answer ... that's a mystery.

The question predates Burton, of course. In fact, *Mystery of the Sacred Shroud* was actually the second Weirdumentary on the subject, the first being *Is It Christ?* (1975), a particularly obscure sixty-minute movie directed by Mort Fallick and narrated by James Earl Jones. *Variety*'s review claimed:

> *Film is well photographed, and documented, and lures viewer curiosity. Interviews with photographers who have lensed the Holy Shroud, and discussions of positive and negative images and medicos are fascinating, especially the medical interviews. ... Producer George Suski, who came up to Boston for the unveiling of his docu, said he plans to adapt and expand* Is It Christ? *into a full-length motion picture for commercial showing.*

But that was not to be. Those involved moved on to other projects. And *Is It Christ?* became less visible than the image on the shroud.

Now back to our previously scheduled programming: After describing the shroud, Richard Burton discusses the second international conference and symposium on the relic, which was held in 1978. That's when he goes full-on weird: "An icon depicting the shroud that had been covered for decades was discovered accidentally by painters cleaning the building. Mere coincidence, or an omen of what is to come?"

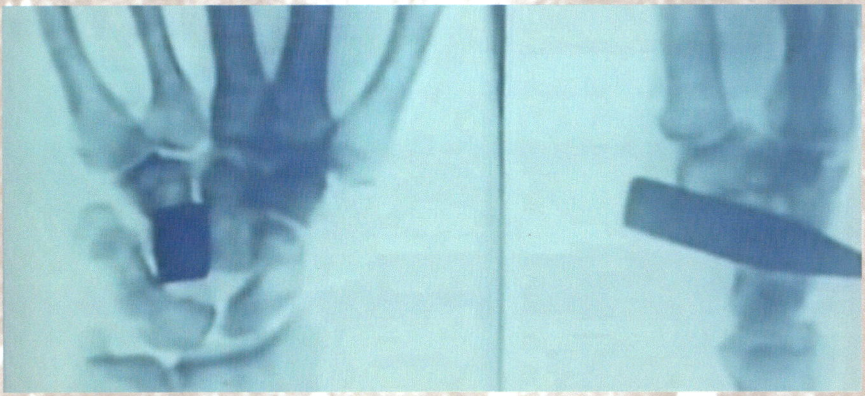

But the emphasis, not surprisingly, is on the shroud photographs. Expert Leo Valla tells us:

> *Unlike most images, the image on the shroud is a negative image ... the strange image of a few rather indeterminate smudges turned out in the darkroom to be a photographic image, a positive image, of very high quality, but at the negative stage. And the quality of the photograph was absolutely superb. The negative itself was very well graded, sharp, although of course a lot of the sharpness was the texture on the cloth, but it was in completely clear focus, the gradation was perfect, the lighting appeared to be soft, good portrait lighting, and the resultant positive was a portrait of just tremendous photographic quality.*

Valla concludes by declaring that the shroud is a "true photographic image," one that was "not made by man."

Though it came three years after *Is It Christ?, Mystery of the Sacred Shroud* was the first time the Roman Catholic Church allowed the actual relic to be filmed.

Music by William Loose and John Caper, Jr. is beautiful. Burton's voice is tremendous. His casting was interesting, given that he was an atheist. And at times he reads the script way too fast. Inexplicably fast, actually.

As for the shroud, it remains enigmatic. "It must mean something," Burton says, but exactly what? "We leave that to you," he adds.

The film's experts generally agree on the shroud's authenticity, but also spoke before it was radiocarbon-dated to the thirteenth–fourteenth centuries.

Whatever its origins, the shroud is at minimum a photographic negative created centuries before the advent of photography. And that, brothers and sisters, qualifies as weird.

North American Film Enterprises released *Mystery of the Sacred Shroud,* which received a G rating. Texans were among the first to see it during the Christmas season of 1978. The traveling salvation-and-shroud show went on to win the Film Advisory Board's "Award of Excellence."

Writer-director Harry Mastrogeorge was responsible for much more quality entertainment than just this Weirdumentary. He also directed episodes of *The Mary Tyler Moore Show, The Love Boat, Hart to Hart, Miami Vice,* and *Scarecrow and Mrs. King.* Amen to that.

In Search Of Historic Jesus

(1979)

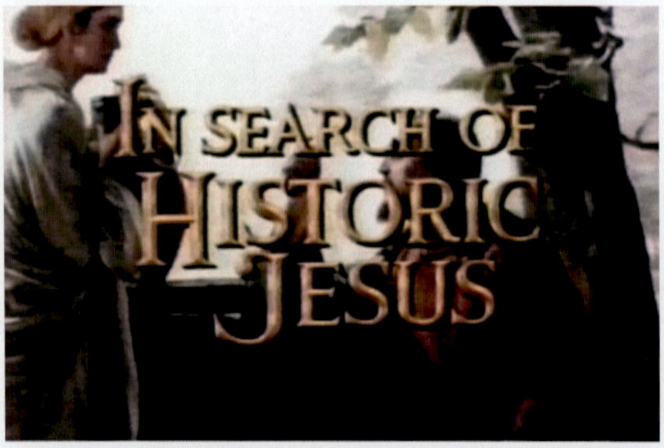

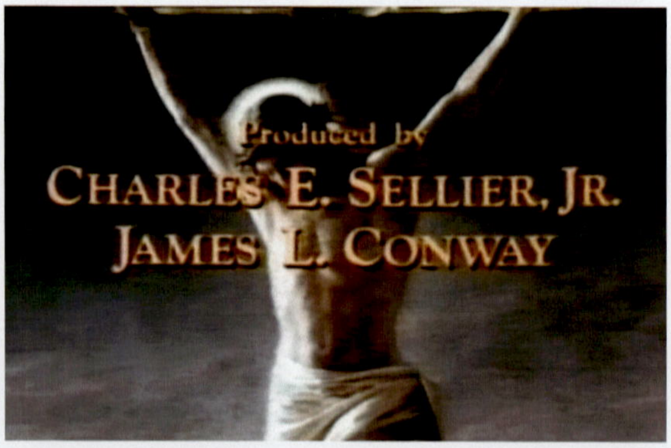

Let us give thanks. Brad Crandall is back, on-camera and on mission.

Originally titled *In Pursuit of the Historic Jesus*, this Sunn Classic film features not only our Crandall as our reliable host, but also John Rubinstein as the Lord of Hosts. Lawrence Dobkin, who had appeared in *The Ten Commandments* (1956), plays Pontius Pilate, and John Anderson (the title character in *The Lincoln Conspiracy*) plays Caiaphas. Charles E. Sellier, Jr. and James L. Conway co-produced; Henning Schellerup directed.

Did Jesus exist? Was he the Son of God? "In search of answers, we have interviewed scores of scientists and scholars, spent years in research, and sent film crews around the world." Thus spake Crandall, in words co-authored by Academy Award nominee Malvin Wald, screenwriter of *The Naked City* (1948).

But that isn't quite true, alas. What we largely get are recycled clips from *In Search of Noah's Ark* (1976), some other stock footage, and a large number of dramatizations depicting the early life, ministry, and crucifixion of Jesus Christ. Along the way, we also learn that director Schellerup was not a disciple of greatness, though admittedly he was hampered by a less-than-bountiful budget.

When the shepherds appear in Bethlehem, their "flocks" number a total of only two sheep. And when the tomb opens at the time of the resurrection, the ground kinda-sorta quakes, which really means the camera shakes and the actors wobble. The scene is not of Biblical proportions.

As far as proving anything about the historical Jesus, the film presents little evidence. It ignores tales of Constantine's mother and her early search for holy relics. And it doesn't mention artifacts like the Sudarium of Oviedo. Instead, Crandall visits an observatory and conducts an interview about the Star of Bethlehem, for which there is "scientific support."

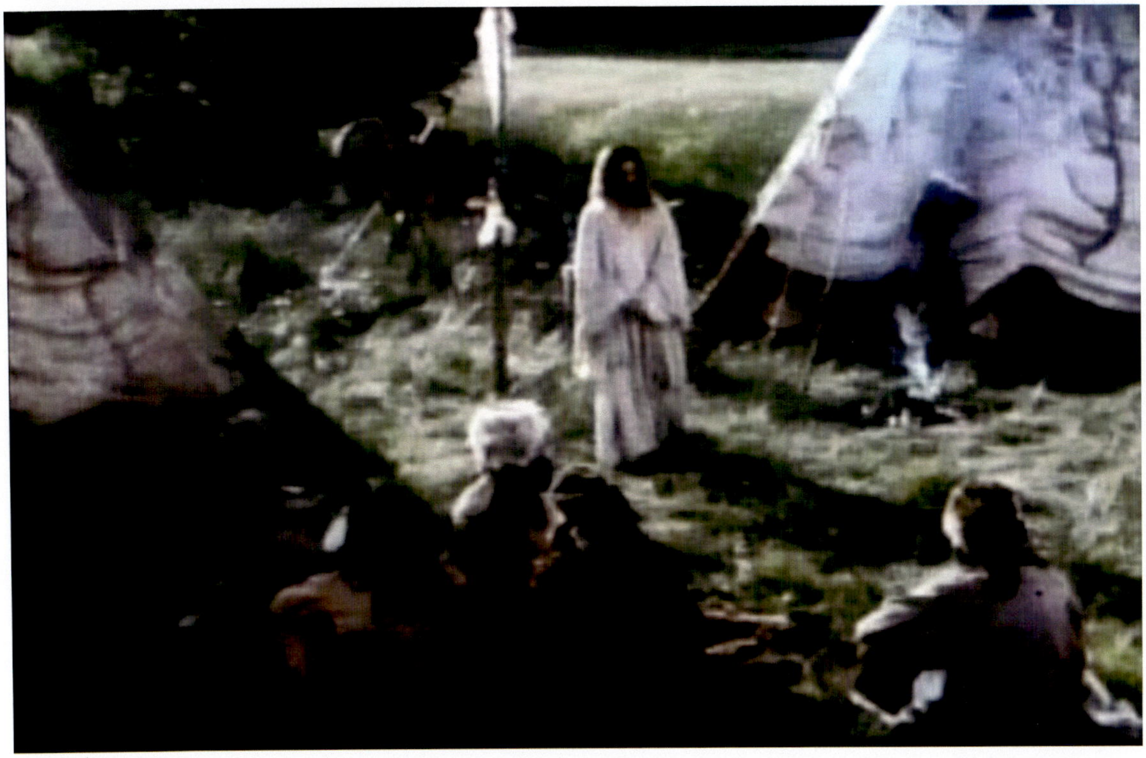

And most of all, he discusses the Shroud of Turin, which makes a good deal of sense since it was at the center of a major research project in 1978.

In Search of Historic Jesus has two highlights. One is Michael Ruud playing an overweight John the Baptist. The other is the film's suggestion that Jesus appeared in the New World, not only to Mormons, but also to "Indians in North and South America" in the guise of the "bearded white god." This allows Crandall to compare a sculpture of Quetzalcoatl to Jesus. Both had beards. Of course, so does Crandall, so perhaps the bloodline continues. [Note to self: Ask Erich von Däniken when next we meet.]

Variety asked, "Some may consider such an exercise in pictorialized rhetoric as harmless; others may see exploitation of the mass audience in a deplorable sense." My rejoinder? Might not a film do both? Therein dwells the essence of the Weirdumentary. Thou hast done well, or well enough.

In Search of Historic Jesus was extremely successful. "Sunn has the family together and ready for immediate delivery," a full-page ad in *Variety* promised exhibitors. And they were right. *In Search of Historic Jesus* became a hit, grossing well over $22 million at North American theaters in 1979 and throughout 1980. Amen to that.

But we are all sinners, and that leads to confession. Gene Siskel, film critic and famed partner of Roger Ebert, reported that Sunn Classic ran ads in Chicago announcing the film *In Search of Historical Jesus* would play one week only. "Last Day," ads reiterated on the seventh day, but instead of resting, Sunn Classic went ahead and held the film over at nineteen area theaters. The *Chicago Tribune* felt that the "Last Day" ads potentially misled its readers. Sunn Classic asked for forgiveness, promising in the future to use the phrase "Last Day at Some Theaters."

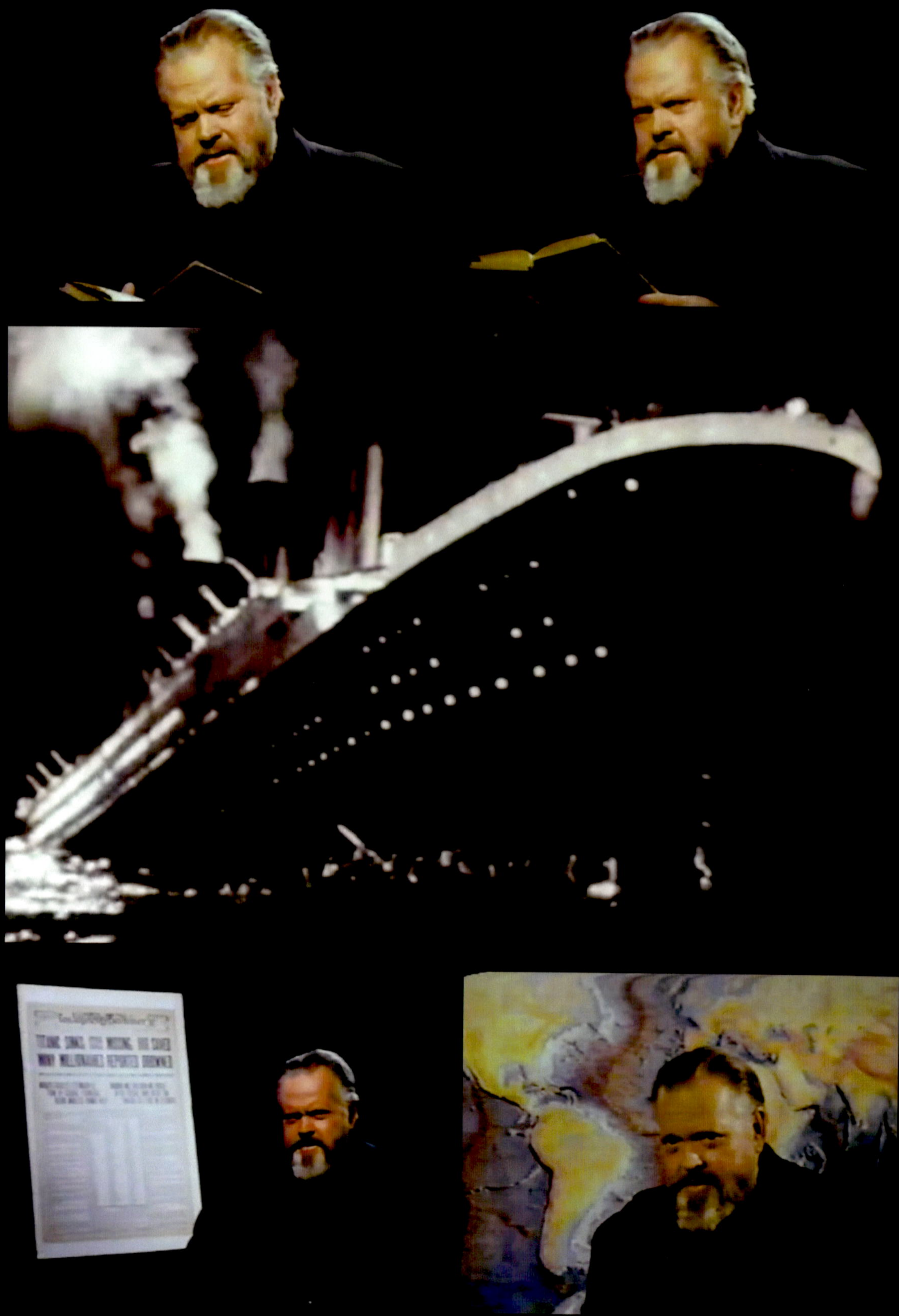

Search for the Titanic

(1981)

"Reality has more than once been foreshadowed by fiction. Here, just for example, is something that goes beyond, far beyond, anything we might ascribe to mere coincidence. In 1898, a little-known author named Morgan Robertson wrote this remarkable piece of fiction about a luxurious ocean liner, larger than any ship existing in its time, filled with wealthy passengers and a rich cargo. On its maiden voyage, this ship, labeled unsinkable, struck an iceberg one starry April night, and sank in the cold waters of the north Atlantic."

Orson Welles speaks those words as our on-camera host, the Robertson novel being so very prescient of the 1912 maritime tragedy. "The similarities of size, speed, and fate are truly incredible, but the most startling parallel of all: Robertson named his fictional ship the *Titan*; its real-life counterpart, as well all know, was the *Titanic*." (Now that's weird, y'all.)

In the twenty-first century, it's easy to be so sick of the *Titanic* as to forget how awe-inspiring the ship was, and how truly epic its sinking. Thankfully, this Weirdumentary returns us to an era before James Cameron and Leonardo DiCaprio, before the sickness that I have termed "I'm king of the world!"

Search for the Titanic spends about five minutes showing us archival footage of the *Titanic* and dramatizations from an old movie. No narration, just music and sound effects and the tiniest bit of character dialogue. Whether Welles watched the final product is unknown, but if so, he probably admired this section. He was, after all, the man who got into a physical fight with Ernest Hemingway as to whether narration was needed in another documentary, narration that Welles believed redundant to what was being shown on-screen.

Then Welles speaks again: "No other modern event has inspired such a steady and overwhelming flow of books and novels and poems and songs and movies. Lost in the depths of a dark and frozen sea, it's captivated the public imagination for decades, and now has inspired a daring of team of scientists and explorers to launch an unprecedented expedition of historical discovery."

Produced and directed by Michael Harris, of *Deadly Fathoms* (1978) fame, this forty-five-minute film—also known as *In Search of Titanic*—chronicles the first major effort to locate the *Titanic*'s remains. We are not only before James Cameron, but also Robert Ballard, who went on to rediscover the *Titanic* in 1985.

Texas oilman Jack Grimm, a "daring investor, well known for backing adventurous and difficult expeditions," financed the journey, which was "five years in the planning." When he wasn't drilling wells, "Cadillac Jack" spent a good part of his life in pursuit of Bigfoot, the Loch Ness Monster, and Noah's Ark.

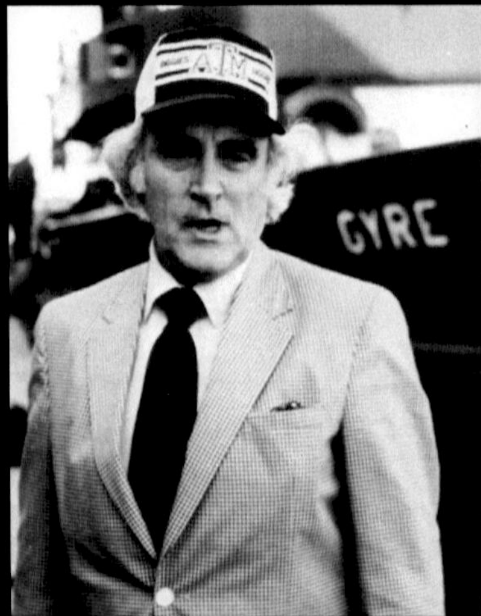
GYRE

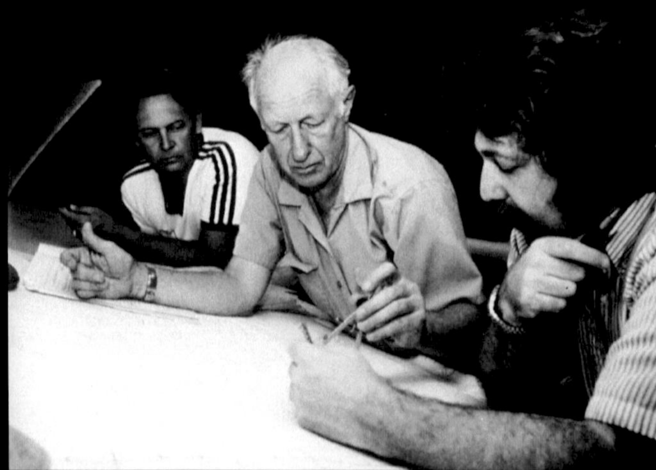

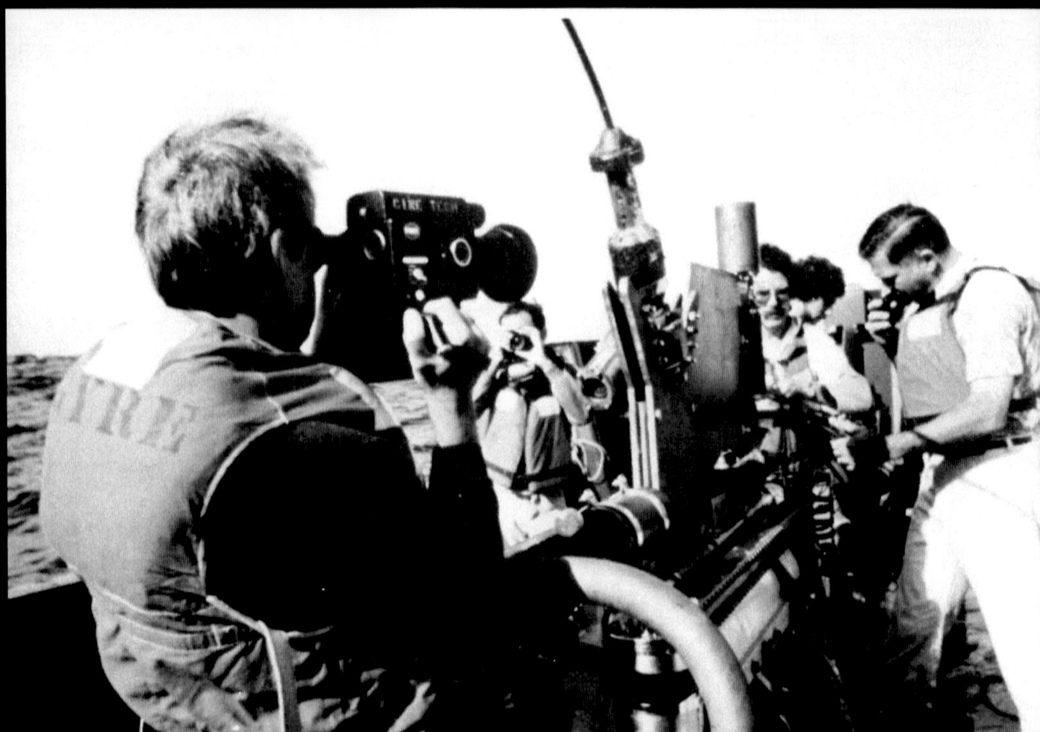

In his 1998 obituary, the *New York Times* wrote: "Mr. Grimm all but took over the [*Titanic*] project, raising several million dollars, arranging for reputable scientists to accompany the expedition with advanced sonar equipment, and even hiring the William Morris Agency. . . ." Grimm himself once said, "My life has been one continuous search for the unknown."

Unfortunately, Grimm was also cheap. In his book *Titanic Life* (2011), Mike Harris describes the team of experts he originally put together to undertake the voyage, one being Robert Ballard. But Rent-a-Cadillac Jack insisted on another crew because they could be had for half the money.

After a presentation at the Explorer's Club in New York City, the ship and film crew cast off. "Thirty-nine men, aided by the most advanced technology that science has available, setting out to unlock the mysteries of a glorious old ocean liner once thought to be indestructible."

Totally sinkable is the awful and strangely upbeat song we hear on the film's soundtrack: "We're gonna find the *Titanic*, in her cold and lonely grave. Yes, we'll find the *Titanic*, with the cowards and the brave." Such dreck might have led some viewers to root against Harris and Grimm.

Anyhow, one newspaper wrote, "With sonar, the Grimm party hopes to locate the ship in about ten days, but, given possibly bad weather and the scope of the search, it could take longer."

In their effort to locate the lost vessel, the crew dropped transponders and used a magnetometer in the area where the *Titanic* transmitted its final call for help, at the area where its lifeboats were rescued hours later.

Unfortunately, Harris and Co. faced a hurricane and a gale, some of their precious time at sea being lost. They do not find the ship, alas.

Welles explains: "Now, at the bottom of a dark, forbidding sea, she is tenaciously protected by the very force that put her there, engulfed in a haze of mystery and speculation, she resides, seductively, just beyond our grasp."

How true that would be, even when Mike Harris made his second voyage and his second documentary on the subject, the hour-long *Return to the Titanic* (1981). Cadillac Jack was back, and that's a fact, but unfortunately Welles wasn't.

The new host was James Drury, who had appeared in *Forbidden Planet* (1956) and who played the title character in TV's *The Virginian* (1962–1971). Joining the crew on the voyage, he explains, "the ocean is so vast, and we have so little time."

It was Weirdumentary enough to call the new film *Return to the Titanic* when the group had never found the ship to begin with.

But in the fishiest of ways, the film discusses Grimm's rediscovery of what *might* have been a *Titanic* propeller blade. "Its immediate impression caught the eye and froze the mind."

It wasn't a blade at all, though; it was just a geological formation. But Cadillac Jack told the press otherwise, suggesting it had fallen off the *Titanic* once ship met iceberg. Such speculation serves as the film's shaky conclusion. (Is it possible to sink lower than the bottom of the ocean floor?)

As *Return to the Titanic* explains, the second expedition was "at war with the North Atlantic." They lost.

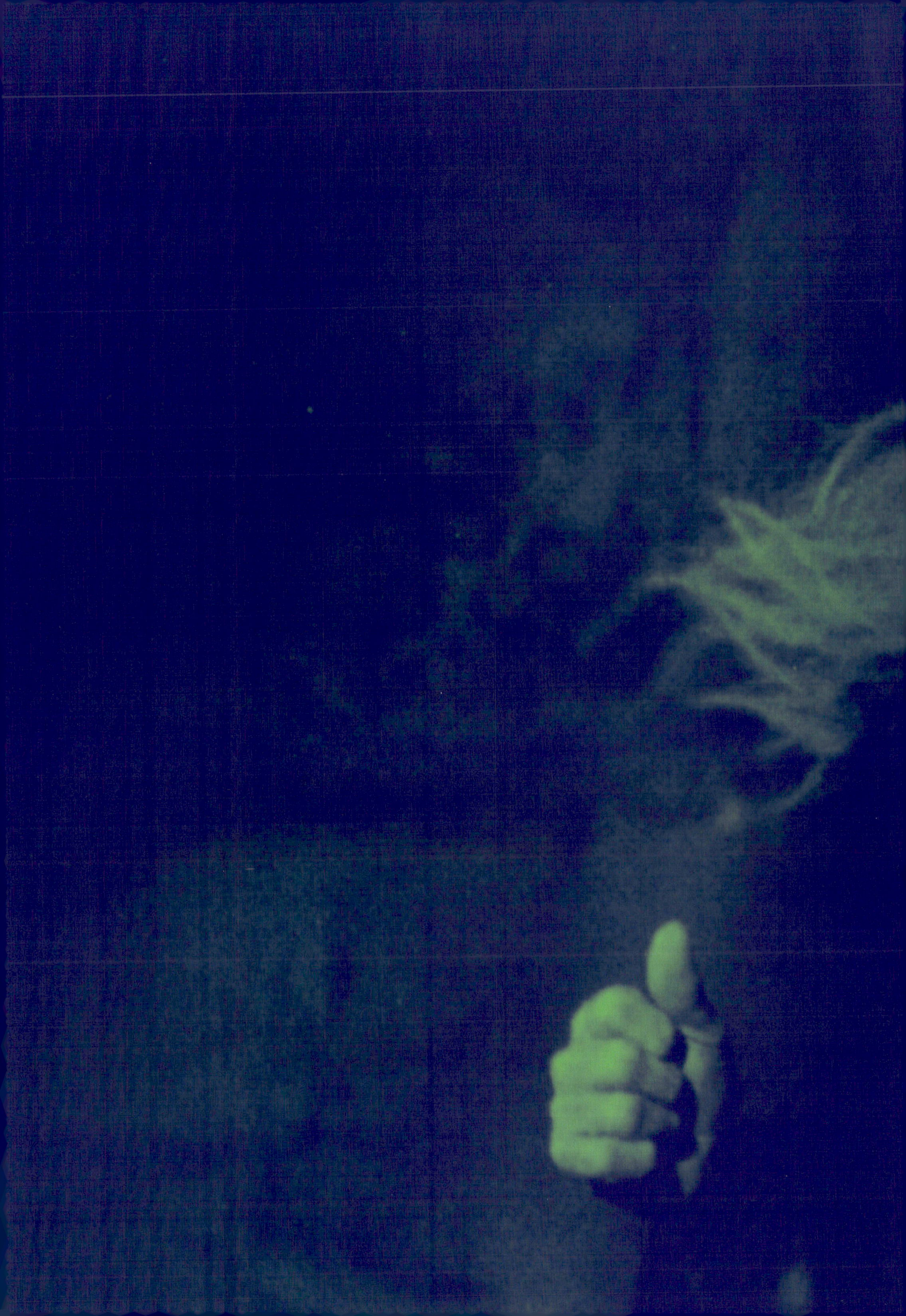

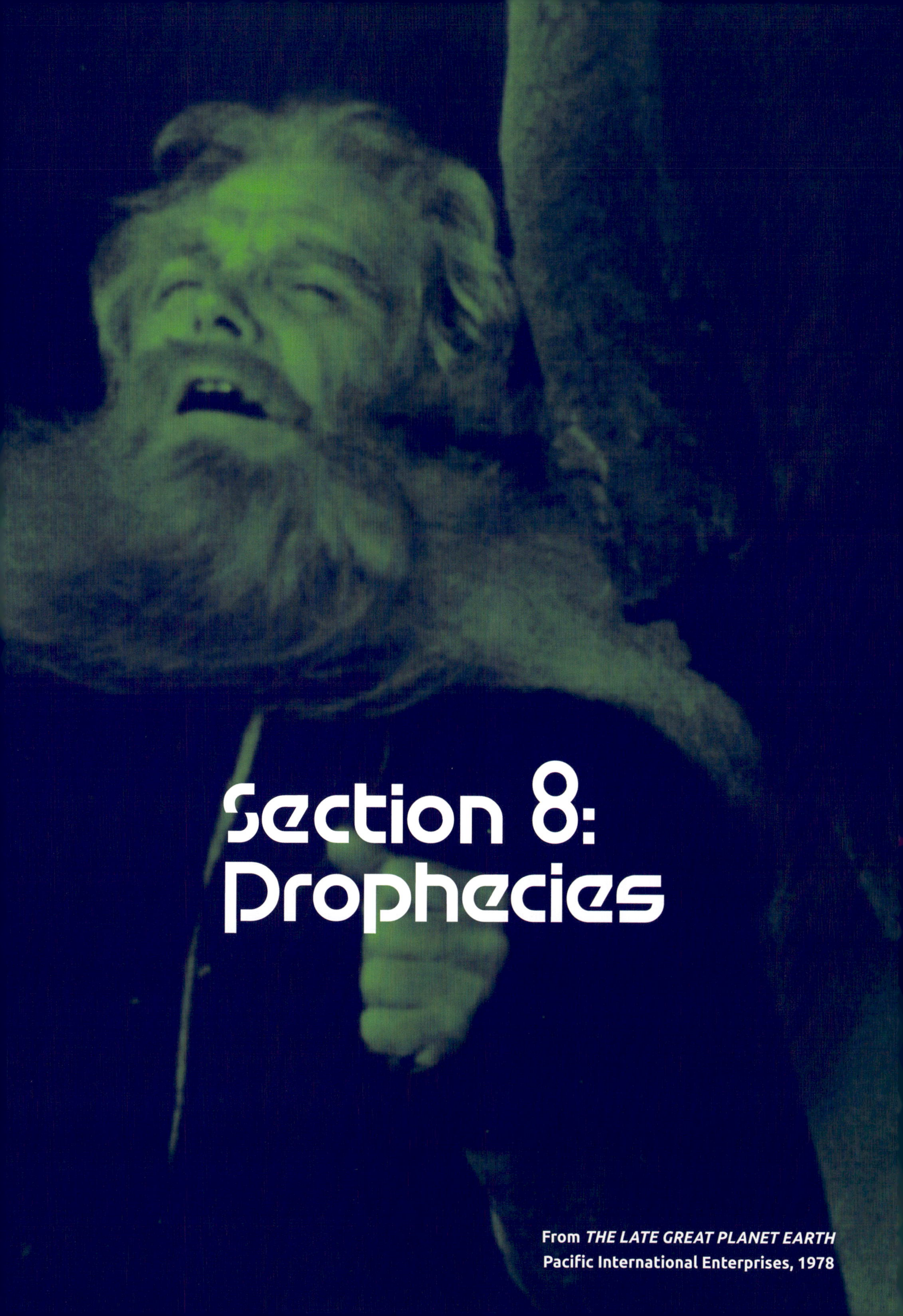

Section 8: Prophecies

From *THE LATE GREAT PLANET EARTH*
Pacific International Enterprises, 1978

The Hellstrom Chronicle

(1971)

The projector starts. Roll credits! Yes, indeed. Roll *end credits*. Well, kinda-sorta. *The Hellstrom Chronicle* begins with a list of thank-yous of the type generally reserved for the end of a movie. "The producers wish to thank the following institutions for their assistance in the production of this film."

In fairness, the list is impressive, so as far as it goes: "U.S. Atomic Energy Commission and University of California at Los Angeles; Griffith Observatory; California Institute of Technology; Lorquin Entomological Society; Entomological Society of America; Anti-Locust Research Center, London; National Museum, Kenya." And lest there be any doubt, all of these are real entities, including the Anti-Locusts in England, their numbers helping to keep Great Britain great.

Why begin this way, even before we see the film's opening title? Con game? Not necessarily. More of a confidence-building exercise, before we viewers fall backwards into the producers' ever-lovin' arms. Trust them. And trust me: this'll only hurt a little bit.

Next, we hear the voice of God, or perhaps the Godless: "The Earth was created, not with the gentle caress of love, but with the brutal violence of rape." Cue footage of lava geysers, a Hell-storm for a Hell-strom. Then we see images of crystals forming, and cellular life. Yes, life, having the very time of its life, growing and multiplying.

"In evolution's greatest irony, one of the first creatures to appear would be the last to remain, for incubating in the darkened womb of prehistory was a seed of grotesque variation, a fetus with the capability to dominate all."

What is this creature? The insect, of course. Vile and horrible, chocolate-covered, deep-fried, or smashed underfoot.

Just what does the word "Hellstrom" have to do with bugs? We learn right after the opening title finally appears. "In Association with Nils Hellstrom, M.S., Ph.D." The word is a person, but maybe not vice versa, but that's getting ahead of ourselves. Anyhow, Hellstrom appears on-camera:

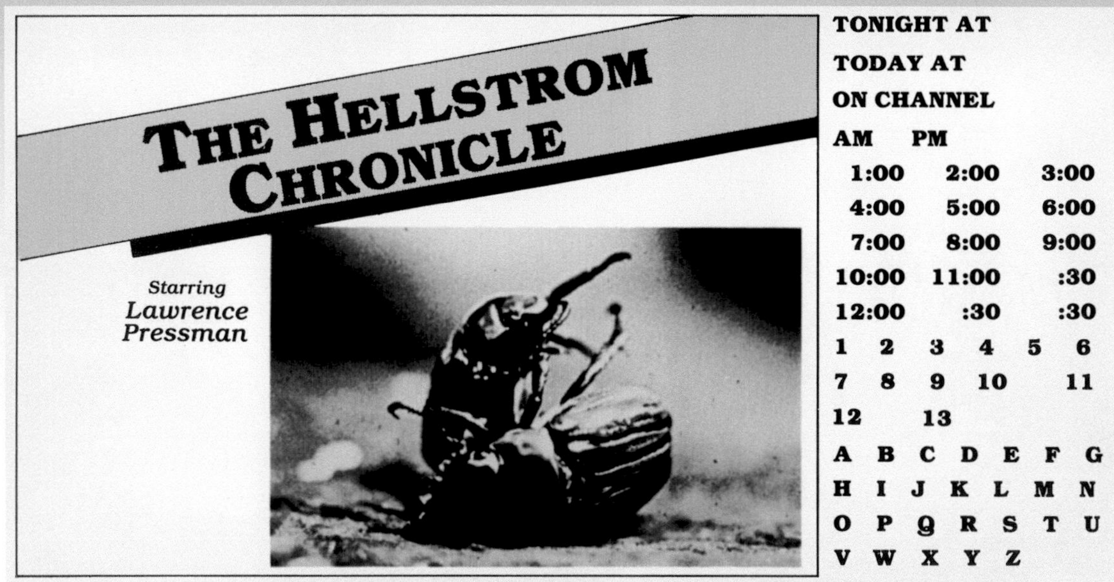

> *If [my] name rings a bell at all, it's probably in connection with the words 'fanatic, lunatic, heretic.' Actually, I'm a scientist, and these other descriptions have come as a result of my dedication and my work, my obsession, some have called it, with certain findings I've made. It's not easy to be obsessed. The past eighteen months, it's cost me two fellowships, one assistant professorship, and even a few friendships. I don't care about that, really. In a way, it's kind of flattering. What I really regret is that after nine years of concentrated work, I've learned something that no one wants to hear, but unless someone does hear, unless someone is at least exposed to it, we as a species might pass from existence, without ever knowing why.*

Later, he makes himself sledgehammer-clear: "If any living species is to inherit the earth, it will not be man. ... Yes, I'm talking about insects. And if you at this moment dare to think this is lunacy, I invite you to remain in your seat, draw your own conclusion, and learn the inevitable destiny of ignorance."

The lord of flies will not be a human, not a demon, but flies themselves, apparently. Why so? Humans are staring into the face of so many disasters, from radiation to pollution, from ignorance to selfishness.

By contrast, insects are up for anything, and always will be, because of their "frightening tour-de-force of adaptability," which ranges from methods of disguise to means of defense, attack even, in the form of "battalions." They can crawl, fly, communicate, metamorphose, and generally freak you out.

And so, humankind and insects—not fish or fowl—will have to fight for supremacy of our shared blue world. "Man, because he is the only creature with the ability to radically change the Earth, and the insect, because he is the only creature that can adapt to whatever changes man can make."

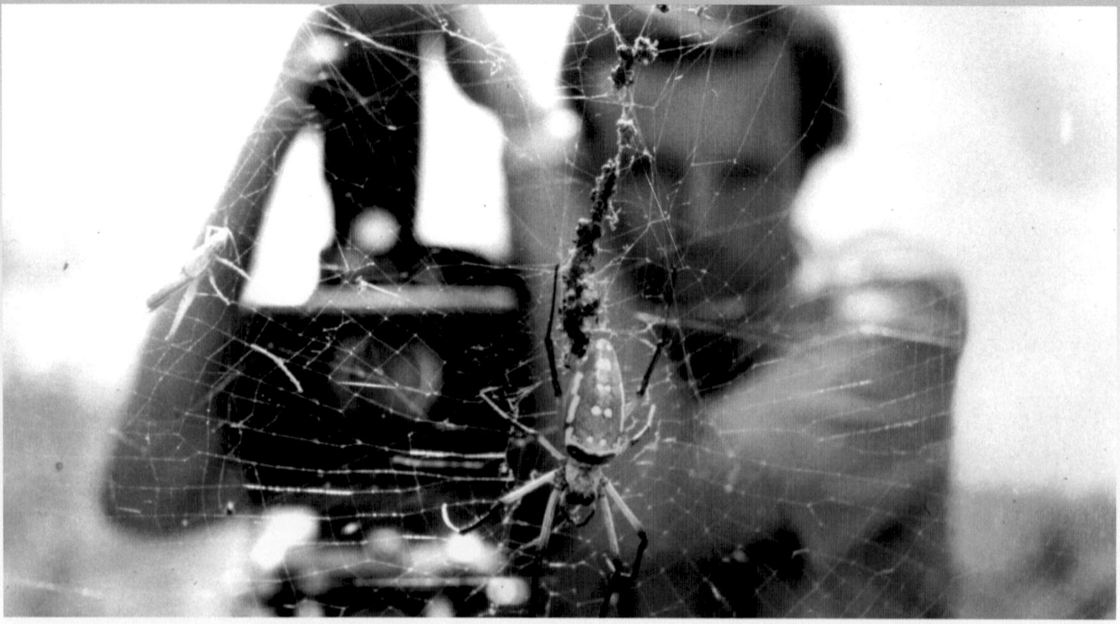

If all this sounds like a 1950s sci-fi flick, then you're on the right wavelength. At one point, Hellstrom even sits in a movie theater watching the giant ants in *Them!* (1954).

The data about bugs is probably accurate, even if presented in sometimes colorful language. Locusts, for example, aren't just destructive; they are part of a "monstrous flight into hell."

Thanks to science or urban legends, we all know cockroaches will survive the same mushroom clouds that will annihilate us. But Hellstrom's discussion transforms into one that is definitely Us versus Them, mano-a-buggo.

The insects will win. We will lose. Hellstrom even brings up dinosaurs in an apparent comparison to what we will become. Here is what *Variety* called the film's "lugubrious, provocative but frightfully convincing contention." And here is what I call the film's Weirdumentary credentials.

When we see Hellstrom on-camera, it is in the expected halls of credibility. He speaks at Griffith Observatory in Hollywood, at the Radiation Laboratory at Rock Valley, Nevada, and in front of some cutting-edge computers at the California Institute of Technology.

He also briefly interviews a farmer who describes how quickly bugs become resistant to new insecticides. The farmer—if he really is a farmer and not an actor, and I have my doubts—is the only other person who talks in the film.

But we do see other people, particularly in a segment where Hellstrom shows us how much humans hate insects, placing them on food at grocery stores and restaurants and filming customer reactions to them, allegedly without their knowledge.

Directed by Walon Green and written by David Selzer, this David L. Wolper production is more than worth the price of admission, being better scripted, directed, and edited than most films covered in this humble tome.

The film's cinematography is superb, and its use of sound to emphasize growing plant life and insects on the prowl is beautifully eerie. Lalo Schifrin's soundtrack should be on everyone's playlist, some of it beautiful, some of it eerie.

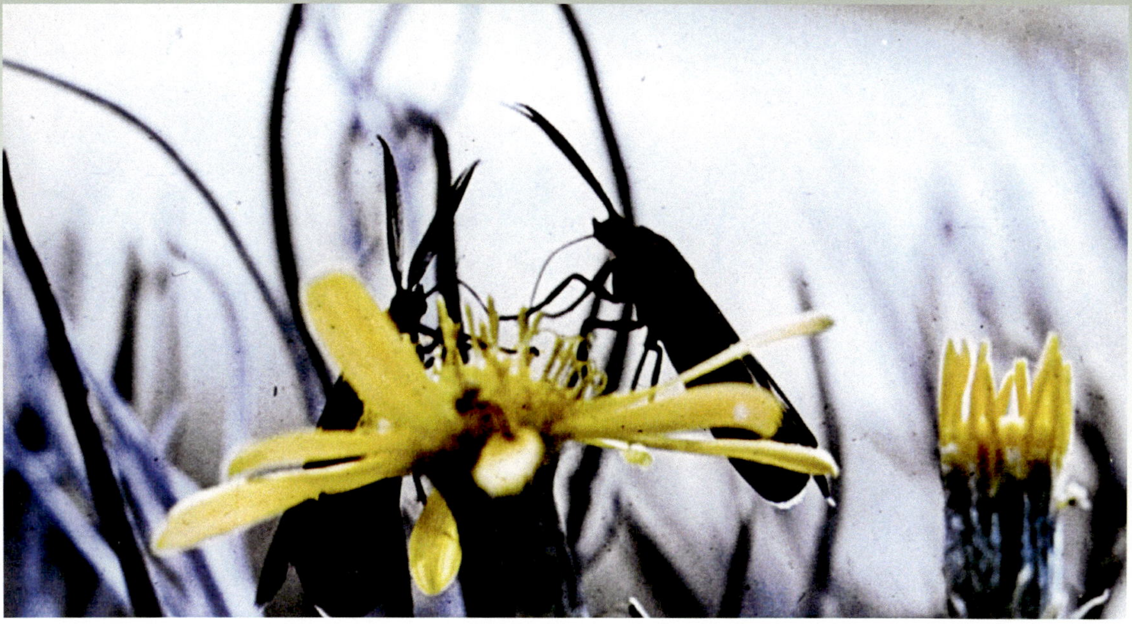

Out with it, then: *The Hellstrom Chronicle* is assuredly the most cinematic, the most well achieved of all Weirdumentaries.

And that ain't all. "There has never been a movie quite like this," film critic Gene Shalit observed. Yes, sir, because—spoiler alert—we must now reveal what the film only tells us when it concludes:

> *Nils Hellstrom is a fictional character who was portrayed by Lawrence Pressman.*
>
> *His statements relating to the impermanence of the human species have been synthesized from contemporary opinions. All statements about the insect world are factual and have been reviewed by Roy Snelling, Ph.D., and by Charles Hogue, Ph.D., of the Entomology Department, Los Angeles County Museum of Natural History.*

Pressman is a great actor and makes a completely believable Hellstrom. The film's lie—or, if you prefer, its withholding of the truth—makes it into something like a mockumentary. Certainly that's how critics have described it in the twenty-first century.

Then there's the fact that one person seen in the montage of bug revulsion sued the producers, claiming "fraud and deceit" had been used to get him to appear in the film. Move over, Borat. Hellstrom was here first.

In all seriousness, though, *The Hellstrom Chronicle* doesn't quite fall into the mockumentary category. The periphery, maybe, but not over the edge. To be sure, the data we hear is true. The key to the film is an exaggerated tale—dare I say, a weird tale—of creepy crawlies vying for dominion over the likes of us.

And to nonbelievers, I will simply say, stop buggin' me. *The Hellstrom Chronicle* is the only Weirdumentary to win the Academy Award for best documentary.

In Search Of... Prophecies

(1976-1982)

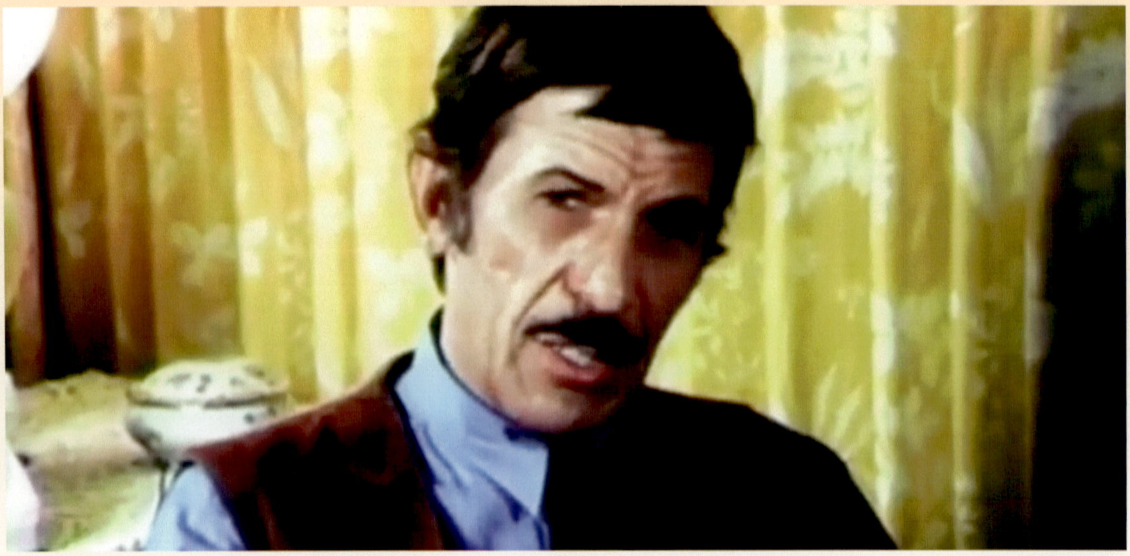

Over the course of six seasons, *In Search of...* racked up a total of 144 episodes. In terms of sheer numbers, Alan Landsburg and Leonard Nimoy had become the Kings of Weirdumentaryland.

Most of the topics were fascinating, even though some don't quite fit this book. For example, there were Vikings, Josef Mengele, the Elephant Man, killer bees, sharks, Nazi plunder, Inca treasure, Dead Sea Scrolls, Pompeii, cryogenics, tidal waves, hurricanes, tornadoes, and earthquakes.

No problemo, Alan. One can't be all weird, all the time. And there's more than enough episodes to keep all of us Weirdumentarists happy, including a few particularly good episodes about prophecies. (Wanna take a stab at predicting what I'm about to talk about?)

Season 2, Episode 5, *Astrology*: "What strange influence does the moon have on the behavior of man?" Or the stars, for that matter?

Some interviewees convey belief in astrology and horoscopes, others skepticism. In any event, for thousands of years the heavens above have helped allegedly predict the earth below. The zodiac reveals all, or maybe reveals nothing. In any event, there's lots of money in them thar stars.

One scientist spends his time decrying astrology, much more than is usually allotted to nonbelievers in a Weirdumentary. But never fear. Plenty of other interviewees counter his claims, having discovered evidence strong enough to convince themselves.

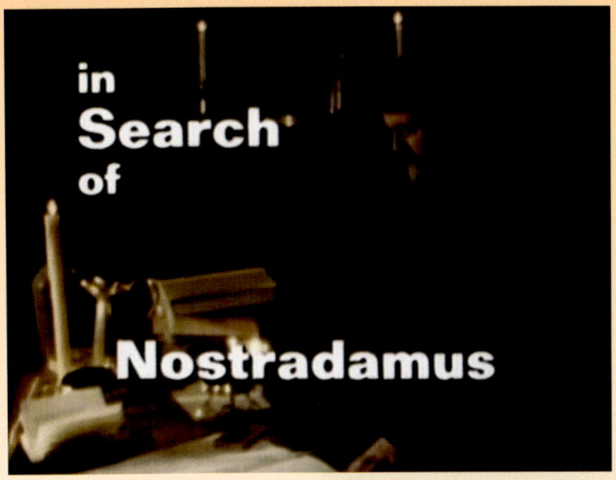

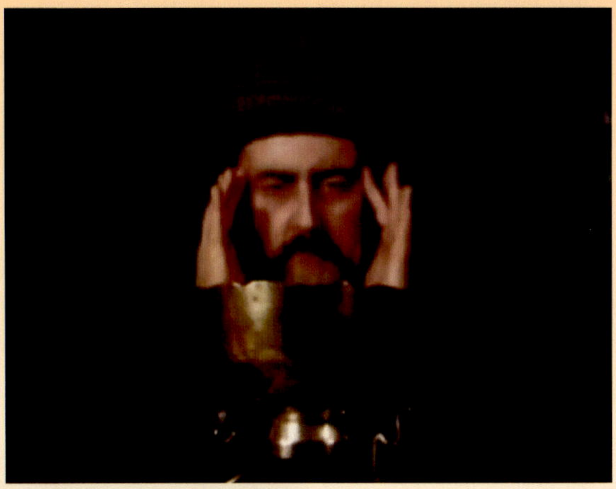

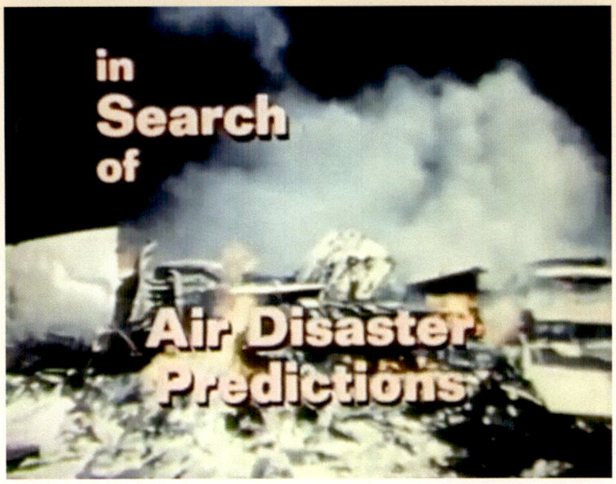

Season 4, Episode 21, *Air Disaster Predictions*: People dream of airplane crashes before they occur. "Were these dreams just nightmares, or will they prove to be prophecy?"

Perhaps ESP and precognition occur when we go beddy-bye. "How many of us are glimpsing the future in our ordinary dreams and nightmares?"

"Skeptics will say no" to such ideas, but that's why they call them skeptics. And hey, if this power could be harnessed, think of how many disasters could be averted, how many lives could be saved.

Some of the stories we hear are intriguing, even convincing, but are they true, or mere coincidence? Search me, I say to those in search of.

Season 6, Episode 15, *Nostradamus*: Here we go again, gang. From Carey D. Wilson through Basil Rathbone to Orson Welles, Nostradamus has been one of the most popular Weirdumentary subjects of them all.

The old boy wrote cryptic quatrains, but do they mean anything? Did they foretell the future? Is it time to say kudos, or who knows?

Time won't tell, I reckon, because eventually the vagueness of what he said will match up to the vagaries of whatever happens. He probably can't lose.

Now, since so many others have gotten to make prophecies, I shall claim my birthright to do the same. I predict that—no matter how long we search—there'll never be another Weirdumentary television series as great as *In Search of...*

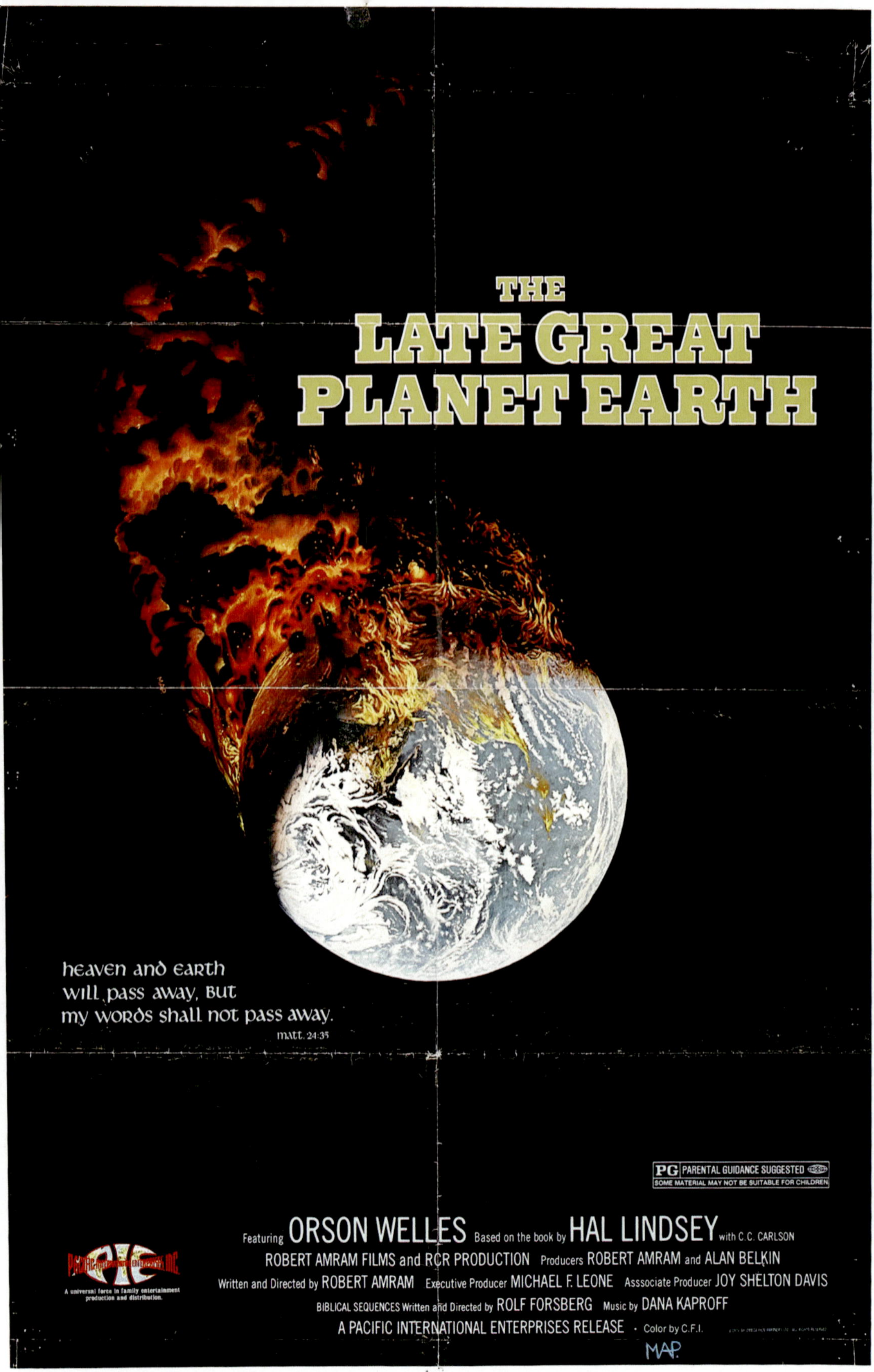
THE
LATE GREAT
PLANET EARTH
heaven and earth
will pass away, but
my words shall not pass away.
matt. 24:35
PG PARENTAL GUIDANCE SUGGESTED
SOME MATERIAL MAY NOT BE SUITABLE FOR CHILDREN
Featuring ORSON WELLES Based on the book by HAL LINDSEY with C.C. CARLSON
ROBERT AMRAM FILMS and RCR PRODUCTION Producers ROBERT AMRAM and ALAN BELKIN
Written and Directed by ROBERT AMRAM Executive Producer MICHAEL F. LEONE Asssociate Producer JOY SHELTON DAVIS
BIBLICAL SEQUENCES Written and Directed by ROLF FORSBERG Music by DANA KAPROFF
A PACIFIC INTERNATIONAL ENTERPRISES RELEASE · Color by C.F.I.
A universal force in family entertainment production and distribution.
MAP.

The Late Great Planet Earth

(1978)

Hal Lindsey's book *The Late Great Planet Earth* (1970) sold 12 million copies during the seventies. Transferring it to the big screen was foretold by somebody. It must have been, given those kinds of sales. And that prophecy was just the first of many. Trailers for the film adaptation promised moviegoers, "It may change your life forever."

The Late Great Planet Earth owes a great debt to Sunn Classic, imitating as it does that company's signature style. Writer and director Robert Amram's dramatic recreations are credible, and Orson Welles as an on-camera host is as good as it gets.

In fact, the film's best moment is likely in the opening scene, when those two elements converge. Angry Hebrews push a false prophet (Beaumont Bruestle) off a cliff to his death. Once his corpse turns to a skeleton, Welles arrives at the very location—two or three thousand years later—to pick up his skull. Alas, poor Beaumont, Orson didn't know you well. You probably weren't on set long enough to get his autograph.

From there, we learn that "3,000 years of history prove that the prophets of Israel spoke the truth. Not everyone wants to believe them, but they cannot be ignored." Folks appearing on-screen include scientists and the vox populi, who include a random fellow eating ice cream, or perhaps low-cal yogurt. More often than anyone else, though, we see author Hal Lindsey, spouting his reasons to believe the end is nigh. Stock footage seems to authenticate his fears.

Welles explains, "Seventy percent of all the prophecies written in the Bible have already been fulfilled. If the visions of the disciple John are truly prophetic, the remaining events are expected to be fulfilled in our lifetime." Lindsey portentously adds, we are "racing on a countdown to the end of history as we know it."

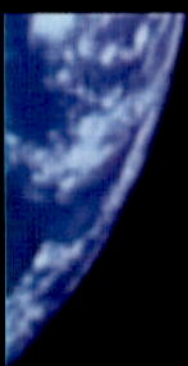

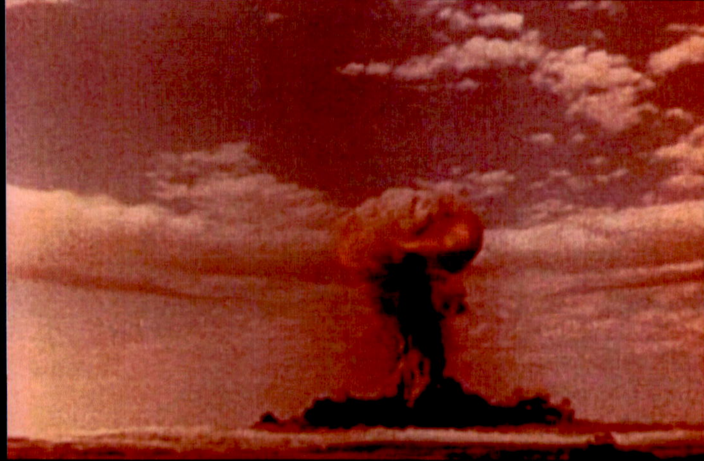

THE
LATE GREAT
PLANET EARTH

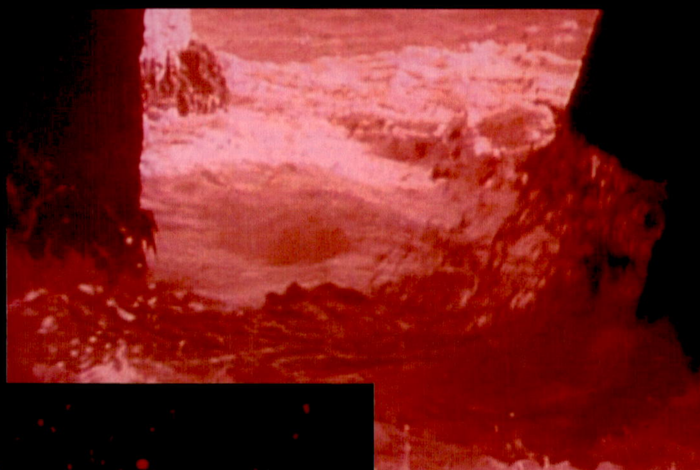

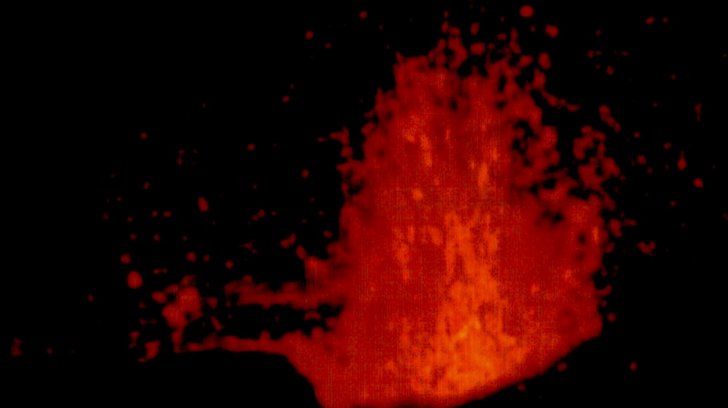

The signs are many, from the state of Israel and the Six-Day War to the arms race, the oil crisis, the increase of natural disasters, and the growth of atheism. And then there's the "Jupiter Effect" as described by author John Gribbin, an alignment of the planets that would create untold disasters in 1982. "As we examine the evidence," Lindsey determines, "it's hard to escape the inevitable conclusion" that the beginning of the end now appears before our very eyes." Mayhap, but another inevitable conclusion is that the Jupiter Effect was ineffective: nada happened on its specified date of doom.

Anyhow, the film really comes alive when Welles speaks anything, whether it be commentary or verses from the Holy Bible. He sounds at his ominous best when reading from the Book of Revelation. Dana Kaproff's musical score comes in at a close second.

An advertisement in *Variety* claimed *The Late Great Planet Earth*—"the most sobering film ever made"—would reach theaters at Christmas 1976. It was to be a "dramatic documentary." By June 1977, the trade press claimed it was "awaiting release." One month later, a revised account claimed it was being readied for distribution later in the year.

The delay came in part from Orson Welles' desire to see a rough cut before joining the cast. It also resulted from co-producer Alan Belkin's idea to shoot new dramatizations for both the beginning of the film and its conclusion, all part of an effort to save a "problem" picture.

Welles, who had already worked with Amram on *Sentinels of Silence* (1971), completed his filming for *The Late Great Planet Earth* in the summer of 1977. The great man required only one take each for his on-camera appearances. And while he worked in front of the camera at the Vasquez Rocks in California (which had served as "Transylvania" for the 1931 version of *Dracula* with Bela Lugosi), Welles recorded his voiceover at his own house.

The MPAA gave *The Late Great Planet Earth* a PG rating in the fall of 1977, presumably due to some gruesome disaster footage. It appeared at theaters by January 1978, and then four-walled its way across America slowly the rest of the year and into 1979 and even 1980.

Screen International believed the film would appeal to "all who like to have their flesh made to creep." As for its critique, the publication confided:

> *This brings to my mind a splendid cartoon ... which showed a sandwichboardman carrying the words 'Prepare to meet thy Doom. If thou art already prepared, ignore this message.' We've had it chums, and those that die before the holocaust will be the lucky ones. The message comes over loud and clear. All very convincing it is, too, as the one-sided argument is put over with the help of corroborative newsreel footage and the pontificating of experts. Mercifully, the agony is piled on so thick that it acquires the macabre black humor of the Grand Guignol. I have a wicked desire to nick all the prints before they go out and add a coda of Woody Woodpecker's 'That's All Folks!'*

Daily Variety was perhaps more pointed: "There's clearly an audience for this kind of fare, but if *The Late Great Planet Earth* is to be believed, there won't be for long."

As for the dearly departed, our own beloved planet, I can only say, "rest in pieces."

The Doomsday Chronicles

(1979)

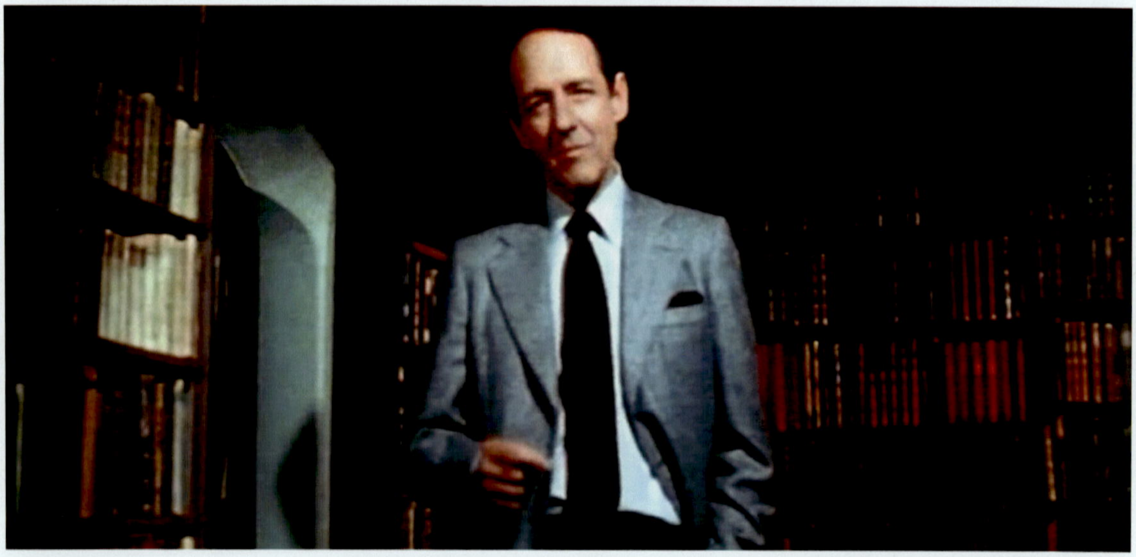

"One day it will be gone. There will be no more dawns and sunsets, and no more spring times to end the frozen winter. No more blue skies. No more starry nights. No more fears and no more joys. Doomsday will have come and gone. And the Earth will be no more."

Spoken in a calm voice by William Schallert, an actor best remembered as the dad on ABC's *The Patty Duke Show* (1963–1966), these words seem all the more petrifying than if read by the likes of Bela Lugosi.

Standing in the Office of Knowledge, the mild-mannered Schallert adds that Doomsday might be coming soon to a planet near us. "Why is there such a strong feeling that we stand on the brink of catastrophe?"

Cue the stock footage, and we'll come to learn the answer: nuclear war, the fuel crisis, epidemics, natural calamities, finite resources in the face of population growth. Things are disastrous, even though Joel Goldsmith's soothing synth music backs up Schallert's words.

Though copyrighted in 1979, *Doomsday Chronicles* seems to have first appeared on TV stations in 1980 and then again in 1981. Thankfully, the world existed long enough to witness a rebroadcast.

"Has the countdown to doomsday indeed already begun?" Schallert asks. Mayhap, given the unrelenting images of earthquakes, volcanos, tidal waves, electrical storms, hurricanes, and tornadoes. Best not to go outdoors, but then staying inside is fraught with problems

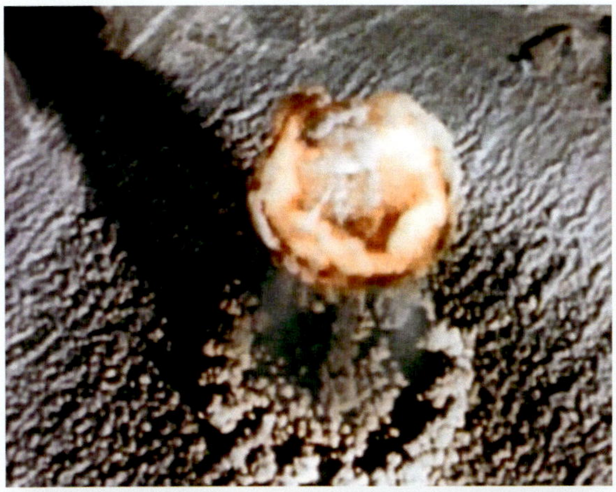
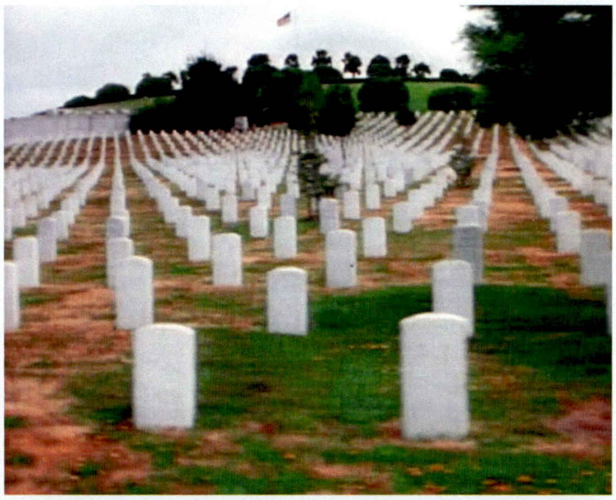
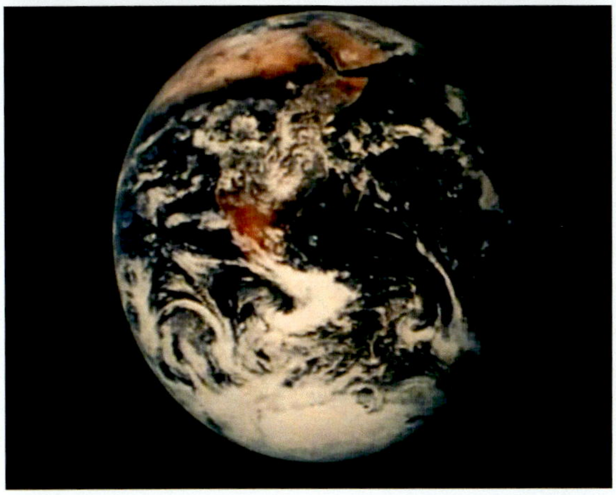
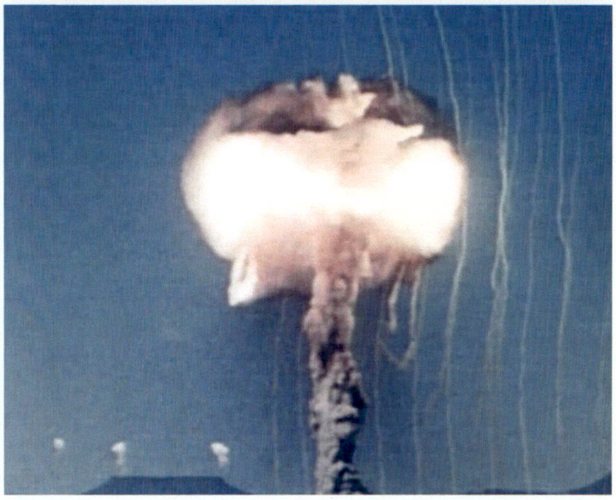

too. After all, Doomsday might be triggered simply by humans driving themselves "mad with the ever-increasing complexity of [their] society."

Target dates for our collective demise include 1999, thanks to some welcome divinations from Nostradamus. But that's when the film seems to hurtle closer to impending doom than our beloved planet Earth.

The script, written by Kenneth J. Morris, Xavier Reyes, and John C. Purvis, pulls a fast one on us, quickly dumping centuries-old prestidigitation for modern know-how. Interviews with real experts detail authentic concerns, to an extent that in retrospect the film seems prescient, whether it's talk of climate change or of nuclear disaster that extends beyond the Superpower nations. "Imagine a terrorist organization or a lone assassin aiming not a rifle at a nation's leader," Schallert asks us rhetorically, "but a nuclear weapon targeted for a capital city."

Scary indeed. Truly. But the "truly" part is what went wrong. Too much of the film is fully baked. Not even a surprise interview with Daniel Ellsberg, of Pentagon Papers fame, can rescue us from serious science. After Nostradamus, there just ain't enough weirdness here to qualify as a fully formed Weirdumentary. Send complaints and/or praise to producer Jerry Johnson and director James Thornton.

As for Doomsday? "It could happen within our lifetime." A repeat viewing of *Doomsday Chronicles*? Not a chance.

Encounter with Disaster

(1979)

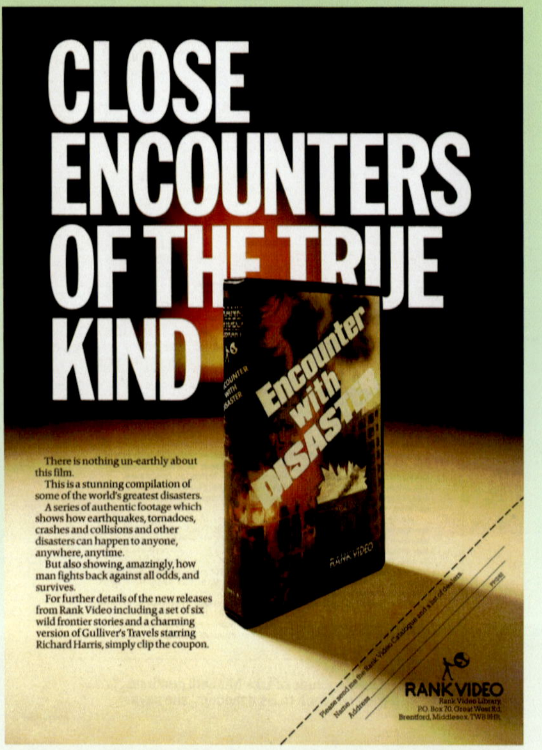

"If you think you will never personally encounter disaster, you may be very wrong, for there is no immunity from disaster, no place safe enough to be out of its reach," Brad Crandall's voice earnestly explains. Words to the wise, Brad, words to the wise.

Encounter with Disaster is unique among the Sunn Classic Weirdumentaries, even though some of the usual suspects hover overhead, including producers Charles E. Sellier, Jr. and James L. Conway.

The key difference is the sole reliance on stock footage. No dramatizations unfold. An aesthetic choice or a financial one? To guess is to ponder, no bad thing as we bide time till Doomsday.

Archival films depict the 1933 earthquake in Long Beach and the 1964 earthquake in Alaska. Then we meet Hurricane Camille, a "pinwheel of fantasy forms" that left destruction in its path in 1969. Of a volcanic eruption in Sicily in 1971, our solemn host notifies us: "Like a seething cauldron, its crater continues to boil a superheated brew down the mountainside."

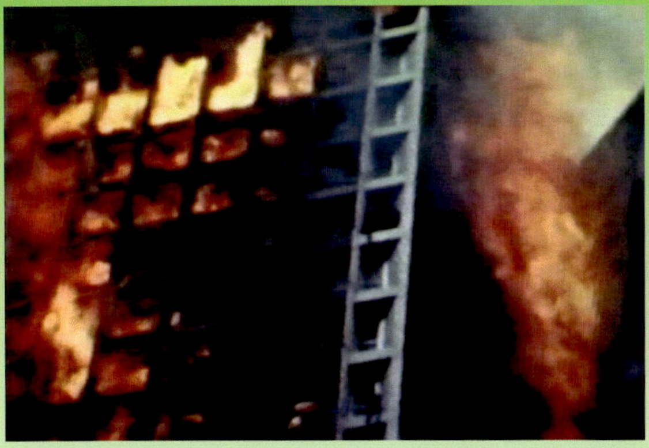

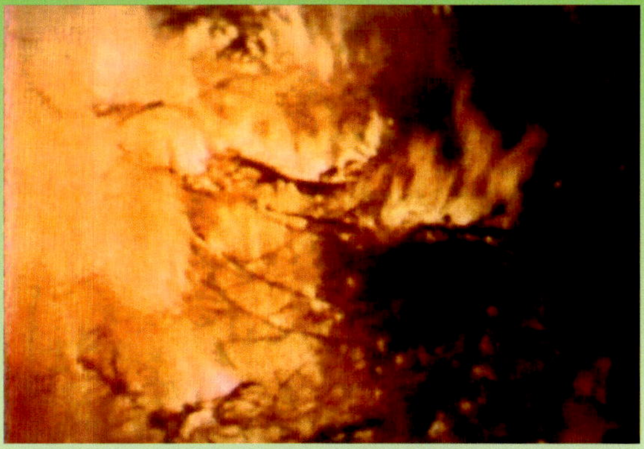

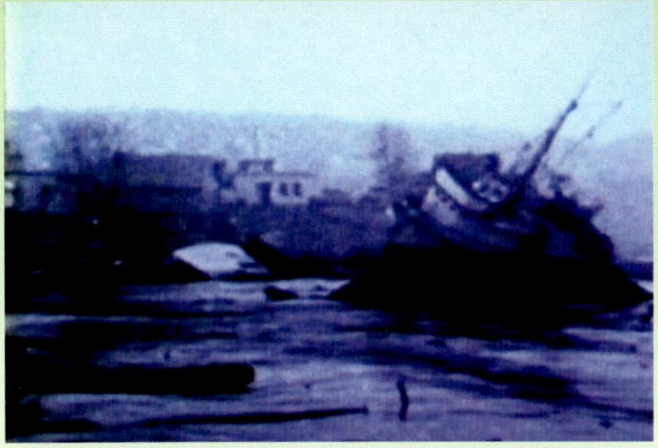

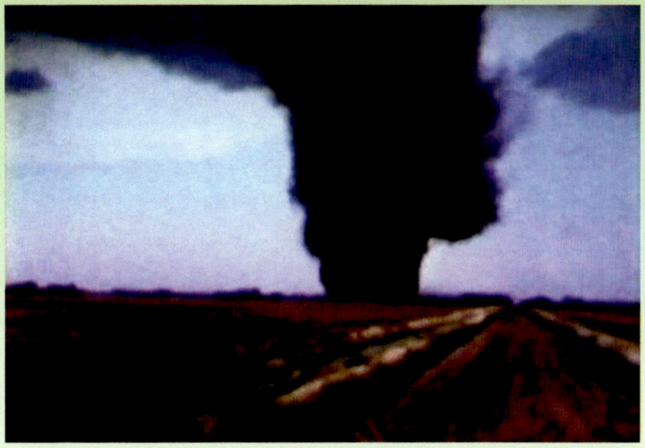

Most of the film's ninety-minute running time depicts man-made disasters. Here we endure the 1937 *Hindenburg* explosion, the 1955 disaster at Le Mans, the 1956 sinking of the S.S. *Andrea Doria*, the 1974 Joelma Building fire in São Paulo, and the 1976 Teton Dam catastrophe.

What else does this footage mean? Well, for the MPAA, it meant slapping *Encounter with Disaster* with a PG rating in January 1979. Real people flinging themselves to their deaths out of blazing infernos did not portend a General Audience.

Oh, to be a monger: Warmonger, Whoremonger, Fishmonger ... or, in the case of Sunn Classic, a Deathmonger. But we can't fault them or San Andreas, really. During the seventies, the major studios had cashed in on disaster time and again, from *Airport* (1970) and *The Poseidon Adventure* (1972) to *Earthquake* (1974), *The Towering Inferno* (1974), and *The Hindenburg* (1975). The pre-Copernican in me feels obliged to explain that, for this Weirdumentary, the Sunn was merely orbiting Planet Hollywood.

Wallace Bennett's script ties together the various tragedies, which detail the past far more than the future. Supervising Sound Effects Editor Jim Bryan helmed a team of five colleagues to produce an audio track worthy of the best.

And Brad Crandall does a magnificent job, though entirely off-camera. Is he in a safe house, far from the dangers that lurk? One can only hope.

As his closing narration explains, "The new potentials for disaster are increasing, slowly, insidiously, and while they provide us with the things that make for the good life, they also provide dangers, many of which may become a threat to our very existence." Cue mushroom cloud.

Then Brad foretokens, "The next victim could be you." I take that to mean us, dear readers. We have been warned.

The Prophecies of Nostradamus

(1979)

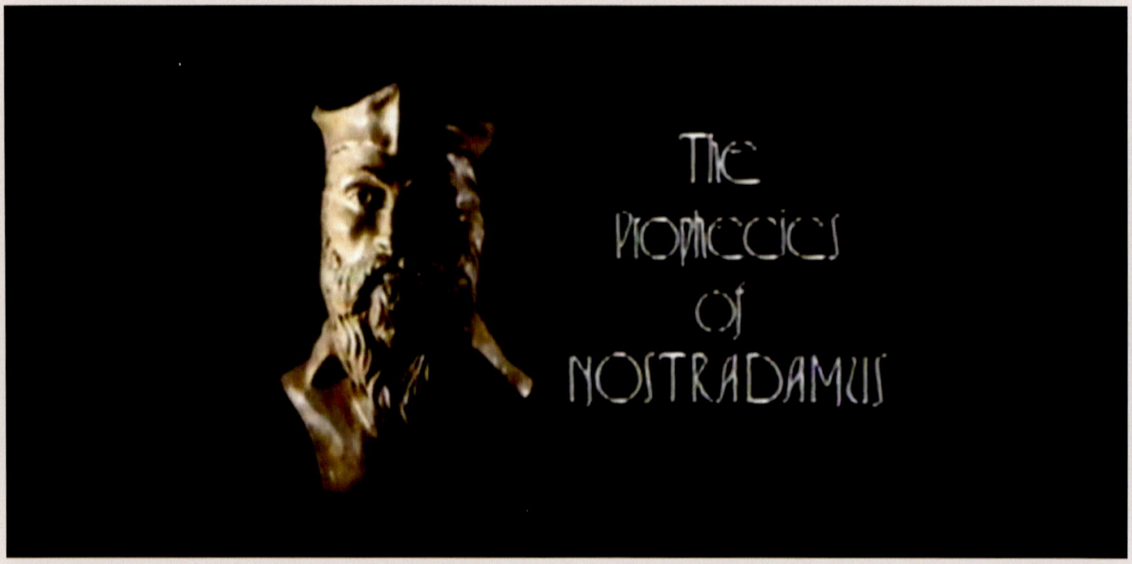

Three drunken French soldiers dig up a grave in the middle of the night. They disinter the remains of Nostradamus. Legend has it that anyone who drinks from his skull will inherit his powers, but will also die. Opening his coffin, the trio is shocked to see a plaque around the prophet's neck reading May 1791. He had died in 1566. The date on the plaque accurately predicted when his grave would be opened. After guzzling wine from his skull, a soldier falls dead, the result of a stray bullet. And, it would seem, the fulfillment of one of Nostradamus' myriad predictions.

Paul Drane's *The Prophecies of Nostradamus* opens with this recreation, as well as effective theme music composed by Warren Morgan. Overall, the ninety-six-minute documentary unfolds like an effective imitation of the Sunn Classic formula. Notable Australian actor John Waters gives a brief history of Nostradamus before devoting the bulk of the running time to his predictions. These we learn through recreations, stock footage, and interviews with a few "experts," among them writers Erika Cheetham and Charles Neilson Gattey.

Half of Nostradamus' quatrains have already come true, Waters informs us while wearing a seventies-era shirt with collars almost as big as the prophet's reputation. He explains the "tragic accuracy" of the predictions, which included the Great Fire of London, the French Revolution, the American Revolution, the Russian Revolution, and World War II. Not only

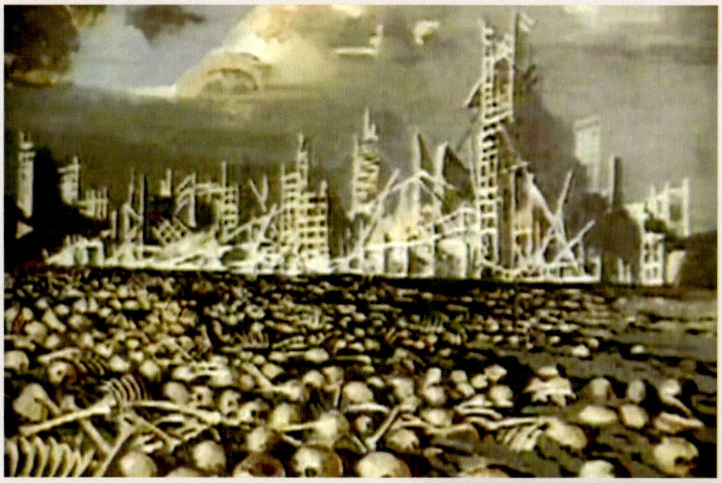

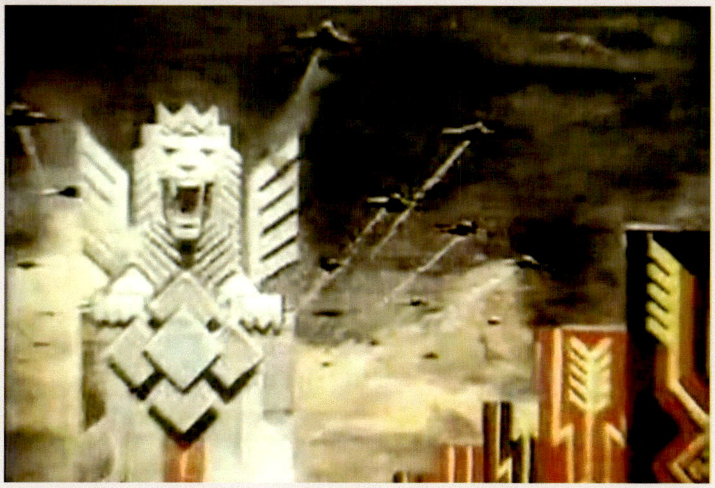

did Nostradamus foretell the assassination of JFK, but he also had advance knowledge that psychic Jeanne Dixon would prognosticate the same. The quatrains hold so much meaning that they might be better described as five-trains or six-trains, Midnight Specials shining their ever-loving light on the dark days ahead.

At a given point, having bombarded us with so much "accuracy" and "obvious" evidence, Waters hedges his bets: "At this point we must stress that this program is concerned with merely bringing together the evidence of the experts and does not take a stand on its validity or otherwise."

With that proviso out of the way, Waters moves on to predictions that had not yet come to pass. Between 1981 and 1999, a third world war will engulf the Earth. Nuclear power unleashed, the victims will suffer famine leading to rampant cannibalism. In hindsight, I'd argue these events didn't get the press they deserved, either in headlines or in food reviews.

Some favorite moments: A rapid-fire montage that depicts the penalties for witchcraft in the sixteenth century. Along with engravings and woodcuts, we see a few shots of Christopher Lee as Dracula. Later, when we learn Nostradamus predicted Franco, the dictator's name repeats over and over again, complete with echo effect.

Paul Drane made *The Prophecies of Nostradamus* in 1979 with funds "lent" to him by the Australian Film Commission. The Sunn Classic wannabe later played on American TV.

"It is ultimately up to you whether or not you believe it."

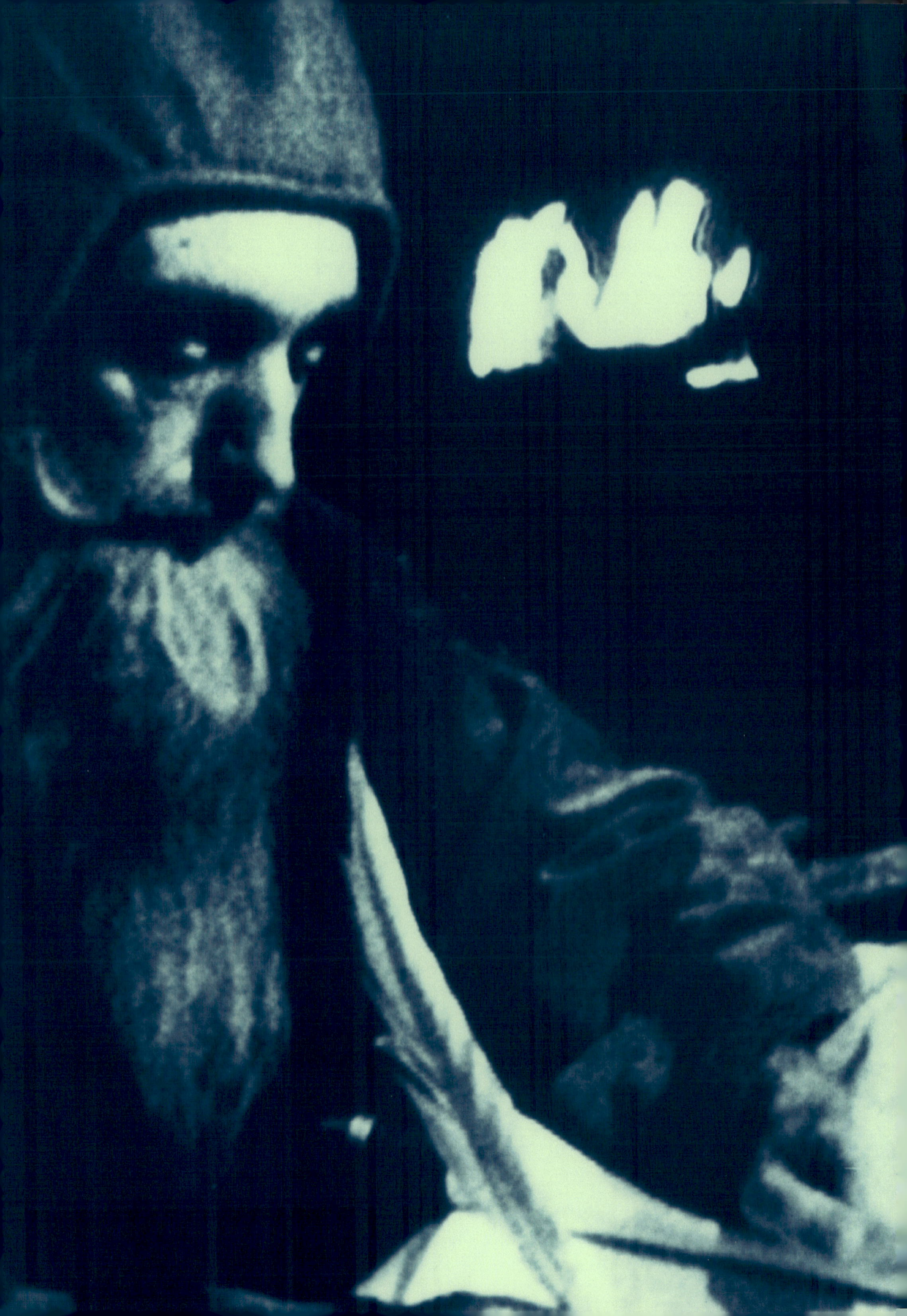

The Man Who Saw Tomorrow

(1981)

"It's clear right from the start that this is going to be another one of those 'gee whiz, could it really be true?' pseudo-documentaries so widely popularized by Sunn Classic Pictures. But this is not a Sunn Classic release; it's Warner Bros. And the significance of that surely must be that the majors, having successfully invaded the horror exploitation field once left to indies, are now looking for new territories to conquer. If this succeeds, look out."

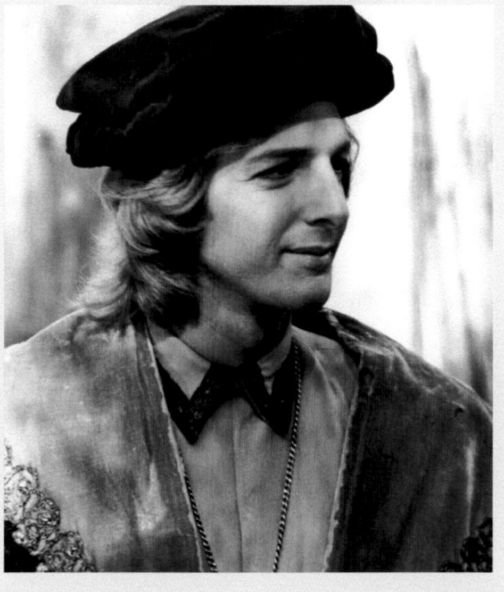

When *Variety* issued that declaration in February 1981, it presumably defined success in financial terms. The trade could scarcely have predicted that *The Man Who Saw Tomorrow* would become the final act of the Weirdumentary show in movie theaters. As prognosticator, *Variety* had nothing on Nostradamus.

As for the film, careful viewers will notice credits for Robert Guenette (director), Guenette and Alan Hopgood (screenplay), William Loose and Jack Tillar (music), as well as the following statement: "Suggested by the production *The Prophecies of Nostradamus* produced and directed by Paul Drane."

Like Nostradamus, Drane had become harbinger of Things to Come. The basic structure of *The Man Who Saw Tomorrow* follows Drane's earlier documentary, with Drane himself getting additional credit as producer of the new project alongside Guenette and Lee Kramer.

The similarities not only include beginning with the story of the trio of graverobbers who disturbed the sleeping seer, but also extensive reuse of dramatizations filmed for *The Prophecies of Nostradamus*. And so it goes for much of the new film, as it probes auguries that have already come true and those that still lie ahead.

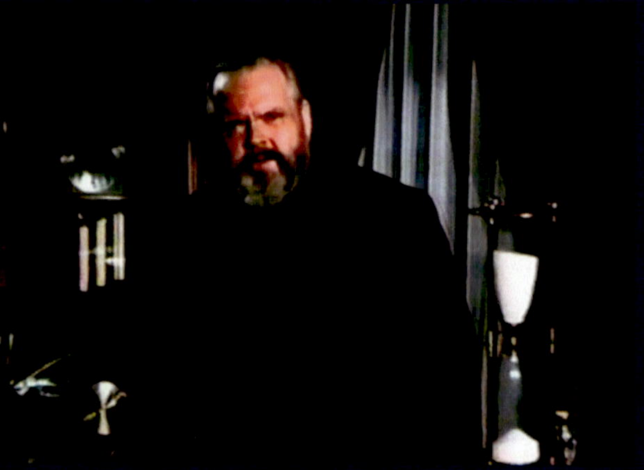

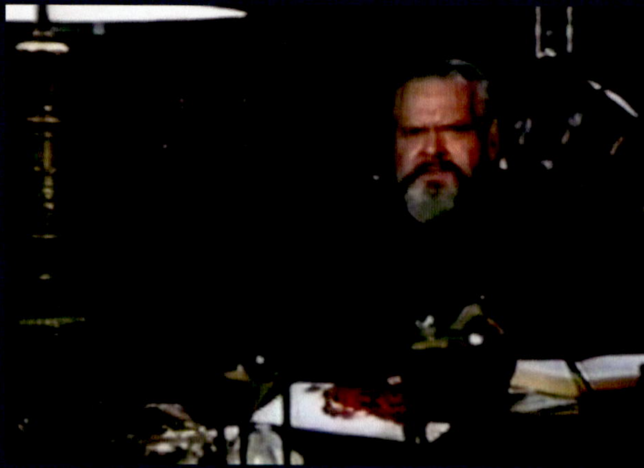

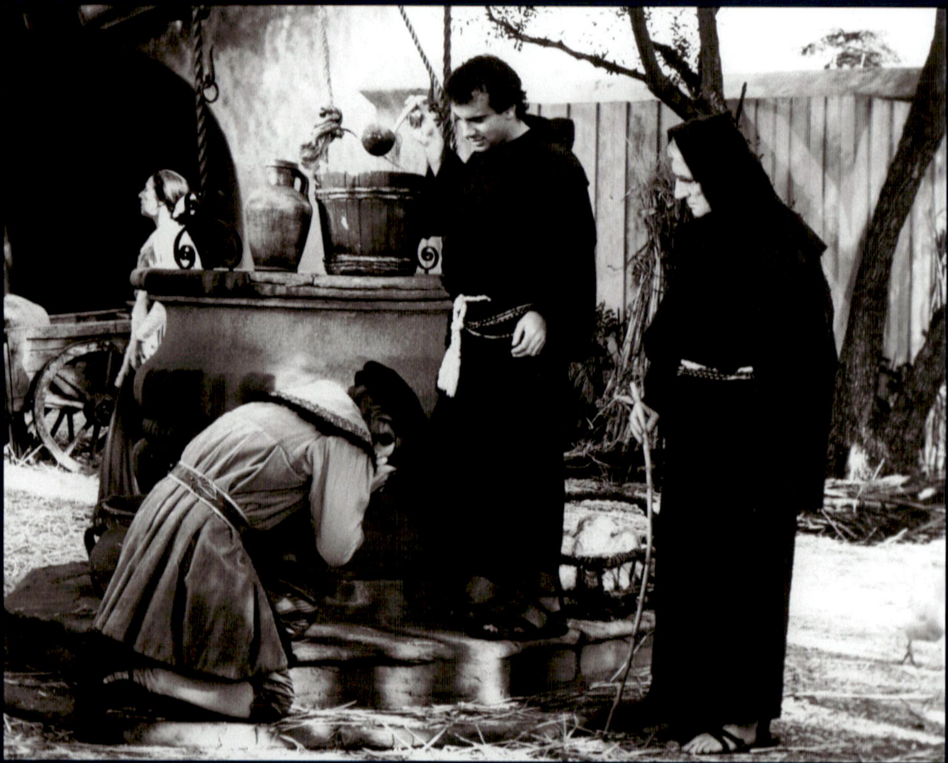

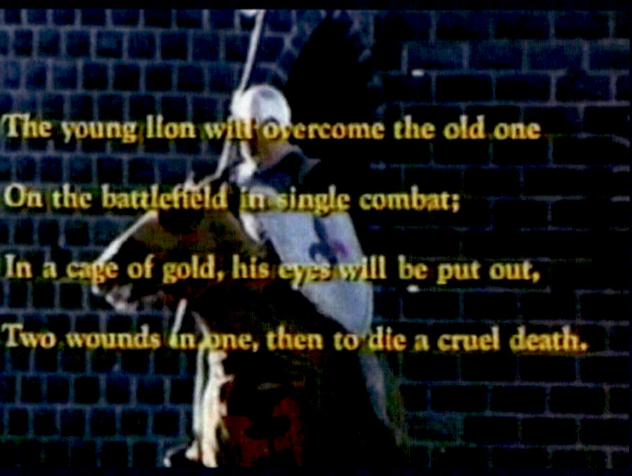

The prophecies of Nostradamus can be interpreted many different ways. This motion picture has presented only some of them. They are not the opinions, judgments or interpretations of the producers of this film.

None of this kept Warner Bros. publicity from heralding the newness of a largely old project. The pressbook claims producer David Wolper (who apparently appeared on the scene after *The Man Who Saw Tomorrow* was finished) spent five hours a day for over five months combing through footage. I say sooth that those proclamations be false.

Thankfully, though, one real difference with *The Prophecies of Nostradamus* exists, and that is the great man himself. No, not the sixteenth-century clairvoyant, but instead the twentieth-century wunderkind: Orson Welles. His weight, metaphorical and literal, elevates *The Man Who Saw Tomorrow* into peaks it otherwise would never have reached, even with Guenette's involvement.

Smoking a cigar and seated in an Office of Knowledge that features a burning fireplace, Orson asks, "Was he a quack, this Nostradamus, a charlatan, or was he a true prophet, a man with a gift to see what others cannot see? We're going to let you judge for yourselves." And later, "Can we dismiss old Nostradamus and all we've just seen as coincidence or facile interpretation, or is there just possibly some real substance and credibility to what he's written?"

And when he describes how Nostradamus received his visions—"by a subtle spirit of fire, by a voice coming from limbo"—the voice that speaks with the greatest authority is definitely Orson's.

Not unexpectedly, much of the narration finds Orson exquisitely spouting qualifiers like "seems," as well as shifting the blame onto others: "some experts believe" and "the Nostradamus proponents say."

Most pivotal of all, though, is his following dialogue: "Let me warn you now that the predictions of the future are not at all comforting, and I might also add that these predictions of the past, these warnings of the future, are not the opinions of the producers of this film, and they're certainly not my opinions."

Who am I to disagree with Citizen Kane? After all, his myriad writing credits never included fortune cookies.

The MPAA saddled *The Man Who Saw Tomorrow* with a PG rating in February 1981 just before Warner Bros. picked it up for theatrical release.

"It's been a long time since WB released a film as cheap-looking as this one," *Variety* bemoaned, explaining: "Visually, *Tomorrow* is a horrible hodge-podge of clips from old feature films, newsreels, talking-head interviews, nature footage and hoaky dramatized scenes without audible dialog. And special effects. Oh, the special effects are wonderful. If *Star Wars* represents 100 on the scale of the art, *Tomorrow* struggles to hit a -4."

Boxoffice was more to the point, calling the Weirdumentary a "curious bit of fluff." No, sir! I won't have it, not in my presence. Orson Welles never qualifies as fluff. And if Guenette might be, he is fluffery of the very best kind.

By 1982, *The Man Who Saw Tomorrow* appeared on The Movie Channel. Then it became a staple at mom-and-pop video stores.

As for the film's predictions of World War III beginning in 1994 and lasting for "Seven and Twenty Years," meaning 2021, well, whether you're Orson or Nostradamus, you can't win them all.

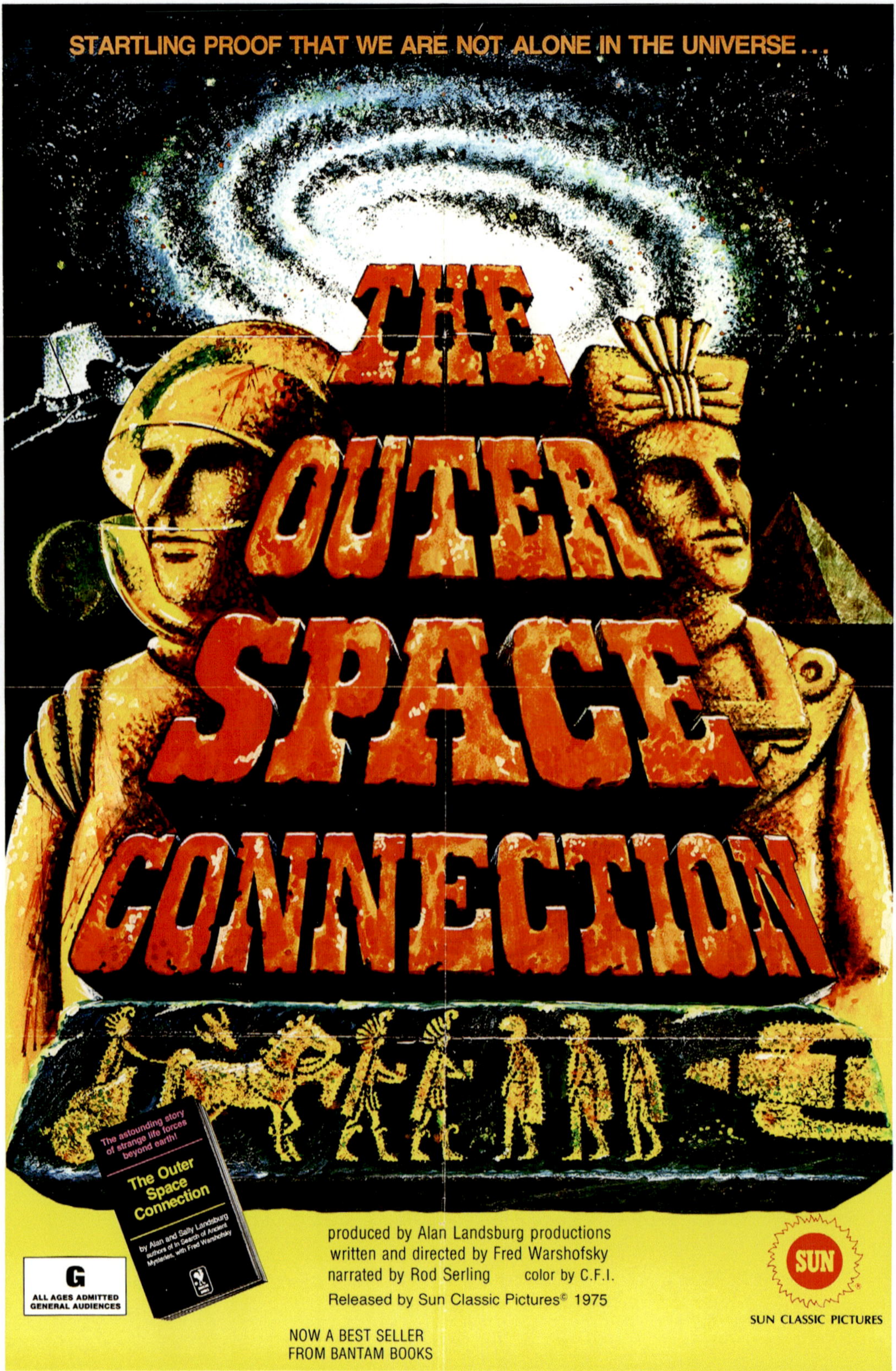
STARTLING PROOF THAT WE ARE NOT ALONE IN THE UNIVERSE...
THE OUTER SPACE CONNECTION
The astounding story of strange life forces beyond earth!
The Outer Space Connection
by Alan and Sally Landsburg authors of In Search of Ancient Mysteries, with Fred Warshofsky
G
ALL AGES ADMITTED GENERAL AUDIENCES
produced by Alan Landsburg productions
written and directed by Fred Warshofsky
narrated by Rod Serling
color by C.F.I.
Released by Sun Classic Pictures© 1975
NOW A BEST SELLER FROM BANTAM BOOKS
SUN
SUN CLASSIC PICTURES

Conclusion

**"In this book, I assemble some of the data that I think are of the falsely and arbitrarily excluded.
The data of the damned.
I have gone into the outer darkness of scientific and philosophical transactions, ultra-respectable, but covered with the dust of disregard.
I have descended into journalism.
I have come back with the quasi-souls of lost data.
They will march."**

— Charles Fort, *The Book of the Damned* (1919)

Harald Reinl, Alan Landsburg, Robert Guenette, Charles E. Sellier, Jr., James L. Conway: to these filmmakers and their colleagues, we salute you.

The Weirdumentary is indeed its own genre, inaugurated with the Academy Award nominee *Chariots of the Gods* in 1970. The curtain closed in 1981 with *The Man Who Saw Tomorrow*, released by Warner Bros., one of Hollywood's biggest studios. If there was an encore, it was the final season of *In Search of…* (1981–82).

Nevertheless, the subject matter lives on. As one character explains in John Carpenter's *The Thing* (1982), "Chariots of the gods, man! They practically own South America. I mean, they taught the Incas everything they know."

And interest in these subjects obviously continued, including on television in such programs as *Arthur C. Clarke's World of Strange Powers* (1985) and *Arthur C. Clarke's Mysterious Universe* (1994). But most of them—like *Ancient Aliens*, which began airing on A&E in 2010—are pale imitations of the Weirdumentary, bastard children without a name to call their own. These descendants are nothing more than troglodytic TV, poorly imitating an art form created by the Weirdumentarists.

Exceptions do exist, most notably *Alien Autopsy: Fact or Fiction* (1995), but they are like bloody steaks: rare, and certainly not well done.

By contrast, the Weirdumentary was a triumph of its era and a triumph of the feature film. It was a hot medium, as McLuhan would say, but it was also a cool large, as I would say.

The programs chronicled in these pages are a coherent collection of incoherence, pseudo-science in authentic cinema. The Real Unreal Deal.

May the gods and the ancient aliens bless them, each and every one. ■

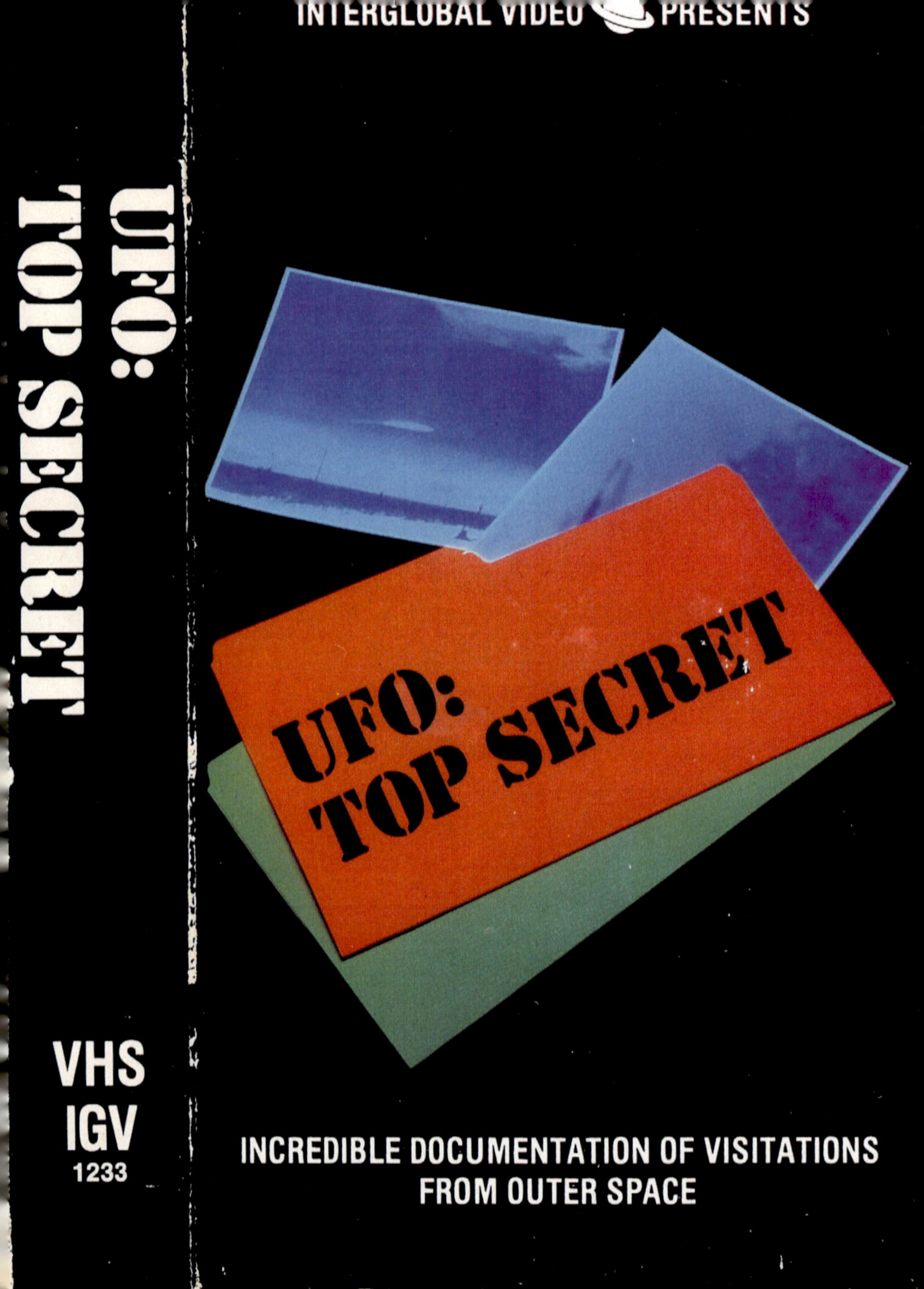

Video box art, *UFO: TOP SECRET*

Interglobal Video, 1986

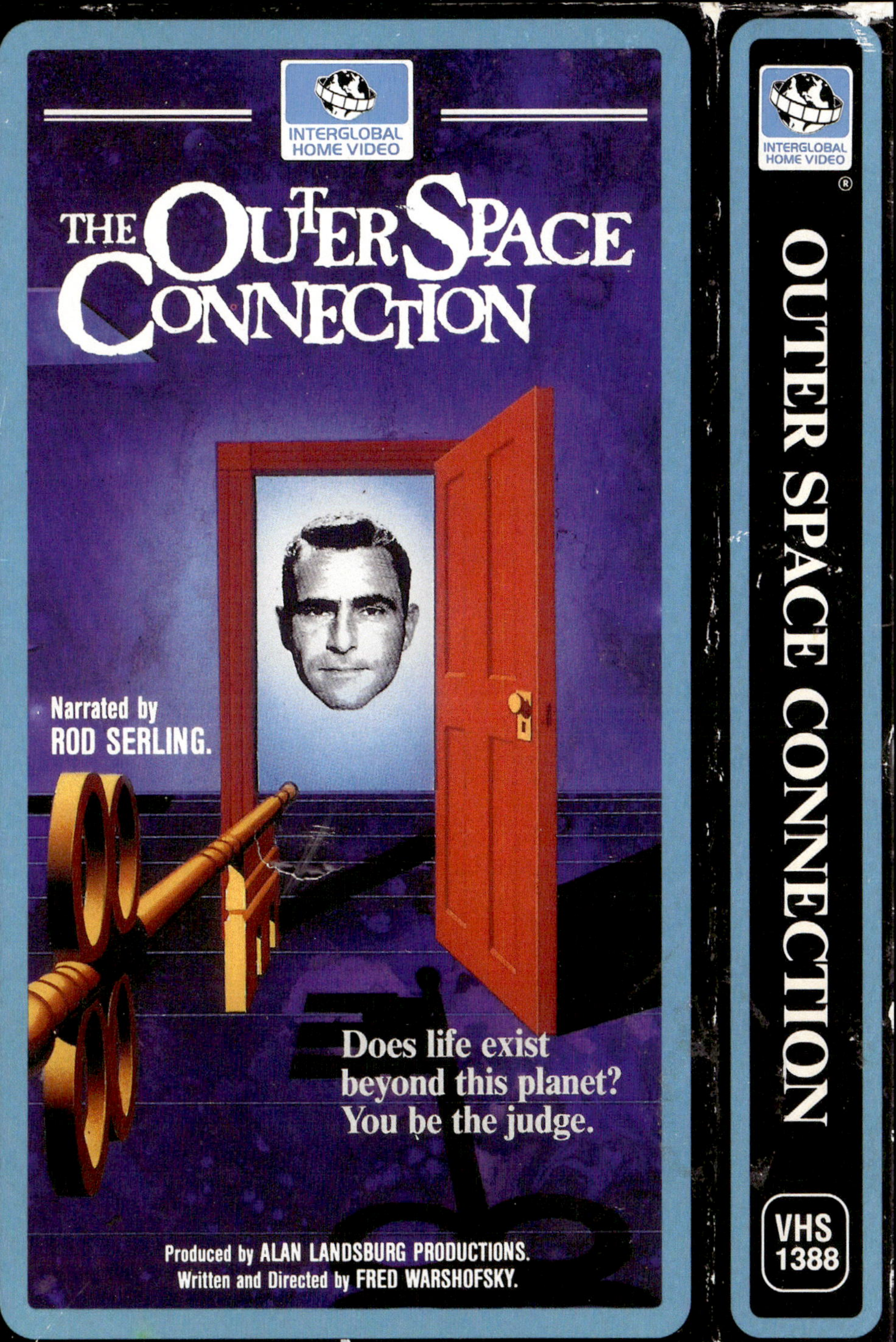

Video box art, *THE OUTER SPACE CONNECTION*
Interglobal Home Video, formerly known as Interglobal Video, 1988

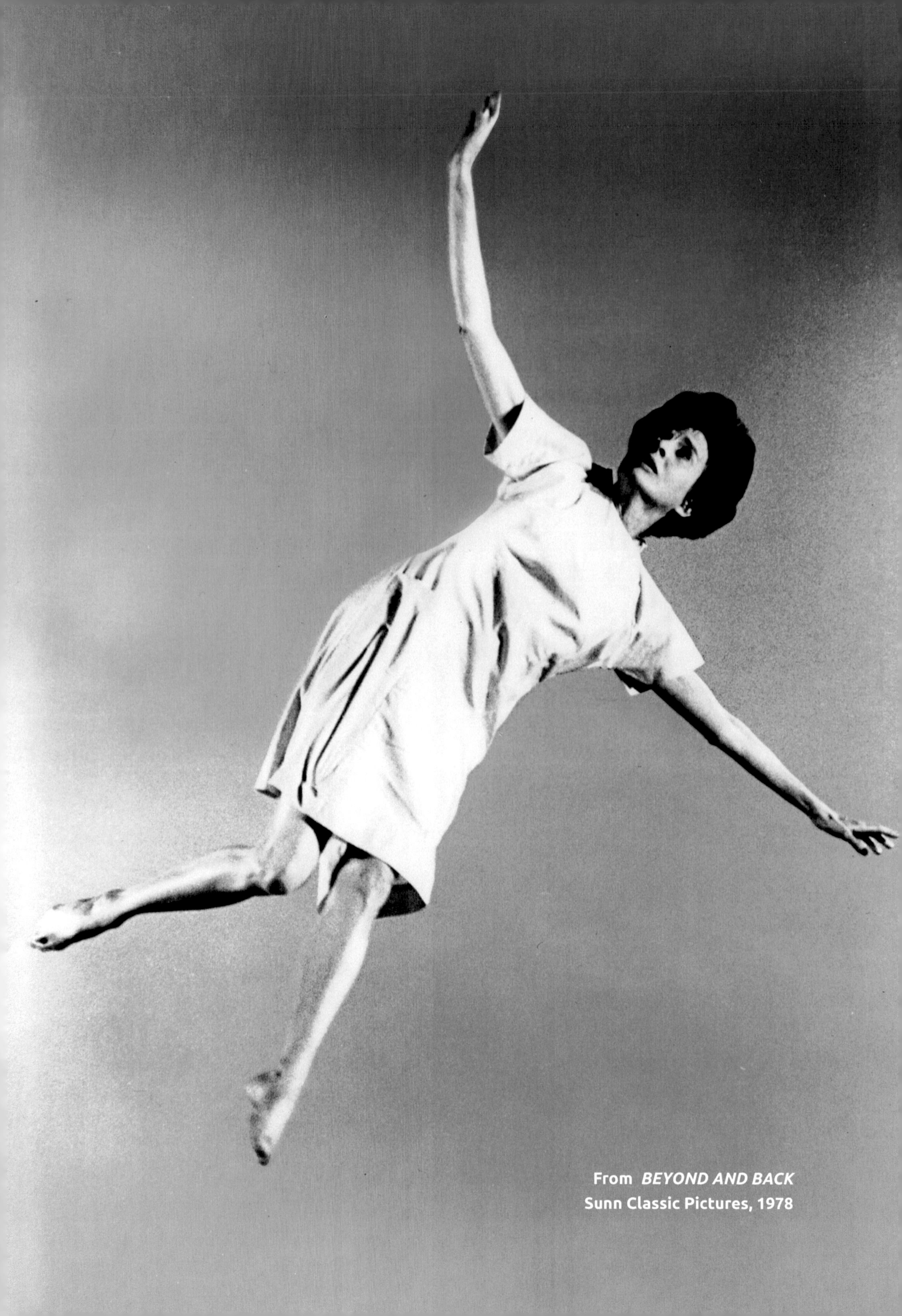

From *BEYOND AND BACK*
Sunn Classic Pictures, 1978

Acknowledgments

Gary D. Rhodes would like to express appreciation to the various archives, libraries, and universities that assisted during the research phase of this book: the Ardmore Public Library of Oklahoma, the Bancroft Library at the University of California at Berkeley, the Billy Rose Theater Division of the New York Public Library, the British Film Institute, the Champion Public Library of Ardmore, Oklahoma, the Cleveland Public Library of Ohio, the Free Library of Philadelphia, the Harry Ransom Center at the University of Texas at Austin, the Library of Congress of Washington, D.C., the Los Angeles Public Library, the Margaret Herrick Library of the Academy of Motion Picture Arts and Sciences, and the Media History Digital Library.

In addition, Rhodes would like to convey his gratitude to the following individuals: the late Forrest J Ackerman, Scott Alexander, John Antosiewicz, Buddy Barnett, Larry Blamire, Bronagh Black, the late Ray Bradbury, Tom Brannan, Mario Chacon, Bill Chase, George Chastain, the late Ned Comstock, Michael Copner, Madison Cox, Tracy Cox, Patrick Crain, Robert Cremer, Richard Daub, the late Jack Dowler, the late William K. Everson, Sander Feinberg, the late Rob Fields, the late Phillip Fortune, Beau Foutz, Christopher R. Gauthier, Donald F. Glut, Argyle Goolsby, Art Greenhaw, the late Gordon R. Guy, G.D. Hamann, Jan Henderon, Matt Horton, Pat Horton, Troy Howarth, the late Alan Hoyt, Cortlundt Hull, Roger Hurlburt, Peter "Magic" Johnston, Larry Karaszewski, Larry the Wolf of the Manimals, Anthony Kerr, Roy Kinnard, Richard Klemensen, the late Howard W. Koch, Matt Ledbetter, Michael Lee, Mark Martucci, Bernard McCarron, Chance Newman, Henry Nicolella, Victor Pierce, Desmond O'Rawe, Frank Percaccio, Mark Redfield, Donald Rhodes, Phyllis Rhodes, Zoran Sinobad, Phillip Sipiora, Anthony Slide, Carter Smith, John Soister, Matthew Sorrento, Billy Stagner, David Stenn, the late Brian Taves, Al Taylor, Mario Toland, John Ulakovic, David Wentink, Stephen B. Whatley, Galen Wilkes, Laurie Williams, Matthew Devin Williams, Leo Wiltshire, and the late Robert Wise.

Rhodes would particularly like to thank the help and encouragement of Stephen R. Bissette, George Chastain, Kristin Dewey, Jeremy Gossett, Roberty Guffey, Mark Martucci, Robert Singer, Michael L. Shuman, and Tom Weaver. He would also like to recognize the ongoing friendship and assistance of Bill Kaffenberger, including research work that importantly helped date some of the films herein accurately: too many internet sources cite the wrong years of release/broadcast for some of them. Some of these films were either not copyrighted or not screened until a year or two after their copyright registration. Here is the reason that a small number of release years herein intentionally deviate from online sources.

Lastly, Rhodes wishes to thank Ron Kretsch, Jessica Parfrey, Christina Ward, and everyone at Feral House for their kindness and support. He is very happy and proud to be associated with this publisher.

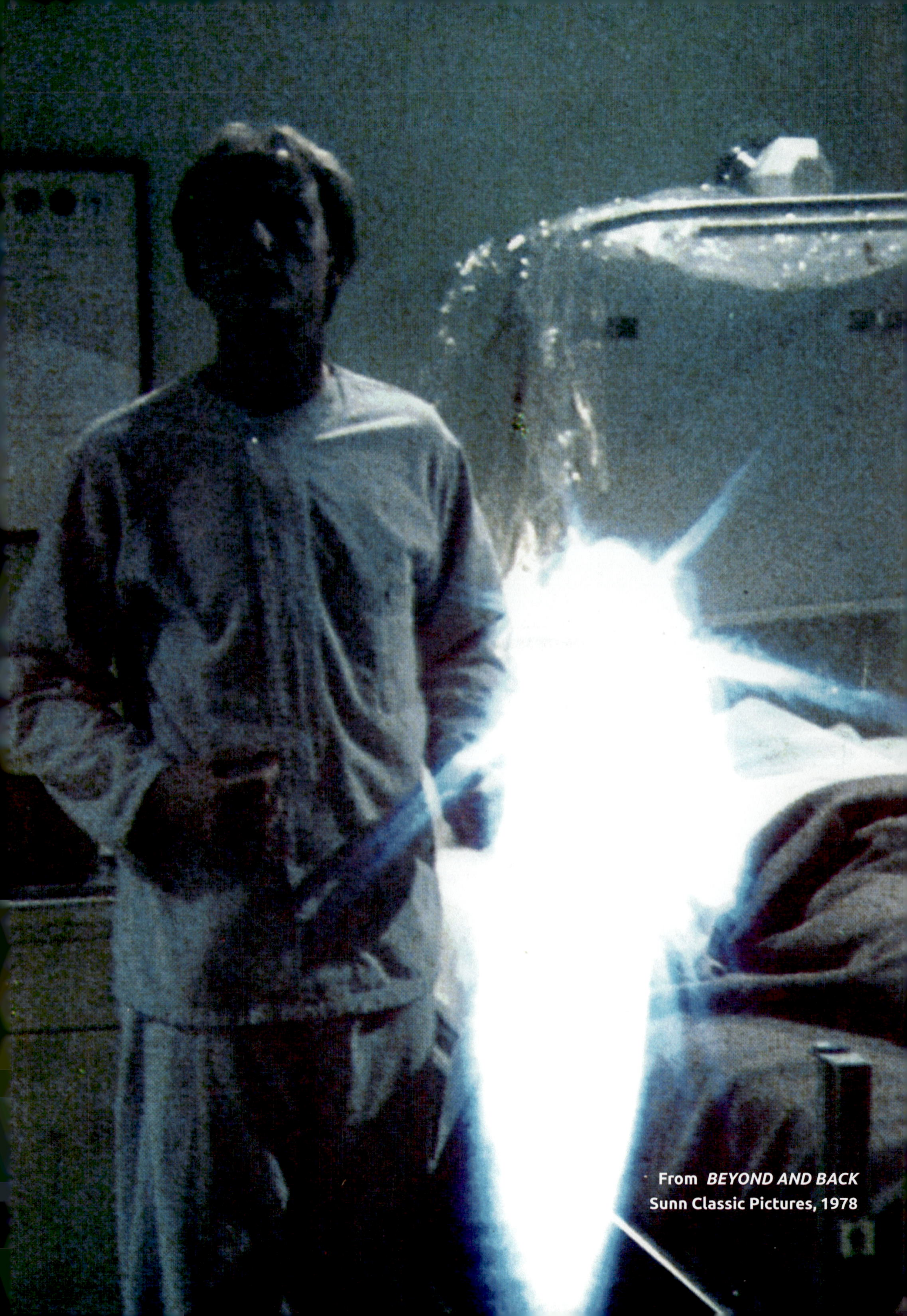

From *BEYOND AND BACK*
Sunn Classic Pictures, 1978

Index

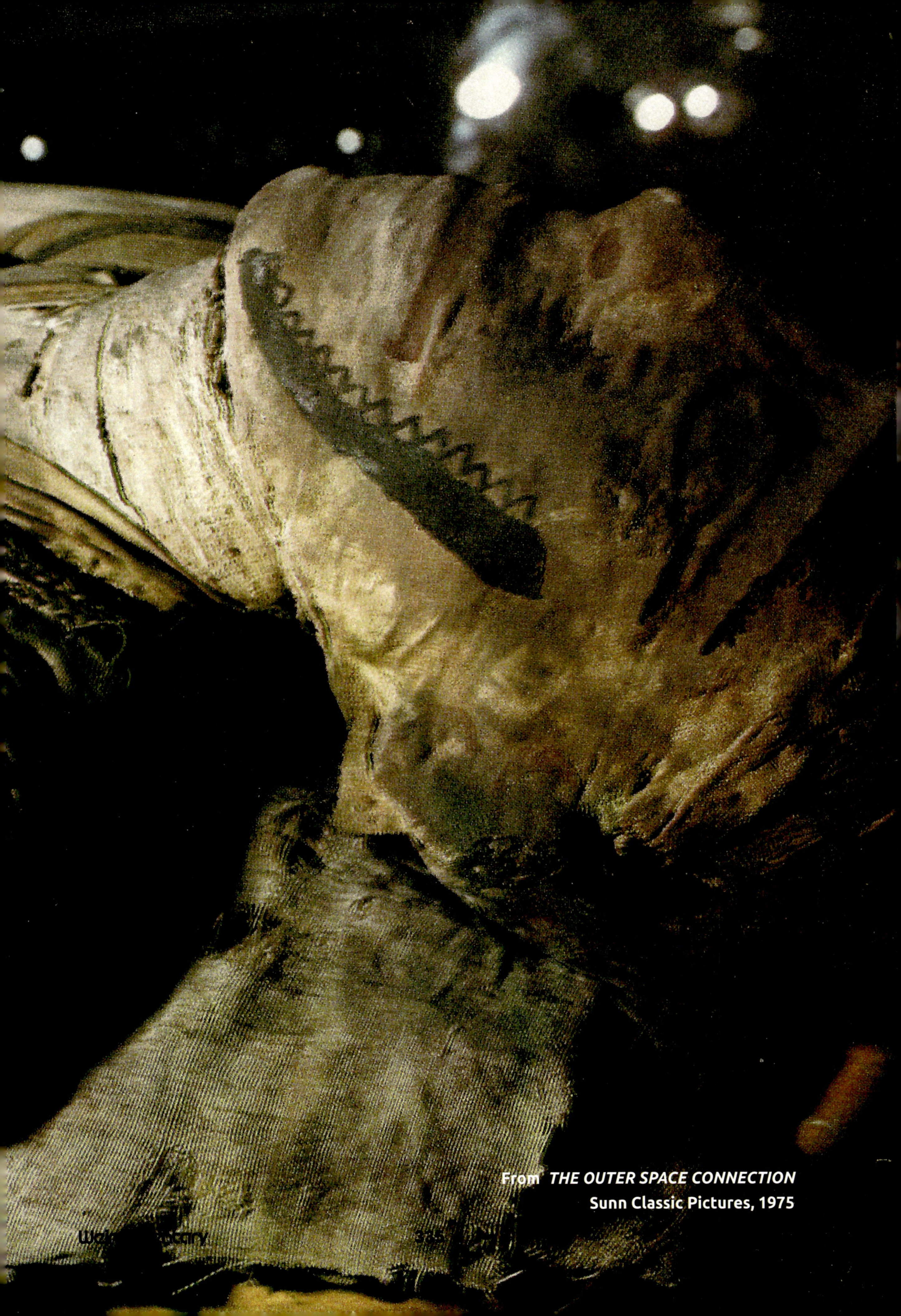

From *THE OUTER SPACE CONNECTION*
Sunn Classic Pictures, 1975

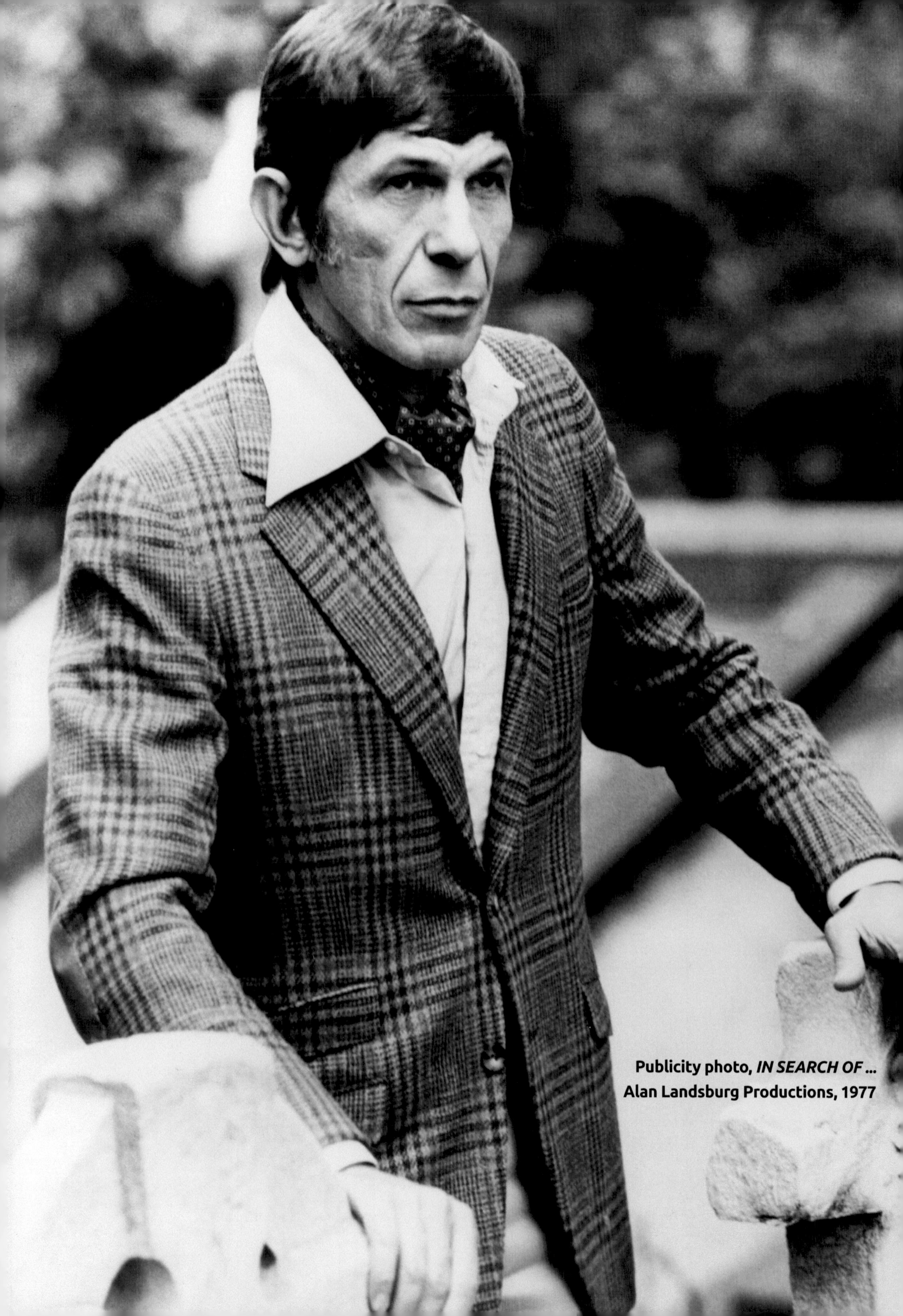

Publicity photo, *IN SEARCH OF ...*
Alan Landsburg Productions, 1977